COMPLETE BOOK OF
FORTUNE TELLING

GRAMERCY BOOKS

New York

Copyright © 1998 by Gramercy Books

All rights reserved under International and Pan-American
Copyright Convention.

No part of this book may be reproduced or
transmitted in any form or by any means electronic or
mechanical including photocopying, recording, or by any
information storage and retrieval system, without permission
in writing from the publisher.

This 1998 edition is published by Gramercy Books®,
an imprint of Random House Value Publishing, Inc.,
201 East 50th Street, New York, N.Y. 10022.

Gramercy Books® and colophon are registered trademarks of
Random House Value Publishing, Inc.

Random House
New York • Toronto • London • Sydney • Auckland
http:/www.randomhouse.com/

Library of Congress Cataloging-in-Publication Data

The Complete book of fortune-telling.
        p.   cm.
      ISBN 0-517-20262-X
1. Fortune-telling.   I. Gramercy Books (Firm)
        BF1861.C63 1998
    133.3—dc21   97-52030
                                    CIP

Printed in the United States of America

8 7 6 5 4 3 2 1

PREFACE

As the world hurtles toward the Millennium, we strive more and more for control over our lives, control over our futures, which in these startlingly unpredictable times seem frighteningly uncontrollable.

When we are feeling good with our lives, we seek the forces of divination to gain confidence that the good times will last. When we are unsure, concerned, and confused, we seek the forces of divination to gain confidence that there is nothing to fear. And at any time, when we feel life spinning away from us, when it seems that our families, our friends, our lovers, our careers loom like giant mysteries which we cannot unlock, we seek the forces of divination to teach and guide us.

COMPLETE BOOK OF FORTUNE-TELLING is a book for all such times. Here are the ancient mystic arts of tea-leaf reading, crystal-gazing, and astrology. Here is the remarkable science of phrenology, the reading of the skull, and the equally fascinating art of physiognomy, the reading of the face. There is palmistry, too, so that we can look at the people we know and learn about them, and learn about ourselves in relation to them. Handwriting analysis or graphology is today used by corporations as part of their pre-hiring steps, so accurate has it become as a gauge to a person's character. From first names to flowers to stones, everything around us has meaning if we but know how to read it, and that is what makes COMPLETE BOOK OF FORTUNE-TELLING so timely and so timeless.

The future is a mystery that unfolds every day. With this unique volume, the mystery can be understood, appreciated, and enjoyed.

J. L. Smythe
New York
1998

CONTENTS

PART ONE

FORTUNE-TELLING AND CHARACTER READING

PAGE

Fortune-telling by Playing-cards 13
Divination by Dice and Dominoes 58
Reading the Tea-leaves 61
Divination by Crystal-gazing 115
Oniromancy: Dreams and Their Interpretation . . . 137
The Dream Oraculum 183
Napoleon's Book of Fate 250
Numerology: The Science of Numbers 269
The Art of Physiognomy 295
The Science of Phrenology 319
Chirognomy and Chiromancy: The Art of Reading the Hand . 335
The Science of Graphology 386
Oracles, Omens and Popular Superstitions:
   Oracles 425
   Omens 436
   Popular Superstitions 467

PART TWO

THE MYSTIC MEANINGS OF THINGS

Talismans and Amulets 497
The Meanings of First names 515
The Virtues of Precious Stones 545
Florigraphy: The Language and Meanings of Flowers . . 570
Colours and Their Significance 582

PART THREE

THE SCIENCE OF ASTROLOGY

The Science of Astrology 589

Part One

FORTUNE-TELLING AND CHARACTER READING

FORTUNE-TELLING BY PLAYING-CARDS

IT is safe to affirm that no pastime in the history of the world has exercised such a deep fascination over the mind of man as card-playing. From their obscure and far-off beginning in the mysterious East—home of so many of the world's most significant inventions, throughout the centuries to modern times, when the use of playing-cards is universal—mankind has found an unfailing and irresistible allure in the manifold hazards and combinations that are possible in cards.

Contrary to what might have been expected, however, cards were not generally known in Europe until a comparatively late period. There is an old legend that Odette de Champdivers, the mistress of Charles VI, the mad king of France, was responsible for introducing them into the French court in the course of her efforts to find a means of distracting her royal lover during his recurring fits of insanity.

It is said that Charles soon fell under the fascination of gambling and started a fashion which spread throughout France and the rest of Europe. It is certain, at least, that a painter, Jacquemin Gringonneur, was commissioned in 1392 to make three packs for the king's own use.

The manufacture of playing-cards was among the earliest uses to which the woodcut was adapted, while some of the foremost painters of the Renaissance—including, it is said, the great Mantegna himself—considered it no indignity to their art to apply it to the designing of cards.

In place of the suits that are usual to-day, the earliest European cards bore hearts, bells, acorns and leaves. Later packs, like the tarot (afterwards to be described), were marked with cups, deniers (or money), staves and swords; while the modern devices of hearts, diamonds, clubs and spades did not appear until the sixteenth century.

Concerning the rational basis of cartomancy, as the art of divination by cards is known, we shall content ourselves here with suggesting that in some way, which is a complete mystery even to advanced students of occult science, the vast psychic power that fills all space and time exerts a magnetic influence upon the nervous system and the fingers of the person who shuffles, cuts, chooses or arranges the cards (who thus becomes essentially a medium), and so opens wide—in all its marvellous clarity and significance for those who have eyes to read—the Book of Life and Fate.

For the benefit of sceptics we would say that cartomancy, like phrenology and palmistry, is claimed to be an empirical science; that is to say, its revelations are based upon the portents and consequences that, throughout the ages, have been observed to accompany or follow the fall of the individual cards and their various groupings.

Perhaps the two most celebrated card-diviners of more recent times were Etteilla and Mlle. Lenormand. The former, who is often called "the father of cartomancy" (a title which might have some justification if card-divining were not an art which flourished centuries before his time), was a barber and wigmaker in Paris, whose real name was Alliette—"Etteilla" is "Alliette" read backwards, in cabbalistic fashion. This remarkable man devoted thirty years to a profound study of cards, and especially of the tarot in all its subtleties, and his methods of divination gave rise to an enormous popularity of the science towards the end of the eighteenth century.

Mlle. Lenormand displayed great intuitive power in her readings, and some remarkable anecdotes are related of her predictions. On one occasion, in January, 1804, Bernadotte, one of the great Napoleon's generals, and his aide-de-camp repaired under the guise of business men to the house of Mlle. Lenormand, where Bernadotte begged to be told of the outcome of some supposed commercial ventures. Mlle. Lenormand, on consulting the cards, promptly remarked, "You are no merchant, but an officer of high rank." This the general strenuously denied, but the sibyl, again scrutinizing the cards, once more affirmed, "You are not only of high rank, but you are, or will be, related to him who will be emperor."

Continuing to read the fateful cards one by one, she went on, "Yes, he will become emperor of France . . . see how his star is in the ascendant! And you . . . you, too, will be a king!" History tells us that Napoleon became emperor at the end of

1804, while in 1818 Bernadotte himself was crowned king of Sweden and Norway as Charles XIV.

It should be assiduously born in mind that cartomancy is governed by the same esoteric influences as other psychic phenomena, and successful prognostications cannot be expected unless a few simple rules are observed.

The most reliable results are said to be obtained in the early evening, at that hour when the stress and turmoil of the day are half forgotten, and the world of Nature is calmly awaiting that long period of reflection, peace and repose which comes with the night.

It is not for nothing, we may add, that the night has ever been universally regarded as a time of mystery, when occult powers are at their height. Night, known to the ancient Egyptians as Nut, the mother of Osiris, represents the negative and occult part of each twenty-four hours, and is the dominion of the passive and contemplative moon; while day, the realm of the ardent and fiery sun, is strongly positive in its magnetic value.

There are two days of the week, Monday and Friday, that are considered to be especially favourable for divining, which, moreover, should only be attempted in calm, clear weather, when Nature is at her best and the psychic forces and magnetic currents which surround the earth are pursuing a normal and undisturbed course.

How the Omens should be Regarded

At this point we wish to make it quite clear to the reader that, according to an invariable law which runs through all the occult sciences, the extent of the revelations granted by the cards is proportional to the degree of faith and enthusiasm with which they are consulted; and while sceptics or those who approach cartomancy in a light-minded fashion may obtain much harmless amusement from it, it is to the earnest student alone that serious revelations will be made.

It should be understood. too, that the omens received are not bound infallibly to be fulfilled; they should be regarded more as indications—straws in the wind—which point out the turn that one's life will take, unless conscious efforts are made to divert it towards another direction.

For fortune-telling by means of the ordinary pack, as distinct from the tarot, it is usual to discard the deuces, threes, fours, fives and sixes of each suit, the remaining cards thus forming the piquet pack of thirty-two.

It is also usual to identify a particular card with the inquirer —he or she whose fate is being told. This is to be done upon the following lines:—

A young, fair man is represented by the king of hearts.
An elderly, fair man is represented by the king of diamonds.
A young, dark man is represented by the king of clubs.
An elderly, dark man is represented by the king of spades.

A young, fair woman is represented by the queen of hearts.
An elderly, fair woman is represented by the queen of diamonds.
A young, dark woman is represented by the queen of clubs.
An elderly, dark woman is represented by the queen of spades.

White or pronouncedly grey hair is to be regarded as fair.

The Meanings of the Cards

The four suits have the following significations:—

Hearts denote love and all that concerns the affections, such as friendship, sympathy, peace and family ties.
Diamonds relate to travelling, voyages, business undertakings and connexions.
Clubs are concerned with power, fame, ability and all kinds of money matters.
Spades speak of misfortune, suffering, loss, mourning, treachery, enemies and betrayal.

The following are the meanings traditionally accorded to the individual cards. It will be noticed that a card which presents itself reversed, that is, upside down, has generally an inauspicious meaning, often the opposite of that which it would express if it were in an upright position.

Hearts

Ace (upright): happiness, a letter, an invitation;
    (reversed): strife, lovers' quarrels.
King: a pleasant and easy-going man, fair or grey-haired.
Queen: an affectionate and sympathetic woman, usually fair.
Knave: an upright and faithful young man.
Ten: success, affection, fortune.
Nine (upright): success, a happy result;
    (reversed): worries, obstacles.

Eight (upright): an unexpected present or visit;
    (reversed): disappointment, annoyance.
Seven (upright): someone loves you truly;
    (reversed): a jealous, fickle and worthless infatuation.

DIAMONDS

Ace: an important document or letter.
King: the protection of a man of power and authority.
Queen: a frivolous and light-minded fair woman, a stranger; if she stands next
    to the king of diamonds, she will marry him.
Knave: a soldier or an official in uniform, perhaps a postman bringing a letter.
Ten: an approaching journey.
Nine: a new business deal to be undertaken.
Eight: a large party or a picnic in the country.
Seven (upright): a present;
    (reversed): quarrels, disputes.

CLUBS

Ace (upright): success in business dealings and speculations;
    (reversed): you will give a present or receive one.
King: a dark man who will be of assistance to you.
Queen: a dark woman, wealthy and affectionate.
Knave: a dark, ardent young man.
Ten: success in business or matters of the affections.
Nine (upright): a wealthy marriage or a large amount of money;
    (reversed): an unexpected present.
Eight (upright): a dark girl, or a small sum of money;
    (reversed): minor losses.
Seven (upright): a dark-haired child;
    (reversed): money worries.

SPADES

Ace (upright): a lawsuit, a business offer, an avowal of love;
    (reversed): unhappiness in love.
King: a judge or a wily lawyer.
Queen: a cunning dark woman, widowed or divorced.
Knave: a dark young man, treacherous and envious.
Ten: a worrying letter, vexation and jealousy.
Nine (upright): illness, misfortune;
    (reversed): the latter omens are reinforced.
Eight (upright): impediments, misfortunes;
    (reversed): danger, temptation.
Seven (upright): burdensome and tedious advice;
    (reversed): failure, hesitation.

THE MEANINGS OF VARIOUS GROUPS OF CARDS

A special significance is attached to two or more cards of the
same value that are grouped together, as is shown below. The

force of the omen increases in a malefic sense in accordance with the number of the cards in the group which appear upside down. Thus:—

Four aces together, in an upright position, denote triumph and success, but the impediments to this success increase in proportion as the aces of hearts, clubs and spades are reversed.

Three aces: you show too much credulity and kindness;
(reversed) which will be taken advantage of.

Two aces: a forthcoming marriage;
(reversed) it will not take place.

It is often considered that two or more aces occurring together in a group indicate a change of life and of surroundings. Other groups of cards of the same value have the following meanings:—

Kings: (four) success and honour in full measure.
(three) slightly less fortunate.
(two) your good fortune will vary according to the efforts which you put forth.

Queens: (four) gossip, slander and backbiting.
(three) the same, but to a lesser extent.
(two) prying and petty gossip.

Knaves: (four) quarrels and strife.
(three) friction, disharmony.
(two) disagreements.

Tens: (four) prosperity, good fortune.
(three) money worries and legal difficulties.
(two) an unexpected windfall.

Nines: (four) a lucky surprise.
(three) a successful issue.
(two) impediments are in the way.

Eights: (four) anxiety, a blending of good fortune and bad.
(three) you will have the backing of your friends and family circle.
(two) a love affair.

Sevens: (four) enemies will lay traps for you; if reversed, you will elude them.
(three) an addition to the family; reversed, loneliness and unhappiness.
(two) you will have a lover; reversed, who will deceive you.

The following are some other positions and groupings, the meanings of which are modified, of course, if one or more of the cards is reversed:—

The card of the inquirer, if he is a man, in juxtaposition with the queen of his own suit means a marriage.

In juxtaposition with the queen of hearts, deep and lasting affection.

With the queen of diamonds, amorous and dangerous intrigues.

With the queen of clubs, remarriage (in the case of a widower), or friendship with a woman of wealth and position.

With the queen of spades, guilt, intrigues and misconduct.

With the knave of hearts, faithlessness.
With the knave of diamonds, a secret love affair.
With the knave of clubs, money troubles, loans.
With the knave of spades, look to the honesty of your servants.

The portents for a woman are as follows:—

If she has as her neighbour a king of the same colour (either red or black), a
marriage.
If she is side by side with the king of her suit, happiness with the man she
loves; but if she has a king of an opposite colour as neighbour, a liaison or
clandestine love affair is foreshadowed.
If she is next to a
knave of hearts, a flirtation.
knave of diamonds, an unimportant love affair.
knave of clubs, foolish conduct in connexion with a young man.
knave of spades, a young man of wicked intentions.
If she has several knaves in proximity, flirtations and minor love affairs.

The aces, placed next to the card of the inquirer, have the
following significance for a person of either sex:—

Ace of hearts: unbroken mutual love and happiness.
Ace of diamonds: news or a letter will lead you to change your mind.
Ace of clubs: a heavy investment in an uncertain and hazardous enterprise.
Ace of spades: treachery, illness, misfortunes of every kind.
(These portents should be reversed if the ace is upside down.)

The meanings of tens, nines, eights and sevens in apposition
with the card of the inquirer (either sex) should be judged from
the tables of the simple meanings of these cards.
We will now give the portents revealed by some specially
significant positions:—

A large number of court cards and aces surrounding or in apposition with the
card of the inquirer signifies that he or she will participate in a gathering of
notabilities or members of the social world.
Ten of diamonds near the card of a male inquirer signifies a journey.
Ten of diamonds near an eight of hearts or diamonds, a sea voyage.
Ten of diamonds near another ten, a legacy.
Ten of diamonds near its ace, a letter from a foreign land.
Queen of diamonds and queen of spades in a ring of clubs, beware of malicious
and slanderous tongues.
Nine of diamonds near the inquirer's card, hesitation and impediments.
Nine of spades near the card of a male inquirer, disease.
Nine of spades near its eight, your health requires attention.
Ace of spades near its nine, you will be left lonely and forsaken.
Ace of spades near its eight, chagrin, vexation, disappointed desires.
Ace of diamonds near a nine of spades, illness.

We repeat that it is important to take into consideration the upright or reversed position of the cards when reading these omens.

READING THE CARDS

There is considerable difference of opinion among occultists concerning whether it is permissible to refer to tables or a text-book of cartomancy while reading the cards, or whether the prognostications cease to be reliable unless the meanings of all the cards and the manifold combinations and positions which they are capable of assuming are committed to memory.

However, in view of the difficulty which the average person is likely to experience in learning the meanings of all the cards at once, we recommend that the student should make as many practice divinations as possible, at the same time constantly referring to these pages. When such a method is adopted, it is surprising how high a degree of speed and facility can be attained in manipulating the cards and interpreting the nature and force of the revelations which they furnish.

As the proficiency of the student increases, printed instructions should be gradually dispensed with, until he arrives at a stage when he can give an accurate and well-judged reading from the resources of his memory and experience alone. This method is certainly preferable to inscribing upon each card its appropriate meaning, a system recommended by some authorities.

METHODS OF DIVINATION

The first method of laying out the cards which we are about to describe is one of the best known and at the same time one which, upon occult grounds, is very highly thought of by professional cartomancers.

Step I

Take up the pack of thirty-two cards (previously described) and shuffle it well. Hand the cards to the inquirer and request him to cut them three times with his left hand, while keeping his mind as far as possible free from any thoughts relating to his fate or any particular question which he would wish to be decided; this precaution is important for an unbiased fall of the cards.

Now deal out the whole pack face downwards from left to right in the form of a fan, and ask the inquirer to select with his left hand thirteen cards in haphazard fashion. As he hands them to you, gather them in a heap in consecutive order, one upon another.

Pick up the remaining nineteen cards and lay them aside, then take the thirteen chosen cards, spread them face upwards from left to right, and search among them for the inquirer's card, on the lines which we have already indicated. Thus, if the inquirer is a young, fair woman, her card will be the queen of hearts; while an elderly, dark man will be represented by the king of spades, and so on.

If, however, the appropriate card does not appear among the thirteen, the seven of the same suit must be taken instead and must be regarded as the inquirer's "guiding spirit"; and if, as happens not infrequently, neither card is found, it must be assumed that the occult powers controlling the divination consider the time and circumstances unpropitious for drawing aside the veil that hides the future, and the divination should be terminated forthwith and undertaken again only after an entire day at least has passed.

Having shifted the card of the inquirer or his "spirit" slightly out of the row in order to distinguish it, consider it as one, the next card to the *right* as two, the next as three, and so on until you come to the fifth card, which should also be set slightly out of the row. Now, reckoning this card as one, repeat the operation of counting up to five, again slightly moving the fifth card so obtained. Repeat this process (including in the counting those cards which have already been moved) until you have indicated altogether five cards by moving them a trifle out of the line.

You should be careful to reckon each fifth card twice, that is as the last card of one count and the first card of the next; and when you reach the right-hand extremity of the whole line, continue from the extreme left hand without terminating or interrupting your counting.

Next ask the inquirer to choose five more cards in haphazard fashion from the pack of nineteen that was set aside in the beginning. The selection should be made with the left hand, as before; and as each one is selected it should be laid upon one of the five cards in the row of thirteen, beginning from the left. Read out the meanings of each of these five pairs of cards.

Step II

Take up the cards in the following fashion: The card at each of the extremities of the row is to be taken with the other, the next two together, and so on, until only the centre card is left; this is to be ignored. As you take them up, read out the omens portended by the cards and by their grouping. If there are two cards together at one end and only one at the other, read these three cards together; if there are two cards at each end of the row, read the two upper ones together and then the two lower ones likewise.

Step III

Reshuffle the eighteen cards in question, cut them three times with the left hand and deal them carefully into three heaps, starting from the left and dealing one card to each heap in turn. After asking the inquirer to choose one of these heaps, spread out the cards it contains and read their omens which will reveal his own future.

A second heap is to be chosen in the same way and likewise interpreted; it will have relation to the inquirer's family circle, relatives, children, friends, associates and environment. The remaining, or "surprise," heap will serve to strengthen or to lessen the force of the portents foreshadowed by the other two, or to settle one way or another any conflicting prognostications which they may present.

The experienced cartomancer will not content himself with a bald and unqualified prediction, but, by meticulously estimating the varying influences of all the cards, will carefully reckon the chances for and against the fulfilment of the prognostications foreshadowed.

Practice and experience will lead, too, to an ability to merge one omen into another upon a simple inspection of the cards, so as to make a logical and connected whole. Thus, instead of predicting from a certain fall of the cards, "a treacherous young man, quarrels, loss of money, a lawyer," it is preferable to say, "Quarrels with a treacherous young man may lead to loss of money and the intervention of a lawyer."

An Old Italian Method

Here is another method, one which has for centuries enjoyed great popularity among the gifted cartomancers of Italy:—

After having shuffled the pack of thirty-two cards, request the inquirer to cut them with his left hand. Now turn up the first three cards on the top of the pack. If they chance to be all of one suit, lay them down one after another in a row from left to right and in the same order in which they appeared in the pack. If, however, they contain only two cards of the same suit, choose the higher of these two; but if the three cards are of different suits, they should all be thrown aside.

Thus, if the three cards taken from the pack happened to be the king, knave and seven of diamonds, they would all be laid in the row; if the queen and the nine of spades appeared, together with the king of hearts, the queen of spades would be chosen; and if the three cards consisted of the king of clubs, the eight of hearts and the ace of diamonds—all different suits—they would all be discarded.

Go through this procedure with all the cards in the pack, taking them in threes. It will be found, of course, that two cards only are left, and unless these are both of the same suit—in which case the higher card is chosen—they should be discarded. Some authorities would reject these two cards in any case, and since there seems to be no outstanding reason why the portents should be affected whichever method is followed, the student may please himself regarding the course to adopt.

When the pack has been exhausted, the rejected cards must be reshuffled and the whole process repeated, and so on until fifteen cards have been extracted. If more than that number are put down, reduce them to fifteen by taking away the requisite number from the *left*. It is important that these fifteen cards should include the card of the inquirer (which is to be identified on the lines already described); and if this card fails to appear, the entire divination must be repeated from the beginning—from the shuffling and cutting of the pack—until the required king or queen materializes.

When the fifteen cards have been assembled in a row, call the inquirer's own card one, and starting from it, from left to right, shift slightly out of the row the third, seventh, ninth and thirteenth cards, reverting to the beginning of the row when you come to the last card on the right-hand side. Read the interpretations of these cards in order, according to the tables previously given.

To complete the divination, take up a card from each end of the row of fifteen, and read the meanings of the pair together. Continue to read the cards in pairs until one card only is left—the "surprise" card—which should be regarded as furnishing the final revelation of the inquirer's fate and fortune.

Two Rapid Methods

The following is an extremely rapid method of revealing a person's destiny, though it is a matter of question whether it is as dependable as the more thorough methods which we have given.

Request the inquirer to shuffle the cards thoroughly, cut them and hand them back to you. Now spread out the pack face downwards upon the table, and ask the inquirer to choose thirteen cards at random. Arrange these cards in a row, face upwards, in the order in which they were chosen, and read out their meanings. A second row of thirteen cards, similarly selected and spread out below the first, will serve to modify or confirm their predictions.

An even shorter method—useful for deciding any single question—consists of dealing the first seven cards of the pack in a row, and reading the omens of the first, fourth and seventh card.

The Temple of Fortune

We have already spoken of Etteilla—*alias* Alliette—the wig-maker of Paris, an ardent student of occult lore, whose ingenious theories and remarkable predictions secured a widespread popularity for the art of cartomancy during the troubled years which preceded the French Revolution of 1789. Etteilla's life work was chiefly associated with the tarot—and especially with the revelation of its occult significance—but the reader may care to avail himself of this celebrated cartomancer's favourite method of fortune-telling by means of the piquet pack of thirty-two cards. It is known as the "Temple of Fortune."

The cards should be well shuffled by the inquirer and cut with his left hand, and then set out face upwards in the order shown in the diagram.

With a little practice, one will soon become skilful in arranging this figure from memory. The Temple of Fortune reveals the past, present and future, the three groups of cards that have a significant bearing upon these realms of time being separated from one another in the diagram by heavier lines. Thus, the future is revealed by the cards that fall in the spaces numbered from 7 to 12, both

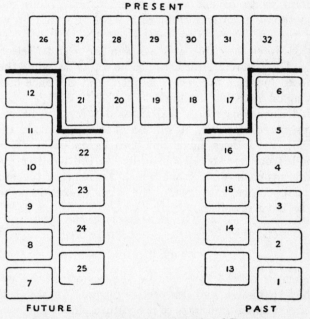

Cards arranged for the Temple of Fortune

inclusive, together with those in spaces 22 to 25; and the same method applies for the past and present.

It should be added that the primary indications are shown by the three outer rows of cards, forming the exterior walls of the temple; while each of the three inner rows—which together comprise Nos. 13 to 25—exerts a modifying or corroborative influence over the omens foreshadowed by its own outer row. In reading the

omens (from the table previously given), the cards should be taken
in the numerical order of the spaces which they occupy, that is
from 26 to 32, and from 17 to 21, and so on.

The Five Heaps

We will now describe a form of divination which furnishes
the inquirer with answers under definite heads.

The thirty-two cards must be thoroughly shuffled and handed
to the inquirer to be cut with his left hand. While cutting the
cards, he should silently formulate a wish of which he would like
to know the outcome. Now spread out the thirty-two cards face
downwards upon the table and ask the inquirer to select thirteen
of them. The remaining cards are to be set aside, while the thirteen
cards chosen must be taken up, shuffled, and cut once more by the
inquirer, again with his left hand.

The diviner must then deal them out from right to left into
five heaps, three of which, it will be observed, contain three cards
each, while the others have but two cards each. These heaps
correspond, from left to right in order, to the inquirer himself, his
home and intimate circle, that which he expects to come about,
surprise happenings, and lastly, the wish whose outcome he was
anxious to have revealed.

THE TAROT

The origin of the tarot cards, the region of the world from
which they emanated, and the precise purpose for which they were
devised are wrapped in a haze of conjecture, doubt and superstition.
The great age of the tarot is, however, unquestioned, as also is the
fact that it was invented for some specific purpose, whether purely
to serve the interests of gaming or whether it was that those who
fashioned these strange designs and symbols did so with the avowed
object of thereby expressing in a concise and ever-living form the
secrets of the highest occult knowledge to which mankind can attain.

The latter theory is supported by the most eminent and profound
occultists, several of whom, including Court de Gébelin, Papus,
Charles Barlet, Oswald Wirth and Eliphas Levi, boldly affirm that

the twenty-two major arcana of the tarot, whose mysterious and apparently fanciful designs still puzzle the uninitiated beholder to-day, are nothing less than the leaves of the sacred Book of Thoth, which contained a summary of the profound occult lore of ancient Egypt. Moreover, these occultists are agreed that the tarot also presents an epitome of the mysteries of the Jewish Cabbala, as well as a key to its mysteries—which is quite consistent when it is remembered that Jewish occultism is largely Egyptian in its origin.

The tarot comprises two main parts:—

1. The major arcana, consisting of twenty-two pictorial and symbolical cards, and
2. The minor arcana, which are composed of fifty-six court and numeral cards, divided into four suits.

The cards of the major arcana follow one another in a regular numerical order that is traditional, and each of them is identified with one of the twenty-two letters of the Hebrew alphabet—which in ancient times were also used for counting. One can often trace the form of the letter associated with a certain card in the design, or part of the design, composing it. Moreover, Egyptian, Hindu and Babylonian symbols can still be recognized, in spite of the variations of form which the cards must inevitably have undergone through the long toll of centuries that have elapsed since they were first devised by the occult masters of the East.

Thus it would seem that the major arcana form a compendium of the esoteric philosophy of many mighty civilizations, from each of which the cards have borrowed certain characteristic attributes, while preserving whole and entire for the spiritual gaze of the initiated those fundamental and eternal truths which form the basis and the resplendent crown of all great religions and systems of philosophy.

The minor arcana of the tarot represent under another guise the familiar suit markings of our modern playing-cards, hearts being represented by cups, diamonds by deniers or money, clubs by staves and spades by swords. The court cards of each suit differ only in design from those in the ordinary pack, although an additional card—the cavalier or knight—is inserted between the queen and the knave. For this reason the minor arcana of the tarot number four cards more than do our packs of modern playing-cards, to which in all other respects they are essentially similar, and of which, centuries ago, they formed the origin.

There is evidence that the tarot has for hundreds of years been one of the most popular mediums employed for divination, and it is in this light that we are chiefly concerned with it here. Below will be found the divinatory meaning which tradition attaches to each of the seventy-eight cards, both of the major and the minor arcana.

The Major Arcana

(1) *The Juggler*, or Magician, points towards Heaven with his left hand, in which he holds his magic wand, while his right arm is directed towards the Earth; thus it will be seen that this figure closely resembles the form of the Hebrew letter Aleph (א), with which it is identified. On the table before him are displayed the cups, deniers and swords of three of the suits of the tarot; staves are represented by the wand which he holds in his hand.

In divining, the Juggler represents the inquirer himself, should the latter be a man; but if the inquirer is a woman, this card must be taken to indicate a change of position, favourable if the card is upright, but unfavourable if it is reversed. If this card is reversed in the case of a male inquirer, it signifies—unless modified by favourable cards in the vicinity—that he will always be more or less at odds with life and the world.

(2) *The High Priestess*, or the Female Pope. In some French packs this arcanum is, quite erroneously, replaced by "Juno." The High Priestess represents the female inquirer, who cannot be regarded as Fortune's favourite if this card is upside down. If the inquirer is a male, however, this arcanum stands for knowledge, occult science, mysticism, divination and esoteric practices. Reversed, it means unhappy consequences resulting from occult studies.

(3) *The Empress*, wearing a golden crown and seated upon her throne, holds a sceptre in one hand and in the other a shield bearing the royal device of an eagle displayed. She represents woman and the female principle embodied in fertility and domestic happiness, and from which spring action, initiative and life itself. Reversed, she presages disharmony and lack of union, leading to stagnation and sterility—conditions which, however, may be modified by any neighbouring cards of favourable influence.

(4) *The Emperor*, holding a sceptre in his hand, is seated in profile on a throne, by the side of which is a shield bearing a charge similar to that of the Empress. This arcanum, which is the complement of the preceding one, represents man, together with his positive attributes, such as will-power, authority, strength and courage. Reversed, it shows the softer aspect of the stern masculine nature, and expresses benevolence, clemency and pity.

(5) *The Pope*, sometimes (erroneously) Jupiter, represents strength, wisdom, inspiration, intelligence, asceticism. Reversed, it counsels the inquirer to be on his guard against craftiness and guile.

(6) *The Lovers*. A young man stands in a state of indecision between two women, one of whom has an air of virtue and dignity, while the other, who lays her hand on his shoulder, is crowned with a bacchanalian wreath. The god of love, flying in a blaze of glory, bends his bow over the three as though seeking at whom to aim. This card expresses love and all that treats of the affections, as well as hesitation, indecision and instability, symbolized by the vacillating attitude of the youth. Reversed, the card shows love troubles, heartache and a broken romance, and extreme inconstancy of purpose.

(7) *The Chariot*. A warrior, crowned and holding a sceptre in his hand, rides in a triumphal car covered with a canopy and drawn by two horses. He wears a golden breast-plate, while on his shoulders are two human masks, which have been taken to represent the Urim and Thummim of the Hebrews. This card symbolizes victory, triumph over snares and obstacles, and the help and protection of Providence. Reversed, it indicates discouragement, quarrels, defeat.

(8) *Justice*. Crowned and seated upon a throne that rises in a column upon either side, the figure of Justice holds the traditional sword and scales; her gaze is directed steadfastly and impartially before her. This card stands for justice, right, integrity, impartiality, balanced judgment and arbitration. Reversed, it means legal trouble, loss and an adverse judgment or decision.

(9) *The Hermit*. A venerable, bearded old man, enveloped in a mantle and supported by a staff, holds a lantern in his extended hand, with which he is seeking after eternal truth. Prudence and wisdom are the leading ideas conveyed by this card; badly aspected by other cards, however, it enjoins the necessity of secrecy, watch-

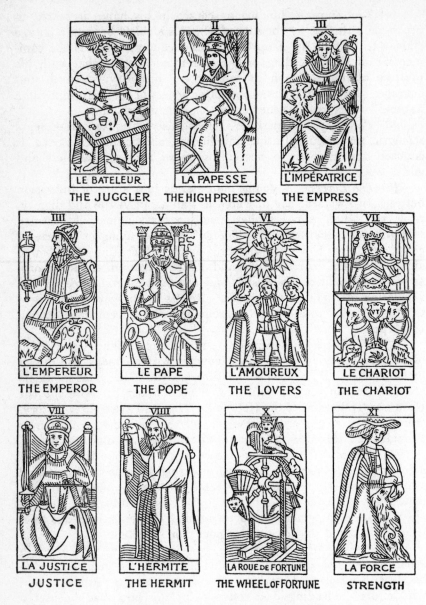

THE TAROT: Cards of the Major Arcana

The Tarot: Cards of the Major Arcana

fulness and caution against hidden enemies and subtle intrigues. Reversed, it signifies timidity, fear and excess of caution.

(10) *The Wheel of Fortune*. This card, which is definitely Egyptian in its symbolism, signifies fate and destiny, and hence, more vulgarly, good and bad luck. It portrays a wheel turning upon its axis; at the summit, armed with a sword, is the inscrutable Egyptian sphinx, symbol of authority and power, and expressing the relentless decrees of fate from which there is no appeal. On either side of the wheel and clinging to its rim are two animal forms, one ascending and the other descending as the wheel revolves; they represent respectively Anubis, the beneficent Egyptian jackal-headed god, and his enemy Set, the god of darkness and the murderer of Osiris, his own brother.

This card, therefore, illustrates how both good and evil in turns have equal shares in determining the destiny of man, and how one may be lifted from obscurity to a pinnacle of good fortune and let fall remorselessly when this apogee has been reached. Thus, in a good position, it is very favourable indeed; but if badly aspected by other cards or reversed, unfortunate influences will delay the achievement of one's aims.

(11) *Strength*. A graceful and elegantly attired young woman, wearing a hat like that observed on the Juggler of the first arcanum, which is the symbol of universal life, is closing with perfect ease the mouth of a roaring lion—a subtle and delightful allegory to express the ideas of invincible strength and dauntless courage which comprise the meaning of this card. It promises victory and the attainment of the end in view to those who know how to direct their natural gifts and will-power into the right channels, and who persevere in their efforts with unflagging energy. Reversed, it means vain and fruitless striving, dissipation of energy and abuse of power.

(12) *The Hanged Man*. A young man, who somewhat resembles the lover of the sixth arcanum, hangs upside down from a cross-beam, to which he is tied by one foot, while his hands are bound behind his back. He represents trials, vicissitudes, charity and, above all, self-denial and personal sacrifice. A reversed card implies that this sacrifice is wasted; it also gives warning of accidents and the risk of violent death.

(13) *Death*. A grinning skeleton mows down humanity with

his merciless scythe, the ground being littered with heads, hands, feet and fleshless bones. This arcanum is a very evil omen, as the number of the card—fateful 13—portends; it threatens serious loss, and should serve as a warning to the inquirer to postpone for a time any important action or enterprise which he may have been contemplating. If the card appears reversed, its portent is more sinister still; the inquirer should look to his health.

(14) *Temperance.* A young woman garbed with angel's wings is pouring a stream of fluid from one vase into another without spilling it. She bears a flower on her forehead, while leaves and plants spring from the earth around her. This beautiful allegory stands for fruitfulness, action, life and vitality, tempered, however, with wisdom and restraint. It is a fortunate card and often foreshadows a rich marriage. When in a reversed position, the symbolism of this arcanum loses its restraint, and fruitfulness degenerates into dissoluteness, vitality and action into mere restlessness and changeability.

(15) *The Devil,* a naked, hideous form, seems to be hovering in the air. Bat's wings flutter from his shoulders; his head displays a pair of branching horns, while his misshapen hands and feet end in the claws of a harpy. On the horizon behind him the sun is just setting in a reddened sky, showing that night, the realm of the Prince of Darkness, is about to begin. At the feet of the Devil, fettered by their necks by means of long ropes, are two naked demons, with tails, horns and long, pointed ears; they represent man and woman, unarmed in their nakedness against the powers of darkness and fettered by their own gross and material desires.

This card is eloquent of temptation—not necessarily itself an evil omen, but evil if the fatal enticement is not resisted. Illness, weakness, and an unprotected condition are also implied. If the card is reversed, the temptation comes with a vast and malign power, and he will be a strong man morally who succeeds in repulsing it.

(16) *The Tower Struck by Lightning,* or the Mad-house. A flash of lightning from Heaven shatters the battlements of a stone tower, while a shower of gold coins, with which the tower has been filled, falls to the earth. Two men are tumbling headlong from the stricken building, the attitude of the one in the foreground curiously

resembling the form of the Hebrew letter Ayin (ע), with which this card is cabbalistically identified.

Surprise is the keynote of this card, symbolized by the flash of lightning. Unhappiness, deception, disgrace and ruin are its portents, and the evil which it brings usually takes the form of a sudden and unforeseen calamity. If reversed, its evil influence is lessened considerably. If placed near a card of deniers, especially a seven, it foreshadows, strangely enough, an unexpected legacy.

(17) *The Star.* A beautiful, naked young woman kneels beneath a sky set with stars, one of which is predominantly brilliant; she pours water from two vases into a spring—a symbolism strongly reminiscent of the fourteenth arcanum. This card is purely Egyptian in its symbolism. The young woman represents Isis regulating the flooding of the Nile, upon which the whole life of Egypt depended.

The resplendent star is Sirius, the particular star of Isis, whose rising at dawn at the time of the summer solstice heralded the beginning of the inundation of the Nile and the commencement of the sacred year of ancient Egypt. An ibis perched upon a flowering tree in the background completes the Egyptian element.

Hope is the spirit breathed by this arcanum. As hope reawakened in the hearts of the ancient Egyptians when the tears of Isis mourning for her lost spouse Osiris caused the annual rising of the Nile and the regeneration of the world, so may fresh faith and renewed courage enter into the hearts of those who have this card well placed.

Reversed, however, it expresses the negation of hope, and presages difficulties and loss.

(18) *The Moon.* An undulating landscape stretches away to the horizon, where it is bounded on either hand by a tower. The moon gazes placidly down upon the earth and scatters upon it shining pearls or drops of gold. Two large dogs are baying at the moon, while below a scarlet crayfish crawls out of a pool in the foreground.

Another Egyptian allegory. Again we see the tears of Isis falling upon a desert country and bringing the naked earth to life where they fall. The towers represent the tropics of Capricorn and Cancer, which limit the course of the sun and moon; while the dogs represent attentive spirits guarding the moon and thus protecting indirectly the life and welfare of humanity. The crayfish rising from its pool is the zodiacal Cancer, the passing of which by the sun and moon coincides with the rising of Sirius and the flooding of the Nile.

Regarded from the divinatory aspect, this arcanum loses all of the beneficent meaning which it was originally intended to convey. Deception, involved and obscure dealings, trickery, hidden enemies and concealed dangers and a generally murky and unsatisfactory state of affairs, represented by the misty and reflective light of the moon, are the meanings accorded to it by tradition.

In a reversed position, its evil influence is strengthened and brought nearer to the inquirer, who will probably come to grief through his own duplicity.

(19) *The Sun.* Two almost naked children—probably the celestial Castor and Pollux, the Gemini of the zodiac—are seen standing in front of a wall. Above them the sun casts down his radiant beams, which fall like drops of gold around them. A very lucky omen, as might be conjectured, signifying peace, contentment and a happy marriage. Even if reversed, this fortunate card does not lose its benign influence, but suffers only a slight lessening in the force of its imports.

(20) *The Judgment.* An angel appears in a blaze of glory, blowing a trumpet from which flutters a small banner resembling that borne by the Paschal Lamb. At the blast of the heavenly clarion, an old man, a woman and a child rise from their tombs with clasped hands.

It is not clear whether this card should be regarded as representing the Last Judgment, as its appearance and traditional title would suggest, or whether the funereal element was added by the fancy of the mediaeval artist who engraved it—in which case it might very reasonably be taken as an emblem of the creation of man, who is seen rising from the earth at the behest of his Creator, while the dark, shadowy hills of a primeval landscape roll away into the distance.

Whatever be its true symbolism, this card heralds a change of position, which may be favourable or otherwise. If reversed, however, this change is definitely unfavourable.

(21) *The World.* A young woman lightly draped in a scarf stands in an attitude suggesting dancing, with her legs crossed like

those of the Hanged Man of the twelfth arcanum. In her left hand she holds a wand resembling that brandished by the Juggler in the first card. An oval laurel wreath surrounds her, while the four corners of the card are occupied by the symbolical figures of the Apocalypse—the Lion, the Calf, the Man and the flying Eagle—who disclosed to the wondering eyes of St. John the four ravening horsemen of Divine judgment.

The dancing figure represents humanity and the world, constantly in motion and surrounded by the zodiac, which is typified by the evergreen wreath (emblem of eternity) marked at the two solstices by crossed bands of red. The four mystical figures stand for the four seasons of the year, the eagle representing Spring, the time of aspiration; the lion symbolizing the heat of Summer; the calf or bull, Autumn, season of ploughing and agricultural pursuits; while the man expresses the idea of Winter, when men are drawn to their fellows in social intercourse.

From the divining point of view, this card is a very happy omen, signifying health, consistent success, fertility and a well-ordered life. If reversed, these good omens will be hampered and delayed in their fulfilment, but not extinguished.

(22) *The Fool.* At first sight this arcanum seems fantastic and devoid of meaning. A gaily dressed man, but with his clothing disarranged and dishevelled, strides negligently across a rocky landscape without appearing to pay any attention to a lynx-like animal which falls upon him from behind with savage fury. The man leans upon a staff, while a bag is suspended from another staff that is slung across his shoulder.

That the carelessness and folly of the man are not due to the natural and passing heedlessness of youth is shown by his short, pointed beard; he is one who has reached mature years, but has succeeded only in dissipating his powers. In a word, he is the same person as the Juggler of the first arcanum, who has chosen the wrong turning when put to the test at the sixth card, and instead of controlling and making use of his natural forces (symbolized by the cups, staves, swords and deniers), has stowed them away uselessly in a bag, although at the same time he cannot help carrying them about with him.

The Fool is the only card of the major arcana which does not bear a number; this is not the result of chance or of oversight on the part of the card-maker, as might at first be imagined, but has a deeper significance. To the student of occultism the major arcana of the tarot symbolize the complete and orderly progression of Heaven, Nature and Mankind through the spiritual, mental and earthly planes. It is impossible, however, to take into account the folly and degradation of man, shown by this card, which, having no fixed place or time of manifestation, being subject to no rules of reason or logic, and violating even the decrees of God and Nature, will fall unexpectedly across even the most carefully ordered life and bring the luckless subject to unhappiness or destruction.

In fortune-telling, the Fool represents want of thought and heedlessness of action, giving rise to unhappiness and leading to degradation. If reversed, it is more unfortunate still, and presages a neurotic condition, disordered mental faculties and insanity.

The Minor Arcana

First of all, a word must be said about reversed cards. Every card of the tarot appearing in a reversed position bears a meaning diverging in a greater or less degree from the normal one. But with some packs of a particular design it is not at all clear, in the case of certain cards of the minor arcana, whether a card is reversed or upright. This is especially so with the majority of the numeral cards of deniers and staves.

The position of the other cards in these suits is often indicated by some detail in their design; for instance, that of most of the cards in the sword suit can be distinguished by the direction in which the weapon is pointing, while other cards have flowers, sprays of foliage, fleurs-de-lis, and so on, from which it may be judged whether or no they are reversed.

With cards that are perfectly symmetrical, however, as are most of the deniers, it is quite impossible to distinguish their position, and so we would suggest that the student make a small mark with pencil or ink at one end of the card, so as to indicate the top or bottom.

In order to yield a true divination, the reversal of the cards should be quite fortuitous and the result of the independent working of fate for each inquirer. It will be obvious, however, that this condition is vitiated and made void when the cards remain in the same relative positions throughout several divinations, perhaps for several different persons; for although the order in which the cards occur will be different when the pack has been shuffled, yet it is impossible by shuffling the cards to have any effect upon their reversal.

Hence we would recommend the student to go through the entire pack before giving a reading, and turn every reversed card into an upright position. The pack should then be shuffled and presented to the inquirer, who must be asked to reverse about one-third of the cards, distributed as evenly as possible through the pack; however, he must not look at the faces of the cards while doing so. The pack should then be thoroughly shuffled once more and given to the inquirer to cut.

Below are the meanings which are to be accorded to the cards of the minor arcana. It will be observed that in fortune-telling by the tarot the ace is not honoured by the pre-eminent position which it takes in the ordinary pack of cards, but instead retains its original value of one, thus being the lowest card in the pack.

CUPS have a general relationship to love, success, happiness, protection.

King. A sympathetic and warm-hearted man, probably fair and a bachelor; also a man of law or of the Church. If reversed, this card counsels the inquirer to be on his guard.

Queen. A fair-haired, friendly woman, probably the object of the inquirer's affections. If reversed, take heed lest she lead you to a course of life which you may come to regret.

Knight. A friendly, fair young man, a lover; also trust, goodwill and a pleasant visit. Reversed, underhand dealings.

Knave. A young, fair person of either sex, probably the bearer of a message. Integrity; also a birth. Reversed, trickery.

Ten. This card stands for the town or place in which the inquirer resides, and also the esteem in which he is held by his friends and acquaintances. Reversed, it shows disputes and friction in his family circle.

Nine. A card of auspicious omen, signifying success and renown. If reversed, the inquirer's success will be somewhat hampered, probably as a result of his own imprudence.

Eight. Disinterested love will receive its reward in a happy marriage, and the inquirer will have true and affectionate friends; if he is a man, marriage with a fair-haired woman is indicated. Reversed, happiness, laughter and gaiety.

Seven. An unexpected stroke of good luck; an enterprise will meet with a success that was not anticipated. Also, success in love. Reversed, good fortune and beneficence.

Six. When upright, this arcanum indicates that the cards which are associated with it in the divination refer to actions that took place in the past. If reversed, they have not yet come to pass, but will do so very shortly.

Five. This card foreshadows a marriage, a happy and triumphal conclusion to a love affair, coupled with a monetary gain. If reversed, it signifies receipt of unexpected news, or the unlooked-for arrival of a friend.

Four. Your love affair is in serious danger of going awry, owing to outside influences. Reversed, a new and very pleasant friendship.

Three. Success bringing brilliant fame; the enterprise you are engaged upon will turn out well, and the hopes you cherish most dearly will be fulfilled. Reversed, disgrace, an accident.

Two. Reciprocated love; at the same time, wealth but miserliness. Reversed, love discouraged or rejected.

Ace. Conviviality, good news and rejoicing. Reversed, an alteration in one's life, probably the beginning of a love affair or the inception of some new enterprise or inspired labour.

DENIERS have a general bearing on money, trade, commercial ventures and material fortune.

King. A fair man, probably unfriendly to the inquirer, and in any case unsympathetic. Reversed, this card symbolizes a hard, cunning and avaricious man who lives a retired life—in a word, a miser and a recluse.

Queen. A wealthy, fair woman leading a retired life; also an urge to make money. Reversed, monetary affairs will not proceed very smoothly.

Knight. A fair young man, unknown to the inquirer; a new arrival. Also, indiscreet behaviour with a member of the opposite sex, engendering worry and scandal. Reversed, a quarrel.

Knave. A young, fair person of either sex, bearing a pleasant message or a letter containing good news. Reversed, bad news and loss of money.

Ten. A gain of money. Reversed, a small gain.

Nine. A fairly substantial income, which will be the result of your own talents and thrift. Reversed, the money will take longer to accumulate, and obstacles will have to be avoided or overcome.

Eight. A well-regulated and tranquil life, coupled with prosperity. Reversed, strife and disorder.

Seven. A monetary gain or gift. A reversal of the card indicates financial worries, which may or may not have serious consequences.

Six. Disputes concerning a sum of money, probably entailing a lawsuit and consequent loss. Reversed, unexpected resources will be placed at your command.

Five. An unhoped-for sum of money, a windfall, which will compensate you for previous losses. Reversed, a slight gain, or one that is fraught with anxiety and legal difficulties.

Four. Social amusements and association with entertaining people, which, if the card is reversed, will probably involve the inquirer in excessive expenditure.

Three. A business proposal or undertaking. If the card is reversed, it is not likely to lead to any significant result.

Two. You will not find it easy to establish your financial affairs satisfactorily. Reversed, a sudden and unlooked-for happening, which may be auspicious or quite the reverse.

Ace. The beginning of a project or enterprise that will entail a monetary gain; also gifts or a legacy. Reversed, a small monetary gain or legacy.

STAVES relate in a general way to enterprise, striving, creation and labour, also commerce.

King. A friendly and sympathetic dark man, most likely a family man; also, successful business dealings. Reversed, danger.

Queen. A dark woman, friendly, prudent and level-headed, probably a married woman with children. Reversed, suspicion, jealousy or mistrust.

Knight. A helpful, dark young man; prudence in money matters. Reversed, ill luck owing to the imprudence of a friend; also carelessness in financial matters.

Knave. A dark-haired child, perhaps the bearer of news or a message from someone closely related to you; also well-regulated financial affairs. Reversed, thriftlessness and extravagance.

Ten. An unfamiliar or foreign town, travels abroad. Reversed, unless care is exercised an undertaking is likely to go awry.

Nine. Frankness, good judgment and integrity, leading to success. Reversed, underhand dealings and disloyalty.

Eight. A dark-haired young woman, of upright character. For a man, a likelihood of marrying the latter. Reversed, worry and deception due to a woman.

Seven. Legacies, business gains and assured success. Reversed, precarious business affairs.

Six. Complete or partial failure of a project. Reversed, vain and fruitless striving or desire.

Five. A love affair; also, a triumph over impediments that threaten the success of an undertaking. Reversed, unreciprocated or even tragic love; badly aspected as well as reversed, illicit love.

Four. Gaiety, pleasure and the enjoyment of congenial company. Reversed, impediments to success and a generally unsympathetic atmosphere.

Three. Wealth and renown are indicated. Reversed, the laying of the foundation of a successful career.

Two. Trouble, crossings in love, unforeseen obstacles in a business enterprise. Reversed, the receipt of a message, probably taking the form of a love-letter.

Ace. The inception of an undertaking of some kind. Reversed, it will be fraught with difficulty, but has a chance of succeeding if care and prudence are exercised.

SWORDS have the most ominous and evil significance of the four suits, relating to strife, loss, worry, sorrow, and the darker passions of the human soul.

King. A man (probably dark) endowed or invested with power, either moral, mental or worldly. If reversed, his power takes on a malign aspect, and it will be directed against the inquirer, who will suffer unhappy consequences.

Queen. A dark woman, evil natured or having an unhappy influence on the inquirer's destiny. Reversed, she will spread scandal and calumnies about him; also, loneliness, abandonment and matrimonial unhappiness.

Knight. A dark young man, able, but treacherous and not to be trusted. Reversed, he will cause quarrelling and strife among your closest friends.

Knave. Evil tidings and impediments; a treacherous rival in love, who will strive to do you harm. Reversed, this rival will prove to be your own supposed friend.

Ten. Unhappiness, sorrow, depression, poverty. Reversed, a slight and transient gain.

Nine. Your credulity will be taken advantage of, and you may be bitterly disillusioned. Be on your guard. Reversed, suspicion, disharmony and rupture, leading to hatred.

Eight. Quarrels, rivalry; also illness. Reversed, a calamity or an accident; bloodshed.

Seven. Business success and bright prospects. Reversed, your enemies will triumph. If you go to law, you may lose your case.

Six. A voyage or the arrival of a traveller or messenger. Reversed, a gain from an unexpected quarter.

Five. Sorrow, loss, and the triumph of one's enemies are betokened, whatever be the position of this card.

Four. Mysticism, occultism, religion, and voluntary seclusion. Reversed, disaster, ruin; loneliness and seclusion that are compulsory to a greater or less degree.

Three. Hatred, strife and disunion. Reversed, separation or divorce, disillusionment; fraud and lies on the part of the inquirer.

Two. Amiability and friendship; probably a former enemy will profess friendship for the inquirer, and may tender a peace-offering. Reversed, do not trust his advances, which are founded merely upon deceit and guile.

Ace. You will incur somebody's enmity, which may have sinister consequences for you. Reversed, you will triumph over this enemy.

It now remains to describe how the tarot should be set out so that its oracular powers may be made use of. Perhaps the most popular method of arranging the cards among professional diviners, and one that at the same time has the great virtue of simplicity, is that which Etteilla himself devised after years of research and deep pondering over the symbolism and traditional meanings of the arcana. It is as follows:—

Shuffle the seventy-eight cards together and give them to the inquirer to be cut three times with his left hand. On their return, deal them out into three heaps, each containing twenty-six cards. The pack must be held face downwards while the cards are being dealt, and one card must be placed face downwards on each of the heaps in turn, working from left to right. Now take the centre heap and set it aside.

Gather up the remaining fifty-two cards, shuffle them well, ask the inquirer to cut them, and in the same manner as before set out three heaps of seventeen cards each, leaving one card undealt. Again remove the middle heap to one side, but keep it separate from the first heap so removed. Once more shuffle the remaining cards, which this time will amount to thirty-five, request the inquirer to cut them three times with the left hand as before, and deal them into three heaps of eleven cards each, leaving two cards undealt. Again remove the middle heap to one side.

Now take up the heap of twenty-six cards that was set aside first of all, and lay out the cards composing it face upwards in a row from right to left. Take the second heap, that of seventeen cards, and arrange it similarly below the first row; and then do the same with the third row of eleven cards, the three rows taking the form somewhat of an inverted pyramid.

Having composed this figure, the diviner is ready to decipher its oracles. He should read each row of cards in turn, from right to left, basing his prognostications upon the interpretations of the individual cards, upon the inferences to be drawn from the proximity of other cards, and from the proportion of the different suits in each row. Reversed cards should be particularly noted; the omens will be the more or less sinister according to the greater proportion of reversed or upright cards.

Moreover, we must mention that in this particular figure the uppermost row of twenty-six cards represents the soul, the psychic development of the inquirer and the mystic and occult powers which mould his character and mark out the lines of his destiny; the middle row relates to his mind and intellectual powers, his interests, affections, abilities and hobbies; while the bottom row has reference to his material life and worldly affairs, his circumstances and surroundings, his health and all that concerns his body and the lower aspects of his nature.

Etteilla's Great Figure of Destiny

Etteilla reached the summit of his powers of divination in the method which he eventually devised and which is known as his Great Figure of Destiny. This can be used either as a method of divination on its own account, or to supplement the method which we have just given and so render it more explicit.

First of all, shuffle the pack of seventy-eight cards thoroughly and ask the inquirer to cut it three times with his left hand. Spread out the pack face downwards and request the inquirer to select a card to represent himself. Place this face upwards in the middle of a large table (the floor may be preferable, since Etteilla's Great Figure takes up a great deal of space).

Reassemble the remaining cards, shuffle them again, once more have them cut thrice, and set them out face upwards round the inquirer's card (as shown in the diagram on this page), laying down the cards carefully one by one from the top of the pack (which should be face downwards) in the exact numerical order which we have indicated.

At this point we must make it quite clear to the student that,

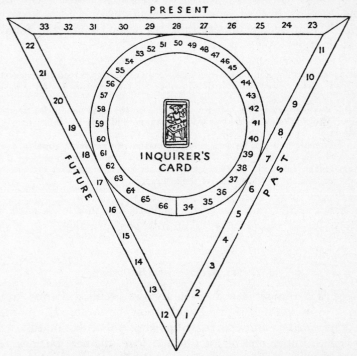

Arrangement of Cards for the Great Figure of Destiny

throughout all the systems we are about to give which utilize numbered spaces for setting out the cards, none of these spaces is necessarily bound to be occupied by a card bearing a corresponding number; indeed, it will be merely coincidence if there is any such correspondence.

For instance, a space labelled five is not necessarily to be occupied by a five of cups, deniers, staves or swords, or by the fifth card (the Pope) of the major arcana; the number attached to the space merely indicates that it is to be occupied by the fifth card in order of those dealt from the pack, which, of course, might be any card.

We have thought it well to emphasize this point, since any misconception on the part of the student resulting in a departure from the established rules of the art of cartomancy will entail a faulty arrangement of the cards and hence an absolutely untrue reading.

All is now ready to interpret the oracle upon the following general lines:—

> The *present* is indicated by the two upper rows of the figure read together, that is, the twenty-third card with the forty-fifth, the twenty-fourth with the forty-sixth, and so on.
>
> The *past* is revealed by the two rows of cards on the right-hand side; thus, the first card is taken with the thirty-fourth, the second with the thirty-fifth, and so on.
>
> The *future* depends for its fathoming upon the two left-hand rows of cards, the twelfth card being read with the sixty-sixth, the thirteenth card with the sixty-fifth, and so on. Observe that the cards in this segment of the circle are read contrary to the order of their numbers.

When thus reading the cards in pairs, the inquirer's card, too, should, as far as possible, be taken into consideration.

A Rapid Method of Divination

Here is a rapid method given by the occultist Papus, author of a very recondite and learned work upon the tarot. By its means revelations can be obtained regarding any particular matter which finds a place under one of four heads: love, finance, business, and a lawsuit or struggle of any kind—a method of division which seems to sum up the principal fields of human activity fairly comprehensively.

According, therefore, to the kind of subject concerning which the prognostications are required, separate the appropriate suit of the tarot from the rest of the pack as shown below:—

> For a love affair take the cups.
> For a money matter take the deniers.
> For a business undertaking, or an enterprise of any kind, take the staves.
> For a lawsuit, or any kind of opposition or struggle, take the swords.

Having shuffled the suit that is indicated, request the inquirer to cut these cards three times with his left hand; throughout the divination the pack is to be held face downwards. Then deal off the first four cards, face downwards, in the following arrangement:—

At this point, take up the *major* arcana, which should previously have been set apart; shuffle them and ask the inquirer to cut them. Spread them out face downwards upon the table and request him to select seven cards haphazard. These seven cards are again to be shuffled and cut; and then, still holding these major cards face downwards, deal off the three uppermost cards into the following arrangement:

$$\begin{array}{ccc}
 & 4 & \\
\text{I} & & \text{II} \\
1 & & 3 \\
 & \text{III} & \\
 & 2 &
\end{array}$$

Arabic numerals stand for the minor arcana, Roman numerals for the major arcana. The oracle is to be deciphered upon the following lines, the cards being exposed one by one in turn:—

	1.	The beginning of the matter in question.
Minor	2.	Its climax, or culminating point.
Arcana	3.	The obstacles likely to impede its progress.
	4.	The conclusion and result of the matter.
Major	I.	Influences affecting the matter in the past.
Arcana	II.	Influences holding sway at the present.
	III.	Influences that will be exerted in the future.

It should be noted that in this method of cartomancy, no particular character, description or appearance, can be attached to any persons who may be indicated. As Papus says, "the king represents a man, without any other distinction, the queen a woman, the knight a young man, and the knave a child."

Papus describes another way of arranging the tarot which is

not so simple as the last, but which furnishes with great reliability general prognostications upon the inquirer's life and destiny, as well as explicit readings upon the progress and result of any particular circumstance.

Separate the major from the minor arcana, shuffle the latter and have them cut by the inquirer as we have previously described. Deal off the first twelve cards, face upwards, and arrange them as is shown below:—

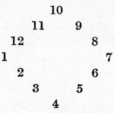

Now shuffle the major arcana, and ask the inquirer to cut them and choose seven cards, the pack meanwhile being kept face downwards. The first four of these cards are then to be placed, in the order in which they were chosen, within and close to all four corners of the parallelogram formed by the first twelve cards, as shown below (the Roman numerals designating the four major arcana):—

The remaining three major cards are then to be placed, in the order in which they were chosen, in the middle of the figure, as is shown by the figures V, VI and VII in the diagram below. The inquirer's card must then be placed in the very centre, the Juggler representing a male inquirer, the High Priestess a female. If either of these cards has already appeared in the figure, it must be removed to the centre, its vacated position being filled by a card of the major arcana which the inquirer is asked to choose haphazard.

The completed figure should then present the following appearance:—

```
                  10
            11    II    9
        12  V    [ ]  VI   8
     1  I         [ ]    III   7
        2        VII     6
            3    IV    5
                  4
```

The figure is now ready to be deciphered. Actually it is not nearly so complicated as it looks.

The twelve minor arcana, whose places are indicated by Arabic figures, relate, in order, to the various vicissitudes and turns of fortune which the inquirer experiences during the course of his life, or which affect any particular enterprise, business matter or event, Nos. 1, 2, 3 referring to the past, Nos. 4, 5, 6 to the present, and Nos. 7–12 (inclusive) to the future. Moreover, the omens revealed by the major arcana Nos. V, VI and VII will give an indication of the particular character of these three realms of time respectively. Further revelations are furnished by the remaining four major arcana upon the following lines:—

I indicates the Beginning of the life, or of the enterprise whose progress and outcome it is desired to determine.

II discloses the influences exerted at the Climax, or culminating point, of the career or enterprise in question.

III relates to the Obstacles that stand in the way of success or fulfilment, and to the dangers that will have to be guarded against.

IV shows the Termination of the life or the ultimate issue of the enterprise.

Italian cartomancers practise a very simple method of consulting the tarot which has the advantage of yielding information upon a number of definite points.

Shuffle the whole pack and ask the inquirer to cut it three times with his left hand; then spread out the cards face downwards upon the table and request him to choose forty-eight of them, laying the chosen cards in order one upon another.

Now, keeping this heap of forty-eight cards face downwards, deal the cards, from the top of the pile, into twelve heaps of four cards each, building up the heaps in rotation. When this operation has been concluded, the heaps are ready to have their meanings read in turn. The twelve heaps refer respectively, and in the order in which they were laid down, to

1. The inquirer himself and the circumstances and influences which surround his life.
2. Monetary affairs.
3. Relatives and family ties.
4. Close relations and their property and concerns.
5. Love affairs and the inquirer's own enjoyment and personal happiness.
6. Friends, acquaintances, associates and fellow workers.
7. Marriage and legal actions.
8. Health, both physical and mental; also accidents.
9. The inquirer's own virtues and abilities, what they will lead to and how they will be rewarded.
10. Good fortune or the reverse which is affecting the inquirer at the present moment.
11. Help, tutelage and protection.
12. Disasters and unhappiness.

FORTUNE-TELLING BY GAMES OF PATIENCE

Wherever patience games are known and played, it has long been traditional that they form a ready means by which the future can be made to yield its secrets. Whether this method of divination —which can be paralleled by an almost endless number of forms of sortilege that were used among ancient peoples—is regarded merely as a particularly charming kind of superstition or amusement, or whether an occult or quasi-scientific basis is seriously claimed for it, it would be unfitting in a treatise on cartomancy to pass by in silence a pastime so universally popular, and one that can at least display a long and unquestioned tradition to affirm its reliability as a means of fortune-telling.

We shall describe only a few games of patience in these pages; the reader may acquaint himself with several hundreds more, in an almost limitless range of complexity, by studying the numerous books that have been especially devoted to patience.

In all the games, the principle is the same. The player mentally formulates a question regarding the issue of some event or the future success of an enterprise, and the cards give an answer propitious or otherwise according to whether the game of patience is satisfactorily resolved or not. Love, business, money, happiness, and the attainment of any cherished hope or desire are subjects upon which the answer of the cards is commonly sought.

A game of patience is usually played by dealing a certain number of cards into a particular arrangement known as the *lay-out*. The cards that remain undealt constitute the *stock*. The object is to build up *families* (consisting of all the cards of one suit) in regular ascending or descending order, or else *sequences*, which follow in the consecutive order of the numbers of the cards (which are not necessarily of the same suit). This procedure is known as *packing*, the original card upon which a family or sequence is built being known as the *foundation*. If a card cannot be played, it is placed in the *rubbish-heap*. Cards that are discarded as taking no part in the game are said to be *dead*.

The patience is successfully resolved when all the families or sequences have been completely built up, or when all the vacant spaces have been filled. When, according to the laws of the particular game that is being played, it is impossible to carry the packing any farther, the cards are said to be *blocked*, or *chockered;* in the majority of cases this marks the unsuccessful conclusion of the patience.

In patience it is usually immaterial whether the pack is held face upwards or with the cards concealed. It must be understood that the cards used for these games are those of the full pack of fifty-two, the sole exception which we shall give here being the example called the Wizard, for which a piquet pack of thirty-two cards is to be used.

We will now give a few specimen games, played with both one and two packs of cards. As previously stated, the inquirer should firmly fix his mind, before playing and while shuffling the cards, upon the particular matter of which he is anxious to learn the issue.

The Carpet

To form the carpet, spread out four horizontal rows, one below the other, of five cards each. The cards must be face upwards. Should an ace be turned up, it is to be laid in a separate row beneath, and its place in the carpet filled by another card from the stock;

the remaining aces, if any, must be removed from the stock and placed side by side with the others to form foundations for families in ascending order. Now search for deuces in the carpet and lay them upon their respective aces. Similarly a three is laid upon the deuce, and so on, the place in the carpet that was occupied by each card that has been removed being filled by another card taken from the top of the stock.

When it is found impossible to continue by reason of there being no cards of the proper value left in the carpet, the cards of the stock must be dealt, face upwards, into a rubbish-heap, each card as it is dealt being scrutinized to see if it can be used to build up a family on its appropriate ace. At this stage of the game any spaces in the carpet should be filled from the rubbish-heap rather than from the stock in hand. A second deal of the heap is not allowed.

A successful issue to the matter in question is indicated when the families are built up on all the aces as far as the kings; if this cannot be done, failure is to be inferred.

The Travellers

This simple game is somewhat of a departure from the usual style of patience. Twelve heaps must first be laid out face downwards, each consisting of four cards. The remaining four cards comprise the stock. These heaps are then to be numbered, mentally, from one to twelve, the ace being taken as number one, while knaves and queens are to be identified with the eleventh and twelfth heaps respectively. There is no heap for kings. A glance at the diagram on the opposite page will make this system of numbering quite clear.

The object of the game is to remove each card in the figure to the heap whose number accords with the value of the card in question. Thus, you will endeavour to assemble all the aces on the first heap, all the nines on the ninth heap, all the knaves on the eleventh, all the queens on the twelfth, and so on.

The game proceeds by turning up the first card of the stock and placing it face upwards beneath that particular heap which agrees with the card's value. Thus a ten of any suit would be placed under the heap which you have mentally labelled ten, while a queen would go under heap No. 12. The top card of the same heap must then be taken up and transferred underneath the heap of its own number; the last-mentioned heap must then yield up its own top card to be similarly dealt with, and so on.

If a king is turned up, however—either from the stock or from the top of a heap—it is to be thrown aside and another card drawn from the stock. The incidence of kings, it will be seen,

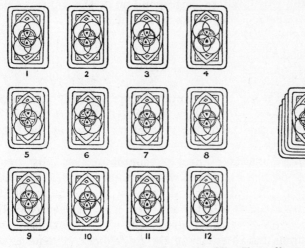

How to Arrange the Heaps for The Travellers

constitutes the only obstacle to success in this game. The patience fails if the stock has been entirely drawn upon without all the cards in the figure having been transferred to their appropriate heaps.

The Wizard

For this patience, a piquet pack of thirty-two cards (previously described) must be held face upwards, so that the cards are observed as they are put down. Deal the first card and call seven, either mentally or aloud; the next card is to be identified with eight, while the following cards as they are dealt are to be called nine, ten, knave, queen, king, ace and then back to seven again. Whenever a card that has been dealt bears the value which you have coupled with it, it must be taken up and set aside.

When the pack has been exhausted, pick up all the cards which have not been set aside and deal them again, the last card of the former deal (unless it corresponded with the value called and so was set aside) being thus the first of the new deal. The calling must be resumed at the point where it was interrupted by the conclusion of the previous deal.

If all the cards fail to correspond with the values called, the patience must be regarded as unsuccessful.

The Clock

Twelve cards are to be arranged face upwards upon the table in the form of the figure on page 53. Should a court card be turned up when setting out the figure, it must be placed at the bottom of the stock.

The game consists of packing simultaneously any two cards in the figure whose combined values total eleven, such as eight and three, an ace and ten, and so on. For instance, if it were desired to cover the two last-mentioned cards, a card from the top of the pack would be laid upon each of them, thus presenting another combination of values in the clock face. Whenever a court card is turned up, it must be placed beneath the other cards in the pack and the next card taken instead.

When all the numeral cards have been placed and only court cards are left to cover the twelve heaps in the figure, the omen is to be regarded as auspicious. If any other cards besides the court cards are left over, the game has failed.

The Four Marriages

Two packs are necessary for this game, and they should be placed together and thoroughly shuffled. Deal out the first thirteen cards from the top of the pack, and if any two of them duplicate one another, return one of them to the pack and take a substitute. These thirteen cards are then placed face upwards in a heap in the order in which they present themselves by chance; they will comprise a complete sequence by value, irrespective of suits.

Now begin to deal the stock on to a rubbish-heap, placing together an ace and a deuce of each suit (making eight cards in all) round the central packet of thirteen cards. These aces and deuces

Arrangement of The Cards for The Clock

are the foundations on which sequences are to be packed in the following order:—

> On each ace—the corresponding ace, the three, five, seven, nine, knave, king, four, six, eight, ten, queen.
> On each deuce—the corresponding deuce, the four, six, eight, ten, queen, three, five, seven, nine, knave, king.

The central packet can be drawn upon for packing by taking its uppermost card; and this card should always be taken in preference to the last card dealt upon the rubbish-heap, in cases where both are eligible.

When you have gone right through the stock, turn over the rubbish-heap and deal it again, and if necessary you can turn it once more.   If the patience is successful, the final figure will display a circle consisting of the king and queen of each suit side by side—whence the title of the game—the central heap of thirteen cards having disappeared one by one.   If this result is not attained within the limit of the three deals allowed, the patience can be said to have failed.

The Star

This is another double-pack patience.   First take out the kings and the aces from both packs.   Place the king of hearts in the middle of the table to form the centre of the star; the remaining kings become dead, and are set aside as being of no use.   The aces, however, must be arranged round the king of hearts in the form of an eight-pointed star, as will be seen in the diagram; they are to form foundations.   The two packs should now be placed together and well shuffled.

The game proceeds by building sequences of the same suit in

Setting of the Cards for The Star

ascending order upon the eight aces, which at the end of a successful game will display the eight queens—since the kings are dead—surrounding the king of hearts.

Begin to deal the cards face upwards, laying one against each point of the star so as to lengthen its rays.   Should a deuce be turned up, it must be placed upon an ace of the same suit; and if the figure contains a three, it is to take its place upon the deuce just played. The vacancies thus made must be filled up, in order, from the stock. When the outer points of the star present no more cards that are eligible for packing, lengthen the rays once more by dealing another circle of eight cards, and continue to pack.

A third and final circle is permitted, and the manipulation of this circle presents some peculiarities. If it contains any two cards of the same suit that are in sequence with one another, the lower card of the two may be placed upon the higher, the vacancy in the ring being filled up from the pack; and when the lower card becomes eligible to take its place in one of the ascending sequences, both the cards may be moved together. Moreover, if you succeed in removing to their proper sequences the three outer cards of the four cards forming any given ray, you may replenish the vacancies with three cards taken from the *extreme points* of any three of the other rays, which in their turn must be replaced with fresh cards from the stock.

If the sequences are completed, so as to display the eight queens, within the limit of the three deals allowed, the patience is successful; if not, the answer to your question is not propitious.

The Windmill

Another two-pack game. Select one of the aces and four kings of different suits, and lay them face upwards on the table, the ace being in the centre and one of the kings at each of the four corners of the table. Shuffle the other cards, and lay out, face upwards, eight more cards in the form of a cross, to make the sails of the mill. A glance at the illustration on page 56 will give a clear idea of this lay-out.

The object of the game is to form four ascending sequences upon the central ace, and a descending sequence upon each of the four kings that flank it, all the sequences being regardless of suit.

First examine the sails of the windmill to see whether there is any card among them that is eligible for packing; for instance, a deuce would be placed upon the ace in the middle of the lay-out, while a queen could be packed upon any one of the kings. A vacancy so caused is to be immediately filled with a card from the stock, and this card may itself become at once of use in sequence building.

When no more cards in the sails are eligible, begin to deal the stock upon the rubbish-heap, the last card dealt being utilized, if

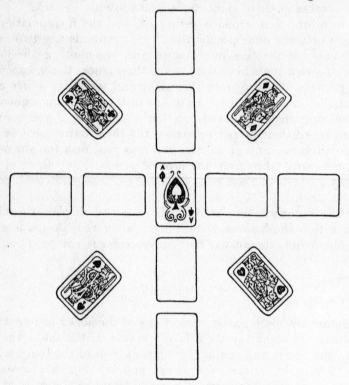

Card Arrangement for The Windmill

eligible, for packing. A successful patience will eventually display a central king in a ring of four aces. No second deal is allowed; so that if the single deal is unsuccessful in completing the figure, it must be taken as an inauspicious omen of fate.

One word of advice may be added. In packing the sequences in this game, should there be any choice in laying a card upon the centre heap or on one of those that have the kings for their foundations, the centre heap should have the preference.

Conclusion

In the course of this treatise we have endeavoured to present to the reader a lucid description of the principal methods of fortune-telling by cards that have been handed down by centuries of tradition. We have introduced him, in the tarot, to the accumulated occult lore of the ancient Egyptians and the Hebrews, and given some representative examples of the fascinating and ever-popular games of patience. For the benefit of the serious student of cartomancy, we would once more emphasize an observation which we made earlier in this treatise; namely, that the prognostications of the cards are not bound infallibly to be fulfilled, but should be regarded rather as signposts of guidance and encouragement, or beacons of warning.

To the Oriental proverb which affirms with the resignation characteristic of the East that "There is no armour against fate" we would oppose Schiller's line, "In thy own breast lie the stars of thy destiny"; for to a large extent the privilege and responsibility of controlling his own fate have been placed in the hands of every rational human being. The fault be his if he fails to direct it in a just and intelligent manner.

DIVINATION BY DICE AND DOMINOES

DICE

THE use of dice for all manner of games of chance dates from time immemorial. In ancient Egypt, classic Greece and the countries of the Far East, cubes of wood, metal, ivory or glass, with their sides numbered from 1 to 6, were popular not only for gaming but also as a means of consultation. Through their medium it was found that future events could be predicted and the turn of fate be made manifest.

Preparation in the traditional style is of the simplest. A circle is drawn in white chalk on the board or table on which the throws are to be made. Any dice which fall or roll outside this circle are not considered, unless they fall on the floor, when it is a presage of violent quarrels.

Three dice must be used and shaken in the box with the left hand. The following are the interpretations of the sum of the numbers which fall uppermost:—

THREE: Good luck awaits you; your wish will be fulfilled or an unexpected and pleasing event will take place.

FOUR: A disappointment is near at hand.

FIVE: Someone as yet unknown to you will bring you much happiness.

SIX: A portion of your worldly goods will be lost, but a gain in spiritual matters is indicated.

SEVEN: The vicious tongue of scandal is wagging; pay no heed to it, the accusations are unfounded.

EIGHT: You are pursuing a course which is both unwise and unjust; be prepared for a reprimand and profit accordingly.

NINE: Success in love affairs; outstanding quarrels will end in reconciliation.

TEN: Great happiness in the family and a progressive step in your business.

ELEVEN: Illness of someone you know, which may cause some anxiety for a time.

TWELVE: You will receive a letter which will call for a quick decision, but do not act without advice from a friend.

THIRTEEN:	Sorrow, which for long will remain uncomforted.
FOURTEEN:	A new friend who will become very dear to you.
FIFTEEN:	Let your conscience guide you; do not become involved in an affair which you suspect to be illegal or unjust.
SIXTEEN:	You are shortly to make a pleasant and profitable journey; let nothing delay you.
SEVENTEEN:	A stranger from abroad will make a suggestion by which you should be guided for future success.
EIGHTEEN:	Great luck and happiness, monetary gain and a rise in position. This will be fulfilled in the very near future.

Mondays, or days when the atmosphere is very heavily charged with electrical forces, as in stormy weather, are bad occasions for consultation, for then the omens are often erratic or inaccurate. The best conditions of all are present in the calm of the evening, about two hours after sundown. Strict silence must be maintained during the shaking and throwing.

If the same number, whatever its denomination, should turn up more than once during a consultation it signifies the advent of important news. To throw the dice so that one remains on top of the other is a warning omen for women, foretelling the deceit of an admirer; for men also it presages a need for great caution.

DOMINOES

A convenient and simple means of home consultation is through the medium of dominoes. In the way that each value of a playing-card is intimately connected with some divinatory significance, so also are the numbers on the face of each domino.

The pieces must first of all be shuffled and left face downwards. Then one is drawn and the number exposed. Do not draw more than three pieces at a single consultation, or on the same day, otherwise you will find yourself badly misled.

These are the omens indicated by each number:—

DOUBLE-SIX:	Great success and an important financial gain.
SIX-FIVE:	You will become a member of some organization formed for the benefit of others.
SIX-FOUR:	Arguments and lawsuits which will result in a loss.
SIX-THREE:	A short journey for your own good.
SIX-TWO:	In a few days you will receive a useful present.
SIX-ONE:	The cause of your trouble will shortly be removed.
SIX-BLANK:	Someone wishes ill of you; beware of a supposed friendship.
DOUBLE-FIVE:	Change of dwelling-place which will bring much happiness.

FIVE-FOUR:	Increase in wealth through a sound investment; do not speculate with your profit.
FIVE-THREE:	An important visit from someone who may help you.
FIVE-TWO:	Birth of a child to a member of your family.
FIVE-ONE:	A passionate love affair which may be attended with unhappy circumstances.
FIVE-BLANK:	Distress for one of your friends; you can be of much comfort.
DOUBLE-FOUR:	Revelry at the house of a stranger.
FOUR-THREE:	Fears of disappointment which are troubling you are quite unfounded.
FOUR-TWO:	You have made the acquaintance of a swindler and hoaxer; women especially should be on guard.
FOUR-ONE:	Financial worries and a settlement of debts which will leave you poor for a time.
FOUR-BLANK:	You have wronged a friend; seek reconciliation without delay.
DOUBLE-THREE:	Rivalry in your love affairs, causing great consternation.
THREE-TWO:	For the next few days you will be unlucky in games of chance; avoid taking risks.
THREE-ONE:	A startling revelation which may be of great help to you.
THREE-BLANK:	Jealousy will be the cause of estrangement from an old friend.
DOUBLE-TWO:	A happy marriage in which you will play an important part.
TWO-ONE:	A loss of personal property in the near future.
TWO-BLANK:	Great joy through meeting one who will become very dear to you.
DOUBLE-ONE:	A bold step taken now will cause you to better your position; do not hesitate.
ONE-BLANK:	A stranger will be coming from abroad to help you.
DOUBLE-BLANK:	An unhappy omen, indicating monetary losses and unforeseen disappointments.

To draw the same domino twice running strengthens the prediction and also denotes an almost immediate fulfilment.

READING THE TEA-LEAVES

I

OF all the many forms of divination—the art of foretelling the future—perhaps the simplest is the reading of the tea-leaves. It is an easily learned method, too; almost anyone who possesses the necessary patience to make a study of the various symbols and their meanings can become proficient in a very short space of time. The widespread belief that the art of reading tea-cups is a closed book to those who are not "psychic" is not justified. It is true, of course, that the "psychic" sense will often enable one to read a deeper meaning into the symbols —but the possession of this strange sense is by no means a necessity.

As in all other methods of divination, there is a certain ritual which must be observed—a ritual which is prescribed by tradition. First, however, let us consider the cup which is to be the vehicle of our destiny.

Although any type of cup may be employed, a greater degree of satisfaction will be attained if it be one with a wide mouth and sides that are not perpendicular. Also, the inside should be white and devoid of pattern, so that the pictures may form clearly. As to the size, it is better to use a large cup rather than a small one; a breakfast cup is the ideal type.

Now a word regarding the tea itself. If a dusty blend is used, then the leaves left in the bottom of the cup will take the form of a confused mass, and it will be impossible to give a coherent and satisfactory reading. Undoubtedly, the best kind of tea for the purpose is China tea, for the pictures it produces are usually extraordinarily well defined.

The ritual traditionally associated with divination by tea-leaves is easily committed to memory. The inquirer drinks from the cup until about one teaspoonful of liquid only is left therein. The cup is then held in the left hand and moved three times in a circular, anti-clockwise direction, during which operation the mind of the inquirer should be concentrated on any particular question, the answer to which he seeks in the tea-cup. The cup is then slowly inverted on the saucer and left there for a minute or so to enable the liquid to drain away.

The ritual is now finished and the task of reading the tea-leaves is about to begin.

On first glancing into the cup—which should be held in the right hand—one may be rather dismayed at the apparently meaningless pattern made by the leaves; if, however, the cup is surveyed carefully from all angles, definite pictures and symbols will begin to appear, and each of these will have some specific meaning.

Nevertheless, it sometimes happens that the cup offers nothing of interest, that the patterns of the leaves are too indistinct and confused to admit of any *true* interpretation; in such cases one must not try to read into the cup what is not there, but must admit, frankly, that the task is hopeless, and explain to the inquirer that it is probably due to the confused state of his mind.

In all readings, it should be remembered that it is as necessary to observe and weigh up the general conditions of the cup as it is to note the separate symbols. The good signs and the bad signs must be set off against each other and a balance struck, for only in this way can it be determined whether the fortune, generally, is propitious or unfavourable.

The handle of the cup represents the inquirer—in fortune-telling by cards it has its analogy in the "house." By this means one is able to distinguish between comings and goings and also to judge relative distances.

As to the timing of forecasted events, one is enabled to do this by noting the position of the various symbols. If they appear near the rim of the cup, the events represented are likely to happen in the near future, while those portrayed in the sides are not so immediate, and those on the bottom are remoter still.

The size of a symbol will afford a clue to its importance or magnitude. Thus, a small representation of an ass would symbolize a small legacy; a large representation, a large legacy. The clarity of a symbol, too, must be taken into account. If it is well defined, then its character, or influence, is emphasized accordingly; if it is misty, or badly formed, its character is diminished.

Sometimes an inquirer will wish to employ the tea-leaves merely for the purpose of obtaining an answer to a specific question; for example: "Shall I receive a letter to-morrow?" In this case a slightly different procedure is followed when reading the signs in the cup: one should not attempt to interpret all the pictures and symbols but should concentrate on those alone which seem to have some bearing on the question.

It may happen, however, that the cup is devoid of such signs. In this eventuality one makes a careful computation of good omens and bad omens, and if the former outweigh the latter then one may predict that conditions are favourable to the fulfilment of the inquirer's wish.

We will conclude this general explanation of the art of tea-cup reading with a warning. Do not consult the same person's cup three or four times a day—if you do, then the fruit of your labours will be disappointment. Either the signs and pictures will be in contradiction to those found in the first reading, or else the general conditions will be so muddled that adequate interpretation will be impossible.

The hand of fate cannot be forced. You will stand a much better chance of success if your inquirings into the future are limited in number to once or twice a week. It should be remembered, however, that this warning does not apply when one is merely desirous of propounding a question to the tea-leaves.

II

HERE, set forth below, you will find an explanation of the various signs and symbols encountered in tea-cup reading. In order to facilitate ready reference, these symbols have been arranged in alphabetical order and are preceded by a classification of some of the more common signs which, through tradition, are associated with good or bad influences.

Symbols of Good Omen.

Acorn; amulet; anchor; angel; ark; basket of flowers; bee; birds; boot; bouquet; bridge; bull; circle; clover; corn; cornucopia; cow; crown; daffodil; dove; duck; eagle; elephant; fig; fish; flowers; garland; horseshoe; oak; palm; rose; ship; swan.

Symbols of Bad Omen.

Arc; bat; black flag; clouds; coffin; cross; dagger; drum; flag; gun; hour-glass; monkey; mouse; owl; rat; raven; scythe; skeleton; skull; snake; square; sword; wreck.

INTERPRETATION OF THE SYMBOLS

A

Abbey.—This symbol predicts a condition of happiness and relates particularly to the disappearance of minor but none the less irritating worries.

Ace.—In the immediate future you will be faced with the necessity of making important decisions. If it is the ace of hearts, the decisions will be connected with your home life or will affect someone you love; if diamonds, it relates to business undertakings, especially to those connected with travel; if clubs, money matters are indicated; if spades, misfortune and sorrow will put obstacles in the even tenor of your way—make your decisions quickly.

Acorn.—At the top of the cup, this symbol predicts good fortune in money matters.

In the middle, continued good health and happiness.

At the bottom, an improvement in health or financial conditions.

Aerial.—If a thin line is observed over a symbol, it should be taken as a warning of gossip or scandal associated with that particular symbol. Be careful to whom you impart any secret knowledge affecting your business or domestic affairs.

Aeroplane.—An unexpected journey awaits you—a journey fraught with risk, and connected in some way with business matters. If the nose of the machine points towards the bottom of the cup, you should exercise great care in making your decision to embark upon this journey, for the project served by it may be unsuccessful.

Airship.—New projects leading towards a definite rise in position are foretold. If the area surrounding the symbol is clear, few difficulties will be encountered in the ascent; if cloudy, many obstacles will have to be overcome. An airship with a broken back or with its nose pointing downwards suggests ultimate failure of the projects and ventures under consideration. See *Balloon.*

Alligator.—Treachery and maliciousness encompass you. Tread warily, otherwise your enemies may do you a great deal of injury. See *Crocodile.*

Alps.—Lofty peaks denote lofty aspirations or ambitions. If the summits are clear of cloud and sharply defined, your endeavours will be rewarded with success. Bars and crosses in the vicinity indicate dangers and obstacles to be overcome.

Amulet.—Whatever form the amulet may take, whether a heart, and anchor, a swastika, or other object, the general interpretation is "protection." Occult influences are watching over you and guiding your footsteps.

Anchor.—If clearly defined, this is indeed a lucky sign.

At the top of the cup, constancy in love and success in business.

In the middle, a voyage bringing conditions of prosperity; if surrounded by dots the prosperity is strengthened.

At the bottom, success linked up with a voyage—social fortune.

When the symbol is obscured by clouds or surrounded by short lines the reverse must be interpreted.

Angel.—An angel in your cup denotes good news, usually of or from someone for whom you bear a deep affection. To the lover, it is a particularly fortunate sign.

Ant.—An emblem of well-directed industry and thrift. Persevere in your labours, for success and honours will come to you only through your personal efforts.

Anvil.—Your strength lies in your stability. Men will avail themselves of your firm qualities in order to fashion new projects. It is unlikely, however, that you yourself will gain materially from being so exploited.

Ape.—See *Monkey.*

Apple.—This symbolizes the desire for knowledge. A cluster of apples foretells an event which demands investigation and study, and which, in some way or other, is connected with commercial gain. An apple tree signifies a change for the better in health or in one's circumstances.

Arc.—This is not a particularly good sign, for it suggests something unfinished—possibly a career suspended through ill-health, or an abandoned project. Unforeseen misfortunes and accidents are associated with the arc.

Ark.—A safe refuge in the midst of dangers. If you are

distressed by domestic or business affairs take heart, for you will soon find a clear way out of your difficulties.

Arrow.—This symbol predicts the receipt of a letter bearing disagreeable news. If the arrow is surrounded by dots, the contents will relate to money matters.

Ass.—If at the top of the cup, fortune will smile on you; should the figure be very clearly formed, a legacy is indicated.

In the middle, it denotes happiness and contentment.

At the bottom, it gives a suggestion of misfortunes overcome by patience and application.

Aviary.—A large cage containing birds is a symbol heralding the advent of many new ideas and projects; these, however, will not be realized easily, for certain restrictions handicap your progress. Endeavour to become more broad-minded, for a limited outlook is also indicated.

Axe.—This presages difficulties in your path. If it appears without a handle, there is a suggestion that your efforts to overcome them will prove of no avail.

B

Baby.—A host of small worries is about to cloud your sky—worries which will hide the sun of contentment for a considerable period. You will be inclined to waste too much time in trying to dispel them—ignore them, and they will disappear as quickly as they came.

If a star surrounded by dashes is observed in the neighbourhood, think carefully before entering into a new agreement or contract.

A baby depicted near the "house" foreshadows a new arrival in the family.

At the bottom of the cup, beware of scandal-mongers and harmful gossips.

Badger.—A badger predicts a long life spent in comfort. To the unmarried man, it foretells a long bachelorhood.

Bag.—If the bag is closed, you must beware of some trap which your enemies have devised; if open, the danger of the trap is minimized, for it points to your escape.

A travelling-bag is a sign of a journey. See *Trunk.*

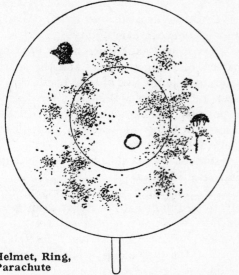

Helmet, Ring, Parachute

In the cup shown on the left three outstanding symbols will be noticed: a helmet, a ring and a parachute. The helmet foretells the offer of a position of trust, one that may involve a certain amount of personal risk; but though the sign itself is clear, which is auspicious, the parachute on the right suggests a providential escape from some danger, thereby conveying to the consultant a warning against extreme recklessness.

The ring at the bottom of the cup predicts a long engagement and, as no unfavourable sign appears in its vicinity, we may conclude that eventually a union will take place and result in great domestic happiness. On the whole, therefore, the cup is a good one, though the success of the consultant in his new sphere of activity seems to depend on his ability to curb his spirit of rashness.

The second cup portrayed on this page is not a good one. In it, also, there are three dominant signs: a bat, on the left; an aeroplane, on the right; a black disk, representing an eclipse, near the handle, or "house." The aeroplane foretells an unexpected journey, in some way connected with business and fraught with danger; and, because the nose of the machine points towards the bottom of the cup, we may assume that the enterprise served by the journey is not likely to be successful. The representation of a bat in the cup strengthens this assumption, for it speaks of strife stirred up by secret enemies, and also of fruitless journeys.

Finally, we must take into consideration the eclipse. This, in itself, is a symbol of ill omen, predicting the temporary overclouding of the sun of contentment, and the failure of health or of investments. The conditions, therefore, are generally unfavourable to the consultant, and we should advise him to exercise great care in the making of important decisions, and to examine his friendships closely.

Bat, Aeroplane, Eclipse

Bagpipe.—Tread carefully in household affairs, for there are indications of trouble through irritating discords and strife. Watch your health, too; especially avoid nervous excitability.

Ball.—Throughout your life you will experience many ups and downs in fortune. In all matters affecting the head and the heart, try to overcome your inclination to take the line of least resistance.

Balloon.—A balloon ascending in a cloudless sky foretells a definite betterment of your position, either financially or socially. It is probable that this ascent will be unexpected, caused by circumstances over which you have no control.

If clouds surround the symbol, your elevation will attract minor worries and difficulties. See *Airship.*

Barrel.—Vain imaginings are retarding your progress in life. Your ambitions are not likely to be fulfilled while words seem more important to you than deeds.

Basket.—This sign, when observed near the "house," foretells a new arrival in the family. At the top of the cup, a basket signifies a gift, or a material increase in one's possessions.

Should the basket be filled with flowers, it is a very good omen; it prophesies a newly acquired happiness, pleasurable events, social gatherings. A ring near this symbol indicates an engagement or a marriage.

A broken basket, or one not clearly defined, means fluctuations in financial affairs.

Bassinet.—See *Cot.*

Bat.—A representation of this creature is a warning to beware of strife and trouble caused by secret enemies. Through their machinations, labours will be brought to naught, journeys will be fruitless. Be more circumspect in your choice of friends.

Bayonet.—Somewhere near you danger is lurking. Rivalry will tend to harm you; sharp, unkind criticism will be levelled at you. A bold front is necessary.

Bear.—This symbol foretells that you are about to enter a zone governed by dangerous conditions; your own stupidity is to blame for this. Exercise great caution. If the bear is turning away from the "house," a long period of travel is indicated.

Bed.—By the state in which the bed appears, you may judge the condition of your mind, and learn the way in which it will affect your fortunes. A neat bed shows a tidy mind—ease and happiness will be your lot in life; if it is untidy, then disorder will breed disorder, and your life will be troublous and unsuccessful.

Bee.—A symbol of industry and prudence. Fate will shower your path with many blessings, of which you will take the greatest advantage; serious financial worries will be unknown to you. A bee also signifies good news.

Near the "house," this symbol predicts active social intercourse, a friendly gathering.

A swarm of bees indicates good luck arising from a large meeting of people. It is a favourable sign to politicians and anyone connected with the law.

Bell.—A pronouncement affecting your fortunes is predicted. If the symbols attending this are favourable, the omen is good; if unfavourable, the reverse must be interpreted.

At the top of the cup, a betterment of position for one holding an official appointment.

At the bottom, sad news, possibly of an illness or a death.

Two bells denote great happiness—to the lover they mean a happy marriage bringing success and wealth.

Birds.—This is a lucky sign to observe in your cup. If they are in flight, good news is on its way; their proximity to the "house" will help you to judge when you are likely to receive the message. At rest, the birds prophesy a successful journey. See also under names of birds, as *Eagle ; Raven.*

Boat.—A boat has two different interpretations: it may foretell a small journey—a removal—or it may symbolize an unforeseen haven of refuge in time of trouble.

If the boat lies at the bottom of the cup, or if it is capsized, beware of dangers arising through misplaced trust. See *Ship.*

Bomb.—An unexpected event will burst upon you with great suddenness, scattering troubles and misfortunes in your path. Underhand methods of your enemies are the cause of this; examine your friendships.

Bond.—If two symbols of a similar nature are connected by a thread or by links, it denotes a strong tie, or bond, drawing two people into close union. The bond may represent friendship, love or business.

Book.—A sign of acquired knowledge. If the book is open, a lawsuit is predicted; if closed, an investigation into an occult science.

Boomerang.—You will reap the reward of that which you have sown. If it be good, then goodness will fly back to you; if evil, then prepare to encounter misfortunes.

Boot.—This, generally speaking, is a lucky symbol. Well-defined, it gives protection from a serious hurt, either physical or financial. A worn and ragged boot predicts disgrace, a set-back in one's career.

If the toe of the boot points away from the "house," an enforced removal is indicated.

If at the top of the cup, a boot suggests disquietude, wanderlust.

If in the middle, a hidden danger; watch your steps carefully.

If the symbol is attended by a ring, a wedding is foretold.

Bottle.—Your health requires closer attention. Do not indulge in any luxury to excess; your constitution is being undermined.

At the bottom of the cup, a bottle prophesies a reverse in fortune; you will be forced to ask aid of others.

Bouquet.—A very lucky sign; it nullifies any symbol of bad omen attending it. You will be blessed with staunch friends, success and wealth. To the lover it has a special meaning—a happy marriage.

To those interested in the arts, it speaks of high honours and ambitions realized. See *Garland*.

Bow.—This symbol expresses hope. If drawn, it denotes expansion of thought, expansion of interests; if slack, lack of self-confidence will prevent you from attaining your object.

If an arrow is fitted to the bow, you may rest assured that your energies are employed in the right direction. You will eventually achieve success.

Bracelet.—A bracelet predicts a union; it may suggest a marriage or a business partnership. If the band is wide, slavery of mind or of body is indicated.

Branch.—This symbol, if it is fully leaved, foretells a new arrival in the family or a new friendship formed. Bare of leaves, fruitless labours, unrealized ambitions.

Bridge.—An event is predicted which will provide you with a short cut to the realization of your ambitions. Seize the opportunity and act fearlessly.

If the symbol is surrounded by dashes, an escape from the dangers that threaten you is indicated.

Bridle.—This sign suggests that you are suffering—perhaps unconsciously—from some restraint, or that someone is using your abilities and energies to his own advantage, but not to yours.

Broom.—Trivial worries which have been affecting your life will be dispersed. Bright days are in store for you.

Bull.—A bull predicts prosperity and good health. Advantageous business associations will be strengthened; you will trample opposition underfoot.

Bush.—Your energies are sprouting in too many directions. Concentrate on one thing at a time and you will achieve a greater measure of success.

Butterfly.—This symbol denotes care-free pleasures and harmless enjoyments. If surrounded by dots, worries caused through the frittering away of money are indicated.

C

Caduceus.—The winged staff of Mercury, messenger of the gods, is a good omen. It speaks of healing and renewed strength, and predicts prosperity from abroad. If near the "house," the receipt of an important letter or message is foretold.

Cage.—Your activities will be restricted through illness or some other misfortune.

To a maid, a cage enclosing a ring indicates a wedding.

Cake.—You will partake in a celebration. If the cake is whole, you will be the founder of the feast.

Camel.—A responsibility, possibly necessitating a certain amount of travel, will be placed on your shoulders. If near the "house," a letter from a tropical country is indicated.

Candle.—The candle symbolizes philanthropy, helpfulness. By your example you will inspire others to do good. If the candle is burning with a strong flame, some kind of missionary work will fall to your lot.

When a moth is observed in the neighbourhood, beware of flattery from false companions.

Canoe.—See *Boat.*

Cape.—See *Cloak.*

Card.—A well-formed visiting-card predicts a new and valuable friendship; badly formed, the friendship is entirely valueless and possibly dangerous.

A playing-card is always interpreted according to its suit and its value, the meanings of which are to be found in that section of this work dealing with Cartomancy. See *Ace.*

Carriage.—This symbol foretells a prosperity attained through the help of others. Your road in life will be made easy for you. To the humble of birth, it predicts a rise in social position.

If near the "house," a carriage denotes a visit from, or an introduction to, an important personage.

Cart.—A cart suggests the conveyance of property. You may benefit by a legacy or a sudden business transaction.

To one of high social position this symbol foretells an unexpected and rapid decline to a lower level of society.

Castle.—You are destined to hold a high position connected with official affairs. Strength of character will prove a valuable asset to you throughout life. An inclination towards intolerance is distinctly implied.

Near the "house," a castle signifies a legacy.

Cat.—This symbol predicts danger from a hidden or an unsuspected enemy. Someone is awaiting an opportunity to injure you—someone who may have ingratiated himself into your confidence. Be watchful.

A cat near the "house," however, foretells domestic contentment and peace.

Catapult.—If the letter Y is observed in the cup, beware of an unprovoked attack on your reputation or credit.

Near the "house," it foretells domestic strife caused through outside influences.

Cathedral.—See *Church.*

Chain.—An unbroken chain denotes an early marriage. If broken, an engagement or a close friendship is likely to be terminated; it also may signify the breaking of a business contract.

Chair.—A betterment in position is indicated. If the symbol is surrounded by a number of dots, financial gain is associated with the new office.

Near the "house," it means a new arrival in the family or a visit from a relative.

Chimney.—This symbol denotes social service. You have

noble qualities in your nature; much of your life will be devoted to the helping of your less fortunate brethren.

Church.—A ceremonial gathering is foretold. If read in conjunction with the attendant symbols it may be possible to predict the nature of the ceremony—whether it is connected with birth, marriage or death.

Cigar.—A burning cigar presages the collapse of some cherished project. Your ambitions will be unfulfilled unless you cut down wasteful expenditure.

An unlighted cigar suggests meanness in money matters.

Cigarette.—You are too fond of indulging in frivolity during hours which should be set apart for hard work. Lack of concentration will make your road through life a stony one and conflicting interests will mar your happiness.

Circle.—This is a fortunate sign to observe in your cup. All your projects will be terminated favourably.

If the circle has a line drawn through it, parting and separation are indicated.

Claw.—Harm from an enemy is foretold. If an animal's claw, it will be directed against the person; if a bird's, the reputation will be assailed.

Cloak.—The cloak is symbolical of deceit. Beware whom you trust; neglect the flattery of business acquaintances. Avoid signing any important contracts or agreements until there is a change of the moon.

Clock.—Do not procrastinate. You are apt to be dilatory concerning small matters connected with business.

If at the bottom of the cup, news of a severe illness.

Clouds.—These foretell unhappiness caused through minor worries. Should dots be observed in the neighbourhood, the troubles are associated with finance.

If near the "house," domestic strife is indicated.

A very cloudy cup reflects the condition of the inquirer's mind: postpone your reading, for nothing of value will be learned.

Clover.—A clover leaf or shamrock leaf is an emblem of exceedingly good omen. Fortune smiles on those in whose cup it is observed, especially so if the symbol be of the four-leafed variety. It nullifies any bad conditions which may attend it.

At the top of the cup, good fortune will be immediate.

c*

In the middle, not so immediate.

At the bottom, remote.

Club.—The attack of an enemy is predicted. Someone may try to worst you in an argument; see that your wits are as sharp as a rapier and you will conquer.

Cock.—See *Fowl.*

Coffin.—This sign does not necessarily foretell a death; it does point, however, to an illness brought on through neglect. Take steps at once to safeguard your health.

If the coffin is surrounded by dots, it means a failure in business or a breakdown in social negotiations.

Coil.—A coil of rope denotes muddled affairs, either business or domestic. If the two ends are not discernible, the condition is likely to last for some time.

Coin.—Monetary gain arising from an unexpected contract or agreement. The sign is strengthened if a head is observed on the face.

A broken coin predicts a financial reverse.

Collar.—This symbolizes servitude. Your lot in life will be to obey, not to command. Try to cultivate greater independence.

If the collar is broken, an escape from servitude and mental slavery is foretold.

Column.—A tall column means that you will attain a high position and be looked up to by your fellow-men. Take heed that in the fulfilment of your ambitions you do not become proud and inclined to disparage the labours of others who are much less fortunate than yourself.

A broken column denotes a failure in business or a breakdown in health. If clouds are observed in the neighbourhood, you will receive news of a death.

Comet.—You will receive a visitor from a foreign land. If stars are noted at the end of the tail, direct commercial gain will be experienced as the result of this visit.

A comet at the bottom of the cup predicts a sudden misfortune, bringing in its train a host of minor worries.

Comma.—This sign suggests a pause in your life's work. It may be due to conditions of health, or, if the attendant symbols are propitious, a holiday is indicated.

A number of commas signifies that you are lacking in determination. Take a bold course; do not vacillate.

THREE main symbols may be observed in the cup on the right: a human figure, an anchor and a moon. The anchor at the bottom of the cup predicts a voyage, but, because the sign is partly obscured and a waning moon is in proximity to it, the project served by the voyage is not likely to be successful. In fact, we should warn the consultant that in the immediate future his affairs will suffer a temporary set-back, for a waning moon denotes waning influences.

The pedestrian, on the left, is walking towards the "house;" this foretells the visit of a friend or a relative, probably in connexion with the adverse conditions described above. It will be seen, therefore, that the immediate future is not auspicious for the consultant, so

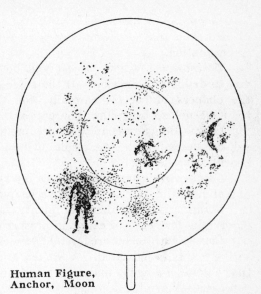

Human Figure, Anchor, Moon

we should convey to him a warning not to embark upon new projects until a better time presents itself.

In the cup on the left there are four outstanding symbols: an umbrella, a swallow, a skull, and a teapot. Though the swallow itself is a good sign, telling of rapid advancement and general good fortune, its auspiciousness is greatly lessened by the skull, which suggests hidden danger in the path of the consultant—a danger connected with ill health. The umbrella denotes that he will have cause to seek assistance from friends, and, as it is open, we may infer that aid will not be denied.

The teapot near the "house" conveys a definite warning against scandal; the consultant's good name is likely to suffer a serious injury. In summing up, we should advise the inquirer to take immediate steps to safeguard his health and to watch his actions carefully, lest he give idle rumour an opportunity to wag her gossip-loving tongue.

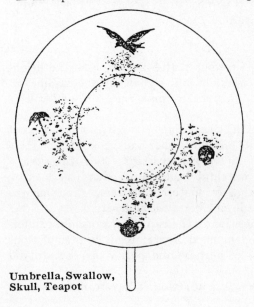

Umbrella, Swallow, Skull, Teapot

Compass.—A mariner's compass is a symbol of travel. If well defined, you may expect many adventures and, possibly, changes of occupation.

Compasses.—A new project will be placed in your hands for you to design and develop. If the angle enclosed is small, calculate the chances of success carefully, for there are indications that they are not so bright as they appear.

Cork.—Buoyant conditions are predicted. Your undertakings will be successful, and the resultant lightheartedness will materially benefit your health.

Corn.—An ear or a head of corn is a symbol of prosperity. Ears of corn near the "house" indicate a festive gathering.

Cornucopia.—The horn of plenty is indeed a lucky sign to observe in your cup. Peace and prosperity will be yours.

Cot.—New projects are foretold. If near the "house," an addition to the family is indicated. A broken or badly formed cot suggests the collapse of a newly undertaken venture.

Cow.—A symbol of prosperity. Your possessions will increase and happiness will abide in your house. To the farmer this sign is especially fortunate; it predicts full granaries and multiplying stock.

If the head of the cow is turned away from the "house," your wealth will come from abroad.

Crab.—See *Lobster.*

Cradle.—See *Cot.*

Crag.—An obstacle lies in your path—according to the height of the crag you may judge whether it be significant or insignificant. If the rock is free from clouds, your triumph is certain and will be accomplished with ease.

Crocodile.—A warning that treachery encompasses you. Do not trust lightly; beware of the "friend" who loads you with flattery or who commiserates with you too spectacularly. See *Alligator.*

Crook.—A symbol of watchful leadership. Men will look to you for guidance in spiritual or material matters. You have a great trust to fulfil in life; do not betray that trust.

Cross.—Whatever its position in the cup, a cross signifies suffering. A self-sacrifice will be demanded of you; trials and tribulations beset your path. Stoutness of purpose and purity of heart will aid you to win through to happiness.

Two crosses indicate a great affliction, a severe illness.

Crow.—See *Raven.*

Crown.—A symbol of temporal authority. Success will crown your endeavours; you will be raised to a high position of trust.

If stars are noted in the neighbourhood, you will reap a rich reward for some self-sacrifice you have made.

A crown near a cross signifies a legacy or some other good fortune resulting from a death.

Cup.—You will shortly receive a reward for services rendered. If dots surround the symbol, the reward will be of a monetary nature.

Cymbal.—This predicts a celebration, the nature of which may be ascertained from the attendant signs. If the neighbourhood is clear, a social gathering is foretold.

D

Daffodil.—A daffodil suggests a condition of happiness. Pleasure and success go hand in hand. If the flower is observed near the bottom of the cup, take care that you do not place too great a store on the social amenities of life to the detriment of your financial well-being. Monetary reverses are indicated.

Dagger.—A secret thrust from an enemy. Treachery and envy are linked up with this sign. Your reputation or your business may suffer considerable damage. Examine newly formed friendships very closely.

Daisy.—An emblem of modesty. Simplicity is the keynote of your personality. If the flower appears at the bottom of the cup, try to cultivate more self-assertiveness.

Dart.—A sudden attack directed from a distance against you or your affairs. See *Dagger.*

Deer.—This symbol foretells the receipt of unexpected news. The attendant signs will show the nature of the news—whether good or bad.

Demon.—Beware of evil influences. A net of treachery is cast beneath your feet. Tread warily.

Dive.—A figure in the attitude of diving suggests impending disaster. If surrounded by dots, give closer attention to your financial investments: a failure is indicated.

Dog.—A symbol of faithful friendship. You will benefit by the advice and support of your companions; in times of adversity they will prove a strong bulwark.

A dog in an attitude of dejection predicts an injustice done to a friend. Keep a close guard on your tongue.

In an attitude of begging, you will receive urgent solicitations for favours.

At the bottom of the cup, a friend is in need of your help.

Donkey.—See *Ass.*

Dot.—A dot strengthens the importance of the sign in whose proximity it is observed.

A number of dots or small circles indicates money.

Dove.—A symbol of domestic peace and happiness. Favourable conditions are predicted regarding any matters affecting your hearth and home.

Dovecote.—To the lover, this signifies a happy marriage. To the elderly, a peaceful rest from their labours—the shelter of a loving home. Ideal contentment is the keynote of this sign wherever it appears in the cup.

Dragon.—A sudden, unreasonable terror will come upon you. Let sanity counsel your actions—this monster is born of your imagination only.

Dromedary.—The one-humped camel foretells a swift and unforeseen journey. If dots are in the neighbourhood, you are likely to experience commercial gain thereby.

A dromedary in an attitude of rest denotes a postponed project, or, if near the "house," a delayed message or visitor.

Drum.—A symbol of bad omen. Scandal is bruited abroad; your good name and integrity are assailed.

If near the "house," domestic discord.

Two or more drums signify public disturbances, riots.

Duck.—Increase of wealth through barter or exchange. To the farmer, especially, this is a sign of excellent omen.

Duel.—The portrayal of a duel suggests a serious personal combat. If the sign is attended by dots, beware of a legal dispute over money or property.

Dumb-bell.—Others will use your abilities and ideas to further their own interests. Do not expect any reward from them, for they will repudiate their indebtedness to you.

Dwarf.—A disappointment due to lack of foresight is indicated. There is a suggestion, too, of some meanness—a malicious action on the part of an underling.

If dots are in the neighbourhood, and the sign is placed near the bottom of the cup, it predicts a financial reverse.

E

Eagle.—The eagle is a symbol of particularly good omen. Through the development of your latent powers you will rise to a high position in life. Men will respect and envy you. Take care that you do not become proud and conceited. You will know few true friendships.

Ear.—Malicious rumours will be borne to your ears; heed them not. There is a danger of your losing a valued friendship through the spreading of scandal.

Earth.—A circle containing a cross symbolizes the earth. If well defined, it suggests that the inquirer rates the material above the spiritual—to the detriment of his character. He may attain much wealth—but not much happiness.

Earwig.—Scandal and idle gossip will cause you distress. If near the "house," your domestic affairs will be affected.

Easel.—To the artist or the artistic, an easel holding a picture predicts success. An empty easel foretells a disappointment.

Eclipse.—A black disk represents an eclipse. For a time your sun of good fortune will be darkened. Harm may come to you either physically or financially. Look to your health and safeguard your investments.

Egg.—A well-formed egg in your cup is a good sign. New projects will be carried out successfully; old ones will yield better fruit.

If the egg be cracked or misshapen, the reverse must be read.

An egg near the "house" predicts a new arrival in the family.

Elephant.—A symbol of sagacity, and physical and moral strength. You will be successful in your undertakings, but your ambitions will not be fulfilled suddenly. You will have to work hard for whatever you attain.

This animal is associated with conditions of good luck; if, however, it appears in thin outline and the enclosed area is clear, there is a suggestion that you are placing too high a value on one of your possessions, either spiritual or material.

Ewer.—A ewer symbolizes help in time of trouble. You will aid your friends and, in turn, receive aid.

Explosion.—A sudden great upheaval in your affairs. If it is observed near the "house," a domestic catastrophe is indicated.

Eye.—A symbol of intelligent perception. A wide-open eye denotes mental alertness and is a warning to you to be on the watch. Tread carefully in business matters.

Near the "house," it suggests a need for a more careful supervision of the family budget. Someone is about to take advantage of your generosity.

F

Face.—If a face having a good-humoured expression is portrayed in your cup, the symbol is of good omen; the opposite must be read if the face is evil or ugly. A smiling expression indicates a condition of happiness.

Two or more faces foretell the formation of new friendships.

Fairy.—This little being from the realms of imagination predicts romantic happenings, fantastic adventures. Your road through life will be joyous.

Near the "house," an addition to the family is foretold.

Falcon.—A falcon signifies a deadly and persistent enemy. Be on your guard—a sudden attack will be directed against your reputation or business interests.

Fan.—A symbol of dissimulation or flirtation. Trouble may be caused by a wrongful concealment of truth, either in business or social affairs. To the lover, it suggests temporary falseness of the loved one; if the fan is fully open, the misdemeanour is intensified.

Feather.—A feather denotes inconstancy, instability. Lack of concentration may prevent you from acquiring success. Do not allow ephemeral pleasures to dull the edge of your appetite for work.

Fence.—Your activities will be limited. Events will place obstacles in your path, but, if you seek carefully, you will discover a way out of all your difficulties.

Fencer.—See *Duel.*

Fern.—Inconstancy of the affections is symbolized by the fern. To the lover, it is a sign portending trouble. Restlessness is strongly bound up with it.

Ferret.—Hidden enemies are at work to destroy your peace of mind. Neglect petty scandals; do not, however, underestimate the strength of your attackers, and thereby be lulled into a false sense of security. They will strike where and when you least expect.

Festoon.—This signifies festivities, a round of harmless pleasures. If near the "house," it denotes a social gathering under your roof.

Fig.—An emblem of prosperity and fertility. Your affairs will prosper exceedingly. Social as well as financial expansion is indicated.

Fir.—The fir cone or fir tree predicts success in all spheres of interest connected with the arts. If the tree is very tall, you will attain a position of great influence and high honour.

Fire.—The portrayal of a fire foretells a sudden burst of anger, bringing in its train disastrous consequences. Do not be hasty; keep close guard over your temper.

Fish.—This is a symbol of very good omen—one of the luckiest you may observe in the cup. It nullifies every evil condition. Peace and plenty attend you always; success crowns your endeavours.

If the fish is surrounded by dots, you will be especially lucky in investments and other financial matters.

Fist.—A closed fist means a menace of some kind. If near the "house," your domestic peace is threatened.

Flag.—Danger from wounds is foretold. There is a suggestion that these are received in the execution of your duty. A fearless heart will prove the stoutest armour.

A black flag is a sign associated with death or severe misfortune. Do not expose yourself to danger unnecessarily.

Flask.—See *Ewer*.

Flower.—A solitary flower in your cup means a request granted, a small kindness done.

See also *Bouquet ; Garland ;* and under names of flowers, as *Daisy ; Rose.*

Fly.—This foretells domestic trials and tribulations. A swarm of flies suggests a host of minor worries. Preserve your equanimity and all will go well.

A fly near the "house" predicts scandal-mongering directed against your wife and children or other dependants.

Foot.—A symbol of sagacity and discreetness. The gift of understanding will smooth out many of the rough places in your life. You will map out a course and stick to it.

If leading away from the "house," excursions into foreign lands are indicated.

Forest.—You will be encompassed by perplexity and see no clear way out of the wood. Endeavour to centralize your interests; do not leap from one unfinished thing to another.

Fork.—A fork in a line predicts some important decision to be made, or suggests the opening up of a new interest. The attendant symbols should be noted carefully, so that conclusions may be drawn as to whether the conditions are favourable or unfavourable.

A table-fork foretells minor worries connected with young domestic affairs.

Fort.—This symbolizes protective strength. You will hold a responsible position, and hold it well. Many will look to you for help.

Fowl.—Your productive labours will be of great benefit to mankind. Do not be too unmindful of your own interests, however, or your rights will be usurped.

Fox.—A fox denotes treachery on the part of a trusted friend. You should beware of flatterers.

Frog.—This symbol indicates false pride. Too much self-importance will embroil you in disastrous arguments. Modesty should be cultivated.

Fruit.—If the fruit depicted in your cup is in season, the omen is generally good. A condition of prosperity is usually foretold. See also under names of fruits, as *Apple ; Pear.*

G

Gallows.—This presages social or financial disaster. Avoid making impulsive decisions. Your judgment is not as sound as it should be.

Garland.—A garland of flowers denotes high honours, success. It is also a token of friendship. See *Bouquet.*

Near the "house," a social gathering or celebration.

Giant.—A gigantic figure in the cup suggests that some strong force is at work in your life; the attendant symbols will enable you

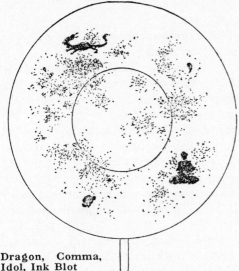

Dragon, Comma, Idol, Ink Blot

Four main symbols are to be observed in the cup on the left: a dragon, top left; a comma, top right; an idol, bottom right; an ink blot, near the handle, or "house." The interpretation of the cup is as follows:—The comma denotes a pause in the life-work of the consultant, which, because of the proximity of the dragon, may be attributed to some unreasonable terror, existing, however, only in his own imagination.

The idol indicates that unfavourable conditions may arise through misplaced trust in a "friend," and the probability that these conditions will somehow affect the good name of the consultant is suggested by the ink blot, which speaks of a sullied reputation. In summing up, therefore, we should advise the consultant to put away childish fears, to allow sanity to counsel his actions, and to be careful in the selection of those friends to whom he confides his dearest ambitions.

In the second cup portrayed on this page we note four outstanding symbols: a square, top; the letter "B" and a spear, left; and a star, near the "house." The square is a sign of ill omen. It indicates restriction, either mental or physical; and, reading it in conjunction with the spear, which signifies the slanderous assault of an enemy, we may predict that if the consultant retaliates he will run the risk of legal restraint. The letter "B" may afford a clue either to the name of the slanderer or to that of the person who indirectly instigates the slander. The star, formed by four lines near the "house," suggests the advent of a domestic disaster, and we may conclude that it is the direct result of the unfavourable conditions predicted by the other signs. Taking all things into consideration, we should warn the consultant to keep a close guard over his tongue and endeavour to overcome his extreme sensitiveness.

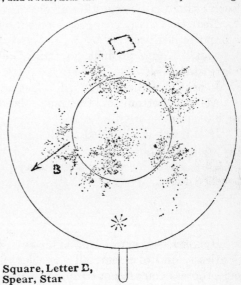

Square, Letter B, Spear, Star

to decide whether the force is for good or evil. Do not let circumstances undermine your will-power.

Gimlet.—You are blessed with keen perception. Success will be yours if you use this gift to advantage.

Glass.—A tumbler indicates integrity. There is a suggestion, however, that your motives are too transparent and that you cannot withstand the hard blows of fortune.

Near the "house," approaching festivity.

Glove.—You will have cause to challenge a decision or an opinion. Do not attack half-heartedly; you have truth on your side.

Goat.—Enemies surround you. Beware of a sudden and unprovoked onslaught on your good name.

Goose.—You are inclined to put too much trust in the leadership of a business acquaintance. Form your own opinions and act according to your own dictates.

Grapes.—Prosperity will attend you. Be careful, however, that you do not acquire too great a taste for material pleasures.

Grasshopper.—This symbol denotes a lack of providence and foresight. You will be brought to want unless you exercise care.

Greyhound.—Strenuous exertions will lead you to good fortune. In the race with your competitors, however, guard your health closely; there is a suggestion of physical exhaustion.

Near the "house," a greyhound foretells the unexpected receipt of important news.

Gun.—A gun predicts an attack delivered against you from a long distance.

If near the "house," it will affect your domestic happiness.

At the bottom of the cup, slanderous and hurtful gossip are indicated.

If a heart is observed in the neighbourhood, damage to your affections is implied.

To a soldier or sailor, a gun may prophesy a call to arms or a cancelled leave.

H

Hammer.—A symbol of industry. You will fashion your fate relentlessly and overcome all obstacles ruthlessly. See to it that in your progress you are not tempted to disregard the finer things of life.

Hand.—A well-formed hand foretells a new friendship leading to success in social or financial matters. If badly formed, the opposite must be interpreted.

A hand pointing towards the "house" foretells good luck arising from the visit of a stranger.

Hare.—This sign denotes timidity. Cultivate self-assertiveness, otherwise your business affairs will be adversely affected. Stand by your own opinions; try to mix with others as their equals, not as their inferiors. The tendency to run away as soon as danger threatens must also be overcome.

Near the "house," a hare predicts a domestic misfortune.

Harp.—Harmony will reign over your domestic affairs. Now is a good time to make fresh social ventures, for success is assured. New friendships are indicated.

To the lover the harp has a special meaning—it predicts a happy marriage.

Hat.—New interests are opening up for you. If the symbol is well defined, good fortune will result. A shabby, dilapidated hat speaks of the failure of a project.

If a heart is observed near the sign, a successful marriage.

Hawk.—Danger from an enemy is threatened. The attack will come like a bolt from the blue; keep your eyes wide open and guard especially the interests and safety of those who dwell beneath your roof.

Head.—The portrayal of a head foretells a betterment of position. You will be placed in charge of certain operations; do not shirk the responsibility. See *Face.*

Heart.—This is a symbol of sincere affection. If attended by a ring, or if there are two hearts close together, marriage is predicted.

If surrounded by dots, money will come to you through a friend.

Fruit depicted near a heart signifies pleasurable pursuits and light-hearted enjoyment.

Heel.—The heel of a shoe or boot denotes a condition of incompleteness. Partnership is essential to your success. To a single person, marriage may be the solution of the problem.

Helmet.—A position of trust will be offered to you. There is an indication that your acceptance of it will involve a certain amount of risk to your personal safety. Good fortune, however, is assured if the sign is clear.

Hen.—See *Fowl.*

Heron.—You are destined to live a somewhat solitary life. Aloofness from your fellow-men stamps you as being rather proud. Endeavour to cultivate sociability.

Hill.—An obstacle will tend to delay your progress. If the hill is clear of cloud, you will surmount it with ease.

Hippopotamus.—This animal symbolizes a coarse, unrefined nature. Animal instincts predominate; exercise more self-control and try to develop spirituality so that your better nature may have an opportunity to assert itself.

Hive.—A hive signifies contentment and orderliness in domestic affairs. If a swarm of bees is attendant, a stroke of good fortune is imminent.

Hoop.—See *Circle.*

Horn.—A symbol of good news. A pronouncement will be made which will materially advance your success. Happiness will light your path.

If at the top of the cup, a legacy is predicted.

Surrounded by dots, good fortune in financial matters.

If the horn is overflowing with flowers or fruit, it is a most propitious sign denoting peace and plenty. See *Cornucopia.*

Horse.—The horse is a symbol of wisdom, faithfulness and social service. Your work in life will be for the betterment of the community: unselfishness will mark all your efforts.

If in a galloping attitude, good news is on its way to you from a beloved friend.

A rider on a horse predicts glad tidings from overseas.

The head of a horse signifies a lover. If well defined, he is constant in his affection.

Horseshoe.—A sign of good luck. Fortune has prepared a pleasant surprise for you; see that you turn it to good account. Dots near the horseshoe indicate that finance is involved.

Near the "house," the luck of the symbol is strengthened and may be connected with matters affecting the heart.

Hose.—Stockings or socks predict a journey. If there appears a pair in good condition, the journey will be successful.

Hour-glass.—This is a reminder that time is on the wing—a warning against procrastination. See that each day's task is finished properly—do not adopt too many new interests.

Near the "house," it foretells some minor domestic tragedy due to lack of foresight.

If at the bottom of the cup, a definite threat of danger arising from neglectful conduct.

House.—A house denotes the safety of material possessions. It is a good sign for the business man to observe, for it speaks of successful conditions governing commerce. Launch out into new projects with confidence and enthusiasm.

To the lover, it predicts the realization of cherished hopes.

At the top of the cup, a change of residence is indicated.

At the bottom, an indication that evil influences will lay siege to your moral principles.

If the symbol is near the handle and surrounded by clouds or dashes, domestic strife or illness is predicted.

Hull.—The hull of a ship foretells the shipwreck of a financial venture. If near the "house," a separation or divorce may take place.

Human Figures.—These must be interpreted according to the attitudes in which they appear. If they seem to be benevolent, they are of good omen; if threatening, evil. Also, observe closely the attendant signs and read them in conjunction with the figures.

Hurdle.—An obstacle in your path. Surrounded by dots, financial worries are indicated.

I

Iceberg.—Danger lies ahead. Progress with caution. Do not be lulled into a false sense of security; the calm waters which surround you hide a relentless enemy.

Idol.—You are placing your trust in someone who is not worthy of it. Take warning before your interests are betrayed.

Ink.—A blot of ink predicts a sullied reputation. Watch your actions and words carefully lest you give the idle tongue of gossip an opportunity to wag.

Insect.—Insects in the cup usually indicate the advent of irritating worries and minor vexations. If you face them light-heartedly and with determination, you will not suffer any serious hurt. See also under names of insects, as *Ant; Earwig.*

Ivy.—This symbol speaks of the faithfulness of friends. If well defined, staunch comradeship will help you materially towards the ultimate goal of your ambitions.

Near the "house," an ivy-leaf represents a devoted lover.

J

Jackal.—A jackal denotes a mischief-maker. You will suffer petty annoyances from idle gossip.

Javelin.—See *Spear.*

Jester.—A symbol of frivolity. Watch carefully; foolish words and actions may lead you into disgrace. Try to cultivate a more serious outlook on life.

Jockey.—If this sign is well defined, success in speculative enterprises is predicted.

At the top of the cup, you will be lucky in a lottery or sweepstake.

Jug.—You will hold an influential position and through it will be able to advance the interests of your friends. Many will turn to you for aid.

If at the bottom of the cup, a jug suggests excessive indulgence in luxuries, leading to severe losses.

Near the "house," good health.

K

Kangaroo.—The kangaroo is a symbol of family affection. Your domestic affairs will run smoothly; you will enjoy the love of dependants and relations.

If near the "house," the meaning is strengthened.

Kettle.—This sign relates to the conditions governing your home life. If clearly defined and near the "house," domestic content-ment is predicted. At the bottom of the cup, family discords.

Key.—A key foretells the advent of new projects. You will gaze upon fresh fields to conquer; the steps which you take will have an important influence on your life. In making decisions, see that your heart is ruled by your head.

Near the "house," a single key denotes domestic happiness. Two or more keys suggest danger from robbery.

Kite.—A symbol of lofty aspirations. If well formed, you will climb to a high position, although in the doing of it you may experience many ups and downs.

Should the kite have no tail, take care that fanciful ideas do not destroy your balance or common sense. There is a danger of your projects being dashed to the ground.

Knapsack.—Many short journeys are indicated. If dots are in the neighbourhood, financial gain will result.

Knife.—This symbolizes separations and strife. According to the attendant signs, broken contracts or severed friendships may be foretold. A knife with a long and pointed blade suggests injury at the hands of an enemy.

If near the "house," a separation or divorce.

Crossed knives signify quarrels, bitter disputes. Surrounded by dots, contentions regarding money matters.

L

Lace.—A pattern suggesting lacework foretells complexities. Complications and perplexities will cloud your horizon. Do not be led into tortuous paths in order to find escape from these. Make bold decisions and have faith in first instincts.

Ladder.—Advancement in position is prophesied. If the ladder is well formed and the top of it clear, success awaits you. There is a suggestion that the advancement comes through your own initiative and labour.

Ladle.—You will receive help from a friend. If dots are near by, the assistance will be financial.

Lamp.—Things which you do not understand will be made clear to you. The gloom encircling you will be swept away.

Near the "house," a lamp predicts a celebration or festive gathering connected with domestic affairs.

Lance.—See *Spear.*

Lantern.—A symbol of guidance and protection. The dark places in your journey through life will be robbed of their terror; good influences will watch over you and light your path.

Laurel.—A laurel leaf indicates high honours. Your labours, whether mental or physical, will be crowned with success.

Leaf.—This signifies the receipt of news. A cluster of leaves foretells happiness, fulfilled ambitions.

A leaf at the bottom of the cup, news of the death of an elderly friend or relation.

Leg.—A symbol of activity. Stirring events will follow quickly on the heels of each other. If the leg is clearly defined and well shaped, they will assist your advancement.

Leopard.—Stealthy enemies are awaiting an opportunity to do you an injury. Act with circumspection; do not be over-trustful in business affairs.

Letter.—The portrayal of a letter predicts that news is on its way to you. The nature of the news may be judged by the attendant signs; if, for example, dots are in the vicinity, financial matters are concerned. When a heart is observed near by, the message is from a loved one. An initial close to or on the letter may afford a clue to the name of the sender.

Letters of the alphabet are often observed in the cup. These may show the surnames of people, and should be read in conjunction with their neighbouring symbols.

Lighthouse.—This symbol promises succour in time of need. You will be saved from shipwreck on the coasts of ill fortune.

Near the "house," it foretells a dangerous journey.

Lily.—A lily denotes purity of thought, word and deed. Your reputation will be irreproachable.

If close to the "house," it predicts a virtuous partner in marriage.

Lines.—These must be interpreted according to their form and position. Generally speaking, they denote progress, either material or spiritual. To be of good omen, they should be clear, straight and free from breaks.

Lines crossing each other indicate important decisions to be made, new ventures to be embarked upon. Double lines always signify journeys; curved lines indicate the dominance of the heart over the head.

Lion.—A symbol of high authority, greatness. If clearly defined, you will rise to a responsible position and receive your due share of honours. Influential friends will aid you in the achievement of this: see that you do not forget their timely help.

If a mace is in the neighbourhood, an official appointment of considerable importance and carrying good emolument is foretold.

THE cup portrayed on the right contains four important symbols: a query, two lines crossing each other, a weather-vane, and a scarecrow. The crossed lines tell us of an important decision about to be made. In proximity to them we observe a query which, symbolizing hesitancy, immediately suggests that the consultant will waver in the making of his decision, and, as a direct result of his irresolution, which is emphasized by the vane, is likely to suffer a loss of some kind. The scarecrow is a definite warning against thriftlessness.

To sum up, the cup generally is not a good one. The consultant should be strongly advised to cultivate firmness and thrift.

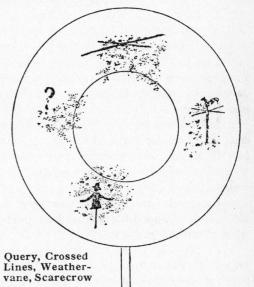

Query, Crossed Lines, Weather-vane, Scarecrow

The four outstanding symbols portrayed in the second cup are a trunk, a horseshoe, a hammer, and a heart. Both the heart and the horseshoe are extremely lucky signs; the former tells of a warm affection influencing the life of the consultant, and the latter heralds a period of good luck. The trunk predicts a sudden change of plans and, noting the dots which surround it, we may assume that the plans are in some way connected with finance. The consultant is evidently a person of great industry, for a hammer appears in his cup, and by this sign we may prophesy that he will fashion his fate relentlessly. In connexion with this last reading, however, we should warn him not to become ruthless in his eager strivings for success, for there is a suggestion that he may be tempted to disregard the finer things of life.

From the general conditions of the cup, therefore, we may assure the consultant that the future holds many good things in store for him, and that through his own initiative and labour he will realize to the full extent many of his most dearly cherished ambitions.

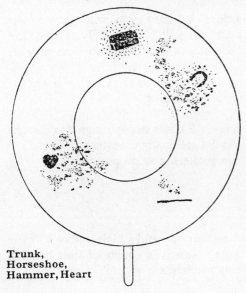

Trunk, Horseshoe, Hammer, Heart

Litter.—If tea-leaves appear in a confused heap or litter, there is a suggestion that herein is reflected the state of mind of the inquirer. Compose yourself and the chaotic conditions will disappear.

Loaf.—A loaf may be of good or of evil import; it must be judged in accordance with the surrounding conditions. As a good omen, it prophesies freedom from want, prosperity; as a bad omen, poverty and hunger.

Lobster.—A lobster, crab, prawn or shrimp denotes a predatory nature. You are inclined to prey upon the fortune of others. Try to rely on your own abilities, and success will reward you. There is a certain viciousness in your general make-up which you would do well to eliminate.

Lock.—An obstacle will bar your progress. If surrounded by dots, lack of hoped-for financial support will delay the carrying out of a cherished project.

Locomotive.—New spheres of interest, mainly connected with travel, will open up before you. The pursuit of these will require much expenditure of energy on your part, but if the sign is well defined nothing but good will result.

Log.—A log of wood suggests inactivity, laziness. Observe the attendant signs to learn whether a mental or physical condition is indicated.

Loom.—Through conscientious industry you will attain your ambitions. The pattern of your life will be smoothly woven and you will bring much joy and brightness into the drab lives of your fellow-workers.

Loop.—A snare has been prepared for you. Look well ahead; do not rush hurriedly into any new ventures.

Lynx.—See *Leopard.*

Lyre.—A symbol of harmony. This is a good sign for anyone connected with the arts; it foretells great advancement.

Near the "house," a festive gathering is prophesied.

M

Mace.—This symbolizes authority and high office. Your position will be a responsible one; you will in course of time become renowned for your sagacity and prudence.

A mace near the "house" suggests an official visit.

Man.—The figure of a man near the "house" foretells the arrival of a guest. If his arm is outstretched, he bears a present for you.

Mask.—A deception will be practised on you. Do not judge hastily; try to penetrate beneath the surface of things.

To a lover, this sign means the infidelity of the loved one.

If appearing near the "house," and the surrounding conditions are good, a mask may be interpreted as an invitation to a dance or some other social enjoyment.

Masonic Symbols.—Whenever signs of this nature appear in the cup they must be interpreted according to the particular meanings assigned to them in the craft. They all, however, denote a condition of brotherly love and centralized interests.

Medal.—You will be awarded some honour or distinction for services rendered; your social position will benefit accordingly. Happy conditions surround you.

Mermaid.—This fairy being of the sea denotes temptation, allurement. Someone will endeavour to attract you from a sane course of action; do not heed his blandishments, or disaster will befall you.

Near the "house," a mermaid predicts domestic trouble caused through a flirtation.

Meteor.—Fame will come to you overnight; your brilliance will attract the eyes of the world. This sign is not wholly good, however, for there is an indication that your fall from fame will be as rapid as your rise. You will suffer much in your career from lack of understanding on the part of your fellow-men.

Mitre.—A high honour awaits you. The excellence of your example will influence the lives of those around you.

If close to the "house," you will receive a present of valuable jewellery or wearing apparel.

Mole.—Enemies are at work to undermine your safe position. Look for danger where you least expect it.

Monk.—See *Priest.*

Monkey.—Mischief is abroad. Pay no attention to those who seek your favours through flattery and imitation of your customs and habits; they do not wish you well.

Monster.—Whatever its form, a monster presages the entry of fear into your heart. Listen to the voice of common sense and the terror will depart, for it is largely a creation of your own imagination.

Moon.—If a full moon is shown in the cup, a love affair is fore-told. Happiness will result from it if the sign is clearly defined and the surrounding conditions are favourable. Dots near by suggest that the attachment is a worldly rather than an ideal one; it may give rise to a marriage of convenience.

A crescent moon—one in the first quarter—predicts new projects; in the last quarter, waning influences will adversely affect your affairs.

Motor-car.—Prosperity awaits you. Do not, however, be too hasty in seeking fortune—the longest path often proves to be the quickest route.

Mountain.—See *Alps.*

Mouse.—This symbol denotes poverty caused through lack of initiative. Do not wait for opportunity to come to you—go out and seek it.

Near the "house," a mouse foretells loss through theft.

Mummy. —The figure of a mummy in the cup indicates that your mental condition is torpid. Take more interest in the things around you, otherwise your prospects are bound to suffer.

Near the "house" and with dashes in the neighbourhood, you will suffer an illness which will suspend your mental activities.

Mushroom.—A mushroom symbolizes sudden growth, expansion. New ideas will blossom into fruitfulness unexpectedly. Should a heart be observed near by, a new love will dawn in your life; but do not, however, be too precipitate in your affections.

At the top of the cup, unsought-for honours will be thrust upon you.

Near the "house," a removal to the country.

N

Nail.—This foretells suffering from maliciousness. Enemies will seek to do you a cruel, heartless injury.

If near the "house," the hurt will be directed against one for whom you have great affections.

Necklace.—A complete necklace signifies the receipt of an honour. If incomplete, damage to your reputation or loss to the affections.

Net.—Snares are spread in your path. Let vigilance be your watchword. Secret enemies are envious of your position.

Noose.—See *Loop.*

Nose.—An advancement in position is indicated. You will be well to the fore in social affairs. If dots are close to it, an investigation into financial matters is predicted.

Nosegay.—See *Bouquet.*

Numbers.—If numbers appear in the cup, they should be interpreted according to their meanings as set forth in the section of this work dealing with Numerology.

Nun.—A sign of deception on the part of one you love. Do not place implicit trust in a newly-found friend until his friendship has been proved.

Nurse.—A figure garbed in the robes of a nurse is a prediction of illness.

If near the "house," have especial regard for the health of your dependants; danger threatens.

If surrounded by dots, a reverse in finance is foretold.

O

Oak.—An oak tree is a lucky sign; it prophesies long life, good health and prosperity. Great strength of character is denoted. Many will seek your protection from the troubles of life.

Oats.—A symbol of simplicity and steadfastness. Though you may not rise to a high position, you will do useful work in the world. The mantle of social service will fall on your shoulders.

Old Man.—You have lost an opportunity to do something great; it may not come again. Make more use of your time; declining fortunes are indicated.

Old Woman.—This sign presages sickness, the enfeeblement of mental powers. See that your substance is not wasted in frivolous living.

Orange.—See *Circle.*

Oval.—See *Egg.*

Owl.—The owl is a symbol of bad omen. Failure in health and business will be experienced unless the greatest precautions are observed.

At the top of the cup and near the "house," misery caused through the unfaithfulness of a loved one.

Oyster.—This sign denotes a secretive nature. You possess valuable assets, but are inclined through being suspicious of your fellow-men to keep them to yourself. You should guard against mental stagnation.

P

Pack.—See *Knapsack.*

Pagoda.—A pagoda symbolizes fatalism. Try to conquer your inclination to take the buffets of fortune lying down. Remember: "the wise man rules his stars, the fool obeys them."

Palanquin.—See *Sedan.*

Palisade.—An obstacle in your path will prove a blessing in disguise. It will afford you protection from your enemies.

Pall.—A disappointment is in store for you. Avoid signing new contracts or agreements.

Palm.—A palm tree or palm branch signifies success crowned with honours. You will realize your ambitions and in doing so earn much respect.

Pan.—A shallow vessel reflects a shallow condition of mind. Contentment may become a vice; rouse yourself to activity.

Pansy.—This is a comforting symbol to observe. You are always in your friends' thoughts. Envy does not embitter them; they wish you well.

Parachute.—A providential escape from some accident or danger is foretold. You possess great ambitions; do not become too reckless in your efforts to climb to the top.

Parasol.—See *Sunshade.*

Parcel.—An oblong tea-leaf in the cup represents a parcel, and predicts a present, or a surprise. The symbols surrounding it may give you a clue to its nature. If dots are in the neighbourhood, it is connected with finance.

At the top of the cup, it is immediate.

In the middle, not so immediate.

At the bottom, remote.

Near the "house," a parcel may foretell a new addition to the family circle.

Parrot.—Idle gossip and scandal will cause you considerable unhappiness. Beware of those who flatter you.

Pawnbroker's Sign.—Three circles arranged in triangular fashion predict a lack of material possessions. Want will drive you to despair unless you develop practicability and thrift.

Peacock.—A symbol of vanity and love of luxury. The chances are that you will have the means to indulge your extravagant tastes; yet there is a danger that you may lose all, for there are many pitfalls in your path and your head is held too high. Flattery will be meat and drink to you; false friendships will cause you much sorrow.

A heart near the sign denotes a rich lover; a ring, a wealthy and happy marriage.

If near the "house," the peacock is of good omen. It foretells a happy home amid beautiful surroundings.

Peak.—See *Alps.*

Pear.—This fruit symbolizes comfort, ease of circumstances. Your labours will be fruitful; no financial worries will ever cloud your horizon.

Pedestrian.—A human figure in a walking attitude predicts the receipt of news. The attendant symbols may reveal the nature of the news.

If walking towards the "house," a visit from a friend or relative is foretold.

If walking away from the "house," a short holiday.

Pencil.—A thick line tapering to a point signifies mental exactitude, fine perception. Your sharp wits will stand you in good stead in your business dealings; do not, however, become too self-confident, for there are indications that some of your most cherished schemes will fail.

Pendulum.—A pendulum is a symbol of regularity. Your domestic and business affairs will be characterized by orderliness. Success will be achieved through persistence of effort. See that you do not become too conventional and narrow minded.

Pentagon.—A five-sided figure symbolizes keen, well-balanced mental powers. You will design your life symmetrically and achieve success through orderliness.

Perambulator.—New projects are foretold. It is probable that these will be connected with travel, and, if the sign is clear, lead to the fulfilment of your ambitions.

Piano.—This is a symbol of harmony. You will exercise a peaceful influence over the lives of those with whom you come in

D

contact, and will bring out the best that lies in the hearts and minds of your fellow-men.

Pickaxe.—A pickaxe indicates a determined, undaunted character. You will hew your path with persistent energy and overcome all obstacles by your directness of attack. There is a danger, however, that in the process you may acquire a certain ruthlessness of heart.

Pig.—This symbol is at once both lucky and unlucky. You will be successful, but greed may destroy your spiritual well-being. Remember to cultivate moderation in all things, and avoid over-anxiety in business affairs.

Near the "house," a pig signifies enmity caused through envy.

Pillar.—See *Column.*

Pincers.—A difficult problem awaits your solution; you will need to muster all your mental energy. Avoid disputes, for there are suggestions of a lawsuit.

Pistol.—A threat will be levelled at you. Circumstances will arise which will call for an immediate decision on your part. Take care that you are not coerced into pursuing a course which you know is morally wrong.

Pitcher.—See *Jug.*

Plumb-line.—This indicates moral rectitude, uprightness. Because of your profound sense of justice your shoulders will bear the weight of many responsibilities. You will be regarded as a benefactor of mankind.

Point.—See *Dot.*

Porch.—A porch foretells new undertakings. You will enter fresh spheres of activity and encounter many adventures affecting both mind and body.

Posy.—See *Bouquet.*

Pot.—A pot of any kind signifies utility. Social service will be the basic principle of your life.

Prawn.—See *Lobster.*

Precipice.—Danger threatens you. A sudden fall in position is indicated. Look well before you leap.

If dots are in the neighbourhood, proceed warily when making new investments.

Priest.—Spiritual leadership is denoted. Through your good example you will influence the thoughts and deeds of others.

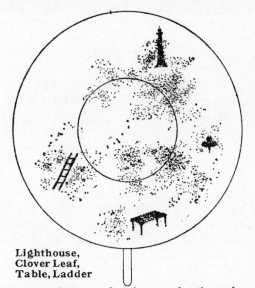

**Lighthouse,
Clover Leaf,
Table, Ladder**

THE cup on the left predicts great good fortune for the consultant. The outstanding symbols are a lighthouse, top right; a clover leaf, right; a table, near the "house;" and a ladder, left. The clover leaf is the most potent and important sign. It foretells a period of good luck and strengthens all the other favourable conditions. The ladder speaks of an advancement in position, through the consultant's own initiative, and, being clear and well formed, suggests that success will crown his efforts.

The lighthouse is a comforting symbol to note, for it promises succour in time of need; while the table near the "house" forms the natural conclusion to the reading: it foreshadows a festive gathering under the consultant's roof—a celebration, without doubt, in honour of his rise in position.

The conditions prevailing in the lower cup are not quite so favourable as those in the one above. The four signs to be noted are a dove, top left; a mountain peak, top right; two parallel lines forming a roadway, near the "house;" and a scabbard, left. The peak suggests that the consultant is fired with lofty ambitions; but because the summit is not clear, being ringed with clouds, we may not predict that their fulfilment will be accomplished without experiencing difficulties.

The empty scabbard points to a very serious fault in the make-up of the consultant—a lack of foresight; this, then, may be the obstacle lying in his path to success. The dove tells us that the domestic life of the inquirer will be blissful; while the two lines forming a roadway signify a short journey. In summing up, we should advise the consultant to cultivate prudence, and to keep his eyes fixed steadfastly on the goal of his ambitions.

**Mountain Peak,
Dove, Parallel
Lines, Scabbard**

Near the "house" and according to the attendant symbols, a birth, marriage or death is foretold.

If the figure appears in monk's garb, a deception of some kind may be indicated.

Profile.—The profile of a face prophesies a new acquaintance formed. It will not be a lasting friendship and very little will be gained from it, though it will, temporarily, exert a great influence on your life.

Pulley.—This signifies advancement through the assistance of friends. Your way will be made easy; you will attain your greatest ambitions speedily.

Pump.—A pump is a symbol of a generous nature. You will place your faculties at the disposal of mankind and so cause much good work to be done in the world. Many appeals for charity will be made to you, and the appeals will not go unheeded. Do not, however, let unscrupulous people take advantage of your warm-heartedness and generosity.

Pumpkin.—This denotes growth and change. Events which will completely alter the course of your life are in preparation. Be ready to seize and to make the best of every opportunity. Your star of good fortune is in the ascendant.

Punt.—See *Boat.*

Purse.—Clearly defined, a purse foretells a gain of some kind, which may be either material or spiritual. If surrounded by dots, financial profit is indicated.

Near the "house," you will benefit by inheritance.

At the bottom of the cup, monetary reverses are predicted.

Pyramid.—A symbol of the desire for immortality. The pyramid gives a warning to the inquirer: concentrate on the doing of good and do not seek reward; be content to leave the acclamation of your noble deeds to posterity.

Q

Query.—A question-mark in the cup denotes indecision. Through hesitancy a loss will befall you. Set your hand to the plough, and, once started, do not look back.

Quill.—See *Feather.*

Quiver.—A quiver of arrows indicates preparedness. Foresight and perception will be of great help to you in the battle of life. The attacks of your enemies will be readily frustrated.

If the quiver contains no arrows, the opposite must be read.

R

Rabbit.—A symbol of a timid nature. Courage is sadly lacking in your make-up; at the least sign of danger you turn tail and run away. Try to cultivate stoutness of heart and learn to face your troubles; you will find the majority of them have existence only in your imagination.

Racket.—A tennis racket foretells a contest of some kind—either mental or physical—and according to the attendant symbols one may prophesy whether it will be of a friendly nature or otherwise.

If the handle points away from the "house," it is a warning not to be drawn into any disputes, for conditions of victory are more favourable to your opponent.

Raft.—You will receive help from a friend. If dots are near by, financial assistance is indicated.

Rainbow.—A symbol of hope. The storm enveloping your life will vanish into sunshine if you yourself will try to look on the bright side of things.

If a foot of the rainbow falls near the "house," it is an exceedingly good omen. It promises realized ambitions—an old age spent in ease and contentment.

Rake.—You would do well to readjust your affairs, paying more attention to detail. Smooth conditions will lead to smooth progress.

Near the "house," a rake predicts trouble caused through the revelation of past misdemeanours.

Rat.—This foretells treachery and malice. You will suffer a loss; be careful in whom you place your trust. Do not turn your back on your enemies and underestimate their vindictiveness.

Raven.—If a raven, crow or rook is portrayed in the cup, there is a suggestion that the inquirer lacks a settled purpose in life. Endeavour to conquer the inclination to profit at other people's expense. Rely on your own abilities and cultivate stability.

Near the "house," strife caused through idle gossip is foretold.

At the bottom of the cup, a slander suit.

Razor.—A razor predicts strife and enmity. If a heart is near by, it denotes a lovers' quarrel, possibly a separation.

Reef.—Hidden dangers beset your course. Let reason rule, accept the advice of those who are experienced, and you will come to a safe anchorage.

Reins.—You will have cause to seek guidance. Place reliance on the counsel you receive; do not let your heart rule your head. You have reached a cross-roads, and whichever path you take you will encounter events which will materially affect your success.

Reptile.—A reptile of any kind in the cup always denotes treachery and deadly malice. Secret enemies seek to do you harm; examine closely any newly formed friendships. See also under names of reptiles, as *Crocodile ; Snake.*

Revolver.—See *Pistol.*

Rhinoceros.—A symbol of a gross and cruel nature. You are lacking in mental and moral refinements, and are inclined to be exceedingly heartless in your dealings with your fellow creatures. This sign, however, is not wholly bad, for it suggests that you possess a strength of character which, if developed, could be put to good use.

Rifle.—See *Gun.*

Ring.—A ring symbolizes lasting friendship, love. It speaks of completion, eternity.

To the lover it is an important sign, prophesying—if clearly defined and unbroken—engagement or marriage. The good omens are strengthened if a heart or flowers are observed in the neighbourhood. An initial appearing close by may offer a clue to the identity of the partner.

At the bottom of the cup, a ring foretells a long engagement; if associated with an unlucky sign, there is a possibility that marriage will not take place.

Clouds surrounding a ring predict an unhappy union.

Two rings near to each other signify the sudden completion of an important contract.

Roadway.—Two parallel lines forming a roadway indicate a journey. The neighbouring signs will help you to form an opinion as to its nature and purpose.

If leading from the "house," a removal is indicated.

Rook.—See *Raven.*

Rope.—This symbol denotes restrictions. Circumstances will arise which will hamper your activities. If the rope is tangled, you will experience many complications in your affairs, the unravelment of which will prove to be an arduous task.

Rose.—A rose is a lucky sign to observe in the cup. It is an emblem of true friendship, happiness and success.

To the lover it speaks of the fulfilment of his most cherished desires; his wedded life will be blissful and of long duration.

To the artist it promises high honours; success will soon attend his endeavours.

To all it signifies that circumstances are propitious to embark upon new projects.

A withered rose foretells the fading of love and the declining of affection.

Rudder.—A symbol of guidance. Providence is watching over your affairs and directing your course. Place implicit trust in your star of good fortune and face the future bravely.

S

Sabot.—A wooden shoe signifies a contented, but somewhat phlegmatic, disposition. Because of a strong domestic streak in your nature you are too inclined to allow the four walls of your house to limit your horizon. Narrow-mindedness and lack of initiative may adversely affect your chances of success.

Saddle.—Events are shaping, which, if taken advantage of in the proper manner, will carry you a long way on the road to success. Be quick to seize your opportunities.

Satchel.—See *Knapsack.*

Saw.—A symbol of discord. Outside influences will destroy the harmony of your domestic circle. Proceed warily in your dealings with strangers.

Scabbard.—A swordless sheath denotes lack of foresight or unpreparedness. You possess limited vision, and, because of this, will be exposed to the attacks of your enemies.

Scales.—A pair of scales symbolizes justice. If they are balanced truly the omen is good and you will be justly dealt with; if unbalanced, evil—you will be weighed and found wanting.

Generally, a lawsuit is predicted.

If at the bottom of the cup, the legal decision will be against you; but if in the middle or at the top—and provided that the associated signs are propitious—the decision will be for you.

A sword in the neighbourhood strengthens the sign.

Scarecrow.—Need will dog your footsteps and frighten away happiness. There is a suggestion that you have only yourself to blame for this condition of things. Exercise thrift, and your days will be long and full of contentment.

Sceptre.—See *Mace.*

Scimitar.—Destruction is suspended above your head. There are indications that these conditions of ill omen are entirely of your own making. Tighten the bonds restricting your passions; think before you speak.

Scissors.—Unhappiness caused through bickerings and disputes is foretold. You will be at cross-purposes with those who seek to advise you; misunderstandings will darken your path and overwhelm you with bitterness.

If near the "house," domestic quarrels are predicted.

If a heart or a ring is close by, a separation of lovers is foretold.

Scorpion.—This is a symbol of deadly vindictiveness. Enemies encompass you. You will feel the poisonous sting of scandal and lying tongues. Advance cautiously but resolutely.

Scourge.—Adversity will lash you with its cruel thongs; vindictive criticism will be levelled against you. Bear yourself boldly and much of your suffering will count for naught. Comfort yourself with the old adage, "No cross, no crown."

Screw.—This is a sign of certain advancement. It may not come quickly, but it will come surely. Put forth all your energies and do not look backwards.

Scythe.—A scythe denotes a sudden cutting off or beating down. It predicts the natural ending of cherished schemes; the failure of health or of flourishing financial investments. Examine yourself and your affairs closely.

Near the "house," it predicts danger to the health of a relative.

At the bottom of the cup, a severe illness; serious danger arising from an accident.

Sedan.—A symbol of progress. You will be carried towards the ultimate goal of your ambitions on the shoulders of others.

Success and honours await you. Do not, however, despise your inferiors through whose labours your advancement is made possible.

See-saw.—Ups and downs will characterize your progress through life. Endeavour to cultivate a perfect mental balance and do not become readily disheartened. "Whom the gods love they chasten."

Serpent.—See *Snake.*

Shamrock.—See *Clover.*

Shark.—Danger threatens from an unexpected quarter. A vicious and sudden attack from an enemy is prophesied. Your life or goods may be endangered. Keep a sharp look-out for signs of trouble, and, when it appears, deal with it quickly. A bold front will scare away the attacker.

Sheep.—This animal symbolizes docility. Your gentle nature will expose you to the rapacious attacks of evil-doers; you will exert much influence, however, through your example of self-sacrifice. Do not always follow where others lead; cultivate initiative and act on your own responsibility.

Near the "house," a sheep foretells prosperity and success.

Shell.—A shell predicts the spreading of news. It will affect your affairs favourably or unfavourably, according to attendant symbols.

Ship.—A sailing ship or steamship, if clearly defined and in good surroundings, is a very lucky symbol. Prosperity and health are on their way to you; your fortunes are assured. If, however, the sign is badly formed, and the sails and rigging are tattered and torn, or the funnels damaged, the reverse must be read.

If the ship is very small and it points away from the "house," a journey is indicated. Pointing towards the "house," a visit from friends or the receipt of news.

Two or more ships foretell the success of commercial enterprises, increasing trade. See *Boat; Wreck.*

Shoe.—The love of comfort prevents you from trudging on determinedly. Remember that the soft and pleasant roads in life often end in adversity. That which is worth having is worth working for.

Shrimp.—See *Lobster.*

Sickle.—A symbol of labour. Your life will be industrious, the fruits of success rewarding the sweat of your brow. The common weal will benefit by your existence. Restrain any ruthlessness which may arise in your nature; it is better to create than to destroy.

D*

Skeleton.—A period of ill health or of need is foretold. Bad luck may affect your well-being, physically or financially, but there are indications that this evil condition is brought about through your own carelessness. Conserve your strength and put your house in order.

Skull.—Danger lies in your path. Avoid unnecessary risks; take better care of your health.

Near the "house," a skull may denote the severe illness and death of a beloved friend or relative.

Sleigh.—A sleigh or sled predicts rapid and easy advancement. Fortune smiles on you; your progress will be free from all jarring obstacles and annoyances. See to it, however, that you do not become cold-hearted and too self-assured.

Slipper.—See *Shoe.*

Snail.—This creature symbolizes a plodding nature. "Slow but sure" is the motto that governs your life; beware, however, lest you become indolent in mind and body and laboriously follow paths that lead nowhere.

Snake.—A snake signifies intense enmity. Someone is plotting to harm you; you will incur much deadly hate.

Near the "house," there is a person in your domestic circle in whom your trust is misplaced.

Sock.—See *Hose.*

Soldier.—You will have much opposition to overcome in your life. Be prepared to face adversity; by your strength of character you will win through.

Spade.—A symbol of hard and conscientious labour. You will attain success, but only by your own unaided efforts, after a difficult struggle. See that all the foundations of your schemes are laid firmly and securely.

Spear.—This signifies the sudden assault of an enemy. Your reputation will suffer hurt through the cruel barbs of slander. Try to overcome your extreme sensitiveness.

Sphere.—See *Circle.*

Spider.—A spider is a symbol of persistence. Whatever ups and downs you may experience—and there is an indication that they will be many—your determination to succeed will remain undaunted. There is a warning in this sign, however, that guile is too strongly developed in your nature; because of this your progress will be retarded, not advanced. Try to cultivate straightforwardness.

THE main symbols appearing in the cup on the right are a comet, top left; a barrel, right; an egg, near the "house;" and a wreck. The wreck is the most important sign. It conveys a warning of disaster, probably a financial crash, for it is surrounded by dots, signifying money. The barrel affords a reliable clue to the cause of the disaster, for it tells of vain imaginings retarding the progress of the consultant, and suggests that he regards words as being of more importance than deeds.

A visitor from abroad, foretold by the comet, may, in some way, be connected with the disaster, or he may be associated with the last symbol, the egg, which predicts a new arrival in the consultant's family.

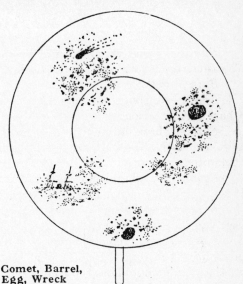

Comet, Barrel,
Egg, Wreck

Taking all things into consideration, the cup does not predict for the inquirer an immediate future blessed entirely with good fortune.

In the second cup the following symbols may be observed: a forest, left; a pistol, top; a rabbit, right; and the letter "E," near the "house." The rabbit denotes that the consultant possesses a timid nature. He will be plunged into a state of perplexity—foretold by the forest—probably as the result of some threat being levelled at him. The latter deduction is suggested by the pistol. The initial letter "E" near the "house" may afford a clue to the name of a person who will exert a great deal of influence on the domestic life of the consultant—an influence which seems to be associated in some way with finance, for the sign is surrounded by dots. In summing up, we should advise the inquirer to endeavour to cultivate stoutness of heart, for it appears that all his troubles are the direct outcome of his inability to face courageously any difficulties that he may encounter.

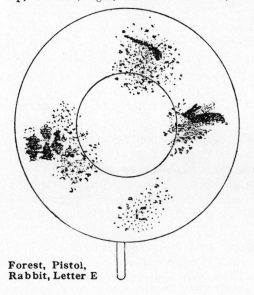

Forest, Pistol,
Rabbit, Letter E

A small spider near the "house" suggests that money is coming to the inquirer.

Spiral.—Your rise in life will be slow but certain. A position of great trust awaits you; maintain faith in your own abilities.

Spire.—See *Steeple.*

Spoon.—A spoon predicts a christening. Two spoons indicate a harmless flirtation.

Spur.—Through your own persistent energies you will gain advancement. Keep a strict watch on your health; continuous attempts to over-ride it will lead to nervous breakdowns.

Square.—A square indicates restriction, either mental or physical. It is a sign of ill omen, suggesting imprisonment or the forced suspension of activities through illness. Ill-considered words or deeds may lead you into serious trouble.

Star.—Three lines crossing each other so as to form a star predict good fortune. Health, wealth and happiness will be yours; see that you do not abuse these gifts.

Four lines forming a star are of evil omen. Expect reverses of fortune, guard well against serious accidents. If near the "house," a domestic disaster is foretold.

A group of small stars close to the "house" signifies happy and contented progeny.

A cluster of five stars denotes success, but not much happiness.

Seven stars mean bereavement, sorrow.

Steeple.—A spire or steeple is a symbol of lofty aspirations, high ideals. You will be raised to an elevated position. Men will look up to you, and by your noble example you will influence their lives.

Stirrup.—You will be helped on to advancement by a friend. Do not belittle his aid.

Near the "house," a stirrup foretells a journey.

Stockings.—See *Hose.*

Stocks.—This predicts restraint. Hindrances will arise in your path; your activities will be confined. There is a suggestion that the condition arises through indiscretion on your part. Put a closer guard on your tongue.

String.—See *Rope.*

Submarine.—Secret enemies seek to do you harm. Do not become over-confident, but look for danger where you least expect it. The calm waters of life often hide the greatest terrors.

Sun.—The sun is a symbol of happiness, power. You will shed brightness around you; many will bask in the warmth of your good-natured protection.

A rising sun predicts successful new enterprises; your fortunes are in the ascendant. Near the "house," an addition to the family.

A setting sun denotes the decline of power; your fortunes are on the wane.

Sunshade.—This foretells a period of happiness. All your affairs will prosper. Make hay while the sun shines.

Swallow.—Rapid advancement, travel, and quick decisions are indicated. A new phase of life approaches—it is laden with good fortune. Strike out rapidly and strongly both in thought and deed. There are indications that new interests abroad will open up for you, necessitating periodical comings and goings.

Swan.—The swan is a symbol of good omen. Your progress will be smooth and graceful; no storms will darken your happiness. In the quiet ways of life you will find great contentment.

If a heart is in the neighbourhood, a faithful lover is indicated.

A ring near by predicts a happy marriage.

Sword.—A sword signifies disputes, the onslaught of an enemy. Be on your guard.

A broken sword foretells a victory for your opponents.

T

Table.—A table denotes a feast, a social gathering. It suggests conditions calling for a celebration. If near the "house," the festivities will occur under your own roof.

A round table prophesies a conference of some kind. If dots are in the neighbourhood, it will relate to money matters.

Talons.—See *Claw.*

Tap.—Social service provides an outlet for your activities. You will bring prosperity into the lives of others, though you yourself may not attain it. If the tap is running, the sign is strengthened. It also denotes an abundance of good qualities.

Tassel.—This is a symbol of frivolity. Luxuries have too great a fascination for you. Endeavour to become more serious-minded, otherwise the real joys of living will assuredly escape you.

Teapot.—Conferences are foretold. You will be asked to give your opinion on matters affecting social conditions; speak your mind openly and fearlessly.

Near the "house," a teapot portends scandal, idle gossip. Your good name will suffer hurt.

Telescope.—This symbolizes acute discernment, perspicacity. Things which to others are indiscernible will be made clear to you. Do not, however, look too far ahead and neglect to take advantage of immediate events.

Tent.—A tent is a symbol of an unsettled life. Your ways will lie in strange places; love of adventure will exercise a strong influence over your career.

Near the "house," a tent predicts a removal or a short holiday.

Thumb.—A thumb denotes power. Someone in authority will proffer you aid; accept it, for circumstances are propitious to your advancement. There is a tyrannical streak in your make-up which must be curbed.

Timber.—See *Log.*

Toad.—This creature signifies flattery. Examine the circle of your acquaintances; a so-called friend is blinding your senses with honeyed adulation. He seeks to gain his own ends at your expense; have no dealings with him.

Near the "house," a toad predicts domestic trouble caused through deceit.

Tomb.—You will suffer a loss. If dots are observed close by, a financial reverse is indicated.

The sign also conveys a warning. Do not dwell too much on past mistakes or failures—look forward to the future.

Tool.—A tool of any kind is a symbol of executive ability. That which is given you to do will be done well. There is a suggestion that others will make use of you to shape their own ends. Do not allow your sense of perception to become blunted.

Torch.—A torch symbolizes learning, progressive work. It is strongly linked up with social service; it predicts that your name will go down to posterity as one who strove unselfishly for the betterment of the human race. Press onwards; do not become disheartened by malicious criticism.

Tortoise.—This denotes a reticent, timid nature. You are very sensitive to criticism and are apt to withdraw into your shell at the slightest provocation. Face facts bravely, and you will discover that you possess a strength of character which will enable you to withstand all the buffetings of fortune.

Mental inactivity must not be encouraged; it will lead to slothfulness and consequent failure.

Train.—See *Locomotive.*

Tramp.—See *Scarecrow.*

Trees.—A clump of trees foretells prosperity. Your ambitions will be fulfilled.

If dots surround the sign, your fortunes will be developed in rural districts. See *Forest.*

See also under names of trees, as *Oak; Yew.*

Trefoil.—See *Clover.*

Trestle.—A symbol of support, this figure, shaped like a capital A, predicts that you will carry a heavy burden of responsibilities on your shoulders. Through co-operation with your fellow-men, you will climb high in life and prove of great service to the community.

Triangle.—According to the position of the triangle, it may denote either good or bad fortune.

If the figure is well formed and has its apex pointing upwards, it is a sign of good omen. You will rise to a high position—all your endeavours will meet with success.

If the base of the triangle is uppermost, it is of evil omen. New projects will come to naught; established schemes will suddenly collapse. You are warned not to let your heart rule your head, for, if you do, certain failure will result.

Trident.—A trident is a symbol of marine authority. To a sailor, or anyone connected with the sea, it promises speedy promotion and eventual leadership.

If the fork is uppermost, successful mercantile enterprises are foretold. Much gain will come to you through anything relating to shipping.

Should the fork point downwards, it has an evil significance. Mercantile projects will fail; losses at sea will be experienced.

Tripod.—This symbol possesses an occult significance. The hidden mysteries of life will be revealed to you; knowledge and power will raise you from the common rut. Take care that you put your extraordinary abilities to a good use. Do not become obsessed by mysticism; it is a good servant but a dangerous master.

Trousers.—Unhappiness caused through scandal. Revelations concerning your past and intimate life are predicted. Face facts with a brave demeanour; let the dead bury the dead.

Trowel.—Conscientious endeavour will assist you to lay the foundations of success. See that you lay them well and truly.

Trunk.—A travelling trunk foretells sudden changes of plans. You will be called upon to make decisions which will alter the course of your existence—the attendant symbols will enable you to forecast whether the alteration will be favourable or unfavourable.

Near the "house," a trunk may predict either a journey or a visitor from afar.

Tumbler.—See *Glass.*

U

Umbrella.—This sign indicates shelter, protection. If open, you will have cause to seek assistance from your friends. Closed, the assistance will be denied.

Unicorn.—See *Dragon.*

Urn.—An urn is a symbol of chance. There are indications that you will be extremely lucky in lotteries, sweepstakes and draws. Do not, however, allow the important things of life to be decided by mere accident; use your own judgment.

V

Valise.—See *Trunk.*

Valley.—A line curving downwards, then rising again, predicts a period when your fortunes will be at a low ebb. It is not an ill-omened sign, however, for a new and higher ascendancy is promised. Seek relaxation, so as to fit yourself for the tasks awaiting you.

Vane.—Inconstancy is symbolized by the weather-vane. You lack concentration and your work will suffer accordingly. Endeavour to do one thing—and one thing at a time—thoroughly. Remember the old saying "A rolling stone gathers no moss."

If a heart is in the neighbourhood, a fickle lover is indicated.

Vase.—Your life will be a useful one. Mankind will benefit by your work. You will shed much happiness around you.

Vessel.—A domestic vessel of any form usually signifies social service. You possess high ideals, and though your position may be lowly, you will accomplish great things, for which your name will be remembered. Material rewards, however, will not come your way—nor will you desire them.

Viaduct.—Through your instrumentality an important deal will be brought about or a contract entered into. It is possible that it will materially advance public welfare.

Violet.—A violet is a symbol of modesty and faithfulness. You have a tendency to become too introspective and thus to develop an inferiority complex. Have faith in your own abilities and try to accept calmly whatever limelight is thrown upon you or your work. It cannot possibly be detrimental to your character.

If a heart is near by, a faithful lover is indicated.

Violin.—This musical instrument signifies independence. Your best work is accomplished without the aid of others. Eliminate the streak of irritability in your make-up, and your life will be harmonious. The sign gives a warning against egotism.

Volcano.—A volcano denotes slumbering passions. Unless you are ever watchful, your lower instincts will suddenly burst forth and wreck your career. Self-control must be practised assiduously.

Vulture.—A symbol of cruelty and theft. Danger is hovering near you. You may suffer from the oppression of one who is in authority over you. Bitter enemies seek to do you an injury. Be on your guard against loss through the dishonest practices of one who envies your position. Burglary is also indicated.

W

Wagon.—See *Cart.*

Wasp.—You will suffer hurt through the persistent machinations of an enemy. Your good name may be injured; scandal-mongers are abroad.

Weathercock.—See *Vane.*

Whale.—A high position of leadership awaits you. The world of commerce is likely to constitute your province. Your keen perception and capacity for administration will stand you in good stead; your energetic nature will override all obstacles in your path.

Wheel.—At each turn the wheel of fortune will bring you advancement. If near the "house," a legacy is predicted.

Windmill.—Only by hard work will you achieve success. Strive cheerfully and manfully; do not be content to leave the grindstone of life to be turned by the winds of chance.

Wings.—A pair of wings foretells a message. According to the conditions governing the sign, you will receive either good or bad news.

Wolf.—Jealous intrigues will mar your peace of mind. Those who envy you are to be feared most. Take precautions against theft.

Woman.—The figure of a woman usually signifies happiness, pleasure. If dots accompany the sign, prosperity is foretold; they may also indicate a large family.

Two or more women, especially if near the "house," suggest scandal directed against you.

Worm.—Secret enemies seek to undermine your position. Probe deeply beneath the surface of things. Examine your friendships.

Wreck.—A shipwreck is a sign of ill omen. Look to your affairs; disaster threatens. If dots surround it, a financial crash is indicated.

Near the "house," domestic troubles. There is danger of a separation from one for whom you have great affection.

Y

Yacht.—See *Ship.*

Yew.—A symbol of longevity. The probabilities are that you will live to a ripe old age and perform much useful work.

If near the "house," a yew tree may predict the death of an aged person, probably a relation.

Yoke.—A yoke signifies a condition of slavery. Someone will attempt to dominate your life. Endeavour to cultivate a greater strength of will; submission will not always repay you.

Z

Zebra.—This animal foretells many adventures in foreign lands. A strong love of travel will exert a great influence over your life. Though you will not attain much success in business affairs, happiness will walk hand in hand with you throughout your life.

DIVINATION BY CRYSTAL-GAZING

THROUGHOUT history man has employed many and various means in order to project his perceptive powers into the boundless realm of the Unknown. Dreams, omens, visions, premonitions, conjurations, hypnotism, table-rapping, cartomancy, palmistry and astrology—all these media and methods have been consulted and practised by the seers and initiates in their efforts to "pierce the veil."

Among such methods of divination, crystal-gazing, in one or other of its several forms, has always been a favourite, for it is at once rapid, reliable and convenient, and rarely involves the clairvoyant in unpleasant or distressing experiences. In addition to these recommendations, crystal vision in a greater or lesser degree is capable of being acquired by practically all who undertake the study of the science with faith, patience, and purity of thought and intentions—by all, that is, save the most grossly material natures, to whom, in any case, the unfolding of a vision of the Infinite would be as unappreciated as pearls which are cast before swine.

The physical properties of crystals exercised the speculative faculties of the ancients to a remarkable degree, the prevalent opinion being that rock-crystal consisted simply of water which had been subjected to an unbelievable degree of cold, far below the temperature of ordinary ice or snow. This was the opinion held by the elder Pliny, who always showed an unquenchable thirst for knowledge regarding the mysteries of Nature; while Claudianus refers to crystal as "ice hardened into stone, which no frost could congeal nor Dog-Star dry up."

Others held, on the contrary, that crystals were the result of the solidification of water by intense heat. Steno, the Danish bishop of Titiopolis, postulated in 1669 the theory that crystals were formed by the continual concretion of matter upon the surface of a six-sided nucleus suspended in a liquid. For other researches which helped to reveal the true nature of crystalline structures, and so laid the basis of the science of crystallography, we are indebted to the microscopists Robert Hooke and Leeuwenhoek, and to Huygens, Sir Isaac Newton, Domenico Guglielmini, Cappeller, Linnaeus, Helmholtz, Faraday, Sir David Brewster, and many other scientific observers.

Crystal-gazing, or one or other of its allied forms of "scrying," was used in very ancient times as a medium of clairvoyance. Saint Augustine informs us that the ancient Persians were the first crystal-gazers. The Greeks of classical days used a clear mirror, a practice which was revived in Europe during the Middle Ages. The celebrated Doctor Dee, who acquired a wide reputation for his magical and clairvoyant powers during the reign of Queen Elizabeth, is variously said to have scried in a crystal, a black mirror, or a slab of polished cannel-coal; the last-mentioned practice is paralleled by the Huille-che tribe of South America, who use a polished black stone for the purpose.

The account which Edward William Lane gives in *The Manners and Customs of the Modern Egyptians* regarding the clairvoyant visions seen by Arab boys in a pool of ink held in the palm of the hand is well known. Elsewhere, scryers have used a hole filled with water, as in the South Pacific, the human fingernail, a drop of blood, the glittering blade of a sword, and similar media, but it is a matter of doubt whether some of the heterogeneous substances that have been used for the purpose will really succeed in invoking true clairvoyant vision. This, however, a crystal, a glass sphere, or a mirror, will certainly do, on account of the peculiar magnetic properties which each possesses, concerning which we shall shortly have more to say.

The genuineness of visions in crystals is so universally acknowledged as to need no vindication, although it may be difficult to put forward a convincing explanation of such phenomena. The *Proceedings* of the Society for Psychical Research and the records of many other learned bodies contain the notes of innumerable cases which have amply demonstrated the power of the clairvoyant to project his subconscious mind through time and space, or in some mysterious way to receive information, often very detailed, which could not be conveyed to him by any non-supernatural means.

William Gregory, M.D., who was professor of chemistry in the university of Edinburgh, in his book *Animal Magnetism*, relates some remarkable cases of crystal clairvoyance which came under his personal notice, one of which is particularly worthy of attention, since it concerns a succession of distant events seen on different days, and all appearing to relate to one connected group of circumstances. In this case, however, the subject, Mr. D., was hypnotized by Dr. Gregory before the crystal-gazing was attempted.

When the globe was placed in his right hand, Mr. D. felt a strong current of cold up his arm; when the crystal was removed to his other hand, a current of heat was felt. Further, the crystal radiated such a powerful effulgence to the subconscious mind of Mr. D. that it painfully affected his sight, even when his eyes were fast closed; and when it was placed above his head, out of range of his eyes, he saw it as plainly and as radiantly as before.

This first dazzling effulgence of the crystal was found in subsequent experiments to be much reduced, and Mr. D. was able to relate in detail the scenes and incidents which he saw while looking into it. These appeared to centre round a tall and picturesquely dressed man—for convenience labelled R.—and to take place in the Balkans or some similar place. This personage was seen on no fewer than twenty different occasions by Mr. D., concerning whom Dr. Gregory writes:—

> From the first observation to the last, he not only never saw the same vision twice, but as he was at that time mesmerized daily, and sometimes twice a day, there was an unmistakable connexion between the separate visions. Thus, one day he saw R. in a wild country, travelling down the course of the river by which the road ran. Next day he was seen in a lower part of the valley, where the country became more cultivated; on the third day he was observed approaching a considerable town, and on the fourth was found in his own home in that town. For about three weeks or a month he was seen every day, often travelling on foot, at other times at home. The various localities were described with singular minuteness. Indeed, the town was so described, and that on many different occasions, that I am sure I should know it were I ever to see it. . . . I conclude that . . . it is possibly near the frontiers of Russia and Turkey, or Transylvania and Turkey.

This connected chain of clairvoyant visions experienced by Mr. D. is impressive enough, especially in view of the obvious sincerity observed in the subject himself, who was a student of medicine, and the unblemished reputation of Dr. Gregory and the impartial and truly scientific spirit which animated his researches. But the following vision is perhaps more striking still, since Mr. D. seemed to be taken, by means of the crystal, an immense distance back into the past, to a school of philosophy in classical Greece. We will once more quote from Dr. Gregory:—

> One day, while observing the town above mentioned . . . he became suddenly silent, and after a short time told me that he was travelling through air or space to a great distance. I soon discovered that he had spontaneously passed into a higher stage; perhaps in consequence of the crystal, which he held in his hand, acting more powerfully than usual, he being then in a very susceptible state.
>
> As soon as he had come to the end of his journey, he began to describe a beautiful garden, with avenues of fine trees, of which he drew a plan. It was near a town, in which he could see no spires. At the end of one principal avenue was a round pond, or fountain, enclosed in stone and gravel, with two jets of water, and close to this fountain or pond stood an elderly man, in what, from the description, seemed to be the ancient Greek dress, the head bare, long beard, flowing white robes, and bare feet in sandals. He was surrounded by about a dozen younger men, most of whom had black beards, and wore the same dress as their master. He seemed to be occupied in teaching them, and after a time, the lecture or conversation being finished, they all left the fountain, by twos and threes, and slowly walked along the avenues.
>
> Looking down these avenues, Mr. D. saw glimpses of the neighbouring hills and of the town. . . . This singular vision also recurred spontaneously two or three times; that is, Mr. D. saw the gardens and the localities, but not again the group at the fountain, although other persons were seen enjoying the walks, and on one occasion two ladies were noticed, whose dress seemed also to be ancient Greek.

Other remarkable instances are cited by Dr. Gregory. Referring to his friend Mr. Lewis, he says:—

> He finds that gazing into a crystal produces the state of waking clairvoyance in him much sooner and more easily [than concentration of thought]. On one occasion, being in a house in Edinburgh with a party, he looked into a crystal, and saw in it the inhabitants of another house, at a considerable distance. Along with them, he saw two gentlemen, entire strangers to him. These he described to the company. He then proceeded to the other house, and there found the two gentlemen whom he had described.
>
> On another occasion, he was asked to see a house and family, quite unknown to him, in Sloane Street, Chelsea, he being in a house in Edinburgh with a party. He saw in the crystal the family in London, described the house, and also an old gentleman very ill or dying, and wearing a peculiar cap. All was found to be correct, and the cap was one which had lately been sent to the old gentleman. On the same occasion, Mr. Lewis told a gentleman present that he had lost or mislaid a key of a very particular shape, which he, Mr. L., saw in the crystal. This was confirmed by the gentleman, a total stranger to Mr. Lewis.

In his book entitled *The Making of Religion,* Andrew Lang gives several striking instances of crystal vision, of which the following personal account is one:—

In February, 1898, Miss Angus again came to the place where I was residing. We visited together the scene of an historical crime, and Miss Angus looked into the glass ball. It was easy for her to "visualize" the incidents of the crime (the murder of Cardinal Beaton), for they are familiar enough to many people. What she did see in the ball was a tall, pale lady, "about forty, but looking thirty-five," with hair drawn back from the brows, standing beside a high chair, dressed in a wide farthingale of stiff grey brocade, without a ruff. The costume corresponds well (as we found) with that of 1546, and I said, "I suppose it is Mariotte Ogilvy,"—to whom Miss Angus's historical knowledge (and perhaps that of the general public) did not extend. Mariotte was the Cardinal's lady-love, and was in the Castle on the night before the murder, according to Knox.

We have not sufficient space within the limits of this treatise to give further instances of the remarkable phenomena of crystal vision, but the student will find an almost unlimited number illustrated in the works of the most impartial of scientific observers.

The reader must make a careful distinction, however, between the genuine crystal-gazer—one who, probably by long and patient striving, has succeeded in developing his or her latent clairvoyant powers—and the commercially-minded sibyl or "professor" of the seaside pier or the fair-ground, who, generally through the medium of a heterogeneous conglomeration of palmistry, crystal-gazing, psychometry, numerology, and a great deal of bluff and deception, will—for a consideration—purport to tell the "fortune" of an almost endless succession of clients, all differing in their circumstances, character and walk of life, but most of them agreeing in the extent of their credulity. The conflicting auras of psychic force after four or five of such sittings must be truly appalling; and one afternoon of this "clairvoyance" would be sufficient to cause severe nervous injury to one who was genuinely and acutely sensitive to occult forces and magnetic emanations.

Setting aside the most obvious frauds, we do not affirm that all such persons who thus contract to reveal the secrets of destiny upon a wholesale basis are devoid of clairvoyant powers; but the greater percentage of these people in whom it does exist have vitiated this divine gift. For it seems to be an inflexible rule of the occult that, whenever any manifestation of psychic power is exploited by human beings for their own commercial benefit, that power, if the greater part of it is not taken away from such unworthy custodians, ceases, at least, to display its deeper and more inspired attributes.

The genuine seer does not force his powers upon the attention of the world—not from fear of ridicule and disbelief, but because the possession of true psychic insight is too precious a gift to be thus publicly paraded. The earnest student who methodically and conscientiously practises the instructions which are given later will reap his own reward in the fuller and more satisfying existence which true crystal vision will bestow upon him. We have thought it well to emphasize these points, for it must be thoroughly understood that the sublimest heights of crystal vision can be attained only by those whose thoughts, intentions, and habits of life are pure in all respects.

We would also warn the student against the belief that any and every picture seen in the crystal must necessarily be of psychic origin. Many eminent men of science who have studied the phenomena of crystal vision have concluded that the peculiar state of the subject when observing in the crystal is nothing more than a self-induced hypnotic trance, the result of concentrating the attention fixedly for a while upon a single point. As we know, it is a commonplace in hypnotism that the mesmeric trance can be induced in this way—by gazing attentively, for instance, at a single point of light, a coin, or a brightly illuminated brass globe.

It is probable, then, that many of the visions seen in the crystal are but projections from the subconscious mind, which, while the subject is in the hypnotic trance, assumes control over the temporarily slumbering conscious mind, in the same way as it does in ordinary dreams. These projections may be the revived memories of incidents and events which the subject has actually experienced, or of which he has heard at some time or other in the course of his life, but which, apparently, he has forgotten— that is, the record of such incidents may have faded completely from his conscious mind, although it has been preserved imperishably in his subconscious mind, and lies there unsuspected by the subject himself until the moment when it is revived and forced upon his attention in the hypnotic sleep. Often, too, impressions originating in the mind of some other person may be unconsciously conveyed to the mind of the subject by telepathy.

This is the theory propounded by many scientists in explanation of part of the phenomena that appear in the crystal. However, many things are seen which cannot be accounted for in this way, and these particular phenomena may be described under two headings:—

1. Direct clairvoyant vision into time and space.
2. Symbolical visions, or the *pictures* of thoughts, feelings and ideas. [Such symbols are not to be regarded in a literal sense, but must be *interpreted* in order that the portent, warning or information which they are meant to convey may be elucidated.]

The student may ask how it is possible for him, when gazing into the crystal, to discriminate between the various classes of phenomena which we have enumerated. We can only reply that it is by *intuition* alone that he will be able to distinguish between telepathic impressions, together with the revivals of old mental experiences that have lapsed into the subconscious mind—profoundly interesting, perhaps, in themselves, but imparting no new knowledge to the gazer and bringing with them no revelation—and those symbolical or prophetic visions which owe their origin to the supernatural.

The former classes of vision should not, indeed, be disregarded, since the degree of intensity and frequency of their occurrence is an index to the sensitiveness of the gazer, while telepathic impressions are in themselves valuable as a form of mind-reading; but the full development of clairvoyance and symbolical vision should ever be the seer's ultimate object. Intuition, we repeat, is the sole signpost to direct him on his way, but it is one that will rarely lead him falsely.

Concerning the Crystal Itself

The globe that was used for scrying in earlier days probably consisted in most cases of natural rock-crystal—either quartz or beryl; and though a few of these crystals still survive, they have become very rare and consequently very expensive. A deep-blue or a yellowish beryl is often found particularly favourable to the production of symbolical visions; while clear, colourless quartz yields the best results with many persons. Dr. Gregory's globe, in which the medical student Mr. D. saw such remarkable visions, seems to have been of natural rock-crystal—probably quartz.

As we have said, however, cost is the principal factor that militates against the employment of natural crystal, so that now-adays the so-called "crystal" generally consists of a ball of clear glass, which must be without specks, flaws or bubbles of any kind. Indeed, the "crystal" used by the alchemist Dr. Dee, whom we have already mentioned, is said to have been of pinkish glass and about as large as an orange. It will be noticed, too, that Andrew Lang refers to the "glass ball" in the account which we have quoted of the vision concerned with the murder of Cardinal Beaton.

An ovoid, or egg-shaped, mass of glass or crystal is sometimes used instead of a sphere, and, indeed, is considered preferable by some clairvoyants. In this case, it is often helpful when endeavour-ing to see events at a considerable distance (either of time or space) to look through the longer axis of the ovoid.

If practicable, then, the student should provide himself with a ball or ovoid of genuine rock-crystal—tinted, it may be, but perfectly transparent. If this lies outside his means, a polished ball of clear glass will make an effective substitute. At all events, the globe should be as large as is conveniently possible, in order to ensure the utmost content of "odyle," a force that will presently be described.

Some sensitive persons can become clairvoyant merely by gazing into a tumbler or hollow glass sphere filled with water. In our opinion, this does not offer such a potent means of attaining psychic vision as does the crystal or the solid glass sphere, but we would certainly recommend the student to try it, since it is an interesting fact that there is a wide difference in the ways in which various persons are affected by various substances, and it is only by experiment that the student will discover the medium which suits him best.

In preparing a glass or globe of water for scrying, the student should use perfectly pure distilled water, though natural water is very suitable if the district is rich in iron. In any case, the water should have added to it enough crystals of pure sulphate of iron —green vitriol—to colour it a distinct green.

Magic Mirrors

Mirrors have been used for stimulating the clairvoyant faculty since a very remote age. The Specularii, or Mirror-diviners, had an established place in the religion of ancient Rome. Dr. Dee's black mirror has already been mentioned, together with its parallel, the polished black stone, probably basalt, of the Huille-che Indians. Every magician and necromancer of the Middle Ages had his magic mirror, in which it was thought possible to conjure up visions of places and personages from another world; while the student need only remind himself of the prominent part which the mirror has played for centuries in the symbolism of the Shinto religion of Japan.

In fact, all over the world and in all ages, instances may be found of the profound psychic significance which men have discerned in the reflecting powers of the mirror. The Zulus, we are informed by Sir James Frazer in *The Golden Bough*, will not look into a dark pool, while (we are quoting from the same eminent authority) "it was a maxim both in ancient India and ancient Greece not to look at one's reflection in water, and . . . the Greeks regarded it as an omen of death if a man dreamed of seeing himself so reflected." Although we are aware that many students of folk-lore would differ from us on this point, we venture to put forth the suggestion that this marked reluctance to peer into what was, in effect, a natural mirror may have owed its origin to the fear of conjuring up a clairvoyant vision, which these races (ever more sensitive to projections from the psychic world than the matter-of-fact European of to-day) well knew from experience was easily induced by gazing into such a medium as a pool of water.

The remarkable instances of clairvoyance by looking into a pool of ink—another form of mirror, in fact—of which E. W. Lane was a personal witness in Egypt, have already been mentioned, but we think his account so worthy of notice, coming as it does from such a dispassionate and erudite observer, that we subjoin the following passages which are taken from it:—

The boy who was to be employed . . . had been called in, by my desire, from among some boys in the street, returning from a manufactory; and was about eight or nine years of age. . . . Taking hold of the boy's right hand, he [the Arab magician] drew in the palm of it a magic square. . . . In the centre, he poured a little ink, and desired the boy to look into it, and tell him if he could see his face reflected in it: the boy replied that he saw his face clearly. The magician, holding the boy's hand all the while, told him to continue looking intently into the ink; and not to raise his head. . . . He then asked him if he saw anything in the ink; and was answered, "No," but about a minute after, the boy, trembling and seeming much frightened, said, "I see a man sweeping the ground." "When he has done sweeping," said the magician, "tell me." Presently the boy said, "He has done." The magician then . . . desired him to say "Bring a flag." The boy did so; and soon said, "He has brought a flag." "What colour is it?" asked the magician; the boy replied, "Red."

He was told to call for another flag; which he did; and soon after he said that he saw another brought, and that it was black. In like manner, he was told to call for a third, fourth, fifth, sixth and seventh; which he described as being successively brought before him; specifying their colours as white, green, black, red and blue. . . .

When the boy had described the seven flags as appearing to him, he was desired to say "Bring the Sultan's tent and pitch it." This he did; and in about a minute after, he said "Some men have brought the tent, a large, green one; they are pitching it;" and presently he added, "They have set it up."

The boy continued to describe in detail the scenes which he beheld in the pool of ink, while the magician burned charms written on paper and muttered his incantations. At this point, Lane describes a vision which was even more remarkable still:—

He [the magician] now addressed himself to me, and asked me if I wished the boy to see any person who was absent or dead. I named Lord Nelson, of whom the boy had evidently never heard; for it was with much difficulty that he pronounced the name, after several trials. The magician desired the boy to say to the Sultan, "My master salutes thee, and desires thee to bring Lord Nelson; bring him before my eyes, that I may see him, speedily." The boy then said so, and almost immediately added, "A messenger is gone, and has returned, and brought a man dressed in a black suit of European clothes; the man has lost his left arm." He then paused for a moment or two; and looking more intently and more closely into the ink, said, "No, he has not lost his left arm; but it is placed to his breast."

This correction made his description more striking than it had been without it, since Lord Nelson generally had his empty sleeve attached to the breast of his coat: but it was the *right* arm that he had lost. Without saying that I suspected the boy had made a mistake, I asked the magician whether the objects appeared in the ink as if actually before the eyes, or as if in a glass, which makes the right appear left. He answered that they appeared as in a mirror. This rendered the boy's description faultless. . . .

A short time since, after performing in the usual manner, by means of a boy, he prepared the magic mirror in the hand of a young English lady, who, on looking into it for a little while, said that she saw a broom sweeping the ground without anybody holding it, and was so much frightened that she would look no longer.

After giving several further remarkable instances, Lane adds the following note regarding the genuineness of the apparitions:—

> That there was no collusion I satisfactorily ascertained by selecting the boy who performed the part above described in my presence from a number of others passing by in the street, and by his rejecting a present which I afterwards offered him with the view of inducing him to confess that he did not really see what he had professed to have seen. . . . The perfumes, or excited imagination, or fear may be supposed to affect the vision of the boy who describes objects as appearing to him in the ink; but if so, why does he see exactly what is required, and objects of which he can have had no previous particular notion?

Following the example of the Arab scryers, the student may try the effect of a pool of black ink poured into a saucer. However, he should be careful that dust and other impurities are not allowed to mar the bright surface of the liquid, and should also guard against shaking the saucer, even in the slightest degree, or breathing upon the pool of ink while he is gazing.

A permanent magic mirror may be made in the following manner: Procure a round-bottomed flask of hard glass, such as is used in chemistry, from three to four inches in diameter. Cut off the neck to within half an inch of the body, by nicking it deeply all the way round with the edge of a file and breaking it off sharply. This operation may be better entrusted, however, to a professional glass-worker. Thoroughly cleanse the interior of the flask with hot water and soap, rinse it out well and allow it to dry.

The flask must now be *completely* filled with black record ink, so that no bubbles or air spaces are left, and tightly corked up. The cork should be sealed with a layer of sealing-wax or melted pitch, when the flask may be inverted and rested upon a low stand of ebony, or black-stained wood. It is preferable to insert the sealed end of the flask into a cavity cut to fit it in the upper surface of the stand, and cement it firmly in place with melted pitch or resin. The outside of the magic mirror must be kept clean and shining; and, when not in use, the globe must be kept in a dark place.

WHY VISIONS ARE SEEN IN CRYSTALS

To lay claim to the ability to assign a conclusive explanation to the wonders of crystal vision would be treading upon thorny ground; and we will not presume to undertake the task of explaining dogmatically a variety of phenomena by which some of the most eminent scientists have admitted themselves baffled. Nevertheless, we will venture to put forth a theory which, though we are far from claiming it as conclusive, has at least the merits of being logical, free from fantasy, and in accordance with observed and accredited facts.

In the middle of the nineteenth century the celebrated Baron von Reichenbach, after long and laborious researches on the phenomena of mesmerism and the properties exhibited by magnets, formulated his theory of *odylic emanation*, in which he claimed to have discovered that all material objects—especially magnets, crystals and the human body—are filled with a peculiar force which they diffuse in the form of an aura or halo that, by sensitive persons, can be seen more or less clearly in the dark as surrounding the object like a cloud of light. This mysterious force Reichenbach named "odyle."

In the course of his subsequent researches and experiments with many different substances, Reichenbach was able to define several of the properties of odyle. He found that, although the velocity with which it moved was less than that of light, it could pass through solid bodies much more rapidly than heat; and, moreover, that it was capable of penetrating all known substances, and of permeating them in the most complete and intimate manner. To persons whom Reichenbach found sensitive, a thick bar of iron shone with such an effulgence of odyle that it became as transparent as glass.

From a prolonged series of observations, Reichenbach was able to deduce that odyle is diffused throughout the universe, as are heat, light, electricity and magnetism. Odylic emanation has unfailingly been observed to accompany chemical action of all kinds; and in this fact Reichenbach saw a perfectly natural explanation of the luminosity which sensitive persons plainly see over graves and tombs—particularly if the interment is a recent one. Without having recourse to the supernatural, it is feasible, he said, to conclude that these dim and eerie glimmers of light are but the odylic emanations occasioned by the chemical changes that are taking place in the dead body.

Moreover, bearing in mind that the earth itself is but a large magnet and therefore particularly rich in odyle, Reichenbach was convinced that in his theory of odylic emanation he had found a reasonable explanation of the aurora borealis—the northern lights which glow and flicker in marvellous radiance round the poles of the earth, sending out their long streamers and curtains of prismatic colours many miles towards the stars. Indeed, by magnetizing a large iron globe, and thus temporarily increasing its odyle content, Reichenbach was able to produce a miniature auroral display, which was plainly perceived by his "sensitiveness." That the aurora borealis has its origin in some form of magnetism is, of course, the universal opinion of scientists to-day.

Now, it was Reichenbach's belief that the human brain—particularly the hinder part of it, known as the cerebellum—is the chief storehouse of odyle for the body, somewhat in the manner of an electric battery or accumulator; and that, whenever the gaze is fixed determinedly upon any object, a ray of odyle streams between the brain and this object.

It is a significant fact that the beryl, the crystal traditionally used for scrying, as well as its various forms, such as the emerald and aquamarine, contains a proportion of iron oxide. An analogy will be at once apparent between these substances and such objects as a sword-blade, a pool of ink, and similar things that are used for scrying in different parts of the world—all of which contain iron in some form or other. Ordinary glass, of which gazing spheres and mirrors are made, also contains iron salts.

The human body likewise contains a certain amount of iron oxides, notably in the blood. Now, a suggested explanation of the phenomena of crystal-gazing is that the crystal itself, by means of the odylic or magnetic properties which it derives in particular from its content of iron, acts as a kind of magnet to the emanations from the spiritual world which surround the gazer and his sitters. These emanations, or psychic impulses, being attracted, as it were, into the crystal, set up vibrations or waves in its odylic force; and these vibrations, by means of the ray or column of odyle which constitutes the gaze of the clairvoyant, are sympathetically reproduced in the odylic content of his brain, thus giving rise to real visual impressions. It will be seen that this action is similar to the working of a telephone apparatus; vibrations set up by sound waves at one end of the line are conveyed along the wire as electrical impulses, and reproduced at the other end as sound waves once more.

In the Middle Ages, as in more ancient days, it was customary for clairvoyants and occultists to assist the invoking of crystal visions by means of magical ceremonies. These usually took the form of elaborate prayers and incantations (some of which would to-day be considered blasphemous in the extreme), the inscribing of magic circles, the burning of perfumes and essences, the reciting of the Hebrew names of the Deity and of his angels and archangels, the use of mystic emblems bearing cabbalistic signs, and other forms of esoteric ritual.

Favourable astrological conditions were also taken into account, and the seer was recommended to imbibe infusions of certain herbs and simples which were supposed to encourage clairvoyance, as well as to perform ablutions before consulting the mirror or crystal.

It was considered essential to success that the moon should be increasing in its light; and this, we may add, is a condition that might still be observed with advantage. The odylic power of the moon has been too well established for its agency to be lightly set aside as unimportant; its strongly marked effect upon lunatics, for instance, being a commonplace that has been observed for centuries. In this connexion, it is interesting to note that, in the opinion of Dr. Gregory, lunacy consists principally of an abnormality in the distribution of odyle in the human body.

We would seriously discourage the student from soliciting the aid of magical practices when consulting the crystal, for, even disregarding the strain which they are likely to impose upon his time and patience, they may be considered not only as unnecessary for the encouragement of lucidity, but even dangerous. No matter how mysterious and inexplicable they may seem to us, the phenomena of crystal vision are, nevertheless, founded upon true science, and are incapable of being explained by any other than perfectly natural and logical means. The practice of crystal-gazing should, therefore, be approached in the purely scientific spirit, which it has been our aim to maintain throughout this treatise.

How to Look Into the Crystal

The student should conduct his experiments in a room that is as quiet as possible, and that can be securely shut off from all disturbing influences. It should be comfortably warmed and ventilated, and the student must be perfectly at ease throughout the whole of his experiments, so that no outside influence may distract his thoughts from the crystal. No bright colours, glittering ornaments or distracting objects of any kind must be allowed to remain within range of his vision.

The light must at all times be subdued by drawing the blinds or curtains, or, if an artificial light is used, by effectively shading its rays from the crystal or mirror. The light of a fire or stove must also be screened off. Direct sunshine must never be allowed to enter the room while the crystal is being used. If the sitting is held in the day-time, the gazer should be placed with his back to the light, which, if possible, should filter into the room from the north.

Moreover, the crystal or mirror itself must never be exposed to bright light, whether natural or artificial; and when not in use, it must be kept securely locked away in a dark receptacle, after having been wrapped in a black silk handkerchief or a piece of black velvet kept specially for the purpose. The reason for this precaution will readily be understood when it is observed that the sun is powerfully charged with negative odyle—as the moon is with positive odyle—and exposure to such a heavy charge of this force is sufficient to upset for a long time the sensitiveness of the crystal.

One of the best times of the day in which to practise crystal-gazing is just before the oncoming of twilight—an hour which, incidentally, is one particularly favourable to occult manifestations of all kinds. An attempt to read the crystal should never be made shortly after a meal.

The crystal or mirror must be placed in front of the observer on a stand or table, the surface of which should be covered with a dull black cloth. A low pedestal of ebony or black boxwood, or a black cushion, may be used with advantage to hold the crystal steady, or it may rest in the folds of a black silk handkerchief. It must be screened from the reflection of extraneous objects by means of a dark handkerchief wrapped partly round it.

Another method is to place the crystal at the back of a partly opened drawer, which must be quite empty in other respects and draped with black, non-reflecting material. A little practice may be needed before the crystal can be adjusted satisfactorily: the

E

ideal position is that in which the crystal or mirror ceases to reflect any object whatever, and its depths, though they appear darkened, are yet quite clear and pellucid.

The gazer should first close his eyes gently and keep them shut for two or three minutes, so as to exclude all disturbing visual images from the retina. He can now begin to look into the crystal or mirror—calmly, steadily and with interest. He must not screw up his eyes in a determined fashion and transfix the unoffending globe with a fierce and frowning glare, as though he is resolved at all costs to wrest from its inscrutable depths the secrets of his destiny. On the contrary, all feeling of tenseness and exertion must be carefully avoided, and the eyes should be blinked at normal intervals, as frequently as is done when they are in use. If a feeling of strain is experienced in the eyes, they must be rested by looking away from the crystal for a moment or two.

It is most important for success that the student should not overtax his powers, and for this reason he should begin his experiments with a short sitting, gradually increasing the time until a space of an hour or more may be spent in gazing without fatigue. We would enjoin the reader not to dismiss this precaution lightly, for success will rarely come to the person who overtaxes his powers at the start. We have even known persons with a weak nervous system to be reduced to a state of temporary hysteria—simply because they failed to observe the golden rule of moderation when beginning the practice of crystal-gazing.

We stress this point because gazing induces such a welcome feeling of calm and rest in both body and mind that the student is often unwilling to relinquish it when the prescribed interval has elapsed. We suggest that the beginner should allow himself ten minutes on the first occasion, and *no more*. This can be increased progressively by four or five minutes at a time, but the student should never be tempted to exceed the period which is indicated for any particular occasion. Moreover, it is very important—at least, until the sensitivity of the gazer has become well developed —that the sittings should be held in the same place, and under the same conditions, and that they should be begun at exactly the same time each day. We have already indicated the early evening, at about the hour of sunset, as being particularly favourable.

We will now describe some of the impressions and experiences which the student may expect to encounter. Probably many attempts will be undertaken before anything at all is seen but the obscure depths of the crystal itself, which, as the eyes begin to grow weary of maintaining a constant focus, will slide suddenly into a double image, which, just as suddenly again, will coalesce into one, a performance that will repeat itself as long as the student continues to gaze. Admittedly not a very encouraging result! But have patience and persevere.

A day will come—perhaps the second or third occasion of gazing, perhaps at the end of a month of patient effort—when, after the usual double image, a faint white cloud will appear to drift slowly across the face of the crystal. After passing repeatedly through the crystal for a while, this white cloud may give place to a greenish or reddish mist, which again will turn to a screen of black or dark grey upon which little pin-points of light keep up an endless, whirling dance. Then the entire crystal, together with its specks of light, will appear to approach close to the eye of the gazer and almost instantly recede again, moving repeatedly to and fro, while the gazer will feel a peculiar tenseness of the nerves all over his body. At this point, he should keep a cool head and continue to gaze calmly and with confidence, for he is now upon the very threshold of crystal vision.

If the gazing is continued, very shortly the crystal will seem to disappear entirely, only to reappear after a second. This it will do for a brief while alternately, until at last a supreme moment comes in which the entire crystal is blotted out by a sea of celestial blue light. Upon this, as upon a beautiful screen or background, will be seen the vision, either direct or symbolic. Usually, it will not seem to the gazer that he is regarding it with his eyes, but rather that the vision has entered his brain, and is being portrayed or enacted there.

The student should try to conquer any fear or surprise occasioned by the contemplation of his first vision; he should watch it calmly and with interest. He will by this time have become oblivious to his surroundings and will be, in fact, in a sort of trance-like state, analogous to deep waking abstraction or even somnambulism. And yet the last vestige of consciousness, registering surprise or even dismay, may bring him back to a fully waking state.

If such a thing should happen, he should make no attempt to return to his new-found visionary world, alluring though it may be, but should put the crystal safely away and, if possible, go to sleep for a time. The experiment should then be renewed upon the next day, or successive days, at the same time and in the same conditions, until the vision returns. Usually on this occasion the student has no difficulty in retaining it vividly before his gaze.

With practice and experience, a time will come when the student will develop the ability of inducing a vision shortly after he has begun to look into the crystal or mirror; when, too, he can so control the emanations from the psychic world of which the crystal vision is a living picture that he can follow its unfolding in detail for a long time and, retaining at will a part of his conscious mind in an almost fully waking state, can describe to another person what he observes in the crystal and answer questions that may be put to him. If any other persons are present, however, it is important that they should not be seated close to the one who is scrying, nor should they converse among themselves. Also, any questions that are put to the gazer must be uttered in a low and gentle but distinct voice. But the first attempts and experiments in gazing should be made only when the student is entirely alone and undisturbed.

Those who are inclined to become discouraged, despondent or sceptical because at first they are not rewarded by a vision of any kind—perhaps not after many attempts—should constantly remind themselves that infinite faith and patience are often necessary in order that the dormant faculty of clairvoyance may be aroused from its long slumber. There are few people who are completely devoid of sensitiveness to occult emanations, and they are chiefly of a very low type of humanity—not necessarily devoid of education or superficial culture, since such attributes are often merely due to chance alone, but bound to a low level of moral and psychical development, and usually brutish, unimaginative, cruel and grossly materialistic.

Admittedly some subjects see visions more clearly and readily than others, while some see them sooner, because their psychic faculties are not in such a state of abeyance. In any case, the extent and value of the visions are proportionate to the degree of faith and of purity of mind and intention with which the science of crystal-gazing is approached; so that confirmed sceptics and those whose thoughts and motives are not good will never succeed in obtaining more than, at the best, confused, fragmentary and meaningless apparitions in the crystal.

When a stage is reached at which clear scenes or images cease to be observed in the crystal, a stage when the void is filled merely with wisps of cloud and drifting shadows or a confused play of lights, you may begin to put questions to the crystal—or rather, to the surrounding psychic aura whose emanations the crystal faithfully reflects. The questions should be put mentally (it is, of course, unnecessary to utter them aloud), and they should be as clear and precise as possible. Then continue to gaze steadfastly into the crystal. Generally, the shadows will clear away and a vision will be presented, which can be taken as the answer of destiny. It was by clairvoyant methods corresponding in essential respects to this kind of divination that many of the celebrated sacred oracles of the ancient world furnished replies to their anxious questioners.

It sometimes happens that fate refuses an answer; and, whether this refusal is absolute or only for the time being, it will have to be respected.

Each of the different colours that appear has its own significance. In general, light colours are of good omen, while the darker shades are inauspicious. Clouds of white, violet, green or blue are good signs, particularly the first. Green is a sign of hope, which increases according to the depth of the tint. Black, on the other hand, has a negative and inauspicious meaning; while red, orange and yellow are very unfavourable colours, the first two of these colours—particularly red—symbolizing hatred, passion, danger and violent emotions, and the last denoting envy, malice and jealousy.

Ascending clouds indicate a response in the affirmative to a question that has been propounded or to a matter over which the scryer or consultant is feeling anxiety. *Descending* clouds imply a negative response.

In scrying for another person, the latter should be given the crystal to hold for a few moments (in order that he may charge it with some of his own content of odyle, which, Reichenbach found, constantly streams from the tips of the human fingers). He should retain it in his left hand and place his right hand on the top of it, and then, returning it to its stand, should seat himself some distance away from the gazer, and observe unbroken silence while the latter peers into the sphere.

As we remarked earlier in this treatise, setting aside telepathic impressions and projections of actual past experiences that have lingered in the subconscious mind, the visions seen in crystals are of two kinds, direct and symbolical. In regard to these two forms of vision, there is considerable obscurity concerning how it is possible to gauge the time at which an event that is represented will take place, or has already taken place if it be in the past. To this we will reply once more with the single word "intuition."

It is a remarkable sidelight on crystal phenomena that some mysterious power is given to the clairvoyant to judge time more or less accurately, while the vision is being unrolled before his eyes. He *feels* instinctively when an event foreshadowed in the crystal is going to be enacted in real life; and, what is remarkable, he can go back in time and declare at what period in the past a particular event has taken place.

Often signs forming part of the visions themselves can be taken to indicate time. Thus, if snow is lying on the ground and the trees are bare, winter is obviously indicated, as equally is summer by a fresh and verdant landscape. Again, visions seen far away in the background usually indicate the distant past or future; those placed midway between the background and the observer relate to events in the near past or future; while those nearest to the observer are the projections of the present or the immediate future. These divisions may serve the student as a general means of judging time; others may arise within his own experience. But, as we have said, intuition must be allowed the chief and final word.

Symbolical visions are attended by still another difficulty— that of their interpretation. They must be regarded as the actual pictures of thoughts and mental impressions, and are in no wise to be taken in a strictly literal sense. The interpretation will most frequently be found, however, to bear some relation to the usual attributes of the symbol, the circumstances with which it is generally connected, or the use to which it is normally put.

Thus, a flaming torch may stand for enlightenment and progress, a serpent for astuteness and cunning, a ship for commerce and travel, the sun for prosperity, success, honour and preferment, the waxing moon for growth and increase of prosperity, the waning moon for ill luck, bad health and loss, and so on. But it is again the gazer's own intuition, or rather that with which he is endowed for the time being, that will determine the real meanings of the symbols with an almost mechanical facility and truthfulness. It is helpful to remember that symbols often appear upon the *right hand* side of the crystal or mirror.

One day, the author, upon looking into the crystal, saw a black dog and a wolf greedily lapping in a clear stream, which immediately became discoloured. A person whom the author recognized as a friend fell into the stream from a bridge and was engulfed in the turbulent and polluted water. At that moment an overhanging branch was seen to fall from a tall and massive oak tree, crushing the dog and the wolf. It settled like a bridge across the stream and enabled the author's friend to climb out safe and sound. The author kept this symbolical vision to himself, apart from warning his friend against malice and calumny, symbolized by the black dog and the wolf.

Nearly a year later, however, the author's friend was involved in serious trouble through the false tongues of calumniators, coupled with the malice and envy of dishonest rivals in business. A plot was set on foot to ruin, in a court of law, his personal reputation and the goodwill of his business; and it had already almost completely succeeded when a third party interposed unexpectedly with evidence that was irrefutable, and at one stroke rehabilitated the innocent victim of this diabolical plot and incriminated those who had formulated it, to their inevitable ruin. It afterwards transpired that the family of which the third party was a member bore a coat of arms in which an oak tree figured prominently! Other remarkable instances could be quoted at length, but lack of space forbids.

The highest plane of crystal clairvoyance to which the student may attain is one that is not reserved for every gazer—even if he be apt at conjuring up lucid visions. This is a state of almost complete trance, in which the scryer seems not so much to be witnessing scenes, visions and symbols from a distance, but actually seems to be a passive participator in such scenes himself. As F. W. H. Myers says in his *Human Personality and Its Survival of Bodily*

Death: "Certain sensations do also accompany these pictures; sensations not merely of *gazing* but sometimes (though rarely) of partial *trance;* and oftener of *bilocation* [the state or faculty of being in two places at once]; of psychical *presence* among the scenes which the crystal has indeed initiated, but no longer seems to limit or to contain."

Those who would aspire to true crystal vision, and particularly vision of that sublime type which we have just described, must strive always to live as cleanly and wholesomely as possible. Ill health, disease, gluttony, sensuality, sloth and materialism, all are incompatible with clairvoyance and that supreme elevation of soul that is attendant upon communion with the world of spirits.

The would-be seer must attend carefully to his health and diet and manner of living. Fresh air, good food (but not too much of it), exercise, and the contemplation of Nature are strong aids towards the attainment of psychic power by furnishing the most suitable ground for its growth and development. For this reason, long walks in the country should be indulged in, alone if possible, or with one or two companions whose minds are in sympathy with that of the student.

Moderation should be observed in all things, especially in eating, drinking and the expression of the emotions. As we have previously remarked, the student should never sit down to consult the crystal shortly after taking a heavy meal; a loaded stomach and high blood-pressure are never conducive to psychical phenomena of any description. An equally important restriction is that relating to the use of alcohol. Absolute abstention is the ideal, but at least moderation must be observed.

Above all, the most earnest efforts must consciously and unremittingly be made towards the cultivation of elevated thoughts and purity of speech and action. Communion with the world of spirits and the ultimate vision of the Absolute are not for him whose thoughts are tainted with worldly lusts and passions, diffusing, like a dank and fetid miasma, the gross breath of materialism. It is only those who can realize the Infinite in their own souls who may hope to become one with it.

DREAMS AND THEIR INTERPRETATION

"A DREAM is the royal road to the subconscious" is one of the chief precepts of the modern psychoanalyst. Since in these days, more than in any other, every intelligent man and woman realizes the supreme importance of the subconscious mind, it is only natural that there should be a general revival of interest in the meaning, or interpretation, of dreams.

The advice contained in the Delphic maxim "Know thyself" has probably never been so greatly valued as it is to-day. People are beginning to appreciate that the greater their knowledge of *why* they think certain thoughts, or *why* they commit certain acts, the better will they be able to obtain a mastery over both mind and body. Thus they can shape their lives in a manner conducive to their own happiness and to that of others.

All this may appear to have little to do with dream interpretation but, nevertheless, it is intimately connected. For it is the subconscious mind which becomes active only when we sleep; we cannot make ourselves aware of it by any effort of the will or act of memory in our waking condition. It manifests itself when our conscious mind is rendered partly inactive. We say "partly" because, if our consciousness becomes wholly inactive, as it does in deep sleep, we can never remember our dreams, for memory is part of the conscious mind. It is a fact that we dream during the whole period of sleep, but we can remember only a very small part of that period.

The dreams which we are able to describe are those which occur just as we are falling to sleep or just as we are beginning to awaken. It is during these times that our conscious mind is partially active and in a state to receive impressions which are retained by the memory. Frequently, however, these impressions are so faint that they are remembered only for a very short time. We may remember a dream for a few minutes when we wake up in the night, but the next day it is entirely forgotten. On the other hand, there are dreams which are so vivid, and which impress themselves so very strongly upon us, that we can recall them and describe them in detail years afterwards.

From the above remarks it will be realized that dream interpretations can be made only when our conscious mind is sufficiently aroused to receive a more or less vivid impression from the subconscious. Regarding the nature of the latter we can say nothing, even to-day, for little is known about it. We know that it is from the subconscious mind that we receive the flashes of intuition and prophetic vision that lie hidden in depths which our conscious mind cannot fathom. During sleep this mysterious underworld of thoughts comes into control, and, because it is unbounded either by time or space, it can reveal to us conditions of our present and future state of which we have no knowledge when we are awake and wholly conscious.

That "dreams go by opposites" is a general belief which is sometimes doubted. With certain qualifications, however, it is a perfectly true statement, although it is only recently that the reason for this has been discovered. There is one peculiarity about the subconscious mind which particularly distinguishes it from the conscious. When we are awake we are constantly making mental contrasts, or thinking in opposites. For instance, we distinguish black from white, large from small, forwards from backwards, joy from sorrow, and so on, by reason of the fact that the one is the direct opposite of the other. Now, when we are asleep we sometimes lose this power of contrast, and there occurs in our mind what is called a "unification of opposites." In other words, we are unable to draw distinctions. When we think we dream of black it may really be white, up may be down, small may be great, sorrow may signify joy. In fact, almost every dream is a puzzle-picture which must be solved with the aid of past experience.

We will not enter into a detailed history of dream interpretation. It is sufficient here to say that the peoples of the earth at all times have attached significance to them.

The Bible contains many examples of dreams—prophetic and otherwise—but perhaps the most famous of them all is the one experienced by Pharaoh, which took the form of a parable that only Joseph could interpret:—

> And it came to pass, at the end of two full years, that Pharaoh dreamed; and, behold, he stood by the river. And, behold, there came up out of the river seven well favoured kine, and fatfleshed; and they fed in a meadow. And, behold, seven other kine came up after them out of the river, ill favoured and leanfleshed, and stood by the other kine upon the brink of the river. And the ill favoured and leanfleshed kine did eat up the seven well favoured and fat kine. So Pharaoh awoke.
>
> And he slept and dreamed the second time: and, behold, seven ears of corn came up upon one stalk, rank and good. And, behold, seven thin ears, and blasted with the east wind, sprung up after them. And the seven thin ears devoured the seven rank and full ears. And Pharaoh awoke, and, behold, it was a dream.
>
> . . . Then Pharaoh sent and called Joseph . . . And Pharaoh said unto Joseph, I have dreamed a dream, and there is none that can interpret it: and I have heard say of thee, that thou canst understand a dream to interpret it. . . . And Joseph said unto Pharaoh, The dream of Pharaoh is one: God hath showed Pharaoh what he is about to do. The seven good kine are seven years; and the seven good ears are seven years: the dream is one.
>
> And the seven thin and ill favoured kine that came up after them are seven years; and the seven empty ears, blasted with the east wind, shall be seven years of famine. . . . Behold, there come seven years of great plenty throughout all the land of Egypt: And there shall arise after them seven years of famine; and all the plenty shall be forgotten in the land of Egypt. . . . And for that the dream was doubled unto Pharaoh twice; it is because the thing is established by God. . . .
>
> And in the seven plenteous years the earth brought forth by handfuls. . . . And the seven years of dearth began to come, according as Joseph had said. . . .

The ancient Chaldeans, Chinese, Egyptians and Hindus, as well as the Hebrews, Greeks and Romans, implicitly believed in dreams as a means of foretelling the future (Plato calls them "prophetic visions"), although they were regarded as "divine messages," as omens of the gods, rather than manifestations of the human mind itself. We owe much to a Roman seer called Artemidorus for our knowledge of divination by dreams as practised by various ancient peoples. He compiled *The Five Books of the Interpretation of Dreams and Visions*, a work which is drawn from various sources and forms a basis of most of the modern "Keys to Dreams."

Naturally, there is much in the beliefs of ancient dream interpreters which must be rejected in the light of the medical knowledge which we possess to-day. For instance, there are many dreams which have purely physical causes, such as those vivid and horrible nightmares which spring from a disordered digestion.

There are also dreams which are "self-suggested;" that is to say, those caused by our thoughts turning either deliberately or unconsciously into certain channels for a few moments previous to sleep.

Let us consider first of all those dreams which arise from physical disorders, and as such have no significance in the prophetic sense. They affect the blood-flow through the brain, and may be caused by a faulty digestion, an abnormal condition of the heart, liver disorders, an increase or decrease in the body temperature, and various other conditions which modify the normal working of the human functions. They need not be regarded as being signs of any serious disorder; most people experience them at some time or other, and they can usually be attributed to over-eating during the previous evening or partaking of some rich food which does not agree with the stomach.

Organic Dreams

Dreams of falling from high places, of running without gaining ground, of being chased or terrified by ghosts and monsters, of screaming with fear (and often awaking at once), of stepping off a kerb or step and of slipping and then waking up with a jerk, of going up or down in lifts, of fields or rivers flowing with blood, of fire and flames, of great stretches of plain or sea, of drowning or any form of suffocation, of murders and wounding, of diseases and dreaming that one is dying—these, and, in fact, any of those dreams which are accompanied by feelings of great terror and which are usually described as "nightmares," are caused by alteration in the flow of blood through the brain; and they must not be regarded as being prophetic, since they do not arise from the subconscious or intuitive mind.

Frequently these nightmares are the result of adopting an unnatural sleeping position. There is no definite rule regarding which side we must lie on when we are in bed. It is always best to adopt the most comfortable position. We are told by medical men, however, that when the body is reclined slightly to the right it then allows the heart, stomach and liver to function quite unhampered by pressure.

Under the title of self-suggested dreams come all those which concern a person or thing which has been prominent in our mind just before falling asleep. Perhaps a book we have been reading may have made a deep impression on us and we may dream about incidents or characters from it. It may be that we have read something in a newspaper or heard some story from a friend, or that we may have seen a film or play. All these things are able to affect us because they are retained by the memory, and are liable to be released when we fall into the sleeping state.

It will be seen that before we attach any divinatory or prophetic significance to a dream we must cast our mind back to make sure that it is not merely the result of something which has occurred to us a day or two previously, and which has been unconsciously reproduced in sleep.

Moreover, there is another type of self-suggested dream. This is the one which is purposely produced. It is a well-known fact that Robert Louis Stevenson was in the habit of *willing* himself, before dropping off to sleep, to dream romantic adventure stories. In this manner, he declares, he received many inspirations for those delightful tales which he gave to the world. Dreams of this type cannot be said to be prophetic, as they are artificially produced.

There is also a type of dream which requires no interpretation, as it is in itself directly inspirational. Such a dream was experienced by Giuseppe Tartini, the great Italian violinist and composer of the eighteenth century.

Tartini had been at work on a beautiful sonata, but had been unable to finish it. Weary and disconsolate he went to bed, pondering on how he could complete his composition. At last he fell asleep, still obsessed by his task, and dreamed a dream. In it the Devil came to him and offered to finish the sonata in exchange for the great musician's soul. Tartini did not hesitate, and joyfully closed the bargain. So the Devil took up a violin and embarked upon a weird yet utterly inspiring trill. The notes were fitted perfectly to the music that Tartini had already written, and when the Devil had finished, the dreamer awakened immediately, rushed to his manuscript and finished the sonata.

Anyone who has heard *The Devil's Sonata* by Giuseppe Tartini, is at once led to remark that the weird, long and unbroken trill contained in it seems to owe its inspiration to something far more mysterious and far more penetrating than the human mind.

One of the most interesting instances of directly inspirational dreams is quoted in *Human Personality and Its Survival After Bodily Death*, by Frederic W. H. Myers. Doctor H. V. Hilprecht, professor of Assyrian in the university of Pennsylvania, had vainly attempted to decipher some inscriptions on two small fragments of agate. He had estimated that they belonged to a certain period of Babylonian history, and had managed to interpret a few words on one of the fragments. These conclusions, together with illustrations, he had set forth in a book which lay before him, ready to be printed. Nevertheless, he tells us, he was far from satisfied, and he was still worrying over the problem on a night in March, 1893.

He went to bed weary and exhausted, and immediately dropped off to sleep. Then he dreamed that "a tall, thin priest of the old pre-Christian Nippur, about forty years of age and clad in a simple abba, led me to the treasure chamber of the temple, on its southeast side." The priest then addressed the professor and told him that his conclusions regarding the fragments of agate were wrong, and he proceeded to relate their real history, saying how he himself was one of the priests who had cut three pieces from an inscribed agate cylinder (of the kind which was used as a votive offering), and that two of these pieces were made into earrings for the god Bel. The third piece, the priest said, would never be found. He then disappeared.

On awakening the professor related his dream to his wife, in order to establish it in his mind. At the first opportunity he once again examined the two fragments and found that they were undoubtedly parts of the same cylinder, and in the light of this new disclosure he was able to piece them together and to decipher them.

This strange dream is undoubtedly a true product of the subconscious mind. It must be noted that all the information imparted by the priest was within the range of the professor's own brain, but it was stifled by his conscious or so-called rational mind; it was necessary for his subconscious mind to gain control, and thus to provide him with the necessary insight and inspiration.

Yet another type of dream requiring no interpretation is that which is caused by mental telepathy. That is to say, if someone with whom we are closely associated is undergoing a severe emotional disturbance, it may sometimes be communicated to our mind during sleep. It is not everyone, however, who possesses this peculiarly receptive power, and it is dangerous to jump to the conclusion that when we dream that a friend is ill or in trouble that this must necessarily be the case. It is true that there are those who, possessing a telepathic mind, have actually seen events in dreams at the same time as their occurrence in reality. On the other hand, we may dream of a friend's death or illness merely because we have a subconscious dread that such an event might occur. There is no need to worry about such dreams unless you know from past experience that you possess the power of receiving telepathic communications.

Those dreams, then, which may be truly regarded as oracular dreams are the ones for which we can find no explanation. They must not be nightmares, or dreams of persons or things we have recently seen or heard about; they must not be those which come to us in illness or from worry or fright. They must be the natural products of untroubled and healthy sleep, when our body is resting in a normal position and we are not affected by adverse conditions of extreme heat or cold.

In the key which follows it must be remembered that the interpretations given are necessarily broad, for it is impossible to enter into detailed descriptions which will agree with every variety of dream. The meanings must be taken as general indications rather than exact prophecies, for when we are dealing with the subconscious mind it is not always easy to arrive at an exact interpretation.

Many dreams may appear to have been overlooked in the compilation of the list, but this is only because no ancient authority or modern psychologist has given them a significance. The reader himself may be able to add to the key. He may find that when he has a certain dream it is followed by a special sequence of events in real life; if both the dream and the events that follow occur with any frequency, it would be safe to suppose that the dream is actually a presage of the reality, and that his subconscious mind had adopted this means of foretelling the event.

It is important to remember that the interpretation of a dream may denote both present events as well as future events, for the two are inseparable. In fact, some philosophers describe the future as the "hidden present," for all those things which occur to-day are leading up to the events of to-morrow. The future is ever in preparation, and it is the peculiar power of our subconscious mind which allows us to see it in the making.

THE DREAM KEY

A

Abandon.—If you yourself are abandoned, a quarrel with a friend is imminent; if you desert someone it betokens the renewal of a friendship.

Abbey.—Present troubles will soon pass away.

Abdication.—To dream of the abdication of a sovereign foretells success for the schemes which you have in mind.

Aboard.—If you dream that you are on board a ship you will gain profit from a hazardous enterprise.

Abroad.—To travel to a foreign country shows an advancement in business; if you dream that a friend or relative goes abroad there is an indication of a future estrangement.

Abyss.—If you are looking down an abyss, you are in some kind of danger but can avoid it if you act swiftly.

Falling down an abyss is an organic dream with no prophetic significance.

Accident.—To be involved in an accident on the road, or to see one, shows a need of great discretion in your affairs; you are trusting others too much.

To dream of an accident to a train is a warning that unless you place a greater confidence in yourself you will meet with failure in the enterprise which you contemplate. Have the courage of your convictions.

Actor.—If you are an actor or actress in real life and dream that you are successful on the stage, it is not a good sign; if you dream that you fail and are hissed off the stage, it presages great success in a future production. If you are not a professional but dream that you are acting, it shows that you lack sincerity and must cultivate a greater respect for the truth.

Adder.—To be bitten by one, lies and treachery coming from a false friend. To kill one, the end of an undesirable friendship.

Aircraft.—To dream of any kind of flying machine signifies that your ambition and courage will lead you onwards to your goal. If you dream of a flying accident, avoid taking business risks for the next few days.

Alligator.—Someone in your circle of acquaintances is a sly and treacherous enemy; you will recognize the person from the exaggerated friendship he displays in an attempt to win your favour and confidence.

Almonds.—If you dream of eating sweet almonds you will shortly go abroad.

To dream of eating bitter almonds foretells a journey with unhappy consequences.

Alms.—If you give them, you will become very prosperous within a year. If you receive them, your wealth will diminish but your happiness will increase.

Alphabet.—If you dream that you are reciting the alphabet, much worry and agitation is in store for you.

Altar.—To dream you are before an altar is an unhappy omen signifying losses and affliction. If you are decorating the altar, however, a happy love affair awaits you.

Anchor.—If you hope and have faith, you will be delivered from your present trouble. If the anchor is dragged, you will embark upon some rash business which will bring you shame.

Andiron.—A sign of great happiness and comfort in the home. If misunderstandings exist at present it lies in your own power to banish them.

Anemone.—See *Flowers*.

Angels.—A particularly fortunate omen for those in love, showing that each is implicitly faithful and that a happy marriage will result. For those who are afflicted it is a sign of comfort and foretells coming joy and consolation.

Anger.—When the dreamer is angry with a friend, the latter may be regarded as being especially faithful. If the dreamer is the object of another's anger, he may rest assured that he is greatly loved.

Angling.—If you are successful and catch many fish, you have ambitions which will soon be realized. No catch at all indicates loss or failure.

Animals.—Domestic animals signify happiness; wild animals —especially the great cats—treachery and cruelty on the part of enemies. (See also special animals under individual names, as *Lion, Tiger.*)

Ants.—If they are seen hard at work upon the ant-hill, it is auspicious for all those engaged in industry, foretelling increased prosperity and expansion of business. Lovers may expect a happy wedded life following this dream. If the ants are flying, the dreamer will journey to a foreign land or pay a visit to a large town. When you stamp on or in some manner destroy the ant-hill it is an ill omen, indicating that your carefully laid plans will result in utter failure and destruction.

Anvil.—To see one, or to hear the ring as a hammer strikes it, foretells great success of the project in hand.

Ape.—Ill fortune as a result of malicious slanders.

Apparel.—See *Clothes.*

Apple.—See *Fruits.*

Apricot.—See *Fruits.*

Arm.—If the arm is strong and healthy, you will have success in an unexpected quarter; if it is weak or diseased, you will suffer a great disappointment.

Arrow.—If it is fired towards you and wounds you, it foretells a betrayal of your confidence. If the dreamer is shooting arrows, he will be led into slanderous utterances in the near future.

Arum Lily.—See *Flowers.*

Ashes.—Unlucky omens denoting coming misfortunes, the chief of which will be money losses.

Ass.—You will overcome your present affliction if you have the patience to wait a little longer. Slowly but surely happiness is approaching.

Assassin.—Within a few days the dreamer will meet one who will help him greatly, especially in financial matters.

Atlas.—If you seize your opportunity, your wish to travel in foreign lands will soon be fulfilled.

Atmosphere.—If it is clear and pure, or tinged with light blue, you are in the happy possession of a good conscience, and your actions will make you universally loved and respected. If you are faced with any problem, the solution is very near at hand; pending lawsuits will result in your favour. Dark or cloudy atmosphere indicates trouble and affliction; quarrels with old friends, misunderstandings, business worries and unsuccessful enterprises.

Attic.—To dream one is in the attic of a house presages the renewal of an old and dear friendship.

Auction Sale.—To the dreamer, this is a subconscious warning that he is living in an extravagant manner. Unless economy is practised great loss or even ruin may result.

Axe.—To wield an axe in a dream tells of great strength of character, which will bring success and much reward.

B

Baby.—A happy omen for a woman, denoting great joy and a true lover. If a man dreams he is nursing a baby, it is a sign of a disappointment in a love affair.

Bachelor.—When a married man dreams he is a bachelor he must take care lest he becomes unfaithful to his wife. To talk to a bachelor in a dream signifies the forthcoming wedding of the dreamer.

Bag.—If one is carrying a full bag, an unimportant loss is to be expected shortly. An empty bag denotes a trifling present from an acquaintance.

Bagpipes.—A dream of ill omen, either to hear them played by another or to play them oneself. It signifies mental conflict, which will result in quarrelling and the breaking of friendship.

Balcony.—To be watching others from a balcony foretells unexpected success. If the balcony gives way, a quarrel with a lover.

Ball.—If you, yourself, are playing with the ball you may expect some exceptionally good news. If you watch others playing but take no part, you will soon become jealous of a friend.

Balloon.—See *Aircraft.*

Banquet.—For both man and woman this is a sign of good times ahead, with much wealth and happiness. (See also *Dining.*)

Bat.—If it is flying at night, some unknown enemy may do you harm. If you dream that you see the bat by day, you will escape a danger which is threatening.

Bath.—To dream that you are in your bath and that the water is warm, you will fail through your own laziness in the task you have undertaken. If the water is cold, success and prosperity will ensue for all those engaged in trading.

Bathing.—If you dream that the water in which you bathe is clear, you may expect your business to improve and your love affair to end happily. When the water is muddy, however, you will have an unexpected misfortune and be crossed in your affections.

Battle.—Violent battles with much bloodshed, causing terror to the dreamer, are organic dreams and have no significance. To dream that one is engaged in or watching a battle, without excessive terror, indicates success in spite of opposition. (See also *War.*)

Beans.—An unfortunate omen indicating serious losses and perhaps sickness, if one dreams of eating them. To see them growing foretells a lover's quarrel.

Bear.—If you are running from the bear, your present happiness is shortly to be marred by a rich, unscrupulous enemy. If you slay the bear, you will prevail against your enemy.

Beard.—If you see a bearded man, you will soon receive some good advice from a friend. For a man to dream that he has a beard denotes that he is engaged on a foolish and fruitless enterprise. If a woman dreams that she has grown a beard, she will be delivered from the attentions of an unwelcome lover.

Bee.—To dream of a bee or bees is exceedingly fortunate; it foretells great domestic happiness, improvement in industry, and faithfulness of friends.

Beggar.—If, in your dream, you refuse to give the beggar money when he asks for it, you may expect a loss. If you give alms, prosperity is in store for you.

Bells.—Tolling bells denote bad news concerning a friend or distant relation. To see a bell which is silent signifies a sudden quarrel, especially for married persons.

Bier.—To see one in a dream is a good omen, foretelling a happy marriage for a member of the family.

Bilberry.—See *Fruits.*

Birds.—To a wealthy person, birds on the wing is an unfavourable sign; it foretells loss of money. To one in humble circumstances, it predicts an upward trend of affairs, bringing happiness and success. (See also under names of birds, as *Jackdaw, Magpie.*)

Blankets.—If you dream that you are buying blankets in summer, a slight illness caused through your own neglect is imminent. If you are buying them in winter, it is a good omen, predicting ease and comfort.

Blind Man.—To dream of leading a blind man signifies that someone whom you trust is, in reality, betraying you. If you dream that you yourself are blind it indicates that you will make a bad choice in selecting a lover.

Blood.—If in great quantity and causing the dreamer to be terrified, blood has no significance, for it is an organic dream. Otherwise, blood symbolizes gold, an increase in material wealth.

Blows.—If the dreamer is giving the blows, he must shortly expect failure in a lawsuit. To receive blows denotes victory in the courts.

Bluebell.—See *Flowers.*

Boat.—If you are in a boat on calm water, you may soon expect a change of residence and occupation. If the water is rough and stormy, be prepared for a great disappointment.

Book.—A good sign, especially if you dream of reading one. You will probably journey to another part of the country and there make a discovery of great value.

Bottle.—A letter containing surprising news is on its way, if you dream of an empty bottle. A full bottle denotes the indisposition of a friend.

Box.—To dream of opening a box means that a secret of the dreamer has been discovered. Closing a box predicts trouble in money matters.

Bread.—If you are eating it, you may expect to enjoy very good health. If you are baking it, it is generally a bad sign, signifying sorrow at home and quarrels between man and wife.

Bridge.—To dream of crossing a bridge indicates that you have been worrying unduly over a matter which is not serious. If the bridge should collapse, you must exercise special care in your financial affairs.

Broom.—To sweep with a broom denotes a change of occupation. A broom lying on the ground signifies desertion by an old friend.

Bull.—If the bull is charging you, enemies are slandering you. If the animal is eating peacefully in a field, great prosperity in store for the dreamer.

Burglar.—To dream of a burglar in one's own house is a sign of a lucky speculation. If you dream that you are a burglar and are arrested, you will defeat an enemy who has been troubling you.

Burial.—A contrary dream, telling of good news from a relative which will affect yourself. To lovers it means a speedy marriage.

Burns.—If the dreamer is burnt, he may shortly expect a present of money. When someone else in the dream is burnt, the dreamer will find a new and faithful friend.

Butter.—To eat or to see it indicates a festive celebration, an invitation for which will reach you within a day or two.

Buttercup.—See *Flowers.*

Butterfly.—Not a favourable dream; it signifies that you are right in doubting the faithfulness of your lover.

Buying.—This is another instance of the subconscious manifesting itself in a contrary manner. Generally, it is an indication of a financial loss.

C

Cabbage.—If you are cutting a cabbage, an intimate friend is jealous of you. Eating cabbage, good health and long life.

Cabin.—If you dream that you are alone in a ship's cabin it foretells domestic troubles and unhappiness. Another person with you in the cabin, however, is a good sign; it denotes advancement aided by one in a good position.

Cage.—If a woman dreams of a cage full of birds, she will shortly have an offer of marriage. If the cage is empty, an elopement owing to family opposition is indicated. For a man, the omen foretells an early marriage.

Camel.—A short journey in connexion with a legacy, if there is only one camel. Several camels mean a large sum of money by inheritance.

Candle.—If it is burning, you will shortly receive a letter bearing good news. Unlighted candles, or snuffing candles, denote a great disappointment and frustrated ambitions.

Canoe.—To be alone in a canoe shows that you will struggle for independence and will meet with much opposition. If someone is helping you to paddle, the contrary is indicated; you are too dependent on another and should learn to fight your own battles.

Caravan.—A journey abroad, probably for business purposes, will greatly increase your prosperity but will be somewhat detrimental to your health.

Cards.—If you are playing and you win, expect a speedy marriage; if you lose, you will shortly be engaged upon a dangerous undertaking. If you are a spectator only, anticipate an attempt to defraud you in some business transaction.

Carnation.—See *Flowers.*

Carrot.—This is an unfavourable omen. It presages a great deal of work with little or no reward.

Castle.—To dream that you live in one foretells that you will shortly be burdened with some great responsibility which will cause worry for a time. To view a castle from a distance is favourable, indicating an improvement in fortune and an appointment to some public office.

Cat.—If you see one walking alone—a journey; a mewing cat —lies will be told about you; a cat which scratches itself—you will be deceived; a purring cat—you will be guilty of hypocrisy. In dreams, the colour of a cat has no significance.

Cave.—If you are hiding in a cave, someone is spreading a scandal about you, which may cause much harm unless you are quick to repudiate it. To see wild animals coming out of a cave indicates the discovery of a secret which will cause misgivings.

Cemetery.—Good news; the restoration to health of a sick friend or relation.

Chapel.—This is a bad sign; a troubled conscience will bring discredit on you, unless you adopt a course of action different from the one which you are now pursuing.

Cheating.—A dream of contraries. If you are cheating someone else, be on your guard against fraud and deception. If you, yourself, are being cheated, you are contemplating a doubtful deal and would be well advised not to go on with it.

Cherry.—See *Fruits.*

Chess.—To dream of playing chess indicates quarrels with friends and the making of several new enemies.

Children.—A happy dream indicating great joy and prosperity. For a woman, it indicates that she has, or will have, a good husband; for a man, complete domestic concord awaits him.

Church.—If the doors are open the omen is good, signifying a rise in position or expansion in business. Closed doors of a church are not lucky—the dreamer may soon expect a bitter disappointment, perhaps a monetary loss.

Cinders.—If the cinders are cold, you will love someone who has no feelings towards you. If they glow, you are loved by a person whom you have not met.

Clock.—To see its face indicates business worries. If heard striking, you will be faced with some minor household problems.

Clothes.—To dream you are well dressed indicates a loss of money, probably through thieves. If you are in rags it is a token of the success of a favoured project. Black clothes denote coming joy; white clothes, much sorrow.

To dream that one is naked has no prophetic significance. This dream, which occurs at some time or other to most people, probably has its origin somewhere in the depths of our subconscious mind, reminding us of the time when earliest man was quite unclothed; for a period in our dream we imagine that we are once more in this primitive condition.

Clouds.—These, if they are dark and threatening, are a symbol of some trouble near at hand. Light and billowy clouds indicate the return of someone who has long been absent.

Clover.—See *Flowers*.

Cock.—If the cock crows, a false friend is planning to do you harm. A silent cock indicates a rival in love who is more formidable than he appears.

Coffee.—Coffee beans, a bad omen, indicating money losses. If you dream of coffee grounds, the sign is favourable; obstacles at present impeding your progress will soon be removed. Drinking coffee, a change of residence which will greatly please you.

Coffin.—A very auspicious dream foretelling the recovery of sick persons and the dispersal of worries. If you dream that you are lying in a coffin, it shows an early marriage either for yourself or a great friend.

Cross.—If you are bound to a cross, you will have some great triumph within a year. To see a cross to which someone else is bound is an unlucky sign denoting disappointment and losses.

Crown.—An ill-omened dream if you wear it yourself, for it presages degradation and punishment. If worn by another, you will soon have a rise in position.

Colours.—It is a good sign to dream of bright or light colours (except white) which are beautiful and pleasing to the eye. It reveals that the subconscious mind is in a happy and harmonious condition; and thus presages joy, freedom, and, perhaps, prosperity. Dark or ugly colours (except black) are unfortunate omens; they denote depression, general unhappiness and failure.

In divination by dreams, certain colours have special meanings, they are as follows:—

Black.—Great joy, probably in connexion with someone very dear to you.
Blue, Light.—Purity and great sincerity bringing happiness.
Green, Dark.—From some source there is evil threatening.
Green, Light.—Calm thoughts and repose, which will cause great contentment.
Purple, Dark.—A mental storm is brewing which may result in sorrow.
Purple, Light.—Inspiration and wisdom.
Red.—Excessive passion causing misery.
White.—Deep sorrow and worry.
Yellow.—Success in love affairs.

Crocus.—See *Flowers.*

Crutches.—To dream that you walk with crutches means that you are about to make a long but profitable journey. To see a friend do likewise denotes a parting attended by sorrow.

Cuckoo.—This is a sign of troubles in love, which will result in quarrels and the arrival of a new lover. If the bird is heard but not seen, you will be deceived by someone who pretends to give you good advice.

Cyclone.—A contrary dream denoting peaceful conditions and financial advancement.

D

Daffodil.—See *Flowers.*

Dagger.—Pointed towards you, it signifies strife and enmity arising from one who is yet unknown to you. If you, yourself, hold the dagger, your cherished wish will not be fulfilled.

Dancing.—If you dream that you are dancing, you will receive an unexpected present from a stranger. To watch others dancing denotes jealousy in love; to dance without a partner foretells a single life.

Darkness.—A dream of walking in darkness is a subconscious manifestation of an uneasy mind; if you have wronged anyone you should endeavour to put matters right, otherwise you will find much unhappiness. If you dream that you walk from darkness to light, you will make an important and profitable discovery.

Death.—An exceptionally happy omen denoting a long and comfortable life. To sick persons, it means a speedy recovery to health. Accompanied by great fear, it is an organic dream and has no meaning.

Deer.—If they run from you as you approach, you will deeply offend your friends by some action. When the deer come towards you, reconciliation with a former lover.

Desert.—To dream of travelling across a hot, dry desert signifies a short journey to a city on a matter of business. If a storm occurs in the dream, the business will have an unsatisfactory conclusion.

Devil.—An unlucky dream foretelling approaching danger and temptation.

Diamond.—If you dream that you find it, a loss of money is to be expected. If you are cutting it, you will prevail over a relentless enemy.

Dice.—Playing at dice indicates business troubles, possibly linked with much adverse speculation.

Digging.—To dig for gold or other treasure in a dream is unlucky and foretells domestic strife or lovers' quarrels. To be digging on cultivated land is a symbol of prosperity signifying increased wealth through labour.

Dining.—An unfortunate dream for married people; quarrels are indicated. For a bachelor or spinster it foretells an unhappy marriage and, perhaps, divorce. (See also *Banquet.*)

Dirt.—To dream that your body or your clothes are dirty denotes coming illness or great worries.

Diving.—If the dreamer is diving into water it is a good omen, signifying a lucky speculation or investment which will bring much wealth. To watch others dive, you will see your friends succeed where you have failed.

Doctor.—The meaning of this dream is a contrary one, indicating that you will enjoy good health and that your ills will be minor ones.

Dog.—To dream of your own dog is lucky; it denotes the fidelity of friends. Strange dogs symbolize enemies who are waiting to ruin you. Mad dogs which attack and bite the dreamer are good omens foretelling the coming of influential and kindly strangers. If you dream that a dog speaks to you, you will learn something from a friend which will be of great benefit to you.

Doll.—Much pleasure and festivity will occur within a few days of the dream, probably at the house of a stranger.

Donkey.—See *Ass.*

Dove.—A dove in a dream is an omen of peace and prosperity, unless you see 't fall to the ground, when it foretells the death of a distant relative.

Dragon.—An indication of a change of residence; if you are in the town you will move to the country, or if you are in the country you will live in a town house.

Dream.—To realize that you are dreaming when you are asleep deprives your dream of all signification, for, in such a case, your conscious mind is in an active state and the subconscious cannot manifest itself in a clear manner.

Dress.—See *Clothes*.

Drinking.—If, in your dream, you drink wine, beer or spirits, you will have a business loss but make a new friend. To drink water is an indication of a disappointment for one who is closely associated with you. If you dream that you are drunk you will soon meet with outstanding success.

Drowning.—A dream of good omen if you, yourself, are drowning. It indicates that someone will render you a valuable service through which you will gain money. To watch others drowning signifies misfortune; if you rescue them, you will be lucky in love.

Drums.—To hear drums foretells family quarrels; only to see them is a sign of reconciliation.

Duel.—If you take an active part in a duel and are the loser, your cherished wish will be fulfilled. To be the winner is unlucky, for it means you will lose a lawsuit. To be a spectator only, anger between friends is foretold.

Dumbness.—Through your garrulity you will commit an indiscretion liable to cause you serious trouble and perhaps bring you into a lawsuit.

Dwarf.—To dream that you have become a dwarf or that you see a dwarf denotes a change of society.

E

Eagle.—If the bird flies high, your ambitions will be realized. If the eagle is nesting or comes down to earth, you will meet with disappointment both in business and love.

Earthquake.—To the married this means discord between man and wife; to the lover it is an indication that he has a favoured rival; to business men it is a warning to proceed with caution.

Eating.—An unhappy dream foretelling strife between friends or lovers. (See also *Banquet, Dining*.)

Eclipse.—To see an eclipse of the sun or moon betokens trouble for a near relation, caused by the dreamer's foolish actions.

Eggs.—Provided they are unbroken, success in business undertakings; if broken, misfortune and quarrels.

Electricity.—A lucky dream foretelling good news from abroad.

Elephant.—A dream denoting prosperity and the making of many new and influential friends.

Entertainment.—If you dream that you are attending any form of entertainment it is a bad sign indicating a broken engagement or the loss of a contract.

Execution.—To be at your own execution presages good; you will achieve success which will make you famous. To watch another being executed indicates that you will help someone with a gift of money or food.

Exile.—If you dream that you are banished, it signifies that you are discontented with your present state of affairs and that you will therefore travel. If your friends are banished, it presages domestic quarrels.

Eyes.—If, in a dream, an eye appears to be sore or infected, it betokens the illness of a close friend. To lose one's eyesight means to lose one's friends.

F

Face.—To see your face in a mirror while dreaming indicates the discovery of a treasured secret; if your face appears pale and drawn, you will suffer by the discovery; if it is swollen and red, you will benefit.

Fairy.—Good news from an unexpected quarter. To lovers, the dream foretells a long and romantic life.

Falling.—A dream which is organic and has no prophetic significance.

Famine.—This signifies great personal comfort and a change for the better in living conditions.

Farm.—To dream that you are on a farm denotes that you will have great success in your business, especially if it involves much mental work. To the lover, the dream is exceptionally lucky, foretelling an early marriage to a good-tempered and devoted partner.

Father.—If you dream of your father it is a sign that he bears the greatest affection for you. If your father is dead, it is a warning of affliction.

Feather.—You will be caused a great deal of worry through the indiscretions or the misfortunes of a relation.

Fig.—See *Fruits.*

Fighting.—If you dream that you fight and lose, you may rest assured that all your troubles will soon be dispersed. In a dream it is unlucky to fight and win, for it shows you have malicious enemies who will succeed in harming you.

Finger.—To cut your finger in a dream means that your recent actions have damaged your character. To see someone else cut a finger, a slander has been spread concerning yourself.

Finger-nails.—To dream that your nails are unusually long denotes business achievements and success in love. If they are exceptionally short or cut right off, it signifies disgrace, estrangement from friends and losses in business.

Fire.—An organic dream, caused by physical disorders. No prophetic significance.

Fish.—To see a single fish is a lucky dream; it denotes increased prosperity, a devoted spouse and a brilliant child. If several fish are seen swimming, many friends are working to help you.

Fishing.—See *Angling.*

Flag.—An omen of danger if the flag is that of a foreign country; your business affairs will pass through a trying period. To see the flag of your own country, a special honour will be awarded to you.

Floods.—A fortunate dream for those who contemplate voyages by water; it foretells calm weather and a safe journey. To all others it is a sign of unfavourable lawsuits.

Flowers.—To dream of gathering flowers indicates a delightful surprise. White flowers, generally, are unlucky, for they presage disappointments, especially in love affairs. Red flowers, generally, are happy omens, foretelling lasting friendships and joyful union.

In dreams, certain flowers have special significations; they are as follows:—

Anemone.—Your love is untrue, seek another.
Arum Lily.—Unhappy marriage.
Bluebell.—You will have a nagging spouse.
Buttercup.—Your business will increase.

Carnation.—A passionate love affair.
Clover.—Someone who is very poor seeks your hand.
Crocus.—Do not trust the dark man who has attracted you.
Daffodil.—You have been unjust to a friend, seek reconciliation.
Forget-me-not.—Be firm, break with your love—he is not suitable for you.
Geranium.—There is no need to worry, your quarrel meant nothing.
Honeysuckle.—Domestic quarrels will cause you sorrow.
Iris.—A letter bearing good news.
Marigold.—A serious failure in business.
Peony.—Your excessive modesty may cause you much sorrow.
Poppy.—A message bringing great disappointment.
Primrose.—You will find happiness in a new friendship.
Rose.—A wedding, perhaps your own, within a year.
Snowdrop.—Do not conceal your secret, you will feel happier if you confide
  in someone.
Violet.—You will marry someone younger than yourself.

Withered flowers are lucky in a dream, for the meaning is contrary; your worries will soon be at an end and you will find a new happiness in life.

Flying Machine.—See *Aircraft.*

Forest.—To be lost in one is lucky; it foretells success and prosperity. If you view one from a distance, you will lose some property.

Forget-me-not.—See *Flowers.*

Fox.—You have a competitor or rival in your affairs who can be outwitted only by your taking immediate and drastic action.

Frog.—To dream of a frog is lucky; it denotes profits for the trader, good crops for the farmer, victories for the soldier and sailor and happy marriage for the lover.

Fruits.—Most fruits in dreams symbolize prosperity and abundance. Certain fruits also have particular meanings; they are as follows:—

Apple.—If red, a present of money within a few days; if green, you will wait
  a month or two for it. Golden apples are omens of greater wealth, but also
  of domestic strife.
Apricot.—Early marriage for the single, dutiful children for the married.
Bilberry.—See *Whortleberry.*
Cherry.—Unhappy circumstances in love affairs.
Fig.—Inheritance of wealth under a will or through a lottery.
Gooseberry.—Beware of a rival.
Grape.—Success for the trader; jealousy for those in love.
Lemon.—Quarrels between man and wife or the breaking off of an engagement.
Melon.—A journey abroad which will bring much profit.
Mulberry.—Through weakness and indecision you will lose a friendship.
Orange.—Exceedingly unlucky in a dream, denoting loss of goods and infidelity
  of a lover. Beware of placing implicit trust in a chance acquaintance.

Peach.—Reciprocal love, good health and many pleasant surprises.
Pear.—An advance in business and a new friendship.
Plum.—Sickness of a friend or relation.
Raspberry.—Great disappointment, but consolation from an unexpected source.
Strawberry.—A visit to the country with someone who loves you.
Whortleberry.—A deception on the part of a friend.

Funeral.—This has a contrary meaning and denotes the marriage of the dreamer, a relation, or an intimate friend.

G

Gallows.—A contrary dream denoting success and many new acquaintances.

Games.—To play them foretells good news; to watch them signifies jealousy, on your part, of a friend.

Garden.—A happy dream meaning marriage with a very beautiful woman or a handsome man.

Geranium.—See *Flowers.*

Ghost.—If of a terrifying and horrible character, this is an organic dream and of no significance.

To dream of talking calmly to a ghost denotes consolation in your troubles.

Giant.—It is a lucky omen to dream of a giant. Commercial prosperity is foretold.

Gipsy.—An omen of domestic happiness, especially if the gipsy is hostile to you. To dream that you are a gipsy means that you will never settle down, but will yield to your subconscious urge to travel and seek your fortune in far-off lands.

Glass.—If the pane of glass is clear, your future will be bright and successful; if it is dark or misty, you may expect some worries in connexion with your private affairs.

Gloves.—To dream of losing them foretells a business loss; to find a pair, a parting from a friend; to wear them, a forthcoming wedding which you will attend.

Goose.—Your expectations will end in disappointment. If you kill the goose, you will achieve startling success.

Gooseberry.—See *Fruits.*

Grain.—A happy dream if you see an abundance of it; respect and much honour will be yours and your household will be full of joy and prosperity.

Grape.—See *Fruits.*

Grass.—You will not prosper in the country; the city is best for your success.

Grave.—A contrary dream denoting health for the sick, riches for the poor, and lovers for the loverless.

Gull.—News from abroad will arrive shortly. If the bird is on the water, the news will be unwelcome.

Gun.—To hear the report but not to see the gun means the death of a distant relative. To fire a gun signifies hurt from an enemy. If you see the gun fired by someone else, you will quarrel with a dearly-loved friend.

H

Hail.—This is a bad dream, denoting disappointed hopes and blighted prospects.

Hair.—If a man dreams that he has long hair, it is a sign that he is weak and wavering. If a woman dreams that she has no hair, she will offend others by her domineering ways. To dream that one's hair is dyed an unusual colour is an omen of worry and affliction.

Halo.—If it surrounds your own head, some disgrace will befall you; surrounding another's, you will reap much honour and glory.

Ham.—This dream has a significance for sick persons only; it denotes a complete and speedy recovery to health.

Hand.—A right hand refers to brothers or sisters; a left hand represents children. To dream that a hand is dirty denotes ill luck for those whom it represents; to injure either hand denotes injury to those whom it symbolizes. If the hands appear to be tied, it foretells the removal of some impediment to success.

Hanging.—If you dream that you are being hanged it is a good omen; a successful career awaits you. To see another being hanged means that a friend or relation will become honoured and famous.

Harvest.—A sign of prosperity for those engaged in business. It also foretells domestic concord and is one of the most favourable of dreams.

Hat.—To wear a new one foreshadows a disappointment; to lose one denotes a present; to find one signifies a trifling loss of money.

Head.—An accident to the head is a forewarning of misfortune for the dreamer. Unseen enemies encompass him.

Hearse.—This is a contrary dream; it denotes a marriage or a similar joyful celebration.

Heaven.—A great change in your life, which will bring you much happiness.

Heel.—If you dream that you injure your heel, expect a minor lover's quarrel.

Hell.—This dream arises from mental strife and usually foretells a change for the better, an improvement in business.

Hen.—A cackling hen is a sign of future joy, but a silent one spells sorrow. To pluck a hen, financial gain; to see one with its chicks, loss and damage.

Herb.—This is one of the many dreams that indicate prosperity.

Hills.—In the distance, they are lucky and denote the realization of ambitions; to climb them, future worries; to run down them, bitter disappointment.

Honeysuckle.—See *Flowers.*

Horns.—If you have grown horns in your dream, you will not marry for love. To see other people with horns, evil influences are exerted over you by your companions.

Horse.—To ride a horse is a good dream foretelling the making of money and true friends; to fall off one denotes a hasty marriage; to beat one means that your aims will be thwarted. To see a number of horses signifies independence and happiness.

Horseshoe.—An omen of ill luck, telling of gambling losses and unrequited love.

Hospital.—A contrary dream denoting good health and freedom from worry.

Hounds.—To dream of following them is lucky; you will reap success. If you are pursued by hounds, your marriage will be an unhappy one. (See also *Hunting.*)

House.—A new or strange house denotes domestic comfort and a contented wife. To see a house fall foretells family quarrels and estrangements.

Hunger.—If you dream of hunger you will never experience it in reality.

Hunting.—To dream of hunting wild animals is a good omen; it shows that you will be fearless in life and will eventually meet with great success. (See also *Hounds.*)

Husband.—If you are single and dream that you have a husband, you will long remain a spinster. To dream of loving the husband of another woman indicates that you will in reality dislike him.

Hyena.—An exceedingly unlucky dream. One whom you have previously trusted will prove an enemy, and will attempt to do you great harm.

Hymn.—To be singing hymns denotes love that will not be returned; to hear others singing them forebodes distress among friends or relatives.

I

Ice.—A bad dream for business people; it denotes failure either of themselves or of those upon whom they are greatly dependent. To those in love it is a sign of a quarrel which may bring an end to the relationship.

Idol.—This is an unlucky omen, especially if you dream that you are worshipping one. It frequently means that you have devoted too much time to material matters and have thereby lost much love and friendship.

Ill Health.—A contrary dream foretelling good health and a long and peaceful life.

Ink.—To spill it is lucky and denotes a surprise present; writing with it foretells business revival.

Inn.—If you are inside one, you will know poverty; if you are outside, you will have a great disappointment.

Insanity.—An omen of great social success. You will possess a faithful marriage partner.

Invention.—To dream of a new invention is a sign of great advancement in business, through your own ability.

Invisibility.—If you dream that you are invisible, you are ashamed of some action which will soon become known to everyone.

Iris.—See *Flowers.*

Iron.—To see a smoothing iron or to be injured by one foretells an accident of a slight nature.

Ivory.—A symbol of prosperity for traders; to lovers it signifies great future happiness.

Ivy.—A fortunate dream foretelling the aid and comfort of a faithful friend.

J

Jackdaw.—To see one flying foretells enemies who will do you harm if they can. If you catch the jackdaw, you will frustrate your enemies.

Jade.—To sick people this signifies a return to health; to the business man it is an unlucky dream, denoting losses.

Jealousy.—To dream that you are jealous means that, in reality, you will have cause for jealousy; to dream that someone is jealous of you is a sign that you are deeply loved.

Jewellery.—Your vanity will bring about many disappointments, especially in love affairs. This is a favourable dream, however, to those who have passed through great grief, for it indicates the healing of wounds and the love of a devoted friend.

Journey.—To make a journey in a dream is a direct prophecy that you will do so in real life. But, if you dream that the journey is bad, in reality it will be good, and vice versa.

Judge.—If you dream that you are appearing before a judge, it signifies an easy conscience and much happiness; to dream that you are a judge indicates that you possess a sharp tongue and will lose a great friend by reason of it.

Juggling.—An unlucky dream, either to see juggling done or to do it oneself. It indicates indecision of mind and probable failure through weakness.

Jumping.—If you dream that you successfully jump obstacles, your life will be full of impediments and disappointments. To fall while attempting to jump is a lucky omen; it denotes the overcoming of difficulties, and eventual success.

K

Keel.—The keel of a ship signifies downfall and failure.

Key.—A single key is a sign of love and marriage; many keys denote prosperity, but little affection.

King.—To dream you are a king is unlucky; it means degradation. If you see a king, you will be helped in life by some rich and powerful friend.

Kissing.—If you dream that you are kissing someone against his will it is lucky; you possess a true lover. If you, yourself, are kissed and resent it, it is unlucky; you will live a life without love.

If the person whom you kiss is responsive, you will never bestow your affections on one only. To dream of kissing enemies is fortunate; it connotes approaching reconciliation.

Kitchen.—Great domestic bliss and a faithful circle of friends.

Kite.—If the kite you are flying soars to a great height, your ambitions will be realized; if it falls to the ground, be prepared for an unpleasant surprise.

Knee.—To dream that one's knee is hurt foretells business worries caused by foolish speculation.

Knife.—An unfortunate dream denoting illness, loss of money and quarrels with relations.

Knight.—If in the dream you are a knight of old, you possess deep-rooted chivalrous instincts which will bring you love and happiness. If you dream of conquering many foes, you will make numerous friends during life.

Knot.—A sign of financial troubles and long lawsuits ending in losses. To dream of tying a knot is an indication of a foolish course of action in business.

L

Lace.—Too much of your time is devoted to frivolity; someone will rebuke you because of this.

Ladder.—If you climb a ladder, you will succeed with the plan you have in mind; if you fall, make certain that your course of action is wise. To see others on a ladder is a good sign; your abilities will be recognized and you will receive your reward.

Lake.—A particularly fortunate dream for lovers, indicating a honeymoon near at hand. To everyone it is a sign of comfort and freedom from financial worries.

Lamb.—A lucky dream, signifying peace and health. More than one lamb, an addition to the family.

Lameness.—If you dream that you see a lame person, it foretells a disappointment. To dream that you, yourself, are lame, is fortunate; you will never know poverty or loneliness.

Lamp.—To carry or to see a brightly burning lamp is lucky; truth and beauty will remain your ideals throughout life. A dim or unlit lamp is unlucky; it suggests that you possess a dull intelligence, which will lead you astray.

Landing.—To dream that you are landing from a ship means

that you have many difficulties before you, but that you will succeed in the end.

Lark.—A happy dream, denoting great joy and exhilaration, a happy partner in marriage, and an abundance of all the good things of life.

Laughter.—If you laugh in a dream, in reality you will cry. If you hear others laugh but do not join in, your prospects are bright and you will find much happiness.

Laurel.—The symbol of achievement, both in dreams and in reality. Few people ever dream of laurel, but those who do become great and famous, outstanding among all men.

Lawsuit.—It is lucky to dream of lawsuits, for, if you do, they will seldom come your way in reality. You may expect a happy and harmonious life, but one rather lacking in adventure.

Lead.—It is unlucky to dream of this metal, especially for those who propose to make a journey. It betokens storms and various mishaps, quarrels with friends and general restlessness and discontent.

Leaves.—To see trees covered with green leaves is a good omen; it refers particularly to the affairs of the heart. Autumn leaves betoken sorrow, probably resulting from the dreamer's own actions; burning leaves tell of a great loss to a friend.

Leg.—A right leg symbolizes parents, a left leg, grandparents. To dream of breaking a leg means that one has deeply offended those whom it symbolizes.

Lemon.—See *Fruits*.

Leopard.—A very unlucky dream; you will have to fight against many malicious influences before success comes your way.

Letter.—If you dream of receiving a letter, you will shortly have occasion to send an urgent one. If you dream that you send a letter, you may expect a valuable present.

Light.—Bright lights foretell riches; dull lights, disappointments. A yellow or greenish light symbolizes the jealousy of a close friend.

Lightning.—A fortunate dream, denoting great success in business and for all those who work on the land.

Linen.—If it is white and clean it presages good news, probably from a large city. Dirty linen, a loss of money, and sickness.

Lion.—This dream foreshadows a rise in power for one of your friends, who will be instrumental in helping you.

Lips.—If you see lips which are red and full, the future is very favourable for you; pale and thin lips denote coming sorrow.

Lizard.—This is an unfortunate dream; it implies bad luck lasting for the next few days. A dishonest business friend may cause you trouble for a time.

Loaf.—See *Bread*.

Lock.—To dream that you are passing through a lock on a river or a canal is very fortunate; it indicates that you will shortly assume a position of responsibility, and will be singularly successful. In addition, you will meet a new and trustworthy friend who will become very dear to you.

Looking-glass.—See *Mirror*.

Love.—Dreams of love often come to those who are lonely and unloved. To them, it is a happy sign foretelling an affair of the heart, probably a marriage. If married persons dream of love, it is an omen of quarrels and domestic strife, as it is also for those who are engaged. To dream that you see others in love also has a contrary meaning; it indicates that they will quarrel or become indifferent.

Lover.—If you dream of an absent lover and he or she appears to be mournful, you may be assured that your lover is faithful; if he or she is happy, you have been deceived by your lover.

Luggage.—If you see your own luggage, it foretells great difficulties to be encountered the next day. To see other people's luggage, a short journey for you.

Lyre.—The ancients generally regarded such a dream as being one of hope, of comfort in difficulties and a general improvement in one's affairs.

M

Madman.—To dream of seeing a madman is exceedingly lucky. It indicates that you will meet someone of great influence who will help you to become prosperous.

Madness.—If you dream that you, yourself, are mad, it is a sign of keen intellect and ability, and portends great success in the future.

Magpie.—This is an omen of a hasty but unhappy marriage. To the trader, a broken contract, implying loss to himself.

Map.—See *Atlas*.

Marigold.—See *Flowers*.

Marriage.—An unlucky dream, implying trouble, anxiety and

loss of money. It was formerly considered to be ominous of death, but there is no authority for this supposition. To those who are about to be married, this dream is merely a natural manifestation of the subconscious mind, and has no unfortunate significance.

Medal.—To dream that you receive a medal for some gallant action has a contrary significance. It indicates that at heart you are too timid and weak and easily influenced. You will probably be led astray unless you seek to eradicate these faults.

Melon.—See *Fruits.*

Milk.—If you are given or sold milk it is a fortunate dream, denoting joy. To sell milk is unlucky; it foretells a great disappointment. To give milk away, a sign of future prosperity.

Millstone.—To see a millstone signifies some hard work which will probably bring you little reward.

Mirror.—To a young woman this denotes scandal; to a young man, great conceit, obstinacy and a bitter disappointment. (See also *Face.*)

Mist.—If you are enveloped in it, the plans which you have in mind will succeed, but not in the way that you expect. To view mist from a distance is not a lucky dream; it betokens troubles and misunderstandings with friends, as well as business losses.

Money.—To lose money foretells unexpected gain; to find it, a heavy loss. To dream that one is very rich, however, is indicative of future prosperity, and is especially fortunate for those engaged in lawsuits.

Moon.—Unexpected happiness and success in love. A new moon is especially favourable to merchants, farmers or lovers. A full moon foretells an approaching marriage.

Mother.—To dream of one's mother is exceptionally favourable, whether she be alive or dead. It indicates wise counsel, kind and loving friends, happy marriage and an honourable position.

Motoring.—If you dream that you are motoring, a short journey is predicted.

Mourning.—A contrary dream denoting great joy.

Mouse.—This foretells busybodies who will attempt to interfere with your affairs. Do not allow them to do so; act as you think fit.

Mouth.—A large mouth shows riches to come; a small mouth betokens poverty. To see someone with a twisted or misshapen mouth foretells a family quarrel.

Mulberry.—See *Fruits.*

Murder.—An organic dream of no prophetic significance.

Music.—If it is harmonious, it foretells good news. Discordant notes signify a journey, with mishaps.

N

Nails.—To be hammering nails is a sign of unexpected news concerning a dearly loved friend. To be drawing them out betokens quarrels with a new acquaintance. If you see a heap of nails, you will shortly visit some place of entertainment.

Nakedness.—See *Clothes.*

Needles.—Lawsuits or arguments concerning your property. If the needles are bright and shining, you will be successful; if they are dull, expect losses.

Nest.—To see an empty nest betokens distress; if it contains eggs or young birds, you will have much domestic happiness.

Nose.—To dream that you possess a very large nose signifies future success and a happy marriage. If your nose is cut off, a relative will bring disgrace to the family. If you see a man or woman with a large nose, it foretells the good influence of a rich friend.

Numbers.—In dreams we are frequently aware of a certain number of objects, or perhaps certain numbers or figures flash vividly before us. Now, these numbers have a significance, but only when they are reduced to the primaries, or those from 1 to 9 inclusive. To reduce any number to a primary, add together the digits of which it is composed, thus: $496 = 4+9+6 = 19 = 1+9 = 10 = 1+0 = 1$. If you dream of the number 24, you must interpret it as 6, for $4+2 = 6$.

In this manner any number can be reduced (*see* the section in this work on the Science of Numbers).

Meanings of Numbers Seen in Dreams

1. You will attain outstanding skill in some trade or art.
2. Complications in business affairs.
3. Your ideas will materialize and bring success.
4. A secure and sheltered life awaits you.
5. You are about to make an important discovery.
6. A sincere love affair is in store.
7. Solution of your problems and dispersal of worries.
8. An advantageous offer, perhaps within a week.

9. Be cautious; you are pursuing a dangerous course.
0. (The cipher has no significance.)

Nun.—A fortunate dream, especially to those in trouble, for it betokens comfort and consolation. Lovers may expect much happiness following this dream.

Nursery.—An omen of prosperity, of wealth earned through labour. To the married it is a direct prophecy, and indicates the birth of a child, probably a son. To those in love but not married it predicts an early wedding.

Nut.—If you dream that you see nuts growing, you will have a rich partner in marriage; if you dream that you are eating nuts, you will become poor through your own extravagance.

Nutcrackers.—To see or to handle nutcrackers foretells that you will receive payment of a debt.

O

Oak.—Oak trees with foliage are a good omen; they signify a calm and untroubled life. A withered or blasted oak forebodes great want and poverty; if the tree falls you will never know prosperity.

Oar.—If you are rowing with two oars, or see another doing so, you will shortly attend some celebration or reunion. To dream of a single oar, or of losing one, denotes the loss of a good friend. A broken oar means a bitter quarrel.

Ocean.—Unlucky if it is rough, signifying disturbance in the household. If it is calm, you will be the means of reconciling two persons who have become estranged; you will also find success in love.

Oil.—For a man to dream of oil in any form is a symbol of disgrace and failure; for a woman, it is fortunate and foretells marriage and honour.

Old Age.—If the elderly dream of old age, they will live long. To younger people the dream signifies prudence and counsel; they would do well to follow the advice of their parents concerning certain affairs.

Olives.—To be gathering olives or to see them on the tree is a sign of peace and happiness, and is especially favourable to sick persons. To dream that you are eating olives indicates a rise in your position and the receipt of a valuable present.

Onions.—Onions, in any form, are an omen of loss of property, and hard work combined with many worries.

F*

Orange.—See *Fruits.*

Organ.—If you hear or see one, you may rest assured that your present trouble will soon pass, owing to help you will receive from a friend. To dream that you, yourself, are playing the organ is very lucky; it predicts immediate advancement and a joyful marriage.

Orphan.—Dreams of orphans denote profits from rich acquaintances, but unhappiness in affairs of the heart.

Ostrich.—A dream of ill omen heralding worries and troubles for yourself and your family.

Owl.—This is a melancholy dream predicting sadness, poverty, and sometimes disgrace.

Ox.—A sign that you will be honest and sincere in all your transactions, and hence will find many friends and succeed in business. White oxen are particularly favourable; they denote riches, power and great honour.

Oyster.—A favourable dream which predicts a comfortable home and many luxuries.

P

Pain.—To dream that you are in pain is an organic dream and has no significance.

Palace.—See *Castle.*

Palm Tree.—The symbol of a journey to a foreign land. If the tree is withered, the journey will be a hazardous one.

Panther.—See *Leopard.*

Paper.—Blank paper foretells a period of grief; paper which bears writing predicts great joy in connexion with a love affair.

Parcel.—To dream that you receive a parcel denotes a loss; to send a parcel foreshadows the arrival of a small present; to be carrying a parcel in the street means that a friend or relation will make a lucky speculation.

Parents.—To dream of your mother or father, whether they are alive or dead, is always fortunate and denotes much joy. Those who have been indiscreet or are in great trouble, and who dream of their dead parents, may take this as a symbol of comfort and guidance.

Park.—To be walking in a park means good health, and fame gained through some sporting contest.

Partridge.—A covey of partridges is a sign of misfortune, but a single bird in the air is exceedingly lucky and foretells prosperity. A sitting partridge predicts that you will receive an angry rebuke from a friend.

Path.—A broad, smooth pathway presages unhappy love affairs and great extravagance; a rough and crooked path is favourable, meaning success and a happy married life.

Peach.—See *Fruits.*

Peacock.—An unfortunate dream indicating loss of money and many heartaches.

Pear.—See *Fruits.*

Pearl.—A prediction that you will acquire riches.

Peas.—To dream of eating them is unlucky, especially if they are hard, for it denotes straitened circumstances and faithlessness in friends. If they are seen growing, you may expect your enterprise to succeed.

Pelican.—You will shortly receive financial help from a friend.

Peony.—See *Flowers.*

Perfume.—See *Scent.*

Pictures.—To dream that you are looking at pictures denotes that the problem which is now troubling your mind will soon be made clear to you.

Pigeon.—If pigeons are flying, it is a propitious sign indicating good news from abroad and a happy surprise at home. If they are roosting, your marriage partner will be faithful and you will live in love and peace.

Pirate.—A happy and romantic omen. It foretells a journey, probably to a foreign land, during which you will meet one to whom you will become very much attached.

Play.—See *Actor, Entertainment.*

Plough.—To dream of a plough or of ploughing is a good omen to a young man; by much labour he will eventually find success and prosperity. To a woman it is a sign of domestic happiness and a loving and contented husband.

Plum.—See *Fruits.*

Poison.—If you, yourself, are taking poison, you will be guilty of an injustice towards a relation. To see another taking poison, you will suffer from the vile tongues of slander.

Policeman.—To dream that you are arrested foretells some honour about to be conferred upon you. If, in your dream, you are a policeman, or if you should see one, you will take part in some profitable transaction.

Poppy.—See *Flowers*.

Potatoes.—To dig for them denotes gain; to eat them forebodes heavy losses and dishonesty in business.

Prayer.—If you dream that you are praying, it betokens happiness; to hear the prayers of others predicts ungracious actions on your part which will bring sorrow to a large number of people.

Precipice.—See *Abyss*.

Primrose.—See *Flowers*.

Prison.—To dream that you are committed to prison is an indication of freedom; your occupation will be such as to allow you much leisure and enjoyment. If you see others in prison, but are not there yourself, it foretells a disappointment.

Profanity.—If, in a dream, you are using profane language, it is a revelation of the evil side of your character which, unless you control it, may cause your downfall. To hear others talking profanely, quarrels and worries.

Prophet.—An unfavourable dream; you will be misled by a false statement.

Purse.—An empty purse is a good omen, denoting success and prosperity; a full purse, sorrow and anger. To lose a purse predicts a trifling gift from a new friend; to find one, good news by letter.

Pyramid.—A lucky dream indicating a large sum of money gained by lottery or speculation.

Q

Quail.—An unlucky omen, portending numerous love affairs which will cause great unhappiness.

Quarrelling.—A contrary dream denoting reconciliation in love.

Quarry.—A sign of much work in hand, especially for those who have been idle; profit and prosperity are indicated. It is a bad dream, however, for those in love, for to them it prophesies misunderstandings and estrangements.

Queen.—If you dream that you are a queen, you will be degraded and humiliated. To see a queen, aid from a rich and influential friend.

Questions.—To hear or to ask many questions denotes a change in circumstances which will be greatly to your advantage.

Quicksands.—To be in them is exceptionally lucky; it predicts a rise in your position and marriage to a rich lover. If you see others sinking in them, the omen is unfortunate; you will meet with troubles and opposition in your business affairs.

R

Race.—To take part in any kind of race means that you will be confronted with a great temptation which must be resisted.

Railway.—You will receive a visit from a long lost friend.

Rain.—If it is falling heavily, it forebodes domestic trouble and business losses; a light shower predicts the success of an undertaking

Rainbow.—A good dream, denoting health and riches. If the rainbow is bright, it foretells a brilliant marriage to someone who is widely loved and famous.

Raspberry.—See *Fruits.*

Rat.—This signifies secret and powerful enemies; you will defeat them if you kill the rat.

Raven.—This bird is a bad omen; you must expect many disappointments, a rival in your affections, and a more or less serious loss of money.

Reaping.—When you, yourself, are reaping, it is a good portent. It denotes an improvement in the conditions of your livelihood, and marriage within a year. Watching others reap is a prediction of a misfortune caused by extravagance.

Rice.—An omen of abundance and domestic concord.

Riches.—See *Money.*

Riding.—If a business man dreams of riding a horse, it is lucky, for it predicts profit; to the lover, it is extremely fortunate, foretelling an early marriage. To watch others riding is also lucky; it portends riches and good health.

Ring.—If you dream that you receive a ring from the one you love, you will soon be married. If a wife dreams of breaking her ring it is unlucky; she will have a bitter quarrel with her husband.

Rival.—To dream of your rival, either in business or love, is exceptionally fortunate; you will soon be successful in your aims.

River.—Smooth-flowing rivers presage love and happiness; swift and turbulent streams, difficulties and misunderstandings.

If you swim across a river you will be successful in business, but possess a fickle, nagging partner in marriage.

Road.—A broad and smooth road is unlucky and predicts family quarrels; a rough and winding road is fortunate; it means that you will have success in your work and happiness in love.

Rocks.—Dangers and difficulties will beset your path; you should tread warily.

Rope.—To be bound with rope denotes that you will soon break a promise to a friend. To see others bound, someone will break his promise to you.

Rose.—See *Flowers.*

Rowing.—To dream of rowing a boat, whether alone or with others, is an omen of success generally, but of commercial success especially. If the boat upsets, you will receive very important news.

Running.—To dream that you are running is very fortunate. It indicates that you will be making a journey in order to meet someone who will help you, and that you will soon increase your income considerably.

Rushes.—Beware of a stranger if you see these in your dream. Someone will try to win your confidence in order to achieve his own ends; you must be discreet.

Rust.—To dream of rusty knives or tools is unlucky; it foretells unemployment and disappointment in love.

S

Saddle.—To be cleaning or repairing a saddle presages a long journey with adventure on the way.

Safe.—If you dream that you are breaking open a safe, you will not marry the person with whom you are now in love. An empty safe denotes an early marriage; a full safe, a late marriage.

Sailing.—This is an omen of success and prosperity.

Sand.—An ill omen denoting many quarrels, disillusionment and loss of money.

Scaffold.—A contrary dream denoting success. (See also *Execution, Hanging.*)

Scent.—An omen of bitter jealousy and of lovers' quarrels with, however, quick reconciliation.

Scissors.—To the unmarried this signifies an approaching wedding; to the married woman it predicts a misunderstanding with her husband.

Sea.—See *Ocean.*

Shark.—An evil dream telling of an enemy who will endeavour to ruin your home life.

Shaving.—To dream that you are being shaved denotes an unfaithful lover; if you are shaving yourself, a financial failure.

Sheep.—To see a flock feeding denotes a faithful lover; to see sheep enclosed in a pen, a disappointment.

Sheets.—These predict great riches which will be gained in a large city.

Shepherd.—A dream of good omen, presaging business successes and the disappearance of worries.

Shield.—A very fortunate dream for the young; it predicts that they will win much honour and fame and the love of someone who is famous. To the elderly it is a warning dream, signifying abuse and the attack of an enemy.

Ship.—See *Boat.*

Shirt.—If you dream that your shirt is torn, malicious lies have been spread concerning you. A new shirt or one of bright colours means a present of money.

Shoes.—New shoes tell of long, unhappy journeys; worn shoes, a meeting with an old friend. If you are shoeless it is a lucky omen, predicting a successful business deal.

Shop.—To a tradesman this is a bad dream, signifying many pressing creditors. To others, who dream they serve in a shop, it is fortunate, denoting much prosperity. If you are buying goods in a shop, a loss of property is foretold.

Silk.—This is an omen of good fortune and joyful love.

Silver.—A prediction of the marriage of a friend or relative.

Singing.—A contrary dream predicting sorrow occasioned by the receipt of unexpected news. (See also *Hymn.*)

Skeleton.—If you are in trouble you will soon receive much comfort, probably from a stranger.

Sky.—See *Atmosphere.*

Smoke.—White or grey smoke predicts that you will offer someone hospitality but will soon regret it. Black smoke, worries connected with domestic affairs.

Snail.—Both a good and a bad dream; it foreshadows a letter bearing good news, but also a conversation which will result in tears.

Snakes.—A bad dream signifying secret and treacherous enemies who will attempt to ruin you. With strength and courage you can prevail against them.

Snow.—If a young girl dreams of snow it denotes that she is about to meet a lover whom she will marry. To others, it is a favourable dream foretelling good news and financial gain. A snow-storm predicts great changes of a satisfactory character.

Snowdrop.—See *Flowers*.

Soldiers.—If peaceful conditions are associated with this dream, you will become involved in a lawsuit or will be persecuted in some manner. To see soldiers fighting is a good omen, denoting success and happiness.

Sparrow.—If you dream that you are feeding sparrows, great domestic happiness will be yours. If the birds fly away from you, however, you will receive an unpleasant surprise concerning household matters.

Spider.—A lucky escape from an accident; if, however, you see a spider spinning, you will receive a sum of money.

Stairs.—To walk up stairs, a disappointment; to walk down them, a surprise.

Starling.—You will be rebuked by a friend because of an unjust action on your part.

Stars.—If you dream of bright stars you will have great success in love and business; dim, fading or falling stars are ill omens denoting quarrels, slander and failure.

Starvation.—A contrary dream foretelling festivities, prosperity and luxurious surroundings.

Stealing.—If you dream that others are stealing from you it is an omen of financial gain; if you, yourself, are stealing, triumph over an enemy is signified.

Stockings.—These are lucky dreams for women, indicating conquests in love; for men they are unlucky, since extravagance or ruination is foretold.

Stones.—To be throwing them presages a visit from a relation; to see others throw them, an omen of sorrow and affliction.

Straw.—To see dry straw is unlucky, for it betokens a loss of money; wet straw predicts a profitable journey.

Strawberry.—See *Fruits.*

Suicide.—If you dream that you are committing suicide, minor worries will cloud your horizon. If you see someone else committing suicide, it is a warning that you have sadly misjudged a genuine friend.

Sun.—If you see it rising, great advancement; setting, disappointed hopes. Bright sunlight signifies the discovery of secrets and much happiness thereby; a darkened sun is an omen of worry and fear. (See also *Eclipse.*)

Sundial.—A lucky dream presaging pleasant surprises conveyed by a letter.

Swan.—If it is white, it foretells great happiness in marriage, and several children. A black swan, a handsome marriage partner.

Sweetheart.—See *Lover.*

Sweets.—To dream of eating sweets is unlucky; you will suffer a bitter disappointment.

Swimming.—This foretells much success in your undertakings, although at first you will have to experience worries and a series of disappointments.

Sword.—To dream that you are wearing a sword signifies that you have been acting in a very high-handed manner; if you persist in your attitude you will meet with a serious set-back.

T

Table.—An omen of domestic comfort; a happy and contented marriage partner.

Tailor.—This signifies weakness of will. Someone will try to persuade you to adopt a course of action which you know to be wrong. Adhere firmly to your principles.

Talking.—If you dream of talking loudly or excitedly to someone, it foretells a sum of money coming to you by way of your business or in the form of a legacy.

Tea.—To dream you are drinking tea denotes a loss of property.

Tears.—Laughter and much joy.

Teeth.—If your teeth are being extracted, you will lose a friend. To dream that they are aching or discoloured, a slight illness.

Telegram.—A pleasant surprise awaits you.

Temptation.—If you are tempted and fall, it is a prediction that the contrary will happen; to be tempted but to resist, you will be led astray by false friends.

Tent.—To dream of a tent predicts security and relief from sorrow and affliction.

Thistle.—Someone in whom you place implicit confidence is disloyal to you.

Thorn.—If a thorn pricks you, it is an omen of a failure leading to success; only to see thorns, the reverse.

Thunder.—If you hear thunder overhead, it foretells great success and the overthrowing of enemies, especially if it is accompanied by lightning. Distant thunder is an ill omen predicting many worries in your domestic affairs.

Tiger.—A warning dream, presaging the arrival of one who will attempt to harm you.

Toad.—This is a prediction of evil, which, however, can be avoided. It may take the form of some great temptation to be dishonest, and the dreamer should arm himself to resist it.

Tomb.—See *Grave.*

Torrent.—A prophecy of great difficulties and misunderstandings.

Tower.—To dream that you are on the top of a tower predicts a reverse in your financial affairs, but a great romance in your life. If you are descending from the summit, you will gain success in business; if ascending, you will suffer a serious set-back.

Trap.—To fall into a trap is a sign that you are too suspicious; you are wrongfully mistrusting someone and will soon regret it. If you are setting a trap of any kind, it is an omen of losses in a lawsuit and great anxiety.

Trees.—In bud, a new love; with luxuriant foliage, a happy marriage and children; without leaves, trouble in matrimonial affairs. Fruit trees are always a lucky omen, meaning great prosperity in business.

Trumpet.—To hear a trumpet denotes that your lover or friend is insincere in his affections; only to see one, indicates a big disappointment.

Tunnel.—If you are walking through a tunnel, you will shortly make a discovery of importance to yourself. To be looking into the mouth of a tunnel foretells a change of dwelling-place and an exciting adventure of a mysterious nature.

Turkey.—You will be involved in trouble over some mistake which you have made, but the consequences of it will have a beneficial effect on your life.

Turtle.—Great domestic happiness and mutual love.

Typhoon.—You will achieve that which will be both profitable and honourable.

U

Umbrella.—To dream that you have lost an umbrella is fortunate, predicting a valuable present from a relation; to find one, a severe loss in business.

Uncle.—To dream of one's uncle implies a visit from a stranger who will bear surprising news.

Undressing.—You will make a grave mistake in your business affairs unless you listen to advice.

Unicorn.—Some correspondence in connexion with official affairs is indicated.

Uniform.—You will make a journey full of adventure, and of special interest to you regarding matrimonial matters.

V

Valley.—To be walking or standing in a valley indicates a new house and a meeting with an old friend. To be looking down on a valley means that you will have cause to regret a past action.

Veil.—If a woman dreams that she is wearing a torn veil, it predicts the revelation of a secret. To see others wearing thick veils, many misunderstandings between friends.

Velvet.—A dream of discord, presaging petty strife and worries in the household.

Vinegar.—You are too jealous by nature and will quarrel with others in consequence.

Violet.—*See* Flowers.

Violin.—A good dream for lovers, suggesting an early marriage and prosperity. To the sick it is an omen of returning health.

Viper.—See *Adder.*

Visit.—If you dream that you are visited by someone, you have been deceived by flattering words and may act foolishly because of them. If you, yourself, pay a visit, it predicts news from an old and dear friend.

Voices.—To hear voices but not to see the speakers betokens sorrow and much worry.

Volcano. —If in eruption, it is a bad sign, denoting passion and angry words. An extinct volcano, reconciliation and the renewal of a love affair.

Voyage.—A direct prophecy of a voyage; if you dream that the conditions will be rough, they will be calm; and vice versa.

Vulture.—See *Eagle.*

W

Wall.—If the wall stands firm and upright, you are in danger; if it leans or falls, you may rest secure, for you are well protected.

Walnut.—An unfortunate dream, denoting losses, worries, disappointments, rebukes and general upheavals.

War.—To dream of a declaration of war is lucky; peace and success in business await you. To a tradesman it foretells the failure of his competitors. (See also *Battle.*)

Wasp.—To dream that you are stung by a wasp tells of envious enemies who will attempt to dishonour you. If you see several wasps flying, a most unpleasant piece of news will shortly be communicated to you.

Watch.—If you are winding up or examining a watch, you will never be independent, and your earnings will be small.

Water.—Clear water means happy love and freedom from cares; muddy water, an evil conscience, quarrels with friends. To be drinking clear, refreshing water, an early marriage; to be drinking bad-tasting water, misfortune.

Waves.—See *Ocean.*

Wealth.—To the poor, it is a good dream, denoting prosperity; to the rich, a sign of losses caused through a craving for much money.

Weapons.—You have enemies who pose as friends, and they will betray your confidence if you continue to trust them.

Weasel.—You will meet with an exceedingly dangerous person.

Wedding.—See *Marriage.*

Weeping.—A contrary dream denoting festivity, joy and laughter.

Wheat.—To the business man, a field of wheat predicts much prosperity and success; to the lover, it is an omen of happy matrimony; to the sailor, a safe voyage; to the married, a comfortable and happy home life.

Whip.—To dream that you are using a whip denotes trouble and sorrow. If you, yourself, are being whipped, you will render a good service to someone.

Whistle.—To hear or to see a person blowing a whistle presages danger and dishonour; if you, yourself, blow one, your enemies will be conquered and much success gained.

Whitewash.—One of your friends is a hypocrite; be careful whom you trust, and do not heed blandishments.

Whortleberry.—See *Fruits.*

Widow.—If a wife dreams that she is a widow, her husband will live long and prosper. If a spinster dreams that she is a widow, she will soon be married.

Wife.—If a spinster dreams that she has married, she will long remain single. If a man dreams of his wife, it is an omen that she loves him deeply and will be faithful.

Wind.—A stiff breeze betokens good news by letter; a gale predicts an unpleasant surprise.

Window.—To dream that you are watching from a window denotes reconciliation after a quarrel. If someone else is looking at you through a window, beware of slanderous accusations.

Wine.—To dream of drinking wine implies a business loss and the making of a new friend. To serve others with wine signifies great domestic enjoyment.

Wings.—If you dream that you have grown wings, you will receive melancholy tidings concerning a friend.

Witch.—A lucky dream. You will find solutions to your problems and also make a useful discovery.

Wolf.—The sign of a treacherous friend who will tell many lies in order to bring discredit upon you.

Women.—For a man to dream of seeing many women is a sign of lies, betrayal and downfall. If a woman dreams that she is in the company of other women, she will have many new clothes.

Worms.—Numerous small worries are awaiting you.

Wounds.—Always a favourable dream, foretelling love to all who are young, and much profit to tradesmen.

Wreath.—A favourable dream predicting the solving of difficulties, and, for the young, happy love affairs.

Writing.—To dream that you are writing a letter denotes that you will receive one from a very old friend. If you are watching others write, it is unfortunate, indicating a violent quarrel with one whom you love.

Y

Yew.—To be sitting under a yew tree predicts the loss of a friend through illness. To see one, a lucky escape from a serious accident is implied.

Yoke.—A sign of a marriage—yours, if you are single, or that of your dearest friend if you, yourself, are married.

Youth.—If an elderly person dreams that he sees a young man or woman, it foretells many more years of health and happiness.

Yule-log.—An omen of comfort and much prosperity.

Z

Zebra.—A change of circumstances; poverty followed by a successful business transaction, which will bring riches.

Zodiac.—To dream of the signs of the zodiac indicates that the dreamer will travel a great deal and eventually settle in a foreign country.

Zoo.—If you dream that you are visiting a zoo, it foretells a change of employment which will bring you much profit and pleasure.

THE DREAM ORACULUM

How to consult the Oraculum. If you wish to know the meaning of any particularly *vivid* or *worrying* dream, the details of which you cannot remember clearly, it is necessary to find the appropriate symbols. To discover the First Symbol write down in figures:—

1. The day of the week on which you dreamed.
2. The day of the month on which you dreamed.
3. The month when you dreamed.
4. Your age.

The figures should be written one under the other and then added up. Now place opposite each number, including the total, *one star if it be odd* and *two stars if it be even*. Let us take an example. Suppose your dream occurred on Wednesday, June 5 (the year does not matter), and your age is twenty-three:—

Day of week   = 4 (Wednesday is the fourth day) sign (even) = **

Day of month = 5 (Fifth of June).............. sign (odd) = *

Month ...... = 6 (June is the sixth month) .... sign (even) = **

Age......... = 23 .... sign (odd) = *

Total .... = 38 .... sign (even) = **

The vertical arrangement of stars on the right-hand side is the First Symbol, and it tells you in which section of the Oraculum the interpretation of your dream will be found. Turn to the pages of the Oraculum at the top of which the First Symbol appears; in our example the pages are 206—207 and the symbol is *****
* * *

It now remains to find the Second Symbol in the following manner: write down:—

1 The *name* of the day in the week (Wednesday).
2. The *number* of the day in the month (Five).
3. The *name* of the month (June).
4. Your age in words (Twenty-three).

Now count the number of letters in each word obtained, write down the numbers vertically, add them up, and proceed as before—placing *one star against an odd number* and *two stars against an even number*.

In the example taken the Second Symbol would be obtained thus:—

Day of week	9	*(number of letters* in Wednesday) .	sign (odd)	=	*
Day of month	4	*(number of letters* in Five, *not* Fifth)	sign (even)	=	* *
Month	4	*(number of letters* in June)	sign (even)	=	* *
Age.........	11	*(number of letters* in twenty-three)	sign (odd)	=	*
Total	28	....	sign (even)	=	* *

The Second Symbols are those ranged down the left-hand side of the pages of the Oraculum. To find the interpretation of your dream, therefore, you must look down the left-hand side of the pages bearing the First Symbol until you find the appropriate Second Symbol, in this case *****   ** * opposite to which is the meaning of the dream: "To those employed in buying and selling, a period of profitable dealing is predicted."

Notice that the day which is taken into consideration is the *one on which you go to bed*, while for the purpose of the Oraculum the new day begins not at midnight but with the rising of the sun.

On page 185 is an index to the pages on which the various first symbols are to be found.

Symbol	Page Numbers	Symbol	Page Numbers
***** *****	186—187	***** **	218—219
***** ****	188—189	***** * *	220—221
***** *** *	190—191	***** * *	222—223
***** ** **	192—193	***** * *	224—225
***** * ***	194—195	***** * *	226—227
***** ****	196—197	***** **	228—229
***** ***	198—199	***** **	230—231
***** * **	200—201	***** * *	232—233
***** ** *	202—203	***** **	234—235
***** ** *	204—205	***** * *	236—237
***** * * *	206—207	***** *	238—239
***** * **	208—209	***** *	240—241
***** ***	210—211	***** *	242—243
***** ** *	212—213	***** *	244—245
***** * **	214—215	***** *	246—247
***** ***	216—217	*****	248—249

***** *****	Care should be taken in making any important decision; the immediate future is uncertain.
***** ****	Your dream indicates the possibility of evil, which may be overcome by taking precautions.
***** *** *	You will experience misfortunes for a while, but none will be of a serious nature; business ventures will be attended with moderate success.
***** ** **	An intimation of coming prosperity, associated with the appearance of one who will become a staunch friend.
***** * ***	If you are well provided with worldly goods you will suffer losses, but if your financial status is poor, improvement is implied.
***** ****	A forewarning of illness, which may be avoided if reasonable care is exercised.
***** ***	There are people around you who intend harm; before acting on the advice of anyone, assure yourself that it is quite genuine.
***** * **	A dream of little importance, but it is advisable to act with every possible caution.
***** ** *	Your dream signifies a period of happiness and change; marriage is suggested.
***** ** *	Temporary losses are foreshadowed, and extreme care should be taken in all financial undertakings.
***** * * *	A dream of happiness combined with prosperity in the very near future.
***** * **	Expect opposition from various sources and guard against a change of fortune for the worse.
***** ***	Travel is indicated by this dream; a new land will be visited and many new friends made. An adventurous future lies before you.
***** ** *	You will receive good news from relations abroad of whom no message has been received for many years; they will soon be returning home.
***** * **	Be prepared for misfortunes; you have unknown enemies who desire to do you harm.
***** ***	An indication of a change for the better in your circumstances; you will receive money from an unexpected source.

✶✶✶✶✶ ✶✶	A short period of unhappiness and lack of success will be followed by a lengthy period of success in all you undertake.
✶✶✶✶✶ ✶ ✶	This is a fortunate dream for those who are contemplating new business ventures; success will attend them from the outset.
✶✶✶✶✶ ✶ ✶	A warning of trouble and danger, especially to those about to travel abroad; a journey by air should be avoided.
✶✶✶✶✶ ✶ ✶	A new and sincere friend will come into your life, and his advice should not be neglected.
✶✶✶✶✶ ✶ ✶	Speedy recovery from illness is indicated by this dream, but every precaution must be taken against a recurrence of the malady.
✶✶✶✶✶ ✶✶	This dream foretells marriage, wealth and a life of happiness and freedom from worries.
✶✶✶✶✶ ✶✶	Good fortune is coming your way; you will be successful in games and sports.
✶✶✶✶✶ ✶ ✶	Changes are about to take place, and the indications are that they will be for the better; accept any opportunity presenting itself.
✶✶✶✶✶ ✶✶	Investments made this year will be attended by good profits; money from other sources is likely to come to you.
✶✶✶✶✶ ✶ ✶	An omen of ill luck; do not be too venturesome during the ensuing month.
✶✶✶✶✶ ✶	Friendships will be made, but not all of them will be for good; avoid dark men.
✶✶✶✶✶ ✶	A visitor you are expecting will be delayed by a minor accident; you will be called to her side.
✶✶✶✶✶ ✶	This dream is favourable to women, but of ill omen to men, who should avoid speculation.
✶✶✶✶✶ ✶	Your efforts to discover secrets into which you are probing will be partially successful.
✶✶✶✶✶ ✶	Improvement in your affairs is assured, and your efforts to attain a higher position will be rewarded.
✶✶✶✶✶	Be on your guard against people you meet daily when travelling; they intend to do you harm.

188

* * * * * * * * * *	A good time awaits you in your business affairs; prosperity lies ahead in the coming year.
* * * * * * * * *	This dream indicates the approach of illness which threatens either yourself or a loved one; beware of taking undue risks.
* * * * * * * * *	Those who are in love have reason to fear disappointment and quarrels; some troubles are already on the way for them.
* * * * * * * * *	You will shortly hear from an old friend of whom you thought to have lost sight for ever.
* * * * * * * * *	Avoid entering upon lawsuits or any form of litigation, as any such attempt would probably end in failure.
* * * * * * * * *	A very auspicious dream, promising good fortune, success and happiness in the future.
* * * * * * * *	You will become the subject of some unpleasant slander, unless you take care to give no cause for it.
* * * * * * * *	Your fears are groundless; proceed with the undertaking you have in mind and all will go well with you.
* * * * * * * *	Beware of putting too much trust in others, as there are those who may prove false.
* * * * * * * *	A busy time lies ahead of you; much business will be transacted, and there is possibility of a journey.
* * * * * * * *	Do not despair if things look dark for the time; the clouds will shortly lift, and happiness and prosperity await you.
* * * * * * * *	You will shortly go on a long journey, but beware of travel by air, as danger from that source is indicated.
* * * * * * * *	A new and very pleasant friendship is predicted by this dream; welcome it, for it may mean much in the future.
* * * * * * * *	It is very probable that you will shortly change your place of residence unless there are many ties to keep you.
* * * * * * * *	A fortunate dream for love affairs; a happy marriage is promised in the near future.
* * * * * * * *	Apparent success awaits you, but do not put too much faith in it, as everything may end in failure.

★★★★★ ★★	Money is on the way to you, probably by means of a legacy; see that you spend it wisely.
★★★★★ ★ ★	Beware of speaking ill of those for whom you care, or friendship may turn to enmity and much sorrow arise therefrom.
★★★★★ ★ ★	Some danger and adversity lie in store for you, but take heart, everything will come right in the end.
★★★★★ ★ ★	Luck in speculations is promised, but be careful not to go too far, or the luck may change and all that was gained be lost.
★★★★★ ★ ★	Change is indicated by this dream, but whether for better or worse is not clear; therefore take care which course you choose.
★★★★★ ★★	Good news is coming through the post; it will mean a change of environment for you.
★★★★★ ★★	You will shortly be offered a splendid opportunity; act on it quickly, or the moment may be lost.
★★★★★ ★ ★	A difficulty will have to be faced shortly; seek advice from your best friend, who will be able to help you out.
★★★★★ ★★	Financial embarrassments are threatened; do not put your money into speculative concerns, as these may fail and bring about your ruin.
★★★★★ ★ ★	You will be offered what seems an easy method of making money; but this has many pitfalls; avoid it at all costs.
★★★★★ ★	Be careful what you say in anger, as the consequences may be extremely unfortunate for you.
★★★★★ ★	An auspicious dream for all those who love an open-air life; health and strength will be yours, also success in all outdoor activities.
★★★★★ ★	You are about to discover a fresh occupation which will prove arduous, but engage your interest more and more in the future.
★★★★★ ★	At all costs avoid speculation during the next week, as much danger lies in wait for you on your financial road.
★★★★★ ★	You will shortly receive a telephone message which is destined to influence you to a large extent in the near future.
★★★★★	Trouble threatens one whom you love; give your assistance, and together you will triumph over the difficulties.

***** *****	You will have good results from business activities, which will take you out of the country for several months.
***** ****	A near relative will suffer a temporary loss of money, and you will be instrumental in recovering it for her.
***** *** *	An omen of ill which, being forewarned, you will be able to avoid; a long railway journey is indicated.
***** ** **	Love and happiness are denoted by this dream, with the possibility of the early marriage of a close friend.
***** * ***	Exercise every care in making important decisions, as your dream is a warning of impending disaster, especially in business.
***** ****	Money is coming to you, and friends from a distance will soon be returning.
***** ***	Beware of one who is interested in your private affairs; although you regard him as honest, he is secretly plotting against you.
***** * **	Both good and evil are indicated in your dream; it is doubtful which will be the more powerful influence, and care should be exercised.
***** ** *	Those who travel by land and sea may expect immunity from danger and a successful issue to their business activities.
***** ** *	There is little meaning in your dream, but if it is repeated in the near future you should act upon anything indicated.
***** * * *	You should not attempt anything rash, as the ensuing months are not propitious for adventurous propositions.
***** * **	Artistic and theatrical people will benefit as a result of this dream; business and professional men should adopt cautious measures.
***** ***	The young will travel and meet with strange and interesting experiences; grown-ups should avoid travelling.
***** ** *	Speculation should be delayed, for financial embarrassment is indicated during the current month.
***** * **	Avoid legal proceedings; they are likely to be unsuccessful and extremely costly.
***** ***	Opposition will arise if you embark on business ventures; adopt a policy of caution for a time.

＊＊＊＊＊ ＊＊	Disputes and conflicts are betokened, but you will emerge unscathed, and the future will be favourable.
＊＊＊＊＊ ＊　＊	You will meet a person who will have a revolutionary effect on your life, but not for worse.
＊＊＊＊＊ ＊　　＊	If you are inclined to embark upon some scheme, do so by all means, as your dream signifies achievement.
＊＊＊＊＊ ＊　　　＊	Make the most of your opportunities if you are artistic, for success will almost certainly attend your efforts.
＊＊＊＊＊ ＊　　＊	Beware of disappointments in sport and business, the influences are temporarily opposed to you.
＊＊＊＊＊ ＊＊	A pleasant change is about to occur in your life, and you will be called upon to leave your home for a short period.
＊＊＊＊＊ ＊＊	This dream is the reverse of lucky; a death from illness is foretold, unless immediate action is taken.
＊＊＊＊＊ ＊　＊	The coming year will bring good fortune and be favourable to you in many ways, especially financially.
＊＊＊＊＊ ＊＊	Do not undertake any speculative ventures; investments will prove profitable, but speculation will end disastrously.
＊＊＊＊＊ ＊　＊	You will receive news from an unexpected source, part of which will bring happiness and part sorrow.
＊＊＊＊＊ ＊	An indication of unsettled conditions; you will suffer fluctuations of fortune which will need your best efforts to remedy.
＊＊＊＊＊ ＊	A domestic change is foreshadowed, and a possibility of steady progress in business affairs during the next few years.
＊＊＊＊＊ ＊	Troubles may occur, due mainly to interference by relatives; avoid entering into discussion with them.
＊＊＊＊＊ ＊	Your dream suggests that hopes on which you are placing reliance may not be fulfilled.
＊＊＊＊＊ ＊	There is an indication of a free flow of money in your direction, and prosperity should attend you, at least for some time to come.
＊＊＊＊＊	Unfortunate for the self-indulgent, a happy omen for those who are generously disposed.

```
* * * * *
* *   * *
```

* * * * * * * * * *	You may expect a certain amount of cares connected with the family to trouble you for a time, but a relation will put things right.
* * * * * * * * *	An event will occur which will have a great effect on your life; guard against illness, as this may cause you to lose an opportunity.
* * * * * * * * *	If you are interested in any competitive pastimes, enter for all the events you can during the next week, for conditions are favourable.
* * * * * * * * *	Avoid high places or slippery roads for a time, as there is distinct indication of danger from a serious fall in the near future.
* * * * * * * * *	The colour red should prove fortunate for you; wear it as much as possible and it may bring good luck.
* * * * * * * * *	For a time do not go anywhere where you cannot be reached by telephone, as news will be conveyed to you by means of it.
* * * * * * * *	Your business affairs are about to take an upward trend; do not let your interest flag, or you may lose a chance to make money.
* * * * * * * *	You are threatened with illness; avoid crowded places for a time, or confined spaces where germs are likely to be picked up.
* * * * * * * *	An offer may be made you to visit a foreign country; consider the proposition well before you accept, as it may involve breaking ties.
* * * * * * * *	Do not believe all you are told; too much credulity may lead you to commit foolish actions for which you will pay dearly later.
* * * * * * * *	Thursday is an unlucky day for you; avoid starting any new undertaking or journey on this day, as the result may prove disastrous.
* * * * * * * *	A great deal of happiness lies in store for you in the country; if you frequent towns, you may lose the chance of it.
* * * * * * * *	Do not allow your artistic side to get the better of you; you must remember to be practical, or your affairs may cause you worry.
* * * * * * * *	A very lucky dream; so long as you do not allow yourself to become selfish, all will go well with you and you will achieve your desires.
* * * * * * * *	You will hear some interesting news in a place where there are trees; take advantage of the knowledge, as it will bring you good fortune.
* * * * * * * *	Trouble is likely to arise through an unfortunate misunderstanding; do not keep silent, but take the first opportunity of putting things right.

* * * * * * *	The letter J has a sinister import in your life; examine closely your friendships with those whose names begin with this letter.
* * * * * * *	Love and good fortune will come to you in the person of a friend whom you will meet in a town with a ruined castle.
* * * * * * *	Danger by fire threatens you in the near future; if you escape injury, however, you will have nothing further to fear from this source.
* * * * * * *	An important appointment will be made during the next month; at all costs be punctual for this, or a splendid opportunity may be lost.
* * * * * * *	Be careful when dealing with articles that have points or sharp edges, as an injury therefrom may prove more serious than you imagine.
* * * * * * *	Take every precaution against burglary or loss through carelessness, as part of your property is threatened.
* * * * * * *	A good dream for all those who are engaged in trading activities, as their business will prosper and many fresh channels be opened up.
* * * * * * *	Take care to control your temper when you feel it rising, as it may lead you into serious trouble and lose you some valuable friends.
* * * * * * *	One whom you believe to be far distant is drawing near, and will bring news of some description, but whether good or bad is not clear.
* * * * * * *	Something you will read in a book will have a great influence on you; beware lest you interpret it in the wrong way.
* * * * * *	Do not seek to deceive others, as in the end you will be found out and lose many friends thereby.
* * * * * *	Your hopes are not based upon a firm foundation; strive to strengthen it by your own efforts and all will be well.
* * * * * *	Much jewellery is not lucky for you; wear little, and its bad influence will not be exercised.
* * * * * *	If possible, make all appointments for the afternoon or evening, as these times are luckier for your undertakings than the morning.
* * * * * *	The sea will favour you in love; attachments contracted on or by it will turn out well.
* * * * *	A parting is near at hand; but take heart, it will not be for long, and much good will come of it.

✱ ✱ ✱ ✱ ✱ ✱ ✱ ✱ ✱ ✱	Care should be exercised in all domestic matters, but business activities are likely to be profitable.
✱ ✱ ✱ ✱ ✱ ✱ ✱ ✱ ✱	Avoid discussing your affairs with friends; their advice, though given in good faith, will be most unreliable.
✱ ✱ ✱ ✱ ✱ ✱ ✱ ✱ ✱	If you have artistic talents, exploit them fully; professional men should act with caution.
✱ ✱ ✱ ✱ ✱ ✱ ✱ ✱ ✱	You will meet an influential person who will desire to help you without disclosing his intentions; act upon his advice.
✱ ✱ ✱ ✱ ✱ ✱ ✱ ✱ ✱	Some whom you regard as friends are not to be trusted, but you will soon be able to discover those who wish you ill.
✱ ✱ ✱ ✱ ✱ ✱ ✱ ✱ ✱	Do not act impulsively; there is danger in taking risks, especially in financial affairs.
✱ ✱ ✱ ✱ ✱ ✱ ✱ ✱	Although you have an anxious period before you, it will be followed by success and prosperity.
✱ ✱ ✱ ✱ ✱ ✱ ✱ ✱	This dream is significant of changes in your life, and marriage in your family is indicated; there are signs of social advancement.
✱ ✱ ✱ ✱ ✱ ✱ ✱ ✱	A reunion with long absent friends is foretold, probably by your leaving home to visit a foreign land.
✱ ✱ ✱ ✱ ✱ ✱ ✱ ✱	For young people of both sexes a successful time in the world of sport will be enjoyed; travel is also indicated.
✱ ✱ ✱ ✱ ✱ ✱ ✱ ✱	Do not worry yourself overmuch about the present state of your affairs; things will right themselves in an unexpected manner.
✱ ✱ ✱ ✱ ✱ ✱ ✱ ✱	A birth is indicated, either in your family or in that of a close friend or relation.
✱ ✱ ✱ ✱ ✱ ✱ ✱ ✱	A good dream for those of a scientific turn of mind; they will distinguish themselves in the immediate future.
✱ ✱ ✱ ✱ ✱ ✱ ✱ ✱	If obstacles seem to deter you, take heed of their warning, and do not pursue the course you have chosen.
✱ ✱ ✱ ✱ ✱ ✱ ✱ ✱	A lawsuit is foreshadowed, but it is not clear whether it affects you personally; accept it as a warning.
✱ ✱ ✱ ✱ ✱ ✱ ✱ ✱	Do not be too anxious to make money at the expense of others, as its acquisition will bring disgrace and loss of friendship.

★★★★★ ★★	Study hard and carefully, as you may shortly be called upon to fill a position of responsibility and importance.
★★★★★ ★ ★	Religion is likely to play an important part in your future life; do not refuse its guidance.
★★★★★ ★ ★	There is the promise of a wedding, but whether the promise will be fulfilled is not clear; if it is, all will be well.
★★★★★ ★ ★	A period of pleasure in a foreign country is at hand, but do not allow this to fill too much of your life, as it will lead to nothing.
★★★★★ ★ ★	Be warned not to gamble in any way, as indulgence in such form of making money would only lead you to ruin.
★★★★★ ★★	Discretion in making decisions is advisable, especially if they are connected with a change of occupation or money matters.
★★★★★ ★★	This is an unlucky dream, and caution is necessary for the remainder of the month, when circumstances will brighten considerably.
★★★★★ ★ ★	There is every prospect of riches coming to you, probably from an unexpected quarter, but also by your own efforts.
★★★★★ ★★	Personal and domestic troubles are indicated, but these may be avoided by exercising precaution.
★★★★★ ★ ★	You will meet many fresh faces, but be careful to exercise care in choosing new friends.
★★★★★ ★	Joy and happiness will be yours, but do not let pleasure interfere with the more serious things of life.
★★★★★ ★	Your long-hoped-for object will be attained if you persevere in your efforts to achieve it.
★★★★★ ★	Difficulties and opposition will beset you, but do not despair of overcoming them; your dream indicates accomplishment in the end.
★★★★★ ★	You are of an ambitious nature, and success is assured if you do not diminish your efforts to attain it.
★★★★★ ★	A good dream denoting profit and happiness both at home and during your travels.
★★★★★	A forewarning of failure in competition with others; success probable in the coming year.

*****
****

***** *****	You will have a long and prosperous life, but occasional worries will try your patience.
***** ****	Joy and sorrow are presaged for you and your family, but joy will predominate.
***** *** *	News of a satisfactory kind will come to you from a distant relation of whom you are unaware.
***** ** **	You will shortly be asked to sign a document which will require mature consideration; legal advice is advised.
***** * ***	Good is indicated by your dream; you will be well advised not to defer any of your plans.
***** ****	Success in the field of sport will be yours if you play whole-heartedly and practise regularly.
***** ***	Financial matters are indicated, but care should be exercised in making new investments.
***** * **	A malicious person is planning to cause you injury, but you will frustrate his designs.
***** ** *	Affairs of the heart will not run smoothly, but you will make a happy marriage all the same.
***** ** *	You will discover enemies among your so-called friends, and make several new and true friends.
***** * * *	Avoid taking a sea voyage for the time being; danger from water is to be inferred from this dream.
***** * **	A good dream for those of an inventive turn of mind; success should crown their efforts.
***** ***	Act warily in all money matters connected with business; a period of loss is foreshadowed otherwise.
***** ** *	This is a propitious dream for those engaged in film work; they will make rapid advance.
***** * **	A promise of improved conditions is contained in this dream; additional income is assured.
***** ***	You will receive an unexpected offer to change your occupation, which should not be rejected.

*****
****

***** **	Letters received from friends will bring you good tidings, and one may contain an offer of marriage.
***** * *	There is little prospect of your dearest wishes being fulfilled for the next few months.
***** * *	Guard against the evil intentions of some of your acquaintances, or you will suffer money losses.
***** * *	A favourable dream, but be warned against tempting providence or you will regret your folly.
***** * *	The next few years have joy, happiness and much good fortune in store for you.
***** **	To those who have ambition to write, this dream portends moderate success after early failure.
***** **	If aviation calls you, answer the call and you will become an accomplished flyer.
***** * *	Changes and misfortune of a temporary nature are indicated, to be followed by much happiness.
***** **	You will shortly be rewarded for all the attempts you have made to improve your prospects.
***** * *	If love and romance have avoided you until now, there is every prospect of a happy change.
***** *	To the romantic and sentimental the prospects are in every way most favourable.
***** *	The year to come will bring with it the fulfilment of many of your fondest desires.
***** *	You have undergone several ordeals, but be assured of a brighter outlook ahead.
***** *	A specially lucky dream to all those who have artistic and musical accomplishments.
***** *	Your worldly expectations will soon be partly realized, but not by any means in the fullest measure.
*****	You have an unfaithful friend whose dishonourable intentions will shortly be disclosed.

✳✳✳✳✳ ✳✳✳✳✳	Money is in your dream, but for the time being there is no indication of your benefiting from it.
✳✳✳✳✳ ✳✳✳✳	You will undergo trials and suffer, but later on will experience comfort and lasting happiness.
✳✳✳✳✳ ✳✳✳ ✳	A letter will reach you with a warning against a so-called friend; do not treat it lightly.
✳✳✳✳✳ ✳✳ ✳✳	Those who have travelled much will cease to do so, and home lovers will be compelled to travel.
✳✳✳✳✳ ✳ ✳✳✳	Discontent and sorrow will be dispelled, and a long period of prosperity and joy will be yours.
✳✳✳✳✳ ✳✳✳✳	A warning of possible affliction which may be avoided if every precaution is taken.
✳✳✳✳✳ ✳✳✳	Talented people will suffer a set-back to their aspirations; the untalented will make progress.
✳✳✳✳✳ ✳ ✳✳	The enterprising should redouble their efforts, for the year will be one of special achievement for them.
✳✳✳✳✳ ✳✳ ✳	Do not hastily enter into matrimony; the indications are favourable to you in other respects.
✳✳✳✳✳ ✳✳ ✳	This dream implies that you are living too extravagantly in view of future happenings.
✳✳✳✳✳ ✳ ✳ ✳	Monetary possibilities are in your favour, but success will come only by great endeavour.
✳✳✳✳✳ ✳ ✳✳	A misunderstanding will arise with one you love dearly, but time will remedy this.
✳✳✳✳✳ ✳✳✳	You have a faithful friend of long standing who will influence your life for good.
✳✳✳✳✳ ✳✳ ✳	Hard work lies before you, but it will bring you honours and fortune in the end.
✳✳✳✳✳ ✳ ✳✳	A dream that is significant of success to those engaged in medicine and science.
✳✳✳✳✳ ✳✳✳	Social events of considerable importance will influence your life in the near future.

***** **	Your dream confirms the old warning, "Marry in haste, repent at leisure."
***** * *	To make important changes at the moment almost certainly would be to court disaster.
***** * *	You will experience new and profitable interests and meet with those who will help you to achieve your ambition.
***** * *	Success in business is foreshadowed, but your love affairs will not run nearly as smoothly.
***** * *	Avoid the company of strangers, there is one who may have an evil influence on your life.
***** **	To those interested in charitable institutions and similar organizations, a year of success is foreshadowed.
***** **	The immediate future is unfavourable for the thriftless; caution should be their watchword in money matters.
***** * *	Success will attend those with literary leanings, after a series of minor disappointments.
***** **	You will travel, and experience gained in a foreign land will be put to great advantage on your return.
***** * *	Apart from some slight domestic troubles, the future holds for you the brightest prospects.
***** *	Avoid signing your name to any important documents; someone is hoping to gain at your expense.
***** *	Musicians should take heart from this dream; it is a good omen for players of stringed instruments.
***** *	A period of adverse fortune is before you, but with courage and perseverance you will re-establish yourself.
***** *	You will shortly change your residence, and this will lead to other changes, of advantage to you.
***** *	Gifts are coming to you, and you will enjoy other benefits from an unexpected source.
*****	The coming spring will be the beginning of a period of great prosperity for you and your family.

✳✳✳✳✳ ✳✳✳✳✳	Accept every opportunity that presents itself, your dream foretells progress and prosperity.
✳✳✳✳✳ ✳✳✳✳	Many cares will be yours, and a period of unsettled conditions is the warning of this dream.
✳✳✳✳✳ ✳✳✳ ✳	Absent friends will communicate with you, and their advice should be gratefully accepted.
✳✳✳✳✳ ✳✳ ✳✳	Riches are portended, but not from the source from which you are expecting them.
✳✳✳✳✳ ✳ ✳✳✳	For young people this is an auspicious dream, denoting success in business and social life.
✳✳✳✳✳ ✳✳✳✳	There is a warning of impending trouble which can be avoided by taking necessary precautions.
✳✳✳✳✳ ✳✳✳	You will incur the anger of a true friend, whom you will convince of its injustice.
✳✳✳✳✳ ✳ ✳✳	A fortunate dream which will change your troubles into contentment and happiness.
✳✳✳✳✳ ✳✳ ✳	This dream, if repeated on the following night, presages a successful forthcoming venture.
✳✳✳✳✳ ✳✳ ✳	You will be approached for financial help which you will be well advised to refuse.
✳✳✳✳✳ ✳ ✳ ✳	You may despair of achieving your object, but perseverance will be rewarded with success.
✳✳✳✳✳ ✳ ✳✳	A dream of considerable importance to all artistic people, especially those about to begin their career.
✳✳✳✳✳ ✳✳✳	The ailing should be encouraged by this dream, for good health and long life are indicated.
✳✳✳✳✳ ✳✳ ✳	You will be the subject of neighbours' gossip, which will cause you annoyance but no harm.
✳✳✳✳✳ ✳ ✳✳	Business advance is foreshadowed by this dream, and years of prosperity will follow.
✳✳✳✳✳ ✳✳✳	Do not place too much reliance on the advice of your friends, but on your own responsibility.

***** **	Your plans are almost certain to be upset; do not despair, you will make others with better results.
***** * *	Disappointment will come to you as the result of receiving news from a far-off friend.
***** * *	A dream that is in every way hopeful, especially to those given to great mental activity.
***** * *	A warning that you should not accept an offer to change your occupation without the fullest consideration.
***** * *	You are enthusiastic and ambitious and will succeed in spite of all the obstacles that will beset you.
***** **	Reduce your expenditure; you will shortly have a splendid opportunity which will require finance.
***** **	A spiteful and determined enemy will cause you annoyance; you will defeat his ends.
***** * *	An omen of peril from sea and air, which should be a warning against taking unnecessary risks during travel.
***** **	Danger by fire is seen in this dream; it can be averted if ordinary care is exercised.
***** * *	Your troubles are nearing the end, and a long period of peace and prosperity is at hand.
***** *	Your desire to venture far afield should be satisfied at the earliest possible opportunity.
***** *	There is money coming to you shortly, but litigation will take place before you receive it.
***** *	You will encounter intrigues, but your wiser self will not allow you to be involved.
***** *	Improvement in your social position is assured, and there are those who will be envious.
***** *	A year of greater achievement lies before you, but not necessarily of greater happiness.
*****	An indication that you should put your spare capital into use, as security appears in the dream.

★ ★ ★ ★ ★ ★ ★ ★ ★ ★	This dream presages better times and a long period free from sorrow and affliction.
★ ★ ★ ★ ★ ★ ★ ★ ★	Your immediate future is bright, but be warned against those who seek to profit at your expense.
★ ★ ★ ★ ★ ★ ★ ★ ★	Enemies are plotting to do you harm, but you will be immune from their evil intentions.
★ ★ ★ ★ ★ ★ ★ ★ ★	You are about to receive a business offer which you should not hesitate to accept.
★ ★ ★ ★ ★ ★ ★ ★ ★	Exercise common-sense in money affairs; advice which is unsound will be offered you.
★ ★ ★ ★ ★ ★ ★ ★ ★	A favourable opportunity presents itself at the moment for launching out in your profession.
★ ★ ★ ★ ★ ★ ★ ★	An auspicious dream for the poor, but of little promise to those possessed of riches.
★ ★ ★ ★ ★ ★ ★ ★	A dream that implies the necessity of caution, especially in affairs of the heart.
★ ★ ★ ★ ★ ★ ★ ★	Accept every opportunity presented, as this dream is full of good omens for you.
★ ★ ★ ★ ★ ★ ★ ★	Unhappiness is presaged, but it will not be of long duration; brighter prospects lie ahead.
★ ★ ★ ★ ★ ★ ★ ★	Avoid conflict with your relations, as disturbances in the home circle figure in your dream.
★ ★ ★ ★ ★ ★ ★ ★	You will meet with many new and desirable friends and journey to a distant country.
★ ★ ★ ★ ★ ★ ★ ★	Care and restraint in money matters are necessary; losses will exceed gains for a time.
★ ★ ★ ★ ★ ★ ★ ★	People will test your generosity, and you will do well to curb your tendency to lend money.
★ ★ ★ ★ ★ ★ ★ ★	A vain and unprofitable dream; a warning of unhappiness if repeated on the next night.
★ ★ ★ ★ ★ ★ ★ ★	Disappointing news will be received by letter from a near relation whom you seldom see.

```
*****
** *
```

***** **	A change in your domestic affairs is near, and a year of success in business.
***** * *	This dream indicates money; a period of suspense will be followed by pleasing results.
***** * *	A forewarning of affliction and sorrow; you will be called upon to travel.
***** * *	Among your friends there is one who will shortly make you a proposal of marriage.
***** * *	Theft is seen in this dream; you should guard your property with the greatest care.
***** **	Danger is indicated, but it may be averted if you are alert to its possibility.
***** **	Damage to property is foreshadowed which will cause you to suffer a loss of money.
***** * *	Beware of two men whom you regard as friends—one tall and the other of medium height.
***** **	You are warned to be practical, and to avoid being influenced too strongly by your heart.
***** * *	Your difficulties will soon recede into the background, and a bright period will ensue.
***** *	Money will come from your own efforts, but others will endeavour to extract it from you.
***** *	You will enter into new undertakings, and you will gain both honour and profit.
***** *	A new friend will come into your life, who will influence your social position.
***** *	Only by studiously attending to your duties will you make progress in your profession.
***** *	A cheerful outlook and an improvement in your financial position may be confidently anticipated.
*****	There will be little of romance in your life, but a happy marriage is assured.

* * * * * * * * * *	By your skill and perseverance you will attain the position for which you are striving.
* * * * * * * * *	Do not place too much reliance on friends, but depend more upon your own ability.
* * * * * * * * *	This dream denotes long life, but there will be alternation between prosperity and adversity.
* * * * * * * * *	News from a distance will reach you and cause a change in your outlook on life.
* * * * * * * * *	You will be faced with many problems that may result in the loss of friends.
* * * * * * * * *	A happy marriage is presaged, and you will be the means of effecting the union of others.
* * * * * * * *	Legal and verbal conflicts should be avoided or you will regret participating in them.
* * * * * * * *	Deception and unknown enemies are indicated and domestic troubles may result.
* * * * * * * *	A period of great activity is near at hand; a journey of some distance will be necessary.
* * * * * * * *	Treachery is implied, but you will avoid danger by acting with every discretion.
* * * * * * * *	Deception and secret enemies are indicated; you should avoid discussing your affairs with others.
* * * * * * * *	Movement from place to place is signified, and a change of occupation may be the reason.
* * * * * * * *	Your wishes will be fulfilled, but do not expect this to happen in the immediate future.
* * * * * * * *	Invalids may take hope, the dream is favourable to an early recovery from illness.
* * * * * * * *	To the married, an indication of lasting domestic happiness; to the single, a portent of delay.
* * * * * * * *	A prominent position is awaiting you, but only by faithful service will you retain it.

★★★★★ ★★	Take little heed of your dream; it has no special meaning, either good or ill.
★★★★★ ★ ★	An unpleasant happening would appear to be imminent; avoid taking any risks.
★★★★★ ★ ★	Benefits in money and kind are on their way; your future is likely to be all you desire.
★★★★★ ★ ★	You will be associated with trouble and sickness, but your near relations will be immune.
★★★★★ ★ ★	A change of environment will bring you many happy experiences and good fortune.
★★★★★ ★★	You have enemies who are at this very moment scheming, but all will end well.
★★★★★ ★★	Achievement is promised by your dream, particularly in your professional career.
★★★★★ ★ ★	This dream is especially favourable to those who are possessed of musical talents.
★★★★★ ★★	Avoid writing letters to other than your friends, or complications will arise and cause you unhappiness.
★★★★★ ★ ★	An exceptionally good dream denoting the probability of receiving unexpected wealth.
★★★★★ ★	You will meet with opposition to your plans, but you should pursue them with greater keenness.
★★★★★ ★	Avoid interfering with the domestic troubles of others, or you will regret having done so.
★★★★★ ★	Help will come to you from an unexpected quarter, and a lasting friendship will be made.
★★★★★ ★	You are expecting to hear from a distant relative; illness will delay the news.
★★★★★ ★	A dream of ill omen; you are advised to delay the completion of your cherished plans.
★★★★★	The artistic and inventive types may take heart of grace; this dream is highly favourable.

★★★★★ ★★★★★	Your long-cherished hopes are shortly about to be realized; money is in the dream.
★★★★★ ★★★★	Be calm and fearless, the troubles you anticipate will then inflict a minimum of harm.
★★★★★ ★★★ ★	To those with literary aspirations, especially in playwriting, a most inspiring dream.
★★★★★ ★★ ★★	A dream that portends a state of happiness, particularly to those who contemplate marriage.
★★★★★ ★ ★★★	Failure in business is in this dream, unless caution is exercised and unwise expenditure is eliminated.
★★★★★ ★★★★	To the studious, distinction is promised; to the manual worker, an improvement in general conditions.
★★★★★ ★★★	Through the help of a stranger you will be enabled to improve your social position.
★★★★★ ★ ★★	You will be well advised to act warily, this dream is a forewarning of danger.
★★★★★ ★★ ★	A friend will inherit a legacy, and you yourself will profit from his good fortune.
★★★★★ ★★ ★	If you have money to invest, take professional advice; your dream indicates pitfalls.
★★★★★ ★ ★ ★	There is illness in your family but, with professional treatment and careful nursing, recovery is certain.
★★★★★ ★ ★★	Riches will come to you, and the indication is that this will happen through marriage.
★★★★★ ★★★	A favourable dream for married women, but some unhappiness is presaged for the unmarried, both men and women.
★★★★★ ★★ ★	To those employed in buying and selling, a period of profitable dealing is predicted.
★★★★★ ★ ★★	Be cautious in everything you undertake; your dream is a warning to all who are impetuous.
★★★★★ ★★★	Interference in love affairs is prophesied by this dream; ignore the advice of those who offer it.

***** **	You will be faced with considerable expenditure, but help will come from an unexpected source.
***** * *	Great changes are about to take place; they will bring you beneficial experience.
***** * *	Most of your aims and projects have reason behind them; exploit them as fully as possible.
***** * *	A dream of mixed blessings; a good omen for business but unfortunate for domestic affairs.
***** * *	There is a suggestion of bereavement, but this will be followed by a happy event.
***** **	Journeying is foreshadowed, mainly for professional reasons, which will bring profit.
***** **	Be resolute and you will have no cause to regret the steps you are about to take.
***** * *	A relation or friend is false to you; misfortune will befall you unless you are cautious.
***** **	An indication that coming events will be unpleasant for those who take unnecessary risks.
***** * *	This dream is a warning against fire; take heed and you will prevent this calamity.
***** *	Both at home and in business a year of satisfactory progress and profit is promised.
***** *	Young people of both sexes are favoured by this dream; the industrious will achieve success.
***** *	There is bridal raiment foreshadowed, but your own marriage is not indicated for the time being.
***** *	A dream that presages continued good health and a long and happy married life.
***** *	A warning against being too optimistic of the outcome of ventures in which you are interested.
*****	Certain disturbing events are about to happen, but they will not inconvenience you greatly.

✱✱✱✱✱ ✱✱✱✱✱	Exercise care and forethought, for there are those who intend to do you some injury.
✱✱✱✱✱ ✱✱✱✱	There are signs of improvement in your affairs, but it will be attained only as a result of determination.
✱✱✱✱✱ ✱✱✱ ✱	Happiness and misfortune will alternate for a few years, but marriage will bring prosperity.
✱✱✱✱✱ ✱✱ ✱✱	This dream portends travel in a far-off land, ending at length in good fortune.
✱✱✱✱✱ ✱ ✱✱✱	One who has hitherto opposed you will prove himself a true and lasting friend.
✱✱✱✱✱ ✱✱✱✱	An indication of a windfall of money; news will reach you of an unexpected legacy.
✱✱✱✱✱ ✱✱✱	Offers of matrimony are coming to you, but you are advised not to act too hastily.
✱✱✱✱✱ ✱ ✱✱	A dream that warns you to observe discretion in affairs relating to money and love.
✱✱✱✱✱ ✱✱ ✱	Good and ill luck are inextricably intermingled in your dream, caution is strongly advised.
✱✱✱✱✱ ✱✱ ✱	Splendid opportunities will come your way; make every effort to profit by them.
✱✱✱✱✱ ✱ ✱ ✱	A bad year for legal matters is implied, and financial speculations should be avoided.
✱✱✱✱✱ ✱ ✱✱	A foreboding of danger from water and fire; take heed and no harm will befall you.
✱✱✱✱✱ ✱✱✱	Avoid borrowing to aid your business affairs, as the dream is a warning against this kind of financial help.
✱✱✱✱✱ ✱✱ ✱	One in ill health—a near relation—will derive a great deal of benefit from seeing you.
✱✱✱✱✱ ✱ ✱✱	By assiduous attention to your duties you will gain the support of those who can influence your progress.
✱✱✱✱✱ ✱✱✱	You will meet with many set-backs, but they will act rather as a stimulus than a deterrent.

★★★★★ ★★	Though you are dubious about the future, you will nevertheless succeed in overcoming all your difficulties.
★★★★★ ★ ★	A forewarning of family afflictions; you will be well-advised to be on your guard.
★★★★★ ★ ★	You will receive news of an inheritance from a totally unexpected source; see that you act wisely.
★★★★★ ★ ★	This dream suggests a continuance of good health and recovery for those who are ailing.
★★★★★ ★ ★	Financial embarrassment is implied, but it will be of a temporary character only.
★★★★★ ★★	Be cautious in your dealings with strangers; there are those who covet your possessions.
★★★★★ ★★	A dream of little meaning except to the artistic, to whom it is exceptionally favourable.
★★★★★ ★ ★	You are hopeful of deriving profit from speculation, but you will be disillusioned.
★★★★★ ★★	A favourable dream for those who contemplate marriage, especially during the present month.
★★★★★ ★ ★	Good news is coming to you, probably from a chance meeting with a former friend.
★★★★★ ★	Your earnest endeavours to secure promotion will be realized in the near future.
★★★★★ ★	A change of residence is signified by this dream; it will entail making a long journey.
★★★★★ ★	If you have projects on hand, proceed with them immediately; the influences favour you.
★★★★★ ★	You place too much faith in one of your friends; act warily or you may suffer at his hands.
★★★★★ ★	There is every indication of a rapid rise in your profession; do not lose the opportunity.
★★★★★	The appointment you have made may end disastrously; you are advised to cancel it.

210

✱✱✱✱✱ ✱✱✱✱✱	You will experience business complications, from which you will emerge successfully but poorer.
✱✱✱✱✱ ✱✱✱✱	A portent of domestic troubles and disappointments that will materially affect your future.
✱✱✱✱✱ ✱✱✱ ✱	People in whom you have every faith are planning against you, but they will not gain their ends.
✱✱✱✱✱ ✱✱ ✱✱	Delays and rebuffs will be met with, but by patience and perseverance you will effect your purpose.
✱✱✱✱✱ ✱ ✱✱✱	The coming year will bring you prosperity if you avail yourself of the opportunities presented.
✱✱✱✱✱ ✱✱✱✱	Financial loss is almost certain; but there will be compensations that will more than make up for it.
✱✱✱✱✱ ✱✱✱	You will be called upon to make an important decision regarding your business affairs; take professional advice.
✱✱✱✱✱ ✱ ✱✱	Good health and happiness are in your dream, also moderate success in your business.
✱✱✱✱✱ ✱✱ ✱	A message of great importance will be received from one of whom you have not heard for some time.
✱✱✱✱✱ ✱✱ ✱	This dream presages departure from your present pursuits and the likelihood of much travelling.
✱✱✱✱✱ ✱ ✱ ✱	A specially lucky dream, particularly for those employed on work of government importance.
✱✱✱✱✱ ✱ ✱✱	You will not gain greatly from the schemes you have in hand; none has a solid foundation.
✱✱✱✱✱ ✱✱✱	You are destined to travel, and this will be the result of a change of occupation.
✱✱✱✱✱ ✱✱ ✱	An unfavourable dream for new ventures; there is every indication that they will end in failure.
✱✱✱✱✱ ✱ ✱✱	Avoid writing to other than your friends, or your correspondence may lead to unexpected trouble.
✱✱✱✱✱ ✱✱✱	The next few months will bring you many joys, among them an improvement in your financial position.

***** **	Do not be too trustful of your friends; your dream is a suggestion of the duplicity of someone.
***** * *	By your mental efforts you will achieve a position of considerable value and importance.
***** * *	Take every precaution against road accidents, which are strongly indicated in your dream.
***** * *	Your troubles are nearing the end. and there is prospect of a prolonged period of comfort and happiness.
***** * *	Adventures in a distant land are probable; be warned against taking too many risks.
***** **	Your ambitions will receive a temporary check, but there is every indication of eventual success.
***** **	A warning against extravagance; a time is approaching when you will need financial strength.
***** * *	Emotional tangles are reflected in this dream; extreme caution in love affairs is advised.
***** **	Fortune is about to smile on you; your dream indicates money, and its arrival will not be long delayed.
***** * *	Put forth every effort to further your projects, the opportunity was never more favourable.
***** *	There are those taking an interest in your love affairs who wish to do you an injury.
***** *	An influence for good is in this dream, but take care that others do not exercise a more powerful influence for evil.
***** *	Travel and adventure may be expected, but there is a distinct warning against being impetuous.
***** *	You will experience losses and disappointments, but a time of even greater success and happiness will follow.
***** *	A change from your daily routine will soon occur, and this will bring an increase in your financial resources.
*****	Avoid interfering in the domestic affairs of your friends, or you will regret having taken such a step.

★★★★★ ★★★★★	A sea voyage is almost assured, but there is no indication of permanent residence abroad.
★★★★★ ★★★★	You will soon form a romantic attachment, but marriage in the near future is extremely doubtful.
★★★★★ ★★★ ★	Put a curb on your impatience; only by diligent attention to your duties will you achieve your ambition.
★★★★★ ★★ ★★	You will profit by the advice of friends, but caution is advised against others who seek to do you harm.
★★★★★ ★ ★★★	A year of success and prosperity is foretold for those engaged in scholastic and literary professions.
★★★★★ ★★★★	Your fortunes will take a turn for the better, and you should avail yourself of every opportunity presented.
★★★★★ ★★★	A warning against taking risks of any kind, and more especially risks with your health.
★★★★★ ★ ★★	Loss is presaged, but whether of property or money is not clearly indicated; guard against both.
★★★★★ ★★ ★	For children, scholarship success is foreshadowed; for adults, success in the world of music.
★★★★★ ★★ ★	Avoid speculation and all forms of litigation, for which the next few years appear to be most unfavourable.
★★★★★ ★ ★ ★	Danger from water is foretold, and those who are not strong swimmers should not be too venturesome.
★★★★★ ★ ★★	This dream has little significance and is in no way a foreboding of danger or misfortune.
★★★★★ ★★★	Do not worry about the future, there is little or no possibility of your plans being frustrated.
★★★★★ ★★ ★	You are ambitious to succeed, but you will encounter many obstacles before attaining your desires.
★★★★★ ★ ★★	You will meet with many ups and downs both in your love affairs and business dealings.
★★★★★ ★★★	This dream indicates the early fulfilment of some of your long-cherished wishes.

✳✳✳✳✳ ✳✳	Avoid correspondence with the opposite sex during the next few months, or unfortunate consequences may ensue.
✳✳✳✳✳ ✳ ✳	Your work will meet with the approval of your employers, who will show their appreciation to your advantage.
✳✳✳✳✳ ✳ ✳	You will meet with interference in your love affairs, but the effect will be negligible if you act rationally.
✳✳✳✳✳ ✳ ✳	Do not attempt any fresh venture until the present year is ended, or you will fail badly.
✳✳✳✳✳ ✳ ✳	Someone will ask you to sign a document, and you are warned against doing so.
✳✳✳✳✳ ✳✳	A good dream for all who are engaged in sport, either professionally or merely for pleasure.
✳✳✳✳✳ ✳✳	You have few faithful friends, but among them is one who will have a beneficial influence on your future.
✳✳✳✳✳ ✳ ✳	This dream is a forewarning of illness, which may be avoided by care; at the worst, complete recovery is indicated.
✳✳✳✳✳ ✳✳	The interference of well-meaning friends and relations will cause you inconvenience and pain.
✳✳✳✳✳ ✳ ✳	You are placing too much faith in your own abilities; be warned in time and seek reliable assistance.
✳✳✳✳✳ ✳	Misfortune will befall a dear friend, and his loss will prove, ultimately, to be your gain.
✳✳✳✳✳ ✳	This dream implies an unhoped-for inheritance, which will aid you to perfect the plans you have in mind.
✳✳✳✳✳ ✳	A foreboding of difficulties and sorrow, but they will be of a fleeting character only.
✳✳✳✳✳ ✳	Your financial position will be assailed, and extreme caution in your investments is necessary.
✳✳✳✳✳ ✳	By devotion to duty you will gain the esteem of your superiors and profit thereby.
✳✳✳✳✳	You will lose several of your friends, but meet with one who will remain true for the rest of your life.

214

★★★★★ ★★★★★	A somewhat inauspicious dream; some trouble lies ahead, but be prepared to face it bravely, and things may yet work out for the best.
★★★★★ ★★★★	This dream is often the accompaniment of a sense of expectation or waiting; it has no particular significance with regard to the future.
★★★★★ ★★★ ★	Those who are in love must expect some ups and downs in their affairs; avoid jumping to conclusions, as this may lead to sorrow.
★★★★★ ★★ ★★	Be careful of what you write; letters may be misinterpreted and trouble result that will be difficult to put right.
★★★★★ ★ ★★★	Do not allow yourself to be drawn into quarrels about family affairs; keep on good terms with your relations.
★★★★★ ★★★★	It seems that you are pursuing an occupation for which you are not suited; find your right vocation.
★★★★★ ★★★	This is a warning not to worry overmuch; if you do so, you will merely waste your energy.
★★★★★ ★ ★★	You have some subconscious wish that you are suppressing; try to discover what this is, and if possible act in accordance with it.
★★★★★ ★★ ★	You need change; make an effort to get away, or, if you are in business, take occasional week-ends away from your ordinary routine.
★★★★★ ★★ ★	There will be a steady increase in prosperity for the next few months, but added expenses may more than counteract your gains.
★★★★★ ★ ★ ★	A secret will be entrusted to you; do not betray this, or the result will be a loss of opportunity and the break-up of a friendship.
★★★★★ ★ ★★	A long-cherished wish is about to be fulfilled, but do not allow this to upset your mental stability; remain calm.
★★★★★ ★★★	For those under forty, this dream indicates increased success in business or profession; over forty, your affairs will remain as they are.
★★★★★ ★★ ★	Those engaged in professional occupations may anticipate a successful and profitable time during the coming year.
★★★★★ ★ ★★	A person holding a high and responsible position will use his influence to improve your business status.
★★★★★ ★★★	You will undertake an unexpected journey, which will cause you to change your occupation for a more profitable one.

✱✱✱✱✱ ✱✱	Good news is coming to you from one of whom you have seldom heard, but who regards you with great affection.
✱✱✱✱✱ ✱ ✱	Apart from trivial worries, you will enjoy a long, peaceful and prosperous life.
✱✱✱✱✱ ✱　✱	You must be alert and watchful, or you will suffer at the hands of one who wishes you harm.
✱✱✱✱✱ ✱　　✱	Not all your desires will be realized, but your dream is a favourable indication for many of them.
✱✱✱✱✱ ✱　　✱	Avoid putting your money into speculative business, or you will suffer losses; otherwise your affairs will progress well.
✱✱✱✱✱ ✱✱	You will experience a set-back in your love affairs, but it will be of a temporary character only.
✱✱✱✱✱ 　✱✱	Go forward with your plans; there is every likelihood of their being completely successful.
✱✱✱✱✱ ✱ ✱	You will widen your social circle, and meet those who will have a beneficial influence on your future.
✱✱✱✱✱ ✱✱	A most auspicious dream for all who are engaged in the professions; not so fortunate for traders and artisans.
✱✱✱✱✱ ✱ ✱	Much social activity and recognition will be yours during the forthcoming year; enjoy it to the full, as it can do you no harm.
✱✱✱✱✱ ✱	Remain in your own country for your holidays this year; there is indication of trouble in store if you go abroad.
✱✱✱✱✱ ✱	If dreamed by a woman, this is a good omen; but if dreamed by a man, beware, for dangers and difficulties lie ahead.
✱✱✱✱✱ ✱	Concentrate more on your work and less on pleasure, or you may lose an opportunity and regret it all your life.
✱✱✱✱✱ ✱	A tendency to be overbearing with your subordinates will only lose you friends and do no good; cultivate courtesy and tact.
✱✱✱✱✱ ✱	Good news will come to you from friends afar, which will entail a journey being undertaken.
✱✱✱✱✱	A dream that foretells misfortune; guard against the jealousy of those whom you regard as friends.

* * * * * * * * * *	Many of your long-cherished desires will be realized, but there will be unexpected reverses of a minor character.
* * * * * * * * *	Travel is indicated, with the possibility of a desirable and profitable change of occupation.
* * * * * * * * *	Beware of an unfaithful friend who is seeking an opportunity to do you an ill service.
* * * * * * * * *	Illness in your home circle is foretold by this dream, but it will not be of a serious nature.
* * * * * * * * *	You will be called upon to sign an important document which will bring you unexpected good fortune.
* * * * * * * * *	A year of exceptional prosperity and happiness is promised by this auspicious dream.
* * * * * * * *	Only by hard work can you hope to succeed; for you there is no royal road to great achievement.
* * * * * * * *	This dream is a warning that your love affairs will not run as smoothly as you would wish them to.
* * * * * * * *	An auspicious dream for all who have literary talent and are keen to apply it.
* * * * * * * *	The next few months will see a momentous change in your career; exercise care in the choice of any new business venture.
* * * * * * * *	Be cautious in all your immediate undertakings; domestic troubles are seen in your dream.
* * * * * * * *	You are warned not to take unnecessary risks during motor and railway journeys, as danger arising from carelessness is threatened.
* * * * * * * *	Beware of danger from fire; apart from this, the dream presages good fortune in the coming year.
* * * * * * * *	A fortunate dream for young girls and women; an omen of lurking dangers for the male sex.
* * * * * * * *	Your business deals are not likely to succeed just yet, but do not allow this to deter you.
* * * * * * * *	A change of occupation is indicated; progress will be slow at first, but perseverance will bring you just reward.

★★★★★ ★★	You should put a curb on your expenditure; a time is near when your resources will be severely taxed.
★★★★★ ★ ★	An omen of an unfortunate love affair; marriage, however, is fore-shadowed after an interval of time.
★★★★★ ★ ★	Disappointments lie ahead, chiefly in business affairs; but you will win through by perseverance.
★★★★★ ★ ★	You are ambitious, and you will realize your hopes if you are deter-mined and strong.
★★★★★ ★ ★	You will receive an offer of marriage from one whom you had little hope of meeting again.
★★★★★ ★★	Do not tempt providence; act cautiously and you will have every reason to be satisfied with your efforts to achieve success.
★★★★★ ★★	A favourable dream generally, but especially for those who are engaged in the theatrical profession.
★★★★★ ★ ★	A dream that presages money troubles for all who are inclined to let the future take care of itself.
★★★★★ ★★	Do not place too much reliance on the advice of your friends, but act fearlessly on your own initiative.
★★★★★ ★ ★	Many difficult situations will beset you, but there is every prospect that you will surmount them.
★★★★★ ★	Accidents are likely to those taking part in sport, unless they put a curb on recklessness.
★★★★★ ★	Your reputation will be attacked by jealous acquaintances, but you will emerge unscathed.
★★★★★ ★	A difficult year lies before you; do not be disturbed, however, you will rise above all dangers.
★★★★★ ★	To those about to sit for examinations, this is a dream that is full of hope and prophesies success.
★★★★★ ★	Legal affairs figure in your dream, which contains a warning against entering into litigation without due consideration.
★★★★★	You have little to fear from the future, if you put forth every effort to realize your hopes.

✳✳✳✳✳ ✳✳✳✳✳	Minor troubles will disturb your business interests, but affairs of the heart will prosper.
✳✳✳✳✳ ✳✳✳✳	This is a dream of hope for those in ill health, for a speedy recovery is strongly indicated.
✳✳✳✳✳ ✳✳✳ ✳	You have a relentless enemy who seeks to do you harm; act firmly and you will outwit him.
✳✳✳✳✳ ✳✳ ✳✳	Fire and water appear in your dream, and danger from these elements should be guarded against.
✳✳✳✳✳ ✳ ✳✳✳	A warning against extravagance, as there are indications of the need of money for the furtherance of your plans.
✳✳✳✳✳ ✳✳✳✳	Avoid taking risks of any kind for the next few months, especially during journeys by sea and air.
✳✳✳✳✳ ✳✳✳	Those who have an urge for seeking fortune in foreign lands are advised to remain at home for the time being.
✳✳✳✳✳ ✳ ✳✳	You will shortly meet one who will propose marriage, and the offer should not be treated lightly.
✳✳✳✳✳ ✳✳ ✳	Next year you will witness a great change in your business associations and fortune will attend you.
✳✳✳✳✳ ✳✳ ✳	Do not place too much reliance on the advice of your friends, but act upon your own responsibility, especially in money matters.
✳✳✳✳✳ ✳ ✳ ✳	There is little prospect of improvement in your social position this year; nevertheless, a bright future is assured for you.
✳✳✳✳✳ ✳ ✳✳	A change of domicile is presaged, probably as the result of the receipt of news from an absent friend.
✳✳✳✳✳ ✳✳✳	The receipt of money is indicated by your dream, but this will not take the form of an inheritance.
✳✳✳✳✳ ✳✳ ✳	Your happiness is in the balance; be warned against accepting the advice of well-meaning friends.
✳✳✳✳✳ ✳ ✳✳	Both you and your near relations will be the recipients of news that will add to your felicity.
✳✳✳✳✳ ✳✳✳	You will receive a letter containing an invitation; accept it, and you will derive unexpected advantage.

***** **	Do not expect too much from your efforts to achieve improvement in your position; you will succeed, but progress will be slow.
***** * *	Many will flatter you, but do not let this turn your head, or misfortune will befall you.
***** * *	The coming year will present many opportunities to you; take the fullest advantage of them.
***** * *	Friendships will be broken, but others of a more lasting and beneficial character will be made.
***** * *	Your troubles will soon be at an end, and will be replaced by a long spell of happiness.
***** **	Do not put your signature to any documents during the next three days, or a monetary loss will almost certainly be incurred.
***** **	Those who depend upon mental activities may be assured of a period of improvement in their affairs.
***** * *	As the result of legal proceedings you and your family will reap financial benefit.
***** **	Self-advancement is strongly indicated in your dream, but you will need to put forth every effort to attain it.
***** * *	The time is not ripe for exploiting new ventures; persevere with those you have in hand and success will come.
***** *	Your troubles will soon pass away; happiness lies ahead both for you and your relations.
***** *	This dream points to marriage with one whom you have known for some time, but who has so far avoided you.
***** *	It is only by your individual efforts that you may hope to achieve your great ambition.
***** *	Think well before undertaking the journey you have in mind; there are hidden dangers ahead.
***** *	You will receive a surprise inheritance, and as a result a change of residence will become necessary.
*****	Be warned against a disappointment in affairs of the heart; it will not, however, mean a definite break.

✶✶✶✶✶ ✶✶✶✶✶	You will be responsible for arranging a journey, and will probably be a member of the party undertaking it.
✶✶✶✶✶ ✶✶✶✶	A good friend will be lost to you, but another and firmer association will be contracted.
✶✶✶✶✶ ✶✶✶ ✶	By the help of others you will be enabled to complete satisfactorily the ventures in which you are interested.
✶✶✶✶✶ ✶✶ ✶✶	An auspicious dream for those who have inventive ability; money from this source is predicted.
✶✶✶✶✶ ✶ ✶✶✶	A dream that has little meaning for men, but indicates a hopeful turn in the affairs of women.
✶✶✶✶✶ ✶✶✶✶	An unknown friend is interested in you; you will be agreeably surprised at an unexpected change in your outlook.
✶✶✶✶✶ ✶✶✶	Act discreetly or you will suffer loss as the result of the machinations of one who is a secret enemy.
✶✶✶✶✶ ✶ ✶✶	This dream implies movement; it is likely that you will be called upon to leave the country.
✶✶✶✶✶ ✶✶ ✶	You are warned to avoid acting impetuously; there is danger of money difficulties unless you are wary.
✶✶✶✶✶ ✶✶ ✶	A quarrel with a close friend will occur unless you steer clear of one who is secretly planning it.
✶✶✶✶✶ ✶ ✶ ✶	The coming year will bring you a complete change of occupation, which will add materially to your financial position.
✶✶✶✶✶ ✶ ✶✶	You will be the recipient of an exceptionally good business offer, which will entail a temporary absence from home.
✶✶✶✶✶ ✶✶✶	This dream has no significance to those with money to burn, but those who need money may derive benefit in varying degrees.
✶✶✶✶✶ ✶✶ ✶	Do not lose heart; you are about to receive news that will materially improve your social position.
✶✶✶✶✶ ✶ ✶✶	Your dream implies a longing for a life of pleasure, but contains a definite warning against satisfying this desire.
✶✶✶✶✶ ✶✶✶	For those above thirty years of age, there is every prospect of improved circumstances following a period of earnest endeavour.

★★★★★ ★★	Domestic changes are prognosticated, mainly for good; accept any opportunity that may present itself.
★★★★★ ★ ★	Avoid for the present marriage entanglements; the signs are definitely opposed to marital affairs.
★★★★★ ★ ★	An elderly person will interest himself in you, and your business affairs will prosper in consequence.
★★★★★ ★ ★	Your dream foretells sorrow and illness, to be followed by years of happiness and prosperity.
★★★★★ ★ ★	Do not allow love affairs to influence you unduly, or your professional career will be adversely affected.
★★★★★ ★★	A reception of some kind is foretold, probably in connexion with the wedding of a near friend.
★★★★★ ★★	Those who are musically inclined will make exceptional progress in the coming year.
★★★★★ ★ ★	An inheritance upon which you depend will be delayed; you must curtail your expenditure temporarily.
★★★★★ ★★	Promotion is near at hand, but the retention of your position will depend on concentration and hard work.
★★★★★ ★ ★	Speculation and litigation should be avoided; do not act upon the advice of those who would make quick money for you.
★★★★★ ★	The coming months will bring you mixed blessings, but there will be a preponderance of good fortune.
★★★★★ ★	Someone is scheming to do you harm; accept the warning of one who will bring you sound advice.
★★★★★ ★	Do not be discouraged; although appearances are against you at the moment, success lies ahead.
★★★★★ ★	News that you are awaiting from a distant friend is likely to be delayed; do not act with undue haste.
★★★★★ ★	You place too much reliance on a newly-formed friendship; it will soon be terminated.
★★★★★	The studious will find honours awaiting them in the next few years, but fortune will be delayed.

★★★★★ ★★★★★	Unforeseen and sudden changes in your business affairs are fore-shadowed; you may be called upon to go overseas.
★★★★★ ★★★★	The coming months will bring a turning-point in your life, in which your heart affairs will play a part.
★★★★★ ★★★ ★	Avoid coming to definite decisions of any kind for the time being and act with caution generally.
★★★★★ ★★ ★★	Those with money to invest are urged to be careful, as losses are indicated in this dream.
★★★★★ ★ ★★★	You will shortly meet with one who will have a most powerful influence on your future.
★★★★★ ★★★★	Many obstacles will be placed in your way by envious people, but you will not suffer ill consequences.
★★★★★ ★★★	This dream foretells the postponement of marriage, probably for a period of a month.
★★★★★ ★ ★★	Those engaged in creative work of an artistic nature may anticipate both honours and profit.
★★★★★ ★★ ★	New friends will be made, and your relations with one coming from from abroad will be specially cordial.
★★★★★ ★★ ★	Take heart, your disappointments will soon be replaced by the un-expected realization of your fondest hopes.
★★★★★ ★ ★ ★	News of a disheartening character will reach you, and temporary financial embarrassment may occur.
★★★★★ ★ ★★	Information of importance will reach you from one who has been seeking you without success for some time.
★★★★★ ★★★	You are running the risk of losing money; be warned against all ventures of a speculative kind.
★★★★★ ★★ ★	Delay in the realization of your hopes is foreshadowed; persevere, however, and you will eventually succeed.
★★★★★ ★ ★★	Your love affairs will progress smoothly if you disregard the unfounded rumours which will reach you.
★★★★★ ★★★	A lack of enterprise is your chief fault; strike out and you will have no reason for regretting your action.

✶ ✶ ✶ ✶ ✶ ✶ ✶	You will be well-advised to overcome your desire for a life beyond the seas; prosperity will be found at home.
✶ ✶ ✶ ✶ ✶ ✶ ✶	Wedding bells are in this dream, but they are not concerned with your own marriage.
✶ ✶ ✶ ✶ ✶ ✶ ✶	You will hear of the death of a distant relation from whose estate you will derive a small inheritance.
✶ ✶ ✶ ✶ ✶ ✶ ✶	The immediate future has little of hope, but by grit and tenacity you will rise to a position of importance.
✶ ✶ ✶ ✶ ✶ ✶ ✶	The coming year has for you a store of good fortune, if only you will have faith in yourself.
✶ ✶ ✶ ✶ ✶ ✶ ✶	Exercise caution and discretion, or there is every possibility of a rift occurring in your domestic affairs.
✶ ✶ ✶ ✶ ✶ ✶ ✶	This dream is a warning of approaching troubles in home and business life; keep a level head and they will have little effect.
✶ ✶ ✶ ✶ ✶ ✶ ✶	Take measures at once to safeguard your health, or you will probably suffer an illness.
✶ ✶ ✶ ✶ ✶ ✶ ✶	You will make the acquaintance of one who will have a strong and beneficial influence on your future.
✶ ✶ ✶ ✶ ✶ ✶ ✶	Take heed of a warning that will reach you from an unknown source, or misfortune may overtake you.
✶ ✶ ✶ ✶ ✶ ✶	Your talents should be exploited; the time is drawing near for your ambition to be realized.
✶ ✶ ✶ ✶ ✶ ✶	You have seen the last of your troubles; look forward with assurance to a long period of good health and freedom from cares.
✶ ✶ ✶ ✶ ✶ ✶	A dream of ill omen; avoid taking risks, as illness and accidents are strongly indicated.
✶ ✶ ✶ ✶ ✶ ✶	Business ventures will meet with a temporary set-back; otherwise the dream is a favourable one.
✶ ✶ ✶ ✶ ✶ ✶	Do not be over-venturesome for the time being; your dream indicates that failure will attend your projects.
✶ ✶ ✶ ✶ ✶	In your daily travels you associate with several persons who wish to do you an ill service; do not discuss your affairs publicly.

✴ ✴ ✴ ✴ ✴ ✴ ✴ ✴ ✴ ✴	This dream implies a betterment of your business affairs, which should continue to prosper for many years.
✴ ✴ ✴ ✴ ✴ ✴ ✴ ✴ ✴	Sportsmen are likely to have a successful time in all games, but care should be taken against incurring injuries.
✴ ✴ ✴ ✴ ✴ ✴ ✴ ✴ ✴	Good health and bright prospects are presaged; several new and lasting friendships will be made.
✴ ✴ ✴ ✴ ✴ ✴ ✴ ✴ ✴	You will be faced with many obstacles in the coming months, but there is one who will help you to overcome them.
✴ ✴ ✴ ✴ ✴ ✴ ✴ ✴ ✴	A life of ease and luxury may not be for you, but good fortune will attend you in most of your undertakings.
✴ ✴ ✴ ✴ ✴ ✴ ✴ ✴ ✴	Do not relinquish your efforts; your plans will soon meet with the success they deserve.
✴ ✴ ✴ ✴ ✴ ✴ ✴ ✴	You will meet influential people, one of whom will use his influence for your advancement.
✴ ✴ ✴ ✴ ✴ ✴ ✴ ✴	Happiness will come to you through marriage, and your financial status will materially improve.
✴ ✴ ✴ ✴ ✴ ✴ ✴ ✴	Do not despair; your hopes will not be fully realized, but there is every likelihood of an improvement of circumstances.
✴ ✴ ✴ ✴ ✴ ✴ ✴ ✴	You will journey south and be profitably employed in work of an entirely different character.
✴ ✴ ✴ ✴ ✴ ✴ ✴ ✴	Deceit on the part of envious people will cause you inconvenience, but justice will be done you in the end.
✴ ✴ ✴ ✴ ✴ ✴ ✴ ✴	Success, happiness and long life are indicated; not, however, unalloyed by minor troubles.
✴ ✴ ✴ ✴ ✴ ✴ ✴ ✴	There are lucky months ahead, but take care not to be led into making rash speculations.
✴ ✴ ✴ ✴ ✴ ✴ ✴ ✴	A lawsuit figures in your dream; act cautiously, as a successful issue appears to be doubtful.
✴ ✴ ✴ ✴ ✴ ✴ ✴ ✴	Your projects will be hampered by interfering friends; ignore their advice and go forward without fear.
✴ ✴ ✴ ✴ ✴ ✴ ✴ ✴	This dream is an indication of improvement in your business dealings, which should now progress rapidly.

***** **	There will be disturbances in your home circle, but they will not affect you to any great extent.
***** * *	Help from an unknown source is implied, and this will probably affect for good your professional career.
***** * *	You will hear of the death of a very old and faithful friend, and a new friend will be found.
***** * *	Travel is foretold by this dream, which also contains a warning against recklessness while making your journey.
***** * *	Unexpected good fortune is coming to you, probably as a result of a bereavement.
***** **	Do not trust a certain person who is thrusting his attentions upon you, or you will soon have cause to regret it.
***** **	A fortunate dream for those engaged to be married within the next month; happiness and prosperity will result.
***** * *	You will meet with a woman who will have an especially happy influence on your life.
***** **	You will change your residence as the result of domestic differences for which you are not to blame.
***** * *	This dream indicates an unexpected termination to a love affair of long standing.
***** *	Do not pay much heed to the business difficulties foretold by this dream; they will be followed by a period of prosperity.
***** *	Someone is slandering you; do not be drawn into discussion, his evil intentions will react on him.
***** *	Put aside your fears, they are groundless; proceed with your plans and be assured of their success.
***** *	An auspicious dream for those contemplating marriage; lasting happiness is strongly indicated.
***** *	The studious may hope for success in examinations, but there must be no relaxation from hard work.
*****	A long-absent friend, whom you had almost forgotten, will inform you of his intention to return.

★★★★★ ★★★★★	Your mode of living will undergo a change as the result of receiving an unexpected inheritance.
★★★★★ ★★★★	Good news will come to you by telegram, and a new venture will bring you both money and fame.
★★★★★ ★★★ ★	A disturbing element will enter into your love affairs; have faith and no ill consequences will ensue.
★★★★★ ★★ ★★	Do not meddle in the affairs of others, or you will be drawn into troubled waters from which you will find escape difficult.
★★★★★ ★ ★★★	You will make the acquaintance of one who will endear himself to you; marriage is foreshadowed.
★★★★★ ★★★★	Help those around you who are afflicted; at some future date you will need and receive their support.
★★★★★ ★★★	A dream that carries a warning to exercise discretion, especially in money matters and when on a journey.
★★★★★ ★ ★★	Pay no regard to those who advise a waiting policy; go straight ahead and you will be well rewarded.
★★★★★ ★★ ★	Adversity and danger threaten you, but do not despair, the clouds are lined with silver.
★★★★★ ★★ ★	Act with caution and do not place too much reliance on the well-meant efforts made by friends to assist you.
★★★★★ ★ ★ ★	This dream is a warning against the dangers of the road; motorists should exercise every care during the next few months.
★★★★★ ★ ★★	You will experience anxiety of mind and many minor troubles; illness is indicated, but complete recovery is assured.
★★★★★ ★★★	Be warned against entering for the time being into ventures requiring the investment of money; your dream foretells losses.
★★★★★ ★★ ★	There will be delay in completing your undertakings; do not, however, be disheartened, you will eventually be successful.
★★★★★ ★ ★★	Legal matters are implied, probably as the result of the loss of property by stealing.
★★★★★ ★★★	There is a likelihood of removal, but it is not clear that you personally will be concerned.

✶✶✶✶✶ ✶✶	Be careful to avoid one who seeks to do you an injustice; he will make himself known to you shortly.
✶✶✶✶✶ ✶ ✶	The time is ripe for you to strike out; pay no heed to those who advise you to delay taking action.
✶✶✶✶✶ ✶ ✶	By means of the telephone you will receive good news, and in consequence you will be called upon to make a long journey.
✶✶✶✶✶ ✶ ✶	One of whom you are often thinking needs your help; offer him your assistance, as it will be to your mutual benefit.
✶✶✶✶✶ ✶ ✶	Brighter times are in store, but you will experience many cares of a minor character in the immediate future.
✶✶✶✶✶ ✶✶	There is one especially faithful friend to whom you may always turn in misfortune; trust him implicitly.
✶✶✶✶✶ ✶✶	You will meet with many trials, but do not despair, fortune will not always pass you by.
✶✶✶✶✶ ✶ ✶	This dream is a warning of deception on the part of one with whom you are on the closest terms of friendship.
✶✶✶✶✶ ✶✶	Your prospects at home are negligible; venture farther afield and you will prosper and secure happiness.
✶✶✶✶✶ ✶ ✶	A happy omen for those who are suffering; recovery from illness and improvement in financial resources are foretold.
✶✶✶✶✶ ✶	Give more attention to your business affairs, or failure is certain to be your lot.
✶✶✶✶✶ ✶	You have two unlucky days, the ninth and sixteenth; act cautiously on these days or misfortune will attend you.
✶✶✶✶✶ ✶	The ability to succeed is yours; do not relinquish your efforts, and time will bring deserved reward.
✶✶✶✶✶ ✶	Friends whom you have not seen or heard of for many years will return and bring you good news.
✶✶✶✶✶ ✶	A dream that implies love and continued happiness; marriage in the near future is indicated.
✶✶✶✶✶	This dream, if repeated, bodes ill for lovers; their fond hopes will be shattered.

★★★★★ ★★★★★	It is inadvisable to expedite your projects; slow and sure is the message contained in your dream.
★★★★★ ★★★★	Interesting and curious experiences will be yours, following your arrival in a land across the seas.
★★★★★ ★★★ ★	Do not enter into legal proceedings, you may suffer a reverse that will mulct you in heavy damages.
★★★★★ ★★ ★★	An unlucky dream; illness is likely, and your financial resources will be severely taxed.
★★★★★ ★ ★★★	The coming months have good fortune in store for you; make the most of your opportunities.
★★★★★ ★★★★	Interfering relations will occasion you worry; avoid discussion with them, and follow your own dictates.
★★★★★ ★★★	Do not be despondent; although you appear to be the victim of misfortune, good luck will soon come your way.
★★★★★ ★ ★★	A change in your domestic circle is presaged; marriage is possible, and a journey is assured.
★★★★★ ★★ ★	Speculative undertakings should be shunned; pay more attention to business, and good progress will be made.
★★★★★ ★★ ★	A year of comparative prosperity is ahead; do not, however, tempt fortune, or you will regret your action.
★★★★★ ★ ★ ★	Prepare for a little unhappiness in the coming months; you will lose a friend, but will have the consolation of making another.
★★★★★ ★ ★★	Your dream indicates that you will meet with romance in a land beyond the seas.
★★★★★ ★★★	You are too liable to be influenced by others; act more on your own initiative and your affairs will give you less worry.
★★★★★ ★★ ★	Think well before you decide on any change of plans; the future appears to be full of difficulties.
★★★★★ ★ ★★	You will receive an unexpected summons to meet an old friend of whom you were at one time extremely fond.
★★★★★ ★★★	A fortunate dream for all who have artistic tastes; profit and fame are strongly foreshadowed.

✱✱✱✱✱ ✱✱	The coming year will be prosperous for those who will take the opportunities that are presented to them.
✱✱✱✱✱ ✱　✱	Marriage is foretold by this dream; those who marry within the next month may be assured of a happy union.
✱✱✱✱✱ ✱　　✱	Deceit is implied; be warned against one whom you regard as a friend, or misfortune may befall you.
✱✱✱✱✱ ✱　　　✱	Your plans will succeed, but there is a likelihood that profit gained from them may bring mixed blessings.
✱✱✱✱✱ ✱　　✱	A warning of danger from fire and water, which can be avoided if every care is taken.
✱✱✱✱✱ ✱✱	You will be fortunate in your business affairs, but only by concentration and hard work.
✱✱✱✱✱ 　✱✱	A favourable dream from the point of view of money-making, but speculative ventures should be avoided.
✱✱✱✱✱ ✱　✱	A dream of good omen for those between the ages of twenty and twenty-five; they will meet with success in business and love.
✱✱✱✱✱ ✱✱	Danger arising from recklessness is foretold for those who travel during the next few weeks; domestic worries are also in this dream.
✱✱✱✱✱ ✱　✱	Your prospects are exceptionally bright; do not tempt fortune, however, but be discreet in all things.
✱✱✱✱✱ ✱	Do not place too much faith in promises that have been made; depend more upon your own efforts.
✱✱✱✱✱ 　✱	You will experience many surprising events, from one of which you will gain experience that will lead to wealth.
✱✱✱✱✱ 　✱	A letter of considerable importance is on the way to you; act upon its contents if you seek happiness and fortune.
✱✱✱✱✱ 　✱	Your friend needs advice and help; go to his assistance, and it will be to the advantage of both of you.
✱✱✱✱✱ 　　✱	There is one who seeks to harm you; he will unwittingly disclose to you his evil intentions.
✱✱✱✱✱	Across the seas lies prosperity and happiness; the opportunity to make the journey will soon be yours.

***** *****	Avoid any speculative enterprise for the next five weeks; this period is not a fruitful one for you.
***** ****	Some irritating but not very serious domestic trouble is indicated; beware of treating it in a harsh or unrelenting manner.
***** *** *	Be not too sanguine about money matters; a pound in the bank is worth ten ventured in a speculative scheme.
***** ** **	Danger on the high road is foreshadowed; take every care not only of yourself but of those living with you.
***** * ***	You will soon be called upon to make a fateful decision, but do not fear to follow the course that will seem clear to you.
***** ****	The health of a child is endangered; if it does not apply to yourself, it is intended that you should pass on the warning.
***** ***	Do not take shelter under trees during a thunderstorm; peril from the skies is indicated by this dream.
***** * **	Someone you will meet shortly has designs upon you; do not be misled by this false friend.
***** ** *	Avoid making important decisions during the next ten days; defer such matters if possible.
***** ** *	You will shortly meet a person who will have a great influence upon your life; take care not to mistake another for this well-wisher.
***** * * *	By bold and steadfast courage you may hope to improve your fortune; avoid rashness, however.
***** * **	In the newspaper you should soon see something of great interest and importance; be prepared for any opportunity that may come.
***** ***	Your dream is somewhat obscure; be guarded in your actions and await other information.
***** ** *	You may receive inducement to change your station or position, but it is by no means clear that such action will be of advantage to you.
***** * **	A suitor is indicated whose claims need close scrutiny; if the message is not for you personally, you should pass it on.
***** ***	If this dream recurs you should be prepared for a change of fortune; by itself it denotes little.

✶✶✶✶✶ ✶✶	Something you have long desired may soon come about; it depends largely upon yourself.
✶✶✶✶✶ ✶ ✶	Beware of danger on the fourth, ninth, and sixteenth of the month approaching; take no personal risks on those days.
✶✶✶✶✶ ✶ ✶	A matter that has long troubled you will soon be brought to a happy and satisfactory conclusion.
✶✶✶✶✶ ✶ ✶	Success from a recent investment is indicated, but be not therefore rash in financial matters.
✶✶✶✶✶ ✶ ✶	A far-away relative is thinking of you, and it will be to your advantage not to repel any advances he may make.
✶✶✶✶✶ ✶✶	It would be wise to forget old grievances and to forgive any injuries you have suffered.
✶✶✶✶✶ ✶✶	You will be asked an important question to which the wise answer will be in the negative, though it may cause some heart-burning.
✶✶✶✶✶ ✶ ✶	Danger by water attends you for a few days; with care and prudence you may circumvent it.
✶✶✶✶✶ ✶✶	Beware of danger arising from personal carelessness in association with stairs, ladders, lifts and high places for the next two weeks.
✶✶✶✶✶ ✶ ✶	Someone near and dear to you is in danger through a neglected chill; pass on the warning.
✶✶✶✶✶ ✶	The numbers three, eight and seventeen are lucky for you if you can rightly interpret this information.
✶✶✶✶✶ ✶	Though tempted to spend freely, you will do well to resist, for a time is approaching when you may need every penny.
✶✶✶✶✶ ✶	You will shortly receive an invitation which you should accept, since it is offered in a spirit of friendship and helpfulness.
✶✶✶✶✶ ✶	Do not let your good nature cloud your business instincts; your duty to those with first claim upon you should make you more careful.
✶✶✶✶✶ ✶	A course you are pursuing is fraught with danger to health or prosperity; it may even be both that are imperilled.
✶✶✶✶✶	If you act wisely and with prudence, your fortune should improve during the next few months.

* * * * * * * * * *	Though there are disappointments in store, you will win through if you go on steadfastly and boldly in the course that seems clear.
* * * * * * * * *	Do not embark upon any important scheme during the next four days; money matters are pointed to especially by this dream.
* * * * * * * * *	An offer or an invitation from the West is predicted, which you would do well to ponder over carefully.
* * * * * * * * *	The coming twelve months should see a change in your occupation and an improvement in your prospects.
* * * * * * * * *	A disappointment is foretold; but you should persevere in your endeavours and not on any account become disheartened.
* * * * * * * * *	The influence of someone of the opposite sex should prove very helpful to you in the near future; see that you act wisely.
* * * * * * * *	Trouble is likely to arise through the act of sons or daughters, nieces or nephews, but it will blow over and no lasting harm will follow.
* * * * * * * *	You are too complacent, and should assert yourself more; retain control of your own affairs.
* * * * * * * *	You may be inclined to neglect the warnings of conscience in a certain matter, but such a course will be disastrous.
* * * * * * * *	Though the skies are cloudless, there is a storm brewing in the air, threatening one you love; advise him to be cautious.
* * * * * * * *	In some way you are courting danger, and the precise details may reach you in a subsequent warning for which you should be ready.
* * * * * * * *	There is a pleasant surprise in store for you; an apparently trivial happening will add much to your future happiness.
* * * * * * * *	You will receive a message from abroad; be not sceptical, for the matter is important to you and yours.
* * * * * * * *	You will encounter someone whom at first you will be inclined to distrust; closer acquaintance, however, will alter your opinion.
* * * * * * * *	If you go abroad this year do not embark upon any hazardous enterprise; danger of an unspecified nature is presaged.
* * * * * * * *	There is a likelihood of danger arising from the soil; if you are bent on gardening you should protect your hands.

✶✶✶✶✶ ✶✶	Success will come to you sooner if you ascertain the sign under which you were born, and then wear the appropriate stone or colour.
✶✶✶✶✶ ✶ ✶	To a man, this dream spells fulfilment; to a woman, it is a warning that caution is needed in current affairs.
✶✶✶✶✶ ✶ ✶	If you have courage enough to sever ties that hold you to the homeland, a successful future awaits you overseas.
✶✶✶✶✶ ✶ ✶	This dream means that you should proceed with any schemes you are considering; a fair measure of success is to be anticipated.
✶✶✶✶✶ ✶ ✶	Be wary of entering upon any plans for the purchase of land or houses; the present time is not very auspicious for such a project.
✶✶✶✶✶ ✶✶	For those with musical or theatrical interests this dream is an encouragement to renewed effort, and promises success.
✶✶✶✶✶ ✶✶	Your prospects should improve in the near future, but caution is needed and thrift is essential.
✶✶✶✶✶ ✶ ✶	Think twice before entering into any financial obligations that tie your hands; you may need your freedom in order to attain success.
✶✶✶✶✶ ✶✶	Though the past few years have not been free from troubles and trials, a happier and more prosperous time is predicted.
✶✶✶✶✶ ✶ ✶	Do not surrender control of your affairs to another, even if large rewards are promised for so doing.
✶✶✶✶✶ ✶	A period of trial is foretold, through which you will pass unharmed if you act with wisdom and prudence.
✶✶✶✶✶ ✶	Do not take unnecessary risks during the next three days; danger from an unexpected source seems to be indicated.
✶✶✶✶✶ ✶	Beware of taking a chill, for such an illness during the coming month might have serious consequences.
✶✶✶✶✶ ✶	An apparently attractive business proposal may be put before you; you should investigate it closely, for it might arouse false hopes.
✶✶✶✶✶ ✶	To persons born in the third, ninth and eleventh months, this dream promises success in enterprise.
✶✶✶✶✶	Be on your guard against any new acquaintances made during the month before and month following the date of this dream.

★★★★★ ★★★★★	This dream suggests that you are not careful enough about your health, and that disaster may overtake you unless you take heed.
★★★★★ ★★★★	You are wronging by your unmerited suspicions someone who wishes you well; try to remedy this injustice.
★★★★★ ★★★ ★	To those whose fortune lies on the water this dream is an augury of good news.
★★★★★ ★★ ★★	Numbers with eight or nine in them are likely to be unfortunate for you this month.
★★★★★ ★ ★★★	An important letter is on the way to you; do not treat too lightly the information it contains.
★★★★★ ★★★★	Should an opportunity arise of changing your dwelling, you would do well to avail yourself of it.
★★★★★ ★★★	Do not lend your aid to a scheme that will shortly be put before you, or misfortune may attend you.
★★★★★ ★ ★★	A plan to which you attach much importance will prove a disappointment; you should, however, await another opportunity to promote it.
★★★★★ ★★ ★	Avoid speculative transactions of all kinds during the coming month, which is not a lucky period for you.
★★★★★ ★★ ★	This dream suggests that you are pursuing a foolish course; it will probably be repeated, and if so its warning is all the more emphatic.
★★★★★ ★ ★ ★	A warning of infelicity impending through your own actions; care and consideration for others will ward it off.
★★★★★ ★ ★★	Beware of doing business with one born in the same month as yourself but some years your senior.
★★★★★ ★★★	You can attain honour and profit in your calling only by paying more attention to things of prime importance.
★★★★★ ★★ ★	You are under the close observation of one who can do much to make or mar you; see that you appear at your best.
★★★★★ ★ ★★	Someone is seeking to injure you, but is unlikely to succeed unless you are careless or negligent.
★★★★★ ★★★	Your dream signifies little of importance unless it should be repeated in the near future, when it denotes, probably, a delay of some kind.

＊＊＊＊＊ ＊＊	Danger affecting health or wealth is betokened; with care and foresight it may be avoided.
＊＊＊＊＊ ＊　＊	Though you are likely to suffer chagrin and disappointment, you have the power to minimize the effect by taking appropriate measures.
＊＊＊＊＊ ＊　　＊	Better health awaits you, but you should guard against risks and protect yourself.
＊＊＊＊＊ ＊　　　＊	A change of abode is predicted, which should improve your prospects and free you from material cares to some extent.
＊＊＊＊＊ ＊　　＊	You are more likely to attain success by patient plodding than by some brilliant stroke; the reward is sure in the end.
＊＊＊＊＊ ＊＊	Suspicion and mistrust will be encountered from those you love, but in due time the clouds will pass.
＊＊＊＊＊ ＊＊	You have but to grasp opportunities that will present themselves and success will be yours.
＊＊＊＊＊ ＊　＊	To those engaged in cultivating the soil, this dream brings a promise of success and prosperity.
＊＊＊＊＊ ＊＊	Take no drastic step of any sort until the week is out; the time is an unfavourable one.
＊＊＊＊＊ ＊　＊	If the digits of the numbers indicating the day, month and year of your birth add up to 30, 34, or 36, this dream spells encouragement.
＊＊＊＊＊ ＊	Someone whom you scarcely know is going to play a great part in your life in the near future.
＊＊＊＊＊ ＊	This dream is a warning against stock and share dealings, betting transactions, and other speculative ventures.
＊＊＊＊＊ ＊	You will receive an unexpected offer of marriage, but you are advised not to give it too hasty consideration.
＊＊＊＊＊ ＊	To those in the legal and the literary world this dream is a happy one and promises advancement.
＊＊＊＊＊ ＊	Pay more regard to future needs and spend less on the pleasures of to-day; some pecuniary losses are envisaged.
＊＊＊＊＊	Advancement through marriage—either your own or that of a near relation—is hinted at by this dream.

✱✱✱✱✱ ✱✱✱✱✱	The dream suggests that you should journey west rather than east or south; it is probably a matter of health that is referred to.
✱✱✱✱✱ ✱✱✱✱	April and May are unlucky months for you this year, but August and October are favourable.
✱✱✱✱✱ ✱✱✱ ✱	A dream that conveys a warning; await clarification by a later one, meanwhile acting with due caution.
✱✱✱✱✱ ✱✱ ✱✱	An eminently favourable dream; your affairs should prosper exceedingly if you exercise thrift and foresight.
✱✱✱✱✱ ✱ ✱✱✱	Money is hinted at, but it will not be gained without courage and perseverance.
✱✱✱✱✱ ✱✱✱✱	Peril arising from personal carelessness in connexion with steps or ladders, lofty trees, and roofs; keep away from precipices.
✱✱✱✱✱ ✱✱✱	You will be parted from one dear to you; whether for a long or a short period is not clear.
✱✱✱✱✱ ✱ ✱✱	Danger is to be apprehended from personal carelessness in connexion with a motor-car, a speed-boat, or an aeroplane.
✱✱✱✱✱ ✱✱ ✱	Do not invest in house property until and unless a more auspicious dream gives an indication of success.
✱✱✱✱✱ ✱✱ ✱	This dream presages both favourable and unfavourable influences; the outcome depends very much upon your own actions.
✱✱✱✱✱ ✱ ✱ ✱	You will soon hear from one who has been separated from you for a great many years.
✱✱✱✱✱ ✱ ✱✱	Act with courage and promptitude upon information that will reach you, and a favourable result should follow.
✱✱✱✱✱ ✱✱✱	A change of residence is indicated, following a change in occupation; the future has good things in store for you.
✱✱✱✱✱ ✱✱ ✱	A dream that portends great happiness, especially to those who are engaged to be married.
✱✱✱✱✱ ✱ ✱✱	Much hard work lies before you; face the future courageously and you will attain your cherished ambition.
✱✱✱✱✱ ✱✱✱	Be on your guard against a stranger who will seek to make your acquaintance shortly; no good will come of such a friendship.

✻✻✻✻✻ ✻✻	A warning of peril arising from personal carelessness in connexion with a two-wheeled or three-wheeled vehicle.
✻✻✻✻✻ ✻ ✻	Happiness and success are on the way to you, and a friend of yours will play a large part in procuring these benefits.
✻✻✻✻✻ ✻ ✻	This dream conveys a warning regarding recklessness to bathers and swimmers; on no account should it be disregarded.
✻✻✻✻✻ ✻ ✻	You have made a serious mistake, but adverse results can be minimized by great care in future conduct.
✻✻✻✻✻ ✻ ✻	Should you receive a warning from a soothsayer, pay due heed to it and act upon the information given.
✻✻✻✻✻ ✻✻	A dream that speaks of travel both by land and sea, and a change of occupation; await further news.
✻✻✻✻✻ ✻✻	Do not repel an outside influence that is coming into your life for, if encouraged, it may be beneficial.
✻✻✻✻✻ ✻ ✻	Matrimonial troubles seem to be indicated, of someone near to you or of yourself; the black clouds will blow over.
✻✻✻✻✻ ✻✻	You may suffer a slight set-back in business; or the failure of another may affect your own prosperity.
✻✻✻✻✻ ✻ ✻	Choose your holiday resort with care, for a momentous event may depend upon a wise selection.
✻✻✻✻✻ ✻	Any business of a speculative nature in which you may engage during the month is unlikely to be successful.
✻✻✻✻✻ ✻	Undue haste or lack of prudence at this juncture in your affairs might be disastrous; proceed with caution.
✻✻✻✻✻ ✻	A concern in whose affairs you have an interest is likely soon to encounter bad times; the set-back will be merely a temporary one.
✻✻✻✻✻ ✻	Do not invest money during the next three weeks, since this period is not a favourable one for you.
✻✻✻✻✻ ✻	A long-cherished desire is likely soon to be fulfilled if you seize opportunities that present themselves.
✻✻✻✻✻	A favourable dream; your plans should prosper and your expectations be satisfied.

*****
*

***** *****	Do not neglect any illness, however slight, since this dream predicts a period of lowered physical resistance.
***** ****	Do not undertake financial obligations, guarantees or security of any kind for anyone in the near future, or you will risk loss.
***** *** *	He from whom you are expecting help will fail you, and you will have to depend upon your own endeavours.
***** ** **	The future is by no means clear; safeguard your position and exercise thrift until matters are straightened.
***** * ***	This dream indicates that relatives by marriage may endeavour to make mischief, but by circumspection you may counter them.
***** ****	Do not yield to sudden impulses or you will do great harm to your future prospects.
***** ***	Promotion and advancement are indicated by this dream, contingent upon your own co-operation.
***** * **	If someone in your family has musical tastes, he or she is likely to do well; fame is signified by this dream.
***** ** *	A crisis in your fortunes is approaching; there are possibilities of great good or much harm, according to the outcome.
***** ** *	Act with great care on the fifteenth of next month, for your dream suggests that this is a critical date.
***** * * *	An improvement is indicated in your health or your fortunes—the dream does not specify which.
***** * **	The course you are at present pursuing, though pleasurable, is hardly a profitable one.
***** ***	You are too impetuous, and unless you act with more prudence and moderation in future, you may do lasting harm.
***** ** *	This dream suggests that there is an unhelpful friendship which you should terminate at once.
***** * **	A person of the opposite sex is about to enter your life, with beneficial results upon your career.
***** ***	It is not in your best interests to accept an offer which will be made to you very soon; weigh your actions carefully.

*****
*

***** **	Of itself this dream signifies little, but it will be followed by another that will give information of importance.
***** * *	You will make fresh contacts, and some of your new acquaintances will be very helpful to you in business.
***** * *	Ill success in affairs of the heart, but better fortune in those of business is foretold by this dream.
***** * *	You are courting disaster by persistence in a certain course; be warned in time and thus avoid a calamity.
***** * *	Though you will succeed to a degree, the full measure of achievement will be withheld for a space.
***** **	To a lover this dream is a warning that "all is not gold that glitters," and that investigation is called for.
***** **	Your fortunes will improve this year, and the future holds much in store for you.
***** * *	First a meeting and then a parting is foretold, but after a short time a permanent reunion will follow.
***** **	Social success and advancement in other spheres are promised by this dream.
***** * *	An acquaintance whom you have taken at his own valuation is seeking to exploit you.
***** *	A project upon which you have set your heart will fail to materialize; but this is all to the good, since little benefit would have come of it.
***** *	A time of strife and contention is predicted; do not enter into litigation, but make the best bargain you can out of court.
***** *	According to this dream, fortune is about to smile upon you; success will not come, however, without courage and effort.
***** *	Abandon the scheme you have in mind and await a more favourable time to forward it.
***** *	Investments made during the coming month should be productive; anything in the nature of gambling, however, is doomed to failure.
*****	It would be unwise to pledge your resources in advance; a period is foretold when money will be greatly needed.

***** *****	Though you will encounter opposition and hindrance, you can win success if you persevere and hold fast to your own plans.
***** ****	Aid is coming to you from a distant relative of whose existence you had no knowledge.
***** *** *	Your efforts will achieve fulfilment, but you are pursuing a somewhat mistaken course.
***** ** **	Avoid, for a time, food that comes from the water, for the dream tells of special risk to you from this source.
***** * ***	Be on your guard against a trivial injury for, if neglected, it may have grave consequences.
***** ****	An encouraging dream; your plans, of whatever nature, should prosper exceedingly during the next month.
***** ***	The death of a person of eminence will have a far-reaching effect upon your life and prospects.
***** * **	The clouds obscuring your horizon will suddenly vanish; look well ahead and go forward steadfastly.
***** ** *	A broken engagement and a death are suggested in the near future; in both events to someone outside your immediate circle.
***** ** *	Your fortunes will suffer a change in the autumn, but whether a favourable one or the opposite is not indicated.
***** * * *	Someone is seeking to undermine your influence in a certain quarter, but you have the power to frustrate the attempt.
***** * **	Proceed with caution; this year is a critical one in your life and a false step would entail much harm.
***** ***	You have but to go forward with courage, and your dearest wishes will come within sight of fulfilment.
***** ** *	A journey will be proposed to you, but there are indications that you would do better to remain at home.
***** * **	Danger from boiling liquid is foretold; care in all dealings with substances of this kind will preserve you from harm.
***** ***	This dream suggests that in cards clubs are your lucky suit; probably there is a further meaning which only you will discern.

✶✶✶✶✶ ✶✶	The wheel of fortune has turned to your advantage; see that you seize every opportunity that presents itself.
✶✶✶✶✶ ✶ ✶	Disappointment in love or a set-back in business is presaged by this dream; the unfavourable conditions, however, will soon be dispelled.
✶✶✶✶✶ ✶ ✶	Games of chance are best left alone during the next ten days; if you gamble, you do so against great odds.
✶✶✶✶✶ ✶ ✶	You will receive news from an unsuspected quarter in a strange manner before the week is out.
✶✶✶✶✶ ✶ ✶	Unless you yield to your impulse to fare farther afield, the inclination and the opportunity will be lost for ever.
✶✶✶✶✶ ✶✶	Though you seek social advantage you would be better advised to consider matters relating more to your future security and happiness.
✶✶✶✶✶ ✶✶	A warning against a too materialistic view of life; be not sceptical, we know very little of the future.
✶✶✶✶✶ ✶ ✶	A voice that has spoken in vain before; an injustice is indicated that you can remedy.
✶✶✶✶✶ ✶✶	An inimical influence is seeking to enter your life; mistrust new acquaintances.
✶✶✶✶✶ ✶ ✶	You are about to incur an obligation for another, and this dream suggests that you look carefully to your security.
✶✶✶✶✶ ✶	Good fortune profits a man little unless he passes on its benefits; pay more regard to the needs of others.
✶✶✶✶✶ ✶	If you are needy, this dream promises better times, with opportunities of improving your position.
✶✶✶✶✶ ✶	Aspirations and ambitions long cherished are to be brought nearer to achievement by an event prognosticated for the coming month.
✶✶✶✶✶ ✶	A dream with some favourable omens and others of less value; opportunities that arise should be seized.
✶✶✶✶✶ ✶	To those in middle life, a dream of good import; to younger persons, a warning that efforts should not be relaxed.
✶✶✶✶✶	A dream of little moment, which will be repeated shortly if it has any significance to you.

★ ★ ★ ★ ★ ★ ★ ★ ★ ★	This dream indicates that someone dear to you is desirous of receiving a letter from you.
★ ★ ★ ★ ★ ★ ★ ★ ★	A dream of consolation to those who are ailing, with a promise of a speedy recovery if care is taken.
★ ★ ★ ★ ★ ★ ★ ★ ★	Monetary affairs should prosper; see that you do not place all your eggs in one basket.
★ ★ ★ ★ ★ ★ ★ ★ ★	To a young person of either sex a warning is conveyed against too much pleasure-seeking.
★ ★ ★ ★ ★ ★ ★ ★ ★	Someone in your immediate circle wishes you ill; examine your friend-ships closely and without bias.
★ ★ ★ ★ ★ ★ ★ ★ ★	The plea you have made will be successful, but the benefits gained must be wisely used.
★ ★ ★ ★ ★ ★ ★ ★	Unfavourable conditions are predicted; they will pass away in three weeks and all will then be well.
★ ★ ★ ★ ★ ★ ★ ★	The person whose affairs cause you much concern will shortly cease to worry you.
★ ★ ★ ★ ★ ★ ★ ★	Pay no attention to your dream, which, unless it recurs within three days, has no especial significance.
★ ★ ★ ★ ★ ★ ★ ★	A relation by marriage will suffer a loss of money; the suggestion is, however, that the loss is only temporary.
★ ★ ★ ★ ★ ★ ★ ★	A time of worry and anxiety is approaching, but the outcome will be favourable.
★ ★ ★ ★ ★ ★ ★ ★	The machinations of a female relative are likely to embitter family affairs; steer clear of embroilments.
★ ★ ★ ★ ★ ★ ★ ★	Good news will reach you in a short time from or about someone whom you love.
★ ★ ★ ★ ★ ★ ★ ★	Immediate fulfilment of your wishes is impossible at present; another opportunity will arise later.
★ ★ ★ ★ ★ ★ ★ ★	A matter of some importance to you and yours is likely to be decided within the month.
★ ★ ★ ★ ★ ★ ★ ★	To those born in spring or autumn the dream brings encouragement; it is not so favourable for others.

***** **	Avoid all risks to health or to wealth during the next few weeks, for special danger is foretold.
***** * *	It is futile to hope for aid from others; depend on your own efforts, and good should result.
***** * *	Little harm can come from the pursuit of your present plans, but the future is not especially favourable for their success.
***** * *	Happiness is predicted and a prosperous and fruitful union; your choice is a wise one.
***** * *	Danger arising from personal carelessness in connexion with edged tools and swift-moving wheels; the risk will endure until the new moon.
***** **	You are entitled to a legacy, but whether you receive it or not depends on a person whose feelings are in some doubt.
***** **	Your fears concerning the future are groundless; persevere and you will gain prosperity.
***** * *	Postpone any drastic or decisive action until another dream directs your endeavours.
***** **	To women in middle life this dream conveys a warning; greater care should be observed in matters of health.
***** * *	To workers in wood or metal a warning regarding carelessness is conveyed; it refers especially to machinery.
***** *	Salesmen and commercial travellers to whom this dream is vouchsafed may look forward to a profitable season.
***** *	To those concerned in the making and sale of beverages, a time of prosperity is indicated.
***** *	Your dream suggests a spell of luck in games of chance and in investments; domestic happiness is also foreshadowed.
***** *	The message of this dream is "Orange blossoms," either for yourself or for someone dear to you.
***** *	A good omen for one about to get married; happiness and comfort are predicted.
*****	A mistaken choice is implied; perhaps it is not too late to investigate the matter further.

* * * * * * * * * *	Loss of money is foretold; though it is too late to avoid the consequence of past action, the experience will be of value in the future.
* * * * * * * * *	Even numbers, according to the dream, are favourable for you, especially numbers in which "two" occurs.
* * * * * * * * *	Risk from fire, matches and lamps is implied; with care and foresight any evil events from this source can be avoided.
* * * * * * * * *	A summons to another sphere of life is predicted; bonds will be broken and new ties formed.
* * * * * * * * *	The next two years of life are fraught with great possibilities, both for good and evil; common sense will direct you.
* * * * * * * * *	Beware of someone to whom you will be linked by that person's marriage; scandal and mischief-making are likely.
* * * * * * * *	Conflicting interests to which you are subjected will make choice difficult in a matter you must settle for yourself.
* * * * * * * *	Your dream is a warning of some unspecified risk to yourself during the next few days; tread warily.
* * * * * * * *	An aged person dear to you, though unrelated, will suffer a slight illness in the near future.
* * * * * * * *	Your fortunes will shortly undergo improvement and a change of residence is implied also.
* * * * * * * *	Much will depend upon your choice in a matter soon to come before you for decision.
* * * * * * * *	Financial responsibilities are likely to be thrust upon you in connexion with the indisposition of a relative.
* * * * * * * *	Marriage at the present juncture would be unwise, and a more favourable period should be awaited.
* * * * * * * *	To a man this dream means little, but to a woman it implies that ardent hopes are to be fulfilled.
* * * * * * * *	Lack of constancy on the part of some person in your family circle is suggested.
* * * * * * * *	You will make a friendship that will have a potent and lasting influence upon your future.

✶✶✶✶✶ ✶✶	Regard with suspicion one who will shortly seek to become on friendly terms with you; that person is influenced by selfish motives.
✶✶✶✶✶ ✶ ✶	Not a favourable dream; it tells of illness and hardships to someone whom you know well.
✶✶✶✶✶ ✶ ✶	The immediate future is somewhat unpropitious, but there are indications of better times to follow.
✶✶✶✶✶ ✶ ✶	Financial assistance will be offered, but it will be subject to conditions that require close consideration.
✶✶✶✶✶ ✶ ✶	You may become involved in a quarrel not of your own seeking; tact and forbearance will extricate you.
✶✶✶✶✶ ✶✶	The dream indicates that the hopes on which you have placed much reliance are illusory.
✶✶✶✶✶ ✶✶	An acquaintance you have made recently is seeking to profit by your misfortune.
✶✶✶✶✶ ✶ ✶	The ensuing year should be one of prosperity and good health for you; your star is in the ascendant.
✶✶✶✶✶ ✶✶	Hold fast to your intentions; there is every prospect that the designs will be carried out.
✶✶✶✶✶ ✶ ✶	March and May are favourable months for your schemes, according to this dream.
✶✶✶✶✶ ✶	Litigation or an unpleasant dispute is threatened, unless tact and prudence are exercised.
✶✶✶✶✶ ✶	A friend overseas is thinking a great deal about you; not knowing your address, the person cannot communicate with you.
✶✶✶✶✶ ✶	An unfavourable time for speculative dealings is implied by this dream; the influence holds until the new moon.
✶✶✶✶✶ ✶	In the choice of friends you are on the point of preferring the less worthy to the one who can be really helpful.
✶✶✶✶✶ ✶	There is little hope that your expectations of monetary help will be fulfilled for the present.
✶✶✶✶✶	A slight accident will befall a friend; it should receive careful attention, or serious harm may result.

✳✳✳✳✳ ✳✳✳✳✳	Accept help that will be proffered you in the immediate future; the contact is one of great value.
✳✳✳✳✳ ✳✳✳✳	A dream that emphasizes the need for caution in the circumstances in which you find yourself at present.
✳✳✳✳✳ ✳✳✳ ✳	A warning against impetuousness and an encouragement to proceed systematically with your enterprises.
✳✳✳✳✳ ✳✳ ✳✳	Speculation is discouraged for the present by this dream, but ordinary investment is likely to be successful.
✳✳✳✳✳ ✳ ✳✳✳	Your stubbornness in certain matters is offending someone whose good-will it would be very unwise to lose.
✳✳✳✳✳ ✳✳✳✳	A forewarning of failure; you should abandon your scheme and await another opportunity.
✳✳✳✳✳ ✳✳✳	Matters over which you have no control are hindering the realization of your desires.
✳✳✳✳✳ ✳ ✳✳	There is a likelihood of danger from illness or from accident; you can avoid the risk by exercising extreme care.
✳✳✳✳✳ ✳✳ ✳	Those interested in the produce of the soil should proceed with their schemes; the coming month is especially favourable.
✳✳✳✳✳ ✳✳ ✳	An auspicious dream to those who get their living by the manufacture or sale of woollen materials in any form.
✳✳✳✳✳ ✳ ✳ ✳	This dream portends some danger arising from fog, mist or dust; disease germs are indicated as the offending agents.
✳✳✳✳✳ ✳ ✳✳	A warning against ill effects of sun-rays, to which the dreamer is specially liable for some weeks.
✳✳✳✳✳ ✳✳✳	Black or yellow objects are associated with some peril to you; both animate and inanimate things are involved.
✳✳✳✳✳ ✳✳ ✳	A good dream, which is specially encouraging to those who make their living—or aspire to do so—by the arts.
✳✳✳✳✳ ✳ ✳✳	Delay is urged; any plans of importance ought to be postponed until at least the rising of a new moon.
✳✳✳✳✳ ✳✳✳	To buyers and sellers of food commodities, the dream promises a time of prosperity and profit.

✱ ✱ ✱ ✱ ✱ ✱ ✱	The dream indicates danger arising from personal carelessness in connexion with vehicles or machines driven by electricity.
✱ ✱ ✱ ✱ ✱ ✱ ✱	An adverse influence is about to enter your life; since it comes in the guise of love and affection, it will be difficult to detect.
✱ ✱ ✱ ✱ ✱ ✱ ✱	Wedding-bells will ring for a man, but a disappointment is predicted for a woman.
✱ ✱ ✱ ✱ ✱ ✱ ✱	One who goes merrily to the altar will rue it within a year and a day; this applies to a woman.
✱ ✱ ✱ ✱ ✱ ✱ ✱	A secret ambition is devouring you; unattainable at present, unless cast out it may wreck two lives.
✱ ✱ ✱ ✱ ✱ ✱ ✱	Success in your case must be wooed, and cannot be compelled; be patient though persistent, and your wishes will be granted.
✱ ✱ ✱ ✱ ✱ ✱ ✱	Your dream is not the most propitious for new undertakings, but you are likely to have a fair measure of success.
✱ ✱ ✱ ✱ ✱ ✱ ✱	Two other persons are bound up with your happiness, and neglect of either will rebound upon yourself.
✱ ✱ ✱ ✱ ✱ ✱ ✱	A temporary set-back is portended by this dream, but the consequences need not be grave unless unwise or imprudent action is resorted to.
✱ ✱ ✱ ✱ ✱ ✱ ✱	A dispute is foretold in which there will be blows struck; do not intervene, for the dream indicates danger to you from such action.
✱ ✱ ✱ ✱ ✱ ✱	Wings are symbolized by the dream; the reference is probably to the badge of an airman.
✱ ✱ ✱ ✱ ✱ ✱	A favourable message, portending good health and prosperity in the near future.
✱ ✱ ✱ ✱ ✱ ✱	An alliance is foretold; in the case of a man it will be a business association, and in the case of a woman one of affection.
✱ ✱ ✱ ✱ ✱ ✱	A crisis is approaching in your affairs; there are both favourable and adverse possibilities.
✱ ✱ ✱ ✱ ✱ ✱	Business ventures should prosper, but affairs of the heart go less well, during the coming month.
✱ ✱ ✱ ✱ ✱	Peril is to be apprehended from a conflagration caused by personal carelessness; the danger will endure for eight days.

* * * * *

* * * * * * * * * *	Your future is bright and the stage is set for important developments; only carelessness can lose you the benefits that are due to you.
* * * * * * * * *	If you play cards for money during the next week, you must expect to lose; wagers also will be unprofitable.
* * * * * * * * *	A dream of fruitfulness; investments made now will be productive, and new undertakings should flourish.
* * * * * * * * *	Exercise care regarding fish food; some danger to health is indicated as imminent from this source.
* * * * * * * * *	Disagreement and misunderstandings between lovers; patience and forbearance on your part will mend all.
* * * * * * * * *	You are shortly to meet one who will thereafter be associated with you for many years.
* * * * * * * *	A parting and a journey of some thousands of miles are expressed in this dream, applicable personally to a man.
* * * * * * * *	First for weal and then for woe, and then for weal again; an alliance is predicted that in the outcome will be a happy one.
* * * * * * * *	Black garments will be worn; perhaps those of ceremony, but more likely those of mourning.
* * * * * * * *	Hope on; though present disappointments may torment you, there are better times ahead.
* * * * * * * *	Do not neglect your health or nutrition, for a period of weakened resistance is foretold.
* * * * * * * *	This dream suggests that temperance and moderation are vitally important to the man to whom the message comes.
* * * * * * * *	You are likely to become embroiled in a quarrel not of your choosing; an extreme course is to be avoided.
* * * * * * * *	Financial commitments are discouraged by this message, which hints at a period of stringency ahead.
* * * * * * * *	Though of little significance, the dream conveys a warning that applies more to a woman than a man.
* * * * * * * *	Any change of employment or occupation would be very untimely and improvident at present; await a further message.

***** *

***** **	A dream of obscure import; it refers to the autumn and a physical danger then to be feared.
***** * *	Beware of attaching your fortunes too closely to those of a certain person in a higher position; if he falls he will drag you down also.
***** * *	You are too ambitious, and should be content to work harder and exercise greater patience.
***** * *	You will shortly make a friendship that will have an important bearing upon your future happiness.
***** * *	A minor disappointment is foretold by this dream, which at the same time augurs well for the not too-distant future.
***** **	A death and, later, a birth are foretold by the dream; the first applies to a very aged person.
***** **	A propitious dream for investors and those beginning new enterprises; it predicts prosperity and success.
***** * *	Peril is foretold from a slight injury, which ordinarily would be disregarded; with care all ill-effects can be avoided.
***** **	Change of station in the case of a woman, and change of fortune in that of a man are indicated by this dream.
***** * *	An important decision having far-reaching consequences is to be made in the near future, either by you or on your account.
***** *	An opportunity of improving your prospects will be presented, and should be taken advantage of.
***** *	A more kindly and charitable attitude towards certain others will be greatly to your advantage.
***** *	Investments made on the fourth and eighteenth of the month should turn out well, but fortune will not smile on speculations or gambles.
***** *	Stone steps and pavements are indicated by the dream as being sources of possible danger to you for a few days; tread warily.
***** *	The unhappiness of someone to whom you are related will cloud your own future for a while.
*****	An omen of good luck, which should pervade all transactions until the moon changes.

NAPOLEON'S BOOK OF FATE

AFTER Napoleon I had been defeated at Leipzig, in the year 1813, he left behind him a "Cabinet of Curiosities," among which the following Oraculum was found by a Prussian officer. This Oraculum, discovered in one of the royal tombs of Egypt during the French military expedition of 1801, had been translated, at the order of the emperor, into the German language by a celebrated German scholar and antiquarian. From that time forth it remained one of the most treasured possessions of Napoleon. He never failed to consult it upon every important occasion, and it is said that it formed a stimulus to his most speculative and most successful enterprises.

The version which we give here is an exact translation of Napoleon's copy, for we have not deemed it either necessary, or desirable, to effect any elaborations or additions. Although the number of questions is not large, they cover an enormously wide field of human activity. We can do no more than to say that not only the emperor but numerous other people of fame and ability have found this Oraculum, by reason of the astounding accuracy of its answers, an invaluable help in the shaping of their destinies.

METHOD OF WORKING THE QUESTIONS

MAKE marks in the following manner, either more or less in the four lines:—

```
* * * * * * * * * * *
* * * * * * * * * * * *
* * * * * * * * * * * * *
* * * * * * * * * * * * * *
```

250

This being done, you must then reckon the number of marks in each line; and if the number is *odd*, you must mark down one star, and if *even*, two stars. When the number of marks in any line exceeds nine, only the surplus marks are to be taken into account.

The number of marks in the lines of the example are:—

First line	.	.	.	.	*	
Second line	.	.	.	.	*	*
Third line	.	.	.	.	*	
Fourth line	.	.	.	.	*	*

To obtain the answer to your question, you must refer to the table called the Oraculum, at the top of which you will find a column of stars similar to those you have produced: guide your eye down the same column until you come to the letter ranging with the figure of the question you are trying; refer to the page having the same letter at the top, and, level with the symbol corresponding with yours, you will find the answer to your question.

Note: The symbols appearing on the pages devoted to the interpretation of the Oraculum are set horizontally; in the Oraculum itself, however, they are set vertically.

The following are days on which none of the questions should be worked :—

Month	1	2	4	6	11	12	20
January	1	2	4	6	11	12	20
February					1	17	18
March						14	16
April					10	17	18
May						7	8
June							17
July						17	21
August						20	21
September						10	18
October							6
November						6	10
December					6	11	15

N.B.—It is not right to try a question twice on the same day.

ORACULUM

Numbers	QUESTIONS	1 • • • •	2 : • • •	3 • : • •	4 : : • •	5 • • : •	6 : • : •	7 • : : •	8 : : : •	9 • • • :	10 : • • :	11 • : • :	12 : : • :	13 • • : :	14 : • : :	15 • : : :	16 : : : :	Numbers
1	Shall I obtain my wish?	A	B	C	D	E	F	G	H	I	K	L	M	N	O	P	Q	1
2	Shall I have success in my undertakings?	B	C	D	E	F	G	H	I	K	L	M	N	O	P	Q	A	2
3	Shall I gain or lose in my cause?	C	D	E	F	G	H	I	K	L	M	N	O	P	Q	A	B	3
4	Shall I have to live in foreign parts?	D	E	F	G	H	I	K	L	M	N	O	P	Q	A	B	C	4
5	Will the stranger return from abroad?	E	F	G	H	I	K	L	M	N	O	P	Q	A	B	C	D	5
6	Shall I recover the property stolen?	F	G	H	I	K	L	M	N	O	P	Q	A	B	C	D	E	6
7	Will my friend be true in his dealings?	G	H	I	K	L	M	N	O	P	Q	A	B	C	D	E	F	7
8	Shall I have to travel?	H	I	K	L	M	N	O	P	Q	A	B	C	D	E	F	G	8
9	Does the person love and regard me?	I	K	L	M	N	O	P	Q	A	B	C	D	E	F	G	H	9
10	Will the marriage be prosperous?	K	L	M	N	O	P	Q	A	B	C	D	E	F	G	H	I	10
11	What sort of wife or husband shall I have?	L	M	N	O	P	Q	A	B	C	D	E	F	G	H	I	K	11
12	Will she have a son or a daughter?	M	N	O	P	Q	A	B	C	D	E	F	G	H	I	K	L	12
13	Will the patient recover from his illness?	N	O	P	Q	A	B	C	D	E	F	G	H	I	K	L	M	13
14	Will the prisoner be released?	O	P	Q	A	B	C	D	E	F	G	H	I	K	L	M	N	14
15	Shall I be lucky or unlucky this day?	P	Q	A	B	C	D	E	F	G	H	I	K	L	M	N	O	15
16	What does my dream signify?	Q	A	B	C	D	E	F	G	H	I	K	L	M	N	O	P	16

* * * *	What you wish for, you will shortly obtain.
* * * * *　　*	Signifies trouble and sorrow.
* * * * 　*	Be very cautious what you do this day, lest trouble befall you.
* * * * *　　*	The prisoner dies, and is regretted by his friends.
* * * * * * *	Life will be spared this time, to prepare for death.
* * * * * *　*	A very handsome daughter, but a painful one.
* * * * *	You will have a virtuous and religious woman, or man, for your wife, or husband.
* * * * * *	If you marry this person, you will have enemies where you little expect.
* * * * 　　* *	You had better decline this love, for it is neither constant nor true.
* * * * 　　　*	Decline your travels, for they will not be to your advantage.
* * * * *　 * *	There is a true and sincere friendship between you both.
* * * * 　* * *	You will not recover the stolen property.
* * * * * *	The stranger will, with joy, soon return.
* * * * 　*	You will not remove from where you are at present.
* * * * *　 *	The Lord will support you in a good cause.
* * * * * * * *	You are not lucky—pray to God that He may help you.

— B —

****	The luck that is ordained for you will be coveted by others.
**** * *	Whatever your desires are, for the present decline them.
**** *	Signifies a favour or kindness from some person.
**** * *	There are enemies who would defraud and render you unhappy.
**** ***	With great difficulty he will obtain pardon or release.
**** ** *	The patient should be prepared to leave this world.
**** *	She will have a son, who will be learned and wise.
**** **	A rich partner is ordained for you.
**** **	By this marriage you will have great luck and prosperity.
**** *	This love comes from an upright and sincere heart.
**** * **	God will surely travel with you, and bless you.
**** ***	Beware of friends who are false and deceitful.
**** **	You will recover your property—unexpectedly.
**** *	Love prevents his return home at present.
**** * *	Your stay is not here: be therefore prepared for a change.
**** ****	You will have no gain, therefore be wise and careful.

* * * *	With the blessing of God, you will have great gain.
* * * * * *	Very unlucky indeed—pray to God for His assistance.
* * * * *	If your desires are not extravagant, they will be granted.
* * * * * *	Signifies peace and plenty between friends.
* * * * * * *	Be well prepared this day, or you may meet with trouble.
* * * * * * *	The prisoner will find it difficult to obtain his pardon or release.
* * * * *	The patient will yet enjoy health and prosperity.
* * * * * *	She will have a daughter, and will require attention.
* * * * * *	The person has not a great fortune, but is in middling circumstances.
* * * * *	Decline this marriage, or else you may be sorry.
* * * * * * *	Decline a courtship—which may be your destruction.
* * * * * * *	Your travels are in vain: you had better stay at home.
* * * * * *	You may depend on a true and sincere friendship.
* * * * *	You must not expect to regain that which you have lost.
* * * * * *	Sickness prevents the traveller from seeing you.
* * * * * * * *	It will be your fate to stay where you now are.

— D —

****	You will obtain a great fortune in another country.
**** * *	By venturing freely, you will certainly gain doubly.
**** *	God will change your misfortune into success and happiness.
**** * *	Alter your intentions, or else you may meet poverty and distress.
**** ***	Signifies that you have many impediments in the accomplishment of your pursuits.
**** ** *	Whatever may possess your inclinations this day, abandon them.
**** *	The prisoner will escape this time.
**** **	The patient's illness will be lingering and doubtful.
**** **	She will have a dutiful and handsome son.
**** *	The person will be low in circumstances, but honest-hearted.
**** * **	A marriage which will add to your welfare and prosperity.
**** ***	You love a person who does not speak well of you.
**** **	Your travels will be prosperous, if guided by prudence.
**** *	He means not what he says, for his heart is false.
**** * *	With some trouble and expense, you may regain your property.
**** ****	You must not expect to see the stranger again.

— E —

****	The stranger will not return as soon as you expect.
**** * *	Remain among your friends, and you will do well.
**** *	You will hereafter gain what you seek.
**** * *	You have no luck—pray to God, and strive honestly.
**** ***	You will obtain your wishes by means of a friend.
**** ** *	Signifies that you have enemies, who will endeavour to ruin you, and make you unhappy.
**** *	Beware—an enemy is endeavouring to bring you to strife and misfortune.
**** **	The prisoner's sorrow and anxiety are great, and his release uncertain.
**** **	The patient will soon recover—there is no danger.
**** *	She will have a daughter, who will be honoured and respected.
**** * **	Your partner will be fond of liquor—and will debase himself thereby.
**** ***	This marriage will bring you to poverty, be therefore discreet.
**** **	This love is false to you and true to others.
**** *	Decline your travels for the present, for they will be dangerous.
**** * *	This person is serious and true, and deserves to be respected.
**** ****	You will not recover the property you have lost.

I

— F —

* * * *	By persevering you will recover your property.
* * * * * *	It is out of the stranger's power to return .
* * * * *	You will gain, and be successful in foreign parts.
* * * * * *	A great fortune is ordained for you—wait patiently.
* * * * * * *	There is great hindrance to your success at present.
* * * * * * *	Your wishes are in vain at present.
* * * * *	Signifies there is sorrow and danger before you.
* * * * * *	This day is unlucky—therefore alter your intention.
* * * * * *	The prisoner will be restored to liberty and freedom.
* * * * *	The patient's recovery is doubtful.
* * * * * * *	She will have a very fine boy.
* * * * * * *	A worthy person, and a fine fortune.
* * * * * *	Your intentions would destroy your rest and peace.
* * * * *	This love is true and constant—forsake it not.
* * * * * *	Proceed on your travels, or journey, and you will not have cause to repent it.
* * * * * * * *	If you trust this friend, you may have cause for sorrow.

— G —

****	This friend exceeds all others in every respect.
**** * *	You must bear your loss with fortitude.
**** *	The stranger will return unexpectedly.
**** * *	Remain at home among your friends, and you will escape misfortunes.
**** ***	You will meet no gain in your pursuits.
**** ** *	Heaven will bestow its blessings on you.
**** *	No.
**** **	Signifies that you will shortly be out of the power of your enemies.
**** **	Ill luck awaits you, it will be difficult for you to escape it.
**** *	The prisoner will be released by death only.
**** * **	By the blessing of God, the patient will recover.
**** ***	A daughter, but of a very sickly constitution.
**** **	You will get an honest, young, and handsome partner.
**** *	Decline this marriage, else it may be to your sorrow.
**** * *	Avoid this love.
**** ****	Prepare for a short journey, you will be recalled by an unexpected event.

— H —

****	Commence your travels, and they will go on as you would wish.
**** * *	Your pretended friend hates you secretly.
**** *	Your hopes to recover your property are vain.
**** * *	A certain affair prevents the stranger's immediate return.
**** ***	Your fortune you will find in abundance abroad.
**** ** *	Decline the pursuit, and you will do well.
**** *	Your expectations are vain, you will not succeed.
**** **	You will obtain what you wish for.
**** **	Signifies that on this day your fortune will change for the better.
**** *	Cheer up your spirits, your luck is at hand.
**** * **	After long imprisonment he will be released.
**** ***	The patient will be relieved from sickness.
**** **	She will have a healthy son.
**** *	You will be married to your equal in a short time.
**** * *	If you wish to be happy, do not marry this person.
**** ****	This love is from the heart, and will continue until death.

****	The love is great, but will cause great jealousy.
**** * *	It will be in vain for you to travel.
**** *	Your friend will be as sincere as you could wish him to be.
**** * *	You will recover the stolen property through a cunning person.
**** ***	The traveller will soon return with joy.
**** ** *	You will not be prosperous or fortunate in foreign parts.
**** *	Place your trust in God, who is the disposer of happiness.
**** **	Your fortune will shortly be changed into misfortune.
**** **	You will succeed as you desire.
**** *	Signifies that the misfortune which threatens will be prevented.
**** * **	Beware of your enemies, who seek to do you harm.
**** ***	After a short time your anxiety for the prisoner will cease.
**** **	God will give the patient health and strength again.
**** *	She will have a very fine daughter.
**** * *	You will marry a person with whom you will have little comfort.
**** ****	The marriage will not answer your expectations.

— K —

* * * *	After much misfortune you will be comfortable and happy.
* * * * * *	A sincere love from an upright heart.
* * * * *	You will be prosperous in your journey.
* * * * * *	Do not rely on the friendship of this person.
* * * * * * *	The property is lost for ever; but the thief will be punished.
* * * * * * *	The traveller will be absent some considerable time.
* * * * *	You will meet luck and happiness in a foreign country.
* * * * * *	You will not have any success for the present.
* * * * * *	You will succeed in your undertaking.
* * * * *	Change your intentions, and you will do well.
* * * * * * *	Signifies that there are rogues at hand.
* * * * * * *	Be reconciled, your circumstances will shortly mend.
* * * * * *	The prisoner will be released.
* * * * *	The patient will depart this life.
* * * * * *	She will have a son.
* * * * * * * *	It will be difficult for you to get a partner.

— L —

✴ ✴ ✴ ✴	You will get a very handsome person for your partner.
✴ ✴ ✴ ✴ ✴ ✴	Various misfortunes will attend this marriage.
✴ ✴ ✴ ✴ ✴	This love is whimsical and changeable.
✴ ✴ ✴ ✴ ✴ ✴	You will be unlucky in your travels.
✴ ✴ ✴ ✴ ✴ ✴ ✴	This person's love is just and true. You may rely on it.
✴ ✴ ✴ ✴ ✴ ✴ ✴	You will lose, but the thief will suffer most.
✴ ✴ ✴ ✴ ✴	The stranger will soon return with plenty.
✴ ✴ ✴ ✴ ✴ ✴	If you remain at home, you will have success.
✴ ✴ ✴ ✴ ✴ ✴	Your gain will be trivial.
✴ ✴ ✴ ✴ ✴	You will meet sorrow and trouble.
✴ ✴ ✴ ✴ ✴ ✴ ✴	You will succeed according to your wishes.
✴ ✴ ✴ ✴ ✴ ✴ ✴	Signifies that you will get money.
✴ ✴ ✴ ✴ ✴ ✴	In spite of enemies, you will do well.
✴ ✴ ✴ ✴ ✴	The prisoner will pass many days in confinement.
✴ ✴ ✴ ✴ ✴ ✴	The patient will recover.
✴ ✴ ✴ ✴ ✴ ✴ ✴ ✴	She will have a daughter.

— M —

* * * *	She will have a son, who will gain wealth and honour.
* * * * * *	You will get a partner with great undertakings and much money.
* * * * *	The marriage will be prosperous.
* * * * * *	She, or he, wishes to be yours this moment.
* * * * * * *	Your journey will prove to your advantage.
* * * * * * *	Place no great trust in that person.
* * * * *	You will find your property at a certain time.
* * * * * *	The traveller's return is rendered doubtful by his conduct.
* * * * * *	You will succeed as you desire in foreign parts.
* * * * *	Expect no gain, it will be in vain.
* * * * * * *	You will have more luck than you expect.
* * * * * * *	Whatever your desires are, you will speedily obtain them.
* * * * * *	Signifies you will be asked to a wedding.
* * * * *	You will have no occasion to complain of ill luck.
* * * * * *	Someone will pity, and release the prisoner.
* * * * * * * *	The patient's recovery is unlikely.

— N —

* * * *	The patient will recover, but his days are short.
* * * * * *	She will have a daughter.
* * * * *	You will marry into a very respectable family.
* * * * * *	By this marriage you will gain nothing.
* * * * * * *	Await the time, and you will find the love great.
* * * * * * *	Venture not from home.
* * * * *	This person is a sincere friend.
* * * * * *	You will never recover the theft.
* * * * * *	The stranger will return, but not quickly.
* * * * *	When abroad keep from evil women, or they will do you harm.
* * * * * * *	You will soon gain what you little expect.
* * * * * * *	You will have great success.
* * * * * *	Rejoice ever at that which is ordained for you.
* * * * *	Signifies that sorrow will depart, and joy will return.
* * * * * *	Your luck is in blossom, it will soon be at hand.
* * * * * * * *	Death may end the imprisonment.

— O —

****	The prisoner will be released with joy.
**** * *	The patient's recovery is doubtful.
**** *	She will have a son, who will live to a great age.
**** * *	You will get a virtuous partner.
**** ***	Delay not this marriage, you will meet much happiness.
**** ** *	None loves you better in this world.
**** *	You may proceed with confidence.
**** **	Not a friend, but a secret enemy.
**** **	You will soon recover what is stolen.
**** *	The stranger will not return.
**** * **	A foreign woman will greatly enhance your fortune.
**** ***	You will be cheated out of your gain.
**** **	Your misfortunes will vanish, and you will be happy.
**** *	Your hope is in vain, fortune shuns you at present.
**** * *	You will soon hear agreeable news.
**** ****	There are misfortunes lurking about you.

****	This day brings you an increase of happiness.
**** * *	The prisoner will quit the power of his enemies.
**** *	The patient will recover, and live long.
**** * *	She will have two daughters.
**** ***	A rich young person will be your partner.
**** ** *	Hasten your marriage, it will bring you much happiness.
**** *	The person loves you sincerely.
**** **	You will not prosper from home.
**** **	This friend is more valuable than gold.
**** *	You will never receive your goods.
**** * **	He is dangerously ill, and cannot yet return.
**** ***	Depend upon your own industry, and remain at home.
**** **	Be joyful, for future prosperity is ordained for you.
**** *	Depend not too much on your good luck.
**** * *	What you wish, will be granted to you.
**** ****	That you should be very careful this day lest any accident befall **you.**

— Q —

****	Signifies much joy and happiness between friends.
**** * *	This day is not very lucky, but rather the reverse.
**** *	He will yet come to honour, although he now suffers.
**** * *	Recovery is doubtful, therefore be prepared for the worst.
**** ***	She will have a son, who will prove forward.
**** ** *	A rich partner, but a bad temper.
**** *	By wedding this person, you ensure yourself happiness.
**** **	The person has great love for you, but wishes to conceal it.
**** **	You may proceed on your journey without fear.
**** *	Trust him not; he is inconstant and deceitful.
**** * **	In a very singular manner you will recover your property.
**** ***	The stranger will return very soon.
**** **	You will dwell abroad in comfort and happiness.
**** *	If you deal fair, you will surely prosper.
**** * *	You will yet live in splendour and plenty.
**** ****	Make yourself contented with your present fortune.

THE SCIENCE OF NUMBERS

WE know that all things in the universe are subjected to rule. The movements of the planets, the sequence of the seasons, and the structure of physical bodies are not determined by chance or by coincidence but by mathematical laws. A knowledge of these enables the scientist to foretell certain occurrences. Thus the astronomer can predict when a comet will be seen, when the sun will be eclipsed, or when the full moon will shine.

In effect, it may be said that the whole universe is governed by numbers, and, since this is so, we may naturally conclude that human beings are no exception to Nature's laws. It is the science of numerology which applies the laws of mathematics to mankind, and teaches the art of interpreting those numbers by which the character of an individual is influenced.

The ancient Egyptians attached great importance to the significance of numbers and employed them as a means of foretelling the future; but it is chiefly to the Greeks and the Hebrews that we owe the foundation of modern numerology. Pythagoras, the Greek mathematician and philosopher, stated that "Numbers are the first things of all of Nature," and believed that all natural phenomena could be reduced to terms of geometry and arithmetic. He founded a school of philosophy on this doctrine, his followers being known as the Pythagoreans. The Hebrews, from a set of beliefs called the "Cabbala"—those tenets "received by tradition" —associated certain numbers with letters of their alphabet, and thus formed the basis of the interpretation of names.

In numerology, the art of which can be very quickly mastered, we are concerned with the reduction of everything under consideration to the form of an arithmetical figure. The figure can then be interpreted by reference to the traditional meanings of numbers. These interpretations are older than history; they date back to the time when the dawning intelligence of primitive man first visualized the *meaning* of number and associated it with a spiritual significance.

The revelations of character which can be obtained by means of numerology are not infallible, for what science can claim to account for all the wonders and vagaries of Nature? Yet general indications can nearly always be obtained from the interpretation of numbers, which will give us a clear indication of the part we play in the harmonious arrangement of the wonderful universe.

PRIMARY NUMBERS AND THEIR MEANINGS

Before we proceed farther with this study, it should be understood that figures themselves are merely signs which represent an idea of number. Numerology is not concerned with the outward appearance of these signs, but with the *meanings* of the numbers which they represent.

An Egyptian sage, an Ancient Hebrew, a philosopher of classic Greece, each made a different sign when he wanted to convey the idea of the number 3. But each one *thought* of the same number. Because of this we have been able to apply various interpretations from ancient writings in the Egyptian, Hebrew and Greek to our own numbers, which are Arabic in origin. Numbers are, in fact, a universal language, for they are understood by all rational persons of every race on earth.

Many systems of numerology are in existence, but the one which is considered here, and which springs from the most ancient and reliable source, is based chiefly on the nine primary numbers. These are represented by the figures 1 to 9 inclusive. The cipher, or 0, such as is contained in the number 10, has no tangible significance and, therefore, is not considered. The figure 10 is a form of 1, with certain modifications of which we shall learn later.

All numbers which are greater than 9 can be reduced to one of the primary numbers. Consider the number 26; to reduce it to a primary number we must add together the digits of which it is composed, thus $2+6 = 8$. We see, therefore, that 26 reduces to the primary number 8. In the same way $44 = 4+4 = 8$; $21 = 2+1 = 3$; $63 = 6+3 = 9$; $98 = 9+8 = 17 = 1+7 = 8$; and $789 = 7+8+9 = 24 = 2+4 = 6$. This is the method we must use throughout for reducing large numbers to primary ones.

There are three main points to be considered in order to discover which number exerts its influence over our lives; they are as follows:—

1. The date of our birth.
2. The primary number of the letters in our surname.
3. The primary number of letters in the forename which we commonly use.

First of all, however, it is necessary to learn the traditional significance of the primary numbers, together with the effects which these produce on the human character.

.   .   .   .   .

1. Unity, or the Monad, expressed by the figure 1, symbolizes the Omnipotent Deity, the "oneness" of Divine Purpose, the beginning of all things, the singleness yet boundlessness of the Godhead. It represents the pinnacle or highest point, the focus of the circumference, the hub of the universe, and the single Parent of the whole world. The universal symbol which conveys this idea is a point enclosed by a circle. Because the Deity is generally conceived of as being masculine and the male species is believed to have been created first, the Monad is generally associated with the male rather than the female sex.

Character Influences. Those who come under the influence of the Monad will show great tenacity and a singleness of purpose. It indicates self-reliance, an unswerving desire for action, resolve, ingenuity, concentration, great achievement and possibly genius. Persons controlled by the number 1 can be implicitly relied upon; they seem to take a pleasure in the assumption of great responsibilities. They will not be content to lead aimless, subordinate lives, but will seek new and perhaps hazardous paths which will lead them onward to their goal. Usually they will be friendly and considerate towards others, and will do all they can to assist those in distress.

The less admirable influences which may be exerted by the number 1 are intolerance, narrow-mindedness, conceit, obstinacy. Those who are highly ambitious and resolute may be inclined to depreciate the value of the work or actions of others. They may consider themselves above receiving advice from their friends, and stubbornly persist in an enterprise which is obviously doomed to failure. Thus they may sometimes be disliked by reason of their haughty independence. If you are influenced by the Monad you should attempt to control your self-confidence and be ready to accept the opinions of older and more experienced people.

2. Duality, the number 2, or the Duad as it was called by the Pythagoreans, represents both diversity and equality or justice. The idea of diversity originates from the conception of two opposites, such as night and day, good and evil, riches and poverty, joy and pain, love and hate. Yet, at the same time, for the sake of justice and equality, two sides of a question must always be heard, while the existence of such things as brotherhood and love must necessarily be dependent upon the presence of two persons. Thus the Duad also stands for balance, harmony, concord, sympathy, response. Two points when joined together form the extremities of a line, which, therefore, is the symbol of duality. The number 2, as directly following the Monad, is traditionally associated with women rather than men.

Character Influences. The characteristic of those who are influenced by the number 2 will be that of placidity. They have not the singleness of purpose of those under the Monad, and therefore are capable of showing greater consideration for the feelings of others. Implicit justice and a hatred of all forms of selfishness or egotism are among their chief traits. These people will go out of their way to avoid strife and discord, whether it concerns themselves or not. They are very easy to make friends with, and usually become a great success socially because of their ability to sympathize with all types of character.

There are no *actively* adverse influences of the Duad; the faults sometimes found in those under its influence are mostly *passive* ones. Number 2 may produce a nature that is too sympathetic, a quality which can degenerate into irresolution or changeability. The great contrasts which it presents to the mind of those swayed by it may create a sense of fatalism and indifference, while the distaste for strife may cause a shirking of all worry and difficulties, and a refusal to shoulder responsibility. Such persons would do well to incorporate with their own a little of the character represented by number 1, thus compensating their natural lack of forcefulness.

3. The Ternary, the number 3, or the Triad, was esteemed by many ancient philosophers as the perfect number. The Pythagoreans believed in three worlds—the Inferior, the Superior, and the Supreme—while followers of Socrates and Plato acknowledged three great principles—Matter, Idea and God. The three great virtues necessary for married bliss were considered to be justice, fortitude and prudence. In the Christian religion the Trinity is seen as an outstanding example of the Triad, while the Scriptures tell of three wise men of the East with their offering of three gifts, of three archangels and three godly virtues. Pagan religions abound in threes; victims were led three times round the altar before sacrifice, prayers were repeated three times to ensure their being answered, the priestess of Apollo sat upon a tripod called the "tripod of truth."

There are three dimensions of space—height, length and breadth; three stages of time—past, present and future; three states of matter —solid, liquid and gaseous; and three kingdoms of Nature—animal, vegetable and mineral. The Triad may be said to represent comprehensiveness and fulfilment, and it is symbolized by the triangle— the figure formed by joining three points. Like number 1, it is regarded as being essentially a male number.

Character Influences. Fortitude and freedom are the keynotes of this number. Persons under its influence will usually be forceful and frank, and possess a great talent for "getting on." They will have brilliant successes in all kinds of enterprises, and will become especially notable for their organizing ability. Any novel project or invention will hold a tremendous fascination for them, and their knack of making other people see things from their point of view will make them especially successful as salesmen and promoters of new schemes.

They are generally happy, make cheerful companions, and can adapt themselves to any kind of company. Their enthusiasm may incline them to be talkative, but their high spirits are so infectious that their exuberance is welcomed. Optimism is ever present— no one under the Triad will be depressed for long by business or private worries.

The excessive independence exercised by number 3 may cause an attitude of indifference, which sometimes gives offence. Other people's ideas and cherished projects may be too hastily brushed aside by those of the Triad, for the latter are inclined to be solely occupied with their own schemes. Over-confidence often causes spectacular failures, sudden rises to fame and then a startling downfall; while the versatile enthusiasm displayed may give rise to impatience with any matter which is not progressing as quickly as was hoped, resulting in an inability to carry through any one project to the very end. Tenacity and endurance are the two attributes which should be chiefly cultivated.

4. The Quaternary, the number 4, or the Tetrad was regarded by many of the ancients as symbolic of truth, while the old Greeks considered it to be the root of all things, as representing what were believed to be the four elements—fire, air, earth and water. It is interesting to note that Pythagoras sometimes referred to the Deity as the Tetrad, or the "four sacred letters," owing to the fact that the name of God was Zeus in Greek. We find the word God represented by four letters in many other languages—Dieu in French; Gott in German; Godt in Dutch; Godh in Danish; Goth in Swedish; Deva in Sanskrit; Dios in Spanish; Deus in Latin; Idio in Italian; and we have our own name, Lord.

The four liberal sciences were considered to be astronomy, geometry, music and arithmetic; man was declared to possess the four properties of mind, science, opinion and sense; and there were the four accepted states of death, judgment, heaven and hell. We have the four winds, four points of the compass and the four seasons. The square symbolizes the Tetrad, and it may be said to stand for solidity and reality.

Character Influences. The number 4 produces the stolid type of character which is unwaveringly loyal and imperturbable in almost all circumstances. Great steadiness and tenacity are displayed in work, honesty and ability for undertaking unpleasant or wearisome tasks being dominant traits of this nature. There is also an implicit obedience to authority, and a meticulous regard for all the conventions.

Friends of those influenced by the Tetrad will find them deep and faithful in their affections, and always ready to appreciate the good side of others rather than to condemn their weaknesses. Forcefulness, will-power and abstemiousness are also present, although number 4 never produces the dogmatic or intolerant type. Practical occupations rather than those requiring great imaginative powers are most suitable for those under the Tetrad.

Clumsiness and an inclination towards dullness are the chief faults of those influenced by number 4. They may display a certain lack of initiative and excessive conservatism, which refuses to recognize the unconventional or the extraordinary. In consequence, if these people should find themselves in strange surroundings, they are reluctant to adapt themselves and take long to do so. They may also be rather lacking in personal ideals, and therefore incapable of any really great achievement. Some of the dash and independence of number 3 would greatly assist their progress; combined with their natural attribute of steadfastness, it would help them on their way towards spiritual and material success.

5. The Quincunx, the number 5, or the Pentad was regarded by the followers of Pythagoras, as well as by Jewish and Arabic philosophers, as the symbol of health. The Egyptians saw in it a mark of prosperity, but on the whole the Pentad seems universally to have symbolized marriage, fecundity and propagation. This belief probably had its origin in the idea of 5 being the union of 3 and 2, or a male and female number. In ancient Rome, its significance was emphasized by the burning of five tapers during the marriage ceremony. Many heathen religions included prayers asking help from five gods to instil five virtues into the hearts of prospective wives.

Mohammedanism preaches five religious duties—prayer, fasting, purification, alms and pilgrimage to Mecca. Our own Scriptures contain many indications that the number 5 seems to have been regarded with a particular significance. Benjamin was given five changes of raiment by Joseph; the latter brought five only of his brothers to Pharaoh; and David chose five smooth stones with which to slay the giant Goliath. Moreover, man possesses five senses—sight, hearing, smell, touch and taste; also five digits on each of his hands and feet.

The Pentad is represented geometrically by a regular, five-sided plane figure or else by a pyramid. It also takes the shape of a five-pointed star, which is one form of the ancient Seal of Solomon.

Character Influences. Dash and adventure characterize the 5 type. It signifies a very vivacious spirit and an aptitude for undertaking many and varied tasks—although not necessarily with great success. Courage in face of difficulties is generally displayed, while the bodily and mental health are unusually good. Those under the Pentad have many passionate love affairs, for they are very susceptible; but they also make gay and amusing companions to those of their own sex. They are seldom disheartened by adverse circumstances, for they can find happiness and amusement in the most unexpected places. They are very responsive to the feelings of others, and are quick to grasp the significance of a situation and act accordingly. Great explorers and travellers are usually produced by number 5.

Irresponsibility and rashness are among the adverse significances, and these two faults may be the cause of much unhappiness to others. Although probably sincere at the time, people of the 5 type may embark upon a love affair which they are quick to bring to an end upon meeting a new and perhaps more fascinating companion. They are often lacking in concentration and unable to attend to urgent and commonplace affairs. In consequence, they are sometimes condemned as being unreliable or even untrustworthy. These faults do not lie deep, however, and are the result of thoughtlessness rather than ingrained perversity. The placid and steadying influence of number 2 can do much to counteract the faults of number 5.

6. The Hexagon, the number 6, or the Hexad is represented geometrically by a six-sided, balanced figure. It is also symbolized by two intersecting triangles known as the Seal of Solomon. By the Jews, six was considered a sacred number, for the world was created in six days. Heathen peoples used the double triangle as a charm to ward off evil spirits; it was also employed to denote the two natures of Jesus Christ, and as such was frequently carved in stone or painted on windows in old monasteries and churches. In Nature we find numerous examples of the hexagonal in the form of crystals, which are a complete and very comprehensive class in themselves. On the whole, the Hexad has always been considered one of the happiest of numbers, since it represents perfect harmony and completion.

Character Influences. Idealism is the chief trait of those who come under the influence of number 6. A desire that all things should work smoothly and that no jarring note should be introduced into the harmony of life will be uppermost in their minds. In consequence, they will be strictly honest and careful to act in a manner which they consider to be best for the common good. Selfishness, self-indulgence and intolerance are quite foreign to them, and they will be singularly charitable to all those who are in worse circumstances than themselves. Wealth for its own sake will mean little, but the value of it will be appreciated as a means of benefiting others, especially sick persons or those who have the misfortune to be physically defective.

Hexad types are very cheerful and make good companions. As husbands and wives they are faithful and loving. Being fully aware of their responsibilities, they take great care in the upbringing and education of their children. In business life people of the 6 type can be energetic, although they seldom rise to any great position, as they attach but little importance to material gain.

The unfavourable qualities are few. Sometimes they possess excessive idealism, which may cause the 6 type to display, quite unconsciously, an air of superiority which will frequently give offence. Also they may put too little store by monetary success and miss opportunities which would be of great benefit to themselves and their dependants. The fighting spirit, too, may also be lacking to a certain extent, causing a tendency for these people to assume an air of "martyrdom" rather than to stand up for what they know to be right. If it is a fault, they are sometimes too soft-hearted and allow themselves to be imposed upon. Those under the Hexad should cultivate a practical sense, and avoid allowing kind-heartedness to degenerate into softness and weakness.

7. The Septenary, the number 7, or the Heptad is the most interesting and mysterious of the primary numbers. The Pythagoreans held it in particular veneration as being the highest primary number which was complete in itself and incapable of division by any other except 1. To the Greeks and Romans it was the symbol of good fortune, being connected with periodical changes of the moon; while ancient philosophers saw in it the sign of custody, or world government, through the influence of the seven planets. The seven notes in music gave rise to the philosophy of the "harmony of the spheres" and the depiction of the universe as one vast musical scale.

In numerous religions the 7 attained great significance. There were seven Gothic gods; the seven worlds believed in by the Chaldeans; the seven heavens and seven hells of the Mohammedans; and seven degrees of initiation in various Eastern orders. Christian Scriptures abound in sevens. The seventh day is holy, for on it God rested; the word "Jehovah" itself contains seven letters; there were seven sorrows of the Virgin; seven cardinal sins and virtues; the army of Joshua encircled Jericho seven times on the seventh day, headed by seven priests bearing seven trumpets; and on the seventh occasion the walls of the city fell.

There were seven plagues of Egypt; seven fat kine and seven lean; and "a just man falleth seven times and riseth up again" we learn in Proverbs. Peter asked of Jesus Christ if he should forgive his brother seven times, and the answer was "until seventy times seven." In Revelation we read of seven spirits before the Throne, and the seven stars which are angels of seven Churches. The reader may find innumerable other examples.

The Heptad may be said to be imbued with the qualities of wisdom, endurance, evolution, balance and completion. As a number in everyday life, it is usually considered to be lucky.

Character Influences. The number 7 imparts to its subjects wisdom and discernment. Those who come under its influence are the world's great thinkers, philosophers and writers, of the type called "ascetic," being rigorous in the practice of all forms of self-discipline. Frequently they have to fight to maintain their theories and principles, for they are mentally so long-sighted that they are "ahead of their time," and are often regarded as cranks or reactionaries. They will show great fortitude in the bearing of physical or spiritual pain, and are seldom heard to grumble at misfortune. Pedantry and petty-mindedness are especially distasteful to them, for their love of knowledge lies in the deepest and greatest things of life. Ordinary pleasures and amusements, unless they demand mental exercise which leads into new fields of thought and contemplation, will mean little to these people.

An excessive love of solitude, which may cause morbidness, is the chief danger to those of the 7 type. When they find themselves forced to mix with other people, they often become disgruntled and resentful because their desire for privacy has not been respected. In consequence, they may become over critical regarding the actions of others, always making mental comparisons with what they themselves consider to be the right course of action.

Moreover, they will frequently refuse to make any practical use of the knowledge which they possess, preferring to store it up and to devote their time to acquiring further knowledge. These people should learn to appreciate the value of friendship, and to develop and make use of their brain power as a means of bringing material success.

8. The Octaedron, the number 8, or the Ogdoad was greatly esteemed in ancient Egypt, where it was customary to have eight people in each boat taking part in sacred processions on the Nile. This custom seems to have originated in the belief that there were eight souls saved from the Flood in Noah's ark. By the mathematical philosophers, the Ogdoad was regarded as the first cube, having six sides and eight angles; and as such signified reality and strength. Being the highest of the even primary numbers, it is the ultimate symbol of balance.

Character Influences. Extreme practicality is the chief trait of those whose influence is number 8. They possess in double strength all the good qualities of number 4. They are infinitely more powerful, and possess a greater will to succeed. Organizing ability and a keen business sense are dominant, and they usually rise to the top of all those occupations which call for quick decisions and the seizing of opportunities. In every sense, these people are fitted to be masters of men, controllers of great concerns.

They have no patience with the inefficient or lazy, and are not given to day-dreaming or extravagant ideas; in direct contrast with 6, their chief interests lie in the world about them rather than in mystical ideals. They are essentially kind-hearted, although their charity is administered with prudence and they actively resent any attempt to take advantage of their good nature. It is not easy for them to fall passionately in love, but they prefer to bestow a faithful and constant affection which can bring about great security, contentment and real happiness.

The 8 type should learn to cultivate imagination. Their intense practical sense may make them tactless and blunt at times, causing distress and resentment in the minds of others. They must also be on their guard against scoffing at all those things of a more or less mystical nature which they cannot understand. They should learn sometimes to have faith rather than to demand proof, to consider rather than to condemn hastily.

Above all, they must avoid the danger of being domineering, which danger may arise from their intense desire for activity and material advancement. A display of greater tolerance and a keener interest in and analysis of other people's view-points are necessary to broaden the vision and to assist the mental progress of those influenced by the Octaedron.

9. The Nonagon, the number 9, or the Ennead was known to many of the ancients as Perfection and Concord, and as being unbounded. The latter quality was attributed to it from certain peculiarities manifested by the figure 9 when treated mathematically. If 9 is multiplied by itself, or any single figure, the two figures in the product when added together always equal 9. For example: $9 \times 3 = 27 = 2 + 7 = 9$; $9 \times 9 = 81 = 8 + 1 = 9$; $9 \times 5 = 45 = 4 + 5 = 9$; and so on. Similarly, if the numbers from 1 to 9 inclusive are added together, totalling 45, the result of adding 4 to 5 = 9; if 9, 18, 27, 36, 45, 54, 63, 72, 81 are added the sum is 405 or $4 + 0 + 5 = 9$.

Again, if any row of figures is taken, their order reversed, and the smaller number subtracted from the larger, the sum of the numerals in the answer will always be 9. For example:—

$$74368215$$
$$51286347$$
$$\overline{23081868}$$

and $2 + 3 + 0 + 8 + 1 + 8 + 6 + 8 = 36 = 3 + 6 = 9$.

There are numerous other examples portraying this peculiar property of 9, but those given above will be sufficient to demonstrate why the ancients considered the Ennead to be unbounded. It is called Concord because it unites into one all the other primary numbers, and Perfection because nine months is the pre-natal life of a child.

In ancient Rome the market days were called *novendinae*, for they were held every ninth day; we remember that Lars Porsena "By the nine gods he swore"; the Hydra, a monster of mythology, had nine heads; the Styx was supposed to encircle the infernal regions nine times; the fallen angels in "Paradise Lost" fell for nine days; the Jews held the belief that Jehovah came down to the earth nine times; initiation into many secret societies of the East consisted of nine degrees; and magicians of former times would draw a magic circle nine feet in diameter and therein raise departed spirits.

Character Influences. The conception of perfection, concord and boundlessness, when applied to the human character, must necessarily be intensely modified, for none of these traits, in their fullest sense, is human—they are all Divine. Those under the influence of the Ennead will show great intelligence and a power of understanding and discretion. They will know how to use their knowledge to good account; nevertheless, their chief interests will lie not so much in practical matters as in affairs of the intellect, in logic, philosophy and an appreciation of the fine arts. Success by sheer hard work or slogging is not for them; they become outstanding among their fellow men because of natural intellect and sheer inspiration.

They make good friends and never take a mean advantage of another person; they are always willing to help others to succeed, and are excellent advisers because of their naturally sympathetic understanding. Like number 6, 9 inspires a lofty sense of morals, its subjects being strictly honest in all their thoughts and actions. Frequently the Ennead is the number of genius, although numerology does not stipulate any particular number for this quality—it may be manifested by those influenced by any other of the primary numbers.

The qualities which may handicap the development of the 9 type are similar to those which are present in number 6. Excessive dreaminess and too much value set on knowledge itself, apart from its application, may tend to cause lethargy and lack of progress. These people should learn the value of hard work and concentration, otherwise there is a danger that they may degenerate into clever dilettantes or dabblers, without achieving outstanding success in any particular field. They are fortunate enough to be blessed with natural gifts, and should do all in their power to put these to the best purpose for benefiting both themselves and the world at large.

SUMMARY OF QUALITIES REPRESENTED BY PRIMARY NUMBERS

1. *Independence*, self-reliance, tenacity, singleness of purpose. Intolerance, conceit, narrowness, depreciation, stubbornness.

2. *Placidity*, justice, unselfishness, harmony, sociability. Irresolution, indifference, avoidance of responsibility, lack of forcefulness.

3. *Freedom*, bravery, adventurousness, gaiety, exuberance, brilliance. Indifference, over-confidence, impatience, lack of stamina.

4. *Stolidity*, loyalty, imperturbability, honesty, will-power, practicality. Clumsiness, dullness, conservatism, inadaptability.

5. *Adventurousness*, vivaciousness, courage, health, susceptibility, sympathy. Rashness, irresponsibility, inconstancy, unreliability, thoughtlessness.

6. *Idealism*, selflessness, honesty, charitableness, faithfulness, responsibility. Superiority, softness, unpracticality, submission.

7. *Wisdom*, discernment, philosophy, fortitude, depth, contemplation. Morbidness, hypercriticism, lack of action, unsociability.

8. *Practicality*, power, business ability, decision, control, constancy. Un-imaginativeness, bluntness, self-sufficiency, domination.

9. *Intelligence*, understanding, discretion, artistry, brilliance, lofty moral sense, genius. Dreaminess, lethargy, lack of concentration, aimlessness.

Birth Dates and Name Numbers

To find out to which primary number the character is assigned we must discover:—

a. The birth number.
b. The number of the forename.
c. The number of the surname.

Together *b* and *c* form the Number of Personality. When *a*, *b* and *c* are added together and reduced we obtain the primary number which governs the subject and indicates the Number of Character.

Suppose the subject was born on April 29, 1941. April is the fourth month, the day is the 29th, the year 1941, so we must add $4+29+1941 = 1974$. To reduce to a primary number we add together the digits thus: $1+9+7+4 = 21 = 2+1 = 3$; the Birth Number, therefore, is 3. Similarly, anyone born on November 7, 1934, has 8 as a Birth Number, for 11 (the eleventh month) $+7+1934 = 1952 = 17 = 8$.

Each day of the month has its number; the months of the year have their numbers, ranging from 1 (January) to 12 (December). Before we can find the *characteristic* number of each person, however, we must find the name number, add it to that of birth and, if necessary, reduce the whole to a primary.

The value of each letter of the English alphabet is obtained by referring to and slightly modifying various cabalistic values which have been handed down by tradition throughout the centuries. There are several systems of valuation in existence, but we give here the one which divides the alphabet as far as possible into divisions of the nine primary numbers. This is in keeping with the *simple* methods of numerology as practised by the ancient sages. We may say, as a general rule, that whenever a complicated and scarcely comprehensible system is employed in a numerological treatise it is a sign of charlatanism, the object being so to confuse the reader that he may not perceive the real ignorance of the would-be numerologist.

Here are the numbers corresponding to the twenty-six letters of the alphabet:—

A	=	1	J	=	1	S	=	1
B	=	2	K	=	2	T	=	2
C	=	3	L	=	3	U	=	3
D	=	4	M	=	4	V	=	4
E	=	5	N	=	5	W	=	5
F	=	6	O	=	6	X	=	6
G	=	7	P	=	7	Y	=	7
H	=	8	Q	=	8	Z	=	8
I	=	9	R	=	9			

There are also four pairs of letters which have a special value. This is because they correspond to single letters of the Greek alphabet, the sound of each of which can only be represented in English by two letters. Since the old Greek numerologists gave them a separate number, so also must we. These are as follows:—

English						Greek		
TH	.	.	.	.	.	θ (Thēta)	=	8
PH	.	.	.	.	.	ϕ (Phi)	=	3
CH	.	.	.	.	.	χ (Chi)	=	4
PS	.	.	.	.	.	ψ (Psi)	=	5

When we come across any of the above combinations in a name, they must be valued according to their corresponding *single* number, not as two separate ones. Thus in the name Theodore, for example, the Th must be treated as 8, being equivalent to the Greek Thēta, not T+H.

How to Find the Number of Character

Suppose the forename commonly used is Robert, or, if a woman, Mary, and suppose that the surname is Saunders. Write down the forenames and surnames, giving each letter its equivalent numerical value thus:—

M	=	4	R	=	9	S	=	1	
A	=	1	O	=	6	A	=	1	
R	=	9	B	=	2	U	=	3	
Y	=	7	E	=	5	N	=	5	
		—	R	=	9	D	=	4	
	21	= 3	T	=	2	E	=	5	
		—			—	R	=	9	
				33	= 6	S	=	1	
					—			—	
							29	= 11	= 2
								—	

To find the Number of Personality of Mary Saunders we must write $3+2 = 5$, for Robert Saunders $6+2 = 8$. Suppose Robert Saunders was born on March 4, 1949. Reduce the birth date to figures and a primary number: $3+4+1949 = 1956 = 1+9+5+6 = 21 = 2+1 = 3$. We must now add the Number of Personality (8) to the Birth Number (3). The total comes to 11, which on reduction gives us 2. Robert Saunders, therefore, reacts to the Duad, the characteristics of which can be read in our table of the primary numbers. Mary Saunders, whose Number of Personality is 5, was born on May 4, 1957. By reducing this date to a primary number we obtain 4, which added to 5 gives 9. Mary, therefore, reacts to the characteristics of the Ennead.

Thus the Number of Character = Birth Number + Number of Personality reduced to a primary number.

Let us take another example:—

NAMES				BIRTH
P } H }	= 3	W	= 5	February 7, 1928
Y	= 7	H	= 8	= 2+7+1928
L	= 3	I	= 9	= 1937
L	= 3	T	= 2	= 20
I	= 9	E	= 5	= 2 Birth Number
S	= 1		—	
	—	29	= 11	
	26 = 8			

$8 + 11 = 19 = 10$
$= 1$ Number of Personality

Number of Character
$= 3$

In order to discover the name number of a married woman, both the maiden and the married name must be taken into consideration. For example, if the subject Phyllis White was married and her maiden name was Roberts, the latter name would be added to the analysis and each letter given its corresponding number, just as if it were part of the surname; for, although at marriage a woman's character does not suffer a complete change, her mental condition and outlook are greatly modified, therefore the best means of analysis is to take both the influencing numbers into consideration.

The names used for numerological analysis need not, however, be the birth names. If an individual changes his name early in life, and has been known under the assumed name for a longer period than he was under his real name, then he must take the former as a basis of character analysis. But this does not apply in the case of stage- or pen-names, which must be regarded as being purely artificial, and cannot form a medium for character reading.

SECONDARY SIGNIFICANCES

In the Hebrew alphabet there were twenty-two letters, and to every one of them a certain mystical significance was attached. The method which we recommend in these pages, however, attaches the chief importance to the nine primary numbers, in accordance with systems of numerology more ancient than the Jewish. Nevertheless, the remaining numbers, those from 10 to 22 inclusive (corresponding with letters of the Hebrew alphabet), must not be totally ignored. We prefer to give them a secondary significance, and to treat their influence as being comparatively slight, seeing that each one can be reduced to a primary number. As regards character influences, they are discovered in our *secondary names*, that is, those forenames or middle names which we frequently represent by an initial only, and which are not used except when we sign our full name.

First of all we will consider the significance of the secondary numbers, always remembering that their influences are not so strong or so certain as those of the primaries.

10. This number, composed of 1 + the cipher or nullity, is really a form of the Monad in the primaries. It has little significance, although it may indicate completion or attainment.

11. Sometimes the number of super-intellect or genius. It may generally be regarded as "lucky," and as leading through development to success.

12. Indicates repression, uncertainty and lack of progress. On the other hand, it carries with it the assets of balance and harmony, which may be prevailing.

13. A mysterious number. Those who regard it as a number of good fortune are as numerous as those who condemn it as being unlucky. It indicates material achievement to those whose Number of Character is 4. There is no reason to suppose that it is unlucky

in everyday life, the popular superstition probably arising from the fact that Judas Iscariot was the thirteenth present at the Last Supper. On the whole, the number spells progress in business matters but little spiritual development.

14. Fortitude and the surmounting of difficulties are indicated. It is the number of stoicism and unselfishness.

15. Thoughtlessness and obstinacy are the chief traits, especially when in conjunction with the primary number 5. If combined with 4, the number of stolidity, it somewhat modifies this quality.

16. Not a very happy influence; it appertains to self-sufficiency and excessive confidence.

17. Always a portent of happiness and harmony. It exerts a favourable influence on the imaginative powers, and thus upon authors, painters, sculptors and all creative artists.

18. This number has no additional influence on those whose primary is 9, but it adds strength and achievement to the other numbers. Thus it counteracts, to a certain extent, the unfavourable qualities found in those numbers.

19. Brightness and inspiration are carried with it. It may be responsible for "bright ideas" occasionally manifested by an otherwise rather dull and uninspired character.

20. Like 10, this number has scarcely any influence. It sometimes has a steadying effect on rash and impetuous characters, but seldom prevails against the real "hot-head."

21. It instils a desire for freedom and independence, as well as ambition, in those whose primary number is not 3. On the 3 type it does not exert a favourable influence; it increases in intensity the adverse qualities of impatience and over-confidence.

22. This number, representing the last letter of the Hebrew alphabet, may signify great success and the power of achievement. Its influence is constantly strong; that is to say, it increases the strength of both the good and the bad traits contained in the primaries. It may thus cause outstanding ascendancy or disastrous downfall.

. . . .

To discover which of the secondary numbers influence us through the medium of our secondary forenames or middle names we must proceed first of all in the same manner as we did in ascertaining our Number of Character.

Suppose the second name is a family name; for example, Neil. We set down the letters as before, giving each one its numerical value according to the table:—

N	=	5
E	=	5
I	=	9
L	=	3

22 Secondary Character Influence

The result obtained is 22, which is the last of the secondary numbers. Remember, *we do not reduce the Secondary Character Influence to a primary number*, but refer to the table of secondary numbers which gives us a slight qualification of the significance of the Number of Character. Suppose the person with the middle name of Neil had 5 as a primary number, then the additional influence of 22 would give him a fresh quality of achievement, but at the same time would increase in intensity his traits of adventure, courage, and irresponsibility. It must be remembered, however, that it is the primary number which has the greater influence, and that the secondary influence is often so slight as to be almost imperceptible.

If the middle name or names have a value which falls within the primary numbers, as 8, for example, we must *convert these primaries into secondaries* according to the equivalents given in the following table:—

PRIMARY		SECONDARY
1	converts to	10
2	" "	11
3	" "	12
4	" "	13
5	" "	14
6	" "	15
7	" "	16
8	" "	17
9	" "	18

It will be seen that this is just a reversal of the reduction process, and that the equivalent secondary number is that of which the digits, on being added together, equal the primary.

Let us consider two secondary names—John Stewart (the full name being Henry John Stewart Alderson). As these two names have a valuation of 45, which is greater than 22, or the last of the secondary numbers, we must first reduce 45 to a primary, that is 9. On referring to the table we discover that the secondary equivalent to 9 is 18; therefore 18 is the Secondary Character Influence.

Let us sum up the complete process of deducing character and destiny from numbers:—

To Find the Number of Character

a. Convert the birth date to figures, add together the digits and reduce to a primary number.

b. Convert the commonly used forename and the surname to figures (according to the table given) and reduce to a primary number.

c. Add together the results of *a* and *b*, and if necessary reduce the answer to a primary number.

To Find the Secondary Character Influence

d. Convert the middle or secondary names to figures and reduce *or increase* to a secondary number.

EXAMPLE OF FULL ANALYSIS

Full name and birthday: *ROBERT JAMES WINTER, January 2, 1927.

NUMBER OF CHARACTER		SECONDARY CHARACTER INFLUENCE
Birthday 1+2+1927 = 1930 = 13 = 4		*Middle Name*
Name *(the one commonly used)		
R = 9		J = 1
O = 6		A = 1
B = 2		M = 4
E = 5		E = 5
R = 9		S = 1
T = 2		—
—		*Secondary* = 12
33 = 6		*Character*
		Influence.
W = 5		
I = 9	Total Name Number = 14	
N = 5	Birth ,, = 4	
T = 2	—	
E = 5	*Number of Character* = 18	
R = 9	= 9	
—	—	
35 = 8		

In the above example we see that the Number of Character is 9, which is exceedingly favourable. Nevertheless, there is a Secondary Character Influence of 12 to be considered, which modifies the qualities of number 9 by suggesting repression, uncertainty and lack of progress. Incidentally, these qualities rather serve to confirm the adverse ones given under number 9 in the table of primaries.

Many people possess only one forename and a surname, in which case, of course, there are no secondary influences—their character depends entirely upon a primary number. It is curious to note that those people who have no second names usually possess characters which are comparatively clear-cut and as lacking in complications as their names. Frequently, too, they are most successful people, with vivid personalities—a few selected at random from the pages of history being William Shakespeare, John Milton, Benjamin Disraeli (Lord Beaconsfield), and Arthur Wellesley (Duke of Wellington).

USES OF NUMEROLOGY

When you have discovered the significance of your own Number of Character, and also of your Secondary Character Influence, you should employ to advantage the knowledge so gained. Numerologists do not claim that the individual plays no active part in the formation of his own character, for mankind, unlike other works of Nature, has a rational mind, a soul, and a will; therefore it lies always within our power to correct our faults or to develop our virtues. It follows then that, by exposing your virtues and your weaknesses, numerology should be a material help to you in life.

Moreover, through a knowledge of the significance of numbers you will find it easier to understand people and to sympathize with their attitude towards life. You may be acquainted with one whom you consider to be morbid and unsociable, and perhaps you have had no opportunity of learning more about him. From a numerological analysis you may find that he reacts to number 7, and that morbidity and unsociability are merely the less desirable traits of a character which is really wise, discerning, strong and contemplative. Thus you will be able to cultivate and encourage the better side of his character, and to appreciate him for his virtues rather than condemn him for his faults.

You may know someone of the 5 type, whose qualities of adventurousness, courage and sympathy will make him popular; nevertheless, from your knowledge of numbers you will know that

J

he may possibly be inconstant and unreliable, and you will be well prepared if he exhibits these traits in dealings with yourself or others.

NUMBERS OF THE DAYS AND MONTHS

We have already seen that dates can be reduced to a primary number. Every day in every year reacts according to some number, as also does every month. On the accepted theory that all phenomena of the universe act together in harmony, we may assume that the days or months most favourable for the material or spiritual development of an individual are those of which the primary number is the same as his Birth, Personality or Character Number.

For example, a man born on June 14, 1962, possesses the Birth Number of 2 ($6+14+1962 = 1982 = 20 = 2$), and, we will suppose, the Personality Number of 3 and the Character Number of 6. Now, if on a certain date he contemplates taking some decisive step, either in business or personal matters, it would be a very favourable omen if this date reduced either to 2, 3 or 6.

NUMBERS OF THE DAYS OF THE WEEK

The days of the week also respond to vibrations of the primary numbers, irrespective of the date. Their influence is a minor one, but it is important enough to be taken into consideration. In the table below we give the days, together with the numbers which control them, and their significance. It will be seen that Sunday and Monday each respond to the vibrations of two numbers—1 and 8 and 2 and 9 respectively.

1. 8. *Sunday.* A day of achievement, self-knowledge and purpose.
2. 9. *Monday.* Conflict, indecision and sometimes failure; also calmness, justice, co-operation and balance.
3. *Tuesday.* A day of unexpected successes and general activity.
4. *Wednesday.* Hard work and steady progress, rather lacking in eventfulness.
5. *Thursday.* Great excitement and achievement, especially in matters requiring physical stamina.
6. *Friday.* Thought and inspiration; a day for pondering and philosophy.
7. *Saturday.* A good day for all forms of government and organization, as well as the acquisition of knowledge.

The vibrations of the days of the week may have their effect on a person, irrespective of his Number of Character.

Remember that the individual numbers of the days of the week have no effect when reckoning the Birth Number. For example, if the subject was born on a Friday it is the day of the month and the year which must be considered, not the fact that the day was a Friday. The same interpretations of the numbers of the days also apply, in a minor degree, to the individual months. Similarly, these vibrations are general and do not affect any particular Number of Character.

The months are numbered as follows:—January—1; February—2; March—3; April—4; May—5; June—6; July—7; August—8; September—9; October—1; November—2; December—3. Again, regarding the above numberings, we would remind the reader that he must not use these when reckoning Birth Numbers; for these the ordinary number of the month in the year must be taken as a basis of calculation.

Numbers of the Colours

The light which we receive from the sun consists of seven colours. They are given below, together with the numerical vibration of each colour.

Red	=	1 and 8
Orange	=	2 and 9
Yellow	=	3
Green	=	4
Blue	=	5
Indigo	=	6
Violet	=	7

The numbers of these colours have their effect on the Number of Character of an individual. It is a well-known fact, among specialists who make a study of human mentality, that colour can have a profound influence on a person. Some feel infinitely happier when they are in a room with yellow walls; others find that blue is the most cheerful colour; others still, violet. The general rule appears to be that the colour which has a number corresponding to the Number of Character of a person is the one which is likely to have the best effect upon him.

Thus, if the subject is a 5 type and wishes to live as harmoniously as possible, he would be advised to surround himself with objects which are blue in colour, for this colour is in sympathy with the number 5. If he is a 3 type, yellow will suit him best; if he is a 7 type, violet, and so on.

We must advise the reader against attempting to apply numerology to the numbers of lottery tickets or the names of race-horses, for the numbering or naming is purely artificial and without any traditional significance whatsoever. In such cases the law of chance is in operation; and, so far, this law has remained a total mystery to the mind of man. There are many who claim to have fathomed it, but all have been proved to be either charlatans or sadly misguided cranks. If it were solved it would mean the end of all forms of gambling, for who can imagine a sweepstake or game of chance taking place if it were known beforehand what number would win! Therefore we will not attempt to misguide our readers by professing to uphold some magical system which will bring them vast wealth.

It is worth mentioning, however, that the numbers 3 and 7 are traditionally regarded as being very auspicious, and they have certainly been predominant among the winning numbers of sweep-stake tickets—either in actual figures or else as the result of reducing a large number to one of the primaries.

VERTICAL TABULATION

There is a very ancient system of prediction of the future by numbers which is known as "vertical tabulation."

Suppose, for example, the subject was born in the year 1958; set down his birth date twice as follows and perform a simple addition:

$$
\begin{array}{r}
1958 \\
1 \\
9 \\
5 \\
8 \\
\hline
1981 \\
\hline
\end{array}
$$

The result, which is 1981, is said to indicate a year of great importance in the subject's life. The vertical tabulation can be carried farther, this time taking 1981 as a basis:

$$
\begin{array}{r}
1981 \\
1 \\
9 \\
8 \\
1 \\
\hline
2000
\end{array}
$$

The year 2000, in the same way, is said to hold some special significance. The tabulation can be carried on still further, taking 2000 as a basis, thus indicating the beginnings of various phases or great changes throughout a lifetime. Unlike the ancients, however, the modern numerologists do not place a great deal of faith in this method of prediction; but, nevertheless, there are some historical examples which must be attributed to something more than coincidence. The examples do not necessarily have a birth date as basis, but the date of some important occurrence. They do not tell us so much about individuals as about the life of a nation. For example:—

George I ascended the throne	1714
1+7+1+4	13
George II ascended the throne	1727
1+7+2+7	17
Preparations for Second Jacobite Rising	1744
1+7+4+4	16
George III ascended the throne	1760

It is also curious to note that Queen Victoria was born in 1819, the figures of which on being added give 19, which added to 1819 makes 1838, the year of the queen's coronation.

French history provides us with a famous example:—

Execution of Robespierre	1794
1+7+9+4	21
Final banishment of Napoleon I	1815
1+8+1+5	15
Abdication of Charles X	1830
1+8+3+0	12
Death of the Duke of Orleans, heir to Louis Philippe	1842

The fact that the South African War ended in 1902 (totalling

12) and the World War began twelve years afterwards, in 1914, is often instanced. Again, to refer to French history, Louis XVI came to the throne in 1774 $(1+7+7+4 = 19)$, nineteen years later, in 1793, he was guillotined.

There are many similar cases in history which the reader can discover for himself, and he can apply the same system to his own life and to those of his friends, taking birth dates as the basis of calculation.

It is in the study of the human character, however, that numerology is most valuable. The preceding pages have explained briefly the elements of the great science of numbers, and it now lies within the power of every reader to apply this science for the benefit of himself and his friends. Do not expect infallibly accurate results, for it must be remembered that numerology is based on interpretations as well as calculations, and that the former, obviously, cannot be so exact as the latter. With care and patience, however, there is little room for error in the compiling of an analysis, provided one is quite certain that the birth dates and names are correct.

Not only does numerology enable a deep and penetrating character reading to be made, but it affords innumerable possibilities as a form of entertainment and as an interesting hobby.

THE ART OF PHYSIOGNOMY

PHYSIOGNOMY is the art and science of reading character from the facial and bodily form. Under another aspect it means the divination or interpretation of a person's lineaments in prognosticating his future. Phrenology, or the art of reading the skull, and palmistry are branches of physiognomy, both of which are dealt with in other sections of our work.

The art of physiognomy is of ancient origin, and was held in high esteem by the Greeks, who relied largely upon it in assessing a man's character or fitness for high office. They taught that men might be compared with the animal in their physiognomy and character, some being noble and leonine, others swinish and brute-like, and so on.

We shall have more to say later about these animal comparisons. They were taken a great deal farther by a sixteenth-century Neapolitan, Giovanni Battista della Porta, the first to treat the subject in a really scientific manner. A century or more later a Swiss pastor, Johann Kaspar Lavater, produced a great treatise on physiognomy. Goethe, a friend of the author, wrote one of the chapters.

Lavater was a poet and mystic, but also a man of action. He met an early death as the result of a bullet wound inflicted by a French soldier when Zurich, his native city, was attacked by Masséna. Though Lavater was no scientist, and knew next to nothing of anatomy, his work was valuable because it was based on his observations, and was illustrated by him with hundreds of drawings of faces.

We next come to the studies of Peter Camper, a Dutch anatomist, who tried to show the evolution of the human countenance from that of apes and other animals (1781). A Scotsman, Sir Charles Bell, approached physiognomy from the domain of physiology (1806), showing the connexion between the expression of the emotions and the muscle movements accompanying it. Guillaume

Duchenne, a Paris physician, produced such expressions on people by stimulating certain muscles with an electric current (1862). Thus he obtained at will expressions of pleasure and pain, and others.

Charles Darwin made much use of Duchenne's work in his own book, *The Expression of the Emotions in Man and Animals*, published in 1872. Darwin was not concerned with physiognomy as such, but with the evolution of emotional expression. In his thorough and purposeful manner he spent years in the study of expression and laid down certain laws that are really the principles of scientific physiognomy. We shall state these later. Paolo Mantegazza, an Italian anthropologist, took up the story where Darwin had left off in his book, *Physiognomy and Expression* (1890).

CHARACTER PORTRAYED BY FEATURES

It is a truism that one may read a man's character in his face. We talk of an open face, a frank look, a sinister appearance, or a furtive glance. The impression we get from a person's countenance depends on form and expression. Some faces are beautiful, or noble, even in repose; and others, until lit up by a smile, are dull or even repelling. But the calm, reposeful and dignified face may go with an empty mind, and everyone knows that beauty of a statuesque, classical, placid type often accompanies an intellect unrelieved by flashes of brilliancy or sparks of wit.

The problem of judging character is complicated by the extent to which everyone dissimulates—often quite unknowingly. The repressions and limitations imposed by civilized society ensure that almost from the cradle man refrains from doing many things that he desires to do, or from showing emotions that are unacceptable to people about him.

The training and education of the young is largely concerned with self-discipline, and we all learn to mask our feelings. Some people are more successful in this than others; but when, under stress of strong emotion or great provocation, the control is relaxed, or even abandoned altogether, the observer sees a strange, and sometimes horrible, picture of primal feeling expressed in an unbridled manner.

The measure of the repression is the measure of the ebullition that ensues when control is lost. A person under the influence of drink or drugs, or when recovering from an anaesthetic, may reflect on his face the very depths of his mind, and we see the true man as he is. The calm, proud Juno of a woman may reveal her hidden traits: we learn that instead of a limpid pool, her character is a very maelstrom of conflicting impulses. The man of integrity, who takes a leading part in the religious life of the group to which he belongs, is betrayed, perhaps, as fundamentally a libidinous and sensual pleasure lover.

We must not attempt to judge such persons by these manifestations; rather should we acknowledge that in leading a moral and socially correct life in spite of such underlying impulses—in bravely and sternly combating the hidden urges—they are worthy of the highest praise.

It will now be apparent that in interpreting the physiognomy of a person we must not take everything at its "face" value. On the contrary, we must assess also the hidden factors and the measure in which the picture we see is a natural or an artificial one.

In this we are helped by the observance of certain marks and traits by which even the most correct and well-schooled subject may often betray himself. Since ancient times, too, physiognomists have formulated certain rules for our guidance, by which we can correctly interpret the elements of a person's physiognomy and attempt to appraise the hidden factors.

If we are prepared also to accept the theories of planetary influence and of consonances between human traits and animal features, then we have other gauges with which to measure personality and predilections.

Though up to the present we have spoken mainly of facial interpretation, it must be borne in mind that physiognomy is concerned with the whole body—its anatomy, or architecture, and its morphology, or form. Man owes to his parents and ancestors his basic make-up both physical and mental, but though no one "by taking thought can add one cubit unto his stature," yet everyone can modify his inheritance and play a great part in shaping his body and mind. If we can observe and recognize what our subject has done in this way, we can assess his potentiality both for the present and the future.

The Facial Framework

Overlying the bony case that holds the brain and forms the framework of the head are masses of muscles that move the eyes, lips, nostrils, jaws and cheeks; raise the eyebrows, wrinkle the brows or move the scalp. At a casual glance one skull looks very like another, but there are great variations that are obvious to the accustomed eye. Camper, whom we have already mentioned, invented the system of comparing the "facial angle" in different individuals, and though his system is no longer used, its principle is retained in the one that replaced it in 1882.

Camper measured the angle made with the horizontal by a line that touched the forehead and the jaw. He found that this facial angle was much less in the case of an orang-utan, for instance, than in that of a man.

Another means of comparing heads is to measure the cephalic index—the ratio of greatest width to greatest length. Thus, taking the length of the skull as 100, the width in dolichocephalic, or long-headed, individuals might be 70, and in brachycephalic, or broad-

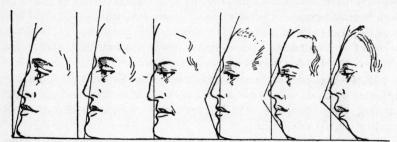

Facial Angle: Ardent; Moral; Dominant; Intellectual; Weak; Degenerate

headed, persons as much as 85. Then there are many variations in the shape of the cranium, as viewed from above; some being roughly oval and others somewhat spherical, with many intermediate forms.

Although these variations of form and angle have special significance in phrenology, they are pointed out here because of their effect upon, and association with, facial types and prevalent expression. A cast of features that might appear to convey an emotional trend might be due to nothing more than some inherited peculiarity of skull conformation.

Here, too, we must touch briefly upon an aspect of physiognomy that treats of the signs of disease—pathognomy. It will be enough for us merely to be aware that certain disorders—notably those connected with the functioning of the endocrine glands—grossly alter the subject's appearance. Acromegaly is a disorder that

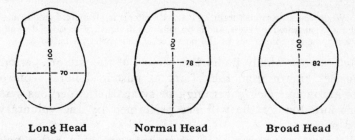

Long Head   **Normal Head**   **Broad Head**

affects the hands and feet and the jaws; the bones become enlarged and the subject's facial appearance changes very remarkably. Another manifestation of disorder in the working of the same gland at the base of the brain is what is known as gigantism or overgrowth. Certain glands in the neck influence diseases that may cause (a) a protruding of the eyeballs and a swelling below the chin, (b) swelling of the cheeks and lips, and thickening of the tongue, with a slowness of speech and action, (c) a dwarfing of growth and the appearance of idiocy or imbecility. These disorders in their early stages may be unrecognized, but may produce effects that mislead the physiognomist, for they affect expression to a very large extent.

A striking comparison may be made between the brain capacity of man and that of his nearest relatives; the index used by men of science is the relation between the brain weight and body weight. A gorilla's brain weighs about one two-hundredth of its body weight, and the brain of an average man one-fiftieth of his body weight. The brain weight of a prehistoric man has been computed from the skull and other bones to be about one-seventieth of his body weight.

Darwin's three principles of physiognomy may be stated briefly as follows:—

1. Certain acts are serviceable in some states of mind to relieve or gratify certain sensations or desires. Whenever the same state of mind is induced,

habit and association of ideas cause the same movements to be performed, though they may not be of the least use. Although some such actions may be checked by the use of the will, the repression will fail to affect certain muscles, and some expressive movements will still be performed despite the inhibition. Moreover, the act of checking certain movements will cause other muscle movements, and the latter are also expressive.

2. Certain mental states lead to related habitual actions, but when directly opposite states of mind are induced there is a strong and involuntary tendency for a reverse action to be carried out, though this, too, is of no service. Movements of this antithetic nature, like those mentioned in (1), are highly expressive.

3. When the sensorium (brain and nerve system) is strongly excited, nerve-force is generated in excess, and is transmitted in certain directions, depending partly on the connexions of the nerve cells, and partly on habit.

Actions not wholly under the control of the will are performed by muscles known from their form as unstriped fibres, controlled by the autonomic (self-governing), or sympathetic, nervous system. Actions initiated by the will are performed by the voluntary or striped muscles.

We must remember that many acts are of a reflex nature, performed without thought or willing. Instances are the blinking of the eyes and the drawing away of the hand from a hot surface. Actions like these, however, are performed also when there is no natural need for them.

Muscular action consists in a contracting of the fibres and a shortening of the muscle. This brings about a temporary puckering or wrinkling of the skin. We know that the more a muscle is used, the more it develops. Disuse of a muscle, on the other hand, causes a weakening of that organ. In course of time the furrows or wrinkles produced by oft-repeated muscle movements of the same sort will become permanent, especially as the skin loses its elasticity in later life. In this way we get the frown lines, the laughter lines, or the down-drooping mouth.

Not only is the skin modified by habitual expression, but the underlying tissues and even the bones themselves may alter in shape from the causes enumerated above. Then there are the innumerable little tricks of habit.

We shall deal first with morphology, or the form of a person's features, and show how to read the various members for the attributes they denote. Later we shall discuss expression, showing what generalizations can be drawn from the prevalent "feeling tones" displayed by face and gesture.

FORM AND FEATURES

In interpretative physiognomy we analyse and examine the different physical peculiarities of a person, assigning to them character values, and sum up the factors favourable and unfavourable. The main headings under which a subject is analysed are given below:—

STATURE, BUILD AND POSTURE				
HEIGHT	FIGURE	BUILD	CARRIAGE	ACTION
Tall Short	Stout Slender	Massive Slight	Erect Stooping	Brisk Leisurely Lethargic

HEAD AND FACE					
FOREHEAD	NOSE		EARS	CHIN	EYEBROWS
High Low Broad Narrow Prominent Receding	Large Small Aquiline Straight Hooked Pointed Retroussé	Thin Fleshy Broad Pinched	Large Small Pointed tops Close-set Projecting Bold rims Poor rims	Projecting Straight Receding Long Short Square Pointed	Arched Flat Oblique /\ Oblique \/

EYES		CHEEKS	MOUTH	HAIR	
Large Small Orbits deep Orbits shallow Lids drooping Lids hooded Bright Dull	Hazel Grey Greenish Blue Brown Black	Full Hollow Fleshy Dimpled Cheek-bones high	Large Small Lips thin Lips thick Lips parted Lips slack Lips tight	Straight Curly Wavy Abundant Thin	Brown, light Brown, dark Black, jet Black, bluish Auburn Red Flaxen Golden White

In order to simplify both the preliminary analyses and the subsequent reading of character we give below a table in which the salient qualities of a person are described by appropriate adjectives. It will be noted that with each attribute is given its opposite.

We may further simplify the process of compiling the character chart by regarding only the first term in each pair, indicating it by a number, and prefixing a minus sign (−) when we wish to denote absence of the attribute. Thus, for example, a prudent person would be distinguished by the index 28, and one whose physiognomy indicated rashness by − 28. A tendency between prudence and

TABLE OF ATTRIBUTES

1.	Moral strength Moral weakness	21.	Voluptuousness Apathy	41.	Despotism Obsequiousness
2.	Intellectuality Unintellectuality	22.	Extravagance Miserliness	42.	Arrogance Meekness
3.	Firmness Indecision	23.	Amorousness Indifference	43.	Jealousy Complacency
4.	Candour Secretiveness	24.	Courage Cowardice	44.	Contentedness Dissatisfaction
5.	Sincerity Insincerity	25.	Loyalty Treachery	45.	Hot temper Even temper
6.	Faithfulness Inconstancy	26.	Uprightness Unscrupulousness	46.	Vindictiveness Forgiveness
7.	Ardour Frigidity	27.	Refinement Coarseness	47.	Love Coldness
8.	Austerity Affability	28.	Prudence Rashness	48.	Affection Coolness
9.	Ambition Unambitiousness	29.	Nobleness Baseness	49.	Benevolence Malevolence
10.	Amiability Surliness	30.	Improvidence Thrift	50.	Nervousness Stolidity
11.	Boldness Timidity	31.	Modesty Shamelessness	51.	Prepotence Impotence
12.	Gentleness Harshness	32.	Docility Obstinacy	52.	Strength Weakness
13.	Kindness Cruelty	33.	Pride Humbleness	53.	Impetuosity Deliberation
14.	Generosity Avarice	34.	Sagacity Unwisdom	54.	Self-indulgence Asceticism
15.	Egotism Unselfishness	35.	Shrewdness Obtuseness	55.	Brilliance Mediocrity
16.	Activity Lethargy	36.	Prudishness Broadmindedness	56.	Artistic nature Inartistic nature
17.	Industry Laziness	37.	Neatness Untidiness	57.	Cunning Artlessness
18.	Sanguineness Melancholy	38.	Ostentation Unobtrusiveness	58.	Vivacity Listlessness
19.	Creativeness Unimaginativeness	39.	Charity Uncharitableness	59.	Passion Self-control
20.	Vanity Diffidence	40.	Frivolity Seriousness	60.	Truthfulness Mendacity

rashness would be shown by the sign ☉ prefixed to the number 28 (☉ 28). The numerical value of ☉ is ½.

It will be noted that this table contains physical, moral and intellectual attributes. The relative extent to which the qualities are present is shown as a numerical value or proportion in the summing up, is explained in the text.

INTERPRETATION OF A PHYSIOGNOMY BY FEATURES

The first step is to observe the *ensemble* of the subject. Is he tall or short, stout or spare, massive or slight, and so on. Does he walk with an erect carriage, moving briskly, or are his actions altogether more leisurely? Age and sex, of course, enter into the calculation, as does the physical condition of the subject. Let us deal first with a man aged from 25 to 45, in normal health. Modifications and allowances for the age factor—to say nothing of those connected with sex—will demand consideration later.

CHARACTERISTICS AND THEIR ATTRIBUTES	
Height	
Tall . . .	14, ☉51
Short . . .	−13, 51
Figure	
Stout . .	7, −16, ☉17, −51
Slender . .	−18, 23, 51
Build	
Massive . .	−8, 52
Slight . .	☉52
Carriage	
Erect . .	1, 28, ☉41
Stooping . .	☉1, −28, −38, −41
Action	
Brisk . .	3, 4, 5, 9, 24, −28
Leisurely .	10, 13, 14, 44, ☉48
Lethargic .	−4, −17, −20, 43
Forehead	
High . .	1, 2, 5, 18, ☉33, ☉51
Low . .	−1, −3, 7, ☉21, ☉27
Broad . .	14, 20, 25, 29, 37, 39, 48, 50
Narrow .	2, 3, 8, 16, 17, 35, 37
Prominent .	2, 9, 16, 25, 34
Receding .	−14, 15, 20, 21, 23, 43, −44, −52

304

Nose

Large	6, −15, 29, 49,
Small	−1, −3, 7, ⊙21, ⊙27
Aquiline	−13, 16, 32, 38, 42
Straight	−3, −6, 13, 48, 51
Hooked	7, 9, 20, 38, −44, 51
Pointed	⊙14, 17, 20, −30
Retroussé	10, 18, 20, 47, 48, 53
Thin	8, −18, −23, 43, −54
Fleshy	7, −14, 20, ⊙21, ⊙27, −37, 43
Broad	9, 15, 25, 48, 54
Pinched	−7, 15, −18, 35, 36, −54

Ears

Large	2, 5, 10, 18, 20, 28, ⊙51
Small	13, 27, 28, 31, −38, 39, 53
Pointed tops	15, 43, 54
Close-set	2, 5, 17, 34
Projecting	7, −13, ⊙14, 15, 20, 23, 35, 43, 54
Bold rims	14, ⊙17, 25
Poor rims	−12, 15, −26, −27, −44, 46, 51, 54,

Chin

Projecting	1, 3, 9, 16, 17, 51, 53
Straight	1, 2, 6, 15, 17, 27, 32, 35
Receding	−4, ⊙13, ⊙14, 15, ⊙27
Long	3, 8, 28
Short	5, 6, 48, 53
Square	1, 8, 18, 26
Pointed	5, 12, −15, 18, 25, ⊙28, 29, 31

Eyebrows

Arched	14, 26, 48, 53
Flat	3, ⊙7, 9, ⊙18, 43
Oblique /\	⊙6, ⊙13, ⊙20, 33, ⊙39, 42, 43
Oblique \/	4, ⊙6, 10, 14, 18, ⊙23, 37, 45, 53

Eyes

Large	5, ⊙7, 16, 18, ⊙23, 25, 48, ⊙51, 55, 60
Small	⊙3, ⊙14, 15, ⊙23, 28, 45, 53, ⊙60
Orbits deep	43, −44, ⊙46, ⊙50, 51, 53, 55
Orbits shallow	5, 10, 14, ⊙16, 39
Lids drooping	⊙17, 23, 33, 43, ⊙48, 54, ⊙55, 56, ⊙60
Lids hooded	⊙4, ⊙6, 7, ⊙13, 15, ⊙21, 35, ⊙46, ⊙57
Bright	4, 10, 14, 16, 18, 25, ⊙45, 48, ⊙50, 51 52, 53, 55, 56, 57, 58, 60
Dull	⊙7, ⊙10, 15, ⊙16, ⊙17, −18, −23, ⊙25, −37, −39, 43, ⊙46, −49, ⊙51, −53, 54, ⊙57, 58

CHARACTERISTICS AND THEIR ATTRIBUTES (*continued*)

Eyes (cont.)	
Hazel . . .	1, 2, ⊙3, 5, ⊙8, 9, 10, ⊙11, 13, 14, ⊙18, 24, 25, 28, 31, 33, 35, 43, ⊙45, 48, ⊙50, ⊙53, 58, 60
Grey . . .	1, 2, 3, 5, − 8, 9, ⊙12, ⊙13, 16, ⊙18, 24, 25, 26, 27, 28, 32, 33, 34, 37, ⊙39, 43, ⊙48, ⊙50, 51, 53, ⊙56, 60
Greenish . .	1, ⊙2, ⊙5, 9, ⊙15, ⊙20, ⊙23, ⊙28, 33, ⊙42, ⊙45, ⊙50, 53, 59
Blue . . .	1, 2, 4, 10, 12, 13, 14, 16, ⊙18, 24, 25, 26, 27, 28, 31, 33, ⊙34, ⊙35, ⊙43, − 46, 48, 51, ⊙53, ⊙55, ⊙58
Brown . . .	1, ⊙2, ⊙3, 4, 6, ⊙7, 8, 10, 12, 13, 14, ⊙16, 18, 24, 26, 29, 31, ⊙32, ⊙34, ⊙38, 39, 43, ⊙44, 45, 48, 50, 51, ⊙53, ⊙56, 60
Black . . .	9, ⊙12, ⊙14, 15, ⊙16, ⊙18, 20, ⊙21, 22, 23, ⊙25, 26, ⊙27, − 28, 33, ⊙34, ⊙37, ⊙38, ⊙42, 43, ⊙44, 46, 47, ⊙48, 51, 52, 53, ⊙54, 55, ⊙56, ⊙57, 59
Cheeks	
Full . . .	4, ⊙7, 11, 13, 18, ⊙20, ⊙25, 47, 48, 50, 51, ⊙55
Hollow . . .	1, − 7, 8, ⊙15, − 18, 20, ⊙22, 28, 31, 39, 43, − 54
Fleshy . . .	7, 15, 18, 20, ⊙25, 32, ⊙37, 43, − 44, ⊙47, ⊙51, 54
Dimpled . .	4, 12, 16, 18, ⊙20, 24, 26, 30, 31, 32, 37, ⊙38, 39, 40, 47, ⊙51, 53, 56, 60
Cheek-bones high .	9, ⊙13, 15, 16, 20, 22, 23, ⊙25, 33, 35, 37, ⊙42, 43, 59
Mouth	
Large . . .	4, 5, 10, 13, 14, 18, 20, 28, 39, ⊙43, 47, − 50, 51, ⊙54
Small . . .	⊙1, 9, 12, 18, ⊙20, ⊙23, 25, ⊙28, 31, 33, 40, 45, 48, 53, 56
Lips thin . .	3, − 7, ⊙8, 15, 17, ⊙24, − 32, −53
Lips thick . .	⊙3, ⊙7, 13, 14, 18, ⊙30, 39, 43, 51, 54, 59
Lips parted . .	8, 12, 18, 25, 38, 39, ⊙40, 44, − 46, 47, 48, − 50, 51, 53, 56, 58, ⊙59
Lips slack . .	− 3, − 6, ⊙13, 21, − 26, − 37, − 39, 43, ⊙47, ⊙51, ⊙57, 59
Lips tight . .	3, − 7, 9, 15, 28, − 32, 41, 46, − 48, 51, − 53
Hair	
Straight . .	3, 12, ⊙16, 17, ⊙18, ⊙20, ⊙40, ⊙45, ⊙50, ⊙53
Curly . . .	⊙3, 5, ⊙8, 13, 16, 18, ⊙20, 30, ⊙32, ⊙33, 51, 52, 53, 54, 56, 59
Wavy . . .	2, 9, 14, ⊙18, 43, 45, 48, 50, 51, 52, 55, 59
Abundant . .	10, 14, 18, 20, ⊙21, 43, 48, 51, 53, 59
Thin . . .	15, ⊙18, 28, − 32, 43, ⊙51, 53
Brown, light . .	1, 2, ⊙3, ⊙7, 12, 15, 43, 45
Brown, dark . .	1, ⊙2, ⊙3, 9, 18, 25, 26, 47
Black, jet . .	1, 3, 6, ⊙7, 18, 20, ⊙21, − 28, − 38, ⊙42, 43, 45, 53, 59

CHARACTERISTICS AND THEIR ATTRIBUTES (*continued*)	
Hair (cont.)	
Black, bluish . .	⊙1, ⊙2, 3, ⊙25, 33, −40, 47, ⊙50, 53, ⊙54, 55, 56
Auburn . .	− 6, 9, 10, 16, 25, 33, 43, ⊙45, ⊙46, 48, 51, ⊙53, ⊙59
Red . . .	⊙6, − 15, 18, ⊙20, 23, ⊙25, ⊙28, 33, 40, 43, ⊙46, 48, 51, 53, 55, 58, 59
Flaxen . .	2, ⊙3, 5, ⊙6, 12, 14, 18, 28, ⊙45, 47, ⊙51, ⊙53, 56, 58
Golden . .	4, 5, 12, 14, ⊙15, ⊙18, 25, 33, ⊙43, 45, ⊙53, 56, 58, 59
White . .	2, 4, 5, 6, ⊙8, 10, 12, 13, ⊙14, ⊙15, 18, ⊙19, 24, 25, 27, 33, 37, 49, ⊙53, 55, 56, 60

A PRACTICAL INTERPRETATION

Our subject for the reading shall be a man aged 25, tall, slender, of slight build. His carriage is erect, his actions somewhat leisurely. His forehead is low, narrow and prominent; his nose small, aquiline and somewhat fleshy. His ears are fairly large, closely set, and with well-defined rims; his chin is straight, short and square. The eyebrows slant downwards to a slight extent, so that in assessing this feature we must take it at about half the tabular value. Eyes are hazel, fairly large, in shallow orbits. Cheeks are hollow, and the cheek-bones fairly high. The mouth is small, with thickish lips that are generally parted. The subject's hair is abundant, dark brown in colour, and wavy. A full analysis of this individual is given in the table that follows:—

PHYSIOGNOMICAL ANALYSIS—MAN, AGED 25	
Tall	14, ⊙51
Slender . . .	− 18, 23, 51
Slight	⊙52
Erect	1, 28, ⊙41
Leisurely . . .	10, 13, 14, 44, ⊙48,
Forehead, low . .	− 1, − 3, 7, ⊙21, ⊙27
Forehead, narrow .	2, 3, 8, 16, 17, 35, 37
Forehead, prominent .	2, 9, 16, 25, 34
Nose, small . . .	− 1, − 3, 7, ⊙21, ⊙27

PHYSIOGNOMICAL ANALYSIS—MAN, AGED 25 (*continued*)

Nose, aquiline	− 13, 16, 32, 38, 42
Nose, fleshy	7, − 14, 20, ⊙21, ⊙27, − 37, 43
Ears, large	2, 5, 10, 18, 20, 28, ⊙51
Ears, close-set	2, 5, 17, 34
Ears, bold rims	14, ⊙17, 25
Chin, straight	1, 2, 6, 15, 17, 27, 32, 35
Chin, short	5, 6, 48, 53
Chin, square	1, 8, 18, 26
Eyebrows, oblique \/	4, ⊙6, 10, 14, 18, ⊙23, 37, 45, 53
Eyes, large	5, ⊙7, 16, 18, ⊙23, 25, 48, ⊙51, 55, 60
Eyes, shallow orbits	5, 10, 14, ⊙16, 39
Eyes, hazel	1, 2, ⊙3, 5, ⊙8, 9, 10, ⊙11, 13, 14, ⊙18, 24, 25, 28, 31, 33, 35, 43, ⊙45, 48, ⊙50, ⊙53, 58, 60
Cheeks, hollow	1, − 7, 8, ⊙15, − 18, 20, ⊙22, 28, 31, 39, 43, − 54
Cheeks, high cheek-bones	9, ⊙13, 15, 16, 20, 22, 23, ⊙25, 33, 35, 37, ⊙42, 43, 59
Mouth, small	⊙1, 9, 12, 18, ⊙20, ⊙23, 25, ⊙28, 31, 33, 40, 45, 48, 53, 56
Mouth, lips thick	⊙3, ⊙7, 13, 14, 18, ⊙30, 39, 43, 51, 54, 59
Mouth, lips parted	8, 12, 18, 25, 38, 39, ⊙40, 44, − 46, 47, 48, − 50, 51, 53, 56, 58, ⊙59
Hair, wavy	2, 9, 14, ⊙18, 43, 45, 48, 50, 51, 52, 55, 59
Hair, abundant	10, 14, 18, 20, ⊙21, 43, 48, 51, 53, 59
Hair, dark brown	1, ⊙2, ⊙3, 9, 18, 25, 26, 47

In reading these features and giving them values we set down on the blank chart the numerical constants found under the names of features on pages 303–306. A positive value given by one feature may be set off by a negative value denoted by some other feature. In such a case we shall add the positives and deduct the numbers prefixed with a minus sign. The value remaining will be that which we have to consider. Let us take an actual instance from our reading:—

Low forehead indicates −1, −3, 7, ⊙21, ⊙27; narrow forehead denotes 2, 3, 8, 16, 17, 35, 37; and prominent forehead indicates 2, 9, 16, 25, 34.

Now we will take the mouth; it is small:

⊙1, 9, 12, 18, ⊙20, ⊙23, 25, ⊙28, 31, 33, 40, 45, 48, 53, 56; the lips are thick:

⊙3, ⊙7, 13, 14, 18, ⊙30, 39, 43, 51, 54, 59; and the lips are parted:

8, 12, 18, 25, 38, 39, ⊙40, 44, −46, 47, 48, −50, 51, 53, 56, 58, ⊙59.

With these characteristics alone we are able to form some idea of the temperament and propensities indicated for our subject.

First set down the index numbers of the attributes in a column, and against each index number write the values obtained from forehead and mouth, putting 1 for each time a positive quality is indicated, $\frac{1}{2}$ for each time the median value ($\odot$) is shown, and -1 for each minus value.

Next, the values are to be summed up for each index number and the total set opposite every one, as shown in the following

PARTIAL SUMMATION OF THE ANALYSIS			
No.	No.	No.	No.
1. .. $-1, \frac{1}{2}$	17. .. 1	33. .. 1	46. .. -1
2. .. 1, 1	18. .. 1, 1, 1	34. .. 1	47. .. 1
3. .. -1, 1, $\frac{1}{2}$	20. .. $\frac{1}{2}$	35. .. 1	48. .. 1, 1
7. .. 1, $\frac{1}{2}$	21. .. $\frac{1}{2}$	37. .. 1	50. .. -1
8. .. 1, 1	23. .. $\frac{1}{2}$	38. .. 1	51. .. 1, 1
9. .. 1, 1	25. .. 1, 1, 1	39. .. 1, 1	53. .. 1, 1
12. .. 1, 1	27. .. $\frac{1}{2}$	40. .. 1, $\frac{1}{2}$	54. .. 1
13. .. 1	28. .. $\frac{1}{2}$	43. .. 1	56. .. 1, 1
14. .. 1	30. .. $\frac{1}{2}$	44. .. 1	58. .. 1
16. .. 1, 1	31. .. 1	45. .. 1	59. .. 1, $\frac{1}{2}$

table. It now remains to decode the index numbers and to set down the total values, when we shall have a picture—instructive, although incomplete—of our subject's character:—

Moral strength ..	..	..	$-\frac{1}{2}$	Pride ..	..	..	1
Intellectuality ..	..	..	2	Sagacity ..	..	..	1
Firmness	..	..	$\frac{1}{2}$	Shrewdness	..	..	1
Ardour ..	..	..	$1\frac{1}{2}$	Neatness	..	..	1
Austerity	..	..	2	Ostentation	..	..	1
Ambition	..	..	2	Charity ..	..	..	2
Gentleness	..	..	2	Frivolity	..	..	$1\frac{1}{2}$
Kindness	..	..	1	Jealousy ..	..	..	1
Generosity	..	..	1	Contentedness ..	..	..	1
Activity ..	..	..	2	Hot temper	..	..	1
Industry ..	..	..	1	Vindictiveness ..		..	-1
Sanguineness	..	..	3	Love ..	..	..	1
Vanity ..	..	..	$\frac{1}{2}$	Affection	..	..	2
Voluptuousness ..	..	..	$\frac{1}{2}$	Nervousness	..		.. -1
Amorousness	..	..	$\frac{1}{2}$	Prepotence	..	..	2
Loyalty ..	..	..	3	Impetuosity	..	..	2
Refinement	..	..	$\frac{1}{2}$	Self-indulgence ..		..	1
Prudence	..	..	$\frac{1}{2}$	Artistic nature ..		..	2
Improvidence	..	..	$\frac{1}{2}$	Vivacity ..	..	..	1
Modesty ..	..	..	1	Passion ..	..	..	$1\frac{1}{2}$

We can easily simplify the interpretation by grouping similar qualities: ardour and prepotence, $3\frac{1}{2}$; gentleness and kindness, 3; generosity and charity, 3; activity and industry, 3; vanity and ostentation, $1\frac{1}{2}$; sagacity and shrewdness, 2; hot temper and passion, $2\frac{1}{2}$; love and affection, 3; impetuosity (after allowing for prudence, $\frac{1}{2}$), $1\frac{1}{2}$. This leaves: intellectuality, 2; austerity, 2; ambition, 2; sanguineness, 3; loyalty, 3; pride, 1; neatness, 1; frivolity, $1\frac{1}{2}$; jealousy, 1; contentedness, 1; self-indulgence, 1; artistic nature, 2; vivacity, 1. Lack of nervousness is indicated (1) and absence of a vindictive nature (1). Attributes of the value of $\frac{1}{2}$ we can ignore altogether.

It will be noted that our system goes a great deal farther than many others; not only does it indicate presence or absence of an attribute, but it applies to the attribute a numerical value by which it can be compared with other qualities. A quick interpretation of a physiognomy may be obtained from the height, figure, forehead, nose, mouth, eyes and hair.

Quickness and accuracy will come with practice. A supply of blank charts (see page 310) can be got from a written or typed copy by use of a duplicator, and the interpretation written in numbers on one of these. From this the result can be indicated on a copy of the Table of Qualities, a tick or cross being placed against the attributes in question. Comparative numerical values need not be used, but predominant attributes might be underlined on the copy.

INTERPRETATION OF EXPRESSION

On the surface it would seem a fairly easy task to interpret a subject's expression, dubbing him benevolent or harsh, cynical or tolerant, frank or secretive, jovial or melancholy, as the case might be. But there is such a thing as duality of personality, with its accompanying duality of expression trend; and there is the case of a prevailing expression that is nothing but a mask.

We know the beautiful woman with a lovely complexion, so placid and unmoved by passing events; she has not, seemingly, a single care in the world. Nevertheless, she *has* one dominant and over-riding care—the maintenance of a youthful beauty unmarred by lines or wrinkles.

We know, too, a man who for years bore a reputation for shrewd wisdom and for keeping his own counsel. Was this not vouched for by his pursed-up mouth and seldom parted lips? And by the fact that he hardly ever spoke unless addressed? The explanation was that he had some years before parted with most of his teeth and had not replaced them by dentures!

Expression, none the less, is a reliable guide to character, although we cannot always appraise it at its "face value." The spoiled little girl pouts unconsciously when she is thwarted; a little later in life she pouts consciously to get her whims satisfied by her doting parents. If she is pretty and attractive, she pouts to bend

BLANK CHART FOR INTERPRETATIONS

Attribute No.	Total	Attribute No.	Total
1.		31.	
2.		32.	
3.		33.	
4.		34.	
5.		35.	
6.		36.	
7.		37.	
8.		38.	
9.		39.	
10.		40.	
11.		41.	
12.		42.	
13.		43.	
14.		44.	
15.		45.	
16.		46.	
17.		47.	
18.		48.	
19.		49.	
20.		50.	
21.		51.	
22.		52.	
23.		53.	
24.		54.	
25.		55.	
26.		56.	
27.		57.	
28.		58.	
29.		59.	
30.		60.	

her sweetheart to her will. All this time she is laying the foundation of wrinkles and lines that will mark her for life as a petulant, hard-to-please woman. By the time she has grown out of these little tricks the marks are ineffaceable.

Another woman makes a little *moue* whenever something surprises or chagrins her. It is not a real pout, for her disposition is a merry, contented one, but it leaves a trace that one can recognize, although it must on no account be confused with the sign just described.

The frowner began as a child by wrinkling his brow in displeasure; he goes on through life "frowning" at all sorts of things. Almost any stimulus will evoke this response. Beware of the mistake of taking this sign, uncorroborated, as a portent of irritability or bad temper.

Some young people cultivate a cynical attitude towards life; though but a pretence, it soon leaves indelible lines on their features. The true cynic may be discerned by other marks, but it is certainly true that one who begins by pretending to be a cynic may sooner or later acquire this unhappy outlook on the world. In like manner, too, the girl who pouts may willy-nilly develop a petulant, peevish temperament.

The would-be "strong, silent man" in his unguarded moments may be anything but silent and self-controlled, and, perhaps, never was strong. In these days some people ape their favourite film stars; starting perhaps with a slight resemblance, they assist Nature by tricks of "beauty-culture," and then simulate the acts and mannerisms of their prototype. It is an innocent aspiration, a seeking after betterment, and we are concerned with the phenomenon here only for the reason that the interpreter of physiognomy must take it into account.

Lavater said: "Faces are as legible as books, only they are read in much less time, and are much less likely to deceive us." We may set off against this a saying of another, that "Faces are as paper money, for which, on demand, there frequently proves to be no gold in the coffer."

We are not expressly concerned here with psychology, but we may say that a person often shows himself forth as he imagines he is. To this extent his face tells a true story, but we may discern, if we read aright, that he falls far short of his aims and aspirations.

Then there is that strange complex that moves a man or a woman conscious of timidity or diffidence to adopt in public an attitude of boldness, hauteur, or even arrogance; and for the naturally quiet, "bookish" individual to assume on occasion the manner of a man of the world or raconteur. This is why even the abstemious man may astonish his family occasionally by coming home tipsy. We see, therefore, that a sign may betoken quite the opposite attribute from that ordinarily associated with it.

As the years go by the expression lines become more emphasized, for the skin loses its suppleness, and after being moved by the muscles a great many times to form furrows and wrinkles it tends to remain in this state. We must not, therefore, take strongly marked lines necessarily to denote strongly marked characteristics, except in comparing two subjects of much the same age. The lines are plainer to see and to read—that is all. A woman's skin retains its elasticity longer, but the ravages of age, when they do at last manifest themselves, are harder to hide.

How Age and Sex Affect the Interpretation

Some attributes are predominantly masculine ones; others are essentially feminine. Intellectuality in women is worth more as an attribute than in men. When it is indicated in a female subject we shall give it a value a quarter as large again as the numerical one. Other qualities that are to be dealt with in this way are candour, faithfulness, vanity, voluptuousness, refinement, modesty, docility, pride, neatness, frivolity, jealousy, love, affection, impetuosity, vivacity and passion. That is to say, in a man and woman whose features indicate an equal numerical value for any or all of these attributes, the woman would be credited with $1\frac{1}{4}$ to the male subject's 1, and so on. There are also certain negative attributes that are stronger in woman. Insincerity, inconstancy, timidity, melancholy, unscrupulousness, obstinacy, meekness, complacency, artlessness and mendacity—all should be increased by a quarter. Then there are attributes that require to be diminished in valuation in a female subject: ambition, avarice, egotism, treachery and self-control are examples. A valuation of 75 per cent is appropriate. With regard to the remainder of the attributes in our table, no discrimination need ordinarily be made for the sex of the subject. It will be useful to set out the result of the above modifications in a tabular form.

INTERPRETATION OF FEMALE PHYSIOGNOMY

POSITIVE ATTRIBUTES TO BE INCREASED IN VALUE 25 PER CENT			
Intellectuality	Voluptuousness	Pride	Love
Candour	Refinement	Neatness	Affection
Faithfulness	Modesty	Frivolity	Impetuosity
Vanity	Docility	Jealousy	Vivacity
		Passion	
NEGATIVE ATTRIBUTES TO BE INCREASED 25 PER CENT			
Insincerity	Timidity	Unscrupulousness	Meekness
Inconstancy	Melancholy	Obstinacy	Complacency
	Artlessness	Mendacity	
ATTRIBUTES TO BE DIMINISHED IN VALUE 25 PER CENT			
Ambition	Avarice	Egotism	Treachery
		Self-control	

We have already warned the physiognomist of the pitfalls to be avoided in reading from expression. A man conceals his identity much less than a woman, and in dealing with the latter the interpreter must seek to discern the basic and underlying truth. Engage the subject in conversation while making an analysis, and watch for unconscious manifestations of character. We must not neglect such other signs as manner and style of dress; use of cosmetics; degree of care betrayed by the hair, skin and hands; extent to which jewellery is worn, and so on. Gloves, stockings and footwear—each has its own story to tell.

THE JUVENILE PHYSIOGNOMY

The interpretation of a child's physiognomy is a much more delicate matter than that of an adult. In some respects it is easier to delineate and in others it is more difficult. The attributes denoted by the features are largely a promise for the future, and only the primary propensities are likely to be manifest at an early age. In youthful subjects we must rely to a greater extent on expression, though here we have to avoid a too hasty judgment or an over-valuation of an attribute.

All healthy children have a fair measure of propensities un-acceptable in an adult: anger, prevarication, mendacity, self-will, a disposition to rebel against authority and a dislike of discipline and restraint—these are met with in the average youngster and we must not regard them as unfavourable. The eyes and lips will furnish signs of great value, since their portents are apparent at a very early age. The face seen in profile will be eloquent in its tale of moral and intellectual attributes.

Since the interpretation, as we indicated, is chiefly a foreshadow-ing of future character, the physiognomist must not be too dogmatic in his prognostications. Attributes that to-day are barely dis-cernible may in a year or two become so strong as to alter the story materially. At the seventh, tenth and thirteenth years of life a truer picture is presented than at intermediate ages, though an interpretation made at seven years may be somewhat different from one six years later.

It is obvious, therefore, that the physiognomist, in dealing with children, must speak of potentialities rather than of qualities—of what the boy or girl should be in the future rather than what he or she is now. The environment of the child a year or two later may affect its character to a great extent; at such a plastic and impressionable period of life it is not possible to do more than indicate lines along which the character should develop, and, even then, the physiognomist's verdict may be upset by later events.

PLANETARY PHYSIOGNOMY

From ancient times certain well-defined types of physiognomy have been invested with astrological significances, and related to the Sun, Moon and Earth, or to the planets Mercury, Mars, Venus, Jupiter, Uranus, Saturn and Neptune.

The types are described below. They are familiar ones, though they may have passed unnoticed hitherto. The physiognomist soon learns that the people round about him can readily be grouped into a few classes, and, as his observation becomes keener and he assimilates the principles of the science, he finds the classes can be subdivided still further.

Again and again he will be struck with the fact that in spite of the seemingly infinite variety in faces, there are some that are essentially very like each other. This physical likeness in unrelated persons is astonishing. Royal persons have their "doubles," as have humbler individuals also. Are not a number of historical romances founded on a striking resemblance between one "born in the purple" and another who saw the light in a peasant's hut? Folk-lore is full of tales of "changelings" and "doubles."

To what degree does this physical resemblance indicate a similarity of character and attributes? Between persons of a like station the resemblance may be very close; in fact, it is sound practice for the physiognomist to ascribe like attributes to such individuals. In his readings of subjects he builds up a fund of knowledge upon which he can draw for a quick interpretation of a person's features. Like the physician he learns from past experience and applies his knowledge to new problems.

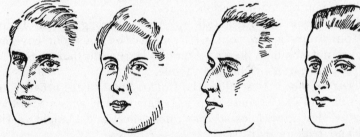

Solar Type Lunar Type Saturnine Type Mercurial Type

The well-marked types that we describe below are real ones, whether or not we accept the doctrine of planetary typology and its astrological significance. The latter theory is an interesting one, and it is remarkable that it has held credence for so many centuries.

Solar type. Tall or medium in height; rounded oval face, not too fleshy; complexion fresh; nose aquiline; fair hair; light eyes; leisurely gait and deliberate actions.

Lunar type. Stature medium to short; broad, rounded, fleshy face; pale complexion; bold, broad forehead; short, rounded nose; light brown hair; grey, moist eyes; action sometimes hesitant and undecided.

Mundane (Earthy) type. Broad, squat figure; prominent bones and squarish face; broad, prominent nose; strong jaws; hair and eyebrows thick and dark, the former growing low on forehead; dark eyes; action brisk but jerky.

Mercurial type. Tall and thin; face long and angularly oval;

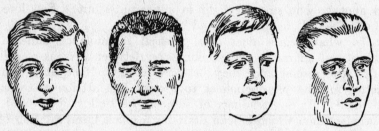

Venusian Type   Mundane Type   Jupiterian Type   Martian Type

long, narrow forehead; dark hair; thin, long nose; eyes dark and sparkling; gait brisk and action smart.

Martian type. Neither tall nor short; strong, broad frame; facial framework square, but well rounded by muscular covering, and hence not angular; nose aquiline; hair generally fair or reddish; eyes green to hazel, bright and mobile.

Venusian type. Resembles the Lunar, but body is broader and not so tall, and face is more elliptical; hair brown; eyes also brown, or may be bluish; complexion clear; nose short and straight; action smart, and tripping gait.

Jupiterian type. Shortish, thick-set body, inclined to corpulence; face oval or hexagonal; forehead high and broad; hair midbrown; eyes blue or brown; nose aquiline, fleshy; complexion fresh, inclined to floridness; gait stately and action deliberate.

Uranian type. Tall and spare in build, conveying an impression of strength; face somewhat angular with rugged, bold features; hair dark; eyes dark and piercing; complexion pale or rather sallow; action brisk.

Saturnine type. Tall, thin; face long and angular; broad forehead; nose aquiline, prominent and bony; high and prominent cheek-bones; dark hair, sometimes black; sallow or pale complexion; gait slow, action deliberate.

Neptunian type. Somewhat short and lean; long, lean face; high forehead; fair hair; light eyes; action nervous; gait jerky.

We give below a list of the qualities and characteristics attributed to the different planetary types, and by decoding the numerical indexes an interpretation can be obtained for each:—

Interpretation of Planetary Attributes
(See table of attributes on page 302.)

Solar: 11, 15, 29, 33, – 40, 41, 42, – 51
Lunar: 6, 9, ⊙18, 23, 32, – 37, 48, – 60
Mundane: 16, 17, – 27, 35, 51, 52
Mercurial: – 8, 16, 17, 35, 55, 57, 58
Martian: 11, 16, 18, 22, 24, 33, 38, 45, 59
Venusian: ⊙7, 27, – 38, 47, 48, 54, 56
Jupiterian: 13, 14, 18, 33, 39, – 40
Uranian: 6, 11, 41, 50, 53
Saturnine: – 4, 6, – 12, 15, 16, – 18, – 23,
    26, 28, 30, 50, 54
Neptunian: – 6, 15, 21, – 26, 50, 53, 54, 56

The above table can be used alone for a reading, or its results can be added to those obtained by a reading of the features in the manner described earlier.

Animal Resemblances

The resemblances with which we shall deal are mainly facial ones, but they can be supplemented by analogies drawn between the habits, gait and bearing of our subject and his animal simile.

We can readily distinguish lion-like and bear-like personalities; the ox-like and sheep-like types are easy to discern also. We talk of a man being bull-headed or sheepish, and describe a surly, gruff man as a bear, or a vindictive woman as a cat; "ass," "pig" and "fox" are terms commonly used of people who merit our ridicule or to whom we have taken a dislike.

There are seventeen chief types, designated by names formed from Latin or Greek words denoting the tribe to which the animal prototypes belong. They are as follows: 1, Leonine (lion-like); 2, Feline (cat-like or tigerish); 3, Canine (dog-like); 4, Equine (horse-like); 5, Ovine (sheep-like); 6, Bovine (ox-like); 7, Ursine (bear-like); 8, Porcine (pig-like); 9, Asinine (ass-like); 10, Lupine (wolf-like); 11, Putorine (ferret-like); 12, Ichthyine (fish-like); and 13, Avian (bird-like). Among the Avian types we may distinguish several varieties; for instance, 14, Corvine (crow-like); 15, Aquiline (eagle-like); 16, Strigidine (owl-like); 17, Psittacine (parrot-like).

Note that some of these are directly associated with the corresponding astrological signs of the zodiac: Leo (1), Aries (5), Taurus (6) and Pisces (12).

ANIMAL TYPES AND ATTRIBUTES
(See table of attributes on page 302)

1. Leonine: 1, 3, 5, 10, 14, 18, 24, 26, 28, 33, − 53, 60
2. Feline: − 5, 6, ⊙13, 20, 30, 43, 47, 50, 53, − 60
3. Canine: 6, − 15, 24, 32, 34, 44, 48, 60
4. Equine: 5, 8, 14, 18, 24, 33, 47
5. Ovine: 5, − 9, − 11, 12, − 15, − 19, − 32, 36, − 48, 50, −55, − 58
6. Bovine: 3, 21, − 32, 43, 53, 54
7. Ursine: 3, 5, 6, 20, 24, 41, 45, 53, 57
8. Porcine: − 5, 14, − 18, 23, 35, − 44, 46, 57
9. Asinine: − 17, − 27, 35, 44, − 50, 54, 55
10. Lupine: − 6, 9, − 10, 11, − 13, − 18, 35, 43, 44, 46, 53, 57
11. Putorine: − 4, − 6, 11, − 14, 15, ⊙24, ⊙25, − 26, − 41, 57, − 60
12. Ichthyine: − 4, 15, ⊙16, ⊙17, − 18, 20, 21, − 22, 30, ⊙57
13. Avian: 2, − 5, − 6, − 48, − 56, ⊙60
14. Corvine: − 6, 11, − 14, − 25, 35, − 49, 57, − 60
15. Aquiline: 3, 11, 15, 24, 41
16. Strigidine: 3, − 13, − 23, − 24, ⊙32, 35, 37, − 47, − 50, ⊙55
17. Psittacine: − 1, − 2, 4, 15, − 27, ⊙49, 53, 54, 57

THE SCIENCE OF PHRENOLOGY

PHRENOLOGY was founded by a physician, Franz Joseph Gall. He was born near Pforzheim, in Baden, in 1758, studied medicine, and later practised his profession at Vienna. While at school he had noticed that some of his playmates who were proficient in certain subjects were marked by various physical peculiarities, and that a difference of physical features often characterized a difference of disposition. Some boys, for instance, were apt at repetition of passages from memory; he observed that such scholars had full, prominent eyes. Gall was thus led to think that a particular aptitude could be discerned by a physical sign that accompanied it. In later life at the university he found much to support his ideas, which he was carefully, though gropingly, trying to build up into a theory.

Earlier philosophers and physiologists had thought that the seat of the dispositions and passions might be located in the chest and abdomen, though the mind or intellect was believed by some to reside in the brain. Gall came to the conclusion that the brain was the organ of mind; that its shape and development varied according to the development of particular regions that were the seat of certain faculties and propensities; and that the shape of the skull or brain-pan roughly corresponded to the convolutions and prominences of the brain itself.

Gall began to lecture on his theories in 1796, at Vienna. Among his students was Johann Caspar Spurzheim, who later assisted Gall in the work and gave his own impress to the young science. Gall examined a great many heads of living individuals, seeking out anyone who was notable for possessing certain traits—good or evil—and endeavouring to trace a consonance between head formation and mental endowment. He visited criminal courts, prisons, and asylums, and examined heads of criminals after execution, and in these and other ways collected innumerable important facts to serve as a foundation for his theory of phrenology.

Gall's propositions met with a good deal of hostility; he was opposed by the Church, who saw in his teachings a danger to her doctrines, and was looked at askance by leaders of his own profession. He went to Paris and there carried on his studies and his educational work. It brought him little honour and scanty material reward, for he died there, almost in poverty, in 1828. Spurzheim did much to spread the knowledge of phrenology in Britain and America; he died at Boston, U.S.A., in 1832.

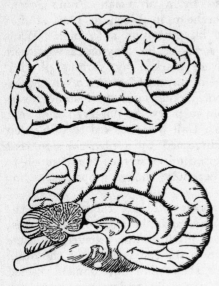

George Combe was one of the earliest exponents of phrenology in Britain. He attended Spurzheim's lectures and demonstrations in Scotland, and though at first he viewed with profound distrust the theories set forth, he later became convinced of the truth of Spurzheim's teachings. Pursuing the investigation further, he contributed to a Scottish magazine a series of essays on phrenology, which he later enlarged into a *System* and published separately, in 1819. Combe, like his predecessors, encountered great hostility in his propaganda; he met with

The Brain

ridicule, abuse and misrepresentation, but his book was widely read and ran into a number of editions.

Combe visited the continents of Europe and America in search of fresh data and facts. He put forward a scheme for the phrenological examination of convicts destined to be transported to the penal settlements, so that those whose propensities showed them to be incorrigible should not be sent to the young Australian colonies, there to become a menace and a corruption to the settlements.

Atrocities perpetrated in New South Wales by some of the felons had inflamed public opinion in the home country, and there was a demand that only the less evilly disposed convicts should be transported; really bad characters, it was urged, should be kept in prison in Britain. Phrenological examination, Combe and his supporters avowed, would disclose which people might safely be sent to the colonies.

It must be remembered that these unhappy people were largely employed in public and private work of all sorts in the settlements,

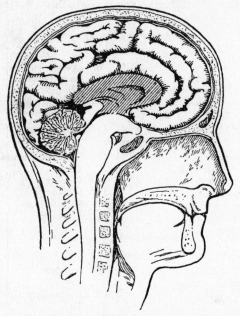

The Brain in Relation to the Skull

and numbers were hired out to the colonists as servants and labourers. Hence arose the danger of indiscriminate transportation.

Combe had many supporters among the medical men and public men of his day. In the course of his studies he examined the heads of prisoners in jails, and without any knowledge of their history he analysed their propensities. When his readings were compared with the prison records, a substantial and remarkable agreement was revealed.

THE PHRENOLOGICAL ORGANS

Gall and Spurzheim located about thirty "organs" that were representative of mental faculties, assigning to them particular

K

regions of the skull. Combe, in the last edition of his *System of Phrenology*, listed thirty-five organs, twenty-one of them affective and fourteen intellectual. In the main, this tabulation has been maintained, though certain modifications have been made by modern phrenologists. An examination of the chart on page 329 will enable the reader to place the different organs, which we list in full below.

AFFECTIVE ORGANS

Propensities

1.	Amativeness	6.	Destructiveness
1a.	Self-preservation	7.	Secretiveness
2.	Philoprogenitiveness	8.	Acquisitiveness
3.	Inhabitiveness	8a.	Alimentiveness
4.	Friendship	9.	Constructiveness
5.	Combativeness		

Sentiments

10.	Self-esteem	16.	Conscientiousness
11.	Approbativeness	17.	Hope
12.	Cautiousness	18.	Wonder
13.	Benevolence	19.	Ideality
14.	Veneration	20.	Mirthfulness
15.	Firmness	21.	Imitation

INTELLECTUAL ORGANS

Perceptive

22.	Individuality	28.	Number
23.	Form	29.	Order
24.	Size	30.	Eventuality
25.	Weight	31.	Time
26.	Colour	32.	Tune
27.	Locality	33.	Language

Reflective

34.	Comparison	35.	Causality

The affective organs include the Propensities (Nos. 1 to 9), and the Sentiments (Nos. 10 to 21). The intellectual organs comprise the Perceptive (Nos. 22 to 33) and the Reflective (Nos. 34 and 35).

The names of some of these faculties need a little explanation; most of them, however, are simple enough.

Amativeness.—This is the love principle, manifested between persons of opposite sex. The size of this region of the skull is a faithful index to this primary faculty in a person. When small it denotes a lack of physical and mental balance and a handicap in life's affairs. When unduly large it betokens a diversion towards the affairs of the heart of life-energy that should be applied to other ends. Some subjects are able to sublimate this propensity—turning it into a passion for charity, for instance—so that love of mankind replaces love of the individual.

Self-preservation.—The organ governing this propensity if, tolerably well developed, imparts nothing more than the natural desire to live. If less developed it may imply a reckless disregard for personal safety, when urged by the influence of other organs to risk life and limb in some cause. Less still would denote a lurking but probably unsuspected trend towards self-destruction, held in check normally by other impulses, but liable none the less to gain the ascendancy if the influence of these inhibiting organs should be relaxed. A large development of the organ of Self-preservation might indicate a hesitance to take risks—amounting almost or quite to cowardice; on the other hand, this state of affairs might denote nothing more than a tenacity of life and a strong power of resistance to disease. By itself it may be difficult to assess, for the synchronous evaluation of other organs is essential to obtain a true picture of the subject's propensity.

Philoprogenitiveness.—This is the instinct of maternity or paternity—shown in love of children. When the subject is deprived of the opportunity for its satisfaction, as by compulsory celibacy, he or she will lavish affection on animals, or even on inanimate things. The male prisoner tames a mouse in his cell, while the unhappy female in like circumstances will make for herself a doll out of rags.

Inhabitiveness.—This trait could well be termed domesticity. It embraces a love of home life, the chimney-corner, the society of spouse and family. In the case of a boy who has this organ poorly developed it will be a waste of money to spend large sums in educating him for a humdrum stay-at-home career. He is likely to roam the world, go to sea, or choose some occupation that allows him to pass from town to town with ever changing scenes and new experiences.

Friendship.—This faculty needs no explanation. Its possessor in marked degree will be loyal and trustworthy, self-sacrificing, generous. Deficiency in this organ implies ambitious self-seeking and little capacity for social life.

Combativeness.—In an average degree this organ denotes nothing more than that pushful, thrusting desire to make one's way, which is characteristic of successful men. Inordinate development, however, betokens a querulous, quarrelsome trend that may land its possessor in trouble. Deficiency means a poorness of equipment for the business of earning a living.

Destructiveness.—If not unduly developed, this faculty, like combativeness, bodes no ill. It denotes impatience with unnecessary delays and barriers to progress; its possessor will not "suffer fools gladly." In an enhanced degree, destructiveness implies unnecessary and unmerited harshness and severity, with, perhaps, vindictiveness and some cruelty. If less than average development is found, the subject may be tardy, mendacious, and procrastinatory.

Secretiveness.—In a moderate degree this implies tact, and a disposition to keep one's own counsel; in a higher degree, equivocation, evasion and prevarication. On the other hand, a deficiency denotes a blunt and almost brutal outspokenness that is calculated to make many enemies.

Acquisitiveness.—A fair measure of this faculty conduces to a wise and thrifty spending, and a proper regard for future needs. In a greater degree, it moves its possessor to "collect" things, such as stamps, furniture, cigarette cards. In excess it implies a miserly and avaricious tendency, or a hoarding for the sake of hoarding. The activities of the sober and steady artisan who acquires by years of thrift a row of houses, and of the foolish woman who goes on predatory "shop-lifting" excursions, are both dominated in different degree by this organ. Its effects are modified, of course, by those emanating from other faculties.

Alimentiveness.—This is one of the primary organs that maintain vitality and well-being. It should be well developed in all, and implies a proper desire for, and delight in, the good things of the table. A lively appetite is necessary for digestion and nutrition; it is no disgrace to like good food and drink. An excess, however, may point to gluttony or drunkenness—or to a sottish way of life—with addiction to gross and sensual pleasures.

Constructiveness.—This faculty may imply a liking for, and proficiency in, manual pursuits; or a similar tendency towards art or science. In excess, the subject may be an ardent though impractical striver after ends that are impossible of attainment. In the young the measure in which this organ is developed is an index and guide to the subject's future. One in whom it is deficient is likely to be a spineless individual who can do little for himself.

Self-esteem.—Midway between bumptiousness on the one hand and a disadvantageous sense of inferiority on the other lies the happy mean of a proper and well-grounded appreciation of one's own talents and imperfections. An average development of this faculty is very much to be desired.

Approbativeness.—This quality means the wish to excel, to do well in one's occupation or one's hobbies. It sometimes involves the cult of hero worship, when the subject patterns his life on that of some public or notable person whom he admires. Extremes lead on the one hand to pomposity and vanity, or on the other to a boorish disregard for the conventions of polite society.

Cautiousness.—The subject in whom this quality is well developed is circumspect in his actions, prudent and discreet. If over developed, it betokens a hesitant and anxious attitude towards life—a fear to take decisive action of any sort. At the other extreme is the dare-devilry and recklessness displayed by one in whom this organ is deficient.

Benevolence.—In excess this faculty leads to a total disregard of the individual's own interests, and a life devoted to philanthropy and charitable service. In deficiency it connotes a selfish lack of interest in other people and an introspective concentration on personal welfare. In moderation, Benevolence indicates success and happiness and a well-lived life.

Veneration.—This quality implies a proper respect for those entitled to it and a reverence for spiritual things. In excess it may lead to a mother idolizing her son or daughter; or to another person becoming afflicted with religious mania. Its deficiency, however, is a misfortune to the subject.

Firmness.—According to the degree in which this region is developed, the subject will be or will become a person of determination, who gains success through persistent endeavours; or he will be an obstinate and unreasonable persister in his own opinions. One in whom the faculty is poorly indicated will be characterized by indecision and hesitancy, allowing his will to be bent by those of firmer mould.

Conscientiousness.—The upright, honest man, the careful

worker, and the faithful servant have this organ well developed. In excess it may indicate a feeling of inferiority and a too censorious conscience. In deficiency it betokens a conscience lulled to sleep and a not too rigid code of behaviour.

Hope.—In mundane matters a good development of this quality indicates a tendency to cheerfulness and healthy optimism. In the spiritual life it implies a depth of religious feeling. In excess it may bring about disastrous speculation, or cause, in financial matters, too credulous reliance to be placed on others. In deficiency it betokens a pessimistic and despondent outlook, with little or no enterprise.

Wonder.—In a healthy measure this quality presupposes a reasoned faith in religion and a belief in a future life. In excess it may lead to a superstitious regard for occult matters, and a fanatical belief in certain tenets. When deficient, a sceptical and materialistic outlook is indicated.

Ideality.—This is the quality of aesthetes, and in normal development denotes a feeling for the beautiful, an appreciation of art, poetry and the finer pleasures of the intellect. If over developed, unless held in check by other faculties, it denotes a fussy and fastidious discontent with the ordinary things of life; perhaps a supercilious and carpingly critical attitude towards material affairs. Deficiency of this organ involves a gross and coarse nature with little taste for the arts.

Mirthfulness.—A proper development of this faculty is necessary to physical and mental balance. One in whom it is deficient cannot see the humorous side of things, and is apt to take himself and others far too seriously. He does not get the best out of life, for he is incapable of tasting its joys to the full. A preternatural solemnity is often observed that ill accords with the subject's youthful age. Excess of the faculty denotes one who is possessed of a caustic and ill-timed wit, often infused with a certain measure of malice or sarcasm.

Imitation.—Since all young people must first learn by copying the work of others, a fair development of this organ is essential in youth. If the organ, however, persists in full growth in after years, it may connote a slavish mimicry of others and a functional lack of self-assertion. Some persons, it is often said, are "born mimics"; this is a mere restatement of a fact known to all phrenologists.

Individuality.—In phrenological terminology this term means perspicacity, the ability to observe and distinguish; when poorly developed an obtuseness and dullness is indicated. A prying interest in the affairs of others is shown by excess of this organ.

Form.—This, like the preceding organ, is one of the perceptive ones. Those in whom the eyes are close together are usually deficient in Form, for its location is at the side of the eye, near the nose. It denotes an ability to memorize shapes, outlines and faces, and when well marked is a sign of linguistic and mathematical ability. It is connected with the memory of words by their shape, as Tune is associated with the recollection of words by their sound.

Size.—Allied to the organ of Form, this enables its possessor to discern and appraise the size and measure of objects. It is necessary in full degree to one who aspires to be a draughtsman; in its mental applications it betokens an ability to sum up and evaluate affairs according to their relative magnitude and importance. To the player of ball games or the marksman its due development is highly important.

Weight.—This organ enables us to appreciate the principles of mechanical motion, of gravity, of force and of resistance. In practical applications, one in whom it is well shown should be balanced physically and mentally, proficient in athletics, with a sound mind in a healthy body. Its effect depends much, however, on the interaction of other faculties.

Colour.—The faculty bearing this name gives ability to judge and appreciate colouring and tone values. To those in whom it is deficient many colours of Nature are non-existent: such people are not able to distinguish the minute gradations of hue that are obvious to other subjects better endowed with the faculty.

Locality.—Simply expressed as "place memory," this faculty denotes a lively recollection of places, and of persons connected with them. It also indicates a liking for travel and the life of the open air.

Number.—Arithmetical aptitude and a dexterity and readiness in calculation are indicated by a generous development of the organ of Number.

Order.—A methodical mind and a neat and tidy disposition are the qualities which this organ betokens. In excess its possessor may be a fretful, painfully "tidy" woman, who makes her house a spotless "museum" instead of a comfortable and happy home; or a man who is spick and span to an extreme degree, prim and proper, and inevitably little-minded withal. Deficiency in this organ denotes a person of slovenly and careless temperament.

Eventuality.—This organ endows the subject with a gift for remembering past events, whether in his own experience or in history. In conjunction with a ripe development of other perceptive faculties, such as Number and Time, it indicates sound intellectual ability and the power of learning well and thoroughly any subjects that are studied.

Time.—This is a sense of chronological perception; under another aspect it indicates a marked sense of rhythm in musical composition. With the four last-mentioned organs it materially influences success in studies.

Tune.—In a musical sense this faculty denotes a feeling for harmony and an appreciation of melodic and rhythmic construction. When well marked the organ indicates an aptitude for music, both in execution and composition.

Language.—Under one aspect this organ should mean a quality of clarity and appropriateness in verbal expression; with certain other organs in fair proportion it gives oratorical gifts. Linguistic aptitude—power readily to learn and speak foreign languages—is another manifestation of the influence of this organ.

Comparison.—Reasoning depends to a great extent upon this organ, which dominates the functions of analysing and comparing facts of experience, and of planning future action from analogies thus drawn. Constructive thinking and the logical operations of induction and deduction are contingent on a proper growth of the organ of Comparison.

Causality.—Sound judgment would be impossible without a due endowment of this organ, which is as necessary to reasoning as the organ of Comparison. A desire to seek out first principles and to explore the mysteries of being is denoted by a marked development of Causality. Reinforced and coloured by the influence of other perceptive organs, it produces the philosopher and the master mind, the constructive statesman, or the great leader.

A Phrenological Valuation

In assessing the value of the phrenological organs the actual size of any one is not important by itself. What matters is the relative size and development as compared with other organs. As

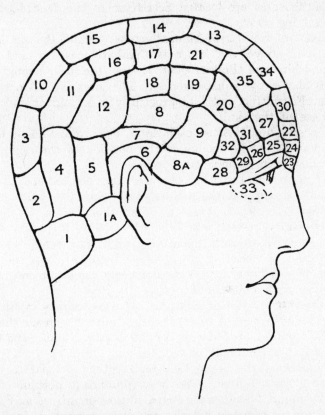

Chart of the Phrenological Organs

one increases it encroaches upon the margins of its neighbours, so that they are of necessity smaller. Certain noticeable peculiarities can be distinguished at a glance; other, lesser, signs need careful scrutiny and comparison in order to determine their value.

The organs of Benevolence, Veneration, Firmness and Self-esteem lie on the top of the head; pairs of other organs, one on each side of the head, join them, so that we have Imitation, Hope, Conscientiousness and Approbativeness in the first row. Then come Ideality, Wonder and Cautiousness. Beneath Ideality lies Constructiveness; below Wonder is found Acquisitiveness; and below Cautiousness are located Secretiveness and Destructiveness, the latter lying above the ear.

In front of the ear is Alimentiveness; behind the ear is Self-preservation; above the latter is Combativeness, behind which are Friendship and Philoprogenitiveness, the last named being bordered above by Inhabitiveness. The organ of Amativeness lies under Friendship and Philoprogenitiveness, and extends down to the base of the skull.

When studying this list each organ in turn should be located on the chart, so as to memorize the position of the regions and their contact with neighbouring organs.

We will now deal with the organs of the forehead and the front of the skull, starting at the mid-line and taking one side. At the top, below Benevolence, come, in order, Comparison, Eventuality and Individuality, the latter adjoining the root of the nose. Counting from above downwards again, below Imitation come the organs of Causality and Locality. In front of Ideality lie in succession Mirthfulness and Time, with Tune bordering the latter and making contact also with Constructiveness.

Around the eye—near the nose—are the organs of Size and Form, and above the eyebrow, counting outwards from the mid-line of the forehead, are those of Weight, Colour, Number and Order. Below the eye is the organ of Language.

In our chart the organs are represented as separate figures enclosed by curved lines. The most prominent portion of each organ, its "bump," denotes the centre of that organ; we may regard it as the summit of a low hillock whose base merges gradually into the surrounding plain. There are no angularities marking the boundaries between the various organs, and we recognize the latter mainly by a careful palpation with the finger, the hair being parted at the same time. A woman's long hair should be loosened when her head is to be "read."

What the Head Discloses

Much information may be gleaned from the shape and con-
figuration of the head; we classify it according to its approach to
one or other of several well-defined types.

We have said something, in the section on physiognomy, about
the comparison of heads by the facial angle, and the cephalic index.
Anthropology teaches us that the head formation in primitive races
is very different from that of the more civilized. In some savage

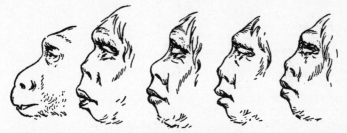

Ancient Man: Gorilla, Java, Neanderthal, Piltdown, Rhodesian

tribes in a low state of development the shape approximates more
to that of certain of the great apes. By comparison of the skulls
of ancient man that have been brought to light we find that the
shape of the human skull has undergone a process of slow change;
during aeons there has been an evolution comparable with, and
related to, man's mental evolution.

In atavistic or degenerate people, even in those that are met
with among civilized races, we see heads that remind us of those
of the apes or of man's ancient forbears. Not only does the skull
itself differ in shape from the normal; the facial angle and the
posture are unlike those of the average individual.

Ancient man was distinguished by heavy and prominent brow
ridges, by an underhung lower jaw and a receding chin. Modern
civilized man has usually a projecting chin and lacks the brow
ridges. Modern man does not require such great power in his jaws,
for it is not necessary for him to rend his food with them; his jaws
and other facial bones are not only finer, but they are also smaller
than those of his early ancestors.

CHART OF PHRENOLOGICAL FACULTIES

No.	ORGAN	VALUE	No.	ORGAN	VALUE
1.	Amativeness		18.	Wonder	
1a.	Self-preservation		19.	Ideality	
2.	Philoprogenitiveness		20.	Mirthfulness	
3.	Inhabitiveness		21.	Imitation	
4.	Friendship		22.	Individuality	
5.	Combativeness		23.	Form	
6.	Destructiveness		24.	Size	
7.	Secretiveness		25.	Weight	
8.	Acquisitiveness		26.	Colour	
8a.	Alimentiveness		27.	Locality	
9.	Constructiveness		28.	Number	
10.	Self-esteem		29.	Order	
11.	Approbativeness		30.	Eventuality	
12.	Cautiousness		31.	Time	
13.	Benevolence		32.	Tune	
14.	Veneration		33.	Language	
15.	Firmness		34.	Comparison	
16.	Conscientiousness		35.	Causality	
17.	Hope				

A = Average. ML = Moderately large. L = Large. VL = Very large.
MS = Moderately small. S = Small. VS = Very small.

When we come across an individual whose head reminds us of the skull of that ancient race which scientists term the Neanderthal, with its heavy brows, low, sloping forehead, and massive jaws, it is natural to look for a mental development of a low order. The animal instincts we should expect to find strongly developed; the intellectual organs we should not be surprised to find poorly indicated. Then, too, a face of the negroid type would warn us to look for greater size in certain organs; and a head with a receding chin and a small facial angle would be an indication of a weak mental development.

These points will help us in a preliminary phrenological estimate, before we examine the organs in detail. Such an analysis could go a lot farther, for among civilized peoples in average development we see broad tribal distinctions. Europe will provide us with long-heads and broad-heads, and with others of an intermediate type; each type has its physical and mental peculiarities that stamp it unmistakably. Even in Britain one can discern the Scottish and the Welsh types, which differ from the Irish and the Southern. When the phrenologist comes across a head of a national type he may expect to find the more strongly marked peculiarities of national temperament.

Often the subject is ignorant of any such nationality in his inheritance; it may be two or it may be twenty generations back that the intermarriage occurred, but the marks of race will crop out sooner or later and tell their story to one who can read it.

On the eastern coasts of England, that were ravaged by the Jutes of old, one may see still the ancient racial type, unmistakable in its virility and physique. After centuries of blending and dilution with the blood of other races, it still stands forth as a distinct type both physical and mental. The same is true of other parts of Britain where there has been an infiltration of alien blood. We can do no more here than indicate the possibilities of this part of our science—which is, in fact, a link between physiognomy on the one hand and phrenology on the other.

Since a phrenological interpretation rests on a judgment of the comparative size or degree of development of the various organs, we need a scale by which to indicate size. Starting with A as the "average" or normal, we denote "moderately large" by ML; "large" by L; and greater magnitude by VL or "very large." In a lesser degree than average we have MS for "moderately small"; S for "small"; and VS for "very small." The results of our reading can be entered on a chart like the one on page 332.

CORRELATION WITH PHYSIOGNOMY

In appraising character by means of a phrenological conspectus the fullest use should be made of other aids to judgment afforded by related sciences. Physiognomy, in its other facets, is especially important; if the phrenologist is able to make a cursory valuation of the subject's features and expression trends, he can, as it were, obtain a background against which to place the results of a reading of the subject's head. Doubts about the value or magnitude of the phrenological organs can be cleared up by reference to the physiognomical indications concerned with like attributes.

The beginner should constantly train and exercise his powers of observation and summation; in trains and buses, in the street, and in all public places he should make a practice of rapidly and unobtrusively examining the heads and faces of people he meets, and of grouping them broadly in the various categories mentioned in this section. Only the widest classification will be possible at first, but later the would-be phrenologist will come to recognize other, lesser, marks of divergence, and to analyse his subjects in more and more detail. Long before he makes a manual examination of a person the reader should be able to recognize the general type of head and any outstanding peculiarities of conformation.

In the case of an actual examination, a preliminary mental summation ought to be made first, and this should be corrected by the information obtained by feeling the head. It will add to the beginner's confidence to observe how he progresses in correctness of mental diagnoses, and his prestige will increase in proportion as he acquires speed and dexterity in his manual examination. The shorter the time taken in palpation the better—provided, of course, it is complete—for a phrenological examination may be something of an ordeal to many subjects.

THE ART OF READING THE HAND

PALMISTRY is a very ancient art; it was practised in the Orient some fifty centuries ago. By the Greeks it was held in high repute, and classical literature is full of references to divination by means of the hand. To this day in the East it is extensively practised—in India, China and Syria, to say nothing of Egypt, that land of mystery.

We should expect an art with such an ancient lineage to possess a well-established basis of rules and procedure, and this is true of palmistry. Its canons were formulated centuries ago, and mediaeval writers on the subject are numerous. One of the earliest printed books is a German treatise on chiromancy by Hartlieb (1448). Another remarkable book on this subject, written by Cocles, appeared in 1504, and the next hundred years or so saw treatises on the art in French, German and Italian.

For nearly two centuries palmistry declined in popularity, but in the middle decades of the nineteenth century two energetic investigators resuscitated it. They were d'Arpentigny and Desbarrolles. The former was concerned mainly with chirognomy, or the discernment of character by the shape and form of the hands; the latter founded the modern art of chiromancy, or divination and prognostication by the lines of the hands.

ANATOMY OF THE HAND

The hand consists of the metacarpal bones and the phalangeal bones. Between the former and the bones of the forearm—the radius and ulna—come the eight carpal bones of the wrist, in two rows. Between the carpals and the fingers, or thumb, come the metacarpals; these resemble the phalangeals, or finger bones, in shape, but are longer. They are enclosed in the muscular envelope of the palm. Jointed to the metacarpals at the knuckles are the bones of the phalanges, in three rows, the bones tapering towards the finger tips.

The thumb has only two phalangeal bones, and these, like its metacarpal, are shorter than those of the fingers. Then, too, the metacarpal of the thumb is capable of free movement, and it is this character that makes the thumb an "opposable" digit and enables man to grasp objects by means of it and the fingers and to use his hand in such complex operations as sewing, writing, drawing and working with tools. There are twenty-seven bones in the hand and wrist—eight carpals, five metacarpals and fourteen phalangeal bones (Fig. 1).

Fig. 1.—Bones of the Hand

One result of the great flexibility of the hand is that on its palmar surface it is seamed and furrowed with lines. The surface is thickly padded in between the lines of flexure, or bending, while at these lines the skin is bound down to the tendons that move the digits, and to the deeper layers. This combination of loose and firm surfaces gives to the grasp that secureness and adaptability which are so necessary. It is obvious that if the padding of the palm were loose and free to slip about, a firm grasp would be impossible.

The "bracelet" lines at the wrist have a similar origin. The monticuli—prominences that we note at the base of the thumb and fingers—are composed of muscle tissue. So, too, are those on the phalanges. Nature, in her wonderful way, has endowed the hand with the characteristics of flexibility and firmness, and has cushioned the palm against shocks that would otherwise injure its framework.

LINES OF THE HAND

With this knowledge of the causation of the lines of the palm we can begin to study the lines themselves and the mounts that lie between them.

On examining the palm with the hand slightly "cupped," a curved line will be noticed enclosing the base of the thumb (Fig. 2, A). This is the *line of life*. Running across the palm from near the base of the first finger to a point roughly midway between the base of the little finger and the wrist is the *line of head* (B). Above is the *line of heart* (C). Extending downwards from the base of the second finger to near the lower part of the line of life is the *line of destiny* (D); and running roughly parallel with it there is a much shorter line stretching from the base of the third finger—the *line of Sun* (E).

An inwardly curved line that starts from near the base of the little finger and finishes near the edge of the palm on that side is termed the *line of inspiration* (F). Above the line of heart, curving from between the first and second to between the third and fourth digits, is the *girdle of Venus* (G). Within the line of life is another curved line roughly parallel with it—the *line of Mars* (H).

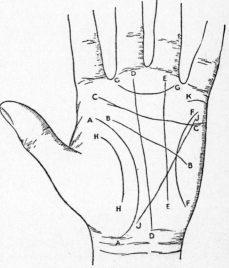

Fig. 2.—Lines of the Hand

Extending diagonally from near the base of the little finger to the lower part of the line of life is the *line of health* (J), or *line of Mercury*. Just above the top of this latter are the short, horizontal *lines of affection* (K), or *marriage lines*. It will be observed that the line of life, line of head and line of health between them form a triangle, which is called the *Great Triangle*. Note also that the line of Sun, line of destiny, line of head and line of heart form the *Quadrangle* at their intersection.

THE MOUNTS

We will now deal with the mounts of the hand (Fig. 3). At the base of the thumb is the *mount of Venus*; opposite is the *mount of Moon,* above which is located the *mount of Mars.* Now, from the little finger inwards, at the base of the digits, are the *mounts of Mercury, the Sun, Saturn and Jupiter,* the last named at the base of the forefinger. According to some palmists, there is another mount of Mars at the opposite side of the palm above the mount of Venus. Between this and Mars-above-Moon is the *plain of Mars.*

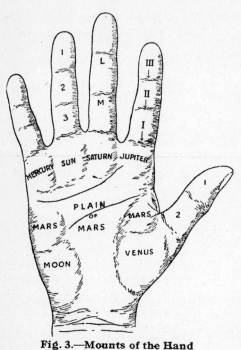

Fig. 3.—Mounts of the Hand

The joints of the digits are numbered from the palm upwards—first, second, third; the phalanges are numbered in the opposite direction — first, second, third. Thus, the second phalange, for example, is bounded by the third joint above and the second joint below; and the third phalange lies between the first joint and the second.

DATE LINES

The chronology used in palmistry is based upon a division of certain of the lines into year-periods. The line of heart, line of head, line of destiny, line of Sun and line of life are those chiefly used for determining ages or dates. The span of man's life can be taken as seventy-five years for the purpose of these readings, and the lines are graduated accordingly. The line of life reads downwards, and the lines of destiny and the sun are read upwards. The lines of heart and head are read from their origin at the thumb side of the palm.

Various more or less fanciful reasons are given for dividing these lines into four-, six-, or seven-year intervals, but we shall adopt a five-year interval. It is more convenient and is at least as well founded as any other date-period. The five date lines, each divided into five-year intervals, are shown in Fig. 4.

SEVEN TYPES OF HAND

By consensus of opinion, palmists have defined seven well-marked types of hand:—

1. The Elemental.
2. The Spatulate or Active.
3. The Conical or Temperamental.
4. The Square or Utilitarian.
5. The Knotty or Philosophic.
6. The Pointed or Idealistic.
7. The Mixed.

The Elemental. This hand (Fig. 5) is the mark of primitive races; it is characteristic of peoples, such as the Laplanders, who inhabit Polar regions, and is a feature also of the Tartar and Slav races. The palm is large, and the fingers short and thick. Intrinsically the hand of the peasant or the serf, it is seen in all lands among those who for generations back have

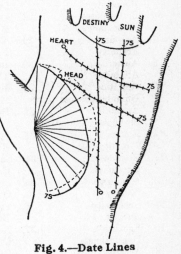

Fig. 4.—Date Lines

come from the stock that furnishes the "hewers of wood and drawers of water." These people have in course of centuries evolved as a type adapted to win a living by hard and rough labour; their acquisitive and self-preservative faculties have developed to predominance, but they lack the finer sensibilities. In Britain the elementals are less numerous than in lands where freedom from serfdom has been but lately won. A few more decades and the type may be a rare survival in these islands.

What significance is to be attached to the possession of an elemental hand in our subject? It depends, of course, on the degree of relation to the archetype, for the pure elemental is uncommon outside those regions that we have mentioned. It will be convenient

TABLE OF ATTRIBUTES

1. Moral strength
   Moral weakness
2. Intellectuality
   Unintellectuality
3. Firmness
   Indecisiveness
4. Candour
   Secretiveness
5. Sincerity
   Insincerity
6. Faithfulness
   Inconstancy
7. Ardour
   Frigidity
8. Austerity
   Affability
9. Ambition
   Unambitiousness
10. Amiability
    Surliness
11. Boldness
    Timidity
12. Gentleness
    Harshness
13. Kindness
    Cruelty
14. Generosity
    Avarice
15. Egotism
    Unselfishness
16. Activity
    Lethargy
17. Industry
    Laziness
18. Sanguineness
    Melancholy
19. Creativeness
    Unimaginativeness
20. Vanity
    Diffidence
21. Voluptuousness
    Apathy
22. Extravagance
    Miserliness

23. Amorousness
    Indifference
24. Courage
    Cowardice
25. Loyalty
    Treachery
26. Uprightness
    Unscrupulousness
27. Refinement
    Coarseness
28. Prudence
    Rashness
29. Nobleness
    Baseness
30. Improvidence
    Thrift
31. Modesty
    Shamelessness
32. Docility
    Obstinacy
33. Pride
    Humbleness
34. Sagacity
    Unwisdom
35. Shrewdness
    Obtuseness
36. Prudishness
    Broadmindedness
37. Neatness
    Untidiness
38. Ostentation
    Humility
39. Charity
    Uncharitableness
40. Frivolity
    Seriousness
41. Despotism
    Obsequiousness
42. Arrogance
    Meekness
43. Jealousy
    Complacency
44. Contentedness
    Covetousness

45. Hot temper
    Even temper
46. Vindictiveness
    Forgiveness
47. Love
    Coldness
48. Affection
    Coolness
49. Benevolence
    Malevolence
50. Nervousness
    Stolidity
51. Prepotence
    Impotence
52. Strength
    Weakness
53. Impetuosity
    Deliberation
54. Self-indulgence
    Asceticism
55. Brilliance
    Mediocrity
56. Artistic nature
    Inartistic nature
57. Cunning
    Artlessness
58. Vivacity
    Listlessness
59. Passion
    Self-control
60. Truthfulness
    Mendacity
61. Musicalness
    Lack of musicalness
62. Aestheticism
    Worldliness
63. Spirituality
    Materialism
64. Devoutness
    Scepticism
65. Sympathy
    Lack of sympathy
66. Superstition
    Incredulity

It will be noted that this table contains physical, moral, and intellectual attributes, which are numbered from 1 to 66. In a list of the qualities of any particular character the numbers alone are used and they can be interpreted by reference to the table. Note that the sign ⊙ represents a median or half-value for the particular quality concerned, while the minus sign denotes the absence of a quality.

to make use here of a table of attributes like that employed elsewhere in this work. In general, we may record a list of attributes such as the following:—

−1, −2, 3, 6, 7, −12, 15, −16, 17, ⊙18, −27, ⊙29, 32, 35, 43, −44, 45, −50, 51, 52, 57, −58, 59, ☽60.

Superstitious, narrow-minded, unintellectual, this type has nevertheless produced on occasion great leaders—in religious persecutions and in the rare and dreadful peasant risings that have stained European history with blood.

The Spatulate or *Active*. This hand (Fig. 6) is large and broad, with blunt, thick fingers broad at the tips. The digits are somewhat long. It is the mark of the man of action rather than the man of thought; of the tireless, restless agitator who seeks to improve the lot of others by his endeavours; of the bold and daring navigator of Polar seas, or of the courageous pioneer who opens up new lands to the world.

People with the spatulate hand have played their part in linking the Atlantic and the Pacific by railway; in cutting canals like the Suez and the Panama; in opening up air routes across continents and oceans. Intolerant of convention, they are original in thought and action; women, especially, of this type are endowed with a large measure of intuition.

We can assign to the spatulate hand the following attributes:—

−1, ⊙2, 3, 4, 5, 6, 7, 10, 11, 16, 17, 18, 24, 26, ⊙28, 34, −36, −38, 51, 52, −53, −54, 56, −59, 60.

In games and athletics they may excel, and usually they are musical. Some of the greatest painters of all time have belonged to the spatulate type. In general, this hand denotes the executive rather than the administrator. Rulers of this group have made history by their failures rather than by their achievements.

The Conical or *Temperamental*. This type of hand (Fig. 7) marks the emotional or temperamental subject—impetuous, impulsive and exuberant. The aesthetic perception is strongly developed, and beauty in all forms and guises appeals strongly to him. Although scarcely artistic in the real sense of the term, he is sensitive to the emotional stimulus of music and pictures. A somewhat unstable nature is indicated, the temperament being coloured by varying moods which never endure long. Sanguine and optimistic generally, he is, however, easily depressed by untoward happenings or by lack of success in trivial enterprises, and the mood of satisfaction may change suddenly to one of black despair.

The content of his mind is coloured by the conversation of any and every person he meets. Unapt at constructive thought, the type with which w̱ are now dealing reflects the moods and opinions of stronger personalities around.

The qualities attributed to persons endowed with the conical type of hand are these:—

⊙1, ⊙2, — 6, 9, 13, 15, 16, ⊙18, 20, 22, 24, — 28, 33, — 37, ⊙41, 43, 45, 48, 50, 51, 53, 54, ⊙56, 58, 59, ⊙60.

The wife or husband of the type is a somewhat difficult person. He or she ill-tolerates discipline or the daily routine of less pleasant duties, and craves for pleasure, excitement—for something new or different. Hot-tempered, such a person would make many enemies but for the repentance that quickly follows an outburst of passion. In religious matters, once a creed is accepted he is steadfast in its practice and support.

The Square or *Utilitarian*. This type of hand (Fig. 8) denotes the methodical, matter-of-fact individual, who is a steady, law-abiding member of society. Though he may not rise to great heights in intellectual matters, he is a plodder who very often reaps the reward due to his industry and perseverance. In contrast to the owner of a spatulate hand, he is conservative in tendency and a sturdy supporter of the existing order of things—in religion, in politics and in business. A suggestion of change calls forth immediate and intense opposition.

A very valuable member of the community, he appears as the successful lawyer, politician, teacher or prelate, making his way in the world as much by the things he abstains from doing as by his deeds. A good soldier but a poor leader, he is nonplussed when his opponent disregards the "rules" or does something contrary to his own experience.

We may summarize the attributes of this type thus:—

1, ⊙2, 3, 4, 5, 6, ⊙7, 8, ⊙11, 13, 16, 17, 18, ⊙20, ⊙22, 25, 26, 33, 35, 36, 37, ⊙38, ⊙39, ⊙41, 43, 44, ⊙45, ⊙48, 50, 51, — 53, ⊙54, ⊙55, 60.

The man of this group makes a good husband to the woman who does not demand much ardour. In matrimony, he is apt to take things too much for granted, forgetting that his partner expects

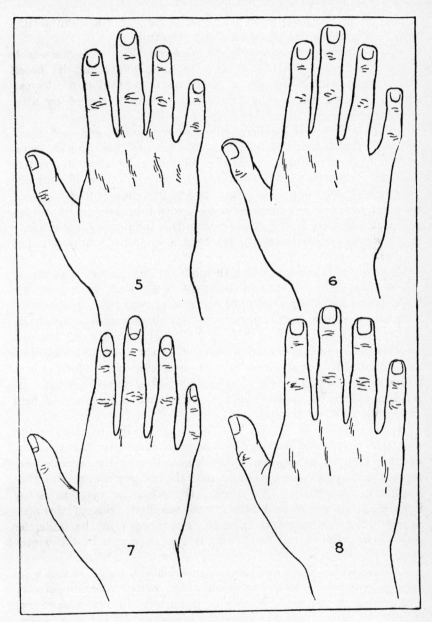

Figs. 5, 6, 7, 8.—Types of Hand

not only a steady devotion to her material wants, but a manifestation of love by little acts of affection and solicitude.

The Knotty or *Philosophic*. This hand (Fig. 9) is noticeable for its bluntly conical finger-tips, its large joints and its broad third phalanges. It denotes a materialistic type of mind, logical, methodical and systematic. This is the hand of the seeker after life's truths.

Such a person is inclined to be reserved and to appear "stand-offish." The latter attribution is undeserved, for reserve arises merely from a profound knowledge of and an interest in matters that only the few care to talk about. In default of like-minded people with whom he can chat, the philosophic is thrown back upon himself, but place him *en rapport* with a kindred spirit and his reserve vanishes. In the young person this temperament inevitably leads to a somewhat introspective tendency, and the subject is not a good "mixer."

To sum up, the attributes of the philosophic type are as follows:— 1, 2, 3, 5, 8, −9, 12, 15, 16, ⊙18, −20, −23, 24, 26, 28, 35, 37, −38, −40, ⊙50, −48, −54, −59, 60.

A hard worker, he is honest with himself as well as with others; he has few delusions about himself. Though he will back his own opinions when he has eventually arrived at them, he keeps an open mind during his investigation or analysis of evidence. Not the best of mates, he is, however, a good though just and stern parent. In religion usually a sceptic, he may nevertheless maintain a firm adherence to some creed.

The Pointed or *Idealistic*. This hand (Fig. 10) marks the possessor as one who worships at the shrine of beauty—not material beauty so much as beauty of the mind, though the artistic perception is usually well developed and the subject appreciates true beauty in everything. As a rule, the idealistic type is rather impractical in mundane matters, and has little idea of thrift or provision for future wants; like the grasshopper in the fable, he sings during the sunny hours, but is like to starve in the winter of life.

Gifted with a vivid and creative imagination, people of this type love verse and *belles lettres;* frequently they write, paint or compose. A marriage of two such persons is usually an ideally happy one, though the parties may have to suffer poverty. On the other hand,

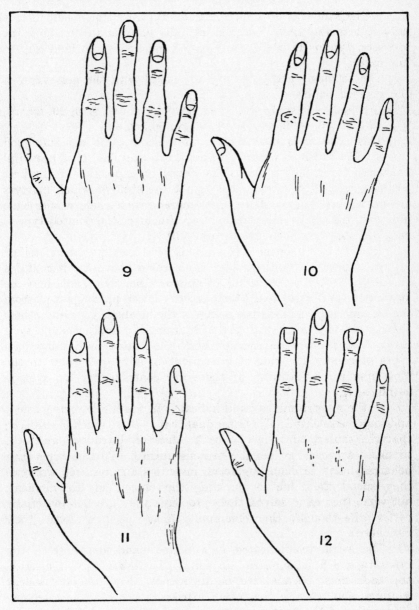

Figs. 9, 10, 11, 12.—Types of Hand

should the similarity of temperament be merely superficial, intense unhappiness may result. Being naturally fickle and inconstant, the idealistic type is in need of a strong bond of love to hold him to his mate.

The following attributes are associated with the possession of the pointed hand:—

⊙1, ⊙2, −3, 4, 5, −6, 7, 10, 12, 13, 15, 16, ⊙18, 20, 22, 23, 27, −28, 29, 30, −32, 43, 45, 48, 53, 55, 56, 59, 60.

This type finds much solace in religious practices and good works. He worships with his whole heart, and feels that beautiful music, pictures, lights and such means of expression fit in best with his idea of devotion. His is not the stuff of which martyrs are made, and religion shorn of its more sensuous side would leave him cold. We take an extreme case, of course; the pointed type is rare, and in its completeness is rarer still.

The Mixed. This hand (Fig. 12) is one that cannot be classified in any of the six groups we have enumerated above, for it contains characteristics of some or all of them. Thus, the palm may be large and the fingers long, thick at the lower phalange and from thence tapering. It thus has points of the idealistic type and others that associate it more with the utilitarian. In another subject we may observe characteristics of both the active and philosophic types of hand. The rule of interpretation is to give value to the most important features. If these are contradictory an average is indicated.

In the main, a mixed hand indicates an adaptable temperament and some versatility. The latter quality may be so much in evidence that the subject turns out to be a "Jack-of-all-trades," and fails to make a success of his life in consequence. To this type have belonged many brilliant engineers, inventors and research workers; they spend their life in pursuing the objects of the moment, but when they have solved their problems they are not materially better off—though the community has profited from their discoveries.

The attributes indicated in a mixed hand are those of the types to which it is nearest in form. There are many varieties, and each must be analysed on its merits. Find out the salient features, and refer to the list of attributes beneath the foregoing description of the type.

A WOMAN'S HAND

Though the female hand as well as the male is classified in the seven types above described, the distinguishing features are not so strongly marked. A woman's hands (Fig. 11) are softer, smoother, and more modelled, but the keen observer can discern the characteristics which we have enumerated.

The elemental hand is rare in the gentler sex, and the spatulate and knotty types are less conspicuous than in the male. When any one of these three *is* found with strongly marked features, the attributes are present in large measure. As to the temperamental and idealistic, the interpreter may here fall into the error of overvaluation, for in many women the hand has something of these features without, however, belonging really to either type. The square or utilitarian type is more easily recognized; and the mixed type, too, can usually be distinguished.

THE HAND IN GENERAL

How often one hears it said that such-and-such a person has a limp or clammy hand: on shaking hands, he lets his own drop directly we relinquish it. Of another subject we say that he has a hearty handshake which inspires confidence and trust and a belief in the owner's integrity. Like many such generalizations, the axiom that you can judge a person by his handshake is well founded. In the main, the limp and soft hand denotes an indolent mind and an easy conscience; if very flabby, it may point also to a lazy or lethargic temperament inclined to sensual pleasures.

An elastic but firm grip points to mental and physical strength, to honest and honourable intention, and to an intuitive and alert brain. If the grip is an "iron" one and the hand is very hard, the indications are those of extreme energy and strength of will; ruthlessness and a strain of cruelty may be present in the subject's make-up.

We must point out that these readings depend very much on degree, and ought to be checked by other signs. It is conceivable that a soft and supple hand might register merely an easy-going, good-humoured temperament; and that a hard, firm handshake would denote an enthusiastic and hard-working individual, with "grit" and determination largely in evidence.

The Thumb and Its Types

The possession of a thumb, that digit which can be placed in opposition to the fingers, differentiates man from all the animals except certain apes and monkeys. It is a most valuable organ, for man could never have uplifted himself above the brutes without it. Ability to make and use crude and rough tools enabled our primitive ancestors to set out on the evolutionary path that has led at last to our civilization of to-day; for with rough tools man could fashion finer and more efficient ones—first of flint, then of bronze and iron—and utilize them to build and construct. No wonder the thumb is such a valuable index to character and temperament!

The characteristics of the thumb, in general, are those of the type of hand to which it belongs; but there are certain special features of the thumb that require notice. First of all, let us mention the rare case where the thumb is absent or is very small; this is a sign denoting a degeneration to a primitive type. Ordinarily the thumb, when placed close to the index-finger, reaches to the joint or just below it. If it does not reach this joint it is a short thumb; if it goes beyond the joint the thumb is said to be long.

The thumb has only two phalanges; the first or topmost one is associated with will-power and executive ability, and the second with logical perception and reasoning powers. The size of the first phalange is important in reading the hand, for if the phalange is large it denotes that other tendencies indicated by the fingers and other parts of the hand are likely to be effective; if the contrary is the case, tendencies remain dormant unless there is enough will-power to ensure that these gifts can be actively employed.

The thumb, then, is a real index to character. By the proportionate size of the two phalanges it denotes whether will or reason will have the upper hand in guiding the actions of the subject; if both phalanges are much the same in size, the individual will employ both these mental faculties equally in determining his way of life. At the base of the thumb is the mount of Venus, indicating the love propensity. If well developed, it shows that the subject is swayed by his heart a good deal in coming to decisions. More will be said about this when we consider the palm of the hand. Palmists sometimes describe the part of the thumb beneath the mount as the third phalange.

If the thumb lies close to the fingers we may state that the owner is careful with money and not too generous. A looser thumb, standing away from the hand, denotes a freer, more open nature. Then, too, we can note whether the thumb is supple at the top joint, or stiff and unyielding. In the former case we may say the subject is broad-minded, generous, tolerant and good-humoured; moreover, he can readily adapt himself to different circumstances. In the man with a stiff-jointed thumb we should expect qualities almost the opposite of those just mentioned; caution, reserve, an obstinate adherence to somewhat narrow views of life and morals, and a determination to obtain what are regarded as rights. With this sign should be considered the relative sizes of the first and second phalange.

It is useful to have some standard by which to measure the relative size of the two phalanges of the thumb. Various proportions have been suggested as the normal one; it may be taken that the first or end phalange should be nearly half the length of the thumb, the second being slightly longer. In the left hand it is likely that the phalanges will show quite a different proportional size; when examining a left-handed subject the left hand should be taken as the representative one.

Sometimes the thumb is broadened and "clubbed" at the tip, which is full and plump. This denotes a passionate, hot-tempered individual, swayed excessively by his emotions and easily roused to intense anger.

Significance of the Fingers

We have elsewhere outlined the characteristics of the different types of hand, depending largely, of course, upon the shape and form of the fingers. Here we will deal with other general considerations affecting the digits.

The length of the fingers can be determined with reference to the length of the back of the hand. Hold out your own hand—the left is most convenient—back uppermost, with fingers clenched, and note the prominence at the outer side that marks the joint of the ulna bone with the wrist. Measure the distance from the centre of this prominence to the end of the knuckle of the third finger. It is convenient to take this measurement in centimetres and millimetres. This length is our standard of comparison (Fig. 13).

Lay the hand on a sheet of paper, palm downwards, and care_

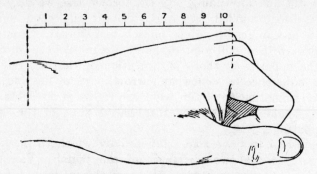

Fig. 13.—Method of Measuring the Hand

fully pencil the outline of the fingers. Now place the end of the pencil between the third and fourth fingers, against the web, and indicate this point by a dot. Rule a line squarely across at the level of the dot. Below this line mark the breadth of the fourth finger, which should be measured outwards from the dot with a pair of dividers or compasses. Rule a second line across at this lower mark, parallel with the line above.

We shall take the lower line as our base or datum, and measure on the diagram the distance from it upwards to the outline of each finger-tip. The index to the length of the fingers as a whole is given by the length from the base line to the tip of the second finger, as compared with the length of the back of the hand.

Let us take an actual diagram obtained from a hand (Fig. 14). The back of the hand measured 10·5 cm., and the second finger 11 cm. The first, third and fourth fingers measured 9·5, 10 and 7·3 cm. respectively. This we should describe as a normal finger length, for the second finger is almost the same length as the

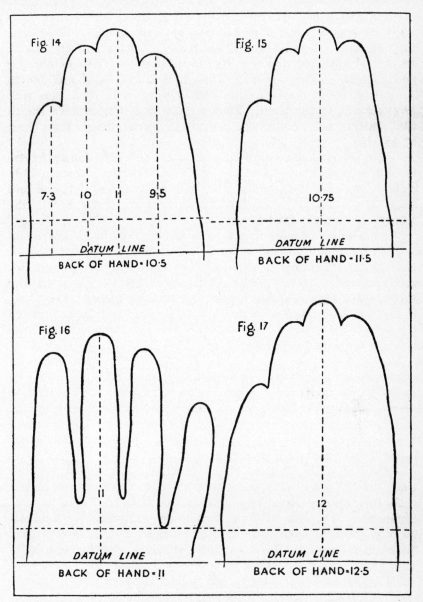

Figs. 14, 15, 16, 17.—Measurement of the Fingers and the Back of the Hand

back of the hand. In three other hands measured in a similar way the results were: Fig. 15, back 11·5 cm., finger 10·75 cm.; Fig. 16, back 11 cm., finger 11 cm.; Fig. 17, back 12·5 cm., finger 12 cm. We should describe Fig. 15 as short; Fig. 16 as normal; and Fig. 17 also as normal. Though the first, third and fourth subjects differ in finger length, the fingers are in each case well proportioned to the hand. Thus we see that it is relative length that matters, not whether one person's fingers are longer than those of another.

The proportional lengths of the first, third, and fourth fingers as compared with the second are, in a normal person, approximately eight-, nine- and seven-tenths. To give an instance, if the second finger is 10 cm. long, the first should measure about 8 cm., the third 9 cm. and the little finger 7 cm.

Long fingers denote a critical and analytical mind, not easily swayed by impulse or moved to do things in a hurry that may be repented of afterwards (see later under "third finger," however, for an exception to this general rule). In affairs of the heart the subjects are somewhat inconstant and hard to please. Very long fingers are associated with an easy conscience and an acquisitive tendency. Such people are often none too scrupulous in their methods of self-advancement.

Short fingers are in general a sign of a more impetuous nature, guided more by heart than head (but see under "third finger" for an exception to this). In a greater degree this attribute results in a marked disregard of convention, and is shown sometimes by the wearing of bizarre and unusual dress. Extremely short digits denote a primitive and elemental type of person, though here one must take the evidence of other signs as well.

Straight, close fingers—unless this sign is modified or contradicted by others—denote a stiff, intolerant nature. A person with this characteristic pays much attention to formality and convention. For fear of doing something undignified or unusual, he often refrains from little acts of kindness and generosity that his heart commends. In morals prudish, in religion bigoted, he is somewhat difficult to get on with.

Fingers that are wider spread indicate a more open temperament. A hand whose digits are well separated shows an easy-going nature—generous, and not afraid to strike out along new paths. A ruggedness or irregularity of shape that is not an actual crookedness denotes a versatility and adaptability of temperament, with some artistic leanings, though here the hand as a whole and the thumb in particular must be interpreted. Crookedness of fingers is an ambiguous sign, often with not very pleasant portents.

As regards flexibility or stiffness, the fingers are interpreted in very much the same manner as the thumb. It must be borne in mind that the lines of interpretation that we follow in dealing with the various parts of the hand are parallel rather than convergent. We may follow any one of them and supplement its story by a reading of some other member. The leading points in chirognomy are the value of the hand as a type, the character foretold by the thumb, and any special indications shown by the fingers generally.

Next to be considered are the attributes denoted by one or more of the digits individually, but they are not so important as those we have discerned by our previous analysis.

First Finger. When short this indicates a somewhat careless attitude and a disinclination to take responsibility. Such a person would sooner work for a wage than be his own master. A long first finger denotes a dominant nature and a capacity for leadership. An impatient and somewhat arrogant intolerance of others' opinions is indicated also when the digit is very long—equal or little less in length than the second finger.

The reader may assume quite justly that the owner of a normal finger (four-fifths as long as the second finger) has a moderate amount of ambition, a capacity for initiative and a good measure of pushfulness.

Second Finger. When this is short the subject has generally an impetuous and imprudent nature. Heart governs head to a very great extent, and the actions are not consistent; a resolve is taken purely according to the emotional stimulus of the moment, and such a person's judgments have seldom a rational basis. Easily moved to laughter or tears, the subject is kind and generous, and a pleasant enough person withal.

A longer second finger suggests more deliberation and caution in action and judgment, with the reason guiding. The possessor may be somewhat self-centred—even introspective—and moody. When the finger is of normal length its indications are to be read as those of a well-balanced judgment and a thoughtful and provident nature.

L

Third Finger. The average or normal length of this digit is nine-tenths of the length of the second finger. If of normal length it denotes a love of and critical appreciation of the artistic and aesthetic in life; also a tendency to take chances in business or in speculation.

When longer it may indicate the gambler, whether in association with the share market or with the turf. Its owner will risk his all in a commercial enterprise, and since the sign carries the attribute of optimism, his judgment is apt to be more sanguine than is justified. An ordinary plodding career is without appeal, and the subject must have a meteoric flight, even if he comes to earth after a brief spell of glory. Artistic leanings also are indicated by the long ring finger. The short-fingered person, though he has not the zest for speculative enterprises, lacks much of the business acumen and shrewdness of one who has the third finger of normal length. He is apt to be too cautious, if anything.

Fourth Finger. A normal digit (seven-tenths as long as the second finger) denotes adaptability and tactfulness, resource in difficult and unpleasant predicaments, and an active habit of mind. A short fourth finger points to a hasty and impetuous person, who easily antagonizes his would-be friends by rashly formed judgments and blatant criticism.

The subject with a long fourth finger is usually well endowed with personal magnetism, has great influence over others, and not seldom possesses the gift of leadership. Whether his powers are applied for the good of others or merely for his own self-advancement is to be read from the signs of the thumb and the hand in general.

The Nails of the Hand

The nails are developed from skin tissues, and so partake of the intimate nature of the flesh. It is remarkable that in people of mixed blood the nails may denote this fact. Even when the foreign blood has been thinned down by marriages with pure-blooded people for a number of generations, the nails may still show the darkening that tells of negro or Indian ancestry. Then, too, the nails show signs of disease, becoming curved inwards in consumption, for example; clubbed fingers are another symptom of this disorder. It is common knowledge that in some cases of poisoning the deleterious substance may show its presence when the nails are subjected to chemical examination.

Long nails denote a calm, phlegmatic temperament; short ones suggest a more impetuous nature. When the finger nails are well formed, with good crescents and a rounded, shapely base, we may expect an equable nature and sound judgment. A broad and curved top, associated with the last-named characteristics, denotes an open, generous and frank mind. Narrow, elongated nails are found on people of somewhat delicate constitution, and are often pale and bloodless or even bluish in colour. When unaccompanied by any signs of ill health, the long and moderately narrow nail suggests a refined and idealistic or psychic type of individual. Nails with a spatulate end, especially when broad in proportion to their length, denote pugnacity. When the nails show a reddish colouring, this attribute is strengthened.

In general, the nails should be pinkish to reddish in hue, and not pale or bluish. Ridged or grooved nails suggest usually a nervous temperament, though this sign may denote nothing more than an alert and sensitive mind. Any irregularities in the shape, form, or colouring of the nails are signs of health defects. Blueness that persists is a sign of some defect of the circulatory system. The nails are of secondary importance to the fingers as an index to character, though they may afford useful indications to health and temperament.

THE THREE WORLDS OF PALMISTRY

The phalanges of the fingers, counting from the tips downwards, are said to represent the world of the mind, the material world, and the animal world respectively. The hand itself is also divided into three "worlds"—the fingers representing the mental domain; the middle part of the hand, the material; and the base of the hand, the animal domain. A predominance of the upper two domains is a more favourable sign than that of the lower two.

In the first case, the business or material side of character will be influenced and held in balance by the idealistic or intellectual side. In the second case, though the sensual side will be restrained by the material, the character will not be of that fineness which is the attribute of the first two domains in equable proportion. Of course, one domain alone may be well developed, and the influence of the remaining two may do no more than act as a check to its full activity, or may even fail to do this. Best of all is a hand with average-sized fingers and an equal development of both other domains; here we have balance, and good proportion of all three kingdoms.

Hands may be observed that show very little of the middle domain, and in such case we may note a predominantly sensual indication, the intellect being applied to aid the lower tastes instead of to check them. We are not stating that there is anything inherently bad in the possession of a predominating lower domain; it may merely signify a pleasure in the less refined enjoyments and gratifications of life.

Chiromancy, or Divination by the Hand

In the previous section we have referred briefly to the lines and mounts of the hand. We propose now to examine the palm in detail, noting the significance of its various traits. We will first examine the mounts.

Venus. The mount of Venus lies at the base of the thumb. It is marked off from the palm by the curved and roughly semi-circular line of life, along which we may set graduations to denote age or time.

A well-developed mount denotes the attributes that follow:—
   7, 12, 39, 47, 48, 51, 52, 56, 61, 62.
When too full and high it indicates:—
   —5, —6, 15, 20, 21, —28, —31, 54, 59.
A mount of Venus that is flat and inconspicuous denotes:—
   —7, —16, —23, —47, —52, —58.

A proper and normal development of Venus is essential to a healthy and balanced nature, both physical and mental.

Jupiter. This mount, at the base of the first finger, is associated with the following qualities:—
   9, 11, 16, 26, 29, 33, 51, 64.
When over-developed there is denoted:—
   15, 41, 42, 66.
An unformed mount of Jupiter indicates:—
   —6, —14, 15, —17, —25, —27, 54, 57.

Though material success is implied by a well-formed mount of Jupiter, an undue growth of this mount is anything but a blessing; a deficient development, on the other hand, is a great misfortune.

Saturn. This mount is located below the second or middle finger. With it are associated the attributes:—

2, 28, 34, —40, —53, —59, 60, 62, 64.

Excessive development denotes:—

8, 15, —18, —23, —54, —58, 59, 66.

Deficiency of the mount of Saturn involves:—

—3, —18, —28, —44, 46, 50, 58, 59, —62.

A poorly marked or a wasted mount tells of misfortunes in the past and in the future. Unless contradicted or modified by other signs it is an ominous token.

Sun. The mount of the Sun, also under the patronage of Apollo, is placed below the third finger. In normal development it presides over many desirable and helpful attributes; in excess it inclines the subject to tendencies that are troublesome but not malevolent. In deficiency it conduces towards a somewhat cold, materialistic, half-lived life.

To deal first with the attributes of the normal, these are:—

1, 2, 5, 6, 7, 13, 14, 18, 24, 26, 47, 56, 61, 62, 63, 64, 65.

Over development denotes:—

21, 22, 23, —28, 29, —36, 48, 59, 66.

Deficiency indicates the following:—

—7, 8, —13, —14, —19, 22, 43, 45, —50, —53, —58.

Mercury. This is located beneath the fourth finger. In normal development it denotes:—

1, 5, 16, 17, 18, 24, 26, 35, 55, 58, 61, 65.

In a greater degree of development we may look for the following attributes:—

9, —14, 15, —22, —26, 57, —60.

When the mount is hardly perceptible the attributes are as follows:—

—1, —3, —16, —17, —19, —35, 50, 53.

Mars. The mount of Mars is to be found above the mount of Moon, opposite the thumb. Another mount of Mars is also spoken of, located above the mount of Venus and opposite the other Martian prominence. Some palmists ascribe a negative influence to the former mount—above Moon—and a positive influence to the latter one, but this is not accepted by others. We shall be wise to assume that the mount of Mars-above-Venus exerts more of a passive influence, whereas Mars-above-Moon endows its possessor with a varying degree of purposive energy, according to its development. It follows, then, that we must take into account both of these prominences when assessing the value of Mars.

When Mars-above-Moon is predominant, the following attributes may be looked for:—

7, 9, 11, 16, 18, 24, —28, 41, 45, 51, 52, 53, 55.

Mars-above-Venus in dominance indicates:—

3, 9, 11, —32, —50, 51, 52, —53, —59.

In the rare event of both mounts being little in evidence the indications are:—

—3, 5, —11, —19, —23, —24, 28, —32, 46, 50, —52.

Moon. This mount is located opposite the mount of Venus. In normal development it endows its possessor with highly valuable powers of imaginative and creative ability in the arts. In lesser degree these qualities are desirable for success in daily life, since lack of imagination is a great drawback in planning a career.

An excessive development of the Moon mount is seen in many of those unfortunate individuals for whom the State is obliged to care in mental hospitals. A deficiency of this mount denotes an unromantic, unsentimental nature, with little appreciation of the finer things of life, and a zest for merely sensual pleasures.

To sum up, a normal mount of Moon indicates:—

13, 14, 18, 19, 26, 29, 48, 51, 55, 56, 58, 61, 62, 63, 64, 65.

Over development in a minor degree denotes:—

—5, —6, 23, —26, 38, 40, 41, 43, 50, 53, 54, 59, 66.

Deficiency in the mount of Moon indicates:—

—1, —3, —4, —7, —11, —18, —19, —23, 50, —56, 57, —58, —60, —64, 66.

SIGNS ON THE MOUNTS

The grille, formed by a number of straight lines crossing others, is a sign that diminishes the value of the attributes belonging to a mount. A cross or an island denotes a similar weakness, the island being less favourable than the cross. Among beneficent signs are the star, the circle, the rectangle and the trident; a clearly marked upright line reinforces the attributes of the mount on which it is located.

It must be understood that in using the words favourable and unfavourable in this connexion, we refer only to the strengthening or weakening of the monticular attributes. These in themselves may not be favourable in the popular sense of the word, but whatever may be the quality associated with the mount, it is reinforced or weakened, as the case may be, by the valuation of the particular signs there present.

The Plain of Mars

Occupying the central area of the palm is the hollow termed the plain of Mars. Upon it we note the Great Triangle, formed by the intersection of the line of head, line of life and line of health—the latter is also called the line of liver or line of Mercury. Above is the Quadrangle, marked out by the crossing of the line of Sun, line of destiny, line of head and line of heart.

If the plain of Mars be very concave it denotes too much passiveness in the subject and a lack of endeavour. When flatter it indicates a bolder, more aggressive spirit.

Significance of the Lines

Some typical formations of the lines are shown in Figs. 18 and 19. Wherever in the following paragraphs a reference is made to the component diagrams the one in question is denoted by a heavy figure enclosed within brackets [1]. This renders identification easy and does not interrupt the text. A full explanation of Figs. 18 and 19 is also printed on the pages facing the diagrams themselves.

Line of Life. This line runs round the mount of Venus, and may be complete in its enclosure of the prominence, or be broken by gaps. On it are measured ages or dates, beginning from the top, near where it is approached or touched or intersected by the line of head. It is divided into fifteen intervals, each of five years. This graduation is merely a matter of convenience, for a claim to determine the date of past or future events with any but approximate closeness would be futile.

Although we make our last interval end at 75, it must be kept clearly in mind that this figure is taken because it represents the mean of longevity. People live, as we know, to 85, 90 or even 100 years, although their line of life would not be longer than in another. The signs that affect early life and old age cannot be dated with such closeness as those that concern adolescence and middle life, and the intervals, though nominally representing periods each of five years, may actually coincide with longer or shorter periods of time.

Typical Formations of the Lines of the Hand, Nos. 1 to 9 (Fig. 18)

1. Gaps in line of life, and a cross upon it.
   Line of health begins independently.
2. Line of life gapped and forked at lower end, one portion merging with line of destiny.
   Line of inspiration, beginning on mount of Moon.
3. Line of life gapped and marked by cross-bars; it is not tied to line of head.
   Line of destiny ends on mount of Sun.
4. Island on line of life which forks at its upper end and sends a branch to Jupiter.
   Line of health has a separate origin.
5. Line of head tied to line of life at origin, and then pursues an undulating course.
6. Line of head soon leaves the line of life and then goes straight across the palm.
   Line of Mars, parallel with line of life.
7. Line of heart springing from Jupiter, and running roughly parallel with line of head.
   Line of destiny stops at line of heart
8. Line of heart springing from Saturn.
   Line of destiny stops at line of head and goes on again from another point on that line.
9. Girdle of Venus.
   Cross on line of destiny, which ends on Jupiter.

Some palmists divide the line unequally, making the early intervals and the last few somewhat longer than those after childhood and up to sixty years. We here adopt equal intervals, with the proviso (mentioned above) that they are of variable time-length. It is unwise, when reading dates of events, to be too dogmatic; the indications of a death, for instance, may be contradicted by signs on other lines or on the mounts. Then, too, the indication in one hand may be different from that in the other.

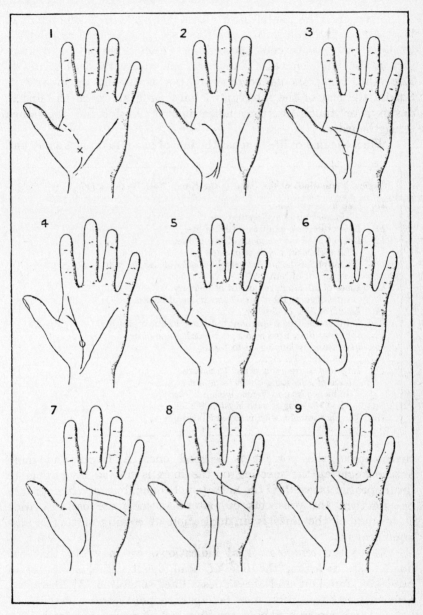

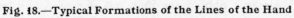

Fig. 18.—Typical Formations of the Lines of the Hand

Sometimes the line of life is double, a sign of a prosperous and happy life. Interruptions in the line [1] are to be read as referring to illness, past or to come, according to their location. A distinct gap in the line denotes a dangerous malady, with peril of death. The other hand should corroborate this testimony or modify it. Should the end of the interrupted line of life approach the line of destiny, or touch it, the indications of misfortune are much strengthened.

When the line of life touches the line of head, making a small and

---

Typical Formations of the Lines of the Hand, Nos. 10 to 18 (Fig. 19)

10. Gap in line of life.
    Undulating line of destiny.
11. Line of destiny loops over line of life.
12. Line of head independent of line of life.
    Line of heart widely separated from line of head.
    Line of Sun begins between lines of head and heart and ends in a fork on mount of Sun.
13. Lines of affection, on mount of Mercury.
    Line of sensuality, parallel with line of health.
14. Island on line of destiny.
    Influence lines from mount of Moon to line of destiny.
15. Influence lines from Venus, one cutting line of head.
16. First rascette looping on to palm.
    The Great Triangle.
17. Line of destiny going direct to Saturn.
    Line of Sun going direct to mount of Sun.
    Influence line on Venus, within line of life.
    The Quadrangle, with Mystical Cross.
18. The Quadrangle, with many small thin lines.

---

sharp angle, the portent is a good one. A larger and more obtuse angle at the meeting of the lines is not so favourable to future prospects; while if the lines do not touch, but merely approach one another, the prospects of material success are bad. A wide separation of the lines is an indication of coming sorrow or disappointment.

As to the temperamental indications, we may say that the line of life touching the line of head denotes the attributes of prudence, foresight and shrewdness; lines separated [3] indicate a deficiency in these gifts; lines far apart, cupidity and covetousness, avarice and vanity. Should the lines not diverge again soon after

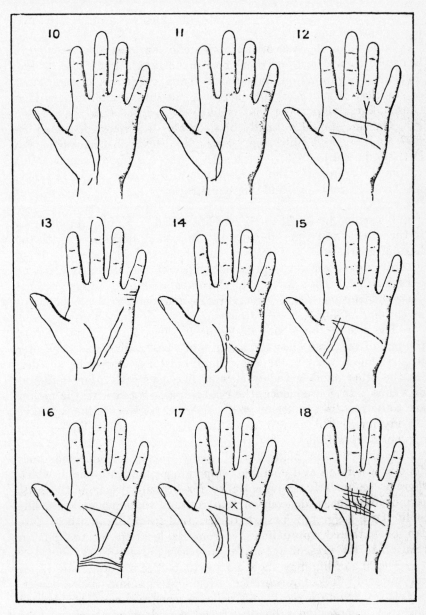

Fig. 19.—Typical Formations of the Lines of the Hand

meeting or approaching, but continue as one, a dullness of mental perception is suggested.

Sometimes the line of life approaches or joins also the line of heart, a token of coming danger or misfortune. If the line of life, instead of beginning on Mars-above-Venus, originates on the mount of Jupiter, it indicates an energetic pursuit of ambitions and a thoroughness of purpose that is likely to reap success.

The line should normally be deep and well marked, a medium pink in hue, and unbroken. Since its length is connected with that of the subject's life, his length of days is implicit in it. But we must regard this sign rather as an indication of his vitality, his physical make-up and his constitution, than as a measure of his years.

If it stood by itself, the line of life would be a faithful indication of the subject's lifetime; but it must be read in conjunction with the lines of heart, head and destiny, and the signs of these interpreted, in order to obtain an approximate idea of the chronology of the person's life. The novice in chiromancy should guard against hasty conclusions drawn from breaks and defects, or other signs, in the line of life.

The size of the mount of Venus is affected by the position of the line of life, and when the latter is of small radius, and lies closer to the thumb than usual, the mount must necessarily be smaller. On the other hand, a widely curving line goes with a larger mount of Venus. In consequence, the qualities associated with the mount are to be read in smaller or greater degree. A double line we have already mentioned; in rare cases there may be a third line—a sign of enormous vitality.

A line of life made up of many short, unconnected lines denotes a nervous and unstable temperament, but also one in which there is an underlying potentiality for brilliant work in the arts. It indicates, too, a delicacy of constitution. A larger gap in a line of life [10], suggests a past or future peril from illness, whose date can be gathered approximately from its location on the line in relation to the present age of the individual.

The line of life may show a succession of short cross-bars [3] or may present a linked appearance. The first sign, known as a ladder, is held to denote a weak and delicate constitution. The chained line, too, denotes poor health at the period corresponding to its location. Both these defects suggest also a weakness of character. Anything which interrupts the course of the line of life is to be read as a defect, or at least as a sign of some change in the subject's health or fortune. Oval or ring-shaped "islands" [4] in the line are sometimes seen; they indicate an epoch in the physical life, and in women may mark the climacteric.

When examining any defects it is well to investigate the line beyond, as its appearance and condition are guides to the outcome of the illness or peril that is foreshadowed; a clear and vigorous line coming after a laddered or chained portion, or after one or more islands, indicates that the obstacle to progress will be surmounted or that better health will follow.

A cross or a star [1] on the line of life means an untoward event— generally an accident or mishap of some sort. When the line appears to split and divides into tiny fibrils, the period concerned will witness a change in the subject's fortune. An upward forking is a better sign than a downward one; a strongly marked fork indicates an important event of far-reaching influence on career or happiness.

A fork at the bottom of the line of life [2] is a common sign; when deeply marked it means the retention of vigour throughout the latter years of life, unless the diverging line strengthens at the expense of the line of life, when the contrary is to be predicted. A number of fine forking lines in this location are a sign of impaired or waning vigour during the twilight of life.

The line of life may send out a branch above [4] towards the mount of Jupiter—a sign of a successful career marked by great energy and ambition. A branch downwards towards the mount of Moon denotes an instability of nature and lack of purpose in the subject's aims. Branches from the line of life downwards across the plain of Mars denote ill fortune or sorrow. A line that is broken or split towards its lower end, with either portion joining the line of destiny [2], is to be taken as a sign of great danger threatening the individual at the period denoted.

Important or striking features in one hand are to be checked and corroborated by the other. If both tell the same story there is no difficulty, but a strong indication in one may be set off against a weaker sign in the other; and in cases of doubt the evidence of other lines or of the digits will show the value that ought to be given to a particular attribute or portent.

Line of Head. This line begins near the start of the line of life, between the thumb and first finger, often making an angle with the curved line of life. It goes across the plain of Mars and ends between the mounts of Mars and Moon, at the part of the palm known as the "percussion." The line of head should be intact, with no gaps, and should be deeply marked. It curves boldly across the plain of Mars and thence slopes gently downwards, to finish on Mars or on the mount of Moon at the upper margin of the latter.

Its length is some guide to the subject's mental endowment— force of will, moral and intellectual power, reasoning ability, self-reliance, and so on. A short line suggests a deficiency in some of these attributes, and a long line indicates an abundance. When both the line of head and the line of life are short, the presumption may be that a brief life is presaged; this indication needs corroboration by other signs, however.

The line should not be tied for long to the line of life [5]; rather should it make an early diversion from the latter [6], going on its independent course as soon as possible after its origin. A delay in thus taking a separate course suggests a rather late maturing of the mental powers. A complete separation from the line of life [12] denotes an early and perhaps precocious dawn of the intellectual powers. A wide separation suggests a varying degree of self-confidence and boldness, which may even tend in excess to careless, reckless and ill-considered action.

The line of head partakes of the attributes of the mount towards which it slopes, to the degree of its descent upon that mount. When it slopes towards Moon, these attributes may range from a vivid imagination with no mean artistic ability to an excess of imagination that leads to day-dreaming and an unpractical attitude towards daily affairs. Should the line be nearer Mars, then the attributes of that mount are foreshadowed in the subject.

The line may have a pronounced upward bulge beneath one or other of the mounts at the base of the digits; in such a case it is influenced by the mount in question, and shares in its attributes. A rising curve under the second finger, for example, would suggest Saturnian characteristics—prudence, discretion, sagacity and wisdom. A curve rising up beneath Mercury, on the fourth finger, indicates tact or, in excess, an adroitness that may amount to double-dealing.

A line of head that goes almost straight across the palm [6] signifies a cold and apathetic temperament, though this may be modified by a contrary sign in the line of heart. An undulating line of head [5], suggests inconstancy or lack of perseverance in pursuit of enterprises; a twisted line leads us to expect duplicity or extreme reserve.

Defects have much the same meaning as those specified for the line of life. Thus, a linking denotes a weakness of constitution; as does, too, a line broken up by cross bars. Forking or branching lines are read by their direction or their approach to the mounts. Those that trend upwards from the line of head are more favourable than any going downwards. Crosses, stars or islands are to be read in the same way as those on the line of life.

The line of head is used as an index to ages and dates, the numbering beginning at the origin on or near the line of life and proceeding by five-year periods to 75.

Line of Heart. This begins beneath Jupiter (first finger) or between Jupiter and Saturn (second finger), curves downwards across the palm and rises again beneath Mercury (little finger) or between Mercury and Mars-above-Moon. In its middle part it may, and often does, run parallel with the line of head below [7]. It may begin and end with a fork, and the direction taken by the limbs of the fork at the beginning is significant. One, for example, may curve round the mount of Jupiter a little way, when the other will probably finish on Saturn. A fork or even a tassel—the latter made up of several short, branching lines—at the termination of the line on the percussion is normal and has no special meaning.

The line of heart is the key to the emotional side of a person's nature—the heart here being regarded in a poetical way as the source from which spring the emotions and passions. At the same time, we must make it clear that it is the mental and intellectual aspect of the affections or feelings that is pointed to by an indication read from this line. When the line originates from Jupiter [7] it suggests ardent, spiritual affection. As a spouse, the subject would make great demands upon his partner for real sympathy and understanding. Though the material and physical side of married life would not be neglected, a union between two such subjects would be primarily one of the heart. A match in which one only of the parties possessed such a line of heart would possibly be fraught with disaster.

A line that begins between Jupiter and Saturn indicates a nature of a sound and solidly sentimental type—free from extremes of passion and inspired by a deep and heart-felt devotion to the subject of his or her affections. The individual may not rise to the heights of passionate love, but neither will he or she fall to the depths of despairing and hopeless misery if affection be unrequited.

Even the quiet person who is content with placid love may, on occasion, be stirred by a convulsing passion. An island on the line of heart is sometimes a sign of such an impending event. Sudden passionate love, when it is experienced later than the first third of life, is usually a catastrophe, for he or she to whom it comes may not be free from marital ties, and the consequences of such an experience, in any case, are devastating.

A line that begins with a fork, one branch rising from Saturn and the other going between this mount and Jupiter, suggests a temperament that is prudent and intellectual, to which the idealistic side of love appeals more strongly than the physical.

When the outer branch of the fork springs from Jupiter, the other branch being on Saturn, there are indications of a nature governed by two main influences—jealous and voluptuous passion of a selfish type, and a longing for idealistic affection. Torn between these conflicting impulses, the subject may fail to find happiness; his ardent nature needs a like ardour in his partner, but he pursues a will-o'-the-wisp in seeking a combination of what would really amount to sensuality on the one hand and to frigid ideality on the other.

An unforked line springing from Saturn [8] is a sign of a temperament to which the physical side of love appeals. If seen in both hands it suggests sensuality—not necessarily to be condemned, however, since it may mean nothing more than a natural vigour of sentiment. When such a line is defective—broken, laddered, or chained—the indications point to a degree of abnormality. This needs to be confirmed by a like sign in the other hand and by the readings of the mounts.

A near approach or a parallelism [7] between the line of heart and the line of head denotes that the former is influenced by the latter—especially during the age-period indicated on the lines. The line of head in such cases is the predominant one. As with other lines, a clear and deep impression shows a healthy state and a fullness of vigour. A thinning down as the line nears the percussion means a diminishing vitality, though often the line is found to be clear and strong right across the palm. It may stop short under the mount of Sun or under Mercury, when its indications would be coloured by the influence of those mounts. It may send down a branch under Saturn to join the line of head —a sign of unreasoning and reckless pursuit of affairs of the heart, the warnings of prudence or the promptings of conscience being unheeded.

Should the line of heart turn downwards after progressing as far as Saturn, and join the line of head, a rash and imprudent response to emotional stimulus is suggested. Heart will rule head, and many hastily conceived plans and ill-considered actions may give cause for regret.

Girdle of Venus. This is a downward bulging curve [9] that begins usually between the mounts of Jupiter and Saturn and terminates between those of Sun and Mercury. That is, it curves down from the intersection of the first and second fingers, approaches and parallels for a short distance the line of heart, and thereafter curves boldly upwards to a point near the origin of the third and fourth digits.

A great deal of nonsense has been written about this line and its significance; it has been suggested that its presence connotes tendencies that are immoral, vicious, or at least voluptuous and libidinous. Women have been advised particularly to avoid a lover whose hand bore the belt of Venus, or *Cingulum Veneris* as the old chiromancers named it in Latin. Criminal tendencies, too, have been attributed to the influence of this line.

Much of this foolishness sprang from the practice of regarding as morally bad any physical manifestation or sign of sexual vigour and maturity. The girdle of Venus is nothing but an index to the subject's physical nature, and by itself denotes merely the state of development of that side of the constitution. As we have pointed out in other sections of this work, a full and proper endowment of the physical attributes of sex is necessary to health, happiness and success. When the girdle is absent we can look to the mount of Venus for information on this aspect of character and temperament; if the girdle is present, it reinforces and strengthens the indications of the mount.

Should voluptuousness or vice be predicted by other signs, then the girdle may be read either as confirming or minimizing these attributes, according to its condition—whether deep or faint, continuous or broken. It is, in a measure, a guide to the state of the nervous system also. A line that is represented only by two broken, split and converging portions coming down from the mounts, and that lacks the middle sector, is a token of a somewhat unstable and perhaps hysterical temperament. If, however, elsewhere in the hand there are strong indications of creative imaginative powers, the above condition of the girdle will probably denote only an emotional and hypersensitive nature, fickle and inconstant perhaps, but frank and honest.

Line of Destiny. This is also called the line of fate and, from its usual termination under or on Saturn, the line of Saturn. It is one of the principal date lines, being divided into five-year intervals, reading from the bottom upwards. It forms a side of the Quadrangle where it crosses the lines of head and heart, and at its lower end runs close to the line of life—indeed, the two lines may coalesce to form one for some part of their course [2].

Instead of going to Saturn the line may end on Jupiter [9], or bend over towards the mount of Sun. The fate of the subject in such cases is much influenced by these mounts: the Jupiterian attributes of ambitious and idealistic striving may predominate, or the Saturnian ones of prudent and well-considered living. If the line of destiny ends on Jupiter, a successful career is suggested for the male subject; for a woman, a good marriage with someone of higher station or degree. If the line ends on or bends towards the mount of Sun [3], it denotes some prospect of success in artistic or literary enterprises. These interpretations, to be of real value, should find corroboration in other signs of the hand.

The line of destiny may stop on the line of heart [7] or go no farther than the line of head [8]; or it may continue, more faintly, from either of these lines; or it will, perhaps, proceed again strongly from another point [8] in the line of head or the line of heart. A termination at either of the lines mentioned suggests some event that results in a virtual end to the person's career; a weak progression of the line of destiny thereafter tells the story of life taken up again with less vigour and energy.

If the line goes on again from a near-by point in the line at which it was interrupted, a new career is referred to that may be as satisfactory as the one that came to an end at the line of head or the line of heart; its valuation depends on its deep or shallow, strong or weak character thereafter. If free of defects, it can be taken as a favourable one. The date of the interruption may be divined from the line where it occurs. A new career started from the line of heart is less likely to be successful than one begun at the lower line, when the subject is in his prime; even so, tokens of energy and virility elsewhere in the palm may make it possible to predict a successful outcome of even a late venture into fresh fields of enterprise.

Before proceeding farther with the various characteristics of the line of destiny, it will be well to say that destiny does not imply fatality. The line shows likely tendencies, and suggests influences that may affect but not necessarily dominate the subject. Man is master of his destiny if he wills, and the line gives a warning of dangers that may beset his path. It also hints at dates when opportunities may arise which should be seized and used to advantage.

A clear and deeply marked line of destiny indicates a history largely influenced by outside forces or personalities; the subject will probably follow his destined career and make little effort to shape out a life of his own. If the line is more faintly impressed, the person is more likely to achieve high ambitions and have a brilliant career, though in consequence he will have to risk an equally great downfall. The outcome is to be read from other signs on this and other lines and on the mounts. A zigzagging or undulating line [10] denotes a changeful or vacillating career, as the case may be. If these signs come only at a particular part of the line, the period when such a condition is most likely is denoted.

The case is mentioned above of a line of destiny running close to, or even uniting with, the line of life at its lower portion; the line of destiny may in rare cases even transgress on to the mount of Venus by a looping over the line of life [11]. There are two indications from this approach to the line of Venus or to the mount itself. The first is that the blood relatives of the subject will be concerned very much in his destiny during the early years—the period may be read in the usual way. The other is concerned with the traditional attributes of the mount, and means that a man, for example, will be aided materially during the years in question by his fiancée, his wife, or some woman friend who cares for and admires him. Of a woman whose hand bore this sign we could predict that she would gain not only happiness, but wealth and social advancement by her marriage.

Other signs of the line, and particularly those given by its later character and trend, are to be taken into account, for the line must be read as a whole. Without going into unnecessary detail we may remark that the degree to which Venus influences destiny is gauged by the nearness to, or merging or looping of, the line of destiny at the mount.

A line of destiny that begins in the middle of the palm, close above the Bracelets, and shapes its course in almost a direct line to the mount of Saturn [17], is one that portrays a self-reliant and ambitious character, one unlikely to be influenced by other personalities except when his own designs are favoured thereby. Sometimes a line, after beginning thus, will fork and split after passing the line of head—a sign of weakening will-power and waning energy. If it becomes broken at the line of heart and merges with the latter, which also is broken or laddered, disappointments and somewhat unhappy later years are suggested. Sons and daughters may bring trouble upon parents at this period, or by their own ill-judged actions cause unhappiness to the elders. When such a line of destiny, after merging with the line of heart, goes on independently to its end upon Saturn, it denotes that troubles have been cured and that happier and more peaceful years ensue.

Crosses [9], stars, or islands [14], on the line of destiny point to mishaps, accidents or set-backs to the person's career. The important matter is to examine the line thereafter for the result of such a defect, and to read the same line on the opposite hand.

Line of Sun. This line is also called the line of success, or of Apollo. It rises from the wrist, from the mount of Moon, or from one of the lines that cross the palm. In some hands it may be difficult to distinguish, or be represented only by a short and irregular line extending from the line of heart, or just below, towards the base of the third finger.

Dates are indicated on this line, and for graduation it is numbered from an imaginary starting-point level with the beginning of the line of destiny; it matters not whether the line of Sun actually begins there or higher up on the palm. The space is divided into fifteen intervals representing five-year periods and ending with 75. Thus it can be determined approximately when the line of Sun begins to influence the individual, for this is denoted by the age-period at which the line first appears on the hand.

The line of Sun is associated with success or with qualities that, unhindered, would contribute to success. Thus it denotes ability, talent and imaginative power. A line that starts from the wrist and progresses boldly to the mount of Sun [17] is a very favourable one, indicating not only a good measure of the qualities just mentioned, but the attainment of fame and material prosperity through them. At the opposite extreme is the case of a line that begins between the lines of head and heart [12] and disappears in a forked or split and faintly-marked manner on the mount of Sun. This means a career not very prosperous in its early years and unproductive in later life.

When the line of Sun makes a late start, but is strong and vigorous thereafter, the indications are much more favourable, for they tell us that fortune smiles on the subject when at last he succeeds in making a definite start in his proper career. A line that began on Venus would denote a feminine influence conducive to success—this in the case of a man, of course. In a woman's hand it would be a confirmation of other signs that pointed to success through marriage. If the line of Sun rises on the mount of Moon, the indications are those of a successful career in one of the arts, other influences being favourable.

The line of Sun may be entirely absent, but this is by no means a bad sign. Generally, in such a case, the line of destiny will be well shown and quite favourable. In any event, the line of Sun manifests only possibilities and potentialities; as regards the future it shows what may or should happen rather than what will occur. Interruptions in the line, unless of an overlapping kind, are not particularly good signs, for they denote a fickleness and inconstancy of purpose; longer gaps tell of periods of failure or poverty. Crosses or stars on the line tell of misfortunes; an island denotes a catastrophe.

Line of Health. Other names for this are the line of Mercury, or the line of liver. Usually it begins on or near the line of life.

It progresses across the hand obliquely towards the percussion where, under Mercury, it may unite with the line of head. The line serves as a guide to the health of the subject. When absent, however, no harm is to be feared, and the indication is favourable rather than otherwise.

Although some palmists claim to diagnose specific diseases from signs on this line, or from its characteristics, we make no such pretension; they speak merely of prevailing trends, and then only in general terms. Age-periods are calculated from an imaginary starting-point at the centre of the hand just above the wrist, and there are fifteen five-year intervals, as is the case with the other date lines.

If the line of health originates on or touches the line of life, a weakness of constitution or propensity to some disease is suggested. It is better for the line of health to take an entirely independent course [4] towards the mount of Mercury, touching only the line of head on the way.

A line of health made up of overlapping, broken portions tells of struggles with ill-health at the dates indicated, though the overlap shows that the defect was in due course repaired. If the line almost disappears between the lines of head and heart it may be taken as a sign of freedom from illness over that part of life's course; the line should thereafter go on clearly to its mount beneath the fourth finger.

When the line of health is separate from the line of life [1] it denotes a freedom from serious illness, though not always a strong constitution. The line of life should always be considered when the line of health is being read; the former is of very great importance in appraising signs on the latter. No definite interpretation should be based, moreover, on one hand alone.

Line of Inspiration. Also known as the line of intuition, this is one of the lesser lines of the hand, and may be absent or scarcely discernible in many hands. It begins usually on the mount of Moon [2], curving first inwards and later outwards, to terminate on the mount of Mercury. It denotes the possession of the faculty of intuition, or foresight; this may be merely what seems a shrewdness of perception, or may appear almost to be clairvoyance. It depends upon the degree of endowment, and this may be gauged from the clarity and continuity of the marking.

Inevitably, such a gift is associated with an instability and hypersensitiveness of temperament. A nature finely attuned to astral manifestations can with difficulty tolerate the shocks and jars of everyday life in busy cities. Though this line may be only very faintly indicated on a hand, it furnishes a highly important clue and should not be underestimated.

Line of Mars. This is a curving line sometimes found within the line of life upon the mount of Venus; it runs roughly parallel with the line of life [6]. It reinforces or modifies by its indications those of the outer line; in cases where the signs of the line of life are unfavourable or indifferent, the interpretation from the line of Mars will profoundly modify them and may put quite a different complexion upon the matter. When the line of life or the mount indicates definite attributes, a strong line of Mars will emphasize and strengthen them.

Lines of Affection. These used to be called marriage lines or lines of union, on the assumption that each one denoted a marriage or a love affair. It is better to regard them as signs of deep attachments formed or to be formed by the party. The lines are found— if at all—on the mount of Mercury, running inwards to the palm from the edge above the line of heart [13]. The age at which these events are indicated is shown only very approximately by the position of the line in the area bounded by the top of the mount and the line of heart beneath. By dividing this area into three intervals of twenty-five years, we can determine in which of them the line of affection is located.

The strength and duration of the attachment are shown by the clarity and depth of the line and its length. Defects on the line denote either a parting or the grave illness or death of one of the parties. A weakening or thinning down of the line as it goes on to the palm, suggests a coolness or a separation. A second and weaker line close below the first may denote the transfer of affections after an indeterminate period of doubt. When such a second line goes on strongly and the first one stops or weakens, the indication of a change of heart is stronger still.

The space in which the affection lines may be found is very small, and it is not easy, therefore, to interpret them with exactitude either as to date or detailed significance. Though they denote marriage, in the popular sense, it may be rather a union of hearts that is referred to; the individual, for example, may be single, or have had no thought of marriage. Generally, however, if he admits the truth, there will be a corroboration of an attachment so strong that in favourable circumstances it would lead to, or would have resulted in, a marriage with the object of his affections. A woman, particularly if her affections are unknown to, or unreciprocated by, the man she likes or loves, is reluctant to admit such a passion even to herself.

Some writers assert that the offspring of a marriage are indicated as to number by little vertical lines arising from the lines of affection. Others go so far as to claim they can read the sex and proclivities of children from marks on these verticals. Even a cursory inspection of the mount of Mercury will show how difficult it would be to attain any accuracy in such investigations; the lines when present are fine and short, a lens being needed to examine them. In some persons there are so many verticals that they would denote an embarrassingly large family! The truth is probably that only the strongest of the lines are to be taken into account. Confirmation of the readings of the lines of affection, or its opposite, can be obtained from influence lines.

Line of Sensuality. This line has an older name—the *Via Lascivia*, or lascivious line. It is sometimes found as a sort of parallel to the line of health [13], but is very often absent. It received its name from an impression that it denoted a strong endowment of the animal instincts and the preponderance of the less pleasant physical attributes. The line, when observed, is to be interpreted merely as a sign of vitality and, unless there are strong indications of sensuality elsewhere in the hand, it will not bear any unpleasant significance.

Influence Lines. These are fine lines that are found on the mounts or that run across the palm in different locations; some connect the mounts to the lines or one line to another. Marriage indications are shown by influence lines that rise on the mount of Moon and extend to the line of destiny [14]. These lines refer, in a general way, to influences brought to bear upon one's fate by other persons. They may be regarded as most favourable when they stop at the line of destiny.

A strong influence line in the twenties or thirties is fairly sure to refer to a marriage. If the line of destiny thereafter is unweakened and no defect appears on it in close proximity, a happy and permanent union is suggested. If the line of destiny is defective soon after it is joined or approached by the influence line [14], an opposite result is foreshadowed. The influence line itself should be free of blemishes in order that a happy union can be foretold.

When the influence line goes through the line of destiny and stops before reaching the line of life, indications are present of a later separation of the parties. Influence lines referring to marriage are also present on the mount of Venus. Apart from the line of Mars, there are other curved lines roughly concentric with the line of life but thinner and less strongly marked [17]; they refer to love episodes or more permanent attachments. Sometimes they may be read as denoting the influence on the subject of a spouse, a mother or a father—rarely of a sister or a brother.

Then there are fine lines which cross the mount more or less horizontally and traverse the line of life, or go farther and cut the line of destiny. These refer to the influence of people having blood ties with the subject. Whether this influence is favourable or unfavourable must be discerned from other signs on the lines of life and destiny. An influence line that cuts both life and destiny is more powerful than one that stops at the line of life.

Influence lines from Venus that cut the line of head [15] or line of heart denote the influence of members of the family in business affairs or matrimonial plans respectively.

Rascettes or *Bracelets*. These are lines at the wrist, and two, or more usually three, are to be seen there. Palmists of days gone by thought that the duration of life could be foretold from their number and that each one accounted for thirty years. It was also said that when the first one rose up in a loop on to the palm it referred to a childless marriage. As an index to longevity the lines are unreliable, but they may be taken as guides to the health and constitution of the individual. They should be clear and well defined for a healthy and favourable indication, but in a youthful subject they may not be very strongly impressed.

The rise of the first line on to the palm [16] is a sign of physical weakness, and is more significant in a woman than in a man. Lines running up to the mount of Moon from the rascettes are said to denote a disposition to travel. The health indications of these wrist lines need corroboration from the line of life.

The Quadrangle. Where the lines of head and heart are crossed by those of destiny and Sun there is formed a more or less rectangular enclosure—the Quadrangle [17]. Some writers understand this term to mean the whole area lying between the line of health, where this bisects the lines of head and heart, and the mount of Mars-above-Venus—enclosed above by the line of heart and below by the line of head. The more this latter area approaches to the rectangular, the more beneficent are the indications. Undue narrowness at the middle part is a sign of a heart easily influenced by the head—a materialistic temperament. A fair separation and an even, regular Quadrangle denote a well-balanced mind in which the emotional and the intellectual sides are consonant.

The presence of a number of small and thin lines in the Quadrangle [18] suggests an irresolute will and a mind easily affected by the dictates or opinions of other persons. Stars and other signs in the Quadrangle have been given various attributions, sometimes favourable and at other times the reverse. A cross (the Mystical Cross), formed by two short lines that intersect in the centre of the palm [17], is said to indicate a leaning towards the occult sciences.

The Great Triangle. This region lies below the line of head and is bounded by the curving line of life on one side and by the diagonally sloping line of health on the other [16]. Its size and conformation depend largely on the location of the line of life, and this latter, of course, upon the size and shape of the mount of Venus. A large Triangle is regarded as a favourable sign.

HOW TO READ THE HANDS

The student will have gathered that palmistry is the reading and interpretation of the hands—not of one hand only. No sound reading can be based on a single hand of an individual, for lines may be absent from the left and present in the right, or vice versa. Fingers and thumbs may show very different signs in the two hands; the mounts may differ; and even the length of the digits may be different. It is imperative, therefore, that any judgment based on examination of the active hand should be modified, if necessary, by the indications shown in the other.

The active hand in a normal person is the right one; in a left-handed subject the left hand is the active one and should first be examined. Glance at the back of the hand for its typological classification into one or other of the seven groups that we have described in an earlier section. Then try the thumb and fingers for flexibility; close the fingers and judge their length by the amount they project over the palm. Or the length of the back of the hand can be taken, as directed elsewhere, and the length of the second finger compared with it. The latter method is recommended when time permits. Examine and bend the thumb.

Now turn the hand palm upwards and scrutinize the lines; examine the mounts for their fullness and note any signs that may be present. The date of any outstanding indication on the principal lines can be gauged by its location. The minor lines and influence lines may now be inspected for any aid they may give in a character analysis or a prognostication. Defects that indicate grave calamities or those connected with the lines of affection, call for confirmation, moderation, or cancellation by signs on the opposite hand.

Hasty judgments or premature declarations are to be avoided, and no interpretation should be given to the subject until the second hand has told its story. In the case of unpleasant or unfavourable indications, the palmist must use his judgment as to how he words his delineation; the age, temperament and physical condition of his client are to be considered.

Warnings about the future are justified, and, indeed, imperative, when the hands indicate a future peril, but an impending event must be referred to in careful and discreet language. The future depends on the inter-relation of a multitude of events—some controllable by man and others that no one can influence—and upon the character of those around us. Who, then, dare foretell, in any but guarded terms, what the future holds in store? Avoid anything approaching fatalism in predictions. Destiny is not immutable, and man is master of his fate.

The active hand portrays our living character and destiny; the opposite or passive hand has impressed upon it our fate and our temperament as it should be, or should have been. We can estimate past achievement or failure by comparing the indications of the passive hand with those of the active one. How far we fall short of attainment can thus be seen; but realization of our imperfections, though it chastens, should not discourage. The past is a closed book, but the present is ours, and the future is a virgin page whereon we may write in letters of gold if we will. A great German poet has said, "What hands have built, hands can pull down." We would rather say, "What hands have wrought, hands can repair."

Interpretation of a Hand (No. 1)

The subject is a young woman. Her hand is of the utilitarian type, though it has many affinities with the philosophic. The thumb is short, with its phalanges fairly equal, and is widely separated from the fingers. The fingers are normal in length, taken as a whole, and they are also normally proportioned. As to the three "worlds," the first and second between them dominate the third.

Mounts. Venus is broad, and the line enclosing it makes a wide curve out upon the palm. The mount is marked with grilles. Jupiter is large and Saturn is normal. Mercury is somewhat flat and the mount of Sun also is not very prominent. The mount of Mars-above-Venus predominates over Mars-above-Moon, and the mount of Moon is large and full.

Lines. The line of life is marked by crosses and intersections. It touches the line of destiny at its lower end and runs close to, but does not join, the line of head. Where the latter line begins it is connected to the line of life by crossing lines from Mars-above-Venus. At its lower end the line of life is forked.

The line of head, which is long, begins boldly, but almost disappears after its junction with the line of Sun; it finishes weakly, low down on the mount of Moon.

The line of heart begins on the mount of Jupiter and for a short space runs parallel with the line of head. Later it diverges and takes an almost horizontal course to the percussion. The divergence of the lines of head and heart is remarkable.

The girdle of Venus is somewhat peculiar. Beginning strongly under Jupiter, it crosses the line of destiny and approaches the line of heart; then it turns upwards, undulates, and ends in a fork. After a separation it goes on again and is marked by two short gaps, continuing then fairly strongly to its end between the mounts of Sun and Mercury.

The line of destiny is forked at its origin and runs up vertically to join the line of life. Soon thereafter there is a gap, but the line continues strongly, crosses the line of head and stops at the line of heart. It takes up its course again at another point, and goes then almost vertically to its end on the mount of Saturn.

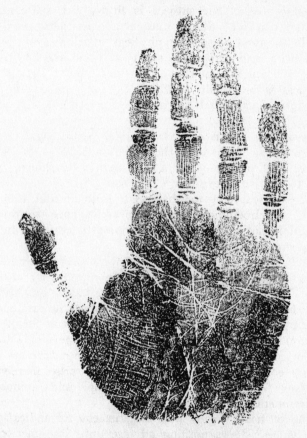

No. 1.—Hand of a Young Woman

The line of Sun begins really on the line of head, though two thin forking lines branch out from it below. It pursues a wavering course to the line of heart and beyond it, where it is met by thin fibrils from a line of affection. There is a bold line of Mars.

The Triangle is small, on account of the low descent of the line of head.

CHARACTER. Reading the hand and fingers from their shape we obtain the following indications regarding the character and ability of the subject:—

Strongest qualities: The subject is firm-willed, self-controlled, deliberate and truthful. She is musical and aesthetic, virile, and is also well endowed with the physical attributes of her sex. Inclined to pride and arrogance, she is despotic and obstinate in asserting her will, and is somewhat austere in manner. An indication of nervousness is practically nullified by other modifying attributions. She is devout, but not a little superstitious. Jealousy is denoted.

Other qualities: She is candid, amiable, gentle, loyal, prudent, shrewd, charitable, contented; there are indications of egotism, extravagance and prudishness. A hot temper is shown, with a disposition to cherish grievances.

The fingers denote a well-balanced, prudent and thoughtful mind; tact, resourcefulness and adaptability are shown; also ambition and initiative, with some boldness in adventuring forth into new spheres of activity.

Past and Future. The line of life shows a *past* career beset by minor troubles *after the first third.* It is connected by criss-cross lines to the line of head at the origin of the latter; and there are indications that the early years of life were spent in circumstances not too happy or prosperous. Alternatively, it may denote early childhood amid scenes of war or famine. The line of life foretells a fairly even career, though mishaps of a minor nature are shown all along its course. These misfortunes may arise merely from an antagonism of the subject towards the people and circumstances of her environment.

The line of head begins well and, except for indications of trivial mischances, shows nothing adverse until its junction with the line of Sun. Here, at the age of 50, is foretold a catastrophe; the line almost disappears for a space, but goes on haltingly with gaps and cross-bars to the base of the mount of Moon. By its length it denotes will-power and great mental ability; it is likely that the crisis foreshadowed may be connected with the mental health of the subject. She recovers, it is apparent, and other signs

—notably those of the line of life—portray a healthy and vigorous middle life and old age.

The line of heart has a Jupiterian origin, and suggests a nature which looks for affection infused with spirituality. It is influenced by the line of head for the first twenty years or so of life, after which there are indications that the subject is swayed less by reason and more by the dictates of her heart. An indeterminate and not very satisfactory love affair is shown at about the age of 20. Seldom have we seen a wider divergence of the lines of head and heart. At 27 years and again near 40 are foreshadowed crises of an emotional kind, but these disturbances of the heart are pacified, and the line of heart pursues its course evenly to the end. Happiness comes somewhat late in life, but is undoubtedly achieved in its fullness thenceforward.

The girdle of Venus denotes a well-matured physical make-up. Well on in life is foreshadowed a crisis of some kind followed by two or three difficult years, after which, however, the line goes on steadily and clearly.

The line of destiny is gapped at about 18 years; an influence line from the line of life touches it soon after it takes up its course again. Some catastrophe is evidently referred to at this age, accompanied by a change of fortune. At the line of heart there is an interruption in the line of destiny, which continues from a point a little to the right and goes on, weakly at first and then stronger, to terminate on Saturn. We can read this as foretelling another crisis in material affairs, this time at the age of about 42. Though a misfortune, it does not become a disaster. Health and wealth are affected, but circumstances soon improve in both directions and the further indications are favourable.

The line of Sun shows a vacillating fortune, and after the age of about 45 is not easy to read in this hand. Influence lines connect it to the line of health, and the latter gives no clear indication of the future. It is missing in the lower part of the hand. There are two squares in the Quadrangle, related perhaps to the misfortunes we have discerned from other signs.

On the whole, the interpretations are favourable; although ups and downs and crises are foretold, the latter part of life should be happy and prosperous, with many opportunities for that self-expression which the character of the subject demands.

INTERPRETATION OF A HAND (No. 2)

The subject is a man in the forties. The hand is of the knotty or philosophic type. Below are listed the chirognomical attributes in their order of magnitude:—

Value 4—Activity; Uprightness; Prepotence. *Value* 3—Sanguineness; Courage; Affection; Brilliance; Musicalness; Aestheticism; Devoutness. *Value* 2—Moral strength; Intellectuality; Candour; Sincerity; Austerity; Gen-

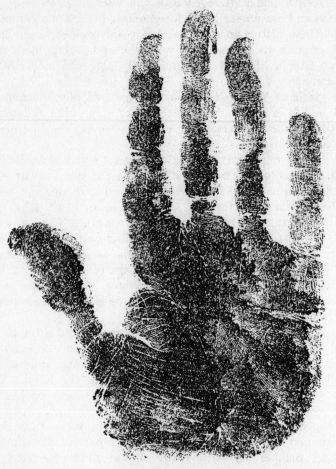

No. 2.—Hand of a Man

tleness; Generosity; Shrewdness; Seriousness; Strength; Artistic nature; Self-control; Truthfulness; Sympathy. *Value* 1—Firmness; Ambition; Boldness; Egotism; Creativeness; Extravagance; Prudence; Nobleness; Pride; Sagacity; Neatness; Jealousy; Hot temper.

READINGS FROM THE LINES

Line of Life.   Prudence, foresight, shrewdness; strong vitality. *No* defects on line.

Line of Head.   Strength of will, self-reliance, intellectual power; bold, independent spirit; imagination and creative ability, infused with energy and practical wisdom; prudence, sagacity and foresight.   *No* defects on line.

Line of Heart.   Stolidly sentimental; matter-of-fact attitude towards problems of daily life.   During the years of middle age— 40 to 50—the head governs the heart.   Undiminished energy and vitality throughout life.

Line of Destiny.   Coalesces with line of life.   From infancy to manhood this subject was under the influence of relatives and had no chance to follow an independent career.   At the age of 25 his career took a fresh turn.   At the age of 35 it was interrupted, and the signs indicate some wavering, but thereafter the line of destiny is favourable, and a successful later life can be predicted.

Line of Sun.   This line is absent from the lower part of the hand.   Starting at the line of heart, it indicates a late beginning of the real career for which the individual was fitted; not until the approach of middle life did he get his chance.

The upper and middle domains of the hand are hardly powerful enough to hold in check the lower, and there are some indications of a sensual nature.

M

THE SCIENCE OF GRAPHOLOGY

FROM the Greek "graphē," which means "writing," and the suffix "ology," which is applied to names of scientific studies, the word graphology is formed. Graphology is the study of a person's character and accomplishments through the medium of his or her handwriting.

At the outset it may be remarked that the extravagant claims frequently put forward by so-called graphologists must be ignored in any scientific treatment of the subject. It has often been declared that not only will the study of a handwriting reveal the writer's character, but it will also enable one to deduce the astral influences to which he is subjected, and thus to foretell what the future holds in store for him!

The true graphologist would not dare to profess such powers, which more properly are part of the divinatory science of astrology. The reader of handwriting bases his studies only on proved facts, the result of years of research and experiment and a careful sifting of the true from the false. He declares that by the study of the general style of handwriting, the formation of letters, alignment, and so on, it is possible to form an idea of the character and mental and physical condition, and possibly of the profession or calling, of the person who penned it. To do more than this is to introduce an element of superstition and vague surmise which is quite foreign to the deductions of the genuine graphologist.

Some of the most outstanding personalities in history have advocated the study of handwriting as being a reliable and valuable method of estimating character. Aesop, Aristotle, Virgil, Cicero, Julius Caesar and, in more modern times, Sir Walter Scott, Disraeli and Robert Browning are only a few of those people of talent and genius who have been keen students of graphology.

It may be said, however, by the general public that the deduction of character from handwriting was formerly regarded either merely as a pleasant and amusing pastime or else as sheer charlatanism unworthy of notice. Not until it began to be advocated by scientists throughout the world was it accepted as a serious study.

To-day graphology is universally recognized by the medical and legal professions, and it has proved so invaluable a help to people in their business and personal affairs that even the hardened cynic can scarcely remain unconvinced.

An intelligent study of the following chapters, the substance of which is endorsed by the leading graphologists of to-day, will not only provide the reader with an entirely new and fascinating hobby, but will also prove of incalculable value in judging the type of person with whom he or she contemplates entering upon a business or personal relationship.

How We Write

The action of writing, once it has been mastered in childhood, quickly becomes spontaneous, requiring very little conscious thought. If you are writing a letter to anyone you will concentrate chiefly on the subject matter, while your pen moves almost automatically across the paper as each new thought occurs to you. The pen itself is under the control of the muscles of the fingers, hand and arm, which, in turn, are directed by the mind. The manner in which the tracings are made by the pen, therefore, must bear a direct relationship to the mind which guides them.

Each variation of movement is unconsciously directed by the brain, and it is because of this that the graphologist can judge the mental state of the writer.

From certain signs, which will be demonstrated later, one can judge will-power and intellect; the extent of the writer's emotions; his or her morals; and, occasionally, profession or calling, as well as the general health of the person concerned.

Preliminary Steps

The first essential in making an analysis of handwriting is to ascertain that it has been made quite naturally and under conditions which have not hampered the ordinary style of the writer.

Every one of us has an accustomed speed with which he writes, and if this is either increased or decreased the result is modification in style. Hasty notes, a scribbled post card, and a carefully copied piece of text are very poor criteria, for in none of these cases is the writing perfectly natural. In each case the habitual writing speed has been varied, and, as a consequence, the style of the writer has undergone alteration.

An ordinary private or business letter forms the best basis of judgment—preferably one which has been written on unruled paper. This stipulation is made because, as we shall see later, there is much to be learned from the natural direction of the writing, without its being guided by ruled lines.

It must also be noted that faulty materials can do much to alter a writer's style. These may consist of badly-flowing ink, a damaged nib, or very harsh paper. If there is reason to suspect such causes, the graphologist should not attempt to form any judgment until he has seen other samples of handwriting written under normal conditions.

CHIEF CONSIDERATIONS

The following are the four main points to be considered:—

1. General style of the handwriting.
2. The shape of individual letters.
3. Various details, such as punctuation, margins and spacings.
4. The signature.

If possible, it is best to take into consideration the writer's age, nationality, education, and so on, all of which may be responsible for peculiarities of style. A very old person, for example, is inclined to write a weak and wavering hand, which would be a sign of a nervous or physical disorder if manifested by one who is young. Misspelt words written by an educated person would betray carelessness, while such mistakes by the uneducated are to be expected, as they are merely the result of ignorance.

Unfamiliarity with the language may cause the writing of a foreigner to appear hesitant or weak, although when writing in his own tongue his style may be progressive and strong. Such details as these do not strictly belong to the science of graphology, but it is essential to take them into consideration if we are not seriously to be misled.

Because so much is indicated by the extent of the pressure used when writing, and its variation, it is always best to judge from ink in preference to pencilled lines. The latter will show a more or less uniform thickness of the strokes, which is seldom a true representation of the force exerted by the fingers.

It should also be noted that it is very difficult to tell a feminine from a masculine hand. Although one frequently hears it asserted that a man writes more vigorously and, owing to his superior physical strength, uses more pressure than a woman, this "rule" has been found to have so many exceptions that it is totally un-reliable as a basis of judgment—at any rate for the amateur.

If the writer under consideration is known to be a woman, then one must make allowances for a little more adornment and, perhaps, a slightly more delicate manner in forming the letters. Otherwise all the advice given in this treatise applies equally to the hand of a man or a woman—we usually refer to the writer as "he" merely for the sake of convenience.

General Style

The person who possesses a normal, methodical mind, devoid of pride and vulgar display, will naturally write in a medium-sized hand. If it is rounded it shows kind-heartedness and a tactful nature, while if it is angular it suggests an inclination towards in-tolerance, and a healthy and brisk mentality.

The large and rounded style reveals one who is very generous and open-hearted. If this large style is angular, however, it indicates pride, maliciousness and frequently deceit.

Minutely small writing generally suggests the precise person, given to pedantry and sometimes petty-mindedness. Normally small writing may be taken as a general sign of carefulness, and a business-like mind. There are, however, so many physical causes which may influence the size of the hand (myopia, or short-sighted-ness, for instance, is often a cause of small writing), that we do not consider this factor so important as the proportionate size of letters.

If the text increases in size as one reads on, it indicates frankness and sincerity. A decrease in size shows cunning and dissimulation, especially if the legibility decreases also, for such a writer is in all probability accustomed to cloaking the real meaning of his words and actions.

Regularity in the size of letters is the result of an orderly, placid and unemotional mind, while great difference in size shows excessive emotionalism and lack of balance. Disproportionate sizing, such as

your luceptung I hope you

Large and Rounded, Large and Angular, and Minute Styles

forming some small letters almost as large as capitals, may mean an aggressive, fault-finding nature; or else it has a purely physical significance and indicates a loss of nerve control owing to disease.

ELABORATION AND NEATNESS

Excessive elaboration in the style is, nowadays, a sure sign of conceit and self-importance. The normal, well-balanced mind finds that all outward show in the form of complicated flourishes and paraphs is quite unnecessary, and will adopt a neat, clear and strictly plain hand. In past centuries it was considered to be a mark of good breeding and education to adorn one's writing in an "artistic" manner, but the rush and bustle of modern life allows little time for such niceties. Some reservation must be made in

Flourished Signature

the case of writing by Latin races, such as the French, Italians and Spanish, among whom a certain amount of flourish is still permissible, although even there the fashion is fast dying out.

A letter which is thoroughly tidy in all respects, written in a plain, medium-sized hand, with the letters and words in good alinement, shows the tidy, well-balanced and logical mind of the writer. A thoroughly untidy and illegible hand is a sign of mental slovenliness and lack of balance, but it does not necessarily mean that the author lacks talent or ability.

If the writing is difficult to read, but at the same time is in good alinement and presents a tidy appearance, one may conclude that the writer is given to dissimulation and ambiguity—he is not anxious that his speech or behaviour should be too clearly understood.

PRESSURE AND SPEED

A rapid scrawl shows nervous precipitation, hastiness and, often, inability for deep thinking; while if the letters are formed in a very wavy manner, provided it is not due merely to old age, it is a symptom of extreme neurasthenia, or some similar serious disorder

it is convenient   History

A Firm, Open Hand, and One that is Weak and Disjointed

of the nervous system, which results in a slackening of control over the motor nerves. Such symptoms are noticeable in one who has led a dissipated life.

The calm and forceful person adopts a strong and clear hand. Very weak lines are made by those who are deficient in physical strength or timid by nature. An abnormally strong hand, however, in which the writing appears to have been slashed on to the page, suggests a passionate person who is unable to control his emotions and is obsessed with his own importance. Meticulous precision in the formation of thick and thin strokes, giving the writing a copy-book appearance, is the sign of a subordinate nature, with little imagination or opinion. Perfectly uniform and very thick lines, displaying little or no distinction between the upstrokes and the downstrokes, denote the unrefined nature.

SLOPE

The slope of the handwriting is one of the most valuable indications of fundamental character, and the information to be gathered from it may be summed up as follows:—

1. Completely upright hand—thoughtfulness and complete self-control combined with an inclination to be rather cold and reserved.
2. Slight slope to the right—sensitive and artistic nature with the emotions well in hand.
3. Exaggerated right slope—great emotional susceptibility and little control over the temperament, sometimes amounting to morbid sentimentality.
4. Slight slope to the left—reserve combined with a certain amount of pride, very little artistic inclination.
5. Abnormal left slope—repression of emotions which may be as strong as those of the writer with a right-hand slope. This results in extreme moodiness and fits of melancholia.

It is important to notice that the slope may vary with the state of mind at the time of writing, for the slope is an indication of the emotions as well as the fixed character. Thus a passionate love letter or a letter written in great anger may contain writing which is infinitely more sloped than is the usual style of the writer.

WORD-SPACING

Well-spaced words and letters suggest generosity and open-heartedness, while an avaricious and mean-minded character will cramp the handwriting. Exaggerated spacing is that of the irresponsible and extravagant type, which totally lacks a sense of proportion. The practice of joining several words together usually springs from the enthusiastic but rather hasty nature, the type of person who has something to say, and loses as little time as possible in saying it. Such a character will be inclined to be rather too frank in expressing an opinion.

LINE-DIRECTION

The general direction of the lines of text and the spaces between them also offer an excellent and ready means of determining both character and emotions.

If the lines run horizontally (without any assistance from ruled paper) it is a sign of an orderly mind, clear and logical and little given to vain hopes or unjustified fears. If the lines slope upwards at the ends this portrays the optimism and great ambition of the writer, who is one who feels well prepared to surmount the obstacles of life. If this upward slope amounts almost to climbing it does not necessarily mean ambition, but great exaltation of mind at the time of writing.

A downward slope at the ends, however, is a bad sign, for it indicates pessimism, fatigue, discouragement, and that sense of fatalism which at once smothers any ambition that might exist. If the downward slope is particularly exaggerated the writer is in a state of complete discouragement, despair and neurotic depression.

When the lines begin horizontally but incline downwards at the middle and resume the normal level towards the end (concave) it indicates a person of stoic outlook, one who will show great courage in facing difficulties which may beset him. On the other hand, if the middle of the line rises above the two extremities (convex) it is a sign of lack of stamina, and also of inability to persevere with an enterprise.

Undulating lines, those in which the words rise and fall, indicate an unstable character, a nature which is frequently inconsistent and which also displays a certain amount of cunning.

SPACING METHODS

The characteristics indicated by the manner of spacing the lines are as follows:—

Moderate and equal spacing—mental equilibrium.
Very little spacing—economy, avarice.
Very wide spacing—generosity, prodigality.
Unequal spacing—artistic nature and versatile ability.

If the size of the paper is such as to cause a cramping together of the lines, it is obviously illogical to take such a letter or document as a standard of judgment; and the same applies to a letter which is very widely spaced in order to spin it out, and to make it appear longer than it really is. If either of these reasons is suspected, it is better to examine further correspondence of the writer and judge from what is his most frequently adopted style.

LINES

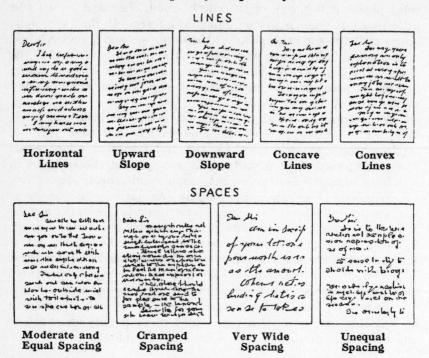

| Horizontal Lines | Upward Slope | Downward Slope | Concave Lines | Convex Lines |

SPACES

| Moderate and Equal Spacing | Cramped Spacing | Very Wide Spacing | Unequal Spacing |

MARGINS

Although they are one of the most outstanding features when examining a letter, for this very reason the true graphologist does not attach a great deal of importance to margins. As the reader becomes more and more acquainted with the elements of the study of handwriting, he will realize that it is not the *obvious* characteristics which betray the writer, but those little details which are a more intimate part of the true self. Nevertheless, it is as well to bear the following general rules in mind, as they have been formulated as a result of years of practical experience and of experiment by experts, and frequently convey useful hints when it comes to summing up the writer's nature.

No margin at all suggests a nature inclined towards meanness.

A single, moderate-sized and regular margin, one which is equal in breadth throughout, is the sign of a well-balanced mind; if *too* regular it discloses a lack of imagination, but great will-power.

Two margins, one on either side of the text, denote the pedant, a man of exacting nature paying a trifle too much attention to detail. It is well to bear in mind, however, that if the writer of the letter is an author, or journalist, or anyone accustomed to writing for publication, the presence of two margins is only the mark of his calling, for it gives a clearer appearance to the text and leaves room for marginal corrections or notes to be made on either side.

A margin which increases in size as the text runs down the page denotes a prodigal nature.

A margin decreasing in size, that is, with the text starting farther to the left as one reads down the page, denotes economy; it is the sign of the shrewd housekeeper.

Very wide margins denote prodigality.

Very irregular margins, with the left extremity of the text running down in a wavy line, denote irresolution and softness and a lack of mental stability.

MARGINS

| Single | Double | Increasing | Decreasing |

REFERENCE TABLE

General Style

SIZE:
Medium—methodical mindedness.
Large—generosity, open-heartedness.
Small—business-like brain, attention to detail.
Minutely small—petty-mindedness, pedantry, myopia.
Increase in size of text—frankness, sincerity.
Decrease in size of text—cunning, dissimulation.
Regularity of size—placidity, lack of emotionalism.

REFERENCE TABLE (*continued*)

Irregularity in size of text—lack of balance.
Disproportionate letters—fault-finding nature, loss of nerve control.

FORM:
Many useless flourishes—self-importance.
Plain—intelligence, good balance.
Untidy and illegible—mental slovenliness.
Neat but illegible—ambiguity, deceit.
Rapid scrawl—precipitation, lack of concentration.
Rounded—kindness.
Wavering—disordered nervous system, old age.
Angular—intolerance.

PRESSURE:
Stressed—forceful will-power.
Weak—timidity or physical weakness.
Slashed—passion.
Uniform and thick—unrefined nature.
Copy-book style—subordination, lack of imagination.

SLOPE:
None (upright hand)—self-control, thoughtfulness, reserve.
To the right—artistic, sensitive nature.
Exaggerated right slope—great emotional susceptibility, little control over temperament.
Slight backward slope—reserve, pride.
Abnormal backward slope—repression, morbidity.

LINES:
Horizontal—orderly, logical mind.
Sloping upwards—ambition, optimism.
Climbing—exaltation.
Sloping downwards—discouragement, pessimism.
Dropping—despair.
Undulating—instability of character.

SPACING:
Words and letters well spaced—generosity.
Words and letters very widely spaced—irresponsibility.
Words and letters cramped—mean-mindedness, greed.
Words joined together—enthusiasm, hastiness, excessive frankness.
Equal between lines—mental equilibrium.
Unequal between lines—artistic temperament versatility.
Very wide between lines—generosity, prodigality.
Cramped between lines—economy, avarice.

MARGINS:
None—meanness.
Moderate and equal—well regulated intellect.
Double—pedantry.
Increasing—extravagance.
Decreasing—economy.
Very wide—prodigality.
Irregular—instability.

Do not be discouraged if some characteristics of style seem to be contradictory when they are interpreted. The mental make-up of every human being is inconsistent to a greater or less degree, and "clear-cut" characters exist only in drama or fiction. Thus, if we are examining a handwriting which is very cramped (denoting greed) but widely spaced between lines (denoting generosity), we must allow the one to modify the other and conclude that the writer is liable to be greedy but will, on some occasions, display a tendency towards generosity.

Again, if margins increase in breadth (denoting extravagance), but the lines are close together (denoting economy), we may gather that the writer is economical in some matters and extravagant in others—quite a natural human trait. One may continue endlessly to combine these various characteristics, and a little common sense is all that is necessary to form a balanced judgment.

INDIVIDUAL LETTERS

As we enter into a deeper study of character from handwriting our powers of observance are put to the test. Although much may be gathered from the first glance at the general style, a more detailed examination is necessary before a complete mental picture of the writer can be formed. Frequently a magnifying glass is necessary to observe the less obvious peculiarities of letters, and we would advise the reader to make use of one if he wishes to take a serious interest in the science of graphology.

We will consider first of all the style and general formation of capital letters:—

CAPITALS

1. Block—preciseness of mind.
2. Simple—good sense, intelligence.
3. Ill-formed—carelessness, indolence, lack of education.
4. Flourished and elaborate—false pride, inferior intellect.
5. Small in proportion to following letters—modesty.
6. Large in proportion to following letters—self-importance, bumptiousness.
7. Broad—boastful nature.
8. Cramped—cunning, apprehensive mind.
9. Passing down well below level of following letters—culture and refinement.
10. Set above level of following letters—conceit.
11. Joined to the next letter—confidence, sequence of ideas.
12. Larger at the head—arrogance.
13. Larger at the foot—pessimistic nature.
14. Beginning with a hook—acquisitiveness, determination to succeed.

15. Beginning with a long curve to the head—reserve, concentration.
16. Ending with a hook—obtuseness, lack of sensitiveness.
17. Underlining the small letters—excessive confidence and self-satisfaction.

In forming capital letters, it is quite possible that a person will adopt an unnatural style for the sake of making an impression. If this has been the case it is quite easy to detect, for (*a*) the capital

CAPITALS

letter will show all the signs of the labour spent in making it, and (*b*) it will be inconsistent with the rest of the style. Very flourished or elegant capitals, for example, are frequently found in a handwriting which is otherwise plain and commonplace in the less conspicuous parts, the latter being the more unconscious and thus more natural style of the writer.

The old-fashioned method of graphology required a minute examination of each letter of the alphabet, accompanied by long lists of each trait of character indicated by the various peculiarities. Modern graphologists consider this to be quite unnecessary and also misleading. Everyone varies his letters slightly, and to form any hard and fast rule results in totally inaccurate deductions being made.

We must judge from the general style rather than individual letters, taking such factors as dimension, shape, slope, openness, joining strokes, and so on, into consideration. There are a few individual letters having special significance and these will be mentioned a little later on.

SMALL LETTERS

The following are the characteristics suggested by small letters in general:—

Broad and low letters—sensitiveness; if very broad—sensuality.
Broad and high—ostentation, showmanship.
Narrow and low—subordination, greed.
Narrow and high—generous nature, charity combined with a business-like brain.
Cramped—avarice, lack of intelligence.
Minute—susceptibility, scientific mind.
Regular—practical-mindedness, physical strength.
Irregular—lack of stability, artistic sense.
Very rounded—joviality, amiability.
Very angular—austerity, spitefulness.
Square—ill temper, domineering nature.
Delicately formed—artistry, gentleness.
Thick—sensuality, worldliness.
Firm—balanced judgment, strength of will.
Broken—indecision, weakness.

We have already mentioned the slope of handwriting in our comments on general style. Sometimes it is found that the letters are irregular in their direction, some leaning towards the right and some towards the left. This is a sign of an inward struggle to suppress the emotions which is not always successful; it denotes the type of person who has occasional bursts of temperamental display followed by a great show of reserve or even sulkiness.

LETTER-STROKES

Upstrokes and downstrokes can indicate much. If they are long and clearly formed, alertness of mind and physical strength is suggested. Shortened strokes are made by those of a cautious nature who are unwilling to commit themselves or express definite opinions.

The strokes which are made above the line, such as those of *t*, *d* and *l*, refer particularly to mental conditions, while those made below, such as in *f*, *g* and *y*, tell of the writer's physical state. Larger strokes above the line show the domination of mind over body, while larger strokes below the line indicate those who concentrate chiefly on the physical side of life, and prefer sport to any kind of study.

The style of writing which dispenses altogether with loops, as in "script," generally indicates a type of person who will be rather more severe and pay greater attention to minor matters than the writer who makes full use of loops and curves. The practice of curving a lower stroke to the left, giving it a hook-like formation, denotes the humorous or whimsical character.

Certain letters, both capital and small, are particularly indicative of the writer's nature:—

M made with three hooks shows culture and an appreciation of beautiful things.
M made with two hooks shows commonplace intellect, a sign of failure.
N made with two hooks shows education, equal temperament.
N made with one hook shows precipitation, conceit.

The Self-symbol

The capital *I* is the symbol of self, and in the same way that we may judge the conceit of people by their use of it in speech, so we can gauge their pretensions from the manner in which they write it.

An excessively large *I*, which is out of all proportion to the other capital letters, signifies intense egotism, for the writer all the while emphasizes this self-symbol and gives it an importance accorded to no other letter. If a large *I* is used to begin with, and decreases in size as one reads on, it shows a person who has little real confidence in himself, but attempts to disguise this shortcoming from his friends and acquaintances.

The normally confident, modest and efficient type of character forms the self-symbol firmly and clearly, and about the same size as the other capitals. The minute and almost indistinguishable *I* shows timidity and weakness; it is the mark of the person who feels too inferior to air an opinion.

Details of Small Letters

Letters which contain a circular stroke, such as *a* and *o*, have a significance in the manner in which the circles, or part circles, are closed. If they are firmly and consistently closed it denotes reserve, a secretive nature; closed with loops shows concentration and will-power; slightly open at the top, frankness, good-humour, lack of affectation; wide open, expansiveness, garrulity; open at the bottom, deceit, fraud, and a general inclination towards criminality; open at the side, indiscretion, tactlessness.

The small *d* is made in a various number of ways, and it can tell the graphologist much regarding the writer's character. Here are the chief variations and their meanings:—

1. Upright copy-book style—subordination, simplicity.
2. Upright but less carefully formed—idealistic nature.
3. Inclined to the right (without hook or loop)—imagination, artistry.
4. Turned to the left—intellectuality.
5. Turned to the right—foresight, intuition.
6. With short loop—precipitancy.
7. Loop or hook covering preceding letters—difficult disposition, love of argument.
8. Several loops—conceit.
9. Loop and hook—dreaminess, lack of practical ideas.
10. Upper part curved back on to or below the line—Egotism, selfishness.
11. Long-loop—strict principles, inclined to narrow-mindedness.

Most revealing of all the small letters is *t*, the cross-stroke of which can be made in such an infinite variety of ways. It would be incorrect to say that one person always crosses his *t*'s in exactly the same way, but a brief examination will quickly show the most frequently used method, which must be taken as the dominant or characteristic. If there is great uniformity it shows the painstaking, methodical qualities of the writer.

The illustration below shows the chief ways of forming a *t* cross-bar, both when the letter is made with two strokes, one for the main body of the letter and another for the bar, and when it is made with one stroke only.

SMALL T's

POSITION

1. Middle of downstroke—mental equilibrium, thoughtfulness.
2. High up—will-power, intellectual energy.
3. On top—domineering character, love of power.
4. Above and not touching—hesitancy, nervousness.
5. Low down—subordination, servility.
6. At the bottom—spite.
7. To the right—expression, a will to succeed.
8. To the left—timidity, repression.
   Crossing downstroke—forcefulness.

LENGTH

1. No cross-bar at all—conceit or ill nature.
2. Long—energy, eagerness.
3. Short—weakness, petty-mindedness.
4. Cross-bar used for more than one *t*—impatience.
5. Cross-bar cutting through letters on either side—maliciousness, spite.

PRESSURE (cross-bar)

1. Fine—delicacy of mind, vivacity.
2. Normal—intelligence, self-control.
3. Thick—strong will.
4. Slashed—vulgarity, greed, passion.

SHAPE

1. Concave curve—sociability, gentleness.
2. Convex curve—materialism, greediness.

3. Beginning with a downward hook—lack of confidence, weariness
4. Beginning with an upward hook—temper.
5. Ending with a downward hook—obstinacy.
6. Ending with an upward hook—tenacity, great endurance.

Direction

1. Inclined upwards—ambition, combative spirit.
2. Horizontal—equilibrium, just nature.
3. Inclined downwards—stubbornness, obstinacy.

One Stroke

1. Middle position of cross-bar—balance.
2. High position of cross-bar—strong will.
3. Low position of cross-bar—hastiness, impatience.
4. Ascending cross-bar—optimism, strength.
5. Descending cross-bar—weakness, indecision.

The *I*-Dots

Dotting the *i* has long since acquired a proverbial significance, although the modern graphologist does not attach so much importance as to the exact manner in which it is done.

In general, a total absence of dots shows intense carelessness, weakness or impatience, while dots placed in their correct position directly over the *i* naturally indicate the methodical, painstaking nature of the writer. A light dot placed high up implies idealism, keen imagination; if it is high and heavy there is an indication of domination and ill temper. When the dot is placed low and is thick it is a sign of vulgarity coupled with a taste for material, worldly pleasures.

The normally intelligent and active person usually places the dot to the right of the *i*; if it is on the left it suggests underdevelopment of the mind and therefore limited intellect. You will notice that all *forward* movements in graphology, such as *t* bars on the right, and *i's* dotted on the right, denote progression, energy, expression, while regressive or *backward* movements show underdevelopment, timidity, repression.

Joining Between Letters

If the words of a handwriting present a thoroughly inharmonious and broken appearance it is generally the sign of inaccuracy, hastiness and impatience, while if each letter is carefully joined to the next it shows diligence, conscientiousness and general efficiency. Nevertheless, it should be noted that this careful joining frequently indicates the artlessness of a subordinate nature, the clerk or typist who pays more attention to the actual appearance of the handwriting rather than the subject matter.

The leaving of a gap between the first letter of a word and those which follow shows an intuitive nature, or one who sees what is likely to happen and makes the necessary preparations. Gaps which occur with regularity, after every three or four letters for example, indicate mental balance and an ability for consistent and logical thought. This peculiarity is frequently found in the handwritings of eminent scientists, lawyers and judges.

A wide, rounded joining is almost invariably the mark of a gentle, placid disposition, that of one who has his emotions well under control. If the joining is narrower, making it more oval or elliptical in shape, it indicates firm-mindedness and a personality of which it is not easy to take advantage.

The exceedingly sharp-pointed and angular connecting link shows brusqueness, and a tendency towards cruelty. At one time this angular style was taught to the children in German schools, but it was later superseded by the flowing, rounded lines of the English copy-book.

It may be taken as a general rule that the more a letter is rounded the greater the degree of kind-heartedness and tolerance on the part of the writer. If the small *n*, for example, is so written as to appear like a *u* it is a sign of benevolence and devotion. On the other hand, letters which have an unusually angular form show inclinations towards intolerance, hardness, or even spite.

First and Last Letters of Words

Many handwritings are characterized by a short line preceding, and joined to, the first letters of words. This is always an affectation as, strictly speaking, it is totally unnecessary and requires to be cultivated. Very often it is an attempt at self-expression. If the line is rather long and rigid it shows a combative nature and one which is given to argument. If, however, the writing itself is generally weak, the writer has probably affected this combative style in order to cover his real weakness and indecision of mind. A curved line indicates vivacity and dash, while an initial hook suggests that the writer possesses a miserly and grasping nature.

Few people form the last letter of a word with as much care as they do the first; there is almost always a slight deformation or difference in alinement which varies in degree according to the character of the writer. The table below gives the chief variations in the formation of last letters and explains their meanings:—

> Shortened or made narrower—economical nature, depression.
> Enlarged—extravagance, generosity, exaltation.
> With straight line—forcefulness, impetuosity.
> With curved line—miserliness, deception.
> Turning back—conflicting ideas, hesitancy.
> Much thicker—strong will.
> Much thinner—modesty, timidity.
> Slightly rising—gratitude, optimism.
> Rising high—equivocation.
> Proper level—kindness, affection, courtesy.
> Slightly descending—practical-mindedness.
> Deeply descending—love of money.
> Hook-like—determination and tenacity.

PUNCTUATION

Early studies in graphology made much of the methods and meanings of various different styles of punctuation. The modern expert, however, does not attach much graphological importance to the manner in which a person forms his exclamation marks, full-stops, commas, and other punctuation marks, or to their position regarding the alinement of the writing.

There are, as common sense indicates, only two ways of punctuation—right and wrong. The writer whose brain is alert, and who realizes the necessity of saying exactly what he means, will conscientiously punctuate his writing correctly, showing the necessary pauses which would take place in speech. A certain latitude must, of course, be allowed, especially in a personal letter, which is usually written at a fairly high speed and with less deliberation then anything which is meant for publication.

Thoroughly bad punctuation is almost an unforgivable sin, for it can cause so much confusion to the reader that it often results in a complete misunderstanding and exactly the opposite meaning of a sentence being taken. Bad punctuation may be a sign of an inconsiderate, muddle-headed brain, of sheer ignorance, or intense nervous precipitation and haste. We all know the rather nervy, excitable type of person who hardly pauses for breath when talking; and the same characteristic is evident when speech is translated into writing.

An unnecessary number of exclamation marks shows the enthusiasm of the young and ardent. Specimen letters from boys and girls at school are found to contain exclamation marks out of all proportion to the significance of the subject matter. An excessive number of commas is the usual sign of the ignorant but conscientious type, who feels that there *ought* to be a few commas scattered about the text, but does not know where or how frequently to place them.

The actual formation and position of the punctuation signs usually follow the general style of the handwriting, and although attempts have been made to classify the various forms according to pressure exerted, alinement, and good or bad outline of question marks, there is so little consistency, even in the same handwriting, that it is impossible, by this means, to deduce anything definite regarding the writer's character.

FIGURES

There are almost as many variations in the formation of figures as there are of letters, and the former must not be overlooked when we examine any piece of writing containing them.

Well-formed figures, made with not more than two strokes of the pen and in a line with the adjoining words, show integrity and frankness. If the figures are placed unevenly, being sometimes above and sometimes below the line, it indicates confusion and a lack of mathematical precision on the part of the writer. When numbers are formed with more than two strokes, that is, in an unnecessarily elaborate manner or with double lines, it is a very strong indication of criminality. This latter characteristic is dealt with later in this study under the section devoted to "The Criminal Hand."

The following figures have a special significance in their formations:—

3, with a horizontal line for the head—accuracy, ruthlessness.

3, formed like a wavy, vertical line—nervousness, inability.

3, looped and very rounded—simplicity.

5, with a single stroke (like an *S*)—dreaminess, lack of practical ideas.

8, squat and fat—sensuality, material greed.

8, high and thin—amiability, artistic sense.

8, with upper circle larger—intellectuality.

8, with lower circle larger—energy, physical strength.

9, with vertical tail—strength of personality and will-power.

9, with sloping tail—mistrustfulness, cautious nature.

9, with curved tail (as in print)—mathematical mind, financial ability.

THE SIGNATURE

Earlier on in this study we remarked on the significance of the personal *I*, and pointed out that because it is the symbol of self the graphologist can judge the conceit or modesty of the writer from the manner in which he forms it. The same may be said of the signature, which is the personality of the writer transformed on to paper. This is, however, usually made with a little more deliberation than ordinary words, for the writer unconsciously feels that from his signature he will be judged.

The number of ways in which one can sign one's name is so great that it would be quite impossible to classify each signature according to its superficial appearance and to list each characteristic betrayed. Such a classification, too, is quite unnecessary, for the graphologist is careful not to judge from the *obvious* appearance, as we have frequently emphasized. He has been able instead, from the study of millions of signatures, to classify the various *basic* features and, from practical experience, he has been able to compile an amazingly complete list of the various signature styles and their interpretations.

Unlike the old belief, lack of flourish in a signature does not necessarily mean mediocrity. Some of the greatest men of to-day sign their name in the simplest manner, without flourish or underlining. As a general rule it may be said that the absence of flourish shows modesty and a quiet confidence in one's own ability, while the complicated signature is that of the pretentious person, probably lacking in a sense of proportion and therefore scarcely likely to possess the makings of greatness. If the signature is so highly ornate as to be almost unreadable, and shows signs of having had much time spent on its elaborations, it is the mark of a fool and an idler.

The following are the chief classifications of signatures and their interpretations:—

1. Absence of any flourish or line—modesty, self-confidence.
2. With an underlining, downward stroke not joined to the name—strong but cautious nature.
3. With a horizontal underlining stroke either straight or with curves—great strength of will.
4. Followed by a dot—prudence, self-consciousness.
5. Followed by a downward stroke joined to the last letter—resolution, and a nature which is quick to take offence.
6. Followed by stroke which curves back horizontally underneath—grudge-bearing, unforgiving nature.
7. Followed by a curved upward stroke—ambition, good humour.
8. Followed by a surrounding stroke, framing the name—secretiveness, wariness.
9. Followed by strokes surrounding the name—affectation, lack of consideration, and disdainfulness.
10. Followed by an almost vertical line—conceit and spite.
11. Followed by a downward stroke of more than one curve—cheerfulness, good nature.
12. Followed by a hooked line—pugnacity.
13. Followed by an angular backstroke—great physical energy, brusqueness.
14. Covered with a curved and complicated flourish—deceitfulness coupled with ability.
15. Underlining curved "corkscrew" flourish—cunning and dishonesty.
16. Underlining wavy line—criminality.

SIGNATURES

17. Followed by or underlined by a knotted lasso—skilfulness, especially in manual work.
18. Followed by an upward line similar to the bass clef—musical ability, artistry.
19. Signature showing signs of retracing—nervousness, a wandering mind.
    Signature larger than ordinary writing—confidence, forcefulness.
    Signature smaller than ordinary writing—modesty, affectation.

PHYSICAL CONDITION

Since handwriting results from a combination of mind and muscle, the physical state of the body must influence the movement of arm, hand and fingers, thus causing the pen to move across the paper in a certain manner. Our nervous system is so sensitive that it is quickly affected by the condition of bodily health, and this condition is registered on paper.

It is well known that a person who is very ill writes in a much weaker style than one whose health is good, for the former has not the strength to use pressure with the pen, a fault which results in wavering and broken lines. After the serious illness of King George V several specimens of his signature were published which gave a clear indication of the various stages of health through which he had passed. When the first symptoms of illness set in he began to sign State documents and letters with a distinctly lighter pressure, while the lines lacked their characteristic firmness of direction; with the increase of sickness the signature became very weak and broken. Then, as he gradually recovered his normal health, the signature increased in force and stability until it was restored to the normal strength.

A common indication of physical weakness is the gradual falling off in pressure as the writing proceeds. The text may begin quite firmly, but soon there is evidence of the writer's fatigue; the upstrokes and downstrokes become wavy and uncertain, while the general legibility gradually decreases. If we have such handwriting under examination it is safe to assume that the writer is not in his normal state of health. But we must not confuse this with the consistently weak hand, which indicates the permanent physical weakness of an invalid or an old person.

We do not claim that it is possible to tell the disease or infirmity from the study of handwriting, but it has been proved that certain peculiarities in the letters made by sick persons bear some relation to the approximate part of the body which is diseased or in an abnormal condition. If a writer suffers from headaches, for example, he will very often make some slight modification in the tops of letters—the top loops of the letters *l* and *h* may be broken or cramped. A person suffering from chest or stomach trouble may unconsciously malform the body of short letters such as *e*, *a* and *o*, while those suffering from leg or foot complaints may unknowingly modify the lower parts of letters, such as the loops of *f*, *y* and *g*.

Generally, however, we do not advise the reader to attempt to state the nature of the illness from which the writer may be suffering, for this belongs to the sphere of an expert known as a Graphic Pathologist, and requires years of study and experience in order to attain any proficiency. It is better to confine oneself to the study of the general indications of ill health which may be listed as follows:—

a. Pressure decreasing in strength.

b. Broken loops and lines.

c. Marks on the paper above or below the lines, showing where the pen has rested.

d. Incomplete words, or those that have indistinguishable letters towards the end.

e. General illegibility which is not characteristic of the writer.

To draw a distinction between the marks of *mental* and *physical* weakness is very difficult, for it is an acknowledged fact that both the mind and the body are affected by ill health. We may take it, therefore, that the symptoms named above do not apply to actual conditions of the body only but are also applicable to an abnormal mental state.

Characteristics of Occupation

The profession or trade of a person is sometimes revealed by his handwriting, although it is not easy to frame any detailed rules regarding this. It is quite obvious, for example, that when a farm labourer sits down to write he is infinitely less familiar with the use of pen, ink and paper than is a university professor or an author.

The man who is accustomed to manual work will be clumsy in holding and manipulating the pen; the absence of education will necessitate his writing slowly and with much thought, and his lack of practice in the formation of outlines will probably cause them to be ill-shaped and inharmonious.

The artist, on the other hand, will write with the delicacy and grace of line that he would introduce into his pictures. Sculptors often "chisel" out their letters as they would marble, giving them a characteristically blocked appearance and great accuracy of outline. An unconscious imitation of print is frequently found in the writing of authors and journalists, while the surgeon delights in fine points and evenly balanced cross-strokes.

Actors and actresses will adopt the "emotional" style, with sloping, flowing lines and occasional flourishes; the architect pays great attention to proportion and usually prefers an upright style to a sloping style. Musicians have often been known to incorporate musical signs into their handwriting, such as a flourish similar in appearance to the bass clef at the beginning of capitals.

Angular joining lines and letters are the mark of the soldier, who portrays the characteristic brusqueness fostered by military discipline. A copying clerk often adopts in private life the "copper-plate" style which he uses for documents, but examples of this are now rare, for the typewriter has taken the place of hand-copied work.

The Criminal Hand

Under this heading we do not propose to make an elaborate study of the handwriting of known and convicted criminals. This calls for expert knowledge acquired by years of experience, and it is of little use to the amateur in graphology. But there are certain characteristics which are almost invariably present in the writing of potential or professed criminals which can be observed almost at first glance. These features of criminality have been ascertained as a result of a careful searching out and comparison of specimens of handwriting that are preserved in police files, and it is curious to observe the consistency which prevails in many of them.

The usual criminal hand presents an uncertain and intimidated appearance, both capital and small letters being broken and their outlines showing signs of shakiness and retracing. Most curious of all is the inclination to make "circular" letters, such as *a* and *o*, with a *clockwise* movement of the pen, instead of *anti-clockwise*, as is the case with the normal person. Such a movement prevents the writing from "flowing," and although the letters may be joined they present a very inharmonious appearance.

The letter *o* is frequently left open at the bottom, a characteristic seldom found in the writing of honest persons. Spacings and margins are usually very irregular, while the lines of text will sometimes rise to excess and sometimes drop at the ends. More often than not capital letters are made with elaborate flourishes; moreover, they show signs of the labour expended in forming them, although their outline is probably far from correct.

The hoaxer or swindler may take pains to assume what he considers to be a "distinguished" hand, full of conceited flourishes, but he lapses into his more natural style in the less conspicuous parts of the text. A close examination will show the great difference between the affected and the natural style.

All figures should normally be made with not more than two strokes of the pen. Three or four strokes usually show dishonesty in money matters, as does a figure presenting an ambiguous appearance, so that it might be taken for another number. Unnecessary flourishes on figures are seldom the sign of an honest man—the handwriting of an embezzler, for instance, often shows a marked inclination towards elaboration in figures.

We must emphasize the fact, however, that a criminal hand in the graphological sense does not necessarily mean that of a person who has committed, or contemplates committing, a crime. It merely describes the *psychological* nature of the writer as being one that has a criminal or dishonest tendency, which, however, may be brought out only by force of circumstance.

Practical Applications

If you have mastered the elementary principles of reading character from handwriting which have been condensed and simplified in the previous pages, you should have no difficulty in analysing

most of the correspondence or documents which may pass through
your hands.

Let us suppose that we have received the following letter from
a prospective employee:—

> Dear Sir
>
> I thank you for your letter
> of January 18th. and will be
> at your offices on Tuesday
> next as requested
>
> Yours faithfully
> J. Simmonds

Our first consideration is the general style, and next the details
of capital and small letters, *t*-bars, *i*-dots, and so on. So let us set
out our analysis under the appropriate headings.

		CHARACTERISTICS
GENERAL STYLE	Neat and of normal size:	*Methodical mind*, business-like brain.
	Letters clear and unambiguous:	*Frankness*, sincerity.
	Stressed pressure:	Forceful will-power.
	Upright:	*Self-control.*
	Moderate, equal spacing:	*Mental equilibrium.*
LETTERS, CAPITAL	Block:	*Preciseness of mind.*
SMALL	Firm:	Practical mind, *physical strength.*
	Upright:	Placidity, *self-control.*
	Firmly rounded:	Amiability, delicacy.
	Lower strokes large and well formed:	*Physical strength*, love of sport.

PERSONAL I	Normal size and firmly formed:	*Confidence,* efficiency.
A and O	Open at top:	*Frankness,* good humour.
SMALL D	Curved to left:	Intellectuality.
T-BARS	High and on the right:	*Will-power,* energy, expression.
	One bar used for two *t's*:	Inclination towards impatience.
	Normal pressure:	Intelligence, *self-control.*
	Inclined upwards:	A m b i t i o n, combative spirit.
I-DOTS	High:	Idealism, keen imagination.
JOININGS	Rounded:	Kindness.
SIGNATURE	Simple, absence of flourish:	Modesty, *self-confidence.*

You will notice that certain of the characteristics displayed are printed in italics. These are the *dominant* traits, or those which occur most frequently, each one confirming and emphasizing the other. Thus, without even having seen our applicant, we are able to deduce first of all that he is methodically minded, frank, balanced, confident, careful, self-controlled, and physically strong—all of which are very desirable qualities in an employee. The other attributes, such as imagination, idealism, placidity, and good humour, are present in a lesser degree, and they all help us to form a vivid mental picture of our man.

Here is one who is to be trusted, and who will work hard, for he is intelligent and ambitious; who is amiable and sociable, so that he would live in concord with his fellow-workers; who is physically strong, and thus unlikely to be absent from his work owing to illness. Although he shows signs of impatience and a combative spirit, these are not dominant traits and therefore are not so influential as to be detrimental to the general character.

What a vast amount of time and money would be saved by a similar analysis of all applications for positions in business! Many employers have been impressed by a personal interview with an applicant, the latter naturally being on his "best behaviour," only to find after engaging him that their judgment has been totally at fault, and that they have employed a dishonest, lazy or entirely inefficient person. Anyone who has mastered the first principles of graphology need never be similarly deceived, for he is well protected from making such mistakes.

Suppose we have received the following letter, also in application for the position mentioned above:—

> Dear Sir
>
> I thank you for your letter of January 18th and will be at your offices on Tuesday next as requested
>
> Yours faithfully
>
> F.H. Warham

After a careful examination we may now go forward with our analysis of the outstanding characteristics.

		CHARACTERISTICS
GENERAL STYLE	Angular:	Intolerance.
	Slope to the right:	Sensitive nature.
	Lines sloping upwards:	*Ambition.*
LETTERS, CAPITAL	Large in proportion:	*Self-importance.*
SMALL	Commonplace in comparison with the capitals:	Inconsistency, *false pride.*
PERSONAL I	Abnormally large:	*Egotism.*
T-BARS	On top:	Domineering character.
	Slashed:	Vulgarity, greed.
	Inclined upwards:	*Ambition*, combative spirit.
I-DOTS	Absent in text:	Carelessness, weakness, impatience.
LAST LETTERS	Dropping:	Love of money.

In the characteristics we see that ambition, pride and self-importance are the dominant traits, while there are general indications of weakness, greed, vulgarity, love of money and impatience. Now, although ambition and pride are not bad characteristics in themselves, in this case we find that they are combined with various adverse qualities. On examining these we may justly conclude that the ambition would be unscrupulous and the pride misguided and false. Altogether not a very happy character is portrayed; the sensitive nature which is suggested by the slope, combined with the other characteristic of false pride, would give rise to "touchiness" rather than true sensitivity. The writer would scarcely make a good employee.

Recently a business man showed an eminent graphologist two letters which he received as a result of advertising for a lady secretary. He had interviewed the applicants, and it now remained to make a final decision. From the interview the business man declared that each appeared as satisfactory as the other; but as the work entailed much which was of a highly confidential nature, and required great accuracy and a cool and collected brain, he wanted to be quite sure of engaging the more suitable type.

The graphologist examined the two letters, and without hesitation proclaimed that of Miss B—— as showing the better qualifications. In the other letter the first thing the graphologist noticed was the exaggerated right slope, showing great emotional susceptibility and little control over the temperament. The capital letters were disproportionately large and flourished, disclosing pride and an inferior intellect. The small letters were thick—the mark of sensuality and worldliness. Most convincing of all, it was seen that the *o's* were left open at the bottom, almost invariably a sign of dishonesty.

Other parts of the letter served to confirm the judgment made on the first few lines, and the business man was advised against engaging this girl. Miss B——'s letter, on the other hand, clearly displayed the qualities of will-power, intelligence, discretion and modesty, and she was accordingly offered the post.

Unfortunately, in the meanwhile, Miss B—— had accepted another position, and as he was anxious to engage someone at once the employer ignored the graphologist's judgment and engaged the other applicant. He was soon to regret his decision. Not only

N

did he find his new secretary exceedingly moody and irritable, but at times she became exceedingly insolent, although her employer was noted for his kindness and consideration. Finally, after she had received her dismissal, she absconded with several pounds in stamps and money from the office cash-box!

This is only one of innumerable examples of the judgment of the graphologist being confirmed by the subsequent behaviour of the writer under examination.

Business men and professional men of all classes have found that the art of reading character from handwriting is of invaluable help to them. Circumstances often prevent our meeting the person with whom we propose to do business; frequently we are called upon to trust or rely on people with whom we have never exchanged a word. In such cases a knowledge of the science of graphology will prevent us from committing ourselves to dealings with dishonest or unreliable persons, and will be the means of saving us time, worry and money.

The handwriting of a person with a business brain and commercial integrity will usually be as clear and as lacking in ambiguity as the writer himself. It may be either upright or slightly sloping, but an excessive slope is undesirable, for the intensely emotional person lacks the asset of cool-headedness.

All the forward movements should be present—small *t*'s crossed and *i*'s dotted on the right-hand side. Block or simply-formed capitals are those of the precise-minded person, and therefore the signs of a good business man. Increasing margins or very broad spacings are adverse characteristics from the commercial point of view, with their signification of extravagance. A slight rising in the lines of the text is favourable, for it shows the optimism and ambition essential for success. Rounded letters, such as *a*'s and *o*'s, left slightly open at the top show the desirable traits of frankness and absence of affectation, but if they are open at the bottom, as we have already seen, it is seldom the mark of an honest or straightforward person.

The general style of a good business handwriting should be brisk and firm and entirely free from exaggerations of any kind. Hoaxing financiers, "confidence men," and other such people frequently adopt an abnormally large or elaborately flourished hand, for their whole life is one of make-believe and deception, a fact which is portrayed consciously or unconsciously when they put pen to paper.

Here are two contrasting examples of commercial handwriting:—

Referring to the 70 bales of wool which

No. 1

Referring to the 70 bales of wool which

No. 2

In specimen No. 1 we may at first be impressed by the "artistic" formation of the capital *R*, but a closer examination will show the inconsistency of the hand. The smaller letters, which are not so conspicuous, are entirely commonplace. The *t's* are made with a single stroke and the cross-bar of one points downwards, indicating weakness and indecision. Cunning and dissimulation are betrayed by a decrease in the size of the letters in the words, while the dropping of the last letter in each word shows a love of money. Notice the figures: the *7* is made with at least three strokes, while the *0* has an unnecessary elaboration at the top.

Specimen No. 2 is very clear and neat. The text shows a distinct tendency towards an increase in size, implying frankness and sincerity, while the simple capital suggests clear-mindedness. The small letters are regular and firm, the mark of a practical nature and physical and mental strength. Although this second specimen may be a trifle commonplace in appearance, we would be more inclined to trust its writer than the author of No. 1.

APPLICATIONS IN PRIVATE LIFE

Graphology may be practically applied not only during the course of business affairs, but also in personal matters. It can enable us to gain valuable information about those who play a part in our private lives. How many young men and women, for instance, have "fallen in love at first sight," made a hasty marriage and then spent the rest of their lives wondering why in the world they ever consented to be bound to someone who is obviously so unsympathetic in temperament? Unfortunately, such cases are only too frequent. They are tragedies which, by a little thought and foresight, could be averted, and have many times been averted, by the practical application of graphology.

Let us take these two specimen handwritings of a young engaged couple:—

Dear Bob Thank you for the

No. 1

Dear Jill I heard from Gerald last

No. 2

No. 1, which is taken from a letter written by the girl, is in a plain, slightly sloping and rounded hand. The pressure is inclined to be stressed, while block capitals are used which pass down below the level of the following small letters. The strokes above the line are considerably larger than those below, the small *t* is crossed to the right, and at about the middle, of the downstroke, and we notice a slight gap between the first letter and the remainder of each word.

From the above clues we may build up some of the girl's characteristics. We can deduce that she is without pride, is kind-hearted and of an artistic, sensitive nature. Pressure inclined to be stressed shows a strong will-power, while the position and shape of the capitals indicate preciseness of mind, culture, and refinement. Great mental ability is indicated by the large upper strokes, and thoughtfulness and expression by the position of the *t*-bar. The gap at the beginning of the words is a sign of intuition.

The character thus portrayed is that of one who is chiefly interested in mental or artistic pursuits rather than physical. Her chief hobby may be painting, writing or music. Nevertheless, she does not let her imagination rule her reason, and manages throughout to keep a clear and intuitive mind. We may rely on her as being kind and sympathetic, and quite ready to tolerate other people's opinions even if she, in her heart of hearts, does not agree with them.

The man's hand is upright and rounded, the capitals are simple and without flourish. Small letters are broad, low and firm. Personal *I* is not so large as the *D*, *J* and *G*. The *o* and *a* are open at the top, the small *d* in Gerald is slightly inclined to the right, the *t*-bar is right-hand, near the middle and straight.

The writer thus shows himself to be generous, open-hearted and amiable, with good sense and stability. The broad and low small letters indicate sensitivity, while their firmness suggests balanced judgment and will-power. We may presume that he is inclined to be modest, as the *I* is on the small side, although not abnormally small; the open letters indicate frankness; the slope of the small *d*, imagination and artistry. The *t*-bars betoken expression and thoughtfulness, while the strongly formed upper strokes indicate intellectuality.

By glancing through the revealed characteristics of the man and woman we can conclude that they would make admirable partners. Both are intellectual, artistic and sympathetic. The common possession of will-power will not cause disruption, as each shows sensitivity and kindness. Altogether the handwritings are those of two people who may be expected to lead a calm, intellectual and harmonious life, devoid of strong passions, but filled with close and consistent affection.

Here are two other specimen handwritings of an engaged couple:—

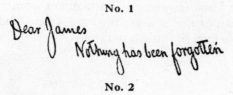

No. 1

No. 2

From the slope of the man's handwriting we see that he is inclined to be emotional. Forceful will-power and an inclination towards mental rather than physical pursuits are shown by the stressed pressure and size of the upper strokes. The small *d* has a loop crossing two of the preceding letters, suggesting a love of argument; the *t* is crossed on the top showing a domineering nature.

In No. 2 the slope is a backward one, indicating reserve and pride; the lower strokes predominate in size, showing a preference for physical rather than mental exercise. The method of crossing the small *t* and the pressure used are similar to the man's style, indicating strong will and domineering temperament.

Thus we have one who is emotional, the other reserved; one who is chiefly intellectual, the other whose interest lies in outdoor amusement. Yet each possesses a domineering nature and would want to command and rule the other. Two such widely differing characters could hardly live happily for long in the matrimonial state.

Of course, it is not essential for two types to be exactly similar in order to harmonize. Quite frequently, in fact, people who are too much alike fail to agree; and because handwriting is a visual representation of the nature of the writer, we can conclude that two handwritings which are almost alike are sometimes those of people whose characters are so similar that they could not be friends. Nevertheless, it is necessary that those who wish to be companions should possess underlying sympathetic traits which will enable them to appreciate the good points of others, and to tolerate or make allowances for the bad points.

We can now begin to see to what a great extent graphology can help us in our private life. Not only have we learnt how, by a little observation, to sum up the character and temperament of our friends and acquaintances, but we have also learnt how to know those persons who are likely to be sympathetic, and those with whom we shall have nothing in common. Instead of having to rely solely on "first impressions," which are usually so misleading, we can now seek out and analyse the basic traits of character which form an intimate part of human nature.

GRAPHIC SELF-ANALYSIS

The question now arises as to whether we really *know ourselves* or whether we only think we do. There are few human beings who have a real knowledge of their own character, and few who even trouble to analyse their mental make-up in a calm, scientific and unbiased manner. With the help of graphology there is no reason why we should not be able to deduce, in a manner quite free from prejudice, our own faults, virtues, temperament and tendencies. By applying exactly the same rules and significations as have been employed in these pages we can all draw up a self-analysis of infinite value.

We have learned that character governs handwriting, but it is also true that handwriting influences character. If, for example, we find in our own writing that *t*-bars are omitted or slope downwards, *i*-dots are omitted or placed on the left, and so on—all of which suggests weakness, stubbornness, hesitancy—by consciously concentrating on a *progressive* style, by forming clear and horizontal right-hand *t*-bars, and dotting the *i*'s correctly, it is possible in time to alter our fundamental character.

As our writing becomes progressive by an effort of will (it is no easy matter to alter one's habitual style), so will we ourselves become more progressive in our other actions. The power of habit is great; a good or bad habit by constant practice soon becomes part of the character, and so the cultivation of good writing habits correspondingly causes an improvement in our mental condition.

The following are graphological characteristics which are specially to be avoided:—

> *t*-bars omitted, sloping downwards or placed on the left.
> *i*-dots on the left or omitted.
> *a* and *o* open at the bottom.
> Very angular or backward sloping writing.
> Excessive slope to the right.
> Lines which slope downwards.
> Figures made with more than two strokes.
> Elaborate or illegible signature.

Here are the chief favourable signs:—

> Rounded and legible writing.
> *a* and *o* slightly open at the top.
> Lines horizontal or slightly sloping upwards.
> Well spaced words and lines.
> *t*-bars and *i*-dots on the right.
> Small *d* with a slight right-hand slope.
> Signature clear and plain or with a single underlining stroke.

Conclusion

We have now come to the end of this brief but important study of reading character from handwriting. The main principles of this fascinating science have all been incorporated in the preceding pages, and they can be so quickly mastered that after a little time the reader will find it unnecessary to refer to the book. It is essential, however, that the beginner should avoid allowing imagination to take the upper hand and interpreting signs which have not been documented by the graphologists.

There are many peculiarities of the pen which, so far as the experts have been able to ascertain, have no particular significance. In our study we have been careful to exclude these; and we advise the reader to do the same, if a genuine result is required.

Keep to the rules as given here, do not jump to conclusions, avoid making sweeping statements which are not justified by the analysis, and you will soon find yourself the master of an art which will be of unparalleled assistance in every phase of your life.

ORACLES, OMENS, AND POPULAR SUPERSTITIONS

WHAT will the morrow bring forth? Will good fortune attend my endeavours, or will bad luck wrap me in its mantle of despair?

For countless years man has been anxious to lift a corner of the veil of the future; eager to catch a glimpse of the shadows cast by coming events; eager to know how to interpret "signs," whether they presage good or evil. In this section we give a few of the methods which man has employed, and still employs, to interrogate the future. Some of them may be well known to you, others strange to you, but all of them have been handed down from generation to generation by the undying hand of tradition.

Remember, however, when seeking to know your fortune by these methods, that the results obtained must be regarded as warnings of what *may* happen—they must not be accepted as conclusive evidence of what *will* happen. You are the master of your destiny; employ the occult advice you receive to make smooth your path of progress.

I

ORACLES

Coffee Grounds

PUT about two teaspoonfuls of finely-ground coffee into a filter, pour on boiling water, then place the filter containing the dregs in a safe place, and leave it there for two or three days so that the dregs may dry thoroughly. Turn the dregs into a shallow saucepan, pour upon them a glass of cold water, place the vessel on a stove and allow the water to heat slowly. Just before boiling-point is reached, remove the saucepan.

Empty the contents on to a flat dish or plate of white unpatterned earthenware or china, which has previously been well cleaned and dried, take the dish in your two hands and, by shaking it carefully and blowing upon it lightly, help the grounds to separate themselves from the water and to coagulate. Gently tip the dish so that the water drains away, then put it on one side, in a place free from air-currents, to dry.

After about half an hour has elapsed, it will be noticed that the coffee grounds, in drying, have formed characters and diagrams of various shapes and sizes. These should be studied carefully with the aid of a magnifying-glass, and interpreted by referring to the alphabetical list of symbols appearing in the section of this work devoted to the reading of tea-leaves.

It is well to remember, however, that in this, as in all other methods of divination, practice makes perfect; do not be dismayed, therefore, if your first attempts at reading coffee grounds meet with little success—try, try, try again.

White of an Egg

Take a fresh egg, separate the white from the yolk, and pour the former into a bowl or large cup that has been filled almost to the brim with water. Set it aside uncovered, in a place free from dust, and at the expiration of twenty-four hours the white of the egg will have formed into clots, which, as in the case of coffee grounds, may be interpreted by making reference to the list of symbols included in the section dealing with divination by tea-leaves.

Germination of Seeds

For this method of questioning the future five seeds of the same species of flower are needed. Plant each one in a separate flower-pot at the same hour of the same day, label each of the pots to correspond with an expected event, and place them where they will all receive an equal amount of sunshine. The events will occur in the order in which the seeds germinate.

Fowls and Grain

With a piece of chalk, draw a circle on the ground. Divide this circle into segments to correspond with the questions it is desired to ask. In each segment and near the rim of the circle place one grain of corn; then, in the centre of the circle, stand a coop containing two fowls—a cock and a hen.

Open the coop so that the fowls may escape at the same time, and watch carefully to see which grains are eaten by the cock and which by the hen. The answer to a question is in the affirmative if the grain in the segment representing it is eaten by the cock, and in the negative if eaten by the hen.

Paper

Take thirteen pieces of paper, write a question on each, and place the slips, unfolded, at the bottom of a bowl. Pour water into the vessel and note the first paper that rises to the surface; the answer to the question on it is in the affirmative.

Water

While repeating quietly to yourself the question which you desire to be answered, drop a small stone into a bowl of water. If the number of ripples caused by the pebble is odd, the answer is "yes"; if even, "no."

Daisy Petals

Take a daisy in full bloom, think of your question, and pluck the petals from it one by one, saying as you do so, "yes," "no," "yes," "no," until the flower is completely stripped. The word which is uttered as the last petal is plucked will give the answer to your question.

This method of divination is much favoured by lovers who wish to discover if their affection is returned. The petals are stripped while the inquirer exclaims "he loves me; he loves me not"; and so on until the last petal, and the answer is reached.

Fire

Write your wish on a small piece of paper. Place this, with the writing face downwards, on a plate, and apply a lighted match to the corner of the slip.

If the whole of the paper is consumed, you will not be disappointed in your wish.

If a part of the paper and the written wish is destroyed, you will not get your wish for some time.

If the writing remains untouched, your wish will be granted.

Apple Peel

With a silver knife, peel an apple in such a manner that the skin comes off in one unbroken strip. Throw the peel over your left shoulder, all the while concentrating on the question you desire to be answered.

If the peel falls on the floor and forms any shape but O or U, the answer is in the affirmative.

Black and White Squares

Cut out of paper two squares of the same size. Colour one of them black, then go to an upstairs window and throw both of them out at the same time. Note carefully which of the squares first reaches the ground.

If it is the black square, the answer to your question is "no"; if the white, "yes."

Dandelion Clock

Blow hard on a dandelion that has gone to seed. If all the seeds fly off, you will get your wish almost at once. If a few seeds remain, some time will elapse before your wish is granted. If many seeds are left, you may not obtain your wish at all.

Cat's Paws

Leave the door of a room slightly ajar, think of the question you wish to be answered, then call in the cat. Observe carefully which forepaw of the animal appears first round the door.

If it is the right forepaw, "yes" answers the question.

If the left, "no."

The Ring

Take a gold wedding-ring and attach to it a piece of black thread. Grasp the thread between the thumb and first finger of the left hand and suspend the ring over a glass of water. Then release your hold.

If the ring in falling to the bottom touches the left side of the glass, the answer to your question is in the negative; if it touches the right side, in the affirmative.

If it touches the side nearest to you or the one opposite to you the oracle refuses to answer; delay further questioning until twenty-four hours have elapsed.

The Book

Think hard of the question you wish to ask, open a book at random, and place the first finger of your left hand upon one of the two pages.

If the figures in the number of the page add up to make an even number the answer is "no"; if they make an odd number the answer is "yes."

Sealing-wax

Procure an old spoon or a ladle, place in it some small pieces of sealing-wax and heat over a flame until the wax is melted. Then pour the wax into a small bowl of clean water and observe carefully the designs and symbols which are formed.

These signs are interpreted in the same manner as are tea-leaves and coffee grounds. If the inquirer so wishes, lead may be used in the place of sealing-wax.

The Arabian Squares

The Arabs—not the least superstitious race among the inhabitants of the mysterious East—have from time immemorial reposed their faith in omens, charms, amulets and every form of divination; and few among them would dream of undertaking any action of importance without having had recourse to astrology or augury, in order to find out whether the time and circumstances be propitious or otherwise.

One of the most popular means of divination used in Egypt and the surrounding lands is the Magic Square known as a "zairgeh," whose origin is attributed to the patriarch Enoch. The Arabs have many forms of "zairgeh," ranging from those of extreme simplicity to others that are very complicated and involved, requiring the use of intricate astrological calculations in consulting them.

We give here two different forms of the simpler Arabian Squares —one giving information concerning matters of love, the other referring to general fortune and worldly success—which have been adapted for English readers from an old Arabic manuscript on divination. The method of consulting the squares is the same in both cases. The consultant firmly fixes his mind upon the matter of which he or she is anxious to know the issue, and then, with closed eyes, selects haphazardly one of the small lettered squares with a pin or the point of a pencil. (The Arabs, before making their choice in this manner, usually repeat various verses of the Koran a prescribed number of times, and perform other ritual which would be tedious to the majority of English readers. But this is quite unnecessary, so long as the attention is concentrated firmly upon the problem in mind.)

The letter contained in the square selected is then written down, and every eighth letter thereafter is set down in its proper

A	M	L	Y	B	D	L	A	H	A	O	O	E	O	O	L
A	N	V	U	F	N	V	O	P	Y	E	M	O	O	O	N
P	W	R	A	R	T	W	G	Y	I	S	Y	E	T	I	A
M	L	D	N	L	R	L	N	A	L	R	E	O	U	L	D
R	A	E	V	N	S	T	H	R	D	A	E	G	T	R	A
I	O	M	R	Y	H	I	P	A	R	S	M	O	I	U	P
G	E	F	A	U	M	M	Y	E	Y	U	R	R	H	P	W
T	O	L	R	L	I	H	E	O	U	F	Y	O	S	O	D
Y	O	I	Y	V	P	V	D	O	N	L	O	E	R	E	E
U	E	L	U	R	O	R	D	R	W	E	R	W	M	D	L
P	I	D	P	I	I	E	I	R	L	W	R	L	S	L	F
E	L	I	E	L	E	A	E	S	G	T	S	C	S	Y	A
E	R	H	E	O	A	A	W	N	I	I	N	M	R	N	A
T	E	N	T	E	E	D	I	L	V	A	L	T	F	D	T
O	E	Y	O	O	A	O	S	V	Y	E	V	Y	L	U	Y
E	O	A	E	O	S	B	O	R	U	R	R	U	E	T	U

An Arabian Square for Love Affairs

order. When the bottom of the magic square is reached, turn to the top row without interrupting the counting, but underline the first letter lighted on. Proceed until you have gone through the entire square, when the final letter that is written down will be the eighth from the one that was set down in the beginning. Now read the answer which the square has given you, starting from the letter that is underlined.

As an example, let us suppose that the reader lights upon the letter L in the fifteenth horizontal line of the square dealing with Love. He will write down L, and then, counting eight squares along, will set down S next to it, continuing with E, D (in the first line), O, N, and so on. The letter D, in the first line, will be underlined, however, since it is the initial letter of the answer.

In order to obtain valid answers from the Arabian Squares, it is important, as we have already stated, to concentrate upon the matter in question, and on no account must the squares be consulted more than once in a month by the same person. After this lapse of time, the astrological influences determining the answers will have

A	S	T	G	H	D	W	Y	F	U	H	O	O	O	O	O
A	C	O	O	N	N	R	U	L	C	U	D	O	O	K	R
S	E	G	L	U	T	H	F	E	S	H	U	R	W	A	A
F	S	T	C	A	O	R	T	R	D	H	K	N	R	D	E
I	E	E	W	D	R	E	W	E	P	R	I	P	Y	R	I
N	E	O	L	R	A	I	L	D	N	A	L	O	L	F	L
S	D	D	P	S	L	Y	B	E	S	B	R	P	W	O	E
E	U	E	E	I	U	T	K	P	H	S	R	L	W	H	
S	O	A	E	I	L	O	E	T	N	R	N	T	C	U	E
O	Y	D	T	Y	O	L	N	D	O	T	L	W	M	D	V
O	U	H	Y	I	E	E	Y	Y	R	E	C	L	R	N	O
O	O	G	O	L	I	J	F	U	W	O	M	B	G	O	O
A	N	A	E	E	H	Y	T	N	E	L	Y	Y	T	S	H
I	F	I	O	O	A	U	E	N	F	S	U	U	T	C	R
J	O	S	R	R	L	C	F	U	R	U	W	L	A	E	O
R	T	R	A	O	S	S	L	Y	S	E	Y	T	T	S	K

An Arabian Square for Success and Fortune

altered sufficiently, with the movements of the heavenly bodies, to furnish another reliable reading.

The Wheel of Fortune

This oracle is capable of furnishing predictions of amazing truth and exactness, so long as it is consulted in a spirit of sincerity. Devised by a gifted occultist, as the result of long experience and mature reflection, it is founded upon subtle astrological calculations, involving the influences of the zodiac, the twelve houses of heaven and the nine planets.

With eyes closed, prick haphazard with a pin or the point of a pencil in the large circle, and note the sign of the zodiac ruling the segment (the space enclosed by any two of the thick spokes) in which the pin or pencil alighted. Then close the eyes again, and in the same manner prick one of the numbers in the same segment. Finally refer to the table, under the sign and number selected, for the oracle's reply.

Aries

1. You will be wealthy and successful in love.
2. Be very careful in your dealings; someone who professes to be your friend is seeking to do you harm.
3. You are passionately loved, even though the name of your lover may not be known to you.
4. Place all your confidence in your own guiding star, and go forward fearlessly to certain success.
5. Think more kindly of your fellow men, if you would have their love and receive their assistance.
6. A long and arduous road lies before you, but it leads to the attainment of your highest ambitions.
7. If you would merit your sweetheart's love, look into your own conduct a little; you may find that it is not above reproach.
8. An approaching change in your life and position is indicated.
9. You should be more prudent in regard to affairs of the heart.

Taurus

1. If you do not guard against impulsiveness, you will have many occasions to regret your actions.
2. You will be happy and blessed in your children, of whom there will be many.
3. There will be a struggle between your will and your desires, and for some time to come your happiness and welfare will be dependent upon your own self-control.
4. Your nature is too vacillating. You must make up your mind with greater determination and go straight to your goal.
5. You will not find true happiness until you have cast out selfishness and excessive love of ease.
6. Fortune will favour you unexpectedly.
7. Do not place too much trust in promises, which may prove false.
8. Love's dreams will be fulfilled before many weeks have passed.
9. An early and happy marriage awaits you.

Gemini

1. Make the most of the opportunities that will shortly come your way.
2. In the near future you are likely to make a number of pleasant and most helpful friends.
3. Your courtship may be long, but its result will be happy.
4. You will have many sweethearts.

5. The success of an enterprise to which you will put your hand is assured.
6. You will have a reunion with an old friend or acquaintance.
7. For some time to come your life will be peaceful and entirely devoid of worry and strife.
8. Joy and festivities in the near future.
9. Be patient; you are in too much of a hurry to attain your object.

Cancer

1. A brilliant future is predicted for you.
2. Some matter is causing you concern, but do not worry unduly, for it will come right in the end.

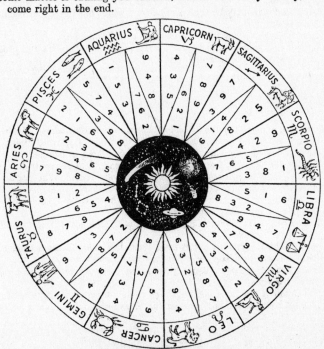

The Wheel of Fortune

3. If you would have the help and esteem of your friends, do not talk about them to their detriment.
4. Your lover is thinking of you.
5. Unless you are very tactful and discreet, a quarrel with one dear to you is foreshadowed.
6. Your business affairs will need care for the next few weeks.
7. You are going to make or receive a proposal of marriage.
8. A business proposition will be put to you shortly. Think it over well before accepting.
9. Wealth and happiness lie at the end of the path that is marked out for you.

Leo

1. Have faith and fear not.
2. You are too credulous and over-willing to believe what is told you, so long as it be pleasant.
3. The course of true love will run smoothly for a long time to come.
4. Travelling is indicated, either for business or pleasure.
5. Your financial position and social status will be improved by marriage.
6. If you are a woman, try the Wheel of Fortune again. If a man, your affection is returned by a dark woman, even though she may not let it appear so.
7. Sorrow and tears may be your portion for a while, but the sun will shine upon you again.
8. Beware lest you allow jealousy to spoil your happiness.
9. You will find your happiness and reward in the high honours and prosperity that will come to your children.

Virgo

1. If you are a man, try the Wheel of Fortune a second time. If a woman, do not place too much reliance in the promises of your admirers.
2. You may lose money through speculation or games of chance.
3. Your life for the next few months will be steady and uneventful.
4. You are going to embark upon a flirtation very soon. Whether or not it develops into a serious love affair is not yet clear.
5. Your emotional life may be a stormy one, but you will come to port at last in a happy and prosperous marriage.
6. To deceive yourself or other people is not in the least likely to advance your own interests.
7. You will shortly receive a gift or a charming compliment which, coming from a certain quarter, will not be unwelcome.
8. Family connexions may cause you trouble; do not become embroiled in petty disputes.
9. For a man: a wealthy woman, older than yourself, will take an interest in you. For a woman: consult the Wheel of Fortune again.

Libra

1. Envious people desire your disgrace and downfall, but have faith in your guiding star, and, if you are discreet, you will have nothing to fear.
2. You will be well advised to restrict your passions and control your temper.
3. Within a day or two you will receive a letter from your beloved.
4. Happiness, joyful news and a gain of money.
5. You will have dreams of love, which are likely to be fulfilled before many weeks have passed.
6. One who has done you a wrong will repent and beg your forgiveness.
7. Put your shoulder to the wheel, for success will come to you only through your own efforts.

8. You are about to commit a foolish action; think well before you take the first step.
9. You are about to go on a short journey, which will have fortunate consequences for you.

Scorpio

1. A passing annoyance will affect you unpleasantly. Do not take much notice of it.
2. You are going to take part in some joyful festivity in a public place.
3. Look after your health, and do not dissipate your powers.
4. Lover's tears; they will soon turn to laughter.
5. A pleasant holiday will be the occasion of meeting a lover.
6. Unless you refuse to believe all that you hear, you may suffer a great loss of money.
7. One of your intimate friends is kind and good-natured, but thoughtless and rash. Take care that his or her actions are not a source of concern to you.
8. Refer to Gemini 6.
9. Your lover is true and constant.

Sagittarius

1. You will have an interview with a business man that may prove rather unpleasant, but the result of it will be favourable to your own welfare.
2. Marriage will relieve you from poverty.
3. Unless you exercise great prudence, you may be the victim of deceit.
4. For a man: your beloved will be innocent and beautiful. For a woman: consult the Wheel of Fortune once again.
5. Favour, happiness and delight will strew your path through life.
6. A surprise is coming to you; it is more than likely that it will be a pleasant one.
7. A new phase of your life is about to begin.
8. Success and failure will mingle in your life during the next few weeks.
9. The impediments standing in the way of your marriage will be unexpectedly removed very shortly.

Capricorn

1. Assistance will come to you from an unexpected quarter.
2. A priest or lawyer will before long play some part in your life.
3. You will suffer from an act of injustice.
4. Though you will not want for money, you will never be very rich.
5. Do not be tempted to gamble during the next few weeks.
6. A gain of money, probably by inheritance.
7. Take your fate into your own hands; you are too much inclined to rely on the results of chance happenings.
8. Beware lest you be induced by gifts or flattery to act in a manner that is not strictly honourable.
9. Some great good luck is coming your way.

Aquarius

1. You are the cause of fierce jealousy and antagonism between rivals for your affection.
2. You are going to lose the friendship of one or more persons; and though you will feel some unhappiness at the time, the loss is not really worth regretting.
3. For a woman: a new lover. For a man: a business development.
4. A bitter quarrel is in store; it will probably "clear the air" of a great deal of misunderstanding and unpleasantness.
5. Refer to Taurus 3.
6. A probable change of residence is indicated.
7. You will be entertained among a numerous and distinguished company.
8. Self-indulgence will prove your downfall; be warned in time.
9. Try the Wheel of Fortune again; if you light upon a 9 of any sign, take it as an omen of the greatest happiness and good fortune.

Pisces

1. You will receive a love letter, or one containing joyful news.
2. If the inquirer is a man, he will obtain the love of a fair young girl. If the inquirer is a woman, she should try the Wheel of Fortune again.
3. Indications of a secret or illicit love affair; be prudent in your conduct.
4. A lucky stroke of business in the near future.
5. The reward will be fully worth the toil.
6. The realization of your dearest wish within a year.
7. Attractive but dishonest proposals will be made to you; summon all your moral powers and reject them.
8. True love will be crowned with marriage and a happy family life.
9. A degree of honour and prosperity that is quite unexpected at present.

II

OMENS

THROUGHOUT the history of the human race, the most implicit trust has been placed in portents and omens. The firm belief that "coming events cast their shadows before"—that future happenings can be foretold by signs actuated by some kind of supernatural power—has been common to mankind since the very earliest days of civilization.

The folklore of practically every race and nation affords numerous instances of man's instinctive faith in omens; while some of the shrewdest people in all walks of life regulate important personal affairs by occurrences that would appear, at first sight, to be trivial and insignificant. Who has not felt pleased when a black cat has crossed his path or when he has met a piebald pony; and who has not experienced a momentary feeling of depression at the sight of the ill-omened cockroach?

This belief in the validity of omens played a prominent part in public and private life during classical times. The College of Augurs at Rome dated from the earliest days of the city's history, and it survived until the might and majesty of the empire had all but passed away, in the fourth century of our era. It was the duty of its members to observe carefully the omens arising from natural causes, as well as those purposely induced by artificial means, and to interpret them on behalf of the rulers, who allowed themselves to be guided implicitly in their policy by the interpretations.

A careful distinction must be made, however, between the augurs and the oracles, such as those of Delphi, Argos and Dodona. An oracle was essentially a place where the god himself—often Apollo or the supreme divinity Jupiter—gave an answer through the mouth of his priest or attendant to the anxious questions of his devotees; while omens were drawn mainly from the phenomena of Nature and everyday life, such as lightning, the flight of birds and the cries of animals.

The Roman *haruspices* practised divination by observing the entrails of slain beasts; the Etruscans were reputed to be particularly expert at interpreting omens in this way. Shakespeare's "Julius Caesar" has a well-known reference to an evil portent that was disclosed by the haruspices which almost immediately met with a tragic fulfilment:—

> Plucking the entrails of an offering forth,
> They could not find a heart within the beast.

This truly monstrous omen, it will be remembered, was supported by those described by Caesar's wife:—

> There is one within,
> Besides the things that we have heard and seen,
> Recounts most horrid sights seen by the watch,
> A lioness hath whelped in the streets;
> And graves have yawn'd and yielded up their dead;

> Fierce fiery warriors fight upon the clouds,
> In ranks and squadrons and right form of war,
> Which drizzled blood upon the Capitol;
> The noise of battle hurtled in the air,
> Horses did neigh and dying men did groan;
> And ghosts did shriek and squeal about the streets.
> O Caesar; these things are beyond all use,
> And I do fear them!

But the great dictator, reposing more faith in his own high destiny than in the portents of the soothsayers, rejected their warnings, and went to his death.

The Roman augurs divided omens into two classes:—

1. Omens received in answer to definite questions.
2. Those unsought and observed by chance.

The signs observed were of five kinds:—

a. Those seen in the heavens, such as thunder and lightning, falling stars, comets and the like.
b. The flight and sounds of birds.
c. The cries of animals and general observations obtained from them.
d. The ways in which birds picked up grain that was spread out for them.
e. Any accidental or unusual happenings.

Special conditions attached to the observing of celestial omens. The augur repaired at midnight to the summit of a hill whence he had an uninterrupted view over the city and the surrounding country-side. Having offered up sacrifice and invoked the guidance of Heaven, he seated himself in a tent with his face turned towards the south, and waited patiently for the answer of the gods. If lightning flickered in the east, on his left-hand side, it was regarded as an auspicious omen, while if lightning was seen on the right it was unfortunate.

A somewhat similar practice seems to have been observed by the Greeks, although among them the right side was considered lucky, the left unlucky. We read that once every year, just before the sacred procession was due to set out on a pilgrimage to the shrine of Apollo Pythius at Delphi, observers were stationed on the city wall at Athens in expectation of seeing lightning flash from the direction of Harma, a phenomenon which was regarded as a divine portent that the pilgrimage was looked upon with favour. In general, however, the Greeks attached greater significance to omens that were casually encountered.

It is not difficult to understand the powerful effect that lightning, shooting stars—veritably "fire falling from Heaven"—and other celestial phenomena had upon the minds of the ancients, who, of course, knew nothing about the natural causes of meteors and atmospheric electricity.

A striking instance of implicit belief in a heavenly omen is afforded by the pilgrimage of the Wise Men of the East to the manger at Bethlehem to worship the Infant Christ, because they had "seen His star in the east." "And, lo, the star which they saw in the east, went before them, till it came and stood over where the young child was," relates the gospel of St. Matthew.

The pages of history furnish us with numberless instances of remarkable omens; we will choose a few of them to show how enduring and widespread was the belief in these supernatural tokens.

In the year A.D. 312, during the later days of the Roman empire, the two rival emperors of the West, Constantine and Maxentius, were struggling for undisputed possession of the throne. Shortly before he was to fight the decisive battle of Saxa Rubra, a miraculous omen appeared to Constantine. A flaming cross made its appearance in the sky at noonday, together with the words, in Greek, "By this conquer."

This vision proved to be the turning-point of the emperor's life. Although his army was inferior in numbers to that of his rival, he swept the latter into the Tiber, and at one stroke became master of the Roman empire. More important still, he became an ardent convert to Christianity and made it the state religion. It is interesting to speculate upon the turn that history would have taken had the emperor Constantine paid no heed to the divine omen that blazed forth in the heavens.

A somewhat similar story is related of Valdemar II, the great king of Denmark. Once, when he was being sadly worsted in a battle with the Estonians in 1219, a red banner charged with a white cross suddenly fell from Heaven on to the battlefield. Taking this as an omen of divine aid, Valdemar rallied his men and, fighting with desperate courage, turned an almost certain defeat into a victory. The miraculous banner, known as the Dannebrog, or Danes' Cloth, was adopted forthwith as the national flag of Denmark.

Everyone has heard the story of how William of Normandy stumbled and fell upon his face when disembarking upon English soil before the battle of Hastings. This incident was immediately taken by his army as an evil omen, and a cry of dismay arose. In spite of the duke's presence of mind in turning the portent to a fortunate significance with the words "Thus I take seisin of (I seize) this land with both my hands," serious misgivings must have remained in the hearts of many of his soldiers.

After a study of historical events, it is not too much to affirm that omens have played as important a part as any other single factor in moulding men's actions throughout the history of the world. Whether there are any solid grounds for placing belief in them is a point upon which we will not dogmatize, lest we be accused of indulging fantasy at the expense of reason; but we would remind the reader that true omens—as distinct from mere superstitions, which are simply the fruit of ignorance—are *empirical* in their nature; that is to say, their significance has been arrived at as a result of centuries of observation of various signs and the occurrences that were found to follow them.

For instance, if time and time again in ancient days the observance of a comet was followed by an outbreak of war, would it not be natural—even logical—to conclude that between these two events there must be some connexion far beyond the range of mere coincidence? In time, therefore, a comet would be regarded as nothing less than the flaming sword of the god of war, and whenever one was observed a specific and evil prognostication would be attached to it.

It is manifestly ridiculous, however, to claim to be able to draw inferences from portents that are deliberately sought, in a way that allows no freedom for the working of fate. For instance, white heather is widely believed to bring good luck, but it would be the height of absurdity to hope surreptitiously to gain the aid of Fortune merely by going into a shop and buying a sprig of white heather. To encounter a goat casually upon the road is a promise of wealth, but only a fool would indulge pious hopes of becoming a millionaire by resorting to a field in which goats were grazing. Although Destiny, for all her inscrutability, occasionally lets fall precious hints and indications of what she holds in store, she is not to be compelled by such trivial devices as these.

The reader may observe a lack of consistency in the interpretations which the ancients attached to the directions in which omens were observed, and which have been handed down to the present day. Thus, while lightning on the left was considered a fortunate sign, a flock of birds on the left was regarded with the greatest disfavour. To reconcile this apparent anomaly, we would remind the reader that the science of omens is an empirical one, and, as such, is dependent entirely upon observed phenomena, which cannot be expected to follow definite rules in their occurrence.

We shall now give a description of some of the most important omens, together with interpretations; and in our arrangement we shall follow as far as possible the system to which reference has already been made, and which was laid down by the Roman augurs —adapting it, however, to include portents which have become established in popular tradition since classical days.

Omens Derived From Birds

It is interesting to note that our word "auspice," meaning an omen or prognostication, is derived from a Latin word meaning "an observer of birds."

Birds seen on the left, especially dark birds, are an omen of ill luck, according to the tradition established by the Roman augurs. To see a "fortunate" bird on the left implies that the good which it promises is considerably lessened. Birds on the right are, on the contrary, a fortunate sign, unless the birds are in themselves unlucky, when the ill luck which they bring is modified.

Birds flying from the left-hand side to the right, across the path of the observer, are fortunate; while birds flying from right to left across his path are unfortunate.

If the birds fly straight towards the observer, they will bring good luck with them; but if they are flying away from the observer, they will take good fortune and happiness away from him.

The height at which a bird or birds are flying has an effect upon the force of the omen—the greater the height, the more favourable being the indication.

If a song-bird sings or utters a cry as it flies, this can be regarded as a good sign; but for a raven, rook, crow or bird of prey to be heard croaking or screaming is an ill omen, unless it happens to be near its nest at the time.

If a bird or birds suddenly change the direction of their flight, the observer should be on his guard against the danger of sudden attacks by an enemy.

If a bird hovers while on the wing, treachery is to be feared, resulting in a sudden and merciless onslaught. This omen is often observed in regard to birds of prey.

As in other methods of divination, discrimination and good judgment are necessary in interpreting the portents revealed by birds, and it is seldom that prognostications can be drawn from a single omen, without reference to other circumstances. For instance, a raven is universally regarded as an inauspicious bird; but if a raven is observed to fly towards the right, past the observer, the evil which it brings in its wake may be considerably lessened, and may be reduced still more if the bird is flying high. On the other hand, a raven flying towards the left, at no great height above the earth, and croaking as it goes, may with certainty be looked upon as a messenger of calamity and evil.

Similarly, swallows are exceedingly lucky birds, and a swallow perching, or flying to the right, can be regarded with joy, especially if, in the latter case, it is high in the heavens. But if it is flying to the left or away from the observer, or skimming the surface of the ground, only slight good fortune is presaged.

Lucky and Unlucky Birds

Buzzard.—An unlucky sign. Beware of danger from hidden enemies and those possessing predatory natures.

Cock.—For a girl to hear a cock crowing while she is thinking of her sweetheart is a portent of good luck. On the other hand, if a prospective bride or bridegroom hears a cock crowing on the wedding-day, strife, bickering and unhappiness in the wedded state are threatened. To meet a white cock is a portent of ill luck. Trouble and danger lie in store for an inmate of any home which it approaches closely.

Crow.—Dark-plumaged birds have always been held to be of evil portent, and the crow and the rook are no exceptions to this tradition. One or more crows or rooks on the left-hand side constitute a definite omen of misfortune, presaging much contention and strife.

Cuckoo.—To hear the call of a cuckoo on the right is a sign of coming prosperity. If the bird is heard on the left the force of the omen is somewhat reduced.

Dove.—A most happy omen, signifying love, happiness and wedded bliss. In classical days the dove was the emblem of Venus, goddess of love, and hence was a favourite bird with lovers, to whom it is exceptionally fortunate.

Duck.—To hear a duck quacking is a fortunate omen, indicative of prosperity. To see this bird flying is an exceptionally good sign, especially for those who are in trouble or sorrow.

Eagle.—Definitely a lucky sign. Among the ancients the eagle was a very important bird, symbolizing the supreme power of Jupiter, who was often represented as being accompanied by an eagle.

Falcon.—Like most birds of prey, the falcon is an unlucky bird, threatening a sudden disaster falling "like a bolt from the blue." If seen or heard on the left, it is still more unlucky.

Goose.—It is a well known tradition that the cackling of geese warned the Romans when the barbarians were making a silent raid upon the Capitol. Ever since then cackling geese have been regarded as a presage of danger and of the advent of secret enemies, and any one who hears them should be cautious in his actions during the following few days.

Gulls.—If sea-gulls settle on any part of a ship in which a person is travelling, or is about to travel, he may expect a happy and fortunate journey. On the other hand, if a sea-gull brushes against a person with its wings or flaps them in his face, it is an omen of death—probably that of a friend.

Hawk.—The sight of a hawk should counsel the observer to be on his guard against others who are more powerful than he. If the bird is hovering on the left-hand side, or, worse still, directly overhead, the gravest possible danger is to be feared from cruel and grasping people.

Hen.—To hear a hen crowing—as distinct from merely cackling —is a warning of serious personal illness.

Jackdaw.—A bird of similar portent to the crow, raven and

rook, foretelling serious ill luck, especially if the bird croaks. (See also *Crow, Raven.*)

Kestrel.—See *Falcon.*

Kingfisher.—To see a kingfisher threatens scandal, calumny, and the public "washing of dirty linen."

Kite.—This bird presages that robbery, extortion and financial losses will be suffered by the person who encounters it.

Magpie.—To see a single magpie, especially if it be upon the left, is a most unlucky sign, presaging death. To encounter two of these birds is very lucky, however, and good fortune should attend you within three days. The omen varies with the number of magpies that are seen in the course of a walk, as is evinced by the well known rhyme concerning these birds:—

> One's sorrow, two's mirth,
> Three's a wedding, four's a birth,
> Five's a christening, six a dearth,
> Seven's heaven, eight is hell,
> And nine's the devil his ane sel.

In Scotland the flight of a flock of magpies past a house is considered to be an omen of the approaching death of an inhabitant. The natives of Devonshire believe that the evil portent of seeing a single magpie is dispelled by spitting three times over the left shoulder, a precaution taken probably in order to propitiate the powers of darkness.

Owl.—The owl is regarded as an ill-omened bird the world over. If you hear an owl hoot three times in succession very bad luck is to be feared. Moreover, it is generally considered unlucky to kill an owl, or indeed, any kind of night bird.

Peacock.—Just as the eagle was the sacred bird of Jupiter, so the peacock was associated by the ancients with Juno, queen of the heavens. To meet a peacock is a happy omen, as might be imagined. If he spreads out his tail before one's eyes, happiness and prosperity are promised. On the other hand, to bring a peacock's tail feathers into a house is considered most unlucky by superstitious people, for they are considered to be representative of the evil eye.

Pigeon.—If a white pigeon is seen flying round a house, the engagement or marriage of one of the inmates in the near future may be inferred.

Quail.—To see a quail or to hear one calling is a fortunate omen, whether the bird be upon the right or left.

Raven.—To see a raven perching on the right, or flying away on the right, may be regarded as an auspicious sign; note, however, that this is not the case if the bird flies from left to right across the path of the observer. If the bird is flying away on the left, bad news may be expected before long. The raven was considered by the ancients to be one of the most ill-omened of birds, an encounter with one foretelling death, illness or other misfortune. This bird's association with death seems universal. History relates that on the day on which Cicero was killed, a raven entered the room in which he was sleeping and, seizing the bedclothes in its beak, pulled them off his couch. It is said that the great orator was deeply impressed by this ominous portent.

There seem to be grounds for believing that when ravens desert the countryside and forests and settle in the neighbourhood of towns, famine and pestilence are in store.

Robin.—The sight of robins near a house or in a garden is an augury of good fortune to those who dwell within.

Rook.—See *Crow*.

Sparrow.—An unfortunate bird as a general omen, but, strangely enough, one that favours lovers.

Stork.—A lucky bird—according to the Roman augurs, one of the most auspicious of all. In Sweden the stork is regarded as a sacred bird, there being a legend that when Christ was being crucified a stork flew round, giving vent to cries of distress. In many countries the stork is encouraged to nest on the house-tops, boxes or even cartwheels being placed in position to form a foundation for the bird's home.

Swallow.—According to the ancients, this bird was one of the most fortunate. It is the symbol of spring and regeneration, birth and awakening; and to see a swallow in the early springtime, before they have become abundant, is a very fortunate omen. If swallows build in the eaves of a house, success, happiness and good luck are promised to all the inmates. To kill a swallow, especially one that has nested under the eaves of your house, may bring the gravest calamity to yourself or your family.

Vulture.—To encounter a vulture—not a very likely happening outside warm climates—foretells the death of a friend or acquaintance. If more than one of these grim birds are seen together, their number indicates the number of days that will elapse before this tragic prognostication is fulfilled.

Wagtail.—To come across a wagtail is a lucky sign, especially if the cheery little bird is walking towards you from the left.

Woodpecker.—A fortunate bird; to encounter one is an omen of success, perhaps as the reward of patient effort.

Wren.—The sight of this charming little brown bird is a promise of good luck; but to injure or frighten a wren in any way, or to take its eggs or young from the nest, is sure to be followed by a calamity of some kind.

Omens Derived From Animals

In drawing inferences from meetings with animals, insects and so on, the reader must bear in mind the injunction already given —that it is foolish to believe in their validity unless the particular creature in question is fairly uncommon in the locality where it is encountered. To regard as being of supernatural significance a meeting that was almost bound to take place is an entirely meaningless superstition.

Ass.—To encounter an ass or donkey is an unfortunate omen, especially if the animal is coming from the opposite direction.

Bat.—To hear a bat squeaking or crying as it flies presages bad luck.

Cat.—It is widely believed that a black cat brings good luck, although there are people who stoutly affirm the opposite. To kill a cat presages the greatest ill luck (among the ancient Egyptians it was a crime, punishable by death), while to tread upon its tail is also regarded by the superstitious as unfortunate. If a cat unaccountably abandons the house in which it lives, some disaster to the inmates is threatened.

Dog.—If a dog bays at the moon or howls outside a house, a death is foreshadowed in the neighbourhood. In Eastern folk-lore a black dog is often regarded as a manifestation of the devil, and classical students will remember the passage of Horace in which he states that the sight of a black dog and its puppies was an evil omen among the ancients. To kill a dog is considered by some people to be almost as unlucky as to kill a cat.

Ferret.—To meet a ferret is a sign that success will attend any enterprise that you are contemplating.

Goat.—A fortunate omen, signifying prosperity and gain.

Hare.—This animal is generally considered to be of evil portent, and at one time there was a belief that the bodies of hares were inhabited by witches. For a hare to cross one's path means disappointment and disaster. If one of these animals is seen running past a house in the country, precautions should be taken against fire. In several parts of the world belief in the evil brought by hares is so strong that persons setting out upon an errand or with an important project in view will turn back immediately upon seeing one of these animals, for they believe that if they continue on their way their project will end in failure.

Hedgehog.—An animal of good omen. To overtake a hedgehog is lucky, while to meet one going in the opposite direction is more fortunate still.

Hog.—See *Pig*.

Horse.—To meet a piebald horse brings good luck, especially to a gamester, but if the observer catches sight of the animal's tail first, ill luck will afflict one who is dear to him. If a pair of lovers encounter a white horse, they may take it as an augury of future happiness.

Lamb.—To meet with a solitary lamb promises peace, happiness and love.

Mouse.—To be presented with a white mouse is an augury of success and happiness in love, unless the donor is aware of the significance of his gift. A brown or reddish-coloured mouse is similarly propitious, though in a less degree; but the gift of a grey mouse brings evil and the risk of danger.

Mule.—An unfortunate omen, denoting financial losses and treacherous business partners.

Ox.—A casual meeting with an ox upon the road brings with it a promise of prosperity and monetary gain.

Pig.—A pig is very unlucky, and to meet one means serious worry. If a wedding party returning from church encounters a stray pig, an unhappy married life for the bride and bridegroom is threatened.

Rat.—This is one of those animals that furnished omens to the Roman augurs. A white rat is auspicious, but a black rat has most unfortunate significance. Depredations wrought by rats are of very evil omen to those whose property they thus assail. A Roman historian tells us that the loss of a battle was foretold by rats gnawing the shields of the army. If you find your personal effects have been gnawed by rats, postpone any business which you may have been contemplating.

Sheep.—To encounter unexpectedly a flock of sheep is a lucky sign, especially if the sheep are coming towards you.

Squirrel.—Meeting a squirrel betokens approaching happiness.

Weasel.—To see a weasel foreshadows domestic discord and worry over family matters.

Reptiles

Lizard.—To find a lizard in a place where it is unusual to do so is an omen of disappointment.

Snake.—An encounter with a snake is a portent of treachery, betrayal and jealousy, directed against yourself if the creature is coming towards you, but against your enemies if it is going away from you. (See also *Viper.*)

Toad.—To kill or injure a toad will bring anxiety or grief upon your head.

Tortoise.—A tortoise is a lucky animal, and to encounter one casually is an omen of tranquillity and protection.

Viper.—To encounter a viper, or adder. indicates a meeting with a woman of questionable character.

Fish

In the East a fish has been looked upon as a fortunate omen for many hundreds of years, being a symbol of wealth and fertility. To see a large fish swimming by itself in the water promises a life of happiness and general prosperity.

Insects

Ant.—To be bitten by an ant foreshadows enmity and quarrelling. If ants make their nest near your threshold, prosperity is indicated.

Bee.—If a bee flies into the house, it is thought to bring luck to the inmates if it is kept prisoner for a short time. In some districts, fishermen believe that the sight of a bee will bring them a good catch if it is flying in the same direction as their boat is moving. To kill a bee presages bad luck. It is a strange thing, however, that to see a flight of bees was considered by the Romans to be a very ill omen. The calamitous defeat of the army of Pompey by Caesar at Pharsalus in 48 B.C. was foretold by a swarm of bees which settled upon the sacred altar.

Beetle.—Ever since the days when the scarab was paid divine honours by the ancient Egyptians, this and other beetles have had a fortunate significance. If a beetle runs across your path when you are on a country walk, regard it as a very lucky omen. The bigger the beetle, the greater the good fortune that it brings. It must be understood, however, that we are not referring here to the common black-beetle, or cockroach, which has a very different significance.

Cockroach.—These disgusting insects are everywhere regarded with repulsion; and not without cause, for if a cockroach appears in a place where it is not generally seen, it is held to presage death.

Cricket.—From time immemorial, and in all parts of the world, these happy little creatures have been regarded as lucky. They betoken peace, prosperity and domestic felicity. If crickets mysteriously abandon a house which they have inhabited for a long time, illness or death is to be feared.

Grasshopper.—These cheerful insects favour travelling and foretell good news.

Ladybird.—This pretty little beetle is everywhere viewed with favour as a harbinger of good fortune. A ladybird bearing seven spots on its back is considered particularly lucky.

Spider.—To see a spider in the evening portends money losses; to see one in the morning is an omen of grief; while at noon it presages trouble and anxiety. To discover a spider upon one's clothes or person is an omen of prosperity. To come upon one that is spinning its web means that a plot is being hatched against you. To kill a spider, particularly at night, is very unfortunate.

o

Wasp.—To be stung by a wasp is a warning to be on your guard against jealousy, deception and danger.

Omens Derived From Plants

Aloe.—This strange plant blooms very seldom, and to come upon one by chance when it is in flower is a forewarning of sorrow and affliction.

Broom.—If a sprig of broom is taken into a house by some heedless person, it will sweep away good luck.

Clover.—To find a four-leafed clover (which is a rare event) presages outstanding good luck and the fulfilment of one's most cherished wishes.

Fir.—It is often regarded as an unfortunate omen to find a fir tree in a locality where they are uncommon. It is a sign of malice and mischief in store.

Heather.—White heather is one of the best known harbingers of luck, but to have any value as an omen it should be discovered or come into one's possession by chance. If the heather, whatever be its colour, is faded, grief of some sort may be expected.

Holly.—This plant has a special connexion with fairies and the supernatural world, and to find a sprig or broken bough of holly foretells an unexpected piece of good fortune in the near future.

Honeysuckle.—It is lucky to find a spray of honeysuckle or to be presented with one.

Laurel.—An omen of peace, love and goodwill.

Rose.—An unexpected gift of a rose is a very lucky omen, while the receipt of a whole bunch of roses is more fortunate still.

Wistaria.—To find a wistaria plant in bloom is a sign that someone who loves you dearly is thinking of you, or is about to send you a letter or message.

Omens Associated with the Human Body

For centuries certain manifestations connected with the human body have been regarded as omens of varying importance, the chief of these being as follows:—

Depression.—To feel depressed for no apparent reason is a sign of unexpected good news.

Hair.—If the hair comes out in unusually large quantities, a severe attack of some affliction is imminent.

Ear.—A ringing in the right ear foretells pleasant news; a ringing in the left ear, unpleasant news. A tingling in either ear signifies that a jealous person is spreading scandal about you.

Itching :—

    Crown of the head.—Advance in position.

    Right cheek.—Someone is speaking well of you.

    Left cheek.—Slander is being spread about you.

    Right eye or eyebrow.—Meeting with an old friend.

    Left eye or eyebrow.—Great disappointment.

    Nose (inside).—Trouble and sorrow.

    Nose (outside).—You will be kissed, cursed, annoyed, or meet with a fool within an hour.

    Lips.—Someone is talking about you with disrespect.

    Back of the neck.—Illness of a relative.

    Right shoulder.—A legacy.

    Left shoulder.—Sorrow.

    Right elbow.—Pleasant and exciting news.

    Left elbow.—Bad news and losses.

    Right palm.—Much money.

    Left palm.—You will pay a debt.

    Spine.—Disappointments.

    Loins.—Reconciliation after quarrels.

    Stomach.—An invitation to dine.

    Thighs.—Change of dwelling-place.

    Right knee.—Happy journey.

    Left knee.—Voyage beset with misfortune.

    Shins.—Unpleasant surprise.

    Ankles.—Marriage or increase of income.

    Sole of right foot.—Profitable journey.

    Sole of left foot.—Journey with losses.

The Meaning of Moles

Belief in the divinatory meaning of moles, birth-marks and similar excrescences upon the human skin has been sanctified by a tradition that originated in very early times. The general opinion seems to be that these strange little growths are, in some way that is at present obscure, impressed upon the body by astrological influences at the moment of birth, or upon the embryo at the time of conception. Whatever may be their cause, there is little room for doubting that they are capable of furnishing interpretations of considerable value concerning the character and destiny of the person upon whom they appear.

The results of the patient and laborious efforts of innumerable workers who have directed their energies over a period of many centuries, to the observation and comparison of moles, and the various traits and happenings with which they seem to be associated in human character and destiny, have been collected by us for the benefit of the reader, and are presented in the following pages. No discrimination need be made between moles and what are commonly termed "birth-marks," for both originated in exactly the same way.

The interpretation of moles and birth-marks depends upon two factors: their actual physical appearance, and the part of the subject's body upon which they appear. Physical appearance is determined by four particulars—size, shape, colour and degree of hairiness, the meanings of which, from the divinatory point of view, are as follows:—

Size.—In general, it may be said that the greater the size of the mole or birth-mark, the greater will be the force of the omen which it indicates, either for good or for evil. Thus a large mole is significant for the light which it throws upon a person's character or destiny; while a very small mole, though not entirely devoid of meaning, cannot be said to have much force, either for good or evil.

Shape.—A round mole or birth-mark is fortunate, but one that is pointed, angular, or straight-sided brings bad luck. An oval mark is moderately fortunate. One that is raised or that stands out prominently is very fortunate indeed, unless it is modified by other circumstances.

Colour.—Light-coloured moles and birth-marks—those that are white, yellowish, honey-coloured, pale brown, or red—have an auspicious significance; while the darker the colour of the mark, the stronger its power for misfortune.

Hairiness.—The more hairs there are on a mole or birth-mark the more unfortunate is its meaning; while a hairless mark can be reckoned as an auspicious sign, unless its influence is affected by modifying circumstances. Long hairs are unfortunate for monetary affairs; thus the shorter the hairs (if any) the brighter the prospects of wealth and prosperity.

The following are the meanings of moles and birth-marks according to the parts of the body on which they are found. These localities are in alphabetical order. In interpreting the meaning of a mole, a balance should be carefully struck of its fortunate and unfortunate characteristics before a definite decision is reached.

Abdomen.—A lazy, selfish, greedy and untidy disposition is revealed by a mole on this part of the body.

Ankle.—A mole on either ankle gives refinement and delicacy to a man, but also foppishness. In a woman, a mark so placed will manifest itself in great energy and ability. She will be brave, optimistic, hard-working and independent.

Arm.—If the mark occurs on the right arm, it presages success in life; most of the enterprises to which the subject puts his hand will have a satisfactory result. If it is the left arm that is so affected, however, anxiety over financial matters will never be absent for long.

Back.—A mole on the back gives an open, frank and generous disposition, with a tendency towards ostentation and display. The subject will also be dignified, brave, arrogant and fond of giving advice in a somewhat patronizing manner. There is a strong romantic strain in his character, which is inclined to degenerate into sensuality and a love of ease and luxury if the mole is located very low down.

Breast.—A mole on the right side of the breast shows that the subject is likely to suffer extremes of fortune. He may rise to a pinnacle of wealth and happiness and enjoy the esteem of his fellow men, only to be reduced to poverty and disgrace as the result of some sudden and untoward occurrence.

A man who has a mole on the left side of the breast will be fortunate in his undertakings, and happy, on the whole, throughout his life. To confidence and ambition he will unite an ardent temperament; he will readily fall in love, and will be most easily and surely approached through his feelings. He will be easy-going, sympathetic and generous, but lacking in decision and constancy of purpose.

A woman who has a mole so placed will be ardent and sincere in love. She should be on her guard lest the warmth of her own feelings and excessive trust in the good intentions of other people lead her to commit an imprudence which she will have cause to regret. She should on no account allow herself to give way to depression.

A mole in the centre of the breast, in either sex, indicates that its possessor will never enjoy wealth, although, at the same time, he or she will never want for the necessities of existence and the requirements of simple comfort.

Cheek.—A mole on the right cheek presages a happy and fortunate marriage; the nearer it is to the mouth, the greater will be the wealth and good fortune brought to the subject by his spouse. In any event, the lucky possessor of a mole on this part of the body will never be reduced to poverty, or anxiety regarding the wherewithal of existence.

A mole on the left cheek is an omen that many difficulties stand in the way of fortune and success. Courage, perseverance and a firm will are needed in the many struggles and vicissitudes that will fall to the lot of the subject. Those who possess these qualities in good measure will win their battles and build up a successful career; but weaker and less resolute spirits will inevitably "go under," for the hand of fate is against them.

Chin.—Fortunate indeed are those persons who have a mole on either side of the chin; it is a sure sign that they will be favoured by destiny in all their undertakings. Even without much effort on their own part, they will be lifted to wealth and prosperity, and will enjoy the affection and regard of those about them.

Ear.—A mole on either ear denotes that the subject possesses a reckless disposition.

Eye.—If the subject has a mole placed near the outer corner of either eye, he will be of a placid, frugal and temperate nature.

Eyebrow.—A mole on the right eyebrow portends an advantageous and happy marriage, very probably at an early age. If the mole is situated on the left eyebrow, the prognostication is not quite so fortunate.

Foot.—A mole on the right foot shows a great love of travelling; and if the subject has a mole on the left foot as well, it is a sign that he will be able to indulge this passion. A mole on the left foot alone shows a quick intellect and well-developed powers of thought.

Forehead.—A mole on the right side of the forehead is a mark of outstanding ability and mental power, which will raise the subject to fame and prosperity. Travelling is also indicated.

If the mole is on the left side of the forehead, however, its possessor will have little notion of the value of money, and is likely to be perpetually in a state of pecuniary embarrassment—if not actual want—owing to his own squandering and extravagance.

A mole in the middle of the forehead is reputed to give its

fortunate owner great success in affairs of the heart. A woman with this mark will count her admirers by the dozen, while a man who is so distinguished will display all the gallantry of a Don Juan.

Hand.—If the back of one or both of the hands is marked by a mole, great natural ability can be inferred. The subject will attain success in life as the fruit of his own talents. If it is the left hand alone that is so marked, the omen has a slightly less fortunate significance.

Hip.—The man or woman who is marked with a mole on the right or left hip will be the progenitor of many strong and healthy children, who will themselves have numerous offspring. If both hips are marked in this manner, the force of the omen is slightly increased.

Jaw.—To have a mole on either side of the jaw is an unlucky sign, showing weak health and a career hampered by illness. The omen is more inauspicious still if the mole is on the left-hand side.

Knee.—A happy marriage is foreshadowed by a mole on the right knee. The subject's wedded life will pass easily and smoothly, unhampered by money troubles or any serious anxieties. If the subject has a mole on his left knee, he will always be inclined to act before he thinks, and will often have cause to regret his rashness. At heart, however, he will be upright and kindly, and he will possess a sympathetic nature.

Leg.—A mole on any part of either of the legs between the knee and the ankle shows a heedless, careless and indolent nature; a person who possesses a mole in this position will most likely be selfish, slovenly and lacking in sympathy towards other people.

Lip.—A mole on either of the lips gives a happy, sunny nature, combined with a certain amount of sensuality and indolence. Those who have a mole so placed are fond of the good things of life, and often turn a deaf ear to duty if it conflicts with the pursuit of pleasure. They are inveterate and ardent lovers, and yet their constancy is not above reproach. If the mole is large and on the lower lip this omen has a more sensual significance; the women who bear this mark are often heartless flirts, the men libertines.

If the mole is on the upper lip, greater delicacy is shown; although the nature of the subject is sensual, it is modified and controlled by refinement and good taste.

Mouth.—See *Cheek*; *Lip*.

Neck.—The subject who has a mole on the side of the neck will suffer remarkable vicissitudes during the course of his life. The progress of his career will at first be slow, but persistence will be rewarded by the attainment of an eminent position. Unforeseen gifts or legacies are indicated, as well as the assistance of devoted friends. (See also *Throat*).

Nose.—A mole on the nose is a very lucky sign. The fortunate person who bears this mark will enjoy success and prosperity, and practically every project which he undertakes will have a satisfactory outcome. Wide travelling and frequent change of scene are also promised. A mole on the side of the nose, especially in women, often gives a voluptuous temperament.

Ribs.—A weak and cowardly disposition is shown by a mole on the right side of the ribs. Those who bear this mark so placed will be indolent, lacking in intelligence and delicacy, and of a brutish nature. If the mole is on the left-hand side, these characteristics will be modified to some extent and also tempered with a little good humour.

Shoulder.—A mole on either the right or left shoulder denotes a life of hard work, with much adversity.

Side.—See *Hip ; Ribs.*

Stomach.—See *Abdomen.*

Temple.—See *Eyebrow ; Forehead.*

Thigh.—A mole on the thigh gives a warm, enthusiastic temperament; and if it is the right thigh that is marked, prosperity and a happy marriage are denoted. If the mole appears on the left thigh, however, the omen is not so auspicious, and the subject will suffer from loss of money, injustice and loneliness; the warmth and frankness of his nature will meet with many rebuffs. It is a singular but very common occurrence that a mole on the thigh is accompanied by one on the ear.

Throat.—A mole on the throat, or front of the neck, is a most fortunate sign, denoting a wealthy marriage or a successful career leading to prosperity and affluence.

Wrist.—The subject who has a mole on either the right or left wrist will have a very interesting and successful career. His own intelligence and the talents with which he is endowed will be his most valuable assets, and they will generally ensure him success in life and lead him to wealth and happiness.

Weather Omens

Popular omens for foretelling the approach of good or bad weather are met with all over the world, and especially in places where the inhabitants lead an open-air life, or where their livelihood is dependent upon favourable weather conditions. That is why fishermen, shepherds and farmers have always enjoyed a universal reputation for the surprising shrewdness of their weather lore, a shrewdness which it is not difficult to understand, since, in a measure, they depend for their daily bread on the sun, the sky, the earth, the sea and the other forces of Nature. These worthies had no knowledge of "anti-cyclones," or "depressions over Iceland," and yet for reliability their predictions would be hard to rival.

It may not be fully realized, however, that the greater number of the popular weather omens that, from familiarity and the frequency of their observation, have passed into trite saws and proverbs are justified in the light of science; and that the first shepherd in ancient days who mentally linked the sight of a rosy sky at sunset with fine weather to come, and an angry red light in the sky at daybreak with the threat of rain and storm, was one of the world's first meteorologists.

In time, the validity of such a prediction would be universally recognized and it would pass into a proverb that would take various forms in different lands. Thus in England people have said for centuries:

> Red sky at night, shepherd's delight;
> Red sky at morning, shepherd's warning.

Other European nations, too, have their own versions of this and similar wise saws.

The old, traditional weather omens and proverbs which we give below have been collected from different parts of the British Isles and from a few other parts of Europe. Many old writers on weather lore have been consulted, as well as shepherds, farmers, fishermen, and outdoor workers in all localities. For the sake of convenient reference, the omens are listed under the heavenly body or phenomenon principally concerned.

Predictions arising from the appearance of the moon, for instance, will be found under the heading *Moon;* those in which the wind is the chief indication, under *Wind*. In conclusion a number of miscellaneous omens are given, all drawn from observations of animals and familiar objects.

Sun.—When the sun is covered with a haze, so that its light appears subdued and sickly, bad weather may be expected. If, however, the rays of the rising sun cannot be seen, but it appears as a bright, shining ball, then good weather will follow.

If the sun goes down in a bank of dark, heavy clouds, the morrow will be wet and stormy.

If the sun comes out while it is still raining, showers will continue for a few days.

A ring round the sun in rainy weather promises a brief spell of fine weather before very long.

A ring round the sun in fine weather shows that rain is not a long distance away.

If the sun as it rises is pale, long continued showers will occur.

It is said, "A red sun in the morning has water in his eye."

> If red the sun begins his race
> Be sure the rain will fall apace;
> If the sun goes pale to bed
> 'Twill rain to-morrow, it is said.

Moon.—If, in fine weather, the moon is encircled by a single misty ring, it is an infallible indication of rain to come. A large circle round the moon threatens rain very soon, while several concentric circles presage a lengthy spell of wet and stormy weather. As an old saying has it, "The moon with a circle brings water in her beak."

When the moon at the full rises into a clear, cloudless sky on the horizon, and the moon itself is a bright yellow colour, a short spell of fine weather is indicated. In winter months a "clear moon brings frost soon."

If the full moon rises amid clouds and the orb itself is pale, wet weather may be expected. Likewise, to see the old moon "in the arms of a new one" is a sign of bad weather to come.

If the full moon rises red, it is a sign of wind.

If the moon either rises or sets during high wind and rain, the force of the storm is likely to abate.

Stars and Shooting Stars.—When the stars blink and flicker and appear to be larger than usual, wet and stormy weather is in store.

If usually small and faint stars cannot be seen at all, the wind will soon rise.

If a large number of shooting stars is seen on a clear night in summer, a fairly long spell of rain is foreshadowed.

Clouds.—A curtain of dark clouds spread uniformly over the sky, together with a drop in temperature, is a sure sign of snow.

If cumulus clouds, that is, white, fleecy, heaped-up ones, float towards the north-western horizon, it is an omen of a fairly long spell of fine weather.

Long streaks of red or crimson cloud in the western sky at sunset presage fine weather, as do clouds that remain in the eastern sky after the sun has disappeared.

If masses of cloud cover the western sky at sunrise and disappear over the western horizon shortly after the sun has risen, a short spell of pleasant weather can be predicted. However, if dark clouds remain in the western sky after sunrise, rain will fall before many hours have passed.

Red clouds round the sun as it is rising threaten rain within the next four hours.

Clouds coming up out of the west denote a shower.

Heavily massed white or grey clouds that constantly increase in size and move at a fair pace across the sky presage thunder.

A uniformly grey sky with dark clouds scudding across it at a lower altitude is a sign of high winds and stormy weather.

If clouds move over the sky in conflicting directions, or rise in spiral formation, thunder and lightning are in store.

The peculiar cloud formation that is popularly known as a "mackerel sky," and which generally occurs in summer, indicates a short period of fine weather. In the words of the old saying:—

> A mackerel sky
> Twelve hours dry.

Little or no rain may be expected to fall from clouds at a very high altitude. This is popularly expressed in the rhyme:—

> Clouds that float high
> Will soon run dry.

Thunder and Lightning.—If lightning flickers in the sky on the evening of a fine day, without any thunder being heard, a spell of fine, clear weather may be confidently predicted.

Thunder in the evening is an omen of several days of very wet and sultry weather.

The truth of the rhyme:—

> Thunder in spring
> Rain will bring

is confirmed by the meteorologists, as also is:—

> Winter thunder
> A summer's wonder.

Rain and Rainbows.—If rain falls from a fairly clear sky, it is likely to continue to fall at intervals.

If rain falls in the early morning, the weather will be fine by noon.

Rain that falls while an east wind is blowing will last another day at least.

A rainbow appearing during a spell of bad weather signifies that the rainy period is nearing its end.

If a rainbow fades rapidly from the sky, fine weather is not far away.

Here is another popular variation of an old weather saw which we have already quoted:—

> Rainbow in the morning, shepherd's warning.
> Rainbow at night, shepherd's delight.

An old shepherd of more than eighty years of age declares that this omen has never once played him false.

Wind.—If the wind comes out of the north for several days on end, fine mild weather may be expected for some time.

If it blows from the south-east, rain will follow.

If a gale springs up suddenly and unexpectedly on a calm evening in summer, it will not be long before thunder is heard.

If the wind drops suddenly and there is an abnormal and unpleasant warmth, a thunderstorm may be expected.

Here are some easily remembered rhymes concerning the four winds; the first one is of Scottish origin:—

> When the wind is in the north
> Hail comes forth,

When the wind is in the west
Look for a wet blast,
When the wind is in the soud (south)
The weather will be gude,
When the wind is in the east
Cold and snaw comes neist.

When the wind is in the east
It's neither good for man nor beast,
When the wind is in the west
It's then the wind is at its best.

Wind east or west
Is a sign of a blast,
Wind north or south
Is a sign of a drought.

When the wind is in the north
A skilful fisher goes not forth.

Mist and Dew.—If high land and the tops of hills are crowned with mist, much rain is in store.

A mist rising over flat fields and marshes in the early morning presages a fine and sunny day.

A widespread mist preceding the sunrise near the period of the full moon indicates a long spell of fine weather.

A damp, sticky mist, driven about by the wind, is an infallible sign of rain to come.

If mists are light and easily dispelled, without accumulating in hollows and valleys, several days of dry and bright weather are promised.

A heavy dew falling at the close of a fine, warm day in spring, summer or autumn is a sign of a fine morrow.

If a warm day is followed by a calm and dewless evening, rain will undoubtedly fall next day.

A light mist rising from the surface of a lake or river and overspreading the surrounding land is an indication of sunny days to come.

Sky.—If the sky opposite the setting sun is suffused with crimson, a good deal of wind can be expected before long.

A red sky in the west at sunset is a sign of fine weather on the morrow.

A red sky at sunrise in summer means heavy rain and a fair amount of wind; if in winter, it is an indication that rain will set in and fall for the greater part of the day.

An old rhyme, well known in the country, sums up the truth of the last two omens thus:—

> Evening red and morning grey
> Send the traveller on his way.
> Evening grey and morning red
> Bring the rain upon his head.

If the south-east sky is red, rain is threatened.

A green sky showing through the clouds in wet weather portends a continuance of heavy rain.

If the sky is suffused with green after sunset, rain and heavy gales are in store; as the old proverb has it, "A green sky means the devil's own weather."

A dark grey sky, with wind blowing from the south, is a sign of frost and cold weather.

A fine, clear sky in the early morning in summer often presages rain clouds before the lapse of many hours; but if the sky is slightly cloudy at this time, the day will probably turn out very fine.

A pale yellow sky in the west is an infallible omen of rain.

General Weather Omens

Animals are universally regarded as providing reliable indications of approaching changes in the weather, and the predictions drawn from their habits and behaviour have been justified beyond all shadow of doubt. It would appear as though some mysterious sympathy, which is denied to mankind, exists between them and future weather conditions. A probable explanation is that the astrological influences which determine the weather react also upon some special, delicately attuned mechanism forming part of the nervous system in animals, and thus confer on them an advance knowledge of the weather with a precision that is usually attributed to instinct.

Spiders are particularly accurate little weather prophets, and regulate the building of their webs to suit the weather from day to day, or even from hour to hour. When they are convinced by some mysterious means that it is going to be fine, they build actively, extending their webs in all directions; but when rain and storms threaten, they confine their operations to strengthening and consolidating their abodes. Thus, if the threads by means of which spiders' webs are anchored to surrounding objects are long, a succession of fine days may be expected; but if the little weavers begin to shorten the threads, the weather will be wet and boisterous.

If spiders begin to alter or rebuild their webs in the evening hours, a calm, clear night is indicated; if they begin building in the morning, the day will be fine and sunny. But if they break down their webs and take refuge in crevices and under leaves, the weather will be bad.

When colonies of *gnats* disport themselves in the evening sunshine, the morrow will be warm and sunny. Large numbers of gnats seen in spring are an omen that the latter part of the year will be mild.

Many *bats* or nocturnal *beetles* flying about indicate that there will be a fine morrow.

When *bees* seem reluctant to leave the hive, rain may be expected very soon.

Fish are very responsive to weather changes. When they swim about just below the surface and come up readily to feed, rain is not far off; but when they avoid the light and lurk at the bottom of deep pools, it will be some time before grey skies and rain are seen.

When *toads* and *frogs* are much in evidence, and their croaking is loud and incessant, heavy rain is in store.

To come upon many freshly-thrown-up *mole hills* portends a lengthy spell of wet and cold weather.

If *cats* rub their paws behind their ears, it is an omen of wet; likewise, if *dogs* roll on the ground and scratch themselves, it portends that rain is imminent.

When *horses* and *cattle* gather in the corner of a field or in the lee of a hedge, rain is on the way. Rain is also indicated when horses, cattle and *sheep* grow frisky and chase one another, or stretch out their necks and sniff the air. If sheep turn their backs to the wind it is a sign of rain.

Birds are very accurate weather prophets. If *rooks* and *crows* croak noisily and fly excitedly about their nests for no apparent reason—especially if they sail with motionless wings, like kites—it is because they sense the coming of rain.

If birds become silent and hushed, as though with fear and foreboding, it will probably thunder before long.

When *robins* hop about near the house for scraps of food, cold weather with much snow and frost may be expected.

Owls have been observed to screech and hoot more vociferously than usual when a change of weather is imminent; so when they are particularly noisy in wet weather, a fine spell may be expected, and vice versa.

Plants are no less responsive than animals to the approach of good or bad weather. *Trees*, for instance, may often be observed to rustle their leaves in calm, still weather. They have divined the approach of life-giving moisture, and are eagerly awaiting its coming. And, sure enough, before very long a few heavy drops of rain herald the advent of a thunder shower.

The pretty little *scarlet pimpernel* is known in the country as the "farmer's weather-glass," on account of its useful habit of closing its petals before the coming of rain, a practice that is shared by several other common flowers, including the beautiful twining *convolvulus*, or bindweed.

Before thunder and rain the leaves of *clover* will be found drawn closely together.

When the *scent of flowers* seems stronger and heavier than usual, it is a sign of approaching rain.

Wet weather may be expected when painted walls and metallic objects are covered with a film of dew, and when distant hills and far-away scenery seem nearer than usual.

When the atmosphere is full of moisture, as it usually is before a period of wet weather, *salt* becomes damp and cakes together, while a strip of *seaweed* that has been hung up dry will be found moist and sticky.

Rain may also be expected if a fall of *soot* from the chimney occurs, and if the *fire* burns in a slow and sluggish fashion. On the other hand, a brightly burning, clear fire foretells cold, clear days.

If *corns* "shoot" and pain occurs in rheumatic joints and old wounds, rain is not far away.

The ominous significance of rain falling upon St. Swithin's day (July 15), is well known:—

> St. Swithin's day, if thou dost rain,
> For forty days it will remain;
> St. Swithin's day, if thou be fair,
> For forty days 'twill rain nae mair.

A similar but less known proverb concerns St. Vitus's day (June 15):—

> If St. Vitus's day be rainy weather,
> It will rain for thirty days together.

Candlemas day falls upon February 2, and it is the subject of two old weather rhymes, both of which have the same import:—

> If the sun shines bright on Candlemas day,
> The half of the winter's not yet away;

and

> If Candlemas day be fair and bright,
> Winter will have another flight;
> If on Candlemas day it be shower and rain,
> Winter is gone and will not come again.

Here is a rhyme concerning St. Vincent's day (January 22):—

> Remember on St. Vincent's day
> If that the sun his beams display
> Be sure to mark his transient beam
> Which through the casement sheds a gleam:
> For 'tis a token bright and clear
> Of prosperous weather all the year.

For the seasons there are these wise saws:—

Spring:

> A late spring
> Is a great blessing.

> As the days grow longer
> The storms grow stronger.

> If the oak's before the ash
> Then you'll only get a splash,
> But if the ash precedes the oak
> Then you may expect a soak.

Summer:

> After a famine in the stall
> Comes a famine in the hall.

> (A bad hay crop precedes a bad corn crop.)

Winter:

> An early winter
> Is a surly winter.

> Who doffs his coat on a winter's day
> Will gladly put it on in May.

> A green winter makes a fat churchyard.

Tradition has also given us the following instructive sayings concerning various months of the year:—

January:

> If you see grass in January
> Lock your grain in your granary.

(If crops come up too early they will be killed by frost and shortage will follow.)

February:

> All the months in the year
> Curse a fair Februeer.

(It is well known that a mild and sunny February precedes a wet and stormy summer season.)

March:

> So many mists in March you see
> So many frosts in May will be.

> March flowers
> Make no summer bowers.

> A wet March makes a sad harvest.

> A peck of March dust and a shower in May
> Make the corn green and the meadows gay

April:

> A cold April
> The barn will fill.

> April showers
> Bring May flowers.

May:

> Water in May
> Bread all the year.

> Till May be out
> Cast not a clout.

(It is held by some that the word "May" in this saw refers to the *blossom*, not to the month.)

> Mist in May, heat in June,
> Make the harvest come right soon.

June:

> Calm weather in June
> Sets the corn in tune.

> If June with bright sun is blest
> The farmer thanks God for his harvest.

July:

> If the first of July be rainy weather
> It will rain more or less for four weeks together.

August:

> Dry August and warm
> Does harvest no harm.

Experience has proved that "A good hay year is a bad fog year," and also "In a year when plums flourish all else fails." Continuous falls of snow make the ground particularly yielding in regard to crops, so the saying has arisen that "A year of snow is a year of plenty."

The proverbial saws contained in these pages are, for the most part, easily remembered, and a mastery of them will not only enable one to avoid disappointment when planning excursions, walks, or picnics, but will also form the means of establishing oneself as a veritable "weather prophet." Much grumbling about the weather would be avoided if only more people took the trouble to study it and heed its clear warnings; but if we are inclined to feel annoyed at having to postpone some pleasant trip owing to stormy conditions, we may find comfort in a philosophy expounded by Charles Dickens: "There's something good in all weathers. If it don't happen to be good for my work to-day, it's good for some other man's to-day, and will come round to me to-morrow."

III

POPULAR SUPERSTITIONS

IN addition to various oracles and omens which we have classified under headings in the preceding pages, there are a number of observances, the origins of which are more or less obscure, that may be described as "popular superstitions." All that may be said of them is that they are traditional, that they have been observed since "time immemorial," and are, therefore, worthy of some notice, even if their only value lies in the fact that they are merely quaint and amusing.

Of chief interest among these, to the readers of the fair sex, at any rate, are the love charms and spells, which deal with all those matters touching upon affairs of the heart. But first of all let us consider a few of the general superstitions that are traditionally associated with lovers.

The Fortune of Lovers

For a girl to meet her sweetheart or to kiss him for the first time under the light of a new moon is considered to be exceptionally lucky, for it means that she will soon become his bride, that their marriage will be blessed with undying love, and that neither of them will know the pinch of poverty. It is also a good omen if, when thinking of her lover, a maiden should hear a cock crow, for it forebodes an early wedding. The same is indicated if, when she is in love, she should fall upstairs.

If it is possible, the meeting-place of lovers should be upon a hillside, especially where there is heather, near a stream or river, on the seashore, or in the heart of a wood, for then, it is said, neither will deceive the other but will for ever remain constant. Poplar trees, however, should always be avoided.

When writing a letter to a sweetheart it is lucky to complete it just as the clock strikes the hour of midnight, and to post the missive while the full moon is shedding its soft light over the house-tops. When you are walking with the one you love, it is said to be particularly fortunate if you meet either a black cat or a white horse or pony.

The best time for an offer of marriage to be made is on a Friday evening, and the engagement should be announced on the Saturday. Blue is notably the best colour for lovers, and the turquoise is their lucky stone. At one time a broken sixpence, of which the man and the girl each kept a piece, was said to ensure that they would never part; and the possession of a lock of the other's hair, tied to form a lovers' knot, was also an assurance of lasting affection.

The superstition has arisen that betrothed persons should not be photographed together, else they will soon be doomed to part, or their marriage will be an unhappy one. Quarrels and inconstancy are near at hand if sweethearts should look together through glass at the new moon. It is unlucky for the banks of canals or ponds, for bridges, valleys or, worst of all, cross-roads to be used as trysting-places, for in such circumstances love and respect are liable to turn to hate and bitter scorn.

Those who wish their love affairs to run smoothly should avoid meeting each other on the stairs, and should on no account kiss or embrace there. Discord is predicted, too, if sweethearts write love letters in ink of any colour other than blue, or in pencil. Should kisses, in the form of crosses, be made at the end of the letter, their number should not be four, seven, or thirteen; three is the luckiest number, and this modest amount is just as sure a sign of love and affection as the swarm of crosses that some people seem to find necessary.

It is unlucky for love letters to be posted either on Christmas Day or on February 29, which occurs once in four years. Great care should be taken not to drop a letter to your sweetheart when you are taking it to the post, for, if you do, the next time you meet you will quarrel. Remember that it is unlucky to receive a pair of gloves as a gift from your lover, for it means a parting; the same applies to a brooch or a knife, but it is said that the ill luck may be warded off if a small coin is given in exchange.

It is very unlucky for a girl to try on her wedding-ring before the ceremony, for it often results in a sudden termination of the engagement or in an unhappy marriage. To lose an engagement ring or wedding-ring is just as ominous, foretelling a break.

The following is the language of rings, and applies both to a man and a woman:—

Ring on the first finger of the left hand	I want to be married.
Ring on the second finger of the left hand	I prefer platonic friendship.
Ring on the third finger of the left hand	I am engaged or married.
Ring on the fourth, or little finger of the left hand	I never intend to marry.

To Find When You Will Wed

The Pea-pod.—Take a pea-pod in which there are nine peas, and suspend it over the doorway by means of a white thread. If the next person who enters by the same door is not a member of the family and is a bachelor or spinster, then your wedding will take place in not more than a year's time.

The Red Rose.—Pluck a full-blown red rose during the month of June, not later than seven o'clock in the morning, and place it in a white envelope. Seal the envelope with wax, and make an impression on the wax with the third finger of your left hand. Now place the envelope under your pillow and carefully note your dreams on the following night. If you dream of water, fields, flowers, mountains, glass, children, parents, organ music, silver, or the moon, you will be married within a year. If in your dreams you see giants, animals, birds, fishes, paper, a looking-glass or the sun, you will wait five years for your wedding. To dream of gold, bells, reptiles, storms or soldiers is unlucky in these circumstances, for it means that you will probably remain a spinster.

The Hair and the Ring.—Take a long hair from your own or someone else's head and pass it through a wedding-ring of gold. Hold the hair, with the ring suspended, between the forefinger and thumb of your left hand, and place your elbow upon the table. Now gently lower the ring until it hangs below the rim and in the centre of an empty tumbler, keeping your hand and arm perfectly still. If the ring does not move at all, it will be long before you marry. But if the ring sways to and fro, and knocks against the side of the glass, you must count the number of times it does so in the space of five minutes and subtract from the total the number of letters in your forename and surname; this will give you the number of years which will elapse before you marry. Should the number result in a minus quantity, your wedding will take place within a year.

The Playing-cards.—To find who, among a company of women, will be the first to marry, deal round an ordinary pack of playing-cards face upwards. The one who receives the king of hearts will be the first to wed. For men the queen of hearts is the significant card.

Any odd number of persons, such as three, five or seven must stand in a circle, at the centre of which is placed a well-shuffled pack of cards in a bag or box. Each member of the company must in turn draw a card until the pack is exhausted. The one who draws the ace of hearts will be the first to marry; the one who holds the two of clubs will be the last to find a husband; while the one who holds the ace of spades will never wed at all.

The Cuckoo.—When you hear a cuckoo for the first time in the year, quote aloud:—

> Cuckoo, Cuckoo, answer me true
> This question that I'm asking you;
> I beg that truly you'll tell me
> In how many years I'll married be.

The number of times which the cuckoo replies is declared to represent the number of years that will elapse before you marry.

The Mirror and the Moon.—The following ceremony should be practised, for preference, on Christmas Eve or Night. Borrow a man's silk handkerchief and take it, together with a mirror, to a pond, lake or stream, and wait, alone, until the moon begins to rise. As soon as the moon rises high enough, turn your back to the water and hold the mirror upwards in such a manner that it reflects not only the moon itself but also the moon's reflection in the water. Now place the silk handkerchief over your face and count the number of moons which you see in the mirror. If there are only two, more than a year will elapse before you wed, but if there are more than two, the total number represents the months that will elapse before your marriage.

The Cherry-stones.—Most people are familiar with the ceremony connected with cherry-stones. The number of these on the plate should be counted, while saying, for the first stone, "this year"; the second stone, "next year"; the third stone, "sometime"; the fourth stone, "never." If the number of stones exceeds four, the incantation is repeated. The word or words occurring at the last stone are said to be a prophecy of your fate as regards marriage. In the same way the petals of a daisy may be plucked, while a similar incantation is uttered until the flower is stripped of all its petals. (*See* Oracles.)

To Find Out Whom You Will Wed

The Ring and Photograph.—Take a photograph of the one you love and hold before it a ring on the end of a thread. Be careful to keep your hand still. If the ring moves in a circle, you will marry the person in the picture soon and will lead a life of bliss; if the ring moves to and fro, it is unlikely you will marry him. Should the ring not move at all, you are likely to remain single.

The Row of Pins.—On the Eve of St. Agnes, that is to say, on the night before January 21, take a row of pins and pull them out, one after the other. Then stick a pin in your sleeve and you will dream of the one you will marry.

Four-leaf Clover.—If you find a four-leaf clover, place it in your right shoe, and the next bachelor of your acquaintance you meet will become your husband.

The New Moon.—This ceremony must be practised on the first night of the new moon. Open wide the windows of your bedroom and sit down on the window-sill, gazing with unblinking eyes at the moon, and at the same time repeating softly and slowly the following incantation:—

> All hail, Selene, all hail to thee!
> I prithee, good moon, reveal to me
> This night to whom I'll wedded be.

Then, it is said, that during the night you will dream of your future husband.

Wedding-cake.—Take a small piece of wedding-cake, pass it three times through a wedding-ring and then lay the cake under your pillow. In your dreams that night your future husband will appear to you.

Place a small piece of wedding-cake under your pillow and put a borrowed wedding-ring on the third finger of your left hand. Before you retire to bed arrange the shoes which you have worn that day in the shape of a T. Then, it is said, your future husband will appear to you in your dreams.

Cherry-stones.—We have already mentioned how cherry-stones should be counted in order to find out when you will wed. The following incantation may be employed to discover whom you will wed: instead of saying "this year," and so on, say "Tinker, tailor, soldier, sailor, rich man, poor man, beggar-man, thief"; the designation of the last stone, it is declared, will be the rank or calling of your future husband. Another, but less familiar incantation, is "Army, navy, peerage, trade, doctor, divinity, law."

Apple-peel.—Peel an apple carefully, so that the peel does not break, and throw the paring over your left shoulder with your right hand. According to the shape which the peel assumes when it has fallen on to the floor, so will be the initial letter of your future husband's first name.

Hallowe'en Ceremonies

Hallowe'en (October 31) derives its name from the fact that in the Christian calendar it occurs the day before All Saints' or All Hallows' Day. It was the last night of the old year according to the ancient calendar of the Celts. On that night it was said that the witches, hobgoblins, warlocks, and other evil spirits walked abroad and devoted themselves to wicked revels. But the good fairies, too, according to some folk-lore, made their appearance at this time, but only from the hour of dusk until midnight. Hallowe'en has always been considered a particularly auspicious occasion for supernatural experiments; it is still celebrated, chiefly in Scotland, by music and merry-making.

The old Celtic custom was to light great bonfires on Hallowe'en, and after these had burned out to make a circle of the ashes of each fire. Within this circle, and near the circumference, each member of the various families that had helped to make a fire would place a pebble. If, on the next day, any stone was out of its place, or had been damaged, it was held to be an indication that the one to whom the stone belonged would die within twelve months. Such a morbid superstition, however, does not find much favour in modern times, and those manifestations which are connected with affairs of the heart are more popularly sought after on the Eve of All Hallows. Here are some of the spells which should be cast only on Hallowe'en.

To See Your Future Husband.—Retire into a dark room with one lighted candle as the only means of illumination. Place the candle in front of a mirror and peer into the glass. At the same time, you must either be eating an apple or combing your hair. After a few moments it is said that the face of the man whom you will wed will appear over your shoulder.

There is an old country superstition which decrees that if a woman should eat a salted herring just before she goes to bed, her future husband will appear to her in a dream, carrying a cup of water with which to quench her thirst.

To Discover Who will be the First to Marry.—Four cups of the same size are set upon a circular table. In one of the cups there is placed a ring, in another a sixpenny-piece, and in another a sprig of orange-blossom or a piece of heather, while the last cup remains empty. Those who wish to take part in the test are blindfolded, and must walk slowly three times round the table and then touch one of the cups on it. The first person to touch the cup containing the orange-blossom or heather will be the first to wed; anyone selecting the cup with the coin will never know want; the cup with the ring represents devoted love; while the empty cup suggests a single life.

A similar test may be made with three saucers. One is filled with clear water, another with ink or muddy water, while the third is left empty. A woman who wishes to know her fortune is blindfolded and led towards the table with her left hand outstretched. She is then told to touch one of the saucers. Should she touch the saucer containing the clear water, she will soon be married to a handsome man; should she touch the saucer containing the ink or muddy water, her future husband will be a widower; if she should touch the empty saucer, she is unlikely to marry at all.

According to custom mashed potatoes are the correct dish for Hallowe'en, and they also offer us a method of divining which member of the company will be the first to wed. Into the heap of mashed potatoes a ring, a threepenny-bit, a button, a heart-shaped charm, a shell and a key are inserted. Then all the lights in the room are turned out, and each guest, armed with a spoon or fork, endeavours to find the hidden charms. The one who finds the ring will marry first; the threepenny-bit signifies wealth; the button, bachelorhood or spinsterhood; the heart, passionate love; the shell, long journeys; the key, great success and power.

To Ascertain if Your Lover is True.—On Hallowe'en select one of the letters which you have received from your sweetheart, especially one which contains a particularly passionate and important declaration; lay it wide open upon a table and then fold it nine times. Pin the folds together, place the letter in your left-hand glove, and slip it under your pillow. If on that night you dream of silver, gems, glass, castles or clear water, your lover is true and his declarations are genuine; if you dream of linen, storms, fire, wood, flowers, or that he is saluting you, he is false and has been deceiving you.

To Discover What Kind of Man You will Marry.—There is a very curious old custom, now practically extinct, which ordains that girls shall go in couples to a field of cabbages and there blindfold themselves. Then each pair, holding hands, shall wander about until they find a cabbage stalk which they pull out of the ground. If the stalk is long, their husbands will be tall; if it is stumpy, their husbands will be short; a crooked stalk indicates a man crooked in mind and body; a soft stalk, a husband who will be weak-willed; a hard stalk, a strong and self-willed man. Earth clinging to the roots of the stalk is a sign of much wealth, while an exceptionally clean stalk indicates poverty.

Another curious spell, which was said to reveal the fortune of a future husband, required pills to be made of grated walnut, nutmeg and hazel-nut, mixed with butter and sugar. Nine of these pills were taken upon going to bed. If the husband were to be wealthy and a man of leisure, the dreams would be of gold, gems, or silks; if he were to be a clergyman, the dreams would be of white linen; dreams of darkness indicated a lawyer; bustle and confusion, a tradesman; thunder and lightning, a soldier or a sailor; rain storms, a clerk or a domestic servant.

To Find Whether Lovers Will be Happy.—The company sit round an open fire and then a man, selecting the lady of his choice, invites her to place a nut in the glowing embers; he, too, does likewise. If the burning nuts merely glow or smoulder, then the couple who placed them there are suited for one another, and will live in harmony and love. But if the nuts should burst, or crackle loudly, or fly apart, then the man and girl will quarrel excessively, for their temperaments are not in sympathy.

"Bobbing" for Apples.—No Hallowe'en is complete without an "apple bob." Each member of the party is given an apple, from which a small piece has been cut, and into which a fortune written on a slip of paper has been inserted. The apples are thrown into a large tub of water and the company invited to duck their heads and retrieve an apple with their mouths. Upon doing so they draw out the slip of paper and read their fortune. These fortunes, which must be brief, give rise to greater interest if they deal with affairs of love, such as "Your husband will be masterful and handsome";

"Your sweetheart is deceiving you"; "Beware of a dark man who professes to love you," and so on.

Hempseed.—A Hallowe'en custom which was very popular decreed that girls should go into a field and there scatter the seed of hemp. While they did so they chanted:—

> Hempseed I sow thee
> Come after me and show me.

Upon suddenly turning round, it was declared that each girl would see a vision of the man who would be her husband.

Wedding Superstitions and Customs

Since in the preceding pages of this section we have spoken of all manner of spells concerning love, it is appropriate that we should now mention some of the beliefs which are connected with marriage.

The word "wed" is derived from the Anglo-Saxon and means "pledge," since the ceremony consists of each party pledging or promising to abide by certain rules, which are made to ensure their ultimate happiness. It is natural that such a solemn occasion should give rise to certain symbolical acts, and that many things connected with it should be based on traditional superstition—the aim always being to ensure that nothing should be done which would be likely to hinder the good fortune of the parties concerned.

June is the most favoured *marriage month*, although most people are probably in ignorance as to the reason for this. It is because the month was dedicated to Juno, the wife of Jupiter, the supreme deity in Roman mythology. She was regarded as the patroness of marriage, and especially as the protector of women. The Romans had a saying that weddings in June were "Good to the man and happy to the maid." Since Roman times, May has been considered an unlucky marriage month.

The *wedding day* is not particularly stipulated by custom, except that Sunday, of course, is not popular. Friday has evil associations for Christians, seeing that it was the day of our Lord's crucifixion, and also, according to tradition, the day on which Adam and Eve ate the forbidden fruit. To the Norsemen, however, Friday was the luckiest day of the week, while the Romans dedicated it to Venus, the goddess of beauty and worldly love. For some reason few people care to be married on a Monday, and preference is usually shown either for a Wednesday or a Saturday. There is an old rhyme concerning weddings which goes as follows:—

> Monday for health,
> Tuesday for wealth,
> Wednesday the best day of all;
> Thursday for losses,
> Friday for crosses,
> Saturday for no luck at all.

In order to ensure wedded bliss, the *bridal trousseau*, with the exception of the gown, was formerly cut out and sewn by the bride herself. The bridal gown was usually made by her friends. They would sew into the hem, or one of the folds, hairs from their own heads, for this was believed to be a means of bringing about their own marriage within a short time.

Because it is the emblem of purity, candour and simplicity, white is decreed to be the correct colour for the bride to wear. The veil worn by the ancient Greek and Roman brides, however, was yellow, and it was made so that it would cover them completely during the ceremony. Green is a colour associated with ill luck, and should not be worn. Blue, as we have mentioned before, is the most fortunate colour for lovers, and the old rhyme decrees that a bride should wear

> Something old, something new,
> Something borrowed, something blue.

The wearing of *orange-blossom* as a decoration is comparatively recent in England. It was introduced from France about the year 1820, the white blossoms being symbolical of innocence, while the tree which produces them signifies fruitfulness. In the same way the *chaplet of flowers* worn on the head and the *bouquet* are used to denote abundance and prosperity. In the Middle Ages ears of corn were worn or carried by the bride.

On the wedding day, lucky is the girl who awakens to the sound of singing birds, for it means that she and her husband will never quarrel, and will for ever remain constant one to another. A spider on the bridal gown or veil is extremely fortunate, for it denotes wealth and plenty. An old practice required that the cat should be fed by the bride before she left for the church, while if it was black and rubbed itself against her legs it was regarded as an exceptionally lucky sign. After taking a final look into the mirror before leaving the house the bride must be careful to add something to her attire, such as gloves; or else, it is said, the marriage will be attended by extremely bad luck.

The bride must not cry before her wedding, for it is not an auspicious omen. On the way to church it is unlucky to meet with a funeral procession; but to see a lamb, a toad, a dove, or a spider on the way is very fortunate. The church should be entered with the right foot first, while to stumble is considered an omen of evil. To ensure happiness the bride and bridegroom should smile at one another when they meet at the altar.

The *bridegroom* is not subject to many superstitions, although he must be careful not to see his bride on the day of the wedding, before the ceremony takes place, or at any rate not to see her in her bridal clothes until she meets him at the altar. For this reason he should keep his back turned while she is coming up the aisle. Once he has set out for the church, the bridegroom must not turn back; if he finds he has left anything behind he must send back the "best man" or another friend to fetch it. He should take care not to drop the ring, and must ensure that he places it as far down as possible on the finger of the bride. If he fails to do this it is taken to be a sign of an early parting, while if the bride has to assist him in putting on the ring it will be she who rules the home.

His *groomsmen*, or bridegroom-men as they were formerly called, are a survival of the times when marriage was made by capture, and he who wanted a wife would set out with a sturdy band of followers to assist him in snatching the maiden from the midst of her people. His *best man*, of course, would be ever at his side to help him in the actual capture.

The *ring* has a history so ancient that it is impossible to trace. At one time it was probably regarded as a talisman of good luck. Since in former days documents were sealed with signet rings, the giving of a ring by a man to a woman upon his marrying her was symbolical of the bride's reception of the authority of her husband. The plain gold (or platinum) circlet may be said to emblematize the never-ending love and devotion which the man promises to bestow upon the woman of his choice.

According to an ancient belief, the third finger of the left hand is chosen as the "wedding finger," and the one on which the ring is placed, because there is said to be a delicate nerve in this finger which connects it directly with the heart.

Rice or *confetti* is showered at the bride and bridegroom on leaving the church. The rice is derived from an Indian custom connected with the throwing of wheat ears, which was once the practice in our country. It is yet another of those symbolical acts at a wedding which are meant to ensure fruitfulness and plenty for the happy couple. Confetti is used because it is less dangerous to the face and eyes than the hard grains of rice.

After the ceremony, the *bridesmaids* usually compete among themselves to obtain a sprig of the bride's bouquet, for the first one to do so is said to be she who will marry soonest. Those who seek the honour of being a bridesmaid, however, should remember the old saw "Three times a bridesmaid, never a bride." Should a bridesmaid be older than the bride she must remember to wear something green, otherwise, it is declared, she will never succeed in finding a husband.

At the reception the wedding-cake forms the chief feature of the feast provided, and this has its origin in the days of the Romans. But the cake such as the ancients ate on these occasions was very unlike the elaborate and almond-pasted confection that is seen to-day. It was originally made of flour, water and salt, and the couple partook of it in the belief that this symbolical act would ensure that they would never know want. Ornament and icing were introduced about the time of Charles II.

To refuse to eat a piece of wedding-cake means that you wish ill of the bride. There is a superstition that the health of the bride must be drunk in wine, spirits or beer. To drink it in a "soft" drink such as lemonade or water is declared to bring her much ill fortune and many troubles.

Sometimes, when the bride is going upstairs to *prepare for the honeymoon journey*, she will throw one of her shoes over her left shoulder, and it is said that the one who catches the shoe will be the first to marry.

When changing her clothes, the bride should be careful to remove all pins which were used in her marriage gown or veil, and to give them to her friends or throw them away. If she uses any of them in her going-away dress or costume, it is said that ill luck will attend her, and that the honeymoon will not be a happy one.

Throwing *an old shoe* at the bride and bridegroom, or, more usually, attaching one to the car in which they drive away, probably had its origin in the days when an Anglo-Saxon father gave the bride's shoe to the bridegroom, who touched her with it upon the head as an emblem of his authority. Some say, however, that the throwing of a shoe is a survival of the time when marriage was made by force, and the bride was carried off amid acts of violence.

The *honeymoon* is so named because the Teutons would celebrate a wedding by drinking mead, a beverage made from honey, for thirty days after the event—the bride and bridegroom taking part in the merrymaking. The young couple must be careful not to break anything while on their honeymoon, especially a mirror. Occasional quarrels during this period are not considered unlucky, it being a superstition that they ensure a harmonious and happy future. The bride may now wear the fateful green, for it is said to bring her good fortune and much love at this time.

The *homecoming* is not attended by a great deal of superstitious custom to-day. There is a Scottish custom that the bride should be carried across the threshold of her new home while her mother-in-law breaks shortbread over her head. There is also an old custom of pouring boiling water over the threshold before a bride enters her house. In some countries it was thought to be lucky if the newly-wed bride placed dough on the door of her house, as an indication that she, in future, would be the housekeeper. In Ireland a cake made of oats is broken over the wife's head in order to ensure that the married couple will never know want.

Superstitions Associated with Children

Babies born at three, six, nine, or twelve o'clock are said to be exceptionally lucky. When they are grown up it is declared that they will be gifted with considerably more insight and ingenuity than the average person. If a child is born with teeth there is a superstition that it will become extremely selfish. For a child to be born with an open hand, however, is a sign of great generosity. Superstition also declares that if a moon is shining at the time of birth, the child will be a male; no moon at all indicates a girl.

When a baby leaves its mother's room for the first time, it should be carried upstairs before it is carried downstairs, in order to ensure its success in the world. For the child to cry at the christening is considered a fortunate sign, for people in the olden days thought that evil spirits were then leaving the baby's body. A baby's tooth, set in a ring or brooch, was sometimes worn in order to bring good luck.

Christmas and New Year Superstitions

The practice of *decorating the house* at Christmas time is not a Christian custom in origin but a heathen one. The feast of Saturn, the Roman god who represented Time, was held in December, and the temples were decorated with various plants and flowers, especially those which were green. As with many other pagan usages, the Christians transferred the idea of decoration to their own festival. The reason why holly is chosen as the chief decoration is somewhat obscure, but it is probably merely because the tree bears its attractive red berries at this time of year.

Mistletoe is considered to be lucky to hang in the house at Christmas, it being a survival of the times when the Druids venerated this parasitic plant, which they discovered growing on the oak tree. It should be remembered that mistletoe is not allowed to be employed as a church decoration because of its pagan associations.

It is lucky to kiss under the mistletoe and unlucky deliberately to avoid the opportunity. The correct method of performing the ceremony is for the man to pluck a berry from the mistletoe for each kiss which he gives the girl, stopping only when all the berries are exhausted. This procedure is seldom strictly observed, however, as it would entail the replacement of the mistletoe after each person had been "caught."

A final word of warning. If you wish to avoid ill luck, make sure that all Christmas decorations are removed before Twelfth Night (January 5).

Charms in the *Christmas pudding* or *cake* are always popular. She who retrieves the ring will be the first to be married. If a girl walks up to bed backwards and places a piece of the cake under her pillow, it is said that her dreams during the night will be of her future husband.

Here are a few *Christmas spells* that have been handed down from generation to generation: Take three leaves of holly and on them prick the initials of three of your admirers. On Christmas Eve place the leaves under your pillow, and it is said that the one whom you will marry will appear to you in a dream.

Sew nine holly-leaves on to your night attire, borrow a wedding-ring and place it on the third finger of your left hand, and then retire to bed. During the night, it is declared, your husband will appear to you in a vision.

Make a chain of holly, mistletoe and juniper, and between each link tie an acorn. You must have two other girls to assist you in doing this. As the clock strikes midnight on Christmas Eve the three of you must go into a room where a fire is lit, lock the door, hang the key over the mantelpiece and open wide the window. Now wrap the chain which you have made round a log and sprinkle it with oil, a few pinches of salt and some earth. The log and chain must be placed on the fire and all lights turned out. Each girl sits round the fire with a prayer-book upon her knees, opened at the marriage service. As soon as the chain has been burnt, it is said that each girl will see the vision of her future husband crossing the room. If such a vision does not appear to a girl, she will never marry; or if she sees a phantom, such as a skeleton, which causes fear, it is also taken to be a sign that she will remain a spinster.

Tie a sprig of holly to each leg of your bedstead, and before you retire eat a roast apple. According to tradition, your future partner in marriage will come and speak to you in your dreams.

The *yule-log* is still burnt in certain parts of the country, and, according to an old custom, this should be lit by a piece of the log used on the previous Christmas. It is said that no evil spirit can then enter into the house. The remains of the yule-log were also considered exceptionally lucky, and if kept in the home would be a protection against lightning or fire. In certain parts of France it is an old belief that the ashes of the yule-log will prevent the crops from rotting if they are scattered over the fields, and the application of them is said to be a cure for chilblains and swollen glands.

The *New Year* is not celebrated in England to the extent that it is in Scotland and countries on the Continent. At one time, in the Highlands, it was customary on "Hogmanay," or New Year's Eve, for a young man to dress himself in cow-hide and, attended by youths who carried sticks to which a piece of cow-hide was attached, to visit the houses of the neighbourhood. Upon reaching a dwelling-place he would run round it three times while the others ran after him, making a great noise and beating against the walls of the house. When they were invited in, the leader would say, " May God bless the house and all that belongs to it, cattle, stones and timber! In plenty of meat, of bed and body clothes, and health of men may it ever abound!"

This strange old custom is now modified into what is known as *first-footing*, when people visit houses just after the clocks have struck midnight, to wish their friends a happy New Year and to hand them gifts, among which are red-herrings and coins for bringing good luck.

If a dark-haired man is the first person to cross the threshold of a house after midnight on New Year's Eve, much good luck will enter with him. In order to ensure such a fortunate visitation, it is not unusual for a member of the household, if he is dark, to go out and come in again just after the hour of midnight.

Squint-eyed, flat-footed, or red-haired men bring bad luck if they are "first-footers," and so does a woman. But a man with a high instep, or one who comes on a horse, is considered particularly lucky. Just as the clock strikes twelve the head of the house should open the door in order to allow the Old Year to pass out and the New Year to come in.

Clocks should be wound up immediately the New Year begins in order to endow the house with good fortune, while all daily cleaning and dusting should be completed early in the day of December 31 in order to avoid the danger of sweeping good luck from the house.

On *New Year's Day* if, on rising, a girl should look out of her bedroom window and see a man passing by, she may reckon to be married before the year is finished.

Children born on New Year's Day bring great fortune and prosperity to all the household.

To *dance* in the open air, especially round a tree, on New Year's Day is declared to ensure luck in love and prosperity and freedom from ill health during the coming twelve months.

Superstitions of the Stage

Some of the most superstitious people in the world are actors and actresses, many of them abiding most religiously by certain rules which are declared to ensure kind treatment from the Fates. The following are some of the more interesting "unwritten laws" of the stage:—

When rehearsing a play, the actors ensure that they are perfect in every line except the last one, or *tag*, as it is called. This is never uttered until the first night of the actual performance, when the success or otherwise of the production is ascertained by the extent of the applause which follows the last line.

If an actress receives *flowers* as a present, she may wear them before or after the performance, but considers it to be very unlucky to wear them when she is actually on the stage. Artificial ones are generally used instead.

When *making up*, an actress regards it as a sign that she will receive a good contract if she accidentally smears some lipstick on to her teeth.

If an actor or actress notices a loose thread of cotton clinging to a person's clothes, he or she will pluck off the thread, pass it three times round the head and then tuck it down the neck of his or her garments. The cotton foretells a new contract and the "magical" rite is said to ensure its receipt.

To *whistle* in the dressing-room is strictly "taboo," as also is the singing of Tosti's "*Good-bye*." Should anyone be guilty of either of these "sins," he or she must go out of the dressing-room, turn round three times and then knock on the door and ask for permission to be admitted.

To quote *Macbeth* is to invite ill fortune to visit you.

All manner of *dolls* and *mascots* are kept in an actress's dressing-room in order to bring her success, while every telegram of congratulation is pinned to the wall and dearly treasured.

Luck at the Card Table

Card players have great faith in their "luck," especially those who gamble and whose success largely depends upon chance and not upon skill. If you have had a run of bad cards it is said *to change your luck* if you lay your handkerchief flat upon your chair and sit on it. In the same way it is said to alter the run of the cards if you turn your chair round three times or walk round it three times. Another method of attracting luck is to blow through the cards when they are being shuffled.

The *luckiest seat* is the one which faces the door; the most unlucky is that which has its back to the fire-place.

When *cutting for deal*, if you turn up the deuce of any suit, good fortune should attend you.

If two packs of cards are used and you are asked with which you wish to deal, always choose the one farthest away from you.

The *most unlucky card* to hold in one's hand is the four of clubs.

When *changing seats* at the table you should always move in a clockwise direction; that is, from right to left.

Never pick up your cards with the left hand, or one card at a time.

It is very unfortunate *to sit cross-legged* when playing cards.

If your partner should lose a game or a trick, never say "*Bad luck!*" or your luck will not change.

Superstitious card players do not like a *dog* in the room when they are playing, for it is said to cause disputes.

Friday is a bad day for card playing, while any *thirteenth day* of the month is considered unlucky. Nevertheless, if you find yourself playing on these days you may always hope that the bad luck rests with your opponents!

Lucky and Unlucky Days

The months or days of the year which may be regarded as auspicious or inauspicious depend chiefly on astrological and numerological calculations, both of which are fully treated in other sections of this work. Nevertheless, there are certain dates, traditionally associated with the varying moods of fortune, that influence the course of human action; and a list of these is given in the following tables of lucky and unlucky days, together with the principal events that may be anticipated.

LUCKY DAYS

JANUARY	3 5 11 19 22 25	Good for business transactions, except speculations. Achievement on the sports field may be expected. Particularly fortunate for young people.
FEBRUARY	1 3 10 19 21 28	Excellent days for intellectual work and all forms of learning. Unexpected good fortune will be the lot of those who are married and have children.
MARCH	3 5 12 17 24 26	People with money worries may expect a turn of fortune. Long-standing quarrels will end in reconciliation and joy.
APRIL	5 9 15 18 21 29	The best time to fall in love and to embark upon new enterprises; also lucky for gamblers and speculators.
MAY	2 4 12 23 25 30	Family gatherings and merrymaking, the renewal of old acquaintances and many pleasant surprises.
JUNE	1 3 11 19 21 23	Conducive to the making of friendships and to marriage. Business successes and a general increase in wealth.
JULY	3 12 15 18 21 31	Successful lawsuits and substantial gains, apart from earnings. Happy endings to previous misunderstandings.
AUGUST	6 11 14 18 24 30	Peaceful days, free from worry and strife. Much benefit derived from meditation and the receipt of wise advice.
SEPTEMBER	1 8 16 17 25 27	Journeys with happy endings, increase of domestic comforts and advances in position.
OCTOBER	15 18 21 24 26 28	Regaining of losses, business expansion and the achievement of cherished ambitions.
NOVEMBER	3 5 7 9 14 22	Consolation for those in trouble. Profitable adventures and the beginnings of love affairs.
DECEMBER	6 12 15 18 25 28	Joy and abundance, good news from abroad and brilliant successes.

UNLUCKY DAYS

JANUARY	2 7 10 15 17 21	Disappointments, losses through gambling and general financial depression.
FEBRUARY	8 17 20 22 25 27	Quarrels with friends, successes of rivals, and domestic troubles.
MARCH	4 7 14 16 20 23	Much scandal will be spread and costly lawsuits may follow. Money losses over broken contracts and unemployment.

APRIL	3 7 8 10 13 24	Separation from an old friend or the appearance of a long-forgotten enemy. Squabbles and petty jealousies in the household.
MAY	3 6 7 15 20 26	Unwise speculations, ill health and much confusion caused through other people's blunders. Particularly bad days for the middle-aged.
JUNE	4 8 9 10 22 28	Disillusionment concerning love affairs and the failure of a cherished project. Shame and anger caused by the betrayal of confidences.
JULY	5 13 16 19 23 25	General discord in business and a small loss of personal property, probably through theft. Worry concerning relatives.
AUGUST	4 7 19 20 21 27	Unrest and disputes in national affairs. Accidents on the road and delayed journeys. Bad news from abroad.
SEPTEMBER	2 4 6 7 12 23	Young people in danger of trouble through thoughtlessness. Broken romances and serious money losses.
OCTOBER	4 6 13 16 17 19	Much labour without reward and dissatisfaction concerning employment. Disappointments over legacies or speculations.
NOVEMBER	6 8 13 16 21 27	Jealousy and the failure of plans. Illness of relatives and animosity from an unexpected quarter.
DECEMBER	9 17 19 21 23 26	Worries brought about by extravagance; increased responsibilities without an increase of income. Disloyalty and a loss of affection.

MISCELLANEOUS OMENS AND SUPERSTITIONS

Bed.—If the head of a bed is placed towards the north it foretells a short life, towards the south a long life, the east riches, the west travel.

Bellows.—It is unlucky to leave bellows lying on the table or on the floor, since in such a position they presage domestic quarrels.

Birthplace.—One's life is prolonged if, in later years, a visit is made to one's place of birth.

Bones.—If you burn beef bones by mistake it is a sign of much sorrow to come on account of poverty. To burn fish or poultry bones indicates that scandal will be spread about you.

Boot.—See *Shoe*.

Bottle.—To break a glass bottle portends misfortune, though it is not so serious as breaking a mirror.   (See also *Glass; Mirror.*)

Bread.—To cut bread in an uneven manner is a sign that you have been telling lies.

Briar.—See *Bush.*

Bush.—To have one's garments caught up by a bush or briar when out walking is a promise of good luck, involving monetary gain.

Buttons.—If you fasten a button into the wrong buttonhole, bad luck awaits you.

Candle.—If a candle falls over, ill luck is not far off.

Caul.—Fortunate indeed is the baby that is born in a caul—which happens only rarely—for the good things of life will come to him easily.   It is a common belief, too, that a person who was born in a caul will never meet his death by drowning.

Coal.—To pick up a piece of coal that has fallen in your path is generally regarded as a sure promise of success and good luck.

Contract.—See *Lease.*

Corns.—The best time for cutting one's corns is when the moon is on the wane.

Door.—If a front door does not face the street, ill luck will attend the house.   You should always close a front door with your face towards it.

Egg.—To let fall an egg and smash it foretells good news; but if the egg is undamaged or merely cracked, bad luck is to be feared. When you have finished eating an egg it is a safeguard against misfortune if the empty shell is crushed with a spoon.   If you burn egg-shells, the hens will cease to lay.

It is unlucky to take eggs out of, or bring them into, a house during the hours of darkness.   Eggs laid on Good Friday never become stale.

Fateful Year.—When a woman reaches the 31st year of her life she may expect some great change to occur.   Frequently it consists of an important journey, some unexpected danger, or some great temptation.   She should be particularly cautious during this period, and take special care in her business and private affairs.

Fire.—Ill luck attends those who *completely* rake out a fire before retiring.   A few embers should always be left.

Fish.—When eating a fish, you should begin at the tail and work towards the head.

Fork.—To cross two forks accidentally is a sign that slander will be spread about you. To drop a fork foretells the visit of a woman friend. To stir anything with a fork is to stir up misfortune. (See also *Spoon.*)

Garter.—It is a warning of treachery if a person's garter comes undone. If a girl loses a garter, a proposal of marriage at an early date is foretold.

Glass.—To break uncoloured glass in any form but that of a mirror or a bottle is a fortunate omen; but if the glass is red, future trouble and anxiety are implied. If green glass is broken, bitter disappointment will be your lot. (See *Bottle; Mirror; Wine.*)

Gloves.—It is unlucky to give a pair of gloves to a friend unless you receive something in exchange.

Grave-digger.—To encounter a grave-digger coming towards you is a very evil portent, usually presaging a severe illness.

Hair.—To attract good fortune one's hair should be cut at the new moon.

Hand.—If you knock your hand accidentally against a piece of wood or a wooden article, it is an indication that you are about to have a love affair. If you knock your hand against iron, however, it must be taken as a warning against treachery.

Handkerchief.—Tying a knot in one's handkerchief is not only useful as a reminder, it is also a means of warding off evil.

Horseshoe.—Finding a horseshoe is an assurance of good luck, but if you give it away or throw it away, your luck will leave you.

House.—If after leaving your house, you turn back to fetch something, you must sit down when you get indoors and count backwards from seven, in order to avoid ill luck. It is unlucky to move into a new house during the months of April, July, and November.

Illness.—If, before you retire to bed, you chant

> Matthew, Mark, Luke and John
> Bless the bed that I lie on,

it will keep away evil spirits and ensure your good health.

There is an old custom which decrees that if someone is lying dangerously ill, a lighted candle should be placed in a shoe and all other lights in the room turned out. Then the name of the complaint from which the person is suffering must be written on a piece of paper and burned in the candle flame, and at the same time the following rhyme should be said three times:—

> Go away death!
> Go away death!
> Life from the flame
> Give new breath!

The candle must then be snuffed with the fingers.

Ink.—To spill ink threatens worry, annoyance, and the failure of a project that is on foot.

Knife.—Crossing two table-knives by accident portends bad luck. The dropping of a knife foretells the visit of a man friend in the near future.

If someone lends you a pocket-knife, return it in the way in which it was given; that is, with the blade open or shut, pointing away from you or towards you. It is unlucky to make a present of a knife or any other sharp instrument unless you receive something in exchange.

Ladder.—Ill luck will attend those who walk under a ladder, unless they cross their fingers while doing so.

Lease.—It brings ill fortune if a lease or any contract is signed in the months of April, July, or November.

Lightning.—Lightning will never strike a person when he is asleep, nor will it visit a house in which a fire is burning.

Lucky Days.—The days of the week on which it is considered most lucky for women to make any important decision or to undertake any great tasks are Tuesday and Friday. For men the fortunate days are Monday and Thursday. (For lucky and unlucky days of the month see pages 486 and 487.)

Matches.—To spill matches is a very lucky sign, and if a girl accidentally upsets an entire box it will not be long before she becomes a bride. Crossing two matches by chance implies that joy and happiness await you.

Mattress.—When you have occasion to turn the mattress of a bed remember that if you turn it "from foot to head, you'll never wed," and also that this task should never be performed on a Friday.

May-blossom.—This must never be cut from the tree and brought into the house before May 1, or ill fortune will attend you.

Meeting.—It is very lucky if, by chance, you meet the same person twice when you are out on business. It is even luckier if you encounter him once when you are setting out and again when you are returning.

Mending.—Never mend a garment while you are wearing it, or misfortune will follow.

Mirror.—Breaking a mirror portends seven years of bad luck. It is also extremely unlucky to receive a mirror as a present. (See also *Glass.*)

Money.—There is an old spell which was once thought to be an infallible means of influencing one's luck regarding money. In order to effect this charm it was necessary to choose a rainy day, and then to go to a place where there was a holly bush, clasp it round the main stem and chant three times,

> Holly tree, O holly tree,
> Let much wealth come to me.

A turn of luck financially was then expected within the course of three months.

Nail-cutting.—There is an old rhyme concerning nail-cutting which goes as follows:—

> Cut your nails on Monday, cut them for news;
> Cut them on Tuesday, a pair of new shoes;
> Cut them on Wednesday, cut them for health;
> Cut them on Thursday, cut them for wealth;
> Cut them on Friday, a sweetheart to know;
> Cut them on Saturday, a journey to go;
> Cut them on Sunday, you cut them for evil,
> For all the next week you'll be ruled by the devil.

New Moon.—It is unlucky to see the new moon for the first time through glass. Upon seeing the new moon you should turn whatever silver you have in your pockets or handbag, and thus ensure prosperity for a month. New enterprises will be fortunate if begun at the time of the new moon.

Pepper.—To upset pepper is an unlucky omen. (See also *Salt.*)

Petticoat.—If a girl's petticoat or slip shows below her dress, she is loved more by her father than by her mother

Picture.—If a picture should fall from the wall upon which it is hung, the death of a relation or friend, illness, or a sudden stroke of bad fortune to an inmate of the house who is about to go upon a journey is foreshadowed. If the glass is broken in the fall, the force of the omen is intensified.

Pins.—Always pick up a pin when you see one lying on the floor, for

> See a pin and pick it up
> All the day you'll have good luck;
> See a pin and let it lie
> Luck will surely pass you by.

To upset a box of pins foretells a surprise, so long as some of them are left in the box; but if none remains, a disappointment will come your way.

Plate.—Breaking a plate is an omen of misfortune, especially if it had not already been cracked.

Purse.—If you give anyone an empty purse he will never be blessed with riches. Place a farthing inside it for luck.

Salt.—It is universally considered unlucky to spill salt; if both salt and pepper are spilt at the same time, the force of this ill omen is doubled. If you help a person to salt, you will help him to sorrow.

Scissors.—Breaking one blade of a pair of scissors is an omen of quarrelling and discord; if both blades are broken at once, a calamity is to be feared. Scissors should always be "sold"; they should never be given.

Seventh Child.—A seventh son possesses many talents and is predestined for worldly success. The seventh son of a seventh son is gifted with the art of healing. The seventh daughter of a seventh daughter possesses the power of second sight.

Sexton.—See *Grave-digger.*

Shoe.—It is unlucky to put on the left shoe before the right, and it is worse still to put the right shoe on the left foot, or vice versa. This belief dates from classical days, and it is related that the emperor Augustus nearly lost his life at the hands of assassins after putting his sandals on the wrong feet.

New shoes should never be left on a table, or ill luck will descend upon the house. If you do not present a new pair of shoes to a poor person at least once during your life, you will go barefoot in the next world.

Shoe-lace.—If your shoe-lace persists in coming untied, take it as an omen that you are about to receive a fortunate letter or some kind of good news.

Sneezing.—To sneeze to the right is a promise of money, but sneezing to the left foreshadows a disappointment. Other divinatory meanings connected with sneezing are contained in the following old rhyme, which is traditional in some parts of the country:—

> Sneeze on a Monday, sneeze for danger;
> Sneeze on a Tuesday, kiss a stranger;
> Sneeze on a Wednesday, sneeze for a letter;
> Sneeze on a Thursday for something better;
> Sneeze on a Friday, sneeze for woe;
> Sneeze on a Saturday, a journey to go;
> Sneeze on a Sunday, see your lover to-morrow.

Sock.—See *Stocking.*

Soot.—If soot burns in a ring at the back of the grate, pleasure and happiness are on their way to you.

Sparks.—Malice and envy are to be feared when sparks jump out of the fire.

Spoon.—Dropping a spoon means that a child or young person is going to call on you. To cross a spoon over a fork presages happiness cut short by grief.

Stairs.—It is unlucky to pass anyone on the staircase.

Stocking.—To put on your stockings or socks inside out is an omen that you will shortly receive a present. If your stocking comes down, your lover is thinking of you.

Stumbling.—A very unfortunate omen. If a person stumbles when leaving his house at the beginning of a journey, or trips or stumbles more than once during the course of the journey, it is advisable to postpone it.

Table.—It is unlucky to sit on a table unless one foot is touching the ground.

Thirteen.—If thirteen sit down to dine, the last to rise will meet with ill fortune.

Tripping.—See *Stumbling.*

Umbrella.—It is unlucky to open an umbrella in the house.

Washing.—To wash in water which has been previously used by someone else means that you will quarrel with him, unless you clasp your hands together over the water when you have finished.

Water.—Never pour water into a tumbler which already holds some, for it is an invitation to evil spirits to visit you.

Whistling.—Women should not whistle, for it encourages evil spirits to visit them.   Remember that

> A whistling maid and a crowing hen
> Are neither fit for God nor men.

Wine.—Spilling wine is an auspicious omen, if it is done accidentally; while to drop a glass of wine and break the glass is a token of a happy marriage and enduring affection.   (See also *Bottle ; Glass.*)

Wood.—If you should be congratulating yourself upon avoiding some form of ill fortune, you should always touch wood when you do so, lest the averted evil should come to pass at some future date.

Words.—When you are talking to someone, and if you should both happen to say the same word or sentence at the same time, you must each clasp the other's little finger and wish.   Then, if you do not disclose your wish, it will be fulfilled.

Part Two

THE MYSTIC MEANINGS OF THINGS

TALISMANS AND AMULETS

THERE are few people who have not, during some period of their life, possessed something which they have described as their "mascot." This belief in the powers of a trinket or symbol is so old, and so universal, that it cannot be dismissed lightly as a silly and ignorant superstition. The most ancient records of humanity clearly indicate that a faith in inanimate objects being endowed with some occult influence has been upheld almost since the time that mankind first began to think. It was an essential part of all early religions. The Chinese, the races of India, the Egyptians, the Greeks, and the Romans are only a few of the early cultured peoples who fervently believed in mascots—some which were created by themselves and others which they received by inheritance.

The word "mascot," which is commonly used nowadays, is comparatively modern in our language. It is borrowed from the French, and probably comes from the Provençal word *masco*, meaning "sorcerer." The more specific terms, which divide mascots into two classes, are "talisman" and "amulet." Frequently these two words are used quite indiscriminately, and no distinction is made between them. This is incorrect, for while a talisman (from the Arabic *tilsam* and late Greek *telesma* = mystery) is some object which brings good fortune and averts danger, an amulet (from Latin *amuletum*) is solely protective; that is, it diverts evil influences from the wearer, but does not necessarily endow him with any particular qualities or attract luck to him.

The chief purpose of amulets in the olden days was to protect the wearer against the "evil eye," which was supposed to be possessed by certain men or women, and to exert a very malign influence upon all who were unfortunate enough to be subject to its glance. It was declared to cause injury, sickness, and even death, as well as moral depravity. Not only were human beings said to be harmed by it, but should a "Jettator" (one possessing the evil eye) look upon cattle or horses they, too, would quickly sicken and die. Crops were doomed to failure under this awful gaze, and even villages and towns might meet with terrible catastrophes.

The amulets worn for personal protection against these ills were very varied. They might consist of grotesque figures, the object of which was to deflect the look of the Jettator from the face of the wearer; or they might be in the form of some charm hidden in the clothing. Because horses were thought to be particularly susceptible, the practice arose of decorating them with tail-ribbons, bells and medallions, a custom which is still prevalent in the case of shire horses.

As a rule, talismans were made when conditions were considered to be particularly favourable to the future owner, probably during a period when his planet was in a position which caused it to be beneficent. The chief purposes of talismans were to induce love, to cure disease, to increase wealth, and to bring success in battle or any adventurous undertaking. They usually consisted of carved or inscribed stone, metal, glass or wood, or pieces of parchment on which were words or diagrams of symbolical significance. There were also, however, innumerable natural talismans, such as powdered toad, to induce love; the mandrake, used for the same purpose; a hyena skin, to make one invulnerable ; and bezoar (a calculous concretion found in the stomach of certain animals), as a cure for all ills affecting the human race.

The origins of certain talismans are so old that the particular purposes for which they were originally made have been forgotten during the course of time. Nowadays, of course, enlightened people no longer believe in the evil eye, but many of the amulets which were used to avert it have come down to us, and are now regarded as talismans or luck-bringers. The cause of the peculiar power which is certainly exerted by many of these amulets and talismans still remains a mystery. The ancients were more interested in effects than causes, but in these days of cold reasoning and scientific research it is natural that many theories should be formed regarding the nature of these potent influences.

Some say that various objects are capable of giving off certain emanations (radium and the magnetic lodestone being taken as known examples) which not only affect the human body, but also the mind. Such a theory may hold good in a case where the virtue of the mascot lies in the fact that it is made of a certain material, but it does not explain why talismans and amulets such as those of parchment, which are based on words or symbols, should also be procurers of good fortune and protectors against ills.

Perhaps the most acceptable explanation is the one given by W. T. and K. Pavitt in their authoritative work *The Book of Talismans, Amulets and Zodiacal Gems* :—

> . . many people are prepared to admit that there may be some active power in a thought made concrete in the form of a Talisman or Amulet which may be made for some specific purpose, or for particular wear, becoming to the wearer a continual reminder of its purpose and undoubtedly strengthening him in his aims and desires.

By accepting this explanation we need not discard the theory that some mysterious, perhaps occult, force is also a powerful factor, but it must be realized that implicit faith in a mascot is the first essential if we wish it to benefit us.

If we believe in talismans and amulets we are following an example set by the most cultured of ancient peoples, and reiterating a faith which has formed an integral part of man's intelligence since the beginning of history. Here are some of the charms which were worn by the ancients and which, in various countries, are in use at the present day.

Beads.—Since the earliest days these have been used as charms and, in fact, it is probable that their sole purpose originally was to protect the wearer from evil influences and bring good fortune. "Eye-beads" are considered particularly lucky. They are made of onyx or, more commonly, glass. The eye is representative of the All-seeing Deity, and the beads are declared not only to avert danger but to bring great success to women in love affairs. The glass ones may be bought at most shops where trinkets or other fancy articles are sold.

In many countries a necklace of amber beads is declared to be auspicious for a bride at her wedding, for it ensures that her husband will be faithful and that she will bear fine children. In Italy necklaces of amber are worn both as a protection against, and a cure for, diseases of the throat; while in some parts of Russia it is thought that all those who wish to live long should adorn themselves with a necklace of this type.

Beads of coral have gained the reputation of warding off misfortune, and are also said to be beneficial to the health. The Romans had a curious custom of making dog-collars of coral and flint in order to protect their animals from the dreaded disease of hydrophobia. For those who suffer from melancholia, necklaces of jet beads have the reputation of inspiring hope and courage, and of banishing the depressing effects of disappointment and worry. All beads which are blue in colour have, since time immemorial, been used as talismans, and are specially to be recommended to those who wish to find a handsome and faithful lover. (For the virtues of precious and semi-precious stones, see pages 545–569.)

Cat.—One frequently sees little charms in the form of a cat, but it is difficult to trace their origin as luck-bringers. To the ancient Romans, the cat was symbolical of liberty, because of its independent nature. In Egypt the cat was sacred; it was regarded as representing the moon, probably because its eyes dilate and contract just as that heavenly body waxes and wanes. Some people find that a black cat talisman is fortunate, others declare it to be thoroughly unlucky—it is, indeed, said to be one of the forms which Satan assumes when he visits the earth.

Because of the cat's legendary "nine lives," it is often adopted as a mascot by those who undertake perilous journeys.

Cross.—The cross was a symbol used by the ancients thousands of years before the coming of Christianity, although the Crucifixion of Jesus Christ has given a special significance to the one known as the Roman cross (†). This is one of the numerous religious talismans, and in Christian countries it is worn more than any other symbolical ornament.

One of the oldest of crosses is the Tau, which is shaped like the letter T. It was formerly worn as a powerful amulet against diseases such as epilepsy, and especially as a preventive of the fatal effects of snake-bite. It is symbolical of eternal life, and was used as a guard over the spirit and as a protection against trouble and affliction.

One of the most popular charms was the cross of St. Benedict, engraved, together with certain letters, upon a medallion. This cross is in the form of what is called the Greek cross (+).

The letters on the medallion stand for Latin words, which are read as follows:—

The four letters in the angles of the cross:	Crux Sancti Patris Benedicti Cross of the Holy Father Benedict
The four letters in the upright bar:	Crux Sancta sit mihi lux O Holy Cross be my light
The four letters in the horizontal:	Ne daemon sit mihi dux Let no evil spirit be my guide
The circle of letters:	Vade retro Satana Get thee behind me Satan Ne suade mihi vana Suggest no vain delusions to me Sunt mala quae libas The things thou offerest are evil Ipse venana bibas Thou thyself drinkest poison

This amulet is said to serve as a protection against all dangers, both physical and spiritual. It can be made of parchment or cardboard, the cross and initial letters being inscribed upon it in ink or paint.

St. Andrew's cross (×), or the *crux decussata*, is likewise regarded as a potent amulet against evil, while the Egyptians paid a special regard to a form of the Tau cross on which was placed a small circle (♀). This was an emblem of many

The Cross of St. Benedict*

of the powerful gods and goddesses, such as Osiris and Isis, and symbolized both life in general and immortality. Crosses are frequently enclosed in a circle, the latter standing for the Eternal Preserver of Life and Eternity. (See also *Swastika*.)

Dragon.—We frequently find this emblem incorporated in coats-of-arms and, as a symbol, it stands for great power and all that is imposing and terrible. At one time, in Britain, it was an ensign of war, and was regarded as being symbolical of victory.

As a talisman, however, it has a more peaceful significance. In China, although it is chiefly emblematical of authority, it has also proved to be a fortunate charm, bringing long life and domestic

---

* The illustrations on pages 501–509 are reproduced from *The Book of Talismans, Amulets and Zodiacal Gems*, by W. T. and K. Pavitt.

happiness. Miniature dragons are carved in wood, stone or metal, and are worn because of this auspicious influence. Such talismans are not very common in Britain, but should we come across one we should regard it as a bringer of longevity, peace and felicity, rather than the emblem of might and conquest.

Eagle.—This is regarded as a talisman of good fortune, and is very widely used as such in China and Japan. It was a device greatly favoured by Eastern emperors, and we find it in the ensigns of the ancient kings of Babylon and Persia. In Christian art the eagle is symbolical of St. John the Evangelist, for it was believed to be able to stare at the sun, just as St. John looked upon the "Sun of Glory."

An image of the eagle is considered to instil into those who wear it great dignity, and quickness of perception. It is thought to be very helpful if one wishes to assume great responsibilities and to attain high rank and authority.

Egyptian Eye Amulet

Eye.—A charm which depicts an open eye is an ancient amulet and talisman of Egypt. It represents the all-seeing eye of gods such as Ra—the sun god—Osiris, Horus and Ptah. Its purpose was to ensure good health, courage and wisdom, and also stability of mind and determination. It was placed either on or in the flesh of dead bodies as a guard over the soul. At one time it was regarded as one of the best protections against the evil eye, and children would wear it as an amulet strung round the neck, or as part of a bead necklace. Sometimes a charm consisting of two eyes would be made as a talisman of great power, the right eye representing the sun, and the left eye, the moon.

In mediaeval days the eye of a cock was used to ward off the influence of witchcraft, while there was a very curious talisman, regarded as a powerful luck-bringer, which consisted of the eye of a woodpecker, the eye of a weasel, a crystal ring, a coin with a hole in it and dust from a meteoric stone, all put into a small bag and hung round the neck.

Fish.—The fish has for long been regarded as a symbol of abundance, riches and—by the Japanese—endurance and pluck.

In Egypt it represented Hathor, the cow-headed goddess, who was supposed to control the rising of the River Nile, which was so necessary to irrigate the crops. It also signified the principle of creation, and thus was a charm for domestic felicity.

The early Christians adopted the fish as the symbol of Jesus Christ, one explanation for this being that "Icthus," the Greek word for "fish," contains the initial letters of the Greek words meaning "Jesus Christ, Son of God, Saviour." In those days, when Christians were cruelly persecuted and were forced therefore to worship in secret, the fish became their secret sign of

Japanese Talisman for Pluck

brotherhood, and they carved it in the catacombs where they gathered together, and on the tombs of those who died. Nowadays one sometimes sees a fish carved of mother-of-pearl and threaded on to a pendant.

Frog.—To the ancient Egyptians the frog represented health and long life; in Rome it was the symbol of Aphrodite, or Venus, the goddess of love, and also a talisman for wealth and fertility. To-day, in Burma, frogs of metal and gilt are worn by children as amulets to protect them against the evil eye, while frogs carved from amber are considered to be good-health charms among Greeks, Italians and Turks.

The frog is a talisman which is exceedingly suitable for lovers. It is said to ensure a happy relationship between them, and to promote mutual ardour and constancy.

Old Egyptian Fish Talisman

Hand.—Among the ancient Egyptians this was the emblem of fortitude, while the Romans regarded it as symbolic of fidelity. It also represents the Deity, and in old paintings one sometimes sees a hand extended from the clouds, two fingers being upraised in the act of benediction.

The ancient Etruscans used a talisman in the form of a hand as protection against bewitchment. To-day, in the Orient, a hand of metal, or of blue glass, is worn to ward off malign influences of all kinds, and especially as a personal protection against the dreaded evil eye. Two hands, sometimes clasped together, stand for concord and friendship; a talisman of this design is worn by lovers to preserve constancy.

In the East there is also a powerful amulet known as the Hand of Fatima (daughter of Mohammed), which is sometimes represented with fingers and thumb outstretched and sometimes by a closed hand. In Christian countries the "Mano Pantea" (Hand of Benediction), represented life size, was frequently kept in a house in order to protect both the goods in it and those who lived there.

Less than a hundred years ago there was a very gruesome superstition rife, especially in Ireland, regarding the hand of a dead man, preferably one who had been hanged. This "Hand of Glory" was supposed to possess many magical properties. If a candle was placed upon it, it was said that the light would be seen only by the one who carried the hand. Hence it was a very popular torch among burglars, house-breakers and other criminals, who, naturally, wished to escape detection.

Hand of Fatima

Heart.—The human heart was supposed to be the seat of the soul, and, therefore, the place whence all affection springs. A model of it is often worn as a talisman to bring love and great joy, while at one time it was used as an amulet to prevent spells of black magic being cast upon the wearer. In *The Book of Talismans, Amulets and Zodiacal Gems*, by W. T. and K. Pavitt, we learn that:—

According to Egyptian lore, at the judgment of the dead the heart is weighed, when, if found perfect, it is returned to its owner, who immediately recovers his powers of locomotion and becomes his own master, with strength in his limbs and everlasting felicity in his soul.

Heart Talisman for Love

Frequently we find that lockets, in which are enclosed a portrait or a piece of hair, are made in the shape of a heart, as an everlasting reminder of someone whom we love.

Horn.—In modern times a charm of this type is not very

common, although one sometimes sees small replica horns used as talismans. The most common kind is the one called the Cornucopia, or Amalthea's Horn of Plenty. According to legend, Amalthea, who was one of the daughters of the king of Crete, nursed the great god Zeus when he was a baby and fed him on goat's milk. When he had grown up, Zeus, to show his gratitude, broke off the horn of a goat and presented it to Amalthea, saying that whoever possessed it should never know want, but should live in abundance for ever. The horn is therefore depicted as overflowing with fruit and flowers, and is said to be a talisman to attract riches and good fortune.

In the East, a piece of horn is sometimes attached to the keys of stables in order to protect horses and cattle from evil spirits. The horn in this case is said to ensure the guardianship of the god Pan, who watches over the forests, pastures and flocks, and is goat-like in appearance.

Cornucopia, or Horn of Plenty

Horseshoe.—This has for long been regarded as a talisman for luck, and since the days of the Greeks and Romans it has been nailed, with the ends pointing upwards, on the doors of houses. The origin of a horseshoe as a charm probably lies in the fact that a crescent moon was the symbol of Isis, the principal Egyptian goddess, who at one time was identified with Greek and Roman deities. Roman matrons wore a replica of the crescent upon their shoes in order to protect themselves from evil influences of the moon, such as madness or hysteria, and also as a talisman to ensure happy motherhood and general good fortune. In time the horseshoe, owing to its shape, assumed the same significance as the crescent, and was regarded as an amulet against malign spirits and a talisman of good fortune.

There is also another explanation of its use as a charm. One day, according to legend, the Devil asked St. Dunstan, who was skilled in shoeing horses, to shoe one of his hoofs. The saint agreed, but caught hold of the Devil so tightly, and gave him so much pain during the course of the work, that he begged to be released. St. Dunstan agreed to let him go only if he would promise to avoid all places where a horseshoe was hung. Hence a horseshoe on the threshold is said to "keep the Devil away."

We know that Nelson nailed a horseshoe to the mast of his ship *Victory*, while the custom is still prevalent among Suffolk fishermen, who believe that it protects them against storms and heavy seas. The horseshoe should never be fixed, or a replica of one worn, with the ends pointing *downwards*, for it is said that the luck will then run out of it. It is considered to be especially lucky to find a horseshoe oneself and to use it as a talisman and amulet for one's own household.

Japanese Key Charm for Wealth, Love and Happiness

Key.—Miniature keys were worn as talismans by the Greeks and the Romans. They represented the god Janus, who was said to be the keeper of the Gate of Heaven, and thus the guardian of all doors. Because the god was two-headed, which enabled him to look into the future as well as into the past, the key talisman was worn to induce foresight, prudence and good judgment.

Key Talisman in the Form of a Ring

The Japanese have a charm representing the keys of a granary; it is much favoured as a talisman for wealth, love, and general happiness.

Ladder.—This is a talisman which is worn in order to assist the wearer to overcome the difficulties and hardships of this world, and eventually to find peace and happiness in the higher realms. It is an old Egyptian symbol of Horus, who was one of the sun gods; he was sometimes described as the "god of the ladder" because he could help man to climb from the darkness of the earth up to the eternal light of heaven.

Ladder Talisman

Lamb.—This is a Christian emblem of the Redeemer. Miniature replicas of a lamb are frequently worn on necklaces and pendants. and it figures frequently in the carvings and sculptures in churches and religious houses. An old religious amulet, which is still seen to-day, consists of a lamb carrying a cross and flag. It is called the "Agnus Dei" (Lamb of God), and is worn as a protection against accidents, storms and diseases.

Lizard.—Images of this reptile were anciently employed both as a talisman and amulet, and the custom still survives in some Mediterranean countries. It was considered invaluable as a charm to induce good eyesight, and also for inspiring wisdom, and was engraved on various jewels and sometimes painted on the walls of houses in order to bring good luck.

The "Agnus Dei," a Christian Amulet

Lotus.—This name has been applied to various kinds of plants, but as a talisman or amulet it refers to that beautiful Eastern flower that grows in the water. In India, carvings and engravings of the lotus are worn as talismans for

good luck, and also as amulets for protection against disease and accident. The plant represents the goddess Lakshmi, the patroness of beauty and fortune. The Egyptians regarded the lotus as an emblem of the sun, inducing insight, clarity of thought and wisdom. Because of its pure beauty, it also became an amulet for the preservation of purity and represented the goddess Isis.

Moon.—Talismans of the crescent moon were worn by Roman women to ensure happy motherhood and protection against evil spirits

Eastern Amulet Containing the Lotus Plant

and sickness. (See *Horseshoe.*)

Palm Branch.—A palm branch was often engraved on gems and metal, and it is a very ancient charm of success. As a Christian talisman (see illustration on page 508) it represented the victory over temptation and evil, and often formed the border surrounding religious symbols.

Peacock.—The feathers of this bird, with their eye-like markings, are considered to attract bad luck to any house in which they are displayed, for they were anciently supposed to be emblematical of the evil eye. The peacock itself, however, or an image

508

of it, was sometimes regarded as lucky; for, as the bird's flesh was thought to be incapable of corruption, it represented the triumph over the grave, and everlasting life. It was used for church decoration as being symbolical of resurrection.

Phoenix.—This mythical bird was said to live for a great number of years, make a nest or funeral pyre of grasses and spices, sing a dirge, and then by flapping its wings set fire to the pyre. Thus the bird was burnt to ashes, but from them a new phoenix was said to arise, whose life would terminate in the same manner.

Ring Talisman with Palm Branch

Anciently, the phoenix was considered to be sacred to the sun, and it is used as a talisman to-day both in China and Japan. In the former country it is worn to promote length of life and married happiness; in Japan it is a talisman for uprightness, faithfulness, justice and kind-heartedness.

Pig.—Small silver charms representing a pig are common. It is difficult to trace the origin of their accredited magical properties, but their use as talismans, especially in China, is very old. The pig was sacred to the inhabitants of ancient Crete because Jupiter, according to some legends, was nourished on the milk of a sow. It is possible that in Christian countries the miniature replicas of a pig are symbolical of St. Anthony, who was the patron saint of swineherds.

Scarab.—This ancient Egyptian talisman, derived from a beetle common in Egypt, was the symbol of Khepera, a form of the sun god, and was therefore a symbol of creation and resurrection. A great number of these scarabs were made. Some, less than an inch long, were carved out of gems and used for rings or pendants; others were immense images of hard stone, such as granite, on the back of which historical events were recorded.

Egyptian Scarab of Stone

As a talisman the scarab was worn to attract good fortune in general, but especially to instil manly qualities into the wearer, such as health and strength, both physical and mental. Not only was this sacred beetle considered to protect the living, but an image of it was placed in the bandages of mummies, and sometimes in the heart of a dead person, as a protection from evil influences during the journey to the other world.

Ship.—A ship was an early Christian symbol universally employed to represent the Church; it signified the wearer's faith in his salvation and protected him against temptation. It is usually found in combination with sacred monograms and various other religious emblems.

Scarab Talisman with Wings Outstretched

Spider.—This is considered to be a very fortunate symbol, and was used by the ancient Etruscans as a talisman to ensure success in business and in all monetary matters. The spider was sacred to the god Mercury, the patron of commerce and science. In the Middle Ages, a spider enclosed in a nutshell, the halves of which were bound together with silk, was hung about the neck in order to protect the wearer from illness.

The Swastika

Swastika.—The swastika, which is one of the oldest and most universal of all the symbolic charms, is found in Europe, Asia, Africa and America. Its name is derived from a Sanskrit word meaning "bringer of good fortune," and it is used to promote happiness, length of life and progress. By many nations it is regarded as a symbol of the sun, and as representing the power of the four winds. It is also called the Wheel of Law, or Buddha's Wheel. Sometimes the swastika is in the form of three, five or six human legs.

Tooth.—In China, a tiger's tooth is looked upon as a good talisman for those who gamble or speculate. In ancient Rome, a wolf's tooth worn on the end of a pendant was said to assist a child during its teething period. In Russia, amulets in the form of imitation teeth are used to ensure the protection of young people against influences of an evil nature, and also as a cure for certain diseases.

Tortoise.—The tortoise talisman is employed in China, Japan and India, and is a symbol of the universe. Its domed shell represents the sky and its body the earth. Owing to the great age which the tortoise attains, it is worn as a talisman to ensure long life, and also as a protection against spells and various evil spirits.

Popular Charms

In addition to those talismans whose origin is steeped in tradition, and which can be traced far back in the history of man, there are a great number of objects which, for reasons more or less uncertain, are considered to bring good luck. One of the most popular of these is the *four-leafed clover*, which, for preference, should be picked at the hour of midnight, on a Friday, and during the first three days of the new moon; or else between the hours of noon and three o'clock on a day of bright sunshine, in a graveyard. Silver charms of four-leafed clover are worn to bring good fortune.

A model of an *anchor* is worn for security and steadiness; it is a Christian symbol of hope. A silver *donkey* is deemed to bring good luck, as also are a *crown*, a model of a *cock*, and a *boot*. An *elephant* is a talisman to promote temperance and power, while a ring of *elephant's hair* has for long been regarded as a charm to ensure prosperity and success in love. The *wish-bone*, or "*merry-thought*," of a chicken is sometimes modelled in metal and worn on a pendant to attract good fortune. A *badger's tooth*, sewn inside the pocket, is said to bring good luck to those who play cards and all games of chance. At one time the *left hind leg of a mole*, enclosed in a silk bag tied with a scarlet thread of silk, was said to ward off ill luck.

One of the strangest amulets is a *caul*, which is greatly valued by sailors because it is said to prevent death by drowning. *Black diamonds*, that is, *pieces of coal*, are considered lucky if found in the street, while *white pebbles* of all kinds are used as charms. A *penny with a hole in it* is thought to attract good fortune; probably some connexion lies between this talisman and the "eye-beads" which we have already mentioned. In the last century the *leek* was used as a protection against lightning, and was grown on the thatches of cottage roofs. *Laurel* was also considered to ward off the disastrous effects of storms. A *hare's foot* is said to afford protection from evil spirits.

Word and Symbol Charms

One of the most ancient of magic words is Abracadabra, which, according to some accounts, is derived from the words in Hebrew "Ha, Brachab Dabarah," meaning, "Speak the Blessing." As an amulet it was written on a piece of parchment in the following form:—

```
ABRACADABRA
ABRACADABR
ABRACADAB
ABRACADA
ABRACAD
ABRACA
ABRAC
ABRA
ABR
AB
A
```

The charm was hung round the neck on a piece of silk, and was said to protect the wearer from disease. Daniel Defoe relates that many of the terror-stricken inhabitants of London wore such an amulet during the time of the Great Plague (1665–66).

A powerful talisman, which was also triangular in shape, consisted of the seven Greek vowels, inscribed on metal or parchment. The seven vowels stood for the seven known planets, and represented force and power and the harmony of the universe. This talisman, which was worn in order to bring success in every enterprise, was made as illustrated on page 512.

Groups of words reading forwards, backwards, upwards and downwards were popular amulets for warding off evil spirits and accidents. Sometimes they were carved on the walls of temples, and often they were worn for personal protection. The following word-charm was at one time widely adopted:—

```
SATOR
AREPO
TENET
OPERA
ROTAS
```

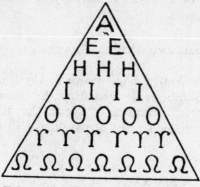

Triangular Talisman composed of
the Seven Greek Vowels

It is difficult to discover the significance of these Latin words,
but the literal translation is: *sator*—the sower; *arepo*—the plough;
tenet—holds; *opera*—works or tasks; *rotas*—wheels.

The Pentacle, or five-pointed star, which is a form of the Seal
of Solomon, has always been credited with great powers in
bringing good luck. It is regarded as a symbol of tremendous
achievement, and also as a protector of bodily health. A popular
modern talisman, which can be made of paper or cardboard, is
based on an old charm incorporating the signs of the planets in the
Pentacle.

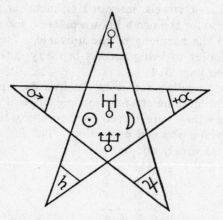

The Pentacle, or Five-pointed Star

The Tetragrammaton

    The Tetragrammaton is a mystic name which was used as a Jewish phylactery; that is, a piece of parchment on which were inscribed certain symbolical words or signs, and which was enclosed in a black calfskin bag and worn on the forehead or left arm. Sometimes the names of the three angels Michael, Gabriel and Raphael were included in a talisman which contained the word Tetragrammaton, which was split into five syllables and included

The Talisman of Venus

in a five-pointed star. This charm was worn for protection, peace and harmony. The talisman illustrated on the preceding page is based upon it.

For those who seek good fortune in love, and journeys free

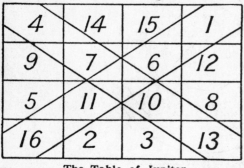

The Table of Jupiter

from misadventure, the talisman of Venus is the most auspicious. It consists of the seal of this goddess, who is also known as Aphrodite, and was said to rule over beauty and love. The charm should be made as shown in the illustration on the previous page.

The Table of Jupiter is a number talisman. It consists of sixteen numbers arranged vertically, horizontally, and diagonally in rows of four, each row adding up to thirty-four. It is worn for riches and peace. The numbers are arranged as shown in the illustration.

One of the most powerful of all word talismans contained the names of the angels who controlled the seven planets. A charm which embodies these, and which may be worn as a symbol of general good luck, is seen on the right.

The names of the angels and the planets they governed are as follows:—

Zaphiel governs Saturn; Zadkiel governs Jupiter; Camael governs Mars; Raphael governs Sun; Haniel governs Venus; Michael governs Mercury; Gabriel governs Moon.

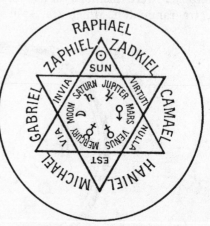

The Talisman of The Angels

In this charm of general good luck is also included the Latin motto *Invia virtuti nulla est via*—there is no way impassable to virtue.

THE MEANINGS OF FIRST NAMES

ONE of the objects of the occult sciences is to seek out and enumerate those influences which have the power, however slight, to sway the character and destiny of mankind. Not the least of these is the personal name by which every man and woman is designated from a few weeks after birth until his or her life on earth is ended.

It is within reason to suppose that a name whose significance is favourable can exert an auspicious influence over its owner, while the bearer of a name which is sordid or evil in its association may be handicapped in his moral and spiritual development; in time, therefore, the name may materially affect the character of the person who bears it.

In the following pages we give a list of first names, their origins and meanings, and the characteristics traditionally associated with them. We do not pretend, however, that the list is exhaustive, the characteristics are positive, or that in every case they are applicable to the individuals concerned. Moreover, it will be observed that in a certain number of cases the name characteristics are diametrically opposed to their original meanings.

MEN'S NAMES

A

Aaron.—Egyptian: "high mountain."
   Ambitious, thorough, successful. Does not understand women. Is at his best among his own sex.
Abel.—Hebrew: "breath" or "fleeting."
   Careless, pleasure-loving, well-mannered. Sometimes displays great physical courage. Can be obstinate and too impatient to take advice.
Abraham.—Hebrew: "father of a multitude."
   Serious-minded, pessimistic, affectionate. Has simple tastes, fond of the open air. Better as a companion than a husband.
Absalom.—Hebrew: "father of peace."
   Bold, cunning, passionate. Seldom a man of peace. He aims at success and has little scruple in achieving his end.

515

Adam.—Hebrew: "red earth."

Lazy, weak, worldly, generous. A name which sometimes brings ill luck.

Adolphus.—Teutonic: "noble wolf." Another form is *Adolphe.*

Benevolent, placid, cultured. Usually handsome and physically strong. Popular with women, but men are inclined to distrust him.

Adrian.—Latin: "from Adria."

Artistic, soulful, frugal, unambitious. Usually makes a successful painter, writer or musician.

Aidan.—Celtic: "little fire."

Strong willed, intelligent. Not always trustworthy in affairs of the heart.

Alan.—Anglo-Norman: "cheerful." Other forms are *Allan, Allen, Alun.*

Sentimental, brave, spirited. Unsuited for sedentary occupations. Thrives on adventure and danger. Usually remains a bachelor, but has love affairs.

Alasdair.—See *Alexander.*

Albert.—Teutonic: "nobly bright."

Thoughtful, tolerant, conservative, hard-working. Suited for all tasks requiring great application and accuracy. Moderate imagination.

Aldous.—Origin obscure.

Sympathetic, charitable. A fine judge of people but lacking in passion.

Alexander.—Greek: "helper of men." Other forms are *Alasdair, Alastair, Alistair* (all Celtic), *Alec, Alex, Alick.*

Daring, quick-thinking, cunning. Often successful in commercial enterprises in which quick judgment and alertness are necessary.

Alfred.—Teutonic: "elf in council" or "wise as a supernatural being."

Practical, moderate, distrustful of women. Usually interested in all forms of sport, either as a player or spectator. Great sense of justice.

Algernon.—Norman: "whiskered."

Spoilt, extravagant, selfish. Over-fond of the opposite sex. Extremely gay, light-hearted and witty.

Ambrose.—Greek: "immortal."

Humorous, placid, musical. Easily flattered, but displays considerable intelligence and gentleness.

Amos.—Hebrew: "burden."

Hard-working, unimaginative, obedient. A good subordinate but a bad leader. Very affectionate but has little passion.

Anatole.—Greek: "eastern."

Cynical, but without malice. Warm-hearted, humane and charitable.

Andrew.—Greek: "a man." Another form is *Andy.*

Powerful, magnetic, simple-mannered, indulgent. Usually interested in medicine and surgery.

Angus.—Celtic: "excellent virtue."

Straightforward, sober, pious, tolerant. Marries young. Chief interests lie in business and domestic affairs.

Anthony.—Latin: "inestimable." Other forms are *Antony, Tony.*

Ascetic, philosophical, lacking in worldly interests. Prefers to be alone but can make a pleasant companion if understood.

Archibald.—Teutonic: "holy prince."

Obstinate, sensual, egotistic. Kind and helpful to his friends. Often extravagantly generous.

Arnold.—Teutonic: "eagle power."
Worldly, pleasure-loving, intelligent. Rather self-centred. He usually makes an unhappy marriage.

Arthur.—Celtic: "high."
Vivacious, industrious, self-opinionated, literary. Seldom takes advice, but profits by his own mistakes.

Aubrey.—Teutonic: "elf ruler."
Disciplined, impartial, scrupulous. Has a good sense of humour and alert judgment. His head rules his heart.

Augustus.—Latin: "venerable." Other forms are *Augustin, Austin.*
Successful, healthy, inclined to bluster. Capable of much deep affection. Covers a soft heart by a stern face.

Austin.—See *Augustus.*

B

Barnabas.—Hebrew: "son of consolation." Other forms are *Barnaby, Barney.*
Honest, genial, lazy. Very gullible and easily influenced by companions. Shy in the company of women.

Barry.—Celtic: "good marksman."
Reserved, strong, true. Rather slow-minded, though possessed of a good memory and sound commonsense. Not emotional.

Bartholomew.—Hebrew: "son of furrows."
Ostentatious, proud, affectionate. Leads a lonely life. Responds gratefully to friendship.

Basil.—Greek: "kingly."
Confident, excitable, obstinate. Sometimes theatrical in behaviour. Seldom a failure. Makes a good husband for a patient wife.

Benedict.—Latin: "blessed."
Decorous, restrained, understanding. Can face hardship and conceal anger or grief. Few really ever get to know him.

Benjamin.—Hebrew: "son of my right hand."
Spoilt, intelligent, gentle, forgiving. Makes a good husband and father.

Bernard.—Teutonic: "firm bear." Another form is *Barnard.*
Unsociable, strong-willed, obstinate. Makes few friends but usually finds a devoted wife.

Bertram.—Teutonic: "bright raven." Another form is *Bertrand.*
Independent, pleasure-loving, dreamy. Usually lacking in strength of mind and concentration.

Blake.—Old English: "fair complexion."
Independent, resolute, successful. Often marries unwisely.

Brian.—Celtic: "strong." Another form is *Bryan.*
Wasteful, luxury-loving, amusing. Possesses great physical strength. Often a confirmed bachelor.

Bruce.—Scottish surname.
Wise, honest, unpredictable temper. Very popular with women.

C

Cameron.—Celtic: "crooked nose."

Artistic, selfish, erratic. A fickle lover, often unable to sustain relationships.

Campbell.—Celtic: "crooked mouth."

Lazy, ambitious, cunning. A considerate husband, but ruthless in financial matters.

Carl.—See *Charles.*

Carmichael.—Celtic: "friend of Michael."

Romantic, persuasive, intelligent. A life of routine does not suit him. He loves all things out of the ordinary.

Cecil.—Latin: "blind."

Well-mannered, proud, careful. Lacks imagination. Calm and collected in an emergency.

Cedric.—Celtic: "war-chief."

Versatile, selfish, talkative. Usually good-looking and passionate in temperament.

Charles.—Teutonic: "man." Other forms are *Carl, Karl.*

Gay, sociable, clever, romantic. Falls in and out of love easily.

Christian.—Greek: "follower of Christ."

Gentle, just, forgiving. Some bearers of this name, however, are entirely unsuited for it; it sometimes implies a merciless, adventurous type, such as the bold Norsemen.

Christopher.—Greek: "Christ bearer."

Loving, enterprising, determined. By his noble example he often inspires others to great deeds.

Clarence.—Latin: "bright" or "famous."

Ingenious, enterprising, impetuous. Possesses great ability for financial matters. A devoted husband and father.

Claud.—Latin: "lame."

Obliging, simple, good-natured. Sometimes mistrustful of women and seldom popular with them.

Clement.—Latin: "merciful."

Merciful, tolerant, frank, kind-hearted. He is deeply sensitive and should be treated with tact and consideration.

Clifford.—Origin obscure.

Reserved, unimaginative, kind, faithful. Possesses great energy and has a diversity of interests.

Clive.—Old English: "cliff."

Highly idealistic, lacking in judgment, given to imaginings. An unsatisfactory husband.

Clyde.—Celtic: "warm" or "heard from afar."

Strong-willed, rebellious, generous. May be led astray by bad companions.

Colin.—Latin: "dove."

Bold, sentimental, passionate. Good looks, but moderate intelligence. Liable to be nervy and irritable.

Conan.—Celtic: "wisdom."

Alert, penetrating, scientific. Rather self-centred. Is unhappy unless working.

Conrad.—Teutonic: "able speech."

Gentle, frank, capable. His judgment is alert, but he lacks ambition. Very shy in mixed company.

Cosmo.—Greek: "order."

Pedantic, exact, truthful, vigorous. Impatient with those who are inefficient or slovenly. A sensitive and devout lover.

Craig.—Celtic: "rock."
Independent spirit, a leader of men. Often acquires great wealth late in life.

Cuthbert.—Teutonic: "well-known splendour."
Level-headed, captivating, contented. Likes music and society. Preferred by women older than himself.

Cyril.—Greek: "lordly."
Jealous, hard-working, competent. Has unhappy love affairs and usually marries late.

D

Damian.—Greek: "tamer." Other forms are *Damien, Damon.*
Ambitions, cold, superficial. A philanderer; rarely successful.

Dan.—Hebrew: "judge." Also used as contraction for *Daniel,* which see.
Humorous, wise, conscientious. Strict in his principles. Invariably to be relied upon.

Daniel.—Hebrew: "God the judge."
Sentimental, affectionate, strong and keen-minded. Can display a powerful temper when roused, but quickly relents and forgives.

David.—Hebrew: "beloved." Another form is *Davy.*
Alert, ingenious, honourable. Usually handsome, graceful and well loved.

Dennis.—Greek: "of Dionysius." Other forms are *Denis, Denys.*
Calm, thoughtful, optimistic. Unromantic and rather fatalistic.

Derrick.—See *Theodoric.*

Desmond.—Origin obscure.
Peaceful, sport-loving, spirited. Faithful in love but inclined to be jealous.

Dominic.—Latin: "Sunday child."
Credulous, honest, staunch. Puts too much faith in women and is often deceived.

Donald.—Celtic: "proud chief."
Sprightly, pleasure-loving, sentimental. Displays great skill in business matters.

Douglas.—Celtic: "dark grey."
Graceful, handsome, talented. Makes many friends of both sexes.

Dudley.—Origin obscure.
Reserved, sincere, egotistic. Inclined to be dull. Possesses keen insight for judging character.

Duncan.—Celtic: "brown chief."
Athletic, jocular, confident. Erratic in his affections.

E

Eamonn.—Old English: "rich guardian."
Shy, determined, miserly. Often achieves eminence, but may have an unhappy private life.

Edgar.—Teutonic: "rich spear."
Prudent, calm, affectionate. Discriminating tastes. Severely critical of the opposite sex.

Edmund.—Teutonic: "rich protection." Another form is *Edmond.*
Good-natured, timid, cheerful. Sometimes artistic in taste but likes nothing which he does not understand.

Edward.—Teutonic: "rich guard." Another form is *Ted.*
Conventional, punctilious, ardent. Capable of loving deeply and lastingly but acutely sensitive.

Edwin.—Teutonic: "rich friend."

 Weak-willed, versatile, sometimes brilliant. Is at his best under the guiding influence of a good friend.

Elias.—See *Elijah.*

Elijah.—Hebrew: "God the Lord."

 Compassionate, intellectual, acute. Often a brilliant speaker. Very fond of company and popular with both men and women.

Emanuel.—Hebrew: "God with us." Another form is *Manuel.*

 Religious, kindly, eloquent. He prefers to remain single but is capable of displaying great affection.

Emile.—Latin: "work."

 Musical, artistic, obliging. Inclined to be obstinate and frequently displays a lack of foresight and common sense.

Enoch.—Hebrew: "dedicated."

 Fearless, just, solitary. Few understand him. He suppresses his passions.

Eric.—Teutonic: "ever king."

 Moody, contemplative, courageous. Given to day-dreaming. Has a high standard of ideals.

Ernest.—Teutonic: "eagle stone."

 Youthful, enthusiastic, trusting. Has great ambitions which he values more than love or friendship.

Eugene.—Greek: "well-born."

 Proud, honourable, inclined to laziness. Makes few friends and often is unhappy when married.

Eustace.—Greek: "happy in harvest."

 Happy, simple, strong, industrious. Suited for an early marriage and a calm, untroubled life.

Evan.—Celtic: "young warrior." Other forms are *Ewan, Ewen.*

 Stalwart, brave, reliable. Possesses great charm of manner. Always placid in his bearing.

Evelyn.—Latin: "hazel-nut."

 Diplomatic, observant, whimsical. A great traveller, becomes restless and discontented if doomed to a settled life.

Ezekiel.—Hebrew: "strength of God."

 Serious, profound, tenacious. He seldom takes any course of action without deep consideration. Many rely upon him for his just and equable judgment.

Ezra.—Hebrew: "rising of light."

 Cordial, veracious, scholastic. Deeply sensitive by nature, he is capable of much sympathy when the feelings of others are hurt.

F

Felix.—Latin: "happy."

 Business-like, cheerful, stern, faithful. Fond of luxury and will work hard to attain his ends.

Ferdinand.—Teutonic: "adventuring life."

 Prudent, imaginative, changeable. Will worry a great deal over small matters.

Fergus.—Celtic: "man of strength."

 Masterful, sincere, virile. Liable to bully if subjected to opposition. Deeply affectionate at heart.

Francis.—Teutonic: "free." Another form is *Frank*.

Skilful, fearless, lively, independent. Inclined to be outspoken.

Frederick.—Teutonic: "peace-ruler."

Peace-loving, versatile, musical, passionate. He is difficult to understand. Reliable and staunch as a friend.

G

Gareth.—Celtic: "gentle."

Lazy, handsome, often plump. Prone to self-indulgence, but often a fine raconteur.

Gary.—Teutonic: "spear."

Wilful, intolerant, clever, courageous. A good friend but a poor husband.

Gavin.—Celtic: "hawk of battle."

Courageous, witty, thoughtless. Light-hearted concerning love. Character lacks stability.

Geoffrey.—See *Godfrey*.

George.—Greek: "husbandman."

Good-natured, vivacious, healthy. Chief fault—tactlessness. Prefers to seek his pleasures in his home circle and is a devoted husband and father.

Gerald.—Teutonic: "spear power."

Firm, unemotional, sometimes merciless. A worshipper of truth. He is seldom interested in women.

Gerard.—Teutonic: "firm spear."

Hot-headed, passionate, intolerant. Inclined to be indiscreet, especially concerning family matters. Never lacks friends.

Gilbert.—Teutonic: "bright pledge."

Brilliant, powerful, active. His friends are numerous and he is susceptible to flattery. The opposite sex finds him somewhat presumptuous.

Giles.—Greek: "with the aegis."

Impulsive, loving, loyal. Hates to be alone. Sometimes garrulous.

Glen.—Celtic: "from the valley." Another form is *Glenn*.

Handsome, creative, athletic. Popular with women, but does not respond well to criticism.

Godfrey.—Teutonic: "God's peace." Other forms are *Geoffrey, Jeffrey*.

Idealistic, retiring, sincere. Often impatient, especially with women. Is more sensitive than he appears.

Gordon.—Scottish place name.

Bold, fiery, seldom handsome. Distrustful of women but a good friend to fellow men.

Graham.—Old English: "gravelly place."

Tight-fisted but good-humoured. Possesses a very masculine charm but is often reluctant to marry.

Gregory.—Greek: "watchman."

Patient, quiet, efficient. Hates insincerity and affectation. He forms few but lasting friendships.

Guy.—Celtic: "sense."

Scientific, worldly, sceptical. Usually shuns society as a whole, but is deeply affectionate towards old friends and relations.

H

Hal.—See *Henry*.

Hamish.—See *Jacob*.

Harold.—Teutonic: "warrior power."

Generous, intelligent, companionable. He is a good fighter and displays brave face even in the most adverse circumstances.

Harry.—See *Henry*.

Harvey.—Celtic: "bitter."

Acrimonious, polished, urbane. Is liable to brood over imaginary worries and impositions. He is at his best when in the company of women.

Hector.—Greek: "defender."

Freedom-loving, conscientious, impulsive. Fond of advising and helping others, but often muddles his own affairs.

Henry.—Teutonic: "home-ruler." Other forms are *Hal, Harry*.

Independent, hard-working, worldly. Inclined to judge people by their financial position rather than their abilities. A faithful husband and extremely fond of children.

Herbert.—Teutonic: "bright warrior."

Pugnacious, rapturous, susceptible. Unsuited for a single life; he should marry early and a woman older than himself.

Hilary.—Latin: "cheerful."

Sympathetic, gay, ingenuous. Never becomes sophisticated, and usually has an air of childish simplicity about him. Idealistic views about the opposite sex.

Horace.—Latin: Origin obscure. Another form is *Horatio*.

Just, benevolent, complacent. Is interested in charitable works and capable of great sacrifices.

Hubert.—Teutonic: "mind bright."

Intellectual, book-loving, indulgent. He is reserved with strangers.

Hugh.—Teutonic: "mind." Another form is *Hugo*.

Stolid, deep-thinking, unemotional. His opinions are conservative and his tastes democratic.

Humphrey.—Teutonic: "support of peace."

Impulsive, rash, loyal, loving. Sometimes self-indulgent. He is popular with his own sex but women fear him.

I

Ian.—See *John*.

Ignatius.—Latin: "fiery."

Inspired, idealistic, self-sacrificing. He is zealous and persistent in the pursuit of good works.

Isaac.—Hebrew: "laughter."

Laughter-loving, proud, generous. Frequently self-opinionated, but hard-working and affectionate.

Isaiah.—Hebrew: "salvation of the Lord."

Ambitious, prudent, cautious. Makes a good leader of men. Usually possesses great physical strength.

Ivan.—See *John*.

Ivo.—Teutonic: "archer." Another form is *Ivor*.

Talented, sophisticated, ostentatious. Possesses literary and artistic talents. Sociable and popular.

J

Jack.—See *John.*

Jacob.—Hebrew: "supplanter." Other forms are *Hamish, James.*
  Versatile, keen, ambitious. The worst types can be treacherous. Generally affectionate but capable of a display of temper. Should be treated with tact.

James.—See *Jacob.*

Jason.—Greek: "healer."
  Elegant, witty, often superficial. Frenetic socializer. Usually remains a bachelor but has many love affairs. Prone to corpulence.

Jasper.—Persian: "treasure-master."
  Materialistic, cynical, sometimes cruel. Little sense of responsibility. Women should beware of him.

Jean.—See *John.*

Jeffrey.—See *Godfrey.*

Jeremiah.—Hebrew: "exalted of the Lord." Other forms are *Jeremias, Jeremy.*
  Enthusiastic, powerful, commanding. A great organizer, though not always popular. He takes himself rather too seriously.

Jerome.—Greek: "holy name."
  Ambitious, logical, practical. Some think him obstinate; actually, however, he is strong-willed.

Jesse.—Hebrew: "the Lord is."
  Courteous, sympathetic, good-tempered. Prefers work to play. Rather dull as a companion.

Joe.—See *Joseph.*

John.—Hebrew: "grace of the Lord." Other forms are *Ian, Ivan, Jack, Jean, Jock.*
  Ingenuous, trusting, honest. Prefers sport to work.

Jonah.—Hebrew: "dove."
  Gentle, forgiving, dilatory. Lacks enthusiasm but shows sincerity in love affairs. A poor business man.

Jonathan.—Hebrew: "the Lord's gift."
  Severe, upright, unforgiving. Possesses a keen sense of duty. His affections are deep and long lived.

Joseph.—Hebrew: "addition." Another form is *Joe.*
  Honest, successful, simple. Lacks originality but remains placid and clear-thinking when others panic.

Joshua.—Hebrew: "the Lord is salvation."
  Placid, firm, forgiving. Beloved by all who know him. Usually marries early in life.

Judah.—Hebrew: "praise of the Lord." Another form is *Jude.*
  Dominating, just, wise. An excellent adviser, for he never speaks without thinking. Devoted husband and father.

Jules, Julian.—See *Julius.*

John.—Hebrew: "grace of the Lord." Other forms are *Ian, Ivan, Jack, Jake, Jean, Jock.*
  Ingenuous, trusting, honest. Prefers sport to work.

Julius.—Latin: "downy-bearded." Other forms are *Jules, Julian.*
  Reticent, introspective, moody, charitable. Few really understand him. He is capable of great affection but shyness often restrains him.

Justin.—Latin: "just."
  Unemotional, truthful, energetic. Usually excels in all forms of sport. Not intellectual, but intelligent and sympathetic nature.

K

Karl.—See *Charles.*

Keith.—Celtic: "wood."
> Well mannered, indolent, awkward. A plodder, but a trustworthy husband and friend.

Kenneth.—Celtic: "comely."
> Handsome, brilliant, serious. Usually a good orator, being diplomatic and imaginative. Prefers intelligence to good looks.

Kevin.—Celtic: "handsome born."
> Quixotic, given to daydreams. Usually of unkempt appearance, but nonetheless a favourite among women.

L

Lambert.—Teutonic: "country's brightness."
> Awkward, blunt, passionate. Despises money and those who possess it. Lives in a dream-world which he will share with the right person.

Lancelot.—Latin: "servant." Another form is *Launcelot.*
> Courteous, faithful, intelligent. Possesses originality of taste. Sometimes acts in rather a rash manner, and may offend conventional people. A devoted and faithful lover.

Laurence.—Latin: "laurel." Other forms are *Larry, Lawrence.*
> Courageous, dutiful, patriotic. Hates deceit and easy virtue. An ideal husband and devoted father.

Leo.—Greek: "lion."
> Ambitious, tactless, thrusting. Usually strong physically but little mental ability. Passionate in love, though inclined to be inconstant and moody.

Leonard.—Teutonic: "lion-strong."
> Strong-willed, ruthless, intolerant. A dangerous person to trifle with, but he is loyal and loving to friends.

Leopold.—Teutonic: "people's prince."
> Sincere, truthful, clear-minded. The type of man whose "word is his bond." He will not forgive deceitfulness or mean-mindedness in others.

Leslie.—Origin obscure.
> Fiery, warm-hearted, forgiving. Do not rely on him too much, he is capricious.

Levi.—Hebrew: "joining."
> Business-like, alert, generous. Realizes the power of money and sets out to attain it. Marries late in life, when he has achieved success.

Lewis.—Teutonic: "famous war." Other forms are *Louis, Ludovic. Lewis* is also an English adaptation of the Celtic *Llewellyn,* which see.
> Heroic, self-sacrificing. He is inclined to be headstrong but has an unimpeachable sense of honour.

Lionel.—Latin: "little lion."
> Staunch, faithful, hot-tempered. Possesses great practical sense but lacks in tact and diplomacy.

Llewellyn.—Celtic: "lion-like" or "lightning."
> Warm-hearted, sympathetic, just. Reserved in company.

Louis.—See *Lewis.*

Lucas.—See *Luke.*

Ludovic.—See *Lewis.*

Luke.—Latin: "light." Another form is *Lucas.*
  Cultured, fastidious, immaculate. Sometimes petty-minded and frivolous. Very variable in temperament.

M

Malcolm.—Celtic: "servant of Columba."
  Liberal, cultured, sparkling. Takes great pride in his personal appearance. Attracted by rich or famous persons.

Manfred.—Teutonic: "mighty peace."
  Persevering, courageous, excitable. Possesses natural understanding of humanity. Always ready to help those in trouble.

Manuel.—See *Emanuel.*

Marcus.—Latin: "of Mars." Other forms are *Mark, Martin.*
  Inspiring, enthusiastic, emotional. Is a great supporter of the weak and defender of the wronged.

Mark.—See *Marcus.*

Marmaduke.—Celtic: "sea-leader."
  Business-like, efficient, brusque. He has great ability to organize and displays an interest in new schemes. Popular with the fair sex.

Martin.—See *Marcus.*

Matthew.—Hebrew: "gift of the Lord."
  Practical, honest, generous. His love affairs are usually unhappy.

Maurice.—Latin: "Moorish." Another form is *Morris.*
  Lazy, dreamy, extravagant. A good companion but seldom rich.

Maximilian.—Latin: "greatest Aemilianus."
  Vigorous, powerful, talkative, kind. Women like him but he is not capable of deep affection.

Michael.—Hebrew: "who is like unto God." Other forms are *Michel, Miguel.*
  Tender, sympathetic, gentle, wise. Often a great traveller.

Miles.—Greek: "crusher"; Latin: "warrior."
  Dauntless, conceited, rash. Lacking in imagination. His pride may bring him to disaster.

Morris.—See *Maurice.*

Moses.—Hebrew: "drawn-out."
  Dutiful, selfless, audacious. Passionate by nature. Very idealistic views concerning the world, but disappointed hopes often cause him unhappiness.

N

Nathan.—Hebrew: "gift."
  Open-minded, vivacious, sociable. Rather too fond of pleasure and constant variety. Naturally indolent.

Nathanael.—Hebrew: "gift of God." Another form is *Nathaniel.*
  Talented, inspired, impulsive. Not very sympathetic. Usually good-looking and healthy.

Neal.—Celtic: "champion." Other forms are *Neil, Nigel.*
  Talkative, sensitive, rational. Makes a good leader.

Neville.—French: "new settlement."
  High spirited, clever, handsome. Unreliable husband but passionate lover. Prone to temper tantrums.

Nicholas.—Greek: "victory of the people."
    Popular, amusing, hard-working, competent. Is inclined to be selfish and to worry unduly.

Nigel.—Latin: "black." It is also the English form of the Celtic *Neal*, which see.
    Athletic, bold, innocent. Easily deceived and often taken advantage of. He prefers home life to artificial pleasures.

Noah.—Hebrew: "rest."
    Silent, strong, slow. Loyal friend and devout lover. Seldom betrays his emotions, except to an intimate friend.

Noel.—Latin: "Christmas."
    Languid, intellectual, highly-strung, retrospective. Little ambition, although usually successful. Cannot always be relied upon.

Norman.—Teutonic: "Niord's man."
    Impractical, placid, courageous. He is fond of good company but makes few intimate friends.

O

Oliver.—Latin: "peace and joy."
    Chivalrous, sensitive, affectionate. He is often thought to be effeminate; in reality, however, he is manly and capable of great bravery and endurance.

Oscar.—Celtic: "bounding warrior."
    Ardent, sagacious, witty. Has little respect for the opposite sex. Often he makes lifelong enemies through misplaced sarcasm.

Oswald.—Teutonic: "divine power."
    Firm, generous, proud, dignified. Admired chiefly by persons older than himself, among whom he finds his friends.

Otto.—Teutonic: "rich."
    Conceited, intelligent, energetic. Women do not admire him, men fear but respect him.

Owen.—Celtic: "lamb" or "young warrior."
    Fearless, faithful, imaginative. Has many friends.

P

Patrick.—Latin: "noble." Other forms are *Paddy, Padraig.*
    Noble, cultured, extravagant. Happier unmarried as a rule.

Paul.—Latin: "small."
    Thoughtful, sentimental, extremely argumentative. Will make a staunch friend, but is irritated by small matters. Possesses no idealistic views concerning women.

Percival.—Celtic: "companion of the chalice."
    Urbane, pompous, audacious. He is charitable at heart but offends many by a display of false pride.

Peter.—Greek: "stone."
    Open, firm, unaffected. Always respected and loved. Marries while young and is devoted to his wife.

Philip.—Greek: "lover of horses."
    Extravagant, commanding, handsome. Cannot be happy without money. He has a loving nature but is somewhat changeable.

R

Ralph. —Old English: "counsel wolf."

Good-humoured, intuitive, complacent. Retains close affections for his parents. Often does not marry.

Randolph.—Teutonic: "house-wolf." Other forms are *Rafe, Ralph.*

Arrogant, humorous, domineering. Does not like to take advice but is always willing to give it. Prefers to mix with people less intelligent than himself.

Raphael.—Hebrew: "healing of God."

Sociable, talented, musical. Hates conceited persons. His best qualities are displayed in adversity.

Raymond.—Teutonic: "wise protection."

Dauntless, care-free, ingenious. Never plays for safety and loves adventure for adventure's sake.

Reginald.—Teutonic: "powerful judgment." Another form is *Ronald.*

Discreet, discerning, imaginative. He makes a good business man and is a lucky gambler.

Reuben.—Hebrew: "behold a son."

Youthful, enthusiastic, ambitious. A born leader and organizer. Rather wary of women unless he knows them well.

Richard.—Teutonic: "stern king."

Witty, energetic, generous. He believes in plain speaking, and sometimes offends. Makes many friends but should not be taken too seriously. Often marries very young.

Robert.—Teutonic: "bright fame." Other forms are *Robin, Rupert.*

Loquacious, successful, susceptible. Often becomes a brilliant speaker. Patience is not his strong point.

Roderick.—Teutonic: "famous king."

Self-reliant, plucky, tenacious. Solid mentality rather devoid of sentiment. Cold imagination.

Rodney. —English surname.

Arrogant, outspoken. Fond of dogs. A devoted and dutiful husband. Often physically vain.

Rodolph.—Teutonic: "wolf of fame." Another form is *Rudolph.*

Insincere, worldly, spoilt, extravagant. He is liked in spite of his faults. Women can influence him.

Roger.—Teutonic: "spear of fame."

Mystic, emotional, just, reasonable. Often achieves fame and amasses great wealth. Marries late.

Roland.—Teutonic: "fame of the land."

Dour, faithful, intelligent, stern. Is self-disciplined and will not give way to his passions.

Ronald.—See *Reginald.*

Rory. —Celtic: "red king."

Sensitive, artistic, spiteful. Popular with other men, but has difficulty in forming close relationships with women.

Ross. —Celtic: "from the peninsula."

Compassionate, imaginative, generous. A leader of men, but ruthless towards his enemies.

Roy. —Celtic: "red haired."

Passionate, athletic, hot-tempered. A faithful husband and a lover of animals.

Rudolph.—See *Rodolph.*

Rupert.—See *Robert.*
Russell.—Latin: "red."
>Crafty, cautious. Independently minded. Slow to love – but loves deeply and passionately when he does.

S

Samuel.—Hebrew: "asked of God."
>Friendly, understanding, unselfish. Is full of original ideas which usually bring him success.
Scott.—Celtic: "tattooed warrior."
>Taciturn, conscientious, miserly. Has a strong sense of responsibility, but must beware of an over-fondness for alcohol.
Sean.—See *John.*
Sebastian.—Greek: "venerable."
>Serious, conventional, conscientious. Suited for married life. If a bachelor, is inclined to become self-centred and irritable.
Silas, Silvester.—See *Sylvester.*
Simeon.—Hebrew: "obedient." Another form is *Simon.*
>Seldom simple. Cautious, non-committal, ambitious. Cannot bear to be idle. His pleasures are few and harmless.
Solomon.—Hebrew: "peaceful."
>Energetic, amusing, competent. Very fond of books and music. Is happier married and takes an interest in the upbringing of children.
Stanley.—Origin obscure.
>Cold, sardonic, handsome. Inclined to overrate his abilities. Very susceptible to flattery although the first to condemn flatterers.
Stephen.—Greek: "crown."
>Refined, amiable, fearless. Lacks in physical strength. Usually makes decisions quickly. Can be obstinate at times.
Stewart.—Celtic: "steward."
>Shy, quietly spoken. Intelligent, without ambition. Often remains a bachelor. Lithe physique.
Sydney.—Origin obscure.
>Excitable, intellectual, eccentric. Has many brilliant successes but also disastrous failures. Often despondent. A delightful and amusing companion when in a good mood. Marries young.
Sylvester.—Latin: "living in a wood." Other forms are *Silas, Silvester.*
>Nature-loving, astute, frugal, passionate. Social functions bore him. Makes one or two deep friendships. Hot-tempered at times.

T

Ted.—See *Edward.*
Terence.—Latin: "tender." Another form is *Terry.*
>Soft-hearted, easily-swayed, unambitious, cultured. Very fond of games. Seldom constant in love, until he marries.
Theobald.—Teutonic: "people's prince."
>Proud, sympathetic, well-mannered. Possesses a vivid imagination. Liable to be snobbish concerning friendships.

Theodore.—Greek: "divine gift." Another form is *Tudor.*
> Upright, honest, pure. Lacks in foresight, living only for the present. Seldom laughs but often smiles. Old-fashioned ideas about women.

Theodoric.—Teutonic: "people's ruler." Another form is *Derrick.*
> Ingenious, versatile, adventurous. Delights in exploration and anything which is new or out of the ordinary. His love affairs are usually stormy and passionate.

Thomas.—Aramaic: "twin."
> Practical, plodding, conscientious. Little imagination but strong passions. Distrustful of matters he does not understand. Prides himself on "plain-speaking."

Timothy.—Latin: "fear God."
> Mischievous, selfish, supercilious. Leads an unconventional life. Rapid talker and full of wild schemes. Has many tumultuous love affairs and settles down late in life.

Tobias.—Hebrew: "goodness of the Lord." Another form is *Toby.*
> High-principled, punctilious, humane. Liable to be priggish. Sometimes displays astounding lack of judgment. Makes a good husband but needs careful managing.

Trevor.—Welsh place name.
> Organised, capable. Often a good employee. Affectionate but taciturn.

Tristram.—Celtic: "sad face."
> Pensive, fatalistic, nervy. Loyal and generous to friends. Mistrustful of the opposite sex.

V

Valentine.—Latin: "healthy."
> Versatile, healthy, vivacious. Full of original ideas. Always busy and has little time for pleasure.

Victor.—Latin: "conqueror."
> Strong, manly, sympathetic. Intolerant of other people's failings. Not very passionate. Prefers platonic friendships to love.

Vincent.—Latin: "conquering."
> Sympathetic, loving, studious. Interesting conversationalist. Somewhat hasty in his judgments.

Vivian.—Latin: "lively" or "alive."
> Discerning, well-balanced, refined, enterprising. Great business talent. Inclined to be somewhat flirtatious.

W

Wallace.—Origin obscure.
> Healthy, powerful, blundering. Lack of tact his chief fault. Often impulsive. Deeply affectionate and wishes ill of no one.

Walter.—Teutonic: "powerful warrior."
> Intellectual, introspective, ambitious. Conservative in his tastes, hating change and novelties. Marries young.

Wayne.—Old English: "cart."
> Even tempered, graceful. Impressive wit and raconteur. Has tempestuous and often unhappy love affairs.

Wilfred.—Teutonic: "resolute peace."
> Religious, forgiving, just. Inclined to be self-centred. Has many hobbies, seldom becomes rich. Makes a faithful and attentive husband.

William.—Teutonic: "helmet of resolution."
> Energetic, susceptible, hospitable. Lacks originality and generally of the plodding type. Prefers home life, although he is not unsociable.

Z

Zachariah.—Hebrew: "remembrance of the Lord."
> Humble, devout, kindly. Usually leads a life of loneliness, but responds happily to friendship and sympathy.

WOMEN'S NAMES

A

Abigail.—Hebrew: "a father's joy."
> Affectionate, sincere, sympathetic. Sees the best side in everyone, and her good nature is liable to be taken advantage of.

Ada.—See *Edith.*

Adelaide.—Teutonic: "noble cheer." Other forms are *Adela, Adele.*
> Self-sacrificing, cultured, gentle. Suited for an early marriage. Has intelligence and will-power.

Adeline.—Teutonic: "noble serpent."
> Passionate, sensitive, unforgiving. Very moody temperament, yet she can be kind and charitable. Usually dark in complexion, and of small stature.

Adrienne.—Latin: "from Adria."
> Fickle, flirtatious, attractive. Causes many broken hearts. Men should not take her seriously.

Agatha.—Greek: "good."
> Brilliant, lively, unemotional. Indifferent to flattery. Prefers to seek her own pleasures in books and music.

Agnes.—Greek: "pine." Other forms are *Aggie, Inez, Nesta.*
> Innocent, resolute, impartial. Rather quiet and sometimes obstinate. Is careful in the choice of friends.

Aileen.—See *Helen.*

Alexandra.—Greek: "helper of men." Other forms are *Alexandria, Alexis.*
> Passionate, bold, enterprising. Charitable heart but faulty judgment.

Alice.—Teutonic: "noble cheer." Other forms are *Alicia, Elsa.*
> Haughty, handsome, commanding. Has a powerful influence over opposite sex. Practical rather than sentimental by nature.

Alison.—Teutonic: "famous war."
> Witty, discreet, courageous. Ambitious nature and eager for fame and honours. Liable to sudden anger, which passes quickly.

Alma.—Celtic: "all good"; Latin: "fair."
> Gracious, forgiving, tender-hearted. Independent spirit. Lofty ideals. Her chief fault is laziness.

Althea.—Greek: "healing."
Artistic, skilful, jealous. Strongly developed maternal instincts. An energetic and well-ordered mind.

Amanda.–Latin: "she who is fit to be loved."
Obstinate, pessimistic, often displays great spiritual strength.

Amelia.—See *Emily.*

Amy.—Latin: "beloved."
Good-natured, brave, gracious. Loved by everyone. Faithful to friends.

Anastasia.—Greek: "who shall rise again."
Thoughtful, competent, patient. Strong-willed if necessary. Rather slow intellect, but tenacity of mind.

Andrea.—Feminine of Andrew.
Clever, often beautiful. Marries young and makes an ideal wife.

Angela.—See *Angelica.*

Angelica.—Greek: "angelic." Other forms are *Angela, Angelina.*
Happy, modest, inspiring. Given to day-dreaming and mystic imaginings. Can be deeply passionate.

Anita.—See *Ann.*

Ann.—Hebrew: "grace." Other forms are *Anita, Anna, Anne, Hannah, Nancy.*
Graceful, merciful, unselfish. Limited intelligence but practical nature. Excellent mother and housewife.

Annabel.—Hebrew: "eagle heroine."
Energetic, impatient, freedom-loving. Usually a "tomboy." Accomplished in all kinds of sport. Loves deeply and fiercely.

Antonia.—Feminine of Anthony.
Graceful, often an artistic nature. Elegant but occasionally shallow and insensitive.

April.—From the month.
Charming, lovable, alert. Healthy appearance, attractive rather than beautiful. Always surrounded by numerous friends.

Arabella.—Teutonic: "eagle heroine."
Austere, spartan, handsome. Leads a life of many interests. Fond of dogs and the open air. Little use for men.

Audrey.—Teutonic: "noble threatener." Another form is *Audry.*
Wise, firm, placid. Selfish when single but a devoted wife and mother. Usually fair and rather plump.

Aurora.—Latin: "dawn."
Unspoilt, quiet, sentimental. Beautiful face and graceful manners. Implicitly faithful companion.

B

Barbara.—Greek: "stranger."
Cold, distant, idealistic. Intellect rather than good looks appeals to her. Marries late in life.

Beatrice.—Latin: "blesser." Other forms are *Beatrix, Trixy.*
Beautiful, cheerful, valorous. Lively imagination. Original ideas.

Becky.—See *Rebecca.*

Belinda.—Italian: "serpent." Other forms *Linda.*
Astute, jealous, graceful. Gives way to her passions.

Bella, Belle.—See *Isabel.*

Berenice.—Greek: "victory-bringing."
Talented, emotional, vain. Inclined to be hard-hearted. Constant in affections.
Bernadette.—Feminine of Bernard.
Adventurous, kind, honest. Lacking in foresight.
Beryl.—From the semi-precious stone.
Intuitive, amiable, seductive. Sometimes hasty in her words and actions.
Love affairs often unfortunate.
Bessie, Beth, Betsy, Bettina, Betty.—See *Elizabeth.*
Beverley.—Old English: "beaver-stream."
Often narcissistic. Strong intellect, emotionally cold.
Biddy.—See *Bridget.*
Blanche.—Teutonic: "white."
Unaffected, candid, animated. Loves company and is the "life and soul" of
a party. Does not take men seriously.
Brenda.—Teutonic: "sword."
Trusting, enterprising, extravagant. Good company and a good wife.
Bridget.—Celtic: "strength." Another form is *Biddy.*
Peaceful, homely, devoted. Can be strong-willed if necessary. Her friends
are liable to impose on her.

C

Camilla.—Etruscan: "servant of the temple." Another form is *Camille.*
Studious, energetic, alert. Fertile imagination. Refined tastes.
Candida.—Latin: "pure white."
Kind-hearted, determined, eccentric. Prone to depression when her affections are
not reciprocated.
Carmen.—Latin: "prophetess."
Passionate, self-willed, intuitive. She "lives on her nerves" and suffers much
anguish from jealousy. Should marry young or not at all.
Caroline, Carrie.—See *Charlotte.*
Catherine, Cathleen, Catriona.—See *Katharine.*
Cecilia.—Latin: "blind." Other forms are *Cecily, Cicely, Sheila.*
Kind, sensitive, musical, entertaining. Lacks will-power and tenacity. Given
to strong passions.
Charity.—Greek: "love."
Calm, forgiving, frank. Melancholy at times, and inclined to "weep she knows
not why." Devoted and loving wife.
Charlotte.—Teutonic: "man." Other forms are *Caroline, Carrie, Lotty.*
Energetic, wise, unemotional. Somewhat manly though attractive in her
bearing. Usually prefers a single life.
Charmian.—Origin obscure.
Sweet-natured, sentimental, attractive. Not a deep thinker but quick to
understand and imitate. Musical and soft-voiced.
Chloe.—Epithet of Greek fertility goddess Demeter.
Unpredictable, impetuous, beautiful. Not always very kind.
Christabel.—Greek: "fair Christian."
Generous, proud, resolute. Simple disposition. Can be obstinate at times.
Christine.—Greek: "Christian." Other forms are *Christina, Kirsteen, Kirsty.*
Introspective, nervous, passionate. Very sensitive nature and easily offended.
Usually pretty and graceful.

Cicely.—See *Cecilia.*

Clara.—Latin: "famous." Other forms are *Clare, Clarice, Clarissa.*
 Straightforward, proud, resourceful. Her personality is a commanding one. Love affairs predisposed to be turbulent.

Clarice, Clarissa—See *Clara.*

Claudia.—Latin: "lame." Another form is *Gladys.*
 Tender, impetuous, flirtatious. She is of the "helpless" type; hence very attractive to men. Usually marries early.

Clemence.—Latin: "merciful." Another form is *Clementina.*
 Sympathetic, generous, practical. Strong maternal instincts. If unhappy she suffers in silence. Quick to respond to affection and friendship.

Columbine.—Latin: "dove."
 Versatile, loving, emotional. Serious nature and rather timid.

Constance.—Latin: "firm."
 Firm, tactful, shrewd. Her tastes are simple. Does not care much about her appearance but possesses natural beauty and charm.

Cora.—Greek: "maiden." Another form is *Corinne.*
 Ingenuous, vague, idealistic. Liable to quarrel violently at times, especially with the opposite sex.

Cordelia.—Celtic: "daughter of the sea."
 Modest, diligent, prudent. Cheerful disposition and great powers of perseverance.

Cressida.—Greek: "gold."
 Passionate, witty, gregarious. Her affections are intense but often short-lived.

Cynthia.—Greek: "of Cynthus."
 Fickle, captivating, mischievous. Pretty ways but seldom sincere.

D

Daisy.—See *Margaret.*

Daphne.—Greek: "bay tree."
 Ardent, moody, compassionate. Independent by nature. Economical and practical as a wife.

Dawn.—From daybreak.
 Sentimental, strong maternal instincts, jealous.

Deborah.—Hebrew: "bee."
 Materialistic, cautious, calm. Averse to any form of quarrelling. Polite and patient by nature.

Deirdre.—Origin obscure.
 Proud, intelligent. Marries well and never lacks luxury.

Delia.—Epithet of the Greed goddess Artemis.
 Beautiful, determined, optimistic. A ruthless rival in love.

Denise.—Greek: "of Dionysos."
 Gentle, placid, capable. Usually of delicate health, dark and attractive.

Diana.—Latin: "goddess."
 Strong, beautiful, passionate. Lover of the open air and the countryside. To please her men must be tall, athletic and courageous.

Dinah.—Hebrew: "judgment."
 Loyal, truthful, affectionate. Slow to take offence and quick to forgive. Good conversationalist and a cheerful companion.

Dolly.—See *Dorothea.*

Dolores.—Latin: "sorrows." Another form is *Lola.*
 Flirtatious, garrulous, extravagant. Amicable and sympathetic spirit.

Donna.—Italian: "lady."

Perceptive, dreamy. Graceful bearing. Lacks ambition, but always content.

Dora.—See *Dorothea.*

Doreen.—Origin obscure.

Reserved, meditative, artistic. Easily hurt. Takes life too seriously.

Doris.—Greek: "of Doris."

Worldly, impatient, handsome. Rather bitter and cynical over love. Her passions are strong but are seldom roused.

Dorothea.—Greek: "gift of God." Other forms are *Dolly, Dora, Dorothy.*

Intellectual, graceful, gifted. Shy and timid in company. Prefers few and intimate friends.

Drusilla.—Celtic: "strong."

Restless, competent, intolerant. Seldom settles down until late in life. Love affairs are numerous and often end unhappily.

E

Edith.—Teutonic: "rich gift." Other forms are *Ada, Aline, Ida.*

Talented, ambitious, sociable. Fond of travel and little inclination towards domesticity. Changeable in love.

Edna.—Hebrew: "pleasure."

Romantic, impetuous, indiscreet. A spendthrift. Men find her irresistible.

Effie.—See *Euphemia.*

Eileen, Elaine, Eleanor.—See *Helen.*

Elaine.—Celtic: "fawn."

Light hearted, inclined to artistic pursuits. Popular with men and women but an inconstant lover.

Eleanor.—See *Helen.*

Elise, Elissa, Eliza.—See *Elizabeth.*

Elizabeth.—Hebrew: "oath of God." Other forms are *Bessie, Beth, Betsy, Bettina, Betty, Elise, Elissa, Eliza, Elsie, Elspeth.*

Resolute, affectionate, intelligent. Somewhat susceptible. Suited for early marriage. Often artistic or musical.

Ella.—Teutonic: "elf friend."

Capricious, dainty, unaffected. Displays great intelligence and wit. Usually an expert needlewoman.

Ellen.—See *Helen.*

Elsa.—See *Alice.*

Elsie, Elspeth.—See *Elizabeth.*

Emily.—Teutonic: "work." Other forms are *Amelia, Emilia, Emmeline.*

Animated, capable, persevering. Independent nature. Cheerful and sympathetic companion.

Emma.—Teutonic: "grandmother."

Maternal, emotional, patient. Marries early. Devotes herself to the affairs of the household.

Enid.—Celtic: "spotless purity."

Pure, stubborn, proud. Has many hobbies. Frivolous pleasures bore her. Attractive and commanding appearance.

Erica.—Teutonic: "ever king."

Contemplative, courageous, disdainful. Jealous concerning those whom she loves. Sometimes quarrelsome and rash.

Esmeralda.—Greek: "emerald."
Slow, silent, wistful. Great personal beauty and graceful manner.

Esther.—Persian: "star." Other forms are *Estelle, Hester, Hetty, Stella.*
Meditative, silent, composed. Taste for drama and painting. Sometimes rather melancholy.

Ethel.—Teutonic: "noble."
Sensible, irresponsive, talkative. Seldom pretty but has attractive ways and a sweet expression.

Eunice.—Greek: "happy victory."
Attractive, resourceful, material. Usually marries young. Her chief interests lie with children and affairs of the household.

Eva.—Hebrew: "life." Another form is *Eve.*
Feminine, wilful, emotional. If dark, of captivating beauty. Fair types are usually plain yet attractive. Always well dressed.

Evangeline.—Greek: "happy messenger."
Happy, confiding, tenacious. Romantic, but always self-possessed.

Evelyn.—Latin: "hazel-nut."
Dreamy, original, ingenious. Possesses a very creative mind, and often wins fame as a poet or author. Changeable temperament.

F

Faith.—From the cardinal virtue.
Chaste, unimaginative, studious. Delicate and dainty appearance. Affections deep and constant.

Fanny.—See *Frances.*

Fay.—French: "fairy."
Intuitive, affectionate, devoted. A gentle and undemonstrative lover and a good cook.

Felicity.—Latin: "happiness." Another form is *Felicia.*
Gay, gracious, impetuous. Inclined to be lazy when young. Seldom remains single though she marries late.

Fiona.—Celtic: "white."
Strong willed, practical. Unromantic but very popular with men. Finds it difficult to settle down.

Flora.—Latin: "flowers."
Pleasure-loving, hard-working, placid. Somewhat commonplace intellect. She takes affairs of the heart exceedingly seriously.

Florence.—Latin: "flourishing." Other forms are *Florrie, Flossie.*
Cheery, brave, charming. Her life may be hard but she never loses her good nature. She makes an ideal companion.

Flossie.—See *Florence.*

Frances.—Teutonic: "free." Other forms are *Fanny, Francesca.*
Pretentious, generous, attractive. She selects her friends with care. Becomes petulant if opposed.

Freda.—Teutonic: "peace." Other forms are *Frida, Frieda.*
Home-loving, placid, intellectual. She makes no attempt to charm, but is attractive nevertheless.

G

Gabrielle.—Hebrew: "hero of God."
Tender, dutiful, uncritical. She has many acquaintances, but few friends. Loving and sympathetic to those in trouble.

Gemma.—Italian: "jewel."
Sensitive, prone to ill health. Often a fine dancer and a peerless conversationalist.

Geneviève.—See *Jennifer.*

Georgina.—Greek: "husbandman."
Domesticated, unromantic, practical. Implicitly faithful in love. Happiest when married.

Geraldine.—Teutonic: "spear power."
Spoilt, selfish, pretty. Spends much time and money on clothes. She is improved by adversity and hardship.

Germaine.—French: "German."
Voluble, capable, restless. A persuasive talker and a lover of gossip.

Gertrude.—Teutonic: "spear maid."
Just, spirited, affectionate. Careless and slovenly by nature and often fails to develop her natural charm. She loves passionately.

Gillian.—See *Julia.*

Gladys.—See *Claudia.*

Gloria.—Latin: "glory."
Radiant, compelling, resourceful. Women are jealous of her but she never bears malice.

Grace.—Latin: "thanksgiving."
Responsive, cool-headed, imaginative. She never forgets those who have helped her. Sets friendship above love and passion.

Greta.—See *Margaret.*

Griselda.—Teutonic: "stone battle-maid." Another form is *Grizzell.*
Stolid, spartan, sincere. Forgiving nature, but impatient with any form of cowardice or disloyalty. Often of handsome and noble bearing.

Gwendolen.—Celtic: "white browed." Another form is *Winifred.*
Mystical, solitary, idealistic. Most people irritate or bore her. Yet she makes a few friends and to them is affectionate and faithful.

H

Hannah.—See *Ann.*

Harriet.—Teutonic: "home-ruler." Other forms are *Henrietta, Hetty.*
Self-willed, rebellious, attractive. Her enthusiasms are many and somewhat varied. Her heart is not easily captured.

Heather.—From the plant.
Light-hearted, active, restless. Makes a good leader and organizer. Rather cold and passionless.

Helen.—Greek: "light." Other forms are *Aileen, Eileen, Elaine, Eleanor, Ellen, Helena, Lena, Leonora.*
Elegant, gentle, cultured. Not necessarily beautiful but always captivating. Sentimental at times.

Henrietta.—See *Harriet.*

Hermione.—Greek: "of Hermes." Another form is *Hermia.*
Determined, elegant, tender. She herself is truthful and never forgives those who deceive her. Implicitly faithful in love.

Hester.—See *Esther.*

Hetty.—See *Esther* and *Harriet.*

Hilary.—Latin: "cheerful."

Subtle, composed. Prone to dishonesty. Attractive in deportment, if not of face.

Hilda.—Teutonic: "battle-maid."

Prudent, brave, thoughtful. Somewhat unenterprising. Distrustful of men.

Honor.—Latin: "honour." Other forms are *Honoria, Nora, Norah.*

Bewitching, greedy, sociable. She thinks more of herself than others. Under the influence of love, however, she becomes noble and self-sacrificing.

Hope.—From the cardinal virtue.

Sensitive, forgiving, lively. Warm and ardent temperament, and exceedingly susceptible in love. Inclined to idolize the object of her affections, and thus sometimes suffers acutely from disillusionment.

I

Ida.—See *Edith.*

Imogen.—Celtic: "maiden."

Something of a hoyden. Quick witted, proud, bold. Should marry young. Often has a very weak constitution.

Inez.—See *Agnes.*

Irene.—Greek: "messenger of peace."

Ardent, radiant, constant. Her intelligence is profound and it is impossible to delude her. She usually marries young.

Isabel.—Hebrew: "oath of God." Other forms are *Bella, Belle, Isabella, Ishbel.*

Modest, eloquent, charming. Usually soft-voiced and dark-eyed. She is sometimes deceitful but suffers remorse.

Ivy.—Teutonic: "clinging."

Tenacious, dainty, irresistible. Her charm is deep but inexplicable, and many fall under its spell. She should not be taken too seriously.

J

Jacqueline.—Hebrew: "supplanter."

Innocent, trusting, honest. Not beautiful, but delicately featured. Constant in affection.

Jane, Janet.—See *Joanna.*

Jasmine.—After the plant.

Fickle, imaginative, daring. Very lively as a companion, but she causes heart-aches for those who love her.

Jean.—See *Joanna.*

Jemima.—Hebrew: "dove."

Handsome, sincere, conservative. Sentimental but not sensitive.

Jennifer.—Celtic: "white wave." Another form is *Geneviève.*

Courageous, graceful, straightforward. Marriage seldom attracts her. She prefers a solitary but selfless life.

Jenny, Jessica, Jessie, Joan.—See *Joanna.*

Joanna.—Hebrew: "grace of the Lord." Other forms are *Jane, Janet, Jean, Jenny, Jessica, Jessie, Joan, Sheena.*

Easy-going, tolerant, attractive. She possesses a retentive memory and is quick to emulate those she admires. Her tastes are rather commonplace.

Josephine.—Hebrew: "addition."

Alert, successful, passionate. Powerful intellect but sometimes displays lack of judgment. Attractive to elderly men.

Joyce.—Latin: "sportive."

Merry, mischievous, inconstant. She takes nothing seriously but is not cold. Unhappy without money.

Judith.—Hebrew: "a Jewess."

Proud, tender, masterful. Displays artistic taste, especially in dress. Attractive and graceful in appearance.

Julia.—Latin: "downy-cheeked." Other forms are *Gillian, Julie.*

Dazzling, amorous, superficial. Only deep sorrow will make her sincere. She lacks imagination and a sense of proportion.

June.—From the month.

Elegant, unaffected, irresolute. She possesses great dramatic ability and is therefore inclined to be very emotional.

K

Katharine.—Greek: "pure." Other forms are *Catherine, Cathleen, Kay, Karen, Kate, Kathleen, Katrina, Kitty.*

Pure, staunch, contented. She makes the best of everything and is never heard to grumble. Affectionate rather than amorous.

Kathleen, Kitty.—See *Katharine.*

L

Laura.—Latin: "laurel."

Timid, amiable, loving. Romantic and sentimental when young.

Lavinia.—Latin: "of Latium."

Intelligent, cheerful, obstinate. Makes a capable wife.

Leah.—Hebrew: "wearied."

Romantic, charming, fatalistic. Inclined to judge only by appearances, and somewhat arbitrary in her opinions.

Leila.—Arabic: "night."

Ethereal, mysterious, moody. Seldom betrays her feelings, which lie very deep. Requires cheerful companionship and loving care to ward off the depression to which she is subject.

Lena, Leonora.—See *Helen.*

Lesley.—Celtic: "from Lesslyn."

Even tempered, generous, charming. Often has a tendency towards stoutness.

Lilian.—Latin: "lily." Another form is *Lily.*

Innocent, imaginative, idealistic. Dependent on others although capable herself. Rather a nervous temperament.

Linda.—Teutonic: "lime tree."

Athletic, romantic, vain. Attractive to men but may have difficulty in finding a suitable partner.

Lois.—See *Louise.*

Lola.—See *Dolores.*

Lorraine.—Teutonic: "people of Lothar."

Captivating, spoilt, radiant. A talented musician in many cases. Unpopular with women.

Louise.—Teutonic: "famous war." Other forms are *Lois, Louie, Louisa.*
> Capable, charming, intelligent. She is a great reader of character. Sometimes unscrupulous to attain her ends.

Lucy.—Latin: "light." Another form is *Lucille.*
> Brilliant, studious, impartial. Never dull though sometimes mysterious. Charm of manner rather than of face.

Lydia.—Greek: "of Lydia."
> Beautiful, graceful, serene. She is seldom moved, although not unsympathetic. Her health is often frail.

M

Mabel.—Celtic: "mirth."
> Mirthful, forgiving, broad-minded. She is loved more than she loves. Rather unimaginative.

Madeline.—See *Magdalen.*

Madge.—See *Margaret.*

Magdalen.—Hebrew: "of Magdala." Other forms are *Madeline, Magdalene.*
> Passionate, truthful, skilful. Romantic when she is young, somewhat egotistical as she grows older.

Maggie, Maisie.—See *Margaret.*

Margaret.—Persian: "pearl." Other forms are *Daisy, Greta, Madge, Maggie, Maisie, Margery, Marguerite, Marjorie, May, Meg, Peggy.*
> Care-free, firm, forgiving. Keen intellect and a brilliant conversationalist. She marries young, and a husband of her own age.

Margery, Marguerite.—See *Margaret.*

Maria, Marie, Marina, Marion.—See *Mary.*

Marianne.—Hebrew: "bitter grace."
> Unsociable, intellectual, determined. Inclined to be too mistrustful of others and cynical over matters of sentiment. Very loyal, however, to her true friends.

Marjorie.—See *Margaret.*

Martha.—Hebrew: "becoming bitter."
> Patient, hard-working, modest. Her value is seldom appreciated. She makes an ideal wife and mother.

Mary.—Hebrew: "bitterness." Other forms are *Maria, Marie, Marina, Marion, Maureen, May, Miriam, Molly, Polly.*
> Placid, gentle, sympathetic. She fears to display emotion. Usually attractive but seldom beautiful. Highly developed sense of humour.

Matilda.—Teutonic: "mighty battle-maid." Another form is *Maud.*
> Proud, headstrong, thoughtless. She has much beauty, and good looks attract her.

Maud.—See *Matilda.*

Maureen.—See *Mary.*

Mavis.—French: "song-thrush."
> Cautious, dedicated, susceptible. A good listener who may have difficulty in imposing her will on others.

May.—See *Margaret* or *Mary.*

Melanie.—Greek: "black."
> Very intelligent, physically strong and brave. Attractive bearing. Tends to remain unmarried.

Mercy.—From the virtue.

Sweet-tempered, sympathetic, simple-mannered. Her life is totally unselfish and she is never more pleased than when employed in helping "lame dogs over stiles."

Michelle.—French: Feminine form of Michael.

Beautiful, depressive, loquacious, stylish. Fond of animals.

Melissa.—Greek: "bee."

Attractive, intuitive, naïve. Her lack of judgement may lead her to make a poor choice of a partner.

Mildred.—Teutonic: "mild threatener."

Daring, hard-hearted, elegant. Clear intellect, unconventional behaviour.

Millicent.—Teutonic: "work-strength."

Wise, calm, amiable. Affectionate nature, seldom passionate.

Miranda.—Latin: "to be admired."

Gentle, unassuming, beautiful. Possesses a dreamy rather than a practical nature. Suited for an early marriage, although a poor housewife.

Miriam.—See *Mary*.

Moira.—Celtic: "soft."

Elegant, composed, amorous. Cultured intellect and great sense of humour.

Molly.—See *Mary*.

Mona.—Celtic: "solitary."

Pensive, reserved, unemotional. Usually attractive in looks but self-willed and, at times, rather cruel.

Monica.—Latin: "adviser."

Vague, dreamy, idealistic. Sometimes unfriendly. She lives too much in a world of visions.

Morag.—Celtic: "great."

Vivacious, attractive, conceited. A good dancer, but has few women friends.

Muriel.—Greek: "myrrh." Other forms are *Myra, Myrtle.*

Practical, timorous, upright. Loves the open air. Little use for sentiment.

Myra, Myrtle.—See *Muriel*.

N

Nadine.—Slavonic: "hope."

Lively, coquettish, quarrelsome. Easily flattered and is often indiscreet.

Nancy.—See *Ann*.

Naomi.—Hebrew: "pleasant one."

Gracious, home-loving, intelligent. Rather lacking in imagination, and inclined to jump too hastily to conclusions.

Natalie.—Latin: "Christmas child."

Shrewd, generous, tactful. A veritable peace-maker, who seems more concerned with the happiness of others than with her own.

Natasha.—Slavonic: origin obscure.

Fine mind, graceful carriage, captivating face. Generous, sympathetic, good humoured.

Nesta.—See *Agnes*.

Nicola.—Feminine of Nicholas.

Anxious, sentimental, forgiving and generous. Enjoys the open air. Requires protective friends.

Nora, Norah.—See *Honor*.

O

Octavia.—Latin: "eight."
Sociable, placid, just. Usually cultivates some hobby, and seeks her pleasures independently of others.

Olga.—Teutonic: "holy."
Alert, sentimental, optimistic. She is very lucky in all her affairs. Often remains unmarried.

Olive.—Latin: "peace and joy." Another form is *Olivia*.
Peaceful, proud, beautiful. Displays charming simplicity although a clear, penetrating intellect.

Ophelia.—Greek: "serpent."
Wistful, romantic, nervous. Seductive manner. She cannot successfully conceal her dislikes.

P

Pamela.—Origin obscure.
Self-indulgent, sweet-tempered, courageous. Possesses artistic tastes and has reserved disposition.

Patience.—Latin: "patient one."
Courageous, delicate, elegant. Very original ideas, and a taste for acting, music and painting.

Patricia.—Latin: "noble."
Noble, forgiving, quiet. Not very passionate but tender and affectionate.

Paula.—Latin: "small." Another form is *Pauline*.
Obstinate, ambitious, attractive. Sometimes inclined to be petty-minded. Lively temperament.

Pearl.—From the gem.
Childish, pure, elegant. Rather self-willed and not very sensitive.

Peggy.—See *Margaret*.

Penelope.—Greek: "weaver."
Faithful, hard-working, loving. Often shows great independence of will.

Philippa.—Greek: "lover of horses."
Sporting, stoical, handsome. As a leader and organizer she is successful and immensely popular.

Phoebe.—Greek: "shining."
Brilliant, passionate, restive. Seductive manner and unforgiving nature.

Phyllis.—Greek: "green bough." Another form is *Phillis*.
Courageous, attractive, determined. Usually marries young and is a devoted wife and mother.

Polly.—See *Mary*.

Priscilla.—Latin: "ancient."
Aristocratic, independent, extravagant. Lacks beauty but possesses charm. Well-developed intellect.

Prudence.—From the virtue.
Austere, reserved, kindly. Attractive looks. She can be sympathetic.

R

Rachel.—Hebrew: "ewe."
Gentle, yielding, impulsive. Economical nature. Excellent housewife.

Rebecca.—Hebrew: "noosed cord." Another form is *Becky.*
Mild, good-natured, hesitant. A rather passive temperament, though she can love faithfully.

Rhoda.—See *Rose.*

Rosalind.—Teutonic: "beautiful serpent."
Confiding, affectionate, idealistic. Frequently remains unmarried, for she seldom finds her true ideal for a partner.

Rosamond.—Teutonic: "famed protection."
Strong, protective, maternal. Intelligence in advance of her years. Great personal charm.

Rose.—Latin: "a rose." Other forms are *Rhoda, Rosa, Rosalie.*
Gracious, charming, beautiful. Her feelings are tempered with self-control and, sometimes, reserve. Implicity faithful in love. Usually marries young.

Rosemary.—Latin: "sea-dew."
Passionate, alert, unaffected. Charming ways and a keen intuitive sense. An ideal wife.

Ruby.—From the precious stone.
Indolent, emotional, neurotic. Very easily offended. She has tempestuous, and sometimes tragic, love affairs.

Ruth.—Hebrew: "beauty."
Dreamy, impassive, good-looking. Leads an independent life, cultivating her own interests and hobbies.

S

Sadie, Sally.—See *Sarah.*

Samantha.—Origin obscure.
Quiet, elegant, wily. Good wife and mother. Practical, but prone to occasional bouts of indecisiveness.

Sandra.—See *Alexandra.*

Sarah.—Hebrew: "princess." Other forms are *Sadie, Sally, Sara.*
Refined, critical, aesthetic. Religious nature. Kind and sympathetic towards those in trouble.

Selina.—Greek: "moon."
Gentle, yielding, wistful. Inclined to be extravagant and flirtatious.

Sharon.—Hebrew: "plain."
Delicate constitution but very strong will. Profoundly intelligent, fond of practical jokes.

Sheena.—See *Jane.*

Sheila.—See *Cecilia.*

Shirley.—Old English: "county clearing."
Practical, limited intelligence but tenacious and full of common sense. Frequently very pretty, but reluctant to marry.

Sibyl.—Latin: "wise old woman."
Whimsical, critical, pure. Makes many friends and is a good organizer.

Sophia.—Greek: "wisdom." Another form is *Sophy.*
Wise, alert, sentimental. Fond of books and quiet seclusion. Rather distrustful of men unless they are open and frank.

Stella.—See *Esther.*

Stephanie.—Greek: "crown."

Headstrong, impatient, sentimental. Fond of all kinds of entertainment, and sometimes insincere in her actions. She is lacking in foresight.

Susan.—Hebrew: "lily." Other forms are *Susannah, Suzanne.*

Pure, graceful, simple. Very trusting and responsive to friendship. She needs someone to advise and help her.

Sylvia.—Latin: "living in a wood."

Unaffected, gracious, healthy. A lover of Nature. Popular with everyone.

T

Theresa.—Greek: "the reaper."

Enterprising, ambitious, spirited. Seldom a failure. Little sentiment but genuine affection.

Tracy.—English surname.

Well-groomed, popular, selfish. Not a deep thinker, but a lover of social amusements and attractive to men.

U

Ursula.—Latin: "bear."

Tactless, vivacious, pretty. Fond of pleasure and company. She seldom troubles to think deeply.

V

Valerie.—Latin: "healthy."

Effervescent, secretive, uxorious. Often a fine dancer.

Vanessa.—Invented by Jonathan Swift.

Clever, modest, attractive. Independent and noble.

Vera.—Slavonic: "faith."

Faithful, sensible, affectionate. Pleasant appearance and simple manners.

Veronica.—Latin and Greek: "true image."

Idealistic, mystical, yielding. Rather unenterprising. Attractive demeanour.

Victoria.—Latin: "conqueror."

Self-willed, intellectual, courageous. Home-loving nature. Keen judgment.

Viola.—See *Violet.*

Violet.—Latin: "modest grace." Another form is *Viola.*

Modest, graceful, imaginative. Her heart rules her head.

Virginia.—Latin: "flourishing."

Robust, cheerful, tender. Seldom downhearted. Suited for an early marriage.

Vivian.—Latin: "alive."

Conscientious, trustworthy, unimaginative. Easily flattered, overly fond of the opposite sex.

W

Winifred.—See *Gwendolen.*

Y

Yvonne.—Teutonic: "archer."
Graceful, inconstant, calm.   Flirtatious nature.   Has little deep feeling.

Z

Zoë.—Greek: "life."
Captivating, impetuous, skilful.   Romantic by nature but intensely practical if necessary.

THE VIRTUES OF PRECIOUS STONES

CUSTOMARILY, gems are classified as precious and semi-precious stones, though this distinction is one made by jewellers and bears no relation to the intrinsic value and attributions of the stones. Precious stones would thus comprise only the diamond, sapphire, emerald and ruby, and semi-precious stones would include the agate, amethyst, aquamarine, blood-stone, cornelian, chrysolite, crystal, garnet, opal, sardonyx, topaz, turquoise and zircon, to name only a few. For our purpose we shall refer to them all as precious stones.

The reasons that have led people to prize gem-stones are varied. Like gold, they have been treasured and preserved as lasting and incorruptible materials that lent themselves to ornamentation and embellishment. Most of them are intensely hard—indeed, even to-day they are valued according to this quality. Many reflect light and refract its rays in such a fashion as to foster the illusion that the stone actually shines with its own light. Associated with this characteristic is that of colour. Certain gems possess the property called dichroism—in different lights they appear differently coloured. Because of this feature, the name dichroite has been given to one stone.

Many gem-stones are rare, or are obtained at great risk or by arduous labour; hence they are costly and valuable in comparison. Some are found in circumstances which lend an atmosphere of romance or mystery to them. For example, on cracking a rough and ugly pebble we may find within a crystal of brilliant and gorgeous colour. Very early in the history of civilization in Egyptian, Chaldean and Mexican lore we find that astrological significance was given to certain precious stones. Amulets and talismans were fashioned out of hard stones even in prehistoric times. Neanderthal man had his amulets, and in Cro-Magnon times ornaments were made from coral, besides shell, horn and ivory. These have their parallel in the ornaments and sacred stones used by primitive peoples of to-day.

Inevitably, precious stones were associated with religious practices; images of the gods were embellished with the most rare and costly gems, or were fashioned from some precious stone itself. Votive offerings of gold or silver and gems were made at the shrines and temples; the garments of the priests and priestesses were ornamented with gems; the exterior and interior of the sacred buildings, too, were encrusted with valuable stones. Any especially large or rare or magnificent stone that was mined was customarily dedicated to sacred uses.

The breast-plate of the Jewish high priest was set with twelve stones arranged in four rows. These gems represented the twelve tribes. In early Christian symbolism certain precious stones were associated with the twelve apostles. The Gnostics of the second and third century made great use of engraved gems.

The beads of rosaries are made from materials of a lasting nature—gem-stones, common stones, or glass; also from less durable objects like the seeds of certain plants. The Hindu rosary is made of crystal or of shell, and the invocation "Om mani padme hom" is repeated while the beads are passed in succession through the fingers. Among the Buddhists the diamond, sapphire, coral, ruby and cat's-eye are held in great esteem for their ritual significance.

In the Middle Ages gem-stones were extensively used as medicines, being crushed to powder and administered to the patient. Besides the mineral stones, others were employed that had quite a different origin: these were concretions, or pebble-like substances, taken from the intestines or other organs of animals. Such stones were regarded very highly, and were set in gold and passed on from generation to generation. Only a tiny portion was scraped off when a medicine or an antidote was needed for some grave disorder; even the carrying or wearing of such a stone was believed to bestow immunity.

Stories are met with, in the old records, of criminals on whom these healing stones were tried after the unfortunate persons had been given a dose of poison. One such narrative relates how the malefactor recovered and was handsomely rewarded by the monarch whose stone had thus been proved to be so potent. Of another, however, who perished miserably in agony, it is recorded that he said he regretted he had not chosen to die by hanging.

From a very early date precious stones were associated with the twelve signs of the zodiac. It can scarcely be doubted that the twelve stones of the Jewish high priest's breast-plate had each an astrological significance. Kosminsky, in his *Magic and Science of Jewels and Stones*, identifies them with the signs and suggests that the stones were those that are given below:—

SIGN	STONE	SIGN	STONE
Aries	Red haematite	Libra	Opal
Taurus	Emerald	Scorpio	Banded agate
Gemini	Marble	Sagittarius	Amethyst
Cancer	Chrysoprase	Capricorn	Serpentine
Leo	Sardonyx	Aquarius	Lapis lazuli
Virgo	Jasper	Pisces	Crystal

Astrologers of to-day identify the stones of the zodiac rather differently, and the table given below shows which gems are now invested with the attributes of the signs.

SIGN	GEM	SIGN	GEM
Aries	Blood-stone	Libra	Opal
Taurus	Sapphire	Scorpio	Aquamarine
Gemini	Chrysoprase	Sagittarius	Topaz
Cancer	Emerald	Capricorn	Ruby
Leo	Chrysolite	Aquarius	Garnet
Virgo	Cornelian	Pisces	Amethyst

Those who are at all familiar with astrology will know that the sun enters in succession the various signs of the zodiac at about the same dates from year to year, so that the appropriate birth-stone of a person can be indicated if we know the date of his birth. Jewellers use a list that suggests a particular stone for each month of the year, but this list takes no account of the fact that Aries, for example, governs, approximately, from March 21 until April 20, and *not* from April 1 to April 30. Later in this section is given a calendar by means of which the appropriate birth-stone for any date can be ascertained.

The Wearing of Precious Stones

Gems should not be worn indiscriminately and without reference to their zodiacal associations. According to the date of birth, certain stones are fortunate, others are harmless, and still others are invested with harmful attributes. It is not sufficient merely to take into consideration the month of birth, for the zodiacal mensems do not coincide with the months of the calendar, and the zodiacal sign changes at a date varying from the 19th to the 24th of the month.

In order to take the fullest advantage of zodiacal influences, a gem should be worn that is in consonance with the sign under which a person was born. An antipathetic stone may have a baleful influence upon its wearer; while, if he uses jewellery containing gems that are not harmful but merely inert, he is missing the benefits that the sympathetic stones would confer.

The ascription of certain attributes to precious stones is an ancient and well-founded practice. Though we may not perceive why or how they can benefit or harm us, it is wise to profit by the lore and experience that have come down to us from past centuries. It has been well said that any deep-rooted and widely prevalent belief must have sprung from a consensus of experience and knowledge. We may laugh at old proverbs and wise saws, but we know in our heart of hearts that they enshrine wisdom and truth.

Many gem-stones are found in the form of crystals. Scientists have measured the angles of crystals, grouped them into classes according to their invariable laws of form, and given these classes names made up of Greek and Latin words—but crystals and crystallization are still very much of a mystery. A crystal of quartz can be made to vibrate by passing through it an alternating electric current. In fact, a crystal of this mineral is used to regulate and check the oscillations of the waves transmitted from a wireless station.

Another wonderful power of some mineral crystals lies in the fact that when certain unlike ones are placed in contact they allow an electric current to pass through them in one direction only. It is to this virtue that wireless reception owed its practical origin. Quartz crystals are utilized, too, in the analysis of chemical substances by means of X-rays. Crystals of other minerals have the faculty of splitting up a ray of light into two rays—on looking at an object through such a crystal it is seen double.

Each of the planets has its own series of light waves or vibrations which proceed from it. Who knows what may be the effect upon humanity of these waves? Knowledge of the effects—curative or harmful—of light rays is only in its infancy. Even sunlight itself may be harmful if the body is not inured to it gradually. Some of the early experimenters with X-rays suffered irreparable injury from these mysterious emanations, for their effects were not fully realized until some years later.

The seers of old taught that for each planet, or each constellation of the zodiac, there were certain harmonious gem-stones and minerals. This harmony might be one of colour—for colour depends on the particular frequency of the preponderant vibration—or might be related to other attributes of the heavenly body. However that may be, the science of the lore and meaning of precious stones is well established. The reader may test its theories for himself, but we urge him to be guided in his choice of jewellery by the precepts set forth in the following pages. A calendar of birth-stones is prefixed for ready reference.

SIGN of the ZODIAC	DATE OF BIRTH	FORTUNATE STONES	STONES TO BE AVOIDED	SIGN of the ZODIAC	DATE OF BIRTH	FORTUNATE STONES	STONES TO BE AVOIDED
CAPRICORN, or THE GOAT	JANUARY 1 2 3 4 5 6 7 8 9 10 11 12 13 14 15 16 17	Ruby Jet Serpentine	Opal Lapis lazuli	AQUARIUS, or THE WATER BEARER	FEBRUARY 1 2 3 4 5 6 7 8 9 10 11 12 13 14 15 16 17	Garnet Jacinth Jargoon	Aquamarine Carbuncle
AQUARIUS, or THE WATER BEARER	18 19 20 21 22 23 24 25 26 27 28 29 30 31	Garnet Jacinth Jargoon	Aquamarine Carbuncle	PISCES, or THE FISHES	18 19 20 21 22 23 24 25 26 27 28 29	Amethyst Rock crystal White sapphire	Agate Topaz

SIGN of the ZODIAC	DATE OF BIRTH	FORTUNATE STONES	STONES TO BE AVOIDED
PISCES, or THE FISHES	**MARCH** 1 2 3 4 5 6 7 8 9 10 11 12 13 14 15 16 17	Amethyst Rock crystal White sapphire	Agate Topaz
ARIES, or THE RAM	18 19 20 21 22 23 24 25 26 27 28 29 30 31	Blood-stone Diamond Haematite	Ruby Jet Pearl

SIGN of the ZODIAC	DATE OF BIRTH	FORTUNATE STONES	STONES TO BE AVOIDED
ARIES, or THE RAM	**APRIL** 1 2 3 4 5 6 7 8 9 10 11 12 13 14 15 16 17	Blood-stone Diamond Haematite	Ruby Jet Pearl
TAURUS, or THE BULL	18 19 20 21 22 23 24 25 26 27 28 29 30	Sapphire Turquoise Amber	Garnet Chryso- lite Sardonyx Jacinth

SIGN of the ZODIAC	DATE OF BIRTH	FORTUNATE STONES	STONES TO BE AVOIDED
TAURUS, or THE BULL	**MAY** 1 2 3 4 5 6 7 8 9 10 11 12 13 14 15 16 17	Sapphire Turquoise Amber	Garnet Chryso- lite Sardonyx Jacinth
GEMINI, or THE TWINS	18 19 20 21 22 23 24 25 26 27 28 29 30 31	Chryso- prase Agate Marble	Cornelian Jade

SIGN of the ZODIAC	DATE OF BIRTH	FORTUNATE STONES	STONES TO BE AVOIDED
GEMINI, or THE TWINS	**JUNE** 1 2 3 4 5 6 7 8 9 10 11 12 13 14 15 16 17	Chryso- prase Agate Marble	Cornelian Jade
CANCER, or THE CRAB	18 19 20 21 22 23 24 25 26 27 28 29 30	Emerald Moonstone Pearl	Opal Lapis lazuli

SIGN of the ZODIAC	DATE OF BIRTH	FORTUNATE STONES	STONES TO BE AVOIDED
CANCER, or THE CRAB	**JULY** 1 2 3 4 5 6 7 8 9 10 11 12 13 14 15 16 17	Emerald Moonstone Pearl	Opal Lapis lazuli
LEO, or THE LION	18 19 20 21 22 23 24 25 26 27 28 29 30 31	Chrysolite Sardonyx Tourmaline	Aqua- marine Carbuncle

SIGN of the ZODIAC	DATE OF BIRTH	FORTUNATE STONES	STONES TO BE AVOIDED
LEO, or THE LION	**AUGUST** 1 2 3 4 5 6 7 8 9 10 11 12 13 14 15 16 17	Chrysolite Sardonyx Tourmaline	Aqua- marine Carbuncle
VIRGO, or THE VIRGIN	18 19 20 21 22 23 24 25 26 27 28 29 30 31	Cornelian Jasper Jade	Agate Topaz Chryso- prase

SIGN of the ZODIAC	DATE OF BIRTH	FORTUNATE STONES	STONES TO BE AVOIDED
VIRGO, or THE VIRGIN	**SEPTEMBER** 1 2 3 4 5 6 7 8 9 10 11 12 13 14 15 16 17 18 19 20 21	Cornelian Jasper Jade	Agate Topaz Chryso- prase
LIBRA, or THE BALANCE	22 23 24 25 26 27 28 29 30	Opal Lapis lazuli Coral	Ruby Jet Pearl

SIGN of the ZODIAC	DATE OF BIRTH	FORTUNATE STONES	STONES TO BE AVOIDED
LIBRA, or THE BALANCE	**OCTOBER** 1 2 3 4 5 6 7 8 9 10 11 12 13 14 15 16 17 18 19 20 21	Opal Lapis lazuli Coral	Ruby Jet Pearl
SCORPIO, or THE SCORPION	22 23 24 25 26 27 28 29 30 31	Aqua- marine Carbuncle Magnetite	Garnet Chryso- lite Sardonyx Jacinth

SIGN of the ZODIAC	DATE OF OF BIRTH	FORTUNATE STONES	STONES TO BE AVOIDED	SIGN of the ZODIAC	DATE OF BIRTH	FORTUNATE STONES	STONES TO BE AVOIDED
SCORPIO, or THE SCORPION	NOVEMBER 1 2 3 4 5 6 7 8 9 10 11 12 13 14 15 16 17 18 19 20	Aquamarine Carbuncle Magnetite	Garnet Chrysolite Sardonyx Jacinth	SAGITTARIUS, or THE ARCHER	DECEMBER 1 2 3 4 5 6 7 8 9 10 11 12 13 14 15 16 17 18 19 20	Topaz Amethystine Sapphire	Jade
SAGITTARIUS, or THE ARCHER	21 22 23 24 25 26 27 28 29 30	Topaz Amethystine Sapphire	Jade	CAPRICORN, or THE GOAT	21 22 23 24 25 26 27 28 29 30 31	Ruby Jet Serpentine	Opal Lapis lazuli

THE MEANINGS OF PRECIOUS STONES

Agate.—This stone is a form of quartz, consisting of chalcedony, amethyst or jasper, and ordinary quartz, disposed in bands or lines. Banded agate shows alternate lines of light and dark, or red and white stone; cat's-eye agate has a peculiar ocellated marking. The variety known as moss agate bears markings resembling trees, ferns, moss and other natural objects.

The wearing of an agate is said to prevent headaches, and to relieve inflammation or tiredness of the eyes. Ground to a powder, the stone was used to check bleeding and to allay the irritation caused by skin diseases. The possession of an agate was held in olden times to bestow the gifts of eloquence, social charm, and good fortune. Agate was one of the stones in the breast-plate of the Jewish high priest.

Agate should not be worn by those born during the periods influenced by Virgo and Pisces; it is, however, a fortunate stone for people born under Gemini. It is supposed to endow its wearer with good health, wealth and longevity. To strengthen its powers the chrysoprase also should be worn.

Amber.—This is the solidified and fossilized resin of trees that grew many thousands of years ago. Owing to its electrical properties it attracted the attention of the ancients.

Amber is sometimes found in large lumps weighing up to twenty pounds. Parts of plants and the bodies of insects are frequently to be seen imprisoned in the yellow mass; they were trapped by the flowing resin long ages ago. Amber is distilled to make a pungent oil—usually mixed with other substances to lessen its strength—that is used for rubbing on the body to cure aches and pains. Powdered amber used to be given for various internal complaints, and the fumes of burning amber were used also. The fossilized gum is a favourite material for amulets, which are worn as a protection from the evil eye, and to prevent danger from plague. A large piece of amber is sometimes worn on the throat to prevent nasal catarrh, hay-fever, and asthma.

Amber is fortunate for people born under Taurus.

Amethyst.—A form of quartz with a beautiful purple or violet hue, this stone takes its name from a Greek word that referred to its supposed power of counteracting the effects of wine fumes. In later times the stone was believed to have a calming and soothing influence. When its wearer became ill the amethyst changed colour; when brought near poisoned food it lost its brightness.

The gem was worn in mediaeval times by doctors of medicine, and was often the stone of choice for the episcopal ring of a prelate. It was also a favourite stone for the beads of rosaries. Amethyst is thought to have been one of the stones set into the breast-plate of the Jewish high priest.

An amethyst wrapped in thin silk and bound lightly to the brows or temples is reputed to be a remedy for nervous headache. The stone should first be warmed in the sun's rays or in front of a fire.

The amethyst is a stone of fortune for those whose birthday falls in the period influenced by Pisces, but may be worn with benefit by all.

Amethystine Sapphire.—This is a variety of corundum with a characteristic amethyst colouring. True amethyst, it may be noted, is a variety of quartz.

The amethystine sapphire was worn on the chest to give relief in lung troubles. Suspended from a necklace, it was a protector of female chastity. Worn at night, it is reputed to bring sweet sleep free from dreams. A delicately coloured stone, its hue may become even paler when the health of its wearer is indifferent.

Amethystine sapphire is a lucky stone for people whose birthday falls under the influence of Sagittarius. Its companion stone is the topaz.

Aquamarine.—This is a stone of the beryl group, its name being taken from Latin words that mean "sea-water" and that refer to its typical bluish-green coloration. History tells of aquamarines that have passed through strange vicissitudes. A notable blue aquamarine that was owned by a daughter of the Roman emperor Titus came later into the hands of Charles the Bald, who gave it to the abbey of St. Denis, where for long it adorned a reliquary. The stone bore an engraved portrait of its first owner, and it is said that in mediaeval times this was erroneously supposed to be the picture of a saint. Another large gem, that came from a papal tiara and was looted by an invading army, found its way again to the Vatican some three centuries later.

Aquamarine partakes of the attributes of the beryl, which are described elsewhere. It is a lucky stone for seafarers, and is supposed to bring harmony into married life.

This gem is best avoided by people born under Aquarius or Leo. For those whose birthday falls in the Scorpio period it is a fortunate stone. It may be worn with the carbuncle.

Blood-stone.—This red-speckled variety of green jasper is symbolical of courage. It is used for seals, cameos and signets, and many of the seals of ancient Babylon were cut in jasper.

Blood-stone was used to staunch the flow of blood from a wound. If worn against the chest it was credited with the power of preventing internal haemorrhage. Ancient writers agree that, once the stone has been worn for such a purpose, it is dangerous to discard it. Since early historic times it has been worn on the abdomen as a strengthener of the digestive system.

There are many legends about the origin of the stone. One says that on the hill of Calvary some of the blood from the crucified Christ fell upon green jasper that lay beneath the Cross, and thus tinged it with red. A much older tradition states that blood-stone was formed when Uranus was wounded by his son Saturn. Magical properties ascribed to the stone include protection from drowning, furtherance of business projects, and the ensuring of victory in battle.

The blood-stone is a fortunate gem for people born under Aries. Worn in a finger ring or as a seal, it enhances and fortifies the influence of the diamond, which is also a lucky stone for those born in this period.

Carbuncle.—This stone is a variety of garnet, of a deep, rich crimson or scarlet hue. It is usually cut *en cabochon*, or with a convex rounded top, instead of being cut with facets in the ordinary manner. The name comes from a word for coal; on account of its brilliant fire and deep colour the gem was likened to a burning coal seen in the darkness. The carbuncle possesses the attribute of hope.

This stone, like so many others, was worn as a protection against plague; its lustre was said to become dimmed when an infected person approached the wearer. A gradually increasing loss of brilliance portended death to him who wore the stone. Another attribute of the carbuncle is that it will protect the traveller from harm on his journeys by land and sea.

Carbuncles are fortunate stones for people born under Scorpio, and can be worn with the aquamarine. Both stones are unlucky for people whose birthday falls under the influence of Aquarius or Leo.

Chrysolite.—This, the "golden stone" of the ancients, is greenish-yellow in hue, although varieties are found with an olive-green or a brighter green colour, which are known as olivine or peridot, as the case may be.

In olden times, this stone was worn at night to banish phantoms and ensure sound sleep. Worn during the day it brought literary or poetical inspiration and dispelled melancholy. It is regarded as an inducement to mental health and as a preventive of madness.

Chrysolite is a fortunate stone for people born under Leo, but should not be worn by those born in the Taurus and Scorpio periods. With the chrysolite a sardonyx may be worn.

Chrysoprase.—This gem is a green form of chalcedony. It was one of the stones in the breast-plate of the Jewish high priest, and symbolizes cheerfulness.

The stone was worn as a remedy for gout and rheumatism, and was used also in the treatment of kidney and bladder troubles. It was said to strengthen the sight of one who gazed long into it. Sunlight causes the colour of the stone to fade.

Chrysoprase is a fortunate stone for people born under Gemini, and with it the agate may be worn. Neither stone, however, should be worn by those born during the Virgo or Pisces periods.

Coral.—This substance is formed by the tiny polyps that build about them a stony habitation. The beautiful and valued pink or red coral comes from the Mediterranean, where it is recovered from the sea floor.

The name comes from a Greek word that means "nymph of the sea." Legend has it that the blood from the head of Medusa, who was slain by Perseus, turned into coral the twigs and branches of shrubs that grew along the seashore; and that the sea-maidens took these petrified branches with them when they returned to their sea caves on the ocean floor.

The wearing of coral was reputed to cure or to prevent many ailments. It lost its rich, deep hue and took on a wan and sickly appearance when the health of the wearer declined. As an amulet coral banished nightmares and warded off demons of the darkness. In many countries, charms of coral are hung round the neck of children to protect them.

Coral is a birth-stone for people born under Libra.

Cornelian.—Properly "carnelian," from the Latin word for flesh, this gem received its name from its pinkish or reddish hue. It is a species of chalcedony, and varies in colour from blood-red to brownish or yellow. The colour becomes deeper in direct sunlight. Since very ancient times cornelian has been used for amulets and talismans, both in the East and in the West. By its aid the Eastern theosophists were said to be able to discern the denizens of the astral plane, and to summon help from that domain. In such cases the stone was gazed at fixedly while the thoughts were focused on the astral.

Worn on the finger or suspended round the neck, the cornelian endows its possessor with contentment, banishes fear, and gives self-confidence. Other talismanic uses were to ward off the baleful effects of the evil eye, and to preserve the body from the dangers of lightning, pestilence and fever. In powdered form the stone was used as a styptic to check bleeding.

The cornelian is a fortunate stone for people born under Virgo.

Persons whose natal day falls under the influence of Gemini or Sagittarius should not wear the stone. Others, however, may wear it with benefit.

Diamond.—This, the hardest of all stones, is a crystalline form of carbon, symbolical of innocence.

There are ancient legends telling of magnificent diamonds whose possession brought misfortune upon all associated with them. Well authenticated cases in more modern times go to show that the possession of unusually large diamonds brings ill luck and disaster. Against this we can set the fact that the diamond is a gem symbolical of purity, of innocence, and of strength.

In Roman days it was bound to the left arm of the warrior to endow him with courage and fortitude. People in mediaeval England wore a diamond as a protection against pestilence. Between lovers, or husband and wife, the stone promoted constancy; a gift of a diamond was a token of reconciliation and a measure towards its attainment.

How, then, can these different influences be explained? It is really a very simple matter; the evil influence of the gem is derived from the evil wrought by men in securing it. A deed of violence deprived the finder, or he to whom the gem belonged by right, of his prize, and its subsequent history—even in our own day—is often one of crime and horror. This tale of evil seems to endure until the stone is removed from the care of the individual and handed over to the State. As long as its possessor holds the gem for his own selfish pleasure, so long does it remain a source of evil influence. It must be placed where men's lust and cupidity, aroused always by the large and magnificent gems, cannot prevail. This is borne out by the story of the great Cullinan diamond— found near Pretoria in 1905—which was bought by the Transvaal government and presented to Edward VII in 1907. Peaceably and lawfully acquired, the stone has no evil aura.

The diamond is a fortunate stone for people whose birthday falls in the Aries period. It may be worn by all others, save only by those whose birth-stone is the emerald. With it may be worn a blood-stone, when the beneficent influence of the diamond will be greatly increased.

Emerald.—This stone is of the beryl group, its colour being a vivid green. Emeralds were prized by the Incas of Peru, who used them as votive offerings at the temples. After the Spanish conquest large numbers of fine stones were brought back to Europe. In India emeralds were used to decorate the temples and the images of the gods. The emerald mines of Egypt were famed in ancient times, and this stone was one of those used in the breast-plate of the Jewish high priest.

An old legend tells how the serpent is blinded by gazing at the emerald. The stone was used in the treatment of inflamed eyes; a lotion was made by steeping a number of the stones in water, or a small quantity of the crushed and powdered stone was put into water and a few drops applied to the eyes. Other medicinal uses of the emerald were as an antidote to poison; a remedy for sores and ulcers; and a treatment for fits. Merely wearing the stone, it was believed, was enough to ward off epilepsy.

The belief that the pangs and dangers of child-birth are lessened by wearing an emerald is a very ancient one; so, too, is the assurance that the gem is a protector of chastity. A broken vow or an unchaste act, the ancients believed, would cause the gem to become dim or lose its colour. An act of gross treachery might even cause the stone to crumble in its setting.

The emerald is a stone of fortune to people born during the Cancer period. With it may be worn the moonstone.

Garnet.—There are several stones that bear this name, though they differ in colour and other features. The almandine, or Bohemian garnet, is deep red; cinnamon stone, or essonite, has a red-tinged golden hue.

Garnets, by changing colour, are said to forewarn their wearer of approaching danger; in India they are worn to ward off plague. The stone is the emblem of constancy and faithfulness; if worn by a friend it is likely to perpetuate the friendship.

A fortunate stone for one whose birthday falls in the Aquarius period, it should not be worn by those born under the influence of Taurus or Scorpio. The companion stone is the jacinth.

Haematite.—This is a form of iron ore, the name being derived from a Greek word referring to its rusty red or blood-like hue.

Haematite is one of the most commonly used medicinal stones. From ancient times to the present day it has been employed in various forms for treating internal ailments. The powdered mineral was mixed with ointment and used as an eye salve. Greek writers termed haematite the blood-stone, but it is usual to reserve this latter name for the variety of green jasper which is blotched and speckled with red.

The haematite is a fortunate stone for those whose birthday falls within the Aries period.

Jacinth.—This stone is known also as the hyacinth, after the Greek youth whose blood was changed into the flower bearing his name. It is a variety of the zircon, and is an orange or cinnamon red in colour.

The ancient myth tells that Hyacinth was killed by a quoit thrown by Apollo, which Zephyr blew against the youth's head. Medicinally the jacinth was worn to prevent or cure disorders of the stomach, and to strengthen the action of the heart. Worn on the third finger it was reputed to bring peace to the mind, and to induce sound sleep at night. As a talisman, jacinth was said to bring happiness and prosperity to its wearer, and to protect him from fevers and poisoning.

Jacinth is a fortunate stone for people born under Aquarius, and may be worn with the garnet. It is not recommended to those whose birthday falls within the Taurus or Scorpio periods.

Jade.—An old name for this stone, derived from its use as a remedy for pains in the region of the loins, is lapis nephriticus, or "kidney stone." Jade ranges in colour from white, through cream and yellowish brown, to a deep green.

The use of jade for kidney troubles, which dates from prehistoric times, was prevalent in many lands. Besides this virtue, jade was reputed to avert epilepsy, to cure the bites of animals, and to be good for eye diseases. Although, generally, the stone was worn against the skin in the region of pain, it was also used occasionally as a medicine, the powdered jade being swallowed. The latter practice was common among the Chinese. Jade is a talismanic stone of the Maoris, who use it also for their weapons and implements. In China, jade amulets symbolizing rulership were buried in the ancestral temple in order to protect the family from ill luck.

Green jade is a fortunate stone for people born under Virgo, but it is not recommended to those whose birthday falls in the Gemini and Sagittarius periods. Cornelian may be worn with jade.

Jargoon.—This gem belongs to the zircon family, and is almost a colourless stone, sometimes of a greyish hue. Though much softer than the diamond, it is sometimes passed off as the latter. It was not used in a medicinal capacity, but was believed to guard its wearer against plague or cholera.

The jargoon is a fortunate stone for people whose birthday comes in the Aquarius period.

Jasper.—This gem-stone is found in various sombre colours, including yellow, green, red and black. The green variety when flecked with red is known as blood-stone. A jasper stone was set into the breast-plate of the Jewish high priest.

From pre-Christian eras to our own time, jasper has been much used for seals. The "Lydian Stone," or touchstone used to test gold, is a variety of black jasper. The custom of wearing an amulet of red jasper over the pit of the stomach as a preventive of digestive pains dates back thirteen centuries at least. The stone is credited with the power of preventing internal bleeding.

Jasper (other than the blood-stone) is a fortunate stone for those born under Virgo.

Jet.—This velvety-black mineral is virtually a hard and compact form of coal, derived from the wood of forest trees of a long past geological era. It is found in the cliffs of Yorkshire, and the chief supply comes from Whitby. Jet used to be picked up in quantity on the shore, but is now obtained from mines in the cliffs.

Jet was once used a great deal for curative purposes. The powdered mineral was taken in wine or water for toothache; or made into an ointment for use in skin diseases; or used as a dental cleanser when the teeth became loose. The fumes of burning jet were believed to repel plague and other pestilences. Other remedial uses of jet fumigation were to cure epilepsy and to cut short an attack of hysteria. Ancient writers state that the fumes of the burning mineral indicated whether a woman were chaste or not; and a prevalent custom decreed the wearing of jet as a cure for female disorders.

Jet had a potency in counteracting magical spells and incantations; it protected the wearer against the bites of snakes and the stings of scorpions. Evil thoughts and the hallucinations of delirium were dispelled by wearing an amulet of this mineral. Jet was dedicated to the goddess Cybele, the "Great Mother of the Gods" in ancient Greek and Roman mythology.

Jet is a lucky stone for people whose birthday falls in the Capricorn period, and may be worn with the ruby; neither gem is recommended to be used by people born under Aries or Libra.

Lapis Lazuli.—This is a deep blue or bluish green mineral whose name—derived from Latin and Arabic words—refers to its coloration. When polished it displays sparkling metallic flecks that are due to particles of iron ore within its matrix. By the ancients it was used for the decoration of buildings, and also to make brooches and other ornaments. In later times it was used in a similar manner in Western countries. Lapis lazuli is thought to have been one of the stones in the Jewish high priest's breast-plate.

The mineral was formerly crushed to make the pigment called ultramarine, which is now prepared by artificial methods. In the Middle Ages lapis lazuli was powdered and made into a paste for use on the skin as a plaster; the powder was also used internally in the form of pills. Lapis lazuli worn next the skin is reputed to cure pain, especially neuralgia. Water in which the mineral had been steeped was used as an eye-wash to allay inflammation.

The stone has been widely employed as a talisman. It was customary to thread a few beads of lapis on a gold or silver wire, and to place them round the left wrist of children to protect the wearers from harm. In an Egyptian papyrus some 3,500 years old, curative necklaces containing beads of lapis lazuli and other magic stones are mentioned. The sparkles of the iron pyrites in the deep blue of the polished lapis lazuli were compared to the twinkling of the stars in the heavenly firmament, and the mineral was hence called the Heavenly Stone.

Lapis lazuli is a stone of fortune to people whose birthday falls under the influence of Libra, and may be worn with opal. Like the latter gem, it is to be avoided by people born during the Cancer or Capricorn periods.

Magnetite.—This is magnetic ore, the lodestone of the ancient navigators, and is black in colour. The name is derived, according to tradition, from a Lydian shepherd called Magnes. One day he found that the iron tip of his crook had become drawn to certain rock upon which he stood, and thus magnetite was discovered. The use of a piece of lodestone for indicating the North, dates back, it is said, to the time of the Phoenicians.

On account of its iron content, magnetite was used extensively in treating various disorders, ranging from rheumatism to the falling out of the hair. It was employed notably as an eye-stone. As a charm, lodestone was worn to acquire wisdom and intuition.

Magnetite is a fortunate stone for people born under Scorpio.

Marble.—Though not a gem-stone, marble is invested with considerable astrological and talismanic virtue, and was one of the stones set into the breast-plate of the Jewish high priest.

All marble is composed of carbonate of lime. The beautiful colouring and veining are due to the admixture of metallic oxides, and to the fusion when the original limestone was altered by the heat of the earth's fire and changed into its new form. Almost every conceivable hue is to be found in marble.

Marble is a fortunate stone for people born in the Gemini period.

Moonstone.—This is an opalescent form of feldspar, resembling in its colour the pale lustrous blue of moonlight. It symbolizes hope.

Moonstone, or selenite, as it is also named, is believed to absorb the rays of the moon, and with them some of the attributes of that heavenly body. It is said to be beneficial in dropsical affections, and is also reputed to allay fever. The stone of travellers, it protects them from evil while on their journey, especially from danger by sea. Its potency increases as the moon waxes, and lessens as that orb declines.

This gem is a fortunate one for people born during the Cancer period, and may be worn with the emerald.

Opal.—Unlike most other gem-stones, the opal is not crystalline in form. It is a variety of silica, is comparatively soft, and owes its beauty to the wonderful play of brilliant colour from its surface. The mineral is formed from the skeletons or the shells of very tiny plant and animal organisms.

The iridescent, rainbow hues of the gem are caused by the irregular refraction of light from its surface, which is traversed by innumerable tiny cracks. In the process of its formation the surface becomes covered with cracks, and these crevices on the opal become filled in with a substance which contains more or less water than the surrounding surface.

Since the extent to which light rays are bent back depends on the composition of the material, we get a great irregularity of refraction and a play of colour that varies according to the aspect from which the gem is viewed. Blue, perhaps, when looked at in one direction, the opal may appear yellow or crimson if we view it from another angle.

Opal symbolizes hope. Though superstition has grown up round it, and it has become regarded as a stone of ill fortune, this error is of comparatively recent date. By the Greeks and Romans the opal was highly esteemed, the former believing that it endowed its possessor with the gift of soothsaying. Another name for the stone was Ophthalmios, or "eye-stone," in reference to its use in treating weak sight.

The opal, as we have said, contains water; it is porous and should not be immersed in water or brought into contact with oils. Though most people would no doubt remove a gem-ring before putting the hands into water containing common soda, we may point out that strong alkaline solutions are especially harmful to the opal, and the stone may be entirely destroyed by such substances.

Opal is a fortunate stone for those whose birthday falls under the influence of Libra, and may be worn with lapis lazuli. People born during the Cancer and Capricorn periods ought not to wear either stone.

Pearl.—This beautiful gem is produced by the nacreous fluid secreted by certain shell-fish round a particle of hard matter that finds its way into the shell of the animal. It is found in the shells of certain freshwater mussels, and also in those of some kinds of oyster. Almost all the bivalves whose shell is lined with nacre, or "mother-of-pearl," produce pearls, but the commercial supplies come from the two we have named. What have come to be known as "cultured" pearls are produced by artificially introducing into oyster shells a grain of some hard substance, around which nucleus, in favourable circumstances, the oyster proceeds to build up a pearl. Pearls are symbolical of purity.

Many charming legends are associated with the pearl. Thus it was said that dew fell into the open shells of the pearl mussel and was transformed into the gem. Probably the explanation is the far more prosaic one that the particle of hard matter causes irritation, and that the coating of nacre built up slowly in the course of years is Nature's remedy for, and protection against, this irritation of the soft tissues of the animal.

In ancient times, as at the present day, pearls were highly valued. The folk-lore of many countries, Oriental and Western alike, is full of references to the gem. Crushed to a powder and taken with water, or dissolved in acids, it was used as a medicine for many complaints. It is said that the native divers who descend to gather pearl oysters believe that the wearing of a pearl wards off evil; and that the gem is even potent enough to protect the diver against the shark and the fearsome octopus.

Not all can wear pearls, for on some persons the gems "grow sick" and lose their brightness. When this happens the pearls should be laid aside for some days until the lustre returns; if, on next wearing them, they lose their lustre again, a longer period of rest must be given. Pearls are *not* unlucky stones, though persons born during the Aries and Libra periods should not wear them. They are the stones of choice for people born under Cancer. With them may be worn the emerald or the moonstone.

Rock-crystal.—This is a colourless, transparent variety of quartz. It is the stone from which the globes of crystal-gazers are fashioned. Of great repute in the Orient, rock-crystal is used for magic purposes in the form of charms and talismans. Sometimes within a crystal will be found water bubbles, and the stone is then known as a hydrolyte. Rock-crystal was one of the stones set into the breast-plate of the Jewish high priest.

The medicinal use of this mineral goes back to early times. A sphere of crystal was used to concentrate the rays of the sun upon diseased limbs or organs of the body. Powdered crystal was treated by distillation to make a medicine for a number of ailments; only very small doses were needed. Powdered rock-crystal was applied as a salve also.

People in many lands use amulets made of rock-crystal, whose beauty and transparency have given rise to many romantic legends. Worn at night, rock-crystal confers on the wearer the boon of sound and peaceful sleep. It is a protection against spells and evil thoughts. Poison poured into a goblet of crystal was said to cause a clouding of the cup; in olden times the stone was much used in the making of fine cups and other vessels.

Rock-crystal is a lucky stone for people whose birthday falls in the Pisces period, and may be worn with the amethyst.

Ruby.—This stone is one of the corundum group, and takes its name from a Latin word referring to its red coloration. In what follows we refer especially to the Oriental ruby. The so-called spinel ruby is a softer stone of different composition. Especially fine rubies are found in Burma and Ceylon, and the gem has for long been esteemed throughout the Orient for its marvellous beauty and the precious gifts it confers upon the wearer or possessor. Its attribute is contentment.

Rubies vary in hue from a pale pink to the deep red of the pigeon's-blood gem. A Cingalese legend calls the stones "tears of Buddha," and the ruby is a sacred gem to the Buddhists. Like certain other gems of rich colour, the ruby is believed to grow paler when illness or other misfortune threatens its wearer. Should the evil be averted, the stone regains its colour. It is said that Catherine of Aragon, first queen of Henry VIII, was warned of her decline from royal favour by a ruby she wore on her finger.

The ruby seems to have been little used in a medicinal capacity —perhaps on account of its high cost, for none but kings and wealthy princes could afford to grind the stone to powder and use it in that way. Worn on the brow the gem was said to give insight and mental power; when applied to the heart its influence on that organ was a stimulating one. Evil spirits were repelled and the phantoms of the night warded off by wearing the ruby. Like other gems it was believed to indicate the presence of poisons by a paling of its hue, and to be of virtue as an antidote against snake venom.

Rubies are fortunate stones for persons born under Capricorn. They are gems of ill augur to those whose birthday comes in the Aries and Libra periods.

Sapphire.—This beautiful blue stone is a variety of corundum. It is credited with the power of ensuring mental health. Sapphires are mentioned in the Scriptures, and in some cases the stone so named was probably the blue sapphire.

The sapphire was used in treating a number of ailments, both in Europe and the Orient. It was a specific for eye trouble, and is said to have been efficacious in drawing particles of foreign matter from the eyeball. Worn over the heart, it strengthened and stimulated that organ. A medicine that was made by steeping the gems in water was given to people stung by scorpions, or those suffering from internal complaints. As an amulet the sapphire gave protection from bewitchment and incantations; it guarded the chastity of the wearer, and by becoming dimmed it warned the latter of evil designs, especially those connected with fraud and treachery.

The blue sapphire is a stone of good omen especially to people whose birthday falls in the Taurus period, but may be worn with benefit by all. If the turquoise be worn also, it will fortify the beneficial power of the sapphire.

Sardonyx.—This stone is composed of sard (cornelian) and chalcedony in layers, the brownish red of the sard showing through the less opaque chalcedony or onyx on top. Sardonyx was one of the stones in the breast-plate of the Jewish high priest. Its attribute is conjugal bliss.

In Roman times sardonyx was one of the favourite gems; since it lent itself to engraving, and its alternations of colour adapted it for cameos, many ancient examples have come down to us. The stone was worn as a protection against plague, and also to ward off the stings and bites of poisonous insects and reptiles. It was said to lessen the pangs of childbirth, and its wearing by a bride was reputed to conduce to marital happiness.

Sardonyx is a fortunate gem for people born under Leo, its companion stone being the chrysolite. Like the latter, it is forbidden to people whose birthday falls in the Taurus and Scorpio periods.

Serpentine.—This is a more or less opaque stone, coloured various shades of green ranging to yellow. The best variety, "noble" serpentine, is somewhat translucent. It was one of those stones set into the breast-plate of the Jewish high priest.

The name of this mineral refers to its use as an antidote for snake-bite, and the stone was worn as an amulet to ward off the attacks of venomous reptiles and insects. Pieces of serpentine bound to the limbs or to the loins were used as a remedy for rheumatism. The stone had also the reputation of drawing to itself the watery liquids that formed in dropsical swellings. Serpentine was used largely by the ancient Egyptians to make scarabs.

This is a fortunate stone for people born under the zodiacal sign of Capricorn.

Topaz.—The topaz is found in several colours, of which the pink, yellow and white are the most highly prized. It is symbolical of faithfulness.

Topaz has been used since ancient times as a medicine for the ailments of women, and for disorders of the lungs, nose and throat. Worn over the region of the stomach, a topaz was used as a protection against affections of that organ and the alimentary system.

It was worn also to avert epilepsy and asthma, and the stones were steeped in water to make a drink for the cure of sleeplessness.

The topaz is said by Eastern seers to enable them to receive messages from the astral plane. It strengthens the mind and preserves from mental disorder. Night terrors are dispelled by wearing this gem, which increases in potency as the moon waxes.

The stone is one of fortune to people whose birthday falls within the Sagittarius period. It may be worn by all whose nativity falls outside the Pisces and Virgo periods. The amethystine sapphire is a companion stone.

Tourmaline.—This gem-stone varies in hue from black to colourlessness, and includes pink, rose, blue, green and yellow shades. It is notable for its optical properties, and has also electrical qualities. When looked at in a certain direction the crystal is transparent: when viewed in a direction at right angles to the first, it is opaque. The effect is due to the polarization of light by the tourmaline.

Tourmaline, like amber, will attract light articles by its electrical property. It is singular that a crystal of tourmaline will act as a magnet if hung on a thin thread of cotton or some other fibre that does not conduct electricity. When heated, however, tourmaline reverses its polarity, and what was the North pole becomes then the South pole. On account of its remarkable properties the gem is used as an amulet, and shaped into various talismanic forms. It is reputed to endow its wearer with perception and wisdom.

The tourmaline is a fortunate stone for people born under Leo.

Turquoise.—This stone comes mainly from Persia, where it is found in veins in the rock. Elsewhere in the East it is found in Syria, China and Tibet; a poorer variety exists in Europe, in Saxony and Silesia. The name is believed to be derived from that of Turkey, whence the stone may have been first brought to the West. It symbolizes prosperity.

Chief among its virtues is regarded that of giving warning of poison, by changing colour. It also enjoys high repute as an eye-stone, being applied to the organ to cure weakness of sight and inflammation. The turquoise is also sometimes applied to the loins or the chest for remedial purposes.

The turquoise does not look its best on all people; on some wearers it may become dim. Unless the stone soon regains its brilliance it should be discarded for some weeks. Magical attributes include

Precious Stones for the Hours of Day and Night

HOUR	SUNDAY	MONDAY	TUESDAY	WEDNESDAY	THURSDAY	FRIDAY	SATURDAY	HOUR
A.M.								A.M.
1	Diamond	Moonstone	Haematite	Jasper	Carbuncle	Coral	Turquoise	1
2	Coral	Turquoise	Diamond	Moonstone	Haematite	Jasper	Carbuncle	2
3	Jasper	Carbuncle	Coral	Turquoise	Diamond	Moonstone	Haematite	3
4	Moonstone	Haematite	Jasper	Carbuncle	Coral	Turquoise	Diamond	4
5	Turquoise	Diamond	Moonstone	Haematite	Jasper	Carbuncle	Coral	5
6	Carbuncle	Coral	Turquoise	Diamond	Moonstone	Haematite	Jasper	6
7	Haematite	Jasper	Carbuncle	Coral	Turquoise	Diamond	Moonstone	7
8	Diamond	Moonstone	Haematite	Jasper	Carbuncle	Coral	Turquoise	8
9	Coral	Turquoise	Diamond	Moonstone	Haematite	Jasper	Carbuncle	9
10	Jasper	Carbuncle	Coral	Turquoise	Diamond	Moonstone	Haematite	10
11	Moonstone	Haematite	Jasper	Carbuncle	Coral	Turquoise	Diamond	11
NOON 12	Turquoise	Diamond	Moonstone	Haematite	Jasper	Carbuncle	Coral	NOON 12
P.M.								P.M.
1	Carbuncle	Coral	Turquoise	Diamond	Moonstone	Haematite	Jasper	1
2	Haematite	Jasper	Carbuncle	Coral	Turquoise	Diamond	Moonstone	2
3	Diamond	Moonstone	Haematite	Jasper	Carbuncle	Coral	Turquoise	3
4	Coral	Turquoise	Diamond	Moonstone	Haematite	Jasper	Carbuncle	4
5	Jasper	Carbuncle	Coral	Turquoise	Diamond	Moonstone	Haematite	5
6	Moonstone	Haematite	Jasper	Carbuncle	Coral	Turquoise	Diamond	6
7	Turquoise	Diamond	Moonstone	Haematite	Jasper	Carbuncle	Coral	7
8	Carbuncle	Coral	Turquoise	Diamond	Moonstone	Haematite	Jasper	8
9	Haematite	Jasper	Carbuncle	Coral	Turquoise	Diamond	Moonstone	9
10	Diamond	Moonstone	Haematite	Jasper	Carbuncle	Coral	Turquoise	10
11	Coral	Turquoise	Diamond	Moonstone	Haematite	Jasper	Carbuncle	11
12	Jasper	Carbuncle	Coral	Turquoise	Diamond	Moonstone	Haematite	12

protection from the evil eye, and from incantations or evil intentions of others. Turquoises are worn by horsemen, because they are reputed to endow the mount with sure-footedness.

The turquoise is a fortunate stone for people born during the Taurus period, but may be worn by all, irrespective of the date of their birth. With it should be worn a blue sapphire, when the influence of both gems is strengthened.

White Sapphire.—White or colourless sapphires are somewhat rare. They sometimes pass for diamonds, since all forms of corundum are intensely hard and the colourless variety of sapphire bears a superficial likeness to the more valuable stone.

The white sapphire bears the attribute of purity, and was worn by young women as a guardian of chastity. On account of its rareness the gem was little used for amulets; it bore, however, the reputation of protecting travellers from peril by land and sea.

White sapphire is a stone of fortune for people whose birthday falls under the influence of the zodiacal sign of Pisces.

THE LANGUAGE AND MEANINGS OF FLOWERS

A S soon as man was sufficiently civilized to have any appreciation of the aesthetic, he became vividly aware of the beauty of Nature's blossoms. There followed a symbolic and mystic attribution to these of qualities and meanings. Beautiful and poetical thoughts were conveyed by the presentation of a sprig of blossom, and whole messages were communicated by bouquets in which each flower chosen betokened a significant idea. Not only love and happiness were the tenor of these floral missives; coquetry, dalliance, prevarication, indifference and coolness; rebuff, refusal, scorn, contempt and insult—all were expressed by a suitably chosen flower.

Needless to say, the practice of using floral emblems was so convenient that it became firmly established in favour near and far. From the Occident to the Orient, these messages were current. A floral love-token handed to the favoured one by a slave or a henchman could tell no tale to irate parent or spouse—at least no such tale as could an intercepted letter.

But the system was open to falsification. The messenger might hand the missive to a person other than the one for whom it was intended; late at night, or in the half-light of dawn, the hopeful knight-errant would appear at the garden gate to carry off his beloved, and she would fail, perhaps, to realize until too late the deception that had been practised upon her. Or the flower might be substituted by another having a meaning that was far different from the one intended, so that unwittingly the maiden would give her admirer his *congé*.

Despite its liability to unhappy breakdowns of this nature, florigraphy has flourished down to our own day, and the modern revival in the sending of valentines has fostered it. Floral cards for birthday messages are also very popular. To the discriminating sender and appreciative recipient, an aptly chosen spray of blossoms may mean much; only the most heedless or uninformed would choose flowers at random.

Let us make it clear that there is a duality in floral tokens. A flower may indicate merely some sweet or lofty sentiment, or it may carry a verbal message. By combining flowers to form a bouquet, a longer message can be composed. The index of attributes given below makes it quite easy both to compose and interpret florigraphic "documents." In selecting flowers for such a purpose, great care should be exercised not to mistake the names; if a florist is commissioned to make up and dispatch or deliver a posy or a bouquet, precise instructions should be written, with a warning not to substitute any other blossoms for the flowers selected. Misguided zeal in trying to secure artistic effects in a floral token may entirely wreck the scheme.

It is worth remembering that flowers can be "telegraphed" to many parts of the world. An order given to a reputable florist in most of our cities will ensure a bouquet being made up at the distant town—even at the Antipodes—and delivered to the person whose name and address are specified. Thus oceans and continents present no barriers to the floral message, and the latest resources of science are pressed into the service of florigraphy—that romantic and poetical language of love which has come down to us from the far-away dawn of civilization.

FLOWERS AND THEIR MEANINGS

A

Aconite.—Misanthropy. "Your attentions are unwelcome."
African Marigold.—See *Marigold, African.*
Agrimony.—Gratitude. "Please accept my thanks for your token."
Almond, Flowering.—Hope. "Your friendship is pleasant."
Alyssum.—Virtue and worthiness. "I admire your noble character."
Anemone.—Estrangement. "Your charms no longer appeal to me."
Angelica.—Inspiration. "Love of you is my inspiration."
Apple Blossom.—Beauty and goodness. "You are as good as you are beautiful."
Arbutus.—Love. "You alone I love."
Arum, Wild.—Ardour. "My heart burns with love for you."
Asphodel.—Mourning. "Even in death our love is not broken."
Aster.—Afterthoughts. "I regret my impetuousness. Do not take me too seriously."
Azalea.—Moderation. "Be more moderate in your actions."

B

Balm.—Fun. "I did not really mean what I said."

Balsam.—Impatience. "I can hardly live till I see you again."

Barberry.—Hot temper. "You are far too hasty in your judgments."

Basil.—Animosity. "I dislike you."

Bee-orchis.—Misunderstanding. "You have misinterpreted my actions."

Begonia. Warning. "We are being watched."

Bell-flower.—Morning. "Meet me to-morrow morning."

Bindweed, Greater.—Persistence. "I cannot accept your answer."

Bindweed, Lesser.—Humility. "I abase myself and ask your forgiveness."

Bird's-foot Trefoil.—Retribution. "Your fickleness will bring its own punishment."

Bittersweet.—Truth. "My words are sincere."

Blackthorn.—Obstacles. "There are difficulties in the way."

Bluebell.—Constancy. "I am faithful."

Bluebottle.—Delicacy. "I worship you from afar, being too timid to approach."

Borage.—Brusqueness. "Your attentions are unwelcome."

Bracken.—Enchantment. "You fascinate me."

Bramble.—Remorse. "I was too hasty. Please forgive me."

Briar, Sweet.—See *Eglantine.*

Broom.—Devotion. "I am ever yours."

Buckbean.—Repose. "May sweet sleep attend you."

Bugloss.—Mendacity. "You are false."

Bulrush.—Rashness. "Pray be more discreet."

Burdock.—Persistence. "I refuse to be discouraged."

Buttercup.—Radiance. "What golden beauty is yours!"

C

Calceolaria.—Money. "Let me assist you."

Camellia.—Loveliness. "How radiantly lovely you are!"

Camomile.—Fortitude. "I admire your courage in adversity. Hope on."

Campion, Meadow.—Poverty. "Though poor and lowly, I dare to admire you."

Campion, Red.—Encouragement. "I should like to make your acquaintance."

Campion, White.—Evening. "Meet me at dusk."

Candytuft.—Diffidence. "You may speak; but do not presume, for my heart is still whole."

Canterbury Bell, Blue.—Faithfulness. "Be not misled; I love you."

Canterbury Bell, White.—Acknowledgment. "I received your gift, and treasure it dearly."

Cape Jasmine.—See *Jasmine, Cape.*

Carnation, Pink.—Encouragement. "Thank you for your charming token."

Carnation, Red.—Passionate love. "I must see you soon."

Carnation, White.—Pure affection. "Chaste love I offer."

Celandine, Lesser.—Reawakening. "Let this harbinger of Spring tell you of my love."

Centaurea.—See *Bluebottle.*

Cherry Blossom.—Increase. "To the ripening of our friendship!"

Chrysanthemum, Bronze.—Friendship. "Though I value your friendship, I cannot love you."

Chrysanthemum, Red.—Reciprocated love. "I love you."

Chrysanthemum, Yellow.—Discouragement. "My heart is given to another."

Chrysanthemum, White.—Truth. "I believe in you."

Cineraria.—Delight. "Your company is delightful."

Cinquefoil.—Sisterly affection. "I regard you as a brother."

Cistus.—Favour. "You are acclaimed the Queen of Beauty."

Clarkia.—Pleasure. "Your company and converse delight me."

Cleavers.—Tenacity. "I am determined to win your love."

Clematis.—Intellectuality. "I pay tribute to your brilliance and cleverness."

Clover, Pink.—Injured dignity. "Do not trifle with me."

Clover, Red.—Petition. "Will you be faithful to me though oceans part us?"

Clover, White.—Promise. "I will be true to you."

Cockscomb.—Foppery. "Your attentions are unwelcome."

Colchicum.—Middle-age. "Youth should mate with youth."

Columbine, Purple.—Resolve. "I shall never give you up."

Columbine, White.—Folly. "It is mere foolishness to press your attentions."

Convolvulus.—See *Bindweed.*

Coreopsis.—Love at first sight. "You have conquered me."

Coriander.—Hidden worth. "Do not judge too much by appearances."

Corn-cockle.—Gentility. "Though appearances may not suggest it, I am of gentle birth."

Cornflower.—Delicacy. "Be not over-impetuous; my heart cannot be stormed."

Cowslip.—Winsome beauty. "You are as winsome as the flowers of Spring."

Crocus, Autumn.—See *Colchicum.*

Crocus, Spring.—Joy of youth. "My heart beats with yours."

Crowfoot.—See *Aconite.*

Currant, Flowering.—Presumption. "We have nothing in common."

Cyclamen.—Indifference. "Your protestations leave me unmoved."

Cytisus.—See *Broom.*

D

Daffodil.—Refusal. "I do not return your affections."

Dahlia, Red.—Rebuff. "You have mistaken my feelings."

Dahlia, White.—Dismissal. "Do not approach me."

Dahlia, Yellow.—Distaste. "Your attentions are distasteful."

Daisy, Field.—Temporization. "I will give you an answer in a few days."

Daisy, Michaelmas.—Farewell. "Do not write or speak to me; I can never love you."

Daisy, Moon.—Autumn love. "Choose a lover of your own age; youth and middle-age may not mate."

Daisy, Ox-eye.—Hope. "I might learn to love you."

Dandelion.—Absurdity. "Your pretentions are ridiculous."

Deadly Nightshade.—Deception. "I believe you to be false."

Dead-nettle, Red.—Coolness. "You have offended me."

Dead-nettle, White.—Coldness. "I do not care for you."

Dog-rose.—Maidenly beauty. "You are as fair and as innocent as this flower."

Dog-violet.—Lad's love. "You are my first sweetheart."

E

Eglantine.—Poetry and fragrance. "These leaves in their sweet fragrance remind me of yourself."

Enchanter's Nightshade.—Double dealing. "Do not play fast and loose with me."

Eschscholtzia.—Petition. "Grant my prayer."

Evening Primrose.—Mute devotion. "Humbly, I adore you."

Everlasting Flower.—Death of hope. "At your wish I go away, to forget you never."

F

Fern, Maidenhair.—Virginity. "I am heart-whole; you have a chance to win me."

Feverfew.—Protection. "Let me shield you."

Flax, Blue.—Gratitude. "You are very kind."

Flax, Red.—Fervour. "I deeply appreciate your kindness." '

Fly-orchis.—Deceit. "You are not true either to yourself or to me."

Fool's Parsley.—Folly. "Do not be so silly; we can be friends."

Forget-me-not.—Remembrance. "Think of me during my absence."

Foxglove.—Shallowness. "You are not really in love."

Fraxinella.—Ardour. "My heart is afire with love."

Fritillary.—Doubt. "Can I trust you?"

Fuchsia.—Warning. "Beware; your lover is false."

Fumitory.—Anger. "I shall never waste another thought on you."

G

Gardenia.—Sweetness. "Like unto this virgin flower are you."

Geranium, Pink.—Doubt. "Explain your actions."

Geranium, Scarlet.—Duplicity. "I do not trust you."

Geranium, White.—Indecision. "I have not made up my mind."

Geranium, Wild.—See *Herb Robert.*

Gilliflower.—Affection. "You are very dear to me."

Gladiolus.—Pain. "Your words have wounded me."

Globe-flower.—Welcome. "You will be welcome."

Golden Rod.—Indecision. "My mind is not made up."

Good King Henry.—Goodness. "You are very good to me."

Goose-grass.—See *Cleavers.*

Guelder Rose.—Autumn love. "He who weds me must be a man in his first youth, not his second childhood."

H

Harebell.—Resignation. "I bow to your will, but still hope on."

Hart's-tongue Fern.—Gossip. "Set a curb on your idle tongue."

Hawthorn.—Hope. "Despite your answer, I shall strive to win your love."

Heartsease.—See *Pansy.*

Heliotrope.—Devotion. "You are my sun."

Hellebore.—Lying tongues. "Do not believe any ill tales of me. I can explain everything."

Hemlock.—Scandal. "I have been maligned and unjustly accused."

Hepatica.—Confidence. "I trust you."

Herb Paris.—Betrothal. "Take this flower as a pledge."

Herb Peter.—See *Cowslip.*

Herb Robert.—Steadfast devotion. "I am your slave."

Hollyhock.—Ambition. "With you as my wife I could achieve great things."

Honesty.—Frankness. "I have told you all."

Honeysuckle.—Plighted troth. "This is a token of my love."

Hyacinth, Blue.—Devotion. "I will give my life to your service."

Hyacinth, White.—Admiration. "I admire you."

Hydrangea.—Changeableness. "Why are you so fickle?"

I

Iris, Purple.—Ardour. "You have set my heart a-glow."

Ivy.—Bonds. "I desire you for my bride."

J

Jasmine.—Elegance. "How dainty and elegant you are!"

Jasmine, Cape.—Spring. "Better times are in store for us."

Jonquil.—Appeal. "Deign to answer my petition; may I hope for your love?"

L

Laburnum.—Neglect. "Why have you forsaken me?"

Larkspur.—Trifling. "Why trifle with my emotions. Give me a definite answer."

Lavender.—Negation. "I like you very much, but this, I am sure, is not love."

Lilac, Purple.—First love. "You are my first love."

Lilac, White.—Innocence. "A tribute to your beauty and spirituality."

Lily, Tiger.—Passion. "My love knows no bounds."

Lily, White.—Purity. "I kiss the hem of your garment."

Lily-of-the-valley.—Maidenly modesty. "Friendship is sweet; talk to me not of love."

Linum.—See *Flax.*

Liverwort.—See *Hepatica.*

Lobelia, Blue.—Dislike. "Like you I do not; love you I could not."

Lobelia, White.—Rebuff. "Your attentions are entirely misdirected."

London Pride.—Flirtation. "Forgive me if I caused you heartache; you can be nothing to me."

Loosestrife, Purple.—Forgiveness. "Take this flower as a peace-offering."

Loosestrife, Yellow.—Peace. "I am sorry; let us forget our quarrel."

Lords and Ladies.—See *Arum, Wild.*

Love-in-a-mist.—Uncertainty. "Your message is ambiguous; what do you mean?"

Love-in-idleness.—See *Pansy.*

Love-lies-bleeding.—Broken heart. "Since you refuse me, life is empty."

Lupin.—Over-boldness. "Who goes softly goes far."

M

Madder.—Calumny. "What you have heard is a vile falsehood."
Magnolia.—Fortitude. "Be not discouraged; better days are coming."
Maidenhair Fern.—See *Fern, Maidenhair.*
Marigold, African.—Boorishness. "Refinement appeals to me."
Marigold, French.—Jealousy. "You are unreasonably jealous."
Marjoram. –Maidenly modesty. "Your ardour brings blushes to my cheeks."
Marguerite.—See *Daisy, Ox-eye.*
May.—See *Hawthorn.*
Meadow-saffron.—See *Colchicum.*
Meadow-sweet.—Uselessness. "I look for a lover who is something more than merely decorative."
Michaelmas Daisy.—See *Daisy, Michaelmas.*
Mignonette.—Dull virtues. "A worthy gem, perhaps; but in an unattractive setting."
Mimosa.—Sensitiveness. "You are too brusque."
Mint.—Homeliness. "Look for a wife of your own age and taste."
Mistletoe.—Kisses. "I send you a thousand kisses."
Mock Orange.—Cancelled wedding. "Your disillusioned bride-to-be has changed her mind but not her degree."
Moneywort.—Fidelity. "Ever faithful."
Monkey Musk.—Coxcomb. "I cannot tolerate a fop."
Monkshood.—See *Aconite.*
Moon Daisy.—See *Daisy, Moon.*
Mullein.—Friendship. "Let us be friends."
Musk.—Over-adornment. "Why not let your natural charm and beauty tell its own story?"
Myrtle.—Fragrance. "Be my sweetheart."

N

Narcissus.—Self-love. "You love no one better than yourself."
Nasturtium.—Artifice. "Beauty unadorned I seek."
Nemophila.—Prosperity. "Congratulations on your success."
Nettle.—See *Dead-nettle.*
Nightshade, Deadly.—See *Deadly Nightshade.*
Nightshade, Enchanter's.—See *Enchanter's Nightshade.*
Nightshade, Woody. See *Bittersweet.*

O

Oak Leaves.—Courage. "Do not despair; love will find a way."
Old Man's Beard.—See *Traveller's Joy.*
Oleander.—Warning. "A false friend has betrayed our secret."
Orange Blossom.—Purity. [*It is unlucky to use these flowers except at a wedding.*]
Orchid.—Luxury. "I will make life sweet for you."
Ox-eye Daisy.—See *Daisy, Ox-eye.*

P

Pansy, Purple.—Souvenirs. "The thoughts of happy days spent together are my greatest treasure."

Pansy ,White.—Thoughts of love. "You are ever in my thoughts."

Pansy, Yellow.—Remembrance. "Though you are absent, I never cease to think of you."

Pasque-flower.—Denial. "I have put aside worldly thoughts and shall never marry."

Passion-flower.—Consecration. "Others have a prior claim upon me."

Pea.—See *Sweet-pea.*

Pelargonium.—Acquaintance. "If you promise not to talk of love I will be your friend."

Peony.—Contrition. "I beg forgiveness for my brusqueness."

Periwinkle.—First love. "My heart was whole until I saw you."

Petunia.—Proximity. "I like you near me."

Phlox, Pink.—Friendship. "I think we might be friends."

Phlox, White.—Interest. "Tell me something about yourself."

Pimpernel.—Meeting. "When and where can we meet?"

Pink, Clove.—Fragrance. "How lovely you are."

Poppy, Red.—Moderation. "My heart cannot be stormed; you must lay siege to it and be patient."

Poppy, White.—Temporization. "I have not made up my mind."

Potentilla.—See *Cinquefoil.*

Primrose.—Dawning-love. "I might learn to love you."

R

Ragged Robin.—See *Campion, Meadow.*

Rest-harrow.—Hindrance. "There are obstacles in our path.

Rocket.—Rivalry. "You have a rival."

Rock-rose.—See *Cistus.*

Rose, Christmas.—Anxiety. "Put an end to my suspense, for pity's sake."

Rose, Dog.—See *Dog-rose.*

Rose, Guelder.—See *Guelder Rose.*

Rose, Moss.—Shy love. "Let me look at you from afar."

Rose, Red.—Love. "I love you."

Rose, White.—Refusal. "I love you not."

Rose, Yellow.—Misplaced affection. "I love another."

Rosemary.—Remembrance. "Never will your memory fade."

S

Salvia, Red.—Passion. "Passionate love is often short-lived."

Saxifrage.—Humility. "Only smile at me and my reward will be great."

Scabious.—Lucklessness. "You are mistaken; I do not care for you."

Snapdragon.—Refusal. "You are nothing to me."

Snowdrop.—Renewed addresses. "I make another bid for your love."

Solomon's Seal.—Simplicity. "Neither rich nor fortunate, I yet dare to love you."

Sunflower.—Ostentation. "Things that glitter do not impress me."

Sweetbriar.—See *Eglantine.*

Sweet-gale.—Encouragement. "I like you a little."
Sweet-pea.—Tenderness. "Your memory is very sweet."
Sweet-sultan.—Happiness. "This is to wish you happiness."
Sweet-william.—Coquetry. "I was only teasing you."
Syringa.—See *Mock Orange.*

T

Tansy.—Rejected addresses. "I am not interested in you."
Thrift.—Interest. "Tell me more about yourself."
Thyme.—Domestic virtue. "I need a wife as capable as you."
Toad-flax.—Reluctant lips. "Be more gentle in your wooing."
Traveller's Joy.—Middle-aged love. "Though not a young lover, my love is sincere."
Trumpet-flower.—Flame of fire. "My heart burns for you."
Tuberose.—Wounding. "I have fluttered near the flame and have singed my wings."
Tulip.—Avowal. "By this token I declare my passion."

V

Valerian.—Merit in disguise. "Conscious of my lowliness, I aspire none the less to wed you."
Verbena.—Enthralment. "You have cast a spell over me."
Veronica.—True love. "Nothing shall part us."
Violet.—Modesty. "Pure and sweet art thou."
Violet, Dog.—See *Dog-violet.*

W

Wake-robin.—See *Arum.*
Wallflower.—Constancy. "Through sunshine and storm I am true to you."
Wind-flower.—See *Anemone.*
Wormwood.—Parting. "The best of friends must part."

THE LOVER'S VOCABULARY OF FLORIGRAPHY

Absurdity.—Dandelion.
Acknowledgment.—White Canterbury Bell,
Acquaintance.—Pelargonium.
Admiration.—White Hyacinth.
Affection.—Gilliflower.
Afterthoughts.—Aster.
Ambition.—Hollylock.
Anger.—Fumitory.

Animosity.—Basil.
Anxiety.—Christmas Rose.
Appeal.—Jonquil.
Ardour.—Arum, Fraxinella, Purple Iris.
Artifice.—Nasturtium.
Autumn Love.—Moon Daisy, Guelder Rose.
Avowal.—Tulip.

Beauty.—Apple Blossom.
Betrothal.—Herb Paris.
Bonds.—Ivy.
Boorishness.—African Marigold.
Broken Heart.—Love-lies-bleeding.
Brusqueness.—Borage.

Calumny.—Madder.
Cancelled Wedding.—Mock Orange.
Changeableness.—Hydrangea.
Coldness.—White Dead-nettle.
Confidence.—Hepatica.
Consecration.—Passion Flower.
Constancy.—Hyacinth, Wallflower.
Contrition.—Peony.
Coolness.—Red Dead-nettle.
Coquetry.—Sweet-william.
Courage.—Oak Leaves.
Coxcomb.—Monkey Musk.

Dawning Love.—Primrose.
Death of Hope.—Everlasting Flower.
Deception.—Deadly Nightshade, Fly-orchis.
Delicacy.—Bluebottle.
Delight.—Cineraria.
Denial.—Pasque Flower.
Devotion. — Broom, Heliotrope, Herb Robert, Blue Hyacinth.
Diffidence.—Candytuft.
Discouragement. — Yellow Chrysanthemum.
Dislike.—Blue Lobelia.
Dismissal.—White Dahlia.
Distaste.—Yellow Dahlia.
Domestic Virtues.—Thyme.
Doubt.—Fritillary, Pink Geranium.
Dull Virtues.—Mignonette.
Duplicity.—Enchanter's Nightshade, Scarlet Geranium.

Elegance.—Jasmine.
Enchantment.—Bracken.
Encouragement. — Red Campion, Pink Carnation, Sweet-gale.
Enthralment.—Verbena.
Evening.—White Campion.

Faithfulness. — Blue Canterbury Bell, Moneywort.
Farewell.—Michaelmas Daisy.
Favour.—Cistus.
Fervour.—Red Flax.
First Love.—Purple Lilac, Periwinkle.
Flame of Fire.—Trumpet-flower.
Flirtation.—London Pride.
Folly.—White Columbine, Fool's Parsley.
Foppery.—Cockscomb.
Forsakenness.—Anemone.
Fortitude.—Camomile, Magnolia.
Fragrance. — Eglantine, Clove Pink, Myrtle.
Frankness.—Honesty.
Friendship. — Bronze Chrysanthemum, Mullein, Pink Phlox.
Fun.—Balm.

Gentility.—Corncockle.
Goodness.—Good King Henry.
Gossip.—Hart's-tongue Fern.
Gratitude.—Agrimony, Blue Flax.

Happiness.—Sweet-sultan.
Hidden Worth.—Coriander.
Hindrance.—Rest Harrow.
Homeliness.—Mint.
Hope.—Almond Blossom, Ox-eye Daisy, Hawthorn.
Hot Temper.—Barberry.
Humility.—Bindweed, Saxifrage.

Impatience.—Balsam.
Increase.—Cherry Blossom.
Indecision. — White Geranium, Go'den. Rod.
Indifference.—Cyclamen.
Injured Dignity.—Pink Clover.
Innocence.—White Lilac.
Inspiration.—Angelica.
Intellectuality.—Clematis.
Interest.—White Phlox, Thrift.

Jealousy.—French Marigold.
Joy.—Crocus.

Kindness.—Mallow.
Kisses.—Mistletoe.

Lad's Love.—Dog-violet.
Love.—Arbutus, Red Carnation, Chrysanthemum, Coreopsis, Purple Lilac, Periwinkle, Primrose, Red Rose, Veronica.
Loveliness.—Camellia.
Lucklessness.—Scabious.
Luxury.—Orchid.
Lying Tongues.—Hellebore.

Maidenly Beauty.—Dog-rose, Marjoram.
Meeting.—Pimpernel.
Mendacity.—Bugloss.
Merit.—Valerian.
Middle-age.—Colchicum, Traveller's Joy.
Misanthropy.—Aconite.
Misplaced Affections.—Yellow Rose.
Misunderstanding.—Bee-orchis.
Moderation.—Azalea, Red Poppy.
Modesty.—Lily of the Valley, Violet.
Money.—Calceolaria.
Morning.—Bell-flower.
Mourning.—Asphodel.
Mute Devotion.—Evening Primrose.

Negation.—Lavender.
Neglect.—Laburnum.

Obstacles.—Blackthorn.
Ostentation.—Sunflower.
Over-adornment.—Musk.
Over-boldness.—Lupin.

Pain.—Gladiolus.
Parting.—Wormwood.
Passion.—Red Salvia, Tiger Lily.
Peace.—Yellow Loosestrife.
Persistence.—Bindweed, Burdock.
Petition. — Red Clover, Eschscholtzia, Marshmallow.
Pleasure.—Clarkia.

Plighted Troth.—Honeysuckle.
Poetry.—Eglantine.
Poverty.—Meadow Campion.
Presumption.—Flowering Currant.
Promise.—White Clover.
Prosperity.—Nemophila.
Protection.—Feverfew.
Proximity.—Petunia.
Pure Affection.—White Carnation.
Purity.—White Lily, Orange Blossom.

Radiance.—Buttercup.
Rashness.—Bulrush.
Reawakening.—Celandine.
Rebuff.—Red Dahlia, White Lobelia.
Refusal.—Daffodil. White Rose, Snapdragon.
Rejected Addresses.—Tansy.
Reluctant Lips.—Toad-flax.
Remembrance. — Forget-me-not. Yellow Pansy, Rosemary.
Remorse.—Bramble.
Renewed Addresses.—Snowdrop.
Repose.—Buckbean.
Resignation.—Harebell.
Resolve.—Purple Columbine.
Retribution.—Bird's-foot Trefoil.
Rivalry.—Rocket

Scandal.—Hemlock.
Self-love.—Narcissus.
Sensitiveness.—Mimosa.
Shallowness.—Foxglove.
Shy Love.—Moss Rose.
Simplicity.—Solomon's Seal.
Sisterly Affection.—Cinquefoil.
Souvenirs.—Purple Pansy.
Spring.—Cape Jasmine.
Sweetness.—Gardenia.

Temporization. — Field Daisy, White Poppy.
Tenacity.—Cleavers.
Tenderness.—Sweet-pea.
Thoughts of Love.—White Pansy.
Trifling.—Larkspur.
True Love.—Veronica.
Truth.—Bittersweet, White Chrysanthemum.

Uncertainty.—Love-in-a-mist.
Uselessness.—Meadow-sweet.

Warning.—Fuchsia, Oleander.
Winsome Beauty.—Cowslip.
Wounds.—Tuberose.

Virginity.—Maidenhair Fern.
Virtue.—Alyssum.

Youth.—Spring Crocus.

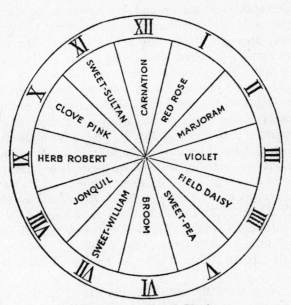

The Lover's Floral Clock

EXAMPLES OF FLORAL MESSAGES

The following are examples of floral messages, but by arrangement between the sender and the receiver, other flowers may be used in place of those given here.

"Meet me": Ivy.
"To-night": White Campion.
"To-day": Pimpernel.
"To-morrow": Buttercup.
"I will meet you": Ivy and White Clover.

"I cannot meet you": Ivy and Lavender.
"Make another appointment": Ivy and Red Clover.
"Meet me to-night at seven o'clock!" Ivy, White Campion, Sweet-william.

COLOURS AND THEIR SIGNIFICANCE

THE perception of colour and the response to its vibrations vary enormously in different persons. People may go almost entirely through life lacking a true appreciation of Nature's beauties, and only the merest chance may awaken them to the fact that their colour sense is deficient.

There are seven colours in the solar spectrum—violet, indigo, blue, green, yellow, orange and red; but some people can distinguish only six, others four, many as few as two. Indigo, or dark blue, in the spectrum is distinguished only by people with an acute colour perception, and most of us have hexachromic, or six-colour, vision. It is important to remember that colour depends on vibration. The only difference between light of different colours is in its wave length, or the rate at which it vibrates. Violet vibrations are the fastest, and red the slowest, but there are other rays beyond these—ultra-violet and infra-red—which, though they accompany light rays, are themselves invisible. The reason that a yellow flower, for instance, "looks" yellow to us is that it absorbs light of all vibrations except the yellow.

Some idea of the influence of the planets upon us can be gained from consideration of the fact that each of these heavenly bodies gives out light of a characteristic vibration. If we wear appropriate colours, and decorate our dwellings with them, we can receive to best advantage the rays proceeding from our birth planet. More about planetary influence is to be found in other sections of this book; here we merely trace the causality. The proper colours for the different zodiacal signs are as follows:—

SIGN	COLOUR	SIGN	COLOUR
Aries	White	Libra	Violet
Taurus	Yellow	Scorpio	Russet brown
Gemini	Red	Sagittarius	Orange
Cancer	Emerald green	Capricorn	Brown
Leo	Golden yellow	Aquarius	Dark blue
Virgo	Pale blue	Pisces	White

For instance, a person born under Gemini would have red as a lucky colour; one whose birthday came under Virgo would have pale blue as the colour of choice. The colours for people born under the various planets are the following:—

PLANET	COLOUR	PLANET	COLOUR
Sun	Orange, Yellow	Mercury	Light green
Moon	White	Venus	Blue
Mars	Bright red	Jupiter	Purple
		Saturn	Black, Dark blue

The following are the colours of the days:—

Sunday—Orange; *Monday*—White; *Tuesday*—Red; *Wednesday*—Green; *Thursday*—Purple; *Friday*—Blue; *Saturday*—Dark blue.

COLOUR IN DRESS

Why does one woman delight to dress herself in red, while another prefers less brilliant hues? Apart from the consideration of the suitability of the colour to the complexion, the colours of preference seem to be chosen for no apparent reason, and one might say with some truth that people are *born* with a liking for red, or mauve, or for quieter colours such as greys and blues. It may be connected with their degree of colour perception, as we have hinted above, and this may be due to the astrological circumstances of their nativity. Whatever the cause, it is established that we all have pronounced likes and dislikes in colour.

One sometimes hears it asked of someone dressed in glaringly bad taste, "Doesn't she *know* what a fright she looks?" Since, in the words of the old Latin tag, "There can be no disputing about matters of taste," it is probable that the lady discussed thinks she looks quite well and fashionably dressed, and thoroughly in harmony with her surroundings.

COLOURS OF MARRIAGE

It is a misfortune for a man or a woman to contract marriage with one whose colour reactions are very different, for such a match is seldom a happy one. The difference of outlook goes far beyond the question of taste in dress, and betokens a fundamental variance of temperament.   Another danger is that of linking up with a person whose nativity colour is one of an antagonistic zodiacal sign.   Thus:—

> *White* should not mate with *Violet*
> *Yellow* should not mate with *Russet brown.*
> *Red* should not mate with *Orange.*
> *Emerald green* should not mate with *Brown.*
> *Golden yellow* should not mate with *Dark blue.*
> *Pale blue* should not mate with *White.*

A person whose nativity colour is found in one column of our zodiacal table should not wear the colour coming opposite in the other column.   That is to say, the second or antagonistic colour should not predominate in any colour scheme, though in small quantity it will do no harm.   When for social reasons the selected colour cannot be worn as an outer garment, it may be used beneath and the same benefit obtained.

The following list gives a useful indication of the colour influence in choosing a partner, and applies just as much to business partnerships as to matrimonial ones:—

> *Violet* should mate with *Red.*
> *Dark blue* should mate with *Orange.*
> *Bright blue* should mate with *Dark green.*
> *Black* should mate with *Yellow.*
> *Purple* should mate with *Sea-green.*
> *Pink* should mate with *Lilac.*

PSYCHOLOGY OF COLOUR

The qualities we attribute to colours are due largely to associations of a religious, traditional or even superstitious nature.   Black is associated with mourning, white with rejoicing; yet white is the negation of colour, and black, as shown in our table, is a colour properly to be worn by those under the influence of the planet Saturn.   There follows a list of the commoner colours together with their attributes: -

> *Black.*—Dignity, solemnity.
> *Blue, bright.*—Friendship, frankness.
> *Blue, dark.*—Truth, sincerity, earnestness.
> *Blue, light.*—Innocence, virtue, steadfastness.
> *Blue, steel.*—Endeavour, ambition, straightforwardness.
> *Green, dark.*—Virility, courage, honesty.
> *Green, light.*—Candour, brilliance, ardour.

Grey.—Modesty, constancy.
Mauve.—Intuition, faith, aspiration.
Orange.—Health, vigour, intelligence.
Pink.—Fervour, modesty, devotion.
Purple.—Power, majesty, fortitude, wisdom.
Red.—Animation, life, success, love.
Violet.—Passion, love, intellectuality.
White.—Innocence, virtue, modesty.
Yellow, golden.—Morbidity, distrust.
Yellow, pale.—High spirits, vivacity, intelligence.

COLOURS FOR ROOMS

A correct choice of colour in the decoration and furnishing of a room may add much to the comfort and well-being of those who use it. For bedrooms, especially, the colouring should be carefully selected. The occupant should choose a light shade of his lucky colour for the predominating hue; but if this is a "cold" colour—for instance, sea-green, pale blue, or grey—a touch of a warmer hue must be introduced into the decoration. If the nativity colour be black, this colour should be used very sparingly against a grey background. If orange or red be the chosen colour, it should be used only for individual features of the decoration, the background being formed of light yellow or pink, respectively.

Part Three

THE SCIENCE OF ASTROLOGY

THE SCIENCE OF ASTROLOGY

ASTROLOGY is the most sublime of all the occult sciences, but at the same time it is one of the most practical, for it divines the human soul itself and indicates the road along which our moral and mental endowments are likely to impel us, thus enabling us to prepare in advance for Life's battles, to avoid the pitfalls that may await us, and to make the utmost of our opportunities.

Astrology is such an ancient science that it is impossible to say with certainty when it was first practised, though it was perhaps in the plains of Chaldea, many thousands of years before Christ, that the earliest astrologers made their observations and formulated their theories. The science was for long cultivated by the priestly caste alone, and its secrets were jealously guarded; but when the ancient civilizations of Egypt, Babylonia and Chaldea fell at length into decay, their sciences—and among them the rules and formulas of astrology—passed to the Greeks and Romans. Among the latter, even with the advent of a sceptical and material age, the most enlightened men, including such thinkers as the philosopher Seneca, continued to believe in the voice of the heavens.

After the classical world had passed away, the Arabs became the chief practitioners of astrology, and to this day it plays an exceedingly important part in the daily life of Mohammedan nations. By means of the Arabs the doctrine of astrology penetrated into mediaeval Europe, which proved a fertile ground for its growth. Kings, emperors, princes of the Church, all had implicit faith in the influence of the stars, and there were few who did not retain their domestic astrologer to advise and forewarn them. Many of the eminent astrologers of those and later times are famous to-day for their achievements in other sciences. They include such celebrated scholars as Regiomontanus, bishop of Ratisbon, who reformed the calendar; Johann Kepler, who discovered the fundamental laws on which the solar system is built; Tycho Brahe, the great Danish astronomer; Jerome Cardan, physician, philosopher and mystic;

Pierre Gassendi, one of the greatest of mathematicians; Philip Melanc-thon, pioneer of the Reformation, and John Flamsteed, the first astronomer royal of England.

Not only was astrology the ardent study of the most learned and powerful minds, but among the masses of the people its authority and guidance were accepted without question, and it was common for a large sum to be paid for the erection of a horoscope, or map of the heavens at the time of birth, which would be consulted at every important period of the owner's life. Two of these ancient maps are reproduced; they are the horoscopes of Henry VIII (page 597) and William Shakespeare (page 605), and to the student of astrology they are documents of absorbing interest, which give un-mistakable indications of the character and fame of the men whose destiny they portray.

But the erecting of a horoscope—though there is no occupation more fascinating or more useful—is apt to prove a long and compli-cated business, and one calling for considerable mathematical ability. Fortunately, however, the basic principles of astrology make it possible for us to assign each person to one of twelve distinct types of humanity, according to the position of the Sun among the signs of the Zodiac at the period of his or her birth. The characteristics imprinted upon the subject at birth accompany him throughout his life, forging his destiny and shaping all his actions, and these vitally important traits can be read in the following pages on merely referring to the zodiacal sign, or signs, corresponding to the period of birth. Provided the birth date is known, the correct zodiacal sign can be found instantly by means of the diagram on page 618.

The marriage prospects and affinities of each zodiacal type will be found particularly valuable; while other important features are the appropriate colours, precious stones, flowers, and so on, which are now regarded as having a powerful effect upon good fortune by attuning the mind to receive harmonious vibrations from the astral force that surrounds us all.

THE "CUSPS" OF THE SIGNS

ONE point should be carefully noted and borne in mind. The Sun enters each sign of the Zodiac on or about the 21st of each month, but it is still influenced to a certain extent by the attributes of the preceding sign, which do not fade away entirely until a week or so has elapsed. For this reason the pure and unmixed attributes of any sign are not manifested until about the 27th of the month. From that date the full force of the sign continues to be exerted until the Sun prepares to enter the next sign, which occurs about the 21st of the next month, and then, mingling with the influence of the new sign, gradually fades away and becomes extinguished in about a week, that is, about the 27th, when the new sign displays its full vigour.

This period—from about the 21st to the 27th of any month—in which the influences of two signs overlap and mingle, is known as the "cusp" of the signs, and persons born at this time partake in a greater, or less, measure of the attributes of *both* signs. In estimating their character and fortune, both signs should be taken into account. For instance, a person who was born on September 25, a few days after the Sun has entered Libra, but with some of Virgo's influence still in force, is ruled by both Virgo and Libra, and the pages devoted to both of these signs should be consulted.

ARIES—THE RAM ♈

March 21–April 21

THE Sun enters the zodiacal sign Aries on approximately March 21 each year, remaining in this sign until about April 21. For the first seven days or so of its occupancy it is still influenced by the gradually declining power of the preceding sign, Pisces; so that persons born between March 21 and 27 are to some extent ruled by Pisces, as well as by Aries.

Aries is known by astrologers as a fiery and positive sign, and is aptly symbolized by the Ram, an animal of great courage and spirit. Aries is ruled by the planet Mars, and those born during this period are notable for their action, energy and initiative. In life's battles they play the part of guides and leaders; they glory in fighting and in surmounting difficulties, and their courage and self-confidence make them pioneers in all kinds of enterprises.

Their aptitude for responsibility and command gains them an ascendancy over others, and they are never so happy or so well employed as when they are supervising or directing a difficult undertaking, and imparting some of their own boundless enthusiasm to their followers and employees. As an example, we will mention Sir John Franklin, the famous Arctic explorer, who was born on April 16, 1786—a man marked out by destiny to be a natural leader of others, and one whose guidance was followed without question to the remotest parts of the earth.

The ambition of persons ruled by Aries knows no bounds, nor does their ability to overcome obstacles. Therefore, provided their interest in their occupation is sustained, they are fated more than all other types to rise to the head of any affairs in which they may be actively concerned. They are, however, impatient and rather capricious, and are apt to lose interest in an undertaking that does not promise to engross all their activities. Moreover, they will not brook the slightest opposition or contradiction; having implicit faith in their own abilities and in the cause which they have espoused —whether it be right or wrong—they will impose their will upon others and override their opinions, and even when proved to be in the wrong they will seldom admit the fact.

Prince Bismarck (born April 1, 1815), the "man of blood and iron," was ruled by Aries, and his autocratic, domineering and fearless character illustrates the truth of what has been stated.

The outstanding defects of Aries subjects are rashness and excessive self-confidence, which often bring about their ruin. Aries people are inclined to outstrip the bounds of discretion in every direction, and they seldom learn restraint from past disasters. By their excessive frankness and boldness of speech they frequently make themselves detested, and by their unwarranted optimism and temerity they bring misfortune upon themselves and others.

Though they are splendid organizers and have the ability to see far ahead, they seldom work according to fixed and well-laid plans; in fact, scheming and subtlety of any kind are foreign to them, and they prefer to be guided by their natural intuition and presence of mind rather than by rules and precedents or a matured course of action.

Aries subjects cannot be led or compelled; but they can easily be deceived or seduced. Having little guile or subtlety in their own make-up, they fail to recognize it in others. Thus they can be influenced by suggestions cunningly made, and are readily deceived by praise and flattery, often of the most gross and obvious kind. Then, inflated by conceit and arrogance, they can be made to view things in a distorted way, and may be impelled to a course of action which, of their accord, they would never have contemplated; whereas any open attempt to control or overrule them would be met with instant, and often violent, opposition. If an Aries subject is convinced that he has been deceived or made to appear a fool, his anger is terrible to behold and the deception is never forgotten, although at other times he is among the first to forgive injuries and slights.

The highest type of person born under Aries is a resolute idealist. He will fight to the bitter end in the cause that he holds dear; he will sacrifice everything for it, and opposition—even persecution—only makes the fire of his conviction burn the brighter.

Idealists of this type were William Booth, the founder of the Salvation Army, and Albert, king of the Belgians; both of them were born under the rule of Aries, and both suffered for convictions which they would not abandon.

Professions and Occupations

Natives of Aries excel in any occupation in which they can organize and take the lead, or in which they can express themselves and give full rein to their abundant intellectual powers. Therefore, they do well as explorers and pioneers, soldiers, leaders of reform and temperance movements, directors and heads of business concerns, political leaders, surgeons, nurses, editors, scientists, inventors and innovators. If they are artistically gifted, they often achieve fame as writers, painters and musicians. Raphael, the great Italian painter, Swinburne, Wordsworth, and Hans Andersen were born under Aries, as also were Johann Sebastian Bach, René Descartes, and William Harvey who discovered the circulation of the blood. All these men were innovators in their several ways, men who refused to be fettered by rules or custom.

Marriage and Friendship

Subjects of Aries are not easy to get on with in married life, especially if their partner refuses to give way in everything, as he or she would be expected to do. Their love of domination makes them domestic martinets, and as parents they are stern disciplinarians.

Moreover, they seem quite at a loss to understand the psychology of the other sex, and their want of tact often causes pain. But they will always rise in arms to defend their spouse and children from the attacks of other people, and they are assiduous in providing for their comfort. Aries folk often suffer acutely through their affections and feelings, though their intense pride impels them to appear unmoved. Women belonging to Aries often gain a distinct advantage, socially and financially, upon their marriage.

The most harmonious partnerships in friendship and marriage for Aries people are formed with those born between July 21 and August 21 and between November 21 and December 21.

Health

Aries rules the head, brain and face, and its subjects are liable to suffer from ailments and accidents affecting these parts, such as headaches, brain fag and brain fever, concussion, apoplexy, disorders of the eyes, nose and skin of the face, as well as cuts, burns, bruises and other head wounds. The stomach and kidneys may also give trouble at times. In other respects, the health is usually good, owing to the strong vital force imparted by Aries and its ruler, Mars.

To Attract Good Vibrations

Those who would obtain the utmost from life should endeavour to attract harmonious astrological vibrations. The native of Aries should wear, and be surrounded with, bright colours, especially bright green, pink and yellow; however, all shades of red are good. White is also fortunate, but should not be worn entirely unrelieved by any other colour.

Stones.—The most fortunate stones for those born in this period are the ruby, bloodstone and diamond. One of these gems should always be worn about the person to ensure good luck. *Lucky Numbers.*—Seven for Aries; nine for Mars. *Lucky Day.*—Tuesday. *Flowers.*—Gorse, wild rose, thistle. *Trees.*—Holly, thorn, chestnut. *Animals.*—Ram, tiger, leopard. *Bird.*—Magpie. *Metal.*—Iron.

TAURUS—THE BULL ♉

April 21–May 21

THE Sun enters the zodiacal sign Taurus about April 21 every year, and remains in this sign until about May 21. For the first seven days or so of this period (until about April 27) the gradually lessening power of Aries continues to exert its influence, and all persons born between April 21 and 27 fall under the rule of Aries as well as under that of Taurus.

Taurus is an earthy sign and is symbolized by the Bull, which represents Nature and fertility. It is ruled by the beautiful and poetic planet Venus, and so it is not surprising that its subjects are usually distinguished by their love of beauty and harmony in every aspect of life, and by their intuition and sympathy with Nature in all her moods. As he accords fittingly with the earthy nature of Taurus, there is much that is elemental in this type—which is not the same thing as being undeveloped. No matter how airy may be their flights of fancy, they never lose contact with the earth and terrestrial matters, and their imaginative and speculative powers are always tempered with sound common sense. This practical outlook is one of the leading traits of Taurus subjects; they are fond of work, and even those of the most refined type are not ashamed to work with their hands. They are particularly fond of gardening and any kind of labour connected with the earth and vegetation, but they are less successful in connexion with animals.

Great pertinacity and fixity of purpose also characterize the sons and daughters of Taurus. They will concentrate all their attention upon a single aim and refuse to be turned aside from their goal. They are usually of a happy and mild disposition and, though acutely sensitive of slights and rebuffs, are slow to anger. When thoroughly roused, however, the whole aspect of Taurians is completely altered, and they give way to furious and ungovernable wrath. Their unyielding determination does not desert them in anger, for they seldom forget an injury, and will fight their enemies unflinchingly to the bitter end. But they will have no part in trickery, deception and underhand dealings, which are quite foreign to their nature, so that all their battles are carried on in the open. As soon as an enemy shows signs of collapse, the Taurian is instantly sorry for him, and in this way frequently makes a fool of himself.

The receptive power of the Taurian mind is enormous; and natives of this sign are more powerfully affected by their associates and environment than are, perhaps, any other type of people. With their natural love of all that is harmonious and beautiful, they are deeply revolted by ugliness, squalor and strife and by coarse companions; and uncongenial surroundings of this kind reduce them to the lowest pitch of misery. On the other hand, they respond instantly to refined and sympathetic surroundings, when they give of their best. They make good and cheerful hosts, and are very successful socially—which is rather surprising, since their nature is usually retiring. Taurians have also a pronounced faculty for imposing their will upon others, which is probably another aspect of their strong intuitive powers.

Robespierre, whose birthday fell within the Taurus period, possessed this power of dominating his associates. It is seen in other types as well, especially in men of unusual intellect who have helped to mould the mind both of their contemporaries and their successors. Foremost among such is Shakespeare (born April 23, 1564), while others of this type include Joseph Addison, Alexander Pope, Machiavelli; Froude, William H. Prescott, Gibbon and Hume, the historians; Thomas Huxley and Edward Jenner, each of whom brought about a revolution in science; Herbert Spencer, the philosopher; and Robert Owen, the social reformer.

Natives of Taurus rarely have difficulty in attracting followers, either in business or for any kind of movement or project, but they should guard against being swayed by other people's advice instead of by their own good sense and intuition. They are often called upon to bear great responsibilities, which they do willingly and well, although not without becoming unduly worried.

Professions and Occupations

Subjects of this earthy sign are suited to any occupation in which their imagination can have full scope. Being naturally musical and artistic, they make good composers, singers and musicians, as well as poets, novelists and painters. Apart from Shakespeare and others already mentioned, Robert Browning, Dante Gabriel Rossetti, Anthony Trollope, Sir James Barrie, Alphonse Daudet, J. M. W. Turner, J. L. Gérôme, Albrecht Dürer, Joseph Haydn and Sir Arthur Sullivan were all born under the rule of Taurus.

The lower types make good gardeners and agriculturists, builders and decorators, and are successful in almost any occupation that is practical and creative. Taurus subjects also excel in ministering

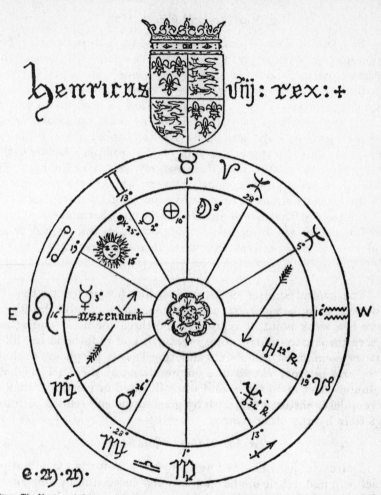

From *The Magic and Science of Jewels and Stones*, by Isidore Kozminsky (Putnam and Sons Ltd).

Horoscope of Henry VIII

to the wants of others and making them comfortable, and hence they make splendid physicians, nurses, matrons, housekeepers and cooks. An outstanding example is Florence Nightingale, "the Lady with the Lamp," who was born on May 12, 1820. Taurians are also congenially employed as house and estate agents, florists, soldiers and government officials.

Marriage and Friendship

Subjects of Taurus have an intense love nature, which refuses to be satisfied with anything less than the entire affection of their marriage partner and friends. Being guided almost entirely by impulse, they frequently make disastrous mistakes in choosing husband or wife. They demand perfection in their mate and are critical and exacting, as well as inclined to be unreasonably and violently jealous, but there is no malice behind their outbursts, which are only the natural result of the interplay between their strong physical nature and their acutely sensitive feelings. This makes them ardent and fascinating lovers, who know how to play at will upon the emotions of their beloved as upon an instrument.

Subjects of Taurus will find that their most harmonious affinities and friendships are formed with those born between August 21 and September 21 and between December 21 and January 21.

Health

The typical subject of Taurus is, like his prototype the bull, endowed with a vigorous constitution and splendid health. If there is a weak point, it is usually the throat or neck, and attacks of sore throat, tonsillitis, quinsy, catarrh and diphtheria are likely. But the commonest complaints afflicting Taurus people are probably those arising from excess and indiscretions of diet. Music has a profound effect upon them, and when ill, tired or run down they are more quickly restored to health by good music and refined surroundings than by any other remedy.

To Attract Good Vibrations

Taurus subjects can attune themselves to fortunate vibrations, which will make their life harmonious and successful, by surrounding themselves with all shades of blue and incorporating it in their clothes. Indigo, too, will be found restful and soothing, but red should be avoided, except, perhaps, the softest shades of rose. All colours should be subdued, for Taurians have little need of stimulants.

Stones.—The lucky stones for Taurus are sapphire, emerald, turquoise, lapis lazuli and moss agate. *Lucky Number.*—Six for Taurus, and for Venus also. *Lucky Day.*—Friday. *Flowers.*—Lily of the valley, violet, rose, myrtle. *Trees.* —Almond, apple, walnut, ash, sycamore. *Animal.*—Bull. *Bird.*—Dove. *Metal.* —Copper.

GEMINI—THE TWINS ♊

May 21–June 21

THE Sun passes into the zodiacal sign of Gemini on approximately May 21, but this sign does not begin to exert its full and unalloyed power until about May 27, since for a week or so its influence is blended with that of the preceding sign, Taurus. Therefore, persons born between May 21 and 27 are also ruled in part by Taurus. Gemini continues in full force until about June 21.

In ancient days Gemini was symbolized by twin children— the Castor and Pollux of Roman mythology. Its astrological symbol consists of two columns united at the top and bottom, an apt illustration of the marked duality of mind and character displayed by those born under this sign. Gemini is known astrologically as an airy sign, and this again accords with the character of its subjects —subtle, intellectual, and versatile, but restless, undependable and diffuse.

The moral and intellectual make-up of a subject of Gemini is like a house divided against itself. This lack of unity is observable in all his actions, and often leads him into the most perplexing situations. Gemini is ruled by the restless planet Mercury, and a Gemini subject is truly "mercurial" in everything, for he seems to be governed alternately by the attraction of two widely different poles. At one time he is full of ardour, energy and enthusiasm, and his wit fairly sparkles; but before long a sudden change comes over him without any apparent cause, and he appears cold, lethargic and unresponsive. He is usually intelligent to a remarkable degree; his intellect penetrates rapidly to the root of any matter and strips it of difficulties, and thus he is extraordinarily apt at acquiring knowledge. But the interest soon wears off, and his attention wanders to something fresh and untried; and for this reason his knowledge, though covering a wide range of subjects, is seldom more than superficial.

In his relations with friends he is most undependable—at one moment affable and effusive, at another, so cold and unapproachable that his perplexed acquaintances are driven to conclude that unwittingly and unintentionally they must have offended him deeply. But when next they meet him he is cordiality itself. However, when the mood suits them, the subjects of Gemini are remarkably good company, being exceptionally witty, merry, generous and—at least, to all appearances—sympathetic and considerate. Actually, however, this itself is only a passing whim or caprice, and they are only kind-hearted when it suits their mood of the moment.

Their nature being what it is, they crave change of scene and activity more than anything, and so are driven on by an insatiable thirst for travel and novelty. They are happy and successful travellers, being able to adapt themselves to any kind of circumstances and environment, though not for long will they make their home in one place, if they can avoid it. The famous African explorer, Sir H. M. Stanley, who was ruled by Gemini, is an outstanding example of this genius for travel.

Gemini people have very fair and unbiased critical faculties. They are able to look dispassionately at both sides of a question, and put themselves in the place of the other person. Their intentions are generally disinterested and honest, but are frequently spoiled by their lack of dependability.

They are often brilliantly clever, ingenious and inventive, and, given some fixity of purpose, there is no intellectual height to which they cannot climb, no depth of thought which they cannot sound. Among the striking instances of this superior Gemini type are Blaise Pascal, the great mathematician and philosopher, George Stephenson, of locomotive fame, Adam Smith, the economist, and William Pitt, who took the helm of State at the early age of twenty-four.

Gemini subjects are usually refined, possessing artistic tastes of a high order, and are gifted with wonderful tact. Their keen penetration extends to their fellow beings, and they are excellent judges of character and ability. Since they readily divine the character and intentions of an opponent, and as a result are able to use his own weapons against him, they nearly always triumph in an argument or a battle of wits.

Their inventiveness and love of change causes them for ever to be devising ingenious schemes or launching money-making projects, but these are often abandoned before they have a chance of coming to fruition. The lower types make clever crooks and sharpers, who usually succeed in evading detection.

Professions and Occupations

Those born under Gemini are most profitably engaged in work calling for mental gifts above the ordinary, as well as tact, subtlety, good judgment, and quickness of wit. They make excellent writers, journalists, teachers, secretaries, lawyers, barristers, magistrates, and diplomats, and are often successful as clerks, financiers, stock-brokers, and surveyors. They are usually very happy in any occupation involving travelling and constant change of scene and interest. People of the Gemini type often display literary ability of a high order, among the many outstanding examples being Lord Lytton, Emerson, Thomas Moore, Pushkin, Walt Whitman, Thomas Hardy, Sir Edwin Arnold and Charles Kingsley.

Marriage and Friendship

The uncertainty of the Gemini temperament does not favour lasting friendship, and is the cause of much friction in married life. Moreover, those ruled by this sign are given to fickleness in their affections; they may lead a double life or commit bigamy. They are little swayed by passion, and the only way to retain their fidelity is constantly to meet their varying moods in a fresh and unexpected manner. All forms of monotony are fatal to success when dealing with Gemini people. Those who can live with them most harmoniously are born between January 21 and February 21 and between September 21 and October 21.

Health

Gemini rules the shoulders, arms, hands and lungs, and its subjects may suffer from disorders and accidents to these parts. But their most common ailments are those affecting the nervous system (governed by Mercury, the ruler of Gemini). They are liable to nervous debility, nervous exhaustion, neuritis, mental strain and intense irritability, and their chief remedy lies in avoiding worry as much as possible.

To Attract Good Vibrations

The colours most in harmony with Gemini are white, silver, yellow and light green. These should be worn on the person, and used freely in light furnishings and decorations.

Stones.—The most suitable stones for this period are agate, chrysoprase, diamond and jade, but all gems that sparkle brilliantly are in harmony with Gemini. *Lucky Number.*—Five. *Lucky Day.*—Wednesday. *Flower.*—Snapdragon. *Trees.*—Elder, filbert. *Animals.*—Dog, squirrel. *Birds.*—Parrot, linnet. *Metal.*—Quicksilver.

CANCER—THE CRAB ♋

June 21–July 21

THE Sun enters the zodiacal sign Cancer about June 21 each year, remaining therein until July 21. However, the power of Cancer is not fully exerted until about June 27, and people born between June 21 and 27 are also controlled to some extent by the gradually declining influence of Gemini, which should be taken into account when their character and fortune are being estimated.

The symbol of Cancer is the Crab, a creature whose habits typify the timid, hesitant yet tenacious disposition of those born under this sign. Cancer is known by astrologers as a watery sign, and it is ruled by the negative and watery Moon. Therefore, it is not surprising that this negative quality is the chief characteristic of those born under Cancer; it can be observed in all their actions and habits of life, making them shy, timid and retiring, constantly anxious over trifles, intensely sensitive, hesitant, romantic, dreamy, but undemonstrative; their tenacity and powers of endurance are, however, little short of amazing. Having once committed themselves —usually after much hesitation—to a definite course of action, they will pursue it resolutely until they have either achieved their goal or perished by the wayside. Of this type were Garibaldi, Mazzini, John Huss, and Calvin, all subjects of Cancer, and all notable for their fixity of purpose.

Few people are as sensitive as those born under Cancer. The least censure, criticism or lack of understanding is taken deeply to heart, but they respond with gratitude to appreciation and encouragement. However, they will not tolerate interference in their affairs or in any project which they have undertaken, preferring to shoulder all the labour and responsibility rather than allow any meddling on the part of others. In uncongenial surroundings, or when tried by much opposition or lack of success, they become morbid and introspective; but they shrink to the last from opening their hearts to others, and jealously keep their worries and grief to themselves.

People of the Cancer type are often dominated by a fear of the future and old age. This may lead them to hoard money, and to become selfish and niggardly. However, they rarely want for money in actual fact, although their business affairs may pass through trying periods. They are very unsuccessful as gamblers, and their wealth—which is often excessive—is usually the fruit of persistent hard work, coupled with shrewdness, economy and foresight. Among the many sons of Cancer who have accumulated vast riches in this way may be mentioned John D. Rockefeller, Cecil Rhodes and John Jacob Astor.

Cancer subjects have most retentive memories, and this gift is often useful to them in their work, whatever it may be. They have also a great respect for convention, and are deeply interested in everything that is old, sacred or historical. At the same time, the freshness of unspoilt Nature appeals to them strongly, and they are never so happy as when wandering in the woods and fields, especially in the neighbourhood of water.

Lower types of the Cancer subject are usually found to be indolent, greedy, mean, intensely selfish, suspicious, morbidly sensitive, and keenly resentful of imaginary injuries and slights. The higher types, however, who are hard-working, peace-loving and devoted to their families, provide one of the most valuable elements in the community.

Professions and Occupations

Those who are ruled by Cancer are generally successful in occupations of a public nature, or those in which they can serve large numbers of people. On this account, they make good government officials, politicians, caterers and hotel proprietors. They often instinctively follow occupations connected with liquids, such as those of publican, wine merchant, barmaid, laundry proprietor and hydraulic engineer.

They are happy when on the sea, and make good sailors and naval officers. Many famous sailors have been born under this sign, including Paul Jones and Admiral Farragut. Success in finance and "big business" often rewards the subjects of Cancer, so long as their activities are free from gambling and speculation. The literary and musical professions, especially if these bring them before the public, are also well suited to their romantic and imaginative temperament.

Marriage and Friendship

Affection runs very deep in Cancer folk, though they seldom wear their heart on their sleeve, so that their lack of demonstrativeness is often taken for lack of sentiment. They are happiest when in the heart of their family, to whom they are intensely devoted, but if, as is frequently the case, they consider that they are not properly understood by those dear to them, they become miserable and dejected, and retire within themselves. Their love affairs and domestic life are often full of worries and difficulties, which, however, are usually overcome by their great pertinacity and patience.

Those born during the Cancer period will find their closest and most enduring friendships with people born between February 21 and March 21 and between October 21 and November 21.

Health

Cancer governs the chest, the stomach and the higher organs of digestion. The most common accidents to which Cancer subjects are liable are chest injuries and broken ribs, while their most frequent ailments are bronchitis, pulmonary tuberculosis, pneumonia, pleurisy, dropsy, rheumatism and all diseases of the stomach. They should always try to exercise prudence and restraint in regard to what they eat, for they are naturally inclined to indulge over-freely in the pleasures of the table, with consequent indigestion and biliousness. Over-indulgence in alcohol should in particular be guarded against, for Cancer subjects are liable to develop into drunkards. Finally, they should do all in their power to resist worry, their most potent enemy.

To Attract Good Vibrations

Emerald green and glistening white are the colours most in harmony with this sign, and people of the Cancer type should always make a point of using these colours lavishly in their dress and in the decoration of their home.

Stones.—The best stones for this sign are emeralds and moonstones, though cat's-eyes, pearls and crystal are also in harmony. *Lucky Numbers.*—Two for Cancer; seven for the Moon. *Lucky Day.*—Monday. *Flowers.*—Poppy, water-lily. *Trees.*—Willow, sycamore. *Animals.*—Otter, seal. *Birds.*—Seagull, owl. *Metal.*—Silver.

LEO—THE LION ♌

July 21–August 21

THE Sun enters the zodiacal sign of Leo on approximately July 21 each year, and remains therein until about August 21. But the full

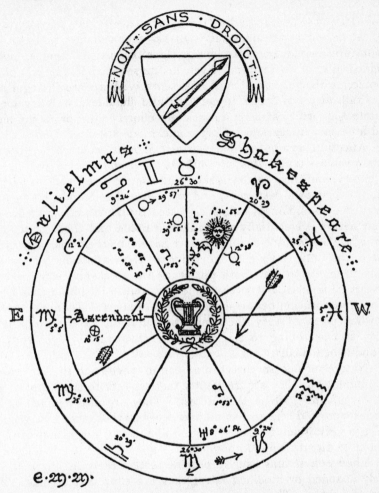

From *The Magic and Science of Jewels and Stones*, by Isidore Kozminsky (Putnam and Sons, Ltd.)

Horoscope of William Shakespeare

influence of this sign does not begin to exert itself until about July 27, being mingled until then with the gradually decreasing force of the preceding sign, Cancer. Therefore, people born on the cusp—between July 21 and 27—are also partly ruled by Cancer, and should study the influence of that sign as well.

Leo is a positive and fiery sign, ruled by the ardent, masculine and strongly magnetic Sun. It is symbolized by the Lion, and the typical person born under this sign has much of the "leonine" in his nature, including great courage, loyalty, energy, dignity, and a decided gift for leadership. Even his personal appearance is often leonine, for the purest and most representative types are distinguished by a tall, vigorous frame, broad back and shoulders, well-developed muscles, an erect carriage, a shock of yellow, golden or tawny hair, and a general appearance of pride and fearlessness.

Affection, sympathy and warmth of heart characterize people who are born under this sign. Their love embraces the whole of humanity, and their loyalty is such that they will defend their friends even to their own detriment, and will never desert one whose cause they have championed, unless disgusted by his treachery or deceit. Their nature is essentially so simple and noble that the least suggestion of guile or double-dealing is more hateful to them than anything, and is the only thing that can alienate their affection. They are utter strangers to fear, both physical and moral, and when roused are terrific fighters, but at the same time they will submit to a great deal of provocation before showing signs of anger. Then, no matter to what pitch of fury they may be wrought, they always fight fairly and according to the rules, and are invariably generous to a vanquished enemy.

Natives of Leo are direct and open in speech and the expression of opinions, but they are frequently tactless—for to them diplomacy savours of guile, which they detest. They are also inclined to be stern, severe and "heavy" in manner, even to those they love deeply, and are very quick-tempered when there is any suggestion of their honour or dignity being impugned.

Their convictions usually become settled early in life, and are rarely changed or modified later; they are expressed dogmatically, even defiantly. The extreme Leo types are often very narrow-minded and bigoted.

Their ambition is great and their strength of will considerable, so that it is not surprising that they usually surmount all difficulties that lie between them and their goal. In obtaining their desires, they frequently appear ruthless; this is seldom the result of wanton cruelty, but springs from the belief that the few must be sacrificed for the ultimate good of the majority. Leo people are born to play the part of leaders, and they have the gift of inspiring rare devotion in those who believe in them.   Striking instances of this type are the emperor Napoleon, Benito Mussolini, Cavour, and Simon Bolivar, all of whom were born under this sign.

In money matters Leo folk are usually favoured by fortune, and they may rise to the position of financial magnates; if they do, it will not be through trickery, but as a result of their own energy and natural gifts.   They will wish to share their wealth with others, and will subscribe freely to charities, but at the same time will surround themselves with all the luxury and refinement that money can command; in the lower types, this will be manifested as vulgar ostentation.   Indeed, a love of display characterizes all Leo subjects, and they have a marked predilection for all that flashes and glitters, especially gold, brass and bright metal objects, strong sunshine and brilliant colours.

The less highly developed Leo subjects may be boastful, vulgar and ostentatious, arrogant and tyrannical, and possessed of a mania for popularity.   They are usually absurdly sensitive on points of dignity, and may also be wasteful and recklessly extravagant.

Professions and Occupations

Leo produces rulers, soldiers, statesmen, church dignitaries, and governors, leaders and managers of every kind.   Financiers, "captains of industry," bankers, jewellers, and goldsmiths are also born under its rays.   On the artistic side, the Leonine love of colour, action and display may produce talent for the stage, literature and painting: famous Leo subjects so gifted being Mary Anderson, the actress, Shelley, Southey, Sir Walter Scott, De Quincey, George Bernard Shaw, Alexandre Dumas, Fénelon, John Dryden, Izaak Walton, and Jean Baptiste Corot, the painter.   The Leo type is not happy when in a subordinate position, and cannot bear to be ruled or given orders; but he makes an able, though exacting, employer or manager.

Marriage and Friendship

Being extremely affectionate themselves, Leo folk are ruled by affection, and they make the finest marriage partners, parents and friends—kind, loyal, and considerate.   They can generally be ruled through their feelings (though not in any other way whatever), and they may be deceived or even led into doing wrong by playing on their sentiments. In love and marriage they make many errors and suffer deeply from them; they are prone to mistake pity and sympathy for love, and may realize their error when too late, but their natural generosity and forbearance often save their married life from shipwreck.

Those born under Leo have the closest ties of affection with people whose birthdays occur between March 21 and April 21 and between November 21 and December 21.

Health

The vitality of Leo folk is boundless; they have the ability to absorb the vivifying power of the Sun to the fullest extent, and sunlight, coupled with fresh air, is their finest tonic and restorative. But they should be careful not to indulge overmuch in violent exercise, for there is danger of the heart being strained or weakened. The heart, spine, back and eyes are the parts of the body most liable to disease or injury. Heart trouble, palpitation, angina, spinal disease, lumbago, meningitis, and disorders of the eyes are among the commonest complaints of the Leo type; but they hate to give way to sickness, and will put up an heroic fight before being prostrated. It is fatal for Leo people to be idle, since they then become morose and gloomy; and when in good health they should be constantly occupied with some interesting employment.

To Attract Good Vibrations

Those born in the Leo period should wear all shades of gold, yellow and orange, while light green and white are also suitable. Gold, and all bright, glittering objects, such as polished brass or copper ornaments, will be found lucky and should be kept about the house.

Stones.—All yellow stones, such as amber, chrysolite, tourmaline, topaz and sardonyx; also ruby. These stones should be set in gold, since this is the metal of the Sun, ruler of Leo. *Lucky Numbers.*—Four for Leo; one for the Sun. *Lucky Day.*—Sunday. *Flowers.*—Marigold, sunflower, cowslip, heliotrope. *Trees.*— Palm, laurel. *Animal.*—Lion. *Birds.*—Cock, eagle. *Metal.*—Gold.

Virgo—the Virgin ♍

August 21–September 21

THE Sun enters the zodiacal sign Virgo on approximately August 21 every year and leaves it on September 21. However, the influence of this sign does not begin to be fully exerted until about a week after the Sun's entry, being diluted by the force of the preceding sign, Leo. Therefore, persons born between August 21 and 27 are also partly ruled by Leo, and should consult the characteristics given by that sign as well.

The negative and earthy sign Virgo is associated with intellectual power, and subjects of Virgo are distinguished by the keenness of their wits and their remarkable discrimination. They are, perhaps, the most calm, level-headed and practical of all the twelve types, for they seldom allow a vestige of sentiment or affection to interfere with, or bias, their judgment or conduct. Indeed, it is probable that sentiment is very shallow in Virgo people, for even the superior types are notable for their selfishness. At the same time, these characteristics have a useful function to fulfil, for they act as a wholesome check upon the more impulsive and expansive types; and, by their critical judgment and cool reasoning ability, natives of Virgo help to avert many errors and catastrophes that would not be foreseen by more rash and emotional people until too late.

Virgo people are pliant and adaptable. They can readily vary their manner and behaviour to suit the company in which they find themselves; while their tactfulness may often amount to servility. But this is not the result of fear; it is usually part of a deliberate plan or scheme, carefully prepared beforehand, and with a definite end in view.

Virgo people are not usually acquisitive, but, should one born under this sign set his heart upon anything, he will stop at nothing to attain it, and, if he is of a lower type, he may display the most extraordinary cunning, hypocrisy and cold-blooded guile. Not even human life stands in the way of a person of the undeveloped Virgo type when once his mind has become fixed upon a definite aim. This type is also capable of displaying greater cruelty than any other; he can commit the most shocking injustices and barbarities in cold blood, and nothing will move him to pity when he is actuated by hatred or self-interest. Of this type were the emperor Caligula, Richelieu, Queen Elizabeth of England, and Abdul Hamid, ex-sultan of Turkey, the "Great Assassin," all of whom were natives of Virgo.

Subjects of Virgo have the love of inquiry developed to the utmost; they are never satisfied to take anything on trust, but must always find out for themselves. Accordingly, under this sign many famous philosophers, mathematicians, and scientific investigators have been born, including Baron Cuvier, John Locke, Tommaso Campanella, Comte de Buffon, Baron von Humboldt, and the Marquis de Condorcet.

Virgo people are modest and reserved; they shrink from publicity, and will not talk readily about their own affairs, preferring to criticize the actions of others and analyse their motives. They are lacking in enthusiasm, and show reluctance to fall in with the plans of others or to assist them in any way. They are entirely individual and quite lacking in camaraderie and the "team spirit." When pursuing their own objects, which they do in a steadfast, practical and matter-of-fact manner, they will listen non-committally to the advice of others, but will seldom act upon it.

Their lack of sentiment makes them very slow to anger, but they are equally slow to forgive, and seldom compose a quarrel of their own accord. But they can swallow resentment and put their pride in their pocket when they consider it to be in their own interests to do so.

Virgo subjects are precise and methodical in all that they do, and have a great respect for law, order and precedent and for the achievements of the past. They are fond of harmony and elegance, and their taste is restrained and austere; but their imagination is decidedly limited, and is far exceeded by their reasoning powers. They are very fond of reading, and are able to remember very clearly a great deal of what they read and see.

The weaker varieties of this type are cunning, capricious and cruel in the extreme, cynical, unduly critical, caustic in their speech and perpetually finding fault. They are also snobbish, servile and excessively selfish.

Professions and Occupations

The critical and analytical faculties with which natives of Virgo are endowed make them well fitted to enter the law or politics. Among well-known lawyers, politicians, and statesmen born under

Virgo were Sir Edward Marshall-Hall, Lord Oxford and Asquith, Bonar Law, Sir Charles Dilke, Lord Burleigh, Sir Robert Walpole, Richelieu, Colbert, Lafayette, Louis Kossuth, President Taft and President Diaz.

Virgo also favours the occupations of literary, music, and dramatic critic, editor, corrector of the Press, doctor, policeman and detective. Mercury, the ruler of Virgo, governs clerical work; therefore the professions of secretary, accountant, schoolmaster, printer and stationer are also indicated. The accuracy and precision of Virgo produce good chemists, engineers and watch and instrument makers.

Marriage and Friendship

Virgo subjects are well suited to married life, being dutiful, faithful and proud of their family, though usually they are quite undemonstrative. The happiness of their union may depend upon their ability to control their proclivity for criticism and fault-finding. Their best affinities for marriage and friendship occur with those born between April 21 and May 21 and between December 21 and January 21.

Health

Virgo rules the abdomen and intestines, and its subjects suffer most commonly from dysentery, colic, diarrhoea, constipation, indigestion and debility. As a general rule, their health is good, though they are prone to worry causelessly over themselves, and to resort to all kinds of patent medicines and quack remedies. A morbid craving for drink or drugs may be experienced, and should be eradicated forthwith.

To Attract Good Vibrations

In order to draw to themselves the right kind of magnetism, those born under Virgo should wear and be surrounded with pale blue, pale gold and yellow. Jade green will also be harmonious, for it is the colour of Mercury.

Lucky Stones.—Cornelian, jade, diamond, jasper. *Lucky Numbers.*—Ten for Virgo; five for Mercury. *Lucky Day.*—Wednesday. *Flowers.*—Madonna lily, cornflower, valerian. *Tree.*—Hazel. *Animal.*—Squirrel. *Birds.*—Parrot, magpie. *Metals.*—Platinum for Virgo; quicksilver for Mercury.

Libra—the Scales ♎

THE Sun enters Libra on September 21, and leaves this sign on approximately October 21. Since the full power of Libra is not exerted until about September 27, when the decreasing influence of Virgo finally ceases, persons born between September 21 and 27 are also partly ruled by Virgo, and they should consult the attributes given by that sign as well.

Libra is an airy sign, and is ruled by the beautiful planet Venus. Its symbol is the scales, typifying balance, justice and harmony, which form the keynote of those born under this sign. Such persons have a natural ability to weigh, compare and estimate facts, and to arrive at an unbiased decision, while it is a remarkable fact that they are able to judge the weight of material objects and can match shades of colour more accurately than people of any other type. Though full of sentiment, they seldom allow their own feelings to interfere with what they consider to be just; and they are broad-minded, tolerant and lenient to the faults of others, realizing that errors and failings are natural to the human race. But they detest injustice, cruelty and unfair treatment, and are always ready to take up arms on behalf of anybody who has been wronged.

In most of the activities of life they are inclined to take a middle course and to avoid extremes of any kind. Under the influence of Venus, the planet of concord and harmony, they constantly crave peace and happy surroundings, and their horror of all strife, worry and unpleasantness makes them invariably pliant, accommodating and complaisant; this trait may easily degenerate into a fault, and it would do the majority of Libra subjects no harm to cultivate some of the tougher moral fibre that distinguishes, for example, natives of Aries and Virgo.

Subjects of Libra are gentle, courteous and affectionate in their manner and speech, and are not easily roused to anger, except by the contemplation of injustice. They cannot maintain a quarrel for long, and seldom feel resentment afterwards. In religious matters they are very tolerant, setting the spirit and relative moral value of any doctrine far above the observance of rites and formulas. They dislike monotony and are fond of change, travelling and seeing interesting and beautiful sights, but if chained by circumstances to one place or occupation, their unfailing good humour enables them to make the best of the situation.

Libra subjects are natural home-makers, and can settle down anywhere, provided their surroundings are congenial; they then hasten to collect around them as many beautiful ornaments, furnishings and other pleasing things as lie within their means.

Intellectually, they are highly developed, and not infrequently of a scholarly turn of mind, with a decided love of the past, which their rich imagination endows with colour and life. However, their tendency to avoid unpleasantness of all kinds may impel them to seek the easiest road through life, with the result that they often turn out indolent and too easy-going, and so neglect and fail to make the best of their fine talents.

The strong imagination of Libra folk makes them intuitive, inventive and ingenious, and when their well-balanced reasoning power is added a strong scientific or philosophic genius may be produced. Of this type were Michael Faraday and G. B. Beccaria, the pioneers of electricity; George Westinghouse and Robert Stephenson, the engineers; Noah Webster, the lexicographer; Hugh Miller, the geologist, and Sir Christopher Wren, the famous architect.

Professions and Occupations

Being apt at learning, adaptable, level-headed and capable of calm decision, Libra subjects can make a success of almost any career. Preferably, however, they should follow some line in which their strong artistic tastes and good sense of proportion have full scope. Thus they make excellent artists, musicians, writers, poets, sculptors, landscape gardeners, florists, and dress designers. As a general rule, they work better when in employment or partnership than when alone. They often find the law congenial, and their strong judicial powers may carry them to great heights. The gift of cool and rapid decision imparted by Libra has also produced many great naval and military commanders, including Augustus Caesar, Pompey, Lord Clive, Lord Nelson, Lord Collingwood, Frederick III of Germany, Lord Roberts, and Marshal Foch.

Marriage and Friendship

Libra subjects make loyal, cheerful and affectionate friends, who are always ready to put their own interests last. They are, as a rule, probably more happy and contented in marriage than any other type, for their deep fund of affection triumphs over difficulties and conflicts of temperament that would wreck the majority of marriages. The most congenial types to mate with Libra people are those born between January 21 and February 21 and between May 21 and June 21.

Health

Libra rules the kidneys, lumbar regions and skin, and its subjects are liable to suffer from disorders affecting these parts, such as stone, Bright's disease, nephritis, diabetes, eczema and skin eruptions. Their nerves, also, are liable to be overstrained, and they should avoid worry and depression of spirits.

To Attract Good Vibrations

Blue and violet are the colours that accord best with Libra, and they should be used freely in order to attract harmonious astral vibrations.

Lucky Stones.—Opal for Libra, lapis lazuli for Venus, its ruler. *Lucky Numbers.*—Eight for Libra; six for Venus. *Lucky Day.*—Friday. *Flowers.*—Violet, white rose. *Trees.*—Almond, walnut. *Animals.*—Hart, hare. *Bird.*—Dove. *Metal.*—Copper.

Scorpio—the Scorpion ♏

October 21–November 21

The Sun enters Scorpio on or about October 21 each year, and leaves it approximately on November 21. Persons born between October 21 and 27 are, however, also ruled to some extent by the preceding sign, Libra, whose influence does not die away entirely until the latter date.

Scorpio, whose symbol is the stinging scorpion, is a negative and watery sign, but is ruled by the fiery planet Mars. Its subjects are a mass of extremes and contradictions, and even at the best are always difficult to size up or classify. Powerfully magnetic, brimful of energy, intense in their emotions, and subtle and involved in their actions and manner of thought, they have perhaps the strangest personalities of all the zodiacal types. The will power which they can exert over other people is enormous. Not only by their gift of rhetoric—in which they excel—but by means of something far deeper, some strange psychological power, they can mould and twist other people to their will, either individually or in the mass.

Scorpio people are nearly always inclined to be haughty, vain, and self-satisfied, and often nourish for their associates a contempt which they do not hesitate to display in harsh and biting words. They often seem to be possessed with a demon of perversity, and they love to impress and "shock" people by some dramatic and unexpected action, usually of an unpleasant nature.

They have amazing powers of tenacity and resistance, and are seldom discouraged when their plans go awry and success seems far away. They will meet the most crushing blows without cringing or changing expression; in fact, they always know when and how to conceal their emotions, although there are few people who live on their emotions so much as those born under Scorpio.

Idealists and humanitarians at heart, the more developed types among these subjects are ever eager to defend and champion the weak and oppressed; but they often speak slightingly of those whom they uphold and protect, and affect a contempt of charity and kind actions. Naturally gifted with dramatic ability, many of them act throughout their daily life and, in a spirit of perversity, seem anxious to give the world an entirely wrong impression of their character and temperament. They have little use for convention, and often fly deliberately in the face of established custom and propriety, a course which seems to afford them keen pleasure.

They are hard workers and never spare themselves, and if they are gifted with ambition—as is usually the case—nothing can stand in the way of its realization. They lay their plans with calm deliberation, meet and overcome obstacles with the greatest coolness and ingenuity, and often look upon other people as pawns to be sacrificed to their own success.

Natives of Scorpio often have pronounced psychic gifts, and feel drawn towards a study of the occult. Many of them can sublimate their intense vital force into religion or mysticism, and this process produces personalities which are outstanding and unique. As examples we may cite Saint Augustine, William Cowper and Samuel Taylor Coleridge, the poets, and Alexander I, tsar of Russia, each of whom had a pronounced strain of mysticism in his nature.

A notable person born under Scorpio is usually remarkable in many other ways than that in which his particular talent or genius has distinguished him; he is the sort of man who is fated to make his mark in the world, no matter how he chooses to do so. This strength of character is observable in Theodore Roosevelt, Captain Cook, Danton, Gambetta, Franz Liszt, Benvenuto Cellini, Martin Luther, Edward VII and William Hogarth, all of whom were born under the rays of Scorpio.

Professions and Occupations

Both Scorpio and its ruler, Mars, favour success in the army and navy. Other congenial careers include those of government official, overseer, magistrate, butcher, iron-founder, brazier, brewer, chemist, photographer, and dentist, while the most skilful of surgeons are produced by this sign. A love of secrecy and intrigue is inherent in the Scorpio nature, and this may produce excellent detectives, spies and secret service agents, as well as prominent freemasons and members of secret societies.

Marriage and Friendship

Those born under Scorpio have an intense love nature, which, if they value their happiness, they must not allow to get beyond control. They should guard against sudden and impulsive attachments that have no basis of real affection. Scorpio subjects are critical and not easy to please, and are liable to become violently jealous with little or no cause, but they may be successfully handled by a tactful partner who knows, and allows for, all the vagaries of their strong personality. Their closest affinities are formed with people born between February 21 and March 21 and between June 21 and July 21.

To Attract Good Vibrations

The deeper shades of red harmonize best with Scorpio, and russet-brown is also beneficial. These colours should be incorporated in the clothes of Scorpio subjects, and in their household decorations, in order to attract the maximum of good fortune.

Lucky Stones.—All red stones are beneficial, especially the ruby; also beryl, topaz and turquoise. *Lucky Number.*—Nine for both Scorpio and Mars, its ruler. *Lucky Day.*—Tuesday. *Flowers.*—Heather and chrysanthemum. *Trees.*— Holly and thorn. *Animals.*—Wolf and panther. *Birds.*—Eagle and vulture. *Metal.*—Iron.

SAGITTARIUS—THE ARCHER ♐

November 21–December 21

The Sun enters the zodiacal sign Sagittarius about November 21, to leave it a month later, about December 21. However, the full power of Sagittarius does not begin to take effect until about November 27, for until that date the influence of Scorpio is also active, though declining. Hence, persons born between November 21 and 27 are partly ruled by Scorpio, and should consult the properties of that sign as well as those of Sagittarius.

Sagittarius is the third of the fiery signs, and is symbolized by an archer, or a centaur, drawing his bow. In magnetism it is positive, and it is under the rule of the benign and expansive planet Jupiter. Natives of this sign are distinguished by frankness, sincerity and optimism; they have a strongly developed sense of justice, and are tolerant, philanthropic and humane. They display great sympathy with human nature, and are generous and charitable to a degree. They like being made a repository of other people's troubles, and are very fond of giving advice, but are apt to become sententious and patronizing, which often lessens the appreciation of their kindness. They are intensely hard workers, though in the pursuit of their aims they are apt to run along a somewhat narrow track, so that much escapes their notice that might be helpful to them.

They are very sociable, and are popular in friendly and convivial gatherings, though they are apt to affront their individual friends by their extreme outspokenness. They are essentially honest and hate deception and trickery in any form, and usually they lead very respectable lives and bow unfailingly to convention. Always ready, and even anxious, to shoulder responsibilities, they are solicitous in their regard for the welfare of those under their tutelage or in their employ.

Being gifted with considerable strength of will, they show great independence and insist on conducting their affairs and living their lives in their own way. They are both versatile and impulsive, and therefore frequently make sudden decisions or change their occupations or interests in a totally unexpected way.

Many people born under Sagittarius are deeply religious, and their faith in moral and spiritual matters seldom falters. Others are fond of philosophizing, and in this direction often display great depth of thought. Examples of the highest type of keen and philosophic intellect given by Sagittarius can be seen in John Milton, Thomas Carlyle, Jonathan Swift, Victor Cousin and Heinrich Heine.

Sagittarians are strangely prone to theorize and make shrewd guesses as to the outcome of events. Indeed, their intuition and

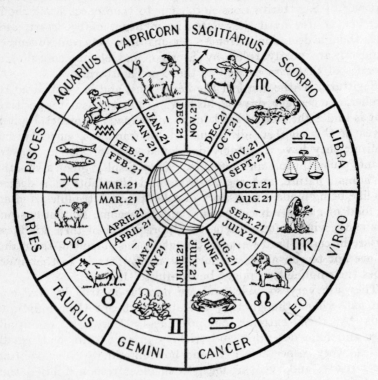

The Circle of the Zodiac.—The sign of the Zodiac by which any person is ruled is shown instantly on referring to the birth period in the innermost ring. The appropriate zodiacal sign should then be consulted. Those born on a cusp—between the 21st and 27th of any month—are also partly ruled by the sign of the preceding month, and therefore both signs should be consulted.

foresight are often considerable, and reliance upon them is amply justified by the success achieved by the higher types of Sagittarians when guided by their own impulses. Many Sagittarius folk display the curious characteristic of completely altering their occupation or habits of life, quite irrespective of advancing age, change of abode and other circumstances, and often without any obvious motive at all; and they are quite as sincere and successful in this new existence as they were in the former. A few notable Sagittarians in whom this peculiarity may be observed are General Monk, who achieved fame first as an able general and then crowned it by restoring the supremacy of England on the sea; Prince Rupert, the dashing cavalry commander, who later became an admiral and eventually retired to the seclusion of the chemical laboratory; and Thomas Becket and Lope de Vega, the Spanish dramatist, both men of pleasure who became rigid ascetics.

Sagittarians are very often of athletic build, with long and well-developed legs, and they are extremely fond of sport; they are at their happiest in the open air and in the company of dogs and horses.

The undeveloped types of Sagittarians are inclined to be pretentious, vain and patronizing. They love to make a parade of any generous actions which they may be called upon to perform, and are full of religious cant and smug self-satisfaction. They do not hesitate to commit the meanest of actions, and are quite unscrupulous in the pursuit of their ambitions; but they endeavour to conceal the unpleasant side of their nature with a cloak of hypocrisy and bluff, for the good opinion of the world is very precious to them.

Professions and Occupations

Sagittarians are naturally fitted for positions of authority in which their advice, aid and judgment can be sought by others. Thus they excel in medicine, the law and the Church, and as employers of labour, naval and military officers, technical experts of all kinds, politicians, missionaries, relieving officers, inspectors, nurses, matrons, modistes and officials of charitable organizations. Many veterinary surgeons and dealers in dogs and horses are found under this sign.

They often have a deep love of music and make excellent musicians. In this connexion it is interesting to note that the great Beethoven was born under Sagittarius, as also were Weber, Rubinstein, Edward McDowell and Sir Hamilton Harty.

Marriage and Friendship

Sagittarians have a great capacity for friendship, and are popular among their associates, but they are apt to lose friends through want of tact. They make good husbands, wives and parents, who never shirk the responsibilities of family life, but they often marry unhappily, probably being carried away by a passing impulse. However, their proud and independent spirit can be depended upon to hide their unhappiness from the eyes of the world, and they will endeavour to make the best of things in order to preserve appearances. They are fond of home life, and take a great pride in the comfort and adornment of their home.

Sagittarius folk mate most harmoniously with those born between March 21 and April 21, and between July 21 and August 21.

Health

The hips, thighs, nerves and arteries are under the rule of Sagittarius, and its subjects may suffer from rheumatism in the lower limbs, as well as from sciatica, gout and nervous disorders. The lungs and throat may be delicate, and the native may be prone to bronchitis and lung troubles. The commonest accidents suffered by Sagittarians are those affecting the lower limbs, such as sprains, dislocation of the hip and fracture of the thigh.

To Attract Good Vibrations

Orange is the colour most in tune with the vibrations of Sagittarius, while mauve and purple harmonize best with Jupiter, its ruler. Good fortune should ensue if these colours are freely used.

Lucky Stones.—Sapphire for Sagittarius; amethyst for Jupiter. *Lucky Numbers.*—Four for Sagittarius; three for Jupiter. *Lucky Day.*—Thursday. *Flowers.*—Carnation and wallflower. *Trees.*—Mulberry and vine. *Animal.*—Horse. *Bird.*—Eagle. *Metal.*—Tin.

CAPRICORN—THE GOAT ♑

December 21–January 21

THE Sun passes into Capricorn on approximately December 21 and leaves it about January 21. People born on the cusp of the sign—

between December 21 and 27—are, however, also influenced to some extent by the gradually declining power of the preceding sign, Sagittarius, and they should consult the qualities given by this sign as well as those with which Capricorn endows them.

Capricorn is an earthy sign, and is ruled by the secretive and restraining planet Saturn. The symbol of Capricorn is the goat, an animal which delights in climbing the highest mountains and the most precipitous rocks. Even so do the patient, persistent and dogged subjects of Capricorn seek the steepest and most arduous paths through life to reach the summit of their worldly ambition or spiritual salvation. Hard work, fatigue, and self-denial are counted as nothing, and all their energies are bent towards one object. Practical, shrewd, and calculating, and of a grave, self-contained disposition, they scorn all forms of extravagance and display and all unnecessary expenditure of energy. They are reserved, secretive and taciturn, and very averse to taking anybody into their confidence or imparting their thoughts and opinions to those around them.

Capricornians scorn effusiveness and are unmoved by flattery, and they seldom express wonderment or surprise; but they are avid of knowledge in all its branches, are keenly interested in science and philosophy, and are impelled towards the study of all that is ancient, such as archaeology, history and folk-lore. They are painstaking and methodical in all they do, and although their researches may be animated by enthusiasm, this is of a quiet and prosaic order and is seldom revealed. Johann Kepler and Sir Isaac Newton, both subjects of Capricorn, are excellent examples of this patient, undemonstrative, but indefatigable spirit of inquiry.

Natives of Capricorn are quick to take the lead in their particular sphere of activity, and their right to do so is usually accepted without question, for their implicit faith in their own powers is rapidly communicated to those about them. If baulked of a position of authority and obliged to work under the domination of others, they become gloomy, morose and mordantly critical.

Though most of them are strongly material, many Capricornians are also idealists at heart, and their love of moral and intellectual freedom often impels them to back up an apparently worthy but hopeless or unpopular cause, even though it is plain that their own interests may suffer thereby. This type of idealism, in a greater or less degree, may be observed in Joan of Arc, Edmund Burke,

Alexander Hamilton, Marshal Ney, W. E. Gladstone, President Woodrow Wilson and the Rt. Hon. David Lloyd George, all of whom, at some period of their life at least, have fought for their convictions in a difficult or apparently losing battle.

Natives of Capricorn are not easily roused to anger, but, on the other hand, they are very slow to forgive, often nourishing their wrongs in secret for years until the time is ripe for the revenge which they never hesitate to reap in full measure, since they are vindictive beyond the ordinary. They are also inclined to be jealous, suspicious and morose. Extreme melancholy and depression of spirits are perhaps the worst enemies of the Capricorn type, and may colour all their thoughts and actions. Edgar Allan Poe is a striking example of this type, as is also, though in a lesser degree, Thomas Gray, author of the *Elegy Written in a Country Churchyard*.

When badly developed, they may become the most hateful of mankind—timid, callous, tyrannical, intensely selfish, miserly, morbid, lustful, and full of low cunning and duplicity. The superior types are, however, among the noblest members of the human race.

Professions and Occupations

Subjects of Capricorn are fitted by their prudence, tact and extreme caution to be diplomats and negotiators of delicate business of all descriptions (Disraeli, Benjamin Franklin and Lord Curzon were all born under this sign). As officials, especially in the government, they are industrious and methodical, and usually rise to a position of authority. Other professions and trades which they may follow with profit are those of editor, actor, detective, architect, farmer, farrier, miner or mining official, metallurgist, dealer in lead or wool, and plumber.

Marriage and Friendship

Subjects of Capricorn make good and true friends, though they are bitter and implacable enemies. In love and marriage, they are capable of deep and passionate affection, though no type is more undemonstrative. They are advised not to marry young, such marriages often proving unfortunate. Much domestic friction can be avoided if they will contrive to overcome their selfishness and cultivate good humour and cheerfulness. Those most in harmony with the Capricorn type, both in friendship and marriage, are born

between April 21 and May 21 and between August 21 and
September 21.

Health

Capricorn folk tend to be weak and ailing in childhood, though
when they reach adult life they usually enjoy good health. The
commonest ills of this type are injuries and diseases affecting the
knees (which are ruled by Capricorn), as well as skin disorders,
chills, rheumatism, constipation, toothache and earache. They
should guard against anxiety and depression, for their complaints
are often induced or aggravated by worry and introspection.

To Attract Good Vibrations

The colours that will bring the most harmonious vibrations to
Capricorn folk are black, grey and violet; all shades of the last two
colours may be used.

Lucky Stones.—Onyx for Capricorn; obsidian and jet for Saturn, its ruling
planet. *Lucky Numbers.*—Three for Capricorn; eight for Saturn. *Lucky Day.*—
Saturday. *Flowers.*—Nightshade and rue. *Trees.*—Pine, cypress and yew.
Animals.—Dog and elephant. *Bird.*—Owl. *Metal.*—Lead.

AQUARIUS—THE WATER-BEARER ♒

January 21–February 21

THE Sun enters the zodiacal sign Aquarius about January 21 and
passes out of it on approximately February 21 each year, but since
for about a week after its entry the influence of the previous sign,
Capricorn, still remains in force, those born on the cusp—between
January 21 and 27—are also ruled by Capricorn, and should consult
the pages devoted to that sign as well.

Aquarius is the last of the airy signs. It is positive in magnetism, and is ruled by the mighty planets Saturn and Uranus; it
is symbolized by a man holding a pitcher of water, which he pours
upon the ground.

Persons born under Aquarius are generally idealistic, generous
and humane, and are quick to relieve the distress or wants of others.
They are very shrewd judges of human nature, and are acutely
sensitive to outside impressions, with a natural gift for immediately

sensing the magnetic auras of any persons or places with which they come into contact.

Seeking eternally after truth and beauty, they are strong champions of progress in every direction, longing to sweep away all that is corrupt and burdensome, even though it may have become sanctified by age and long custom, and to replace it with something more serviceable to the needs and welfare of humanity. Three leading examples of this type are Abraham Lincoln, Charles Dickens, and Philip Melancthon, the reformer.

Though gifted with great insight and intuition, their reasoning powers are also active, and they do not depend upon feeling alone for their impressions or opinions, but must debate everything in their own mind in a logical fashion. When once they have formed their conclusions, however, their opinions are unalterable.

Aquarians are cheerful and reliable friends and are usually very popular, since they have social gifts of a high order. They deeply appreciate the affection of others, and respond eagerly to the least show of friendship; but at the same time, their feelings are easily affronted, and slights and injuries which would leave many people unaffected are nursed and brooded over for a long time.

Aquarians are usually strong intellectually, and though they are eager to welcome fresh and novel ideas, they refuse to take anything on trust, but insist on its being demonstrated fully and satisfactorily before they will accept it. They are keenly attracted by science—especially by electricity and magnetism—and by any invention or new line of thought that promises to increase the happiness of humanity. Among leading scientists, thinkers, and others who have helped the human race, Francis Bacon, Swedenborg, Copernicus, Charles Darwin, Ernst Haeckel, Sir Hiram Maxim and Thomas Alva Edison were all born under the sign of Aquarius.

The dual rulership of this sign—by both Saturn and Uranus—makes its natives contradictory in many ways. Under the influence of Saturn, they may be cautious, indolent, restrained in their passions, and rather slow-going and dull. But at other times, under the sway of Uranus, the same people may surprise their friends by an entire alteration of character for a time, when they defy convention, break old ties and habits, and probably display eccentricity or strange flashes of genius.

Aquarians often have fine talents or incipient genius lying latent and undeveloped in their subconsciousness, and unfortunately it may be on rare occasions only that these are ever called to the surface— usually in emergencies and at the urge of necessity. Many such people, apparently quite ordinary and undistinguished, might rise to a high place in the world if they would but apply themselves to developing these hidden powers.

Inferior or undeveloped sons of Aquarius may be indolent, timid, neurotic, revengeful, dishonest, unscrupulous and false to their word. In financial matters Aquarians are usually fortunate, but, whether they be rich or poor, money is often a worry or a source of misfortune to them.

Professions and Occupations

Aquarians are happy and successful in any kind of scientific research, but especially in connexion with electricity. This sign also produces talented musicians, actors, and poets, such as Mozart, Schubert, Mendelssohn, Madame Patti and Ole Bull, the violinist; David Garrick, Sir Henry Irving, Joseph Jefferson, Lord Byron and Robert Burns were also born under Aquarius.

This sign particularly favours the callings of psychologist, company promoter, aviator, electrician, ship's carpenter and nurse or keeper of the insane.

Friendship and Marriage

Aquarius folk are romantic and idealistic, and are apt to set the object of their affections upon a pedestal, so that they are bitterly disappointed and grieved when their beloved's human frailties become apparent. The consequent disillusionment gives rise to much unhappiness, until the partners become adjusted to one another by the process of time. Usually Aquarians are faithful and loyal in matrimony, but they may be quite the opposite. At the best of times their sudden moods and caprices are liable to cause perplexity and pain to friends and marriage partner alike. They should mate, if possible, with those born between May 21 and June 21 and between September 21 and October 21.

Health

Aquarius rules the legs and ankles, and these members are more prone to injury—by sprains, fractures and the like—than any other part of the body. The circulation of the blood also comes under this sign, and may be liable to disorder. Uranus gives a tendency to electric shocks and danger from lightning. Aquarians are often keenly interested in hygiene, food reform, dietetics and similar subjects, and by practising these things are often able to keep themselves in splendid health.

To Attract Good Vibrations

Electric blue and electric green are the most harmonious colours for Aquarius, and if worn on the person and freely used in other ways they will be found to act as receivers of beneficial astral vibrations.

Lucky Stones.—Zircon and garnet for Aquarius; malachite, ruby, jet and black onyx for Saturn; jacinth and jargoon for Uranus. *Lucky Number.*—Two. *Lucky Day.*—Saturday. *Flowers.*—Snowdrop and foxglove. *Tree.*—Pine. *Animal.*— Dog. *Bird.*—Cuckoo. *Metal.*—Platinum.

PISCES—THE FISHES ♓

February 21–March 21

THE Sun enters Pisces about February 21 and leaves this sign about March 21. Persons born between February 21 and 27 are also partly ruled by the preceding sign, Aquarius, and they should, therefore, study the characteristics given by this sign as well.

Pisces is a watery and negative sign, and is ruled by the two planets Jupiter and Neptune. Its symbol is two fishes, attached yet turning in opposite directions, which typify the dual nature of those born under this sign, who often intend one thing and do another. Gifted with wide vision and a rich imagination, they are capable of conceiving lofty and grandiose schemes; but when they are called on to put them into action, grow timid and lose confidence.

Natives of Pisces are exceedingly romantic, kind-hearted and emotional, but are so lacking in stability and will-power, and are so sensitive to rebuffs and discouragement, that the amount of good which they achieve falls far short of their intentions. They are retiring, vacillating and sadly lacking in ambition, and yet, if constantly urged forward with encouragement and sympathy, they may easily climb the heights of fame and success, for they are often talented, are very apt at learning and accumulating knowledge, and possess a quiet sort of persistence which is peculiar to them.

Pisces subjects readily absorb impressions and take on the psychic auras of people with whom they are brought into contact, and thus their judgment is often clouded and their opinions are unreliable. For this reason, when they are obliged to make an important decision, they should ponder the matter carefully when alone and act resolutely upon their own intuition, without allowing it to be vitiated by the influence of others.

Pisces subjects are fond of comfort and a quiet life, and they will invariably take the easiest path that offers itself. But the superior Pisces folk—and even many of the weaker types—are capable of making the most signal sacrifices when necessity demands, and will then endure an extraordinary amount of suffering and privation without complaint.

A love of order and social convention characterizes those born under this sign, yet they are always ready to find an excuse for the transgressions of others; for, not having much real vice themselves, they simply cannot recognize it in the people around them.

Natives of Pisces are usually fond of animals and children and may have considerable influence over them, ruling them by kindness rather than severity. They may become powerfully attracted towards the study of the occult, and, if very weak, may be completely ruled by superstition. Their telepathic and intuitive powers are often highly developed, and they make good mediums, thought-readers and psychic investigators.

Many of the finest and most enlightened types of mankind are born under Pisces, and many of its natives achieve renown, high rank, honours and riches. But the great majority of those born under this sign are burdened with such a heavy "inferiority complex" that they stand constantly in need of a stimulus to bring them up to the mark.

Professions and Occupations

Travel, especially on the water, seems to exert a great fascination for Pisces folk, and this, coupled with their characteristic love of delving into the mysterious and unknown, may produce a genius for exploration; notable examples are David Livingstone and Arminius

Vambéry. Pisces subjects may also have a strong gift for music, literature and philosophy, occupations in which their intense imagination can have full play, and this sign has produced such great artists and thinkers as Chopin, Handel, Rossini, Michelangelo, Ibsen, Victor Hugo, Longfellow, Montaigne, Cardinal Newman, Ernest Renan, Schopenhauer and Ellen Terry.

Among the more prosaic occupations favoured by this sign are those of commercial traveller, sailor, brewer, fishmonger, teacher, nurse, leather-worker and dealer in boots and shoes; also any occupation connected with children and animals.

Marriage and Friendship

Subjects of Pisces are most deeply in harmony with people born between June 21 and July 21 and between October 21 and November 21. They are full of sentiment, and their sympathy is easily excited. They like to be petted and fussed over, and are often very attractive to the opposite sex. But their vows, promises and affectionate ways are not to be relied on, and a measure of firmness on the part of their partner in marriage is usually desirable.

Health

Pisces rules the feet and toes, and these parts are particularly liable to disease and injury. Among the most common ailments affecting subjects of Pisces are chills, gout, dropsy, sluggishness of the liver and infectious diseases. They should guard also against disorders arising from the pleasures of the table, of which they are usually very fond.

To Attract Good Vibrations

The most magnetic colours for Pisces folk are purple, mauve, and sea-green; these should be freely used in clothing and in household decorations.

Lucky Stones.—Sapphire and emerald for Pisces; amethyst for Jupiter, and coral for Neptune, its rulers. Lucky Numbers.—Six for Pisces; three for both Jupiter and Neptune. Lucky Day.—Thursday. Flowers.—Heliotrope and carnation. Trees.—Willow and elm. Animals.—Sheep and ox. Birds.—Swan and stork. Metal.—Tin.